D1527791

Praise for *New Essays in Japanese Aesthetics*

"A. Minh Nguyen's *New Essays in Japanese Aesthetics* is an important, comprehensive, and fascinating collection. Beginning with historical and systematic overviews of the philosophical tenets of Japanese aesthetics and treatments of central themes in Japanese art and aesthetics, this is a book of enormous scope, including discussions of traditional art forms such as the tea ceremony, calligraphy, haiku, Nō drama, pottery, and the martial arts, quotidian activities such as gift wrapping, flower arranging, cooking, etiquette, and gardening, and contemporary movements in Japanese literature, film, and the visual arts. This is a book that no student of Japanese aesthetics, whether beginning or advanced, should be without."

—Philip Alperson, Professor Emeritus of Philosophy,
Temple University

"A. Minh Nguyen's *New Essays in Japanese Aesthetics* is a kaleidoscope of twenty-seven new contributions on the unrelenting pursuit of elegance across Japanese culture that have been written specifically for this volume by nothing less than a cadre of the world's most distinguished Japanologists. As it is turned in the hand of the reader, it reveals from a bottomless array of angles the different strategies this always unique and yet porous culture has deployed to enchant the human experience, aspiring as it does to transform the ordinary into the extraordinary and the mundane into the sublime."

—Roger T. Ames, Chair Professor in the Humanities,
Peking University

"A. Minh Nguyen's *New Essays in Japanese Aesthetics* is a most impressive collection. This volume provides important information to all who study Japanese aesthetics. I know of no other book that covers the subject so completely."

—Donald Keene, University Professor Emeritus and Shincho Professor Emeritus of Japanese Literature, Columbia University

"A. Minh Nguyen has put together an important volume that gives us, in one place, the tools to understand the knotty subject of Japanese aesthetics. The most notable scholars address these questions from various perspectives: some of them walk us through the history of aesthetics in Japan, others explicate the broad issues and ramifications of these ideas, while others take us deep into particular artists, genres, and works. This is an impressive achievement of long-lived value."

—Doug Slaymaker, Professor of Japanese, University of Kentucky

"Japanese aesthetics, famous throughout the world, is more often revered and celebrated than meticulously analyzed. *New Essays in Japanese Aesthetics* goes beyond surface pleasures to uncover the relations and tensions that shape aesthetic worlds in Japan. Encyclopedic in breadth, the book is a must-have for anyone seeking to better understand this intriguing and elegant domain."

—Kristin Surak, Associate Professor of Japanese Politics, School of Oriental and African Studies, University of London

"A trove of treasures for thinking across the history of Japanese artistic practice and aesthetic thought, ranging from literature and the visual arts to philosophy, politics, and the aesthetics of daily life, this is a compendious work that will return many readers and introduce many more to the most vital topics and motifs of the Japanese cultural tradition with fresh insights and lucid clarifications of complex matters. A perfect text for reading in and for teaching from."

—Alan Tansman, Louis B. Agassiz Chair in Japanese and Director of the Doreen B. Townsend Center for the Humanities, University of California, Berkeley

New Essays in Japanese Aesthetics

New Essays in Japanese Aesthetics

Edited by
A. Minh Nguyen

Foreword by
Stephen Addiss

LEXINGTON BOOKS
Lanham • Boulder • New York • London

Published by Lexington Books
An imprint of The Rowman & Littlefield Publishing Group, Inc.
4501 Forbes Boulevard, Suite 200, Lanham, Maryland 20706
www.rowman.com

Unit A, Whitacre Mews, 26-34 Stannary Street, London SE11 4AB

Copyright © 2017 by Lexington Books

All rights reserved. No part of this book may be reproduced in any form or by any electronic or mechanical means, including information storage and retrieval systems, without written permission from the publisher, except by a reviewer who may quote passages in a review.

British Library Cataloguing in Publication Information Available

Library of Congress Cataloging-in-Publication Data

ISBN 978-0-7391-8081-5 (cloth : alk. paper)
ISBN 978-1-4985-7211-8 (paperback)
ISBN 978-0-7391-8082-2 (electronic)

♾™ The paper used in this publication meets the minimum requirements of American National Standard for Information Sciences Permanence of Paper for Printed Library Materials, ANSI/NISO Z39.48-1992.

To Nhi, Cynthia, and Vivian

Contents

xii   *Contents*

List of Illustrations

Foreword

Stephen Addiss

Japan is a paradox. Sushi and McDonald's are equally popular; Bunraku, Noh, and Kabuki theaters coexist with the latest entertainment technology; traditional forms of literature flourish alongside comic books for all ages; and modern architecture has not reduced the enjoyment of bonsai. This is not a new phenomenon. Throughout its history, Japan has exhibited a series of paradoxes, more than most other countries.

This seeming sense of contradiction is especially true in Japanese arts. They have played an unusually large role in the history and culture of Japan, yet there was no word for art (or aesthetics) until the influence of the West in the modern age. Just to name a few examples of artistic paradox, the seventeenth-century appreciation for the simplicity and rough textures of monochrome *raku* tea bowls coincided with an admiration for highly decorated, technically advanced, and multicolored porcelains. Even in the work of a single artist, Itō Jakuchū (1716–1800), there are a number of large, carefully rendered full-color studies of fish, birds, and plants on silk, as well as many rough ink paintings (usually of roosters) on paper in a style that emphasized bold brushstrokes with very little detail.

Do these paradoxes mean that the study of Japanese aesthetics is hopeless or futile? Surely there are enough qualities that repeat through different ages and different aspects of Japanese art and culture to begin to construct a sense of Japaneseness (including the sense of paradox), as long as we are careful not to try to establish ironclad certainties. One of the ways to discover these common (or sometimes uncommon) qualities is through a series of chapters on individual topics as presented in this publication. However, as these generally focus upon early modern and modern Japan, some historical background may serve as a useful starting point. The Introduction identifies many very important hallmarks for the understanding of traditional Japanese aesthetics, and two major themes can be stressed here.

NATURE

Chief among these significant themes is the well-known Japanese love of and respect for nature. This shows in many (if not most) aspects of traditional Japanese life and culture, but perhaps poetry from different periods is one of the best ways to see how it has continued, as well as changing, in the manner it has been expressed by poets through the centuries.

Although the written history of Japan begins with the Asuka (552–645) and Nara (646–794) eras, there are indications of how important nature was to Japan even earlier. One of the first Japanese books, the *Nihon shoki* (*Chronicles of Japan*, completed in 720), contains a number of poems praising nature. According to tradition, an early example is said to have been composed by Emperor Yūryaku (418–479), who reigned from 456 to 479. Its repetitions and rhythmic nature suggest its origins as a song or chant.

> Secluded
> Hatsuse Mountain—
> departing
> this good mountain—
> running forth
> this good mountain—
> secluded
> Hatsuse Mountain—
> ah how beautiful
> ah how beautiful![1]

By the time of Japan's first major poetry collection, the *Man'yōshū* (*Anthology of Ten Thousand Leaves*, compiled after 759), the great majority of the verses were in the *tanka* (also called *waka* and *uta*) five-part format of 5–7–5–7–7 syllables. Some of these are nature poems, whatever their secondary meanings might imply, such as this verse presented to Prince Yuge (?–699):

> Evening seems to have
> deepened to midnight—
> we hear a wild goose
> calling as it flies, while we watch
> the moon crossing the sky

More often, images from nature are directly compared to human feelings, as in this tanka by Lady Kasa (eighth century, active 730's):

Deep in the mountains
sedges grow among the rocks
with deep roots—
the bond between our hearts
I can never forget

During the succeeding Heian period (794–1185), the Imperial Court was thoroughly established not only as the political but also as the cultural center of Japan and direct Chinese influence waned. At this time, the arts became highly developed; for example, not only fine calligraphy but also the ability to compose (and often improvise) verses became important elements in the popularity and status of court noblemen and noblewomen.

Most common during this era of court dominance were tanka that expressed human emotions emphasized by images from nature, as in this verse from the early-eleventh-century novel of Lady Murasaki (ca. 973—ca. 1014), *The Tale of Genji*:

You cannot know
my deepest feeling—
like the water
that seethes over rocks
its color can't be seen

Since the word for color (*iro*) can also mean passion, the emphasis is more upon love than upon nature, not surprising in the hothouse atmosphere of an elaborate court society.

It was monk-poets who somewhat reversed this trend, particularly Saigyō Hōshi (1118–1190), who spent much of his adult life away from urban centers. He experienced the natural world during his travels, such as during a visit to the island of Shikoku in 1168:

Deep in the mountains
the moon shining through
needles of the black pines
has a violent
and frightening power.

This focus on nature was to become stronger in future centuries, but Japan was to experience a major change in the late twelfth century, when the shift of power from court nobles to samurai was beginning to take place. This was to have a notable effect not only in government but also in aesthetics. In terms of poetry, tanka continued to be important, but another form began to take precedence during the warrior-dominated Kamakura (1185–1333) and

Muromachi (1337–1573) eras. Renga, best known as 'linked verse,' had a natural basis, since the tanka form divides easily into two parts consisting of 5–7–5 and 7–7 syllables. Why not have one poet write the first three segments and another follow with the final two, or continue to add 5–7–5 and 7–7 links, with more poets involved in the process? There are a few examples of two-author tanka as early as in the *Man'yōshū*, so this collaborative form was not new, but on a larger scale it was to engage Japan's finest poets during the medieval period.

Perhaps the most fascinating aspect of renga is that the linking sections were not supposed to join easily or obviously, but rather to expand the poem in new directions. When the number of links could reach 100 or even 1,000, the result was a kind of complexity not seen before in Japanese verse. The subject might change, the season might change, and the emotion might change, yet there had to be some sense of continuity—even if this was often obscure without careful attention. Here are four links (with authors indicated) from one of the most famous renga, composed in 1488 and known as 'Three Poets at Minase':

is the remaining moon
still crossing over
this misty night?
(Shōhaku, 1443–1527)

with frost covering the fields
autumn draws to a close
(Sōchō, 1448–1532)

for the cries of insects
having no compassion,
grasses wither
(Sōgi, 1421–1502)

coming to the hedge,
the path has opened up
(Shōhaku)

While all four links suggest the season of autumn, we have moved from the night sky to the fields to insects to a pathway. As the renga continues, the seasons change and nature is presented in multiple ways rather than serving as illustrations of single human emotions. This constituted a distinct change from what tanka offered, and represented a new way to experience the natural world.

However, it was during the succeeding Momoyama (1568–1600) and Edo (1600–1868) eras that the most popular form of Japanese verse developed, now known as 'haiku.' Poets had already noticed that the first part of a renga, the 5–7–5 syllables called *hokku*, could stand alone, and with the name of *haikai* (later to become known as 'haiku'), it came of age as a unique form of verse, especially in the hands of Matsuo Bashō (1644–1694) and his followers. Compared with most tanka, haiku very seldom mention the emotions of the poet; the images, usually from nature, stand alone. This means that the reader becomes more important to the experience of the poem, since in a fine haiku little is stated but much is suggested. A Bashō poem from one of his travel journals, the *Oi no kabumi* (*Knapsack Notebook*, completed in 1691), is a case in point:

> yellow mountain roses,
> are you falling in rhythm?
> the sound of the waterfall

Does Bashō imply that the falling flowers are somehow related to the falling waters? Or are they two nonrelated things? Is this an example of the Buddhist understanding that each and every person and thing is the center of the universe, yet all things are interconnected? Or is the haiku merely recording what the poet could see and hear in nature? A later essay in this volume (Essay 16, Michiko Yusa's "Bashō and the Art of Eternal Now") will explore the paradox of Bashō's being able to express the universal and the momentary simultaneously, but for now we can note that haiku not only eliminates the 7–7 segments of tanka but also avoids the direct statement of human emotions. Yet, while there is no obvious sentiment in this verse, there is certainly a mood captured—one interpretation might be that the falling flowers represent the melancholy of transience while the waterfall suggests continuity. But the potential meanings in each haiku are left for each reader to experience.

Another verse by Bashō from 1691 can also be understood as a specific observation of nature, but through the mind of the poet it goes beyond pure logic:

> winter wind
> through the cedars
> sharpens the rocks

We can sense the bite of the wind in this poem—the chill of winter is never stated, but it becomes clear nonetheless. Within the uniqueness of our own personalities, we can feel what Bashō felt at this moment; the objective becomes subjective.

Like Saigyō, whom he revered, Bashō took many journeys through Japan, and these certainly stimulated his poetic spirit as a result of his profound experience with nature. Later, haiku poets added their unique vision to the genre, but it was Bashō who made haiku into a major form of verse that is now the best known and most practiced form of poetry in the world.

Over the centuries, moving from praise poems about nature to the more emotional tanka, then on to renga, and finally to haiku, Japanese poets have affirmed their attention to and love of nature. The forms of poetic expression have changed along with the historical and social environments, yet tanka, renga, and haiku have all not only survived but also flourished in the modern era. One may still question how well the Japanese attitude toward nature will continue to endure when most people now live cheek by jowl in crowded cities, but since one of the characteristics of the culture, as noted, has been to welcome the new while preserving the old, there is no reason to expect a cosmic change.

ASSIMILATION

A second vital theme in the history of Japanese art and culture has been its paradoxical ability to absorb large amounts of foreign influence and yet maintain its own unique identity. Although isolated geographically as an island nation, Japan has been seemingly transformed several times by other cultures. Yet, it has maintained, at least for most Japanese, a strong sense of identity expressed in the phrase *ware-ware Nihonjin* ('we Japanese') that seems to exclude foreigners from ever fully understanding the unique nature of their homeland.

The first major wave of influence came from China in the sixth and seventh centuries, in large part through Korea, and brought with it new ideas about government, new medicines, new forms of art and architecture, and, above all, Buddhism and a writing system. These must have seemed overwhelming, yet they were not only accepted and developed by the Japanese but also harmonized with native traditions.

That Buddhism from India entered Japan with other aspects of an advanced civilization certainly helped to advance its cause. Its basic teachings were also very powerful in their message of spiritual liberation and they were to inspire many Japanese. Furthermore, Buddhism became amalgamated with age-old Shintō to the extent that deities from one are believed to have their counterparts in the other. To this day, many Japanese take part in Shintō ceremonies throughout their lives while finding it perfectly natural that their funerals will be Buddhist. Walking through the mountains, one is as apt to come across a Shintō shrine as a Buddhist temple. The sense of *kami*, the manifold gods in nature, is Shintō, yet a fine old tree or a waterfall inspires not only respect but often also reverence, whatever the religious beliefs of the viewer.

For these reasons and more, it was not long before the criticism that Buddhism was a foreign religion quickly faded, and it became thoroughly absorbed in Japanese culture. In addition, different sects appealed to different classes of people. For example, the complex doctrines of tantric sects, with their esoteric accoutrements including elaborate mandalas, fascinated many well-educated court nobles. However, the most popular form eventually came to be Pure Land Buddhism, where the sincere recital of the short mantra *Namu Amida Butsu* ('Praise to Amida Buddha') could ensure rebirth in his Western Paradise. Paintings of Amida descending to take the dying believer's soul up to the heavens conveyed a sense of wonder and compassion that appealed to many Japanese in all stations of life.

The other most significant element brought to Japan in this first wave of outside influence was the Chinese writing system, although it did not fit the Japanese language well at all. With every Chinese word a monosyllable, a single character (or combination of two characters) for each word was sufficient, even though this meant that one had to learn several thousand characters to become educated. Japanese, however, features a variety of extended word endings, particularly in verbs and adjectives, and these became a problem to notate. At first, one Chinese character would be used for the basic verbal stem, and other characters would be added just for their sounds. This was extraordinarily cumbersome, and to know which characters represented meanings and which were merely sounds was difficult. Nevertheless, since this was the only system the Japanese had seen, they used it until something better was devised. The *Man'yōshū* was first written this way and this form of writing Japanese is still called *man'yōgana*. Eventually, in the process of assimilation, a simplified system of shapes (originally derived from Chinese characters) was devised, and written Japanese became a combination of Chinese characters and Japanese syllabic forms called *kana*.

Writing is a notable example of how the Japanese have been able to borrow something from another culture and make it their own, but the respect for Chinese culture remained. At the Heian court, while learning Chinese was not considered appropriate for ladies, many noblemen wrote poems in classical Chinese, a trend that would continue for more than a thousand years. Around the year 1013, a collection called the *Wakan rōei shū* (*Japanese and Chinese Poems to Sing*) was compiled that featured Chinese verses by both Chinese and Japanese masters, as well as Japanese tanka. Whichever the language and poetic style, elements of nature were almost always included, as in this Chinese poem by Minamoto no Shitagō (911–983) as translated by Jonathan Chaves:

> Following the wind, the falling blossoms
> carry soughing sounds;
> frothing against rocks, the plunging falls
> play their lovely lute.[2]

It may seem surprising, but writing poems in Chinese became a Japanese thing to do, especially when a second major wave of Chinese influence came to Japan during the twelfth and thirteenth centuries. Along with some elements of literati culture, this wave brought Zen Buddhism, which was to have a notable cultural impact, perhaps greater than it ever had in China. In addition to its religious effect, Zen brought an increased interest in composing poems in Chinese, which still continues among Zen masters today. As temples were often built deep in the mountains, the sense of nature in these poems is typically very powerful, especially when compared with the Japanese poems of court nobles in earlier centuries.

One of the most remarkable of Japanese Zen masters during this age was Ikkyū Sōjun (1394–1481), who included wine shops and brothels as subject matter in his poems. His sense of his own spirit going beyond life in a temple is expressed in the following Chinese-style quatrain:

> *Straw Coat and Hat*
> Woodcutters and fishermen have everything they need;
> What use have I for the carved chairs and wooden floors of Zen?
> With straw sandals and a wooden hat, I roam three thousand worlds,
> Dwelling in water, subsisting on wind for twenty years.[3]

Comparing Ikkyū's verses in Chinese and Japanese, one finds a somewhat similar idea expressed in paradoxical Zen fashion in one of his tanka:

> In the well not yet dug
> on the water not yet gathered
> there are ripples—
> the man without a shadow
> scoops it up[4]

Both of these poems show Ikkyū as a Zen teacher expressing a heightened state of consciousness, but what are the differences here? First, we can see in the tanka form the Japanese preference for asymmetry, as opposed to the four balanced lines of Chinese. Second, the Japanese poem invokes nature more specifically and directly, even if its meaning lies beyond the everyday world. Third, the tanka presents its subject evocatively, rather than stating its theme as directly as does the quatrain.

A third wave of Chinese influence came, paradoxically, when Japan closed itself almost entirely to the outside world; only the Port of Nagasaki was open to Chinese traders and a small island was reserved for a few Dutch merchants. Nevertheless, starting in 1600, the Tokugawa Shogunate gradually shifted its governmental and cultural focus from Zen to Neo-Confucianism, emphasizing loyalty to the government. This brought about an educational system by scholars who had to be well-versed in Chinese. As on the mainland, these scholars often took up the arts as a means of self-cultivation and self-expression, leading to the literati (*bunjin*) movement that is discussed in a later chapter in this volume—chapter 17, Cheryl Crowley's "Knowing Elegance: The Ideals of the *Bunjin* (Literatus) in Early Modern Haikai."

Many literati wrote poems as well as calligraphy in Chinese. One of the most remarkable of these *bunjin* was Uragami Gyokudō (1745–1820). Not only a poet, painter, and calligrapher, he was also a musician and composer on the Chinese seven-string zither *qin* (Japanese: *kin*), a quiet instrument more suited for contemplation than for public performances. Midway through his life, Gyokudō gave up his hereditary position as a samurai-official to wander through Japan with his *qin* and brushes. His paintings and calligraphy, mostly ignored during his lifetime, are now highly treasured in Japan. His poetry, however, is currently little-known, despite his having published two volumes in the 1790s. Two of his Chinese quatrains express what he has seen, much like haiku, without a direct statement of the poet's emotions. First quatrain:

> The rain clears, surging mountain peaks seem gathered like a kingfisher's plume,
> Fishing boats are moored in a reedy inlet;
> A covey of birds flies past, the waves become still,
> My eyes accompany slanting sunbeams to the half-severed mountains.[5]

Second quatrain (entitled 'Spring Evening Moonlight'):

> The dew shines in the moonbeams,
> Whitening lakeside reeds and mountains;
> A single bird kicks a flower into flight,
> And two or three petals fall to the ground.[6]

A different poet might have made several haiku of these images such as:

> A covey of birds
> flies past—
> the waves become still.[7]

And:

> A single bird
> kicks a flower into flight—
> two or three petals fall.[8]

Gyokudō had certainly assimilated the forms and style of Chinese poetry, yet one might consider that his creative impulse is not dissimilar to the aesthetics of Japanese verse.

CONCLUSION

We have seen through the medium of poetry how over the course of many centuries the Japanese were able to continue to express their strong ties to nature while absorbing three waves of influence from abroad. The fourth wave, of course, has been that of the West since 1868. Of all Asian countries, Japan was the most rapid and successful in responding to the new challenges, becoming a world power within a few decades. This was possible, one may well speculate, because of its history of accepting and transforming new cultural and political elements from abroad without losing sight of its own heritage. Not that this has always been easy; in the later nineteenth century, there were many disputes and even a brief rebellion against the new internationalizing trends. To this day, there remain a number of cultural paradoxes as noted earlier, for example, in the field of poetry, where the new popularity of free verse has not supplanted haiku or tanka; they exist independently.

Perhaps the Japanese have been able to deal with seeming opposites because of their sense of what is appropriate in any situation. One would drink sake rather than whiskey at a sushi counter, while a steak house will serve Western drinks. A scroll painting is appropriate in an alcove, but an oil painting is considered more suited to a wall above a chair. Nevertheless, the history of Japanese culture in the past one and a half millennia has been that of dealing with the significant changes, with their inevitable tensions, that have been taking place. The chapters that follow in this volume are welcome explorations of many different facets of Japanese aesthetics, a field of study that can illuminate both the age-old traditions and the new international elements that coexist in the island nation.

NOTES

1. All translations are by the author unless otherwise indicated.
2. *Japanese and Chinese Poems to Sing: The Wakan Rōei Shū*, ed. and trans. J. Thomas Rimer and Jonathan Chaves, with contributions by Jin'ichi Konishi, Stephen Addiss, and Ann Yonemura (New York: Columbia University Press, 1997), 101.
3. *Zen Sourcebook: Traditional Documents from China, Korea, and Japan*, ed. Stephen Addiss, Stanley Lombardo, and Judith Roitman (Indianapolis, IN: Hackett, 2008), 200.
4. Ibid., 203.
5. Stephen Addiss, *Tall Mountains and Flowing Waters: The Arts of Uragami Gyokudō* (Honolulu: University of Hawai'i Press, 1987), 54.
6. Ibid., 55.
7. Ibid., 54.
8. Ibid., 55.

Preface

What is the Japanese notion of elegance and how does it manifest itself in Japanese life and culture? Does Japanese aesthetics suggest important ways in which aesthetic experiences and activities help to cultivate a moral sensibility in both the practitioners and the appreciators? Why do Japanese writers and filmmakers return to classical aesthetics to cope with the horrors of the post-nuclear age? What is the aesthetic vision of the eminent Japanese philosopher and poet Kuki Shūzō (1888–1941)? Four papers devoted to the above topics were presented at the 108th Annual Meeting of the American Philosophical Association (APA)'s Eastern Division in Washington, DC on December 29, 2011. The three-hour session, entitled 'Japanese Aesthetics,' took place in the main program under the auspices of the APA Committee on the Status of Asian and Asian-American Philosophers and Philosophies. Widely published and respected in the field, the speakers included Peter Leech (University of Otago, New Zealand), Mara Miller (Independent Scholar and Artistic Consultant, United States), Yuriko Saito (Rhode Island School of Design, United States), and Barbara Sandrisser (Architectural and Environmental Aesthetics, Inc., United States). As a committee member with an abiding interest in both aesthetics and Japanese philosophy, I organized and chaired the session and wrote a report for the committee's newsletter—A. Minh Nguyen, "Report on 'Japanese Aesthetics,'" *APA Newsletter on Asian and Asian-American Philosophers and Philosophies* 12, no. 1 (2012): 1–6.

The session was well-attended and the response was positive. After the session, Jana Hodges-Kluck, an editor at Lexington Books (an imprint of Rowman & Littlefield), and I met over coffee at the APA Meeting and brainstormed strategies for developing an edited collection of new essays in Japanese aesthetics. With enthusiasm, she urged me to submit a formal proposal for such a collection and the rest is history.

This collection of twenty-seven new essays by an international panel of experts, with a foreword by Stephen Addiss and a collaborative comprehensive introduction, aims to present high-quality contemporary reflections on Japanese aesthetics. The collection aims to appeal not only to humanities scholars but also to graduate and undergraduate students of Japanese aesthetics, philosophy, arts, literature, culture, and civilization. It attempts not only to advance research but also to serve as a resource for the classroom. Since these wide-ranging essays articulate the contributors' Japanese-aesthetical concerns and their application to Japanese arts (including literature, theater, film, drawing, painting, calligraphy, ceramics, crafts, music, fashion, comics, cooking, packaging, gardening, landscape architecture, flower arrangement, the martial arts, and the tea ceremony), I also foresee its usefulness to non-academic professionals and general audiences.

Presenting twenty-first-century multidisciplinary and interdisciplinary perspectives on Japanese aesthetics, the collection variously complements, challenges, and expands upon previous studies in the field. Such studies include but are not limited to the following: Nancy G. Hume, ed., *Japanese Aesthetics and Culture: A Reader* (Albany, NY: State University of New York Press, 1995); Michael F. Marra, trans. and ed., *A History of Modern Japanese Aesthetics* (Honolulu: University of Hawai'i Press, 2001); Michael F. Marra, ed., *Japanese Hermeneutics: Current Debates on Aesthetics and Interpretation* (Honolulu: University of Hawai'i Press, 2002); and Michele Marra, trans. and ed., *Modern Japanese Aesthetics: A Reader* (Honolulu: University of Hawai'i Press, 1999). While each has its own virtues—for instance, Hume's edited collection contains notes on historical periods and language, a glossary of the major literary and aesthetic terms, and an extensive, annotated bibliography that guides the reader to various materials, ranging from primary sources and critical studies to lists of films and audiovisual works—none of the above collections includes essays published after 2002. Indeed, since the 2002 collection features revised versions of papers originally presented at a conference at the University of California, Los Angeles (UCLA) in 1998, it hardly reflects twenty-first-century multidisciplinary and interdisciplinary perspectives on Japanese aesthetics.

As volume editor, my primary responsibility consisted in soliciting submissions from around the world and ensuring quality and consistency throughout the manuscript. This dual task entailed recruiting topnotch contributors, commenting on draft chapters, asking contributors to make content revisions, and grouping the chapters into thematic categories to allow for a rich interplay and cross-fertilization. Two additional tasks needed to be performed: providing an introduction that puts the twenty-seven essays into context and creating an index for the book after receiving the typeset pages from the publisher.

In editing this collection, I made a number of style choices mostly out of respect for the contributors' personal and professional preferences.

Such preferences had led different contributors to use different terms and different spellings to refer to the same entities, hence some apparent inconsistencies across chapters. Not only terms and spellings vary from contributor to contributor and thus from chapter to chapter, but the use of diacritical marks, italics, and capital letters, as well as title capitalization (especially in the case of citation), also varies. For instance: nō, *nō*, noh, *noh*, Nō, *Nō*, Noh, *Noh*; and *Tōkyō Monogatari*, *Tōkyō monogatari*. For Japanese names, I generally follow the practice of placing the last name (family name) first and the first name (given name) last.

During the last six years, teaching and administrative work prevented me from giving my undivided attention to research for any extended period. I could not have completed the manuscript, therefore, without the generous support of the following individuals and organizations: each and every one of the four members of the APA panel on Japanese aesthetics—Peter Leech, Mara Miller, Yuriko Saito, and Barbara Sandrisser (regrettably, Barbara could not contribute her essay on elegance to the present volume because of contractual obligations); each and every one of the twenty-seven essay authors and coauthors, who contributed not only full essays but also extended abstracts, the latter of which "New Contributions to Japanese Aesthetics," the second part of the introduction to this volume, is based on, adapted from, or inspired by (to avoid an unwieldy number of references to the twenty-seven unpublished abstracts in this introductory essay, I have taken the liberty of paraphrasing or using verbatim a significant number of phrases and sentences without placing them in quotation marks and without further attribution, because the chapter and abstract contributors are coauthors of the essay); Yuriko Saito for contributing "Historical Overview of Japanese Aesthetics," the first part of the introduction; Oxford University Press and Michael Kelly, editor-in-chief of the magisterial *Encyclopedia of Aesthetics*, for granting Yuriko and me the permission to use as part of the introduction her significantly revised and updated entry on Japanese aesthetics, which appears in the second (2014) edition of the encyclopedia; Stephen Addiss for coming out of retirement to contribute the foreword and for allowing us to use his original artwork for the cover; the Office of the Provost, the College of Arts and Sciences, University Programs, and the Honors Program at Eastern Kentucky University (EKU), and the Bluegrass State Intelligence Community Center of Academic Excellence, a partnership among EKU, Kentucky State University, and Morehead State University, for a number of faculty research and development grants; David Coleman, director of the EKU Honors Program, for fulfilling some of my duties as associate director in the summers of 2015 and 2016 so that I could complete the manuscript and deliver it to the publisher on time; David Coleman and Sara Zeigler, formerly dean of University Programs at EKU, now dean of the EKU College of Letters, Arts, and Social Sciences, for sponsoring my Salzburg Global Fellowship in July 2015 at Schloss Leopoldskron, a majestic and serene eighteenth-century castle located on the outskirts of Salzburg, Austria, where part of the manuscript was completed—many thanks to Jochen Fried, Astrid Schroeder, and other staff members of the Salzburg Global Seminar for their extraordinary hospitality; my colleagues and friends in the Department of Philosophy and Religion, the Asian Studies Program, and the Honors Program at EKU, especially Patrick Puckett and Abraham Velez, for their concrete assistance and guidance; Jana Hodges-Kluck for giving me a chance to do the book and guiding me every step of the way, and other members of the editorial staff and the production staff at Rowman & Littlefield (Jayanthi Chander, Liz Garvin, Natalie Mandziuk, Megan Murray, Della Vache, Kari Waters, and Rachel Weydert) for their extraordinary courtesy and professionalism—their patience and good cheer through numerous deadline extensions are gratefully acknowledged; my dear friends and editorial consultants—Nhi Huynh, Erik Liddell, Arie May, Nicole Wells, Ogechi Anyanwu, Sandy Goldberg, Peter Leech, Lauren McCord, Hiroshi Nara, Patrick Puckett, Meera Viswanathan, and Abraham Velez—the first four of whom read and commented on the entire manuscript (some essays several times), offering unfailingly wise suggestions for improvement; and Nhi Huynh, Hoa Huynh, and Lauren McCord for helping me prepare the index. I am forever indebted to my parents, brothers, and sisters for their unbounded love. That they support me for anything I do and take pride in whatever I achieve helps bring out the best in me. Finally, I would like to thank my wife, Nhi, and our daughters, Cynthia and Vivian, for their constant support and encouragement. For two peripatetic decades that included spells in New York, New Jersey, Georgia, and Kentucky, they taught me much about beauty matters and, more importantly, life matters. To them I dedicate this book with joy, gratitude, and love.

A. Minh Nguyen
Richmond, Kentucky
December 2017

Introduction

This introduction comprises two essays on the artistic and aesthetic traditions of Japan: "Historical Overview of Japanese Aesthetics" and "New Contributions to Japanese Aesthetics." The first surveys the history of Japanese aesthetics and the ways in which it is similar to and different from Western aesthetics. The second introduces the contributions to this book. "Historical Overview of Japanese Aesthetics" derives from a significantly revised and updated version of Yuriko Saito, "Japanese Aesthetics: Historical Overview," in *Encyclopedia of Aesthetics*, vol. 2, ed. Michael Kelly (New York: Oxford University Press, 1998), 545–53. Used here by permission of the author and the publisher, Saito's updated and expanded entry on Japanese aesthetics appears on pages 4–12 of volume 4 of the second edition of *Encyclopedia of Aesthetics* (2014), also edited by Michael Kelly and published by Oxford University Press. "New Contributions to Japanese Aesthetics" is based on, adapted from, or inspired by the extended abstracts submitted. A genuinely collaborative effort, it blends the various pieces that the contributors drafted. To avoid an unwieldy number of references to the twenty-seven unpublished abstracts in this introductory essay, the editor has taken the liberty of paraphrasing or using verbatim a significant number of phrases and sentences without placing them in quotation marks and without further attribution, because the chapter and abstract contributors are coauthors of the essay. The editor would like to thank Yuriko Saito and each and every one of the chapter contributors for their decisive contributions to the introduction. He would also like to thank Nhi Huynh, Erik Liddell, Arie May, Patrick Puckett, Abraham Velez, and Nicole Wells for their helpful comments and suggestions. All errors are his own.

HISTORICAL OVERVIEW OF JAPANESE AESTHETICS

Yuriko Saito

The aesthetic traditions of Japan have been established over its long history. The process of Westernization began in the late nineteenth century, and Japan has rapidly transformed itself into an industrialized, technologically advanced culture. It may appear that the traditional (i.e., pre-Westernized) Japanese aesthetic ideas, values, and practices have all but disappeared amidst the skyscrapers and high-tech industries. The indigenous Japanese aesthetic sensibility still exists, however, not only in classical art forms such as the tea ceremony, Nō drama, and haiku, but also in daily activities such as packaging, cooking, and even etiquette. While Japanese aesthetics by no means designates a uniform development, several common themes persist throughout its diverse historical and artistic manifestations. Such themes, discussed here, together comprise what may be termed a uniquely or characteristically Japanese aesthetic tradition.

For the Japanese authors' names, we will follow the practice of placing the last name first and the first name last except when citing their writings in English. We will also observe the custom of referring to classical Japanese authors by their given names rather than by their family names when not stating their full names. For instance, Yoshida Kenkō will hereafter be Kenkō.

AESTHETIC EGALITARIANISM

Perhaps the most prominent aspect of Japanese aesthetics is that aesthetic concern affects every area of people's lives. Both in producing and in appreciating, the object of an aesthetic experience is not limited to what are generally referred to as 'the fine arts' such as painting, music, and literature. Other objects and phenomena, whether made by human beings or natural, are equally celebrated for giving rise to rewarding aesthetic experiences in the Japanese tradition. So are numerous daily practices such as cooking, bathing, and gift wrapping, as well as physical exercises such as archery and swordsmanship. Instead of comprising a special realm divorced from everyday life, aesthetic matters are thoroughly integrated into Japanese life, past and present.

This inclusivity, which may be called aesthetic egalitarianism, extends further. The Japanese tradition does not make the Western distinction between the so-called higher and lower senses, the former generally considered as more legitimate vehicles for conveying aesthetic values. A typical aesthetic experience, according to the Japanese tradition, engages several senses, which together inform the aesthetic value.

The best example of such an experience that does not privilege any particular realm or sense can be found in an artistic medium unique to Japan: the tea ceremony. Established during the sixteenth century, this art form elevates the otherwise mundane activities of serving and drinking tea and eating snacks to a ritualized event. No limit is set on what can become its aesthetic content. Participants are encouraged to attend not only to the tea itself but also to the surrounding environment—the garden, tea hut, privy, and weather, as well as objects such as the tea bowl, flowers, the scroll decorating the alcove, and various utensils for making the tea. Equally important are the host's elegant and seamless bodily movements in preparing and serving the tea, as well as the content of the conversation that ensues spontaneously among the guests.

Furthermore, the participant's experience of each item engages several different senses. For example, the entire body is engaged in walking through the garden, kneeling to cleanse one's hands and mouth in the water basin, crawling into the tea hut through a small entrance, taking one's seat, and lifting the tea bowl. The activity of drinking tea itself involves not only the senses of taste and smell, but also the sound of slurping, the tactile sensations of the bowl's surface texture and the warmth of its contents, as well as its visual effect. The tea hut is also appreciated for its visual and spatial factors, the sound of the water boiling and the leaves rustling in the garden, and the tactile sensations of the wood grain and the weave of the straw mat against one's feet. These elements are valued all the more because of the awareness, encouraged by the philosophy behind this art form, that this specific occasion will never repeat itself. It is literally a once-in-a-lifetime event (*ichigo ichie*).

While the tea ceremony is an explicitly participatory art form, many other Japanese aesthetic activities both entice and challenge. The preferred mode of indirect communication and artistic minimalism (to be explained later) requires that the audience take an active role in facilitating an aesthetic experience.

Several factors, both religious and historical, have contributed to this egalitarianism. Chronologically, the first contribution can be traced to the indigenous Japanese religion, Shintō, according to which the dynamic, ever-changing spirit, *kami*, resides in every natural object. Neither an abstract entity nor an entity existing in the other world, deity is always embodied in concrete objects. This world is viewed as constituting reality itself rather than as a faint shadow or a veil covering reality that transcends this world. The consecration of objects making up this world, nature in particular, provided the foundation for the subsequent Japanese tendency to find aesthetic value in everything. The Shintō worldview also determined the decidedly "this-worldly" characteristic of Japanese representational art. While some Japanese paintings do depict otherworldly mandalas and other symbols associated with the esoteric Buddhist metaphysical worldview, the subject matter of Japanese art is predominantly nature—landscapes, flowers, and animals. Similarly, Japanese literary works generally shun abstract metaphysical speculations and instead deal primarily with concrete objects and events.

This attention to every aspect of experience became firmly established among the nobility during the Heian court period (794–1185), thus setting the standard for cultural sophistication. Supported by landed wealth, the Heian aristocracy could afford to indulge in cultivating sensibility through literature, calligraphy, nature appreciation, music, fashion, courtship ritual, and even incense connoisseurship. In courtship ritual, consisting primarily of exchanging poems, aesthetic sophistication was regarded as the sole criterion for one's worthiness as a lover, as a cultured person, and sometimes even as an ethical individual. The relevant considerations included not only the poem itself and its sensitivity to the season, the weather, and the occasion, but also the calligraphy, the selection of paper, the attachment of a flower or a twig suitable for the poem, and the appropriate fragrance of incense.

Although these specific rituals did not survive beyond the Heian period, this legacy of the keen sensitivity to every aspect of an object or phenomenon has persisted throughout Japanese history. It was first embraced by the warriors who seized political power after the decline of the Heian aristocracy. Commoners by birth, these warriors made a conscious effort to emulate the cultural accomplishments of the aristocrats by training themselves in the arts in addition to their military pursuits. It was under their patronage that many Japanese art forms, such as the tea ceremony, Nō theater, screen painting, architecture, and gardening, flourished.

The spiritual foundation for the medieval warriors' preoccupation with culture and the arts was Zen Buddhism, introduced from China to Japan toward the end of the twelfth century. The warriors embraced Zen Buddhism primarily for its teaching on mental and physical discipline, a requirement for a successful military career, as well as for its accompanying cultural and artistic sophistication. It was Zen metaphysics that furthered aesthetic egalitarianism. Zen metaphysics consists of transcending ordinary discriminations and categorizations in its enlightened experience of the ultimate reality, Buddha-nature. All objects and phenomena are rendered equally real, valuable, and worthy of appreciation simply by virtue of "being such" or "being thus." The commonly held distinctions between sentient and nonsentient, noble and ignoble, valuable and unvaluable are overcome by a thoroughgoing Zen egalitarianism, resulting in the absolute affirmation of the facticity of everything. The thirteenth-century Zen priest Dōgen (1200–1253) thus describes the ubiquity of Buddha-nature by referring to a donkey's jaw, a horse's mouth, the sound of breaking wind, and the smell of excrement, as well as by pointing to grasses, trees, mountains, and streams.

This uncompromising Zen commitment to appreciating the "thusness" of everything is manifested in several Zen-inspired art forms. For example, Matsuo Bashō (1644–1694), the most noted haiku master, sometimes took animals' bodily functions, fleas, and lice as his subject matter and elevated them to aesthetic heights. Similarly, a superb garden design is created by arranging otherwise ordinary rocks and pebbles or by reusing "found objects" such as discarded millstones and abandoned temple foundations in the construction of stepping stones. The same observation can be made regarding flower arrangement, an art form that predates the introduction of Zen Buddhism but one to which Zen subsequently gave a theoretical foundation. The materials for arrangement need not be opulent flowers; in fact, withered twigs or branches with simple, unassuming flowers are often favored.

By the time the common townsfolk started commissioning or supporting popular arts such as Kabuki theater, woodblock prints, and genre literature during the Edo period (1600–1868), aesthetic sensitivity to every aspect of daily life had become entrenched in all segments of Japanese society. This prevalence of the aesthetic sensitivity and its integration with life continue even today amidst the thoroughly modernized, high-tech life. In addition to participating in traditional arts such as the tea ceremony, flower arrangement, and calligraphy, contemporary Japanese lives are still permeated by aesthetic concerns. Seasonal haiku are featured on the front page of major newspapers; both at home and in restaurants, food is carefully arranged on a plate specifically chosen to suit both the food and the season; a package is meticulously wrapped with the appropriate material; and even business letters invariably contain some reference to the beauty of the season.

The possibility of aestheticizing every object and phenomenon, however, raises a question about the feasibility of any criteria for aesthetic value. If anything whatsoever can provide an aesthetic experience, what makes some qualities aesthetically more positive than others? What are some specific aesthetic values, according to Japanese aesthetics?

THE AESTHETICS OF IMPLICATION, SUGGESTION, IMPERFECTION

One such set of criteria of aesthetic value in the Japanese tradition is given by a cluster of concepts: *yojō* (emotional aftertaste in poetry), *wabi* (the beauty of poverty in the tea ceremony), *sabi* (lonely beauty in haiku), and *yūgen* (mystery and depth, primarily in Nō theater).

Yojō refers to the quality of a poem in which the words do not fully reveal the emotion that the poet is trying to express. Frequently likened to the moon hidden behind clouds or autumnal mountain scenery shrouded in mist, this suggestion of lingering emotion through understatement is used as the evaluative criterion for the aesthetic value of a poem.

Landscape imagery also appears in the definition of *wabi* given by tea masters. Takeno Jōō (1502–1555), for example, cites the following poem by Fujiwara no Teika (1162–1241) for illustrating *wabi:*

> Looking about
> Neither flowers
> Nor scarlet leaves
> A bayside reed hovel
> In the autumn dusk.

A little later, Sen no Rikyū (1522–1591) refers to a poem by another poet, Fujiwara no Ietaka (1158–1237), for the same purpose:

> To those who wait
> Only for flowers
> Show them a spring
> Of grass amid the snow
> In a mountain village.

Both poems depict rather desolate and colorless landscapes in contrast to a more typical autumnal landscape with its brilliantly colored leaves or a spring landscape with the lustrous pink of cherry blossoms.

Although applicable to poetry, *yūgen* was primarily developed as the aesthetic ideal for Nō theater by Zeami (also spelled Seami) Motokiyo (1363–1443), as well as for linked verse *(renga)* by the poet-monk Shinkei (1406–1475). The Nō theater consists of a small number of actors, at least one of whom wears a mask, conveying a relatively well-known story of historical figures or supernatural events through minimal, stylized, and usually slow body movements. The drama takes place on a sparse stage with few props, accompanied by both instrumentalists and singers seated on the stage. Linked verse, no longer practiced today, started out as a kind of parlor game involving a number of people, and later developed into an art medium, becoming a precursor of haiku. Each participant takes turns improvising a short verse that builds on the verse made by the previous person by maintaining some continuity of imagery while introducing a new element.

According to Zeami, *yūgen* is the highest and most ineffable beauty achievable in a Nō play, which is illustrated by, among other things, a lonely snowless peak amidst many snow-clad mountain tops and a silver bowl filled with snow, suggesting chillingly exquisite and severe beauty achieved without opulence. Shinkei gives examples of the glimpse of the moon through clouds as well as a single white blossom amidst bamboo, reminding us of both *yojō* and *wabi*.

Derived from both *sabishi* (loneliness) and *sabi* (rust), *sabi* refers to the austere, stark, and rustic atmosphere conjured up primarily in haiku, but also in other literary expressions, the tea ceremony, and Nō theater. Because of its association with rust, it also refers to agedness.

Although initially put forward to describe the genre-specific aesthetic value, these concepts subsequently became more widely applicable. Merging with one another, they indicate some uniform preferences that characterize the Japanese aesthetic tradition. First, they all favor artistic minimalism. For example, the two most celebrated poetic forms in Japanese literature are extremely short: tanka and haiku, which are 5–7–5–7–7- and 5–7–5-syllable verses, respectively. Their brevity both necessitated and encouraged the expression of the poetic content through implication and suggestion. An explicit and comprehensive account is neither possible nor desirable. Similarly, the Nō play conveys deep and rich emotions through restricted body movements, subtle tilts of the mask, a sparsely set stage, and the monotonous, drone-like chanting of the chorus. As for rock gardens and brush ink paintings, they avoid colorfulness and consist of monochrome shading. Their respective spaces are filled with only minimal elements, although their empty spaces are as significant and fertile in expressive power as their filled spaces. Some ink paintings, by Zen priests in particular, consist of only a circle. As mentioned previously, flower arrangement shuns showy bouquets of flowers, instead favoring sparse elements such as a single branch. Finally, while affording multisensory aesthetic experiences through various elements, everything about the tea ceremony underscores simplicity, from the tea hut to the utensils, from the tea bowls to the food accompanying the tea.

The taste for minimalism gives rise to a further preference for indirect communication. This standard was established in the first work of Japanese literary criticism, the Preface to the *Kokin Wakashū* (*Anthology of Ancient and Modern Japanese Poems*), commonly abbreviated as *Kokinshū*, compiled in 905. Its editor, Ki no Tsurayuki (868?–945?), claims that, in a good poem, the emotive content is conveyed in terms of or by way of nature, evoking a certain mood or atmosphere. A straightforward outpouring of feelings and ideas, while it may provide optimal, unambiguous communication, is considered crude and uncouth, hence aesthetically undesirable. Indeed, such directness is still considered aesthetically and even ethically inferior in Japanese discourse, which consistently prefers implication, allusion, and innuendo.

When applied to the visual realm, this preference for suggestion and implication results in appreciating things that are hidden or obscured, rather than fully exposed. If the optimal view of the moon requires a clear sky and unobstructed view, the moon's beauty is heightened by a cloud covering it or a tree blocking its view. Similarly, the allure of distant mountains is enhanced by mist. Hence, when constructing a garden for strolling, one should not make a scenic view visible all at once; rather, the view should be partly hidden, inviting the stroller to follow the path, which will provide a succession of unfolding scenes. This aesthetic sensibility is also manifested in the Japanese fondness for wrapping gifts or packaging objects. Inordinate aesthetic considerations go into engaging people's senses in unwrapping a package one layer at a time.

The historical root of this preference for implied or hidden things can again be traced in part to the Heian sensibility that was developed for courtship ritual. At the initiation of the courtship, the lady is always situated inside a room adjacent to an open veranda with a shade or curtain drawn in-between. This arrangement gives the suitor a glimpse of the bottom of the lady's many-layered kimono peeking out beneath the curtain, a glimpse that is sufficient to display her taste and pique his interest. What began as a means of seduction subsequently became a norm that favors implication and obscurity.

The reason for this preference is the stimulation of the imagination. Implication, obscurity, and hiddenness are considered more attractive than a straightforward expression or unhindered view, because a certain mysteriousness on the surface entices further exploration by engaging the subject's imagination. Appreciation is based not only on what is said or seen, but also on what is not said or not seen, as well as on the manner in which the two are contrasted.

The allure of implication and obscurity, together with artistic minimalism, poses a challenge to the recipient of the aesthetic experience. On the one hand, it is demanded that one be satisfied with whatever is given, no matter how seemingly incomplete or insufficient it may be. On the other hand, participation and the engagement of one's imagination are required to complete the experience. One needs to feel the intense emotion suggested by the subtle tilt of a Nō mask, to explore fully and appreciate the poetic content only hinted at by a poet, and to celebrate the essence of a specific season represented by a single branch in a vase.

Another aspect of the aesthetic preference stemming from *wabi, sabi,* and *yūgen* is the celebration of objects or phenomena falling short of their optimal condition, things not normally appreciated because of their failure to entertain us with opulence or perfection. If cherry blossoms are in prime condition at full bloom, their aesthetic value is increased when they are in decline, that is, when they start falling. If a perfect tea bowl consists of an unblemished surface, a regular contour, and an orderly pattern, an even higher aesthetic value is accorded a chipped, cracked, or discolored surface, an irregular shape, or a disorderly pattern brought about either by accident, by aging, or by design. The tea masters' pursuit of this studied imperfection extends to other implements used in the tea ceremony. One master is said to have replaced the luxurious cloth framing of a scroll painting with shabby material, while another is known for having intentionally broken off the handle of a flower vase. Finally, many other Japanese objects are made with materials that age gracefully. Unpainted wood is used in architecture to show prominent grain resulting from use and weathering, clay pottery exhibits crackles with repeated handling, and lacquerware reveals its inner layer of a different color when rubbing wears off the surface lacquer.

The appreciation of the aged and the imperfect is again a legacy of Zen philosophy. Aging and accident, universal circumstances governing both objects and human beings, are not cause for lamentation but rather are fully embraced in Zen because every state of an entity, including its decline and destruction, expresses its thusness. What started out as paying equal homage to those aesthetic values normally unappreciated or underappreciated has led to an overcorrection of the common tendency and subsequently resulted in an undervaluation of the more popular aesthetic values.

This emphasis on appreciating the defective and the decayed underscores the prevalence of what it sets out to overcome: the preference for beautiful objects in perfect condition. This contrast in taste gave rise to one of the few debates in the Japanese aesthetic tradition. On one side are the advocates for the more challenging aesthetic qualities of impoverishment, obscurity, and agedness, represented most notably by Yoshida Kenkō (1283–1350), a Buddhist monk whose collection of essays entitled *Tsurezuregusa* (*Essays in Idleness*, c. 1330) is often regarded as the manifesto of this viewpoint. In discussing the beauty of falling cherry blossoms and the moon hidden by clouds, Kenkō contrasts such aesthetic appreciations with a more prevalent and "natural" sentiment of people who "commonly regret that the cherry blossoms scatter or that the moon sinks in the sky," and he claims that a person who derives only a negative aesthetic experience from such a situation is "exceptionally insensitive." While recognized as natural and prevalent, the penchant for opulence and perfection is criticized as the taste of the uneducated, unsophisticated common folk. Connoisseurs, according to the advocates of *wabi* aesthetics, will not give in to such easy attractions; a refined and cultivated sensitivity is required for appreciating what may be regarded as the more challenging aesthetic values.

Several centuries later, however, a noted philologist and literary critic, Motoori Norinaga (1730–1801), criticizes the sensibility advocated by Kenkō and his followers. Kenkō's view, writes Norinaga, "does not accord with human feelings but is a fabricated aesthetic taste formed in the impertinent mind of a man ... What that monk said can be described ... as contrived only to make what does not accord with human wishes a refined taste."

Despite their opposing conclusions, both Kenkō and Norinaga seem to agree that it is more "natural" for humans to long for clarity, perfection, and abundance. The aesthetics of imperfection, desolation, and agedness advocates transforming what would normally be a disappointing experience, such as viewing an obscured moon or a shabby scroll, into a positive experience. The appreciation of the imperfect can then be interpreted as an end product of a dialectic movement, a resolution to the disappointment or dissatisfaction in the ordinary context. But why challenge the "natural" aesthetic attraction and advocate what may be considered a subversive aesthetics? Is it simply to exercise one's imagination more?

This aesthetic preference for the obscured, imperfect, and insufficient presupposes certain cultural and economic conditions. For example, the possibility and effectiveness of indirect expression require a background of culturally shared allusions and associations, such as cherry blossoms symbolizing transience and elegance and an autumn dusk evoking desolation and loneliness. The appreciation of an object not altogether visible is based on the possibility of an unobstructed view of the object, such as the moon not covered by clouds. Otherwise, the experience will simply result in frustration and disappointment.

The aesthetics of *wabi* similarly presupposes a ready access to beautiful and expensive objects; it is an aesthetics born out of wealth and privilege. Powerful and wealthy, the advocates of *wabi* aesthetics, ranging from shoguns to tea masters, could afford to emulate the impoverished appearance of peasant life by creating rustic tea huts with stark interiors and ordinary, sometimes defective, tea bowls. For poor peasants who had no choice but to make do with such objects, the look of poverty would only symbolize an ever-unrequited longing. The Japanese penchant for simplicity and insufficiency was thus cultivated as part of an elite aesthetics, first by the aristocracy, then by the warrior class. Both groups were educated in the arts and shared a cultural literacy; at the same time, they were wealthy and powerful enough to indulge in the "fabricated" and "contrived" appearance of imperfection and impoverishment.

This aesthetics sometimes took on a political undertone of appeasing the poor through the aestheticization of poverty. This is most notably illustrated by the development of the tea ceremony. Its increasing imitation of poverty and emphasis on being satisfied with one's lot, no matter how inadequate, paralleled the increasing power and wealth of its patron shoguns.

Although initially cultivated as rather self-indulgent preoccupations supported by wealth and sophistication, the aesthetics of insufficiency came to be entrenched in every segment of society, forming one of the consistent characteristics of Japanese aesthetics. Its appeal to the general populace, both wealthy and poor, stems from its aestheticization of the conditions of life in general—the imperfection and impermanence of existence. As in many other world cultures and traditions, the transience of everything, particularly of human life, poses a challenge to humans because this predicament is difficult to accept. The initial Japanese response to this irrevocable fact of life ranged from resignation and regret to seeking the bliss of nirvana in the Pure Land.

The aestheticization of the aged and the imperfect in the aesthetics of *wabi, sabi*, and *yūgen* became the prevalent mode of affirming one's existential predicament in the Japanese tradition. The aesthetic celebration of imperfection and perishability makes the difficulties of life more palatable and even attractive. Death itself becomes aestheticized as seen in the aura surrounding the medieval ritual of suicide by disembowelment. This *seppuku* (or *harakiri*) is considered not only an ethical act of carrying out one's duty according to the warrior ethic and an act of bravery indicative of both physical strength and mental will, but it is also the final aesthetic act showing how gracefully and elegantly one can take leave of this world, evidenced not only by the physical act itself but also by the calligraphic composition of a parting poem. This aestheticization of death also appeared in the twentieth century. The wartime loyalty to the Emperor was often inspired by the parallel drawn between death and falling cherry blossoms, a traditional symbol of beauty marked by transience and poignancy.

RESPECT FOR THE ESSENTIAL CHARACTERISTICS OF THE OBJECT

Another criterion for Japanese-style aesthetic evaluation, specifically of designed objects, is the attention to and respect for the indigenous characteristics of the subject matter or the material. This principle is best illustrated by a comparison between European formal gardens and Japanese gardens. The geometric pattern of the former is primarily executed with shrubs and plants, irrespective of their native growth patterns, their characteristics, or the genius loci. In contrast, Japanese garden design takes advantage of what the site and the materials have to offer. A distant mountain view, for example, is frequently incorporated into a Japanese garden through a technique called *shakkei* (borrowed scenery). A tree is shaped to articulate its native characteristics through the elimination of those branches and leaves considered to be adventitious and detractive from its essential features.

This principle of garden design was first established in the eleventh-century manual for garden making, *Sakuteiki* (*Records of Garden Making*).

Primarily concerned with rock arrangement, its author, Tachibana no Toshit-suna (1028–1094), reiterates the importance of "obeying the request" in designing a garden. The native characteristics of each rock must be attended to and enhanced in making an arrangement, as if each rock were requesting that its voice be heard and respected.

A further theoretical basis for this respect for each object was supplied by Zen Buddhism. The Zen identification of Buddha-nature, or the ultimate reality, with the thusness or being-such-ness of an object cultivates an atten-tive and respectful attitude toward the characteristics essential to defining its individuality. This Zen celebration of the thusness of each object encourages the artist to lend sympathetic eyes and ears to what the object is prepared to articulate and to assist in distilling its quintessential features.

Art forms other than garden making that also deal directly with nature as the material share the same design principle. The arts of flower arrangement and bonsai consist of discerning the unique characteristics of each plant and shaping it to highlight such individuality by eliminating leaves and flowers, bending stems, and training branches with wires and ropes. Japanese cook-ing is also marked by its methods, presentation, and choice of vessels that accentuate the characteristics of the ingredients. In using materials such as Japanese paper and bamboo to create various artifacts, ranging from packag-ing and ornaments to architectural elements, the characteristics of the materi-als are fully utilized. Furthermore, manufactured materials such as concrete for architecture, plastics and synthetic fabric for clothing design, and artificial flowers for flower arrangement are wholeheartedly embraced by contempo-rary Japanese designers. Following the time-honored principle of respect for the material, they pay homage to, rather than shun, hide, or contradict, the unique features of these new materials. This design canon is thus flexible in accommodating and making creative use of new challenges.

The same principle of respecting the voice of the material applies to rep-resentational arts. For example, Bashō instructs his disciples to "listen to the pine tree" and "enter into the bamboo" when composing a haiku about them. When successful, he claims, the resulting haiku reads as if it "became" rather than having been "composed." If one captures the heart of bamboo into the paint brush, the nineteenth-century painter Tsubaki Chinzan (1801–1854) claims, the painting of bamboo will take form by itself. A similar suggestion is given with respect to acting in a Nō play: if the actor discerns and identi-fies with the essence of the character to be portrayed, the outward expression of imitation will follow naturally. Indeed, the actor's preparation before the performance includes a period during which he meditates on the character of the mask he is to don.

On the other hand, this emphasis on respecting the object's characteris-tics tends to result in a de-emphasis of the artist's unique contribution to the creative process. Consequently, the success of an artwork, judged by the degree to which it conveys the essential features of the object used or depicted, is frequently described by epithets such as 'natural' or 'spontaneous.' A successful work of art should facilitate the audience's appreciation of the material used and the subject matter depicted. In contrast, a design composed primarily as a vehicle for the artist's self-expression, and imposed on the material irrespective of its characteristics, is criticized as appearing "artificial" or "forced."

While these terms refer to the features of the objects, in the Japanese tradition they also refer to some aspects of the artists and their creative acts. In a sense, therefore, the Japanese tradition accepts what in Western aesthetics would be considered an intentional fallacy. What, then, is the relationship between spontaneity as a feature of the artwork and the spontaneity of the artist's creative act?

SINCERITY AND DEVOTION AS CRITERIA FOR INTENTIONALIST CRITICISM

In the Western aesthetic tradition, the controversial nature of the relationship between the artist's state of mind and the work of art is discussed as the problem of the intentional fallacy. Is the design or intention of the artist available or desirable as a standard for judging her artwork? Is the artist's intent or purpose relevant to a correct interpretation and appraisal of her artistic creation? William Wimsatt, Jr. (1907–1975), Monroe Beardsley (1915–1985), and many others think not. According to Japanese aesthetics, however, the inseparability of artists and their artworks is assumed and requires that the evaluation of a work of art refer to the artist's state of mind.

As a powerful and persistent legacy of Zen Buddhism, the Japanese aesthetic tradition considers artistic endeavor to be a secular means of experiencing enlightenment. This is indicated by the fact that most of the artistic disciplines can be referred to as 'the way'(*dō*): *sadō* for the tea ceremony, *gadō* for painting, *kadō* for flower arrangement, *shodō* for calligraphy, *kyūdō* for archery, and *kendō* for swordsmanship. Zen enlightenment requires, among other things, transcendence of oneself because ordinary egocentric concerns render one's experience of the world—mediated by discrimination, conceptualization, and valuation—useful for satisfying self-interest. These, however, hamper the direct experience of the Buddha-nature of everything.

Thoroughgoing devotion and commitment to artistic discipline is one way of continuously transcending oneself. Masterful artists are distinguished from novices not only by their mastery and internalization of skills and techniques but also by their dedication to the process of art-making. Successful artistic training culminates in freedom from one's conscious intent to achieve artistic success.

The "disinterested" attitude in the Western tradition is often proposed as a necessary condition for having an aesthetic experience as an audience member. In contrast, the same notion in the Japanese tradition refers to a requirement for an artist's creating a successful work of art. This highest stage of "no intent" or "no self," which is attained through rigorous training, facilitates an approach to the subject matter or the material with a humble, open attitude, allowing the object to evoke its inner essence to which the artists listen and submit themselves. All of this will in turn be reflected in the "effortless," "spontaneous," "natural," or "unconstrained" appearance of the resulting object or performance. A potter, for example, is expected to form a vessel based on an interaction between the particular clay and his hands rather than forcing the clay to conform to a preconceived shape.

Furthermore, the potter must submit to accepting unexpected reactions of the glaze to the firing. The harmonious atmosphere in the tea ceremony, according to Rikyū, must be generated by the participants' spontaneous cooperation; a conscious effort to create such harmony will fail. The Nō actor's performance invoking *yūgen* is characterized by "effortless proficiency" and "perfect freedom," each of which is achieved only after long, arduous, and rigorous training. The highest compliment paid to an artist can only be expressed paradoxically: the most artful is achieved when the art becomes thoroughly artless. In a sense, then, Japanese-style aesthetic evaluation is intentionalist. The gauge of artistic merit, however, is the degree of the absence (not a mere lack but a positive privation achieved through transcendence) of an artistic intention, the kind of absence that lends an air of spontaneity and artlessness to the product.

The art of artlessness also results from a thorough integration of mind and body. The devotion to and rigorous training in a particular medium will lead the artist to experience a complete harmony between what the mind dictates and what the body executes (sometimes through a certain tool): the mind and the hand of a painter or a calligrapher will need to become one with the brush; no separation can creep in between the sword, the body, and the mind of a warrior; and body movement and its rhythm help determine the design of an object, ranging from pottery to sword, from woven textile to carved wood.

RECENT SCHOLARSHIP ON JAPANESE AESTHETICS

Recent scholarship focuses on the historical context of the formulation of the Japanese aesthetic tradition conceived as comprising the "uniquely" Japanese art forms and aesthetic concepts explained above. In particular, emphasis is placed on how the image of Japan as an aesthetic nation was constructed after

1868, the beginning of the Meiji period (1868–1912), as a way of protecting its cultural identity from the sudden and rapid Westernization initiated by Japan's opening to the West, thereby ending its two and half centuries of self-imposed isolation. Compared to what were considered to be superior Western imports, ranging from technology and educational systems to military and political organizations, it was thought that the only realm in which Japan could take pride was its traditional arts and aesthetics. Their "uniqueness" was praised as being unmatched by the rest of the world, and the celebration of their "superior" aesthetic heritage, recent scholarship claims, subsequently led this cultural nationalism to political nationalism, ultimately providing a justification for the Japanese military progression into Asia as its leader and protector from Western imperialism. A number of seminal prewar writings are interpreted as collectively and cumulatively promoting this nationalistically motivated, retrospective formulation of Japanese aesthetics. The most notable among them are *Bushidō: The Soul of Japan* (1900) by Nitobe Inazō (1862–1933) and *The Book of Tea* (1906) by Okakura Kakuzō (1862–1913), both written and published first in English to introduce these "uniquely" Japanese aesthetic practices to the world. The summation of these sentiments can be found most succinctly and eloquently in "Japan, the Beautiful, and Myself," the 1968 Nobel Prize in Literature acceptance speech by Kawabata Yasunari (1899–1972). His speech provided a springboard for the postwar generation's critique of the classical Japanese aesthetic discourse, exemplified by "Japan, the Dubious, and Myself," the 1994 Nobel Prize in Literature acceptance speech by Ōe Kenzaburō (1935–).

There is no denying that today's understanding of Japanese aesthetics is influenced by the specific modern historical circumstance that gave rise to its systematic construction. Nor can we ignore the fact that Japanese aesthetics thus formulated was appropriated for a political agenda and played a role in the subsequent direction of Japanese history. At the same time, these historical significances of the Japanese aesthetic tradition do not take away its contribution to expanding the general aesthetic discourse, particularly by challenging some assumptions in Western aesthetics.

THE CHALLENGE TO WESTERN AESTHETICS

Studying Japanese aesthetics is valuable both for multicultural explorations of aesthetic issues and for a comprehensive understanding of Japanese culture, which is dominated by aesthetic concerns. It also offers some potentially fruitful areas for comparative inquiry and theorizing—for example, a comparison between the concepts of *wabi* and *sabi* and the eighteenth-century British cult of the picturesque. Both traditions celebrate obscurity and irregularity, the creation of an aesthetic value through iconoclastic acts, an emphasis on the stimulation of the imagination, and a fascination with the passage of time.

Another comparison can be made between the Japanese means of justifying every aspect of one's life through aestheticization (particularly those aspects that are difficult to accept) and the aesthetic justification of life that Friedrich Nietzsche (1844–1900) proposes by which every contingency is given necessity as an ingredient in forming an organic whole. Both recommend a total affirmation of what exists and happens through aesthetic means.

In addition to offering prospects for these inquiries, Japanese aesthetics also challenges some important assumptions in Western aesthetics. For example, the attitude of aesthetic egalitarianism that permeates and defines the Japanese art world challenges the Western paradigm of art production and appreciation, which primarily involves experiencing a fine-art object through one of the higher senses. As explored by the recently emerging discourse of everyday aesthetics, we are compelled to question whether rich aesthetic experiences outside of the fine arts such as those involving ordinary artifacts, the environment, nature, and daily activities can adequately and appropriately be explained by this model.

The Japanese notions of good works of art and successful artists also suggest alternatives to their Western counterparts. In particular, the design principle of respecting the subject matter and the material can be translated into an ecologically desirable attitude that begins with overcoming the view of nature as mere raw material to be used for various human purposes, both practical and aesthetic. This practice may suggest a model of partnership between humans and nature that encourages careful attention to nature's dictates.

The evaluative criteria of spontaneity, both of the works of art and of the artists, can also challenge the competing Western criteria of formal unity and expressive power of the object. Is it sometimes possible that a work of art is valued to the extent that the creator submits his individuality and originality to the demands of the subject matter or the material? Can we sometimes describe successful artists as those who facilitate the experiencing agents' communion with the subject matter represented or the material used in the art objects?

The alternative ideas suggested in Japanese aesthetics should not be regarded as invalidating or replacing Western aesthetic ideas. The challenge they pose, however, can shed light on both the nature and limitations of Western aesthetic concepts and theories for explaining the rich and diverse content of human aesthetic experience.

REFERENCES

Primary Sources

Addiss, Stephen, Gerald Groemer, and J. Thomas Rimer, eds. *Traditional Japanese Arts and Culture: An Illustrated Sourcebook.* Honolulu: University of Hawai'i Press, 2006.

Dōgen. *Shōbōgenzō: Zen Essays by Dōgen.* Translated by Thomas Cleary. Honolulu: University of Hawai'i Press, 1986.

Fujiwara, Teika. "Maigetsushō." In *The Theory of Beauty in the Classical Aesthetics of Japan*, translated and annotated by Toshihiko Izutsu and Toyo Izutsu, 79–96. The Hague: Martinus Nijhoff, 1981.

Hattori, Dohō. "The Red Booklet." In *The Theory of Beauty in the Classical Aesthetics of Japan*, translated and annotated by Toshihiko Izutsu and Toyo Izutsu, 159–67. The Hague: Martinus Nijhoff, 1981.

Hayashiya, Tatsusaburō, ed. *Kodai chūsei geijutsuron (Ancient and Medieval Theories of Art).* Tokyo: Iwanami Shoten, 1973.

Herrigel, Eugen. *Zen in the Art of Archery.* Translated by R. F. C. Hull. New York: Pantheon Books, 1953.

Kawabata, Yasunari. *Japan, the Beautiful, and Myself: The 1968 Nobel Prize Acceptance Speech.* Translated by Edward G. Seidensticker. Tokyo: Kodansha International, 1969.

Keene, Donald, ed. *Anthology of Japanese Literature: From the Earliest Era to the Mid-Nineteenth Century.* New York: Grove Press, 1955.

Kuki, Shūzō. *Reflections on Japanese Taste: The Structure of Iki.* Translated by John Clark. Sydney: Power Publications, 1997.

Marra, Michele, trans. and ed. *Modern Japanese Aesthetics: A Reader.* Honolulu: University of Hawai'i Press, 1999.

Nanbō, Sōkei. "A Record of Nanbō." In *The Theory of Beauty in the Classical Aesthetics of Japan*, translated and annotated by Toshihiko Izutsu and Toyo Izutsu, 135–58. The Hague: Martinus Nijhoff, 1981.

Nihon koten bungaku taikei (Outline of Classical Japanese Literature). 100 vols. Tokyo: Iwanami Shoten, 1958–1968.

Nihon koten bungaku zenshū (Complete Works of Classical Japanese Literature). 51 vols. Tokyo: Shōgakukan, 1970–1976.

Nitobe, Inazō. *Bushidō: The Soul of Japan.* Rutland, VT: Charles E. Tuttle Company, 1969.

Ōe, Kenzaburō. "Japan, the Dubious, and Myself." In *Japan in Traditional and Postmodern Perspectives*, edited by Charles Wei-Hsun Fu and Steven Heine, 313–25. Albany, NY: State University of New York Press, 1995.

Okakura, Kakuzō. *The Book of Tea.* Rutland, VT: Charles E. Tuttle Company, 1956.
———. *The Ideals of the East.* Rutland, VT: Charles E. Tuttle Company, 1997.

Sei Shōnagon. *The Pillow Book of Sei Shōnagon.* Translated and edited by Ivan Morris. New York: Columbia University Press, 1967.

Suzuki, Daisetz T. *Zen and Japanese Culture.* New York: Pantheon Books, 1959.
Tachibana no Toshitsuna. *Sakuteiki (Records of Garden Making).* In *Sakuteiki: Visions of the Japanese Garden,* translated by Jirō Takei and Marc P. Keane, 153–204. Boston: Tuttle Publishing, 2001.
Tanizaki, Jun'ichirō. *In Praise of Shadows.* Translated by Thomas J. Harper and Edward G. Seidensticker. New Haven, CT: Leete's Island Books, 1977.
Tsunoda, Ryusaku, Wm. Theodore de Bary, and Donald Keene, eds. *Sources of Japanese Tradition.* 2 vols. New York: Columbia University Press, 1964.
Yamamoto, Tsunetomo. *Hagakure: The Book of the Samurai.* Translated by William Scott Wilson. Tokyo: Kodansha International, 1979.
Yanagi, Sōetsu. *The Unknown Craftsman: A Japanese Insight into Beauty.* Adapted by Bernard Leach. Tokyo: Kodansha International, 1989.
Yasuda, Ayao, ed. *Nihon no geijutsuron (Theories of Art in Japan).* Tokyo: Sōgensha, 1990.
Yoshida, Kenkō. *Essays in Idleness: The Tsurezuregusa of Kenkō.* Translated by Donald Keene. New York: Columbia University Press, 1967.

Secondary Sources

100 Key Words for Understanding Japan (Nippon o Shiru Hyakusho): SUN Special Bilingual Issue. Tokyo: Heibonsha Ltd. Publishers, 1993.
Brandt, Kim. *Kingdom of Beauty: Mingei and the Politics of Folk Art in Imperial Japan.* Durham, NC: Duke University Press, 2007.
Carter, Robert E. *The Japanese Arts and Self-Cultivation.* Albany, NY: State University of New York Press, 2008.
Ekuan, Kenji. *The Aesthetics of the Japanese Lunchbox.* Edited by David B. Stewart. Cambridge, MA: MIT Press, 1998.
Grilli, Peter. *Pleasures of the Japanese Bath.* New York: Weatherhill, 1992.
Hisamatsu, Shin'ichi. *Zen and the Fine Arts.* Translated by Gishin Tokiwa. Tokyo: Kodansha International, 1971.
Hume, Nancy G., ed. *Japanese Aesthetics and Culture: A Reader.* Albany, NY: State University of New York Press, 1995.
Ienaga, Saburō. *Japanese Art: A Cultural Appreciation.* Translated by Richard L. Gage. New York: Weatherhill, 1979.
Iida, Yumiko. *Rethinking Identity in Modern Japan: Nationalism as Aesthetics.* London: Routledge, 2002.
Ikegami, Eiko. *Bonds of Civility: Aesthetic Networks and the Political Origins of Japanese Culture.* Cambridge: Cambridge University Press, 2005.
Izutsu, Toshihiko, and Toyo Izutsu. *The Theory of Beauty in the Classical Aesthetics of Japan.* The Hague: Martinus Nijhoff, 1981.
Karatani, Kōjin. "Japan as Museum: Okakura Tenshin and Ernest Fenollosa." Translated by Sabu Kosho. In *Japanese Art after 1945: Scream against the Sky,* edited by Alexandra Munroe, 33–39. New York: Harry N. Abrams, 1994.
———. "Uses of Aesthetics: After Orientalism." In *Edward Said and the Work of the Critic: Speaking Truth to Power,* edited by Paul A. Bové, 139–51. Durham, NC: Duke University Press, 2000.

Kasulis, Thomas P. *Zen Action / Zen Person.* Honolulu: University of Hawai'i Press, 1981.

Katō, Shūichi. *Form, Style, Tradition: Reflections on Japanese Art and Society.* Translated by John Bester. Berkeley, CA: University of California Press, 1971.

Keene, Donald. *Landscapes and Portraits: Appreciations of Japanese Culture.* Tokyo: Kodansha International, 1971.

Kerr, Alex. *Lost Japan.* Melbourne: Lonely Planet Publications, 1996.

Kikuchi, Yuko. *Japanese Modernisation and Mingei Theory: Cultural Nationalism and Oriental Orientalism.* London: Routledge, 2004.

Lee, O-Young. *The Compact Culture: The Japanese Tradition of "Smaller Is Better."* Translated by Robert N. Huey. Tokyo: Kodansha International, 1991. Originally published in 1984 by Kodansha International as *Smaller Is Better: Japan's Mastery of the Miniature.*

Marra, Michele. *The Aesthetics of Discontent: Politics and Reclusion in Medieval Japanese Literature.* Honolulu: University of Hawai'i Press, 1991.

Marra, Michael F., trans. and ed. *A History of Modern Japanese Aesthetics.* Honolulu: University of Hawai'i Press, 2001.

———, ed. *Japanese Hermeneutics: Current Debates on Aesthetics and Interpretation.* Honolulu: University of Hawai'i Press, 2002.

Minami, Hiroshi. *Psychology of the Japanese People.* Translated by Albert R. Ikoma. Tokyo: University of Tokyo Press, 1971.

Morris, Ivan I. *The World of the Shining Prince: Court Life in Ancient Japan.* New York: Knopf, 1964.

Oka, Hideyuki. *How to Wrap Five Eggs: Japanese Design in Traditional Packaging.* New York: Harper & Row, 1967.

Pilgrim, Richard B. *Buddhism and the Arts of Japan.* Chambersburg, PA: Anima Books, 1981.

Reeve, John, ed. *Living Arts of Japan.* London: British Museum Publications, 1990.

Richie, Donald. *A Lateral View: Essays on Culture and Style in Contemporary Japan.* Berkeley, CA: Stone Bridge Press, 1992.

Saito, Yuriko. "The Japanese Aesthetics of Imperfection and Insufficiency."*Journal of Aesthetics and Art Criticism* 55, no. 4 (1997): 377–85.

———. "Japanese Aesthetics of Packaging." *Journal of Aesthetics and Art Criticism* 57, no. 2 (1999): 257–65.

———. "Representing the Essence of Objects: Art in the Japanese Aesthetic Tradition." In *Art and Essence*, edited by Stephen Davies and Ananta Ch. Sukla, 125–41. Westport, CT: Praeger Publishers, 2003.

———. "The Moral Dimension of Japanese Aesthetics."*Journal of Aesthetics and Art Criticism* 65, no. 1 (2007): 85–97.

Sandrisser, Barbara. "On Elegance in Japan." In *Aesthetics in Perspective*, edited by Kathleen M. Higgins, 628–33. Fort Worth, TX: Harcourt Brace College Publishers, 1996.

Sokoloff, Garrett. "By Pausing before a *Kicho*." In *Aesthetics in Perspective*, edited by Kathleen M. Higgins, 620–27. Fort Worth, TX: Harcourt Brace College Publishers, 1996.

Tanahashi, Kazuaki. *Brush Mind: Text, Art, and Design.* Berkeley, CA: Parallax Press, 1990.

Tansman, Alan. *The Aesthetics of Japanese Fascism.* Berkeley, CA: University of California Press, 2009.

Ueda, Makoto. *Literary and Art Theories in Japan.* Cleveland, OH: Case Western Reserve University Press, 1967.

Varley, H. Paul. *Japanese Culture.* 4th ed. Honolulu: University of Hawai'i Press, 2000.

NEW CONTRIBUTIONS TO JAPANESE AESTHETICS

A. Minh Nguyen et al.

'A. Minh Nguyen et al.' refers to the editor and each and every one of the chapter contributors to this volume. "New Contributions to Japanese Aesthetics" is based on, adapted from, or inspired by the extended abstracts submitted by the contributors. To avoid an unwieldy number of references to the twenty-seven unpublished abstracts in this introductory essay, the editor has taken the liberty of paraphrasing or using verbatim a significant number of phrases and sentences without placing them in quotation marks and without further attribution, because the chapter and abstract contributors are coauthors of the essay.

The book is divided into six parts: Japanese Aesthetics and Philosophy (chapters 1–5), Japanese Aesthetics and Culture (chapters 6–9), Japanese Aesthetics and Cultural Politics (chapters 10–15), Japanese Aesthetics and Literature (chapters 16–20), Japanese Aesthetics and the Visual Arts (chapters 21–24), and The Legacy of Kuki Shūzō (chapters 25–27). Part I grounds Japanese aesthetics in Asian worldviews (including Buddhism, Daoism, and Shintoism), provides several non-Asian approaches for understanding it (including those inspired by David Hume and Arthur Schopenhauer), and uses the Japanese artistic tradition to address two neglected topics in Western philosophy: the way in which the moral character of an action is determined by its aesthetic dimensions and the role that bodily aesthetics plays in cultivating moral virtues. Part II probes the aesthetics of four Japanese art forms that play a crucial role in constituting Japanese culture and society: nō theater, gardening, cuisine, and the martial arts. Part III explores what is aesthetical about Japanese cultural politics and what is cultural-political about Japanese aesthetics by examining both the theoretical and the concrete in art, culture, and politics that illustrate diverse modes of engagement with one another; among the topics discussed are Ainu philosophy of art, Hellenism's contribution to Japanese self-conceptions and standards of artistic excellence, Japanese exceptionalism and its discontents, strategies for aestheticizing and legitimizing sacrifice during the Asia-Pacific War, Kafū Nagai's aesthetics of urban strolling, and the subversive Afro-Japanese fusion of cool and *kawaii* (cute). Part IV deals with a cluster of issues concerning Japanese literature: the aesthetic, metaphysical, and spiritual principles that inform the poetry and prose of Matsuo Bashō; the ideals of the *bunjin* (literatus or person of taste and discernment) in early modern haikai; the nature and value of *mitate* and *nazorae*, two forms of aesthetic comparison, in the Edo period; aesthetics and the narrative arts of novel, play, and film after the atomic bombings of Hiroshima and Nagasaki; and the aesthetic and ethical implications of the poetic renaissance in Japan in the aftermath of the 2011 Tōhoku disaster. Part V focuses on the Japanese visual arts, attempting to furnish fresh insights into the renowned twentieth-century painter Kishida Ryūsei's theory of realism, the revolt against the beauties of nature (*kachō fūgetsu*) as a thematic corpus in post–World War II Japan, the aesthetics of emptiness in Japanese *avant-garde* calligraphic art and American abstract expressionist painting, and Gilles Deleuze's analysis of Yasujirō Ozu as a Zen cinematic thinker of time. Part VI discusses Kuki Shūzō's seminal contributions to Japanese aesthetics, investigating the phenomenological richness and cultural embeddedness of *iki* (a phenomenon integral to Japanese aesthetic life whose structure he studies in his celebrated text, *The Structure of "Iki"*), the similarities and differences between *iki* and glamour, and olfactory aesthetics in Kuki and Immanuel Kant.

JAPANESE AESTHETICS AND PHILOSOPHY

Many have written that Zen Buddhism is the major source of Japan's distinctive aesthetic sensitivity. Few have gone on to explain how it was that Zen originated this remarkable cluster of qualities of the beautiful. Chapter 1, Robert E. Carter's "A Philosophic Grounding for Japanese Aesthetics," begins with an account of Zen and beauty by Yanagi Sōetsu (1889–1961) and then moves to the philosophies of Nishida Kitarō (1870–1945) and Nishitani Keiji (1900–1990). All three thinkers stressed the importance of "becoming" the object in order to see it clearly, and of enlightenment as the originating source of such becoming and seeing. What enlightenment provides is a transformation of both the "seer" and the "seen." As an ordinary ego-self, the seer is separate and even distanced from the seen. Furthermore, ordinary seeing imposes concepts, categories, comparisons, assumptions, habits, and so on. Such seeing "represents" or mediates seen objects; it is ego-laden. The seeing that enlightenment affords is "unmediated," direct experience of the seen, yielding the object in its "suchness," uncolored by the ego; indeed, so uncolored that the self and the object become one and the same. The result is a seeing that is transformed: the plain or simple stands out against the contrived complexity and adornments of style and fashion. The natural world is a primary aesthetic source just as it is. Rather than the natural and plain appearing dull and drab, it now sparkles with a luster and depth that has hitherto been unknown and unseen. It is this "unseen" that comes to be vividly apparent as a result of the experience of enlightenment.

Chapter 2, David E. Cooper's "Cloud, Mist, Shadow, *Shakuhachi*: The Aesthetics of the Indistinct," aims to articulate and explain a distinctive Japanese aesthetic taste for "indistinct" phenomena such as misty slopes, muffled sounds, and masked scents. It begins by distinguishing different ways in which things may be indistinct: lack of form, occlusion, and "dimming down." The second section argues that, while there is no single and exclusively Japanese taste, sensitivity to the indistinct is a pronounced feature of Japanese tradition that contrasts with the ideal of clarity of form familiar in Western aesthetic tradition. The chapter then turns to explanation of this—for some authors, "unnatural"—taste for the indistinct. In the third section, explanation takes the form of placing this taste within the context of already familiar aspects of Japanese aesthetic sensibility. Not only does appreciation of the indistinct integrate smoothly with appreciation of such qualities as *yūgen*, but it also reflects and enhances both a preference for allusion over explicit reference and a heightened sensitivity to the impermanent or ephemeral. In the final section, explanation takes the form of grounding appreciation of the indistinct in East Asian worldviews, including Buddhism and Daoism, that have helped shape Japanese aesthetic sensibilities. Cooper argues that the taste for the indistinct attests to a rejection of viewing the world as composed of "insistently individualized" objects that stand over against experience, and an acceptance instead of a vision of things as intimately interfused with one another and as emerging in unity with our experience of them. Experiences of the indistinct, one might say, offer insight into the way of things.

Does the theory of taste championed by David Hume (1711–1776) provide a way of understanding Japanese aesthetic thinking? The starting point of chapter 3, Richard Bullen's "Authority in Taste," is a provocative remark by Donald Richie (1924–2013): "The Japanese definition of worth and beauty is much closer to Hume's than to Kant's."[1] The chapter begins with Hume's aesthetic philosophy as articulated in his "Of the Standard of Taste," which proposes a standard of aesthetic judgment identified with the "good judge." According to Hume, the good judge is a person with innate talents in judging art, improved by years of practice. The chapter argues that Hume's theory has parallels in traditions of Japanese aesthetic culture. This is examined through the example of the culture of *chanoyu* (the tea ceremony), specifically the practice of tea masters Sen no Rikyū (1522–1591) and Kobori Enshū (1579–1647). Bullen argues that taste is defined and regulated by tea masters, who act in ways analogous to how Hume proposes good judges act. The chapter introduces the tea world's *iemoto* system, which is grounded in the idea that authority and skill succeeds from parent to child, and which assigns masters the authority to authenticate and appraise works of art. In addition, a master's favoring of selected wares or designs for his own use—for example, through commissions and reviews—sets standards that are to be followed by others. The identification of masters' tastes through the suffix *-konomi* (*-gonomi*), which determines, regulates, and perpetuates standards of taste and the use thereof, is explained. The chapter concludes with correspondences between aesthetic and moral philosophy in Hume's and traditional Japanese systems (for more on the moral dimension of Japanese aesthetics, see chapter 5 in this book).

In chapter 4, Steve Odin's "Beauty as Ecstasy in the Aesthetics of Nishida and Schopenhauer," the author develops a Zen-colored aesthetic ideal of beauty as *muga* (無我). The intended meaning of the expression is self-effacement or ecstasy as explored and articulated by Nishida Kitarō (1870–1945), arguably the most influential Japanese philosopher of the twentieth century and the founder of the Kyoto School of Philosophy. Odin attempts to show how Nishida's initial conception of beauty was influenced by Arthur Schopenhauer (1788–1860). He further endeavors to demonstrate how, like Nishida in Japan, the Chinese philosopher, historian, literary critic, and poet Wang Guowei (1877–1927) forged a synthesis of Zen/Chan Buddhism and Schopenhauer's neo-Kantian aesthetics to arrive at a conception of beauty as *wu-wo* (無我) or ecstasy. Like Schopenhauer's aesthetics, the Zen philosophy of Nishida comprehends beauty as self-forgetting—as losing oneself in an aesthetic experience of art or nature. Odin thus contends that both Nishida and Schopenhauer develop an aesthetic of beauty as a function of ecstasy or selflessness. For Nishida, as for Schopenhauer, the realms of art, religion, and morality are all modes of loss or lack of self. Yet for Nishida, as for Schopenhauer, the aesthetic experience of beauty is an ecstasy of the moment, whereas religious salvation culminates in an eternal ecstasy.

Western ethics is primarily concerned with whether an action is morally right or just or demonstrates care for others, while Western aesthetics tends to focus on the nature of aesthetic value and its kinds such as beauty and sublimity. Not much attention has been paid to the way in which the moral character of an action is determined by its aesthetic dimensions. Neither has the role that bodily aesthetics plays in cultivating moral virtues received serious consideration. Chapter 5, Yuriko Saito's "Bodily Aesthetics and the Cultivation of Moral Virtues," addresses these lacunae in Western philosophy by illuminating aesthetics' contribution to other-regarding moral virtues such as care and respect. The Japanese artistic tradition offers a rich legacy of the way in which artistic training helps nurture the moral character of a practitioner. Furthermore, in the everyday life of Japanese people, moral virtues such as gentleness, thoughtfulness, and consideration for others, whether humans or nonhumans, are practiced by cultivating aesthetic sensibilities. Bodily movements are particularly pertinent to this training, indicated by the Japanese character for "the cultivation of proper conduct," which combines two Chinese characters: "body" and "beauty." Despite the common dismissal of rules of etiquette and proper manners as nothing more than a superficial convention or a means to maintain social hierarchy, Saito argues that graceful bodily movements facilitate an aesthetic communication of social virtues. As such, cultivating bodily aesthetics is indispensable for a good society and the Japanese aesthetic tradition helps highlight this significance of aesthetics in people's everyday activities (for more on the moral dimension of Japanese aesthetics, see chapter 3 in this book).

JAPANESE AESTHETICS AND CULTURE

Zeami Motokiyo (1363–1443) is generally recognized as the greatest playwright and theorist of nō theater, and his treatises inform much of the written discourse on the aesthetic ideals of this art form. But nō performers (*nōgakushi*) juggle a complex assortment of competing artistic and practical demands in the aesthetic choices that they make. Chapter 6, C. Michael Rich's "Beyond Zeami: Innovating *Mise en Scène* in Contemporary Nō Theatre Performance," discusses some of the innovations and subversions that the author has observed contemporary *nōgakushi* deploy in performances, workshops, recitals, and demonstrations. It also relates comments that *nōgakushi* have made to the author about their ideals, goals, and preferences in performance. Rich defines *mise en scène* as the totality of design aspects of a theatrical or cinematic production that are intentionally shown to the audience. While not part of the traditional nō terminology, this critical term helps explain, he contends, the range of options available to nō performers in staging a production and in foregrounding their preferences. Even traditional nō performance practice tolerates wide variation, and innovations in *mise en scène* increase as collaborative opportunities with other musical and theatrical traditions grow in Japan and abroad. The rising independence of acting lineages from school headmasters (*sōke*) is one of the factors that encourage experimentation. Since most contemporary *nōgakushi* depend on dedicated amateurs who pay for lessons and performance opportunities, shrinking audiences and the loss of wealthy patrons have engendered a sense of crisis in the nō world. Some *nōgakushi* attribute this decline to the comparative ease of consumption of popular culture. To counter nō's reputation for difficulty, *nōgakushi* appropriate themes from current television historical dramas, perform in nontraditional spaces, and change other aspects of *mise en scène*. This chapter also discusses many performance variations that have traditionally been practiced in nō and enquires into their effect on the stability of hierarchies and specializations among professional *nōgakushi*. In conclusion, innovative deployment of *mise en scène* constitutes an important creative space for aspiring *nōgakushi* who want nō to remain a vital and relevant theatrical form.

Like China, Italy, France, and England, Japan has a distinguished gardening tradition. There are different kinds of Japanese garden exhibiting different styles and serving different purposes. Some are designed for pleasure and recreation, while others for contemplation and meditation. Japanese gardens present issues concerning aesthetic appreciation. In chapter 7, Allen Carlson's "The Appreciative Paradox of Japanese Gardens," the author attempts to formulate and resolve the paradox named in the chapter title. On the one hand, such gardens lend themselves to easy aesthetic appreciation not unlike much pure art and pristine nature; on the other hand, they are neither pure art nor pristine nature nor even instances of harmonious relationships between art and nature such as English natural gardens. Rather, they involve dialectical relationships between the natural and the artificial, in which nature and art are two distinct and frequently conflicting elements. Entities that involve such dialectical relationships, like earthworks, placement pieces, and topiary gardens, are typically difficult and confusing objects of aesthetic appreciation, yet Japanese gardens are not. The question posed by Japanese gardens is, therefore, how they so successfully manage to avoid being such difficult and confusing entities. Carlson addresses this question by arguing that Japanese gardens are designed to have a particular appearance—a look of inevitability—that allows them to rise above judgment in a way similar to the way in which pristine nature does. This argument faces the objection that in fact we sometimes make aesthetic judgments about Japanese gardens. However, Carlson meets this objection by contending that since Japanese gardens are designed to have an appearance of inevitability of the kind that pristine nature has, in the limiting case in which they approach perfection in achieving this aim, they do indeed move beyond judgment.

Eating is one of the central activities in which we engage. Every culture worthy of the name endows it with ritual significance as a primary mode of social interaction. While there are gourmets in all cultures, the artistry of Japanese cuisine provides especially fertile grounds for aesthetic reflection, and that is the focus of chapter 8, Graham Parkes's "Savoring Tastes: Appreciating Food in Japan." Some of Parkes's reflections on the aesthetics of eating and preparing food in Japan are prompted by the musings of the French literary critic Roland Barthes (1915–1980), and others by the prescriptions from the Japanese Zen master Dōgen (1200–1253). For the traditional Japanese meal, the aesthetics of presentation is more important than it is in Western cuisine, and the modes of preparing, cooking, serving, and eating afford greater possibilities for creative combining of taste experiences, even in the case of modest family-style meals. Factors such as the number and size of serving dishes, the pace and manner in which the meal is served, the use of chopsticks, and the nature of Japanese rice combine to produce an unusually rich aesthetic experience. Japanese *haute cuisine*, in the form of *kaiseki ryōri*, has been influenced by Zen Buddhist ideas and practices, some of which help resolve the inevitable tension between engaging in social intercourse during a meal and paying attention to what one is eating. These practices are easily transferable to the activities of preparing and eating food, in ways that enhance the aesthetic enjoyment of the most humble ingredients as long as they are fresh and natural. The chapter concludes with a reflection on the significance of a correspondingly simple Japanese ritual involved in the drinking of beer or *sake*.

Japan is justly celebrated for its martial arts. Kendō, jūdō, karate, jūjitsu, and aikido each have a large number of practitioners not only in Japan but also throughout the world. But why do we refer to these self-defense or combat systems based on *bushidō*, the martial tradition of the samurai, as 'arts'? To what extent can Japanese *bugei* (martial arts) be understood as an art form? Chapter 9, James McRae's "Art of War, Art of Self: Aesthetic Cultivation in Japanese Martial Arts," explores the aesthetic value of martial arts training. McRae argues that Japanese martial arts have aesthetic value because they contribute to self-development and promote the study of key aesthetic principles. The Zen tradition, which has influenced every aspect of Japanese culture, understands art as a form of moving meditation that provides both artist and audience with an opportunity for self-cultivation. This chapter draws from the aesthetics of John Dewey (1859–1952) and the philosophy of the Zen master Takuan Sōhō (1573–1645) to elucidate how *bugei* treats the character of the practitioner as a work of art that is revealed and cultivated through practice and performance. Contemporary neuroscience and psychology illustrate how Takuan's notion of *fudōshin* (the immovable mind) represents a flow state in which the artist exhibits hyperpraxia, an enhanced state in which he or she achieves optimal performance. Moreover, Japanese martial arts serve as an artistic medium through which core Japanese aesthetic principles are expressed. Martial arts practices such as *kata* (forms) and *randori* (sparring) promote a heightened awareness of the martial artist's spatiotemporal relationship with his or her context, which is illustrated in key aesthetic concepts such as *ma* (the space-time interval between things), *mono no aware* (the tragic beauty of impermanence), and *wabi-sabi* (simple, austere beauty). *Bugei* is thus an art form because it promotes the self-cultivation of martial artists as living works of art and offers a performance medium through which they can express themselves.

JAPANESE AESTHETICS AND CULTURAL POLITICS

The next six chapters address issues at the intersection of Japanese aesthetics and cultural politics. In the inaugural issue of *Cultural Politics*, the editors state that the central aim of their journal—and, by extension, the interdisciplinary field itself—is to explore "precisely what is *cultural* about politics and what is *political* about culture."[2] Thirteen years and thirty-nine issues later, the central aim remains unchanged. A more tendentious but no less influential conception of cultural politics is advanced by Peter Jackson, who writes, "Cultural politics can be defined as the domain in which meanings are constructed and negotiated, where relations of dominance and subordination are defined and contested."[3] Cultural politics occupies a series of "contested terrains," "symbolic spaces," and "negotiated domains" that jointly constitute "a web of social relations characterized by complex patterns of dominance and subordination."[4] Addressing issues at the intersection of Japanese aesthetics and cultural politics, the following sextet of chapters examines both the theoretical and the concrete in art, culture, and politics that exemplify diverse modes of engagement with one another. The topics discussed include the challenge of Ainu aesthetics to the standard aesthetic theory and practice, Hellenism in modern Japan and the cultivation of national pride through the aesthetic appreciation of Japanese traditional art, Japanese exceptionalism and its discontents, Japanese fascism and the aestheticization of death, urban strolling and the aesthetic discourse on the city, and Afro-Japanese cultures and the aesthetics of cool and *kawaii*.

The Ainu are an indigenous people of Hokkaido, Sakhalin, and the Kuril Islands. They were both physically and culturally different from the Japanese until the second half of the twentieth century. Throughout this past century, numerous ethnic Japanese settled on Hokkaido, the northernmost of the four main islands of Japan, and intermarried with the Ainu. Approximately 25,000 Japanese citizens of Ainu descent lived on Hokkaido in the early twenty-first century.[5] Since the Ainu had little in common with the Japanese, either ethnically, linguistically, culturally, or politically, it comes as no surprise that their respective arts and aesthetics also diverged sharply. Traditional Ainu culture did not include many of the features that have shaped Japanese aesthetics. There was no courtly culture, no close ties to hegemonic China or Korea, no Buddhism or Confucianism with their elaborate aesthetics and philosophies of art, no written language, and *a fortiori* no calligraphic tradition with its deep imprint on East Asian mind, spirit, and art—all elements that have profoundly influenced Japanese arts and aesthetics. Chapter 10, Koji Yamasaki and Mara Miller's "Ainu Aesthetics and Philosophy of Art: Replication, Remembering, Recovery," is based upon an extraordinary experiment by scholars, artists, and museum professionals to open up the renowned collection of Ainu art and handcrafts held at Hokkaido University's Natural History Museum in the Botanic Garden to Ainu artists so that they could make replicas of selected objects. The project served three purposes: (1) to allow tactile and kinesthetic contact; (2) to enable Ainu artists to make replicas of the works that they had selected; and (3) to facilitate their discussion with one another and to record their observations, both about the objects and about the processes of discovery and creation as they selected, examined, and replicated the works. The project resulted in a 2009 themed exhibition, *Teetasinrit Tekrukoci: The Handprints of Our Ancestors: Ainu Artifacts Housed at Hokkaido University—Inherited Techniques*, and a catalogue by that name. As gleaned from the participating artists' observations, Ainu aesthetics challenges and changes our understanding of aesthetics and the philosophy of art on four levels: descriptive aesthetics ("accounts of art and aesthetic experience that may be partly narrative, partly phenomenological, partly evocative, and sometimes even revelatory"[6]); categorical aesthetics (the categories of aesthetic experience and evaluation used by a culture, especially the terms in which the culture understands its own works, experiences, and values); implications of these aesthetics for a variety of human activities such as museum practice and daily life; and implications of the first three for our broader understanding of aesthetics and the philosophy of art. Preliminary analysis suggests that Ainu aesthetics takes as its objectives not only the creation and appreciation of pleasure but also the creation and appreciation of meaning, sacrality, community, and knowledge. These latter values become especially important given the threats to Ainu culture posed first by incorporation into the Japanese polity and culture and then by modernization and commercialization. Ainu works of art, therefore, carry special significance as means of conveying to current and future generations not only the aesthetic experiences of the past but also their sacred relations, sense of community, and knowledge. This suggests new roles for art and for museums as they strive to present the works, especially those of Ainu artists, in their full physicality to contemporary audiences.

Why did Greece hold such a fascination for many Japanese intellectuals during the Meiji (1868–1912) and Taishō (1912–1926) periods? What does this phenomenon tell us about Japan's cultural identity, consciousness of its own place in the world, and cultivation of national pride through the aesthetic appreciation of Japanese traditional art? Chapter 11, Hiroshi Nara's "The Idea of Greece in Modern Japan's Cultural Dreams," attempts to demonstrate that the idea of Greece was embraced by Japanese intellectuals and cultural leaders during Japan's modern transformation in the Meiji era and through the interwar years. The fascination with Greece and adoration of what Greek culture represented can be said to have started with art historian and museum curator Ernest Fenollosa (1853–1908) in the 1880s, who observed iconographic similarities between classical Greek art and ancient Japanese Buddhist art. Other intellectuals, including Okakura Tenshin (1863–1913), Uchimura Kanzō (1861–1930), Hori Tatsuo (1904–1953), Aizu Yaichi (1881–1956), and Watsuji Tetsurō (1889–1960), seized Fenollosa's observation and developed it in many different directions. The idea that Japanese Buddhist art was connected with classical Greek culture began with Fenollosa as a result of visual comparison in the 1880s, but it eventually shifted to take on a new ideological charge and function in the service of rising nationalism. Okakura was noteworthy for having deployed it to promote his brand of nationalism and Pan-Asianism. The proposed connection with Greece came to be bantered about in a variety of popular discourses with the purpose of bolstering Japan's stature in the world of politics and culture. Subsequently, the idea of Greece evolved to figure prominently in the works of some writers as it helped define their interior selves. Articulation and defense of the tripartite claim that Japan was connected with Greece in the remote past, that Japan was not unlike the West in many ways, and that Japan possessed a culture that rivaled various Western cultures significantly enhanced the discourse concerning the aesthetic appreciation of Japanese art.

Yashiro Yukio (1890–1975) was an important Japanese art historian. He began his study of Western art in Tokyo and then continued on in Italy with the famous American art critic Bernard Berenson (1865–1959). Yashiro's full-length study *Sandro Botticelli*, published in England in 1925, is still highly regarded. After his return to Japan following the 1923 Tokyo earthquake, Yashiro undertook a systematic and comprehensive examination of Japanese art history using the methods of analysis that he had come to admire in Europe. His investigations resulted in a number of significant publications in both English and Japanese. Convinced that works of art were meant to be directly enjoyed and appreciated by the general public, Yashiro urged art historians to set aside more specialist concerns and help lead their readers to seek to cultivate a direct emotional response to their own experiences of individual artworks. In this effort, he made unacknowledged use of traditional Japanese attitudes toward the intuitive nature of any true approach to beauty that dated back to the Heian period (794–1185). Many of Yashiro's approaches are most apparent in his magisterial book *2000 Years of Japanese Art*, published in 1958 and one of the first large-scale treatments of this historical material in English. His methods seek to turn his readers into connoisseurs, a strategy with a long pedigree in Japanese aesthetics, beginning with early poetic treatises, but one that is often at odds with modern and contemporary strategies of art-historical research. Chapter 12, J. Thomas Rimer's "Yashiro Yukio and the Aesthetics of Japanese Art History," examines Yashiro's contention that an authentic study of any work of art must stem from a strong sense of identification with the work by the viewer. As gleaned from his writings, Yashiro's art-historical research was guided by several principles. First, the art of Japan is part of world art and should not be seen as unique or exceptional. Second, making and making use of imaginative comparisons among the artworks from Japan, China, and the West are legitimate intellectual undertakings. Third, basic aesthetic categories can be validly applied to artworks whatever their cultural provenance. "[I]f we base our appreciation of all art on an assessment of its fundamental quality of beauty," he concludes, "then there should be no difference between east and west."[7] These guiding principles gave Yashiro's art-historical investigations an unusual dimension, and one quite different from a variety of exceptionalist views that many of his Japanese contemporaries championed in their attempt to define their own culture within—or against—the context of the modern world (for more on Japanese exceptionalism, see chapter 11 in this book).

During the Asia-Pacific War (1941–1945), the Japanese mainstream media published numerous *bidan* or stories of good deeds to promote acts of sacrifice by ordinary Japanese. In newspapers, magazines, and books, and on radio, screen, and stage, stories celebrated good deeds such as the generous donation of money and labor to the war effort, the affectionate send-off of loved ones to the battlefield, the military exploits of soldiers overseas, and the long-distance travel to the Yasukuni Shrine to pay tribute to the fallen. In schools, language and ethics textbooks were used to teach similar lessons to children. Chapter 13, Akiko Takenaka's "Aestheticizing Sacrifice: Ritual, Education, and Media during the Asia-Pacific War," explores the culture of wartime Japan in which children came to express in writing their willingness to die for the nation. Takenaka examines rituals practiced in schools and elsewhere, textbooks and other guidebooks instructing teachers and pupils on appropriate behavior, and mass-media representations of such activities. In particular, she examines how the concept of sacrifice was aestheticized through this process. One key strategy prevalent at the time, which Takenaka calls "the manufacturing of desire and gratitude," repackaged and aestheticized the mandates declared and enforced from above (i.e., by the Japanese state) into objects of desire to be dispensed in response to "requests" by individuals or institutions deemed worthy of receipt. The tales of heroism and noble deeds were meant not only to set examples for the readers but also to instruct them on how to think, feel, and act. More importantly, battlefield *bidan* readied the readers for their ultimate sacrifice: death—the dramatic center of this genre of narrative. The value set on war death has been extensively discussed, for example, in relation to the Yasukuni Shrine, where those who fought and died for Japan are enshrined and worshipped as venerable divinities. In addition, the act of dying has been widely aestheticized through an association with the falling petals of cherry blossoms. Less discussed, however, are the ways in which the repetition of smaller sacrifices,

framed by uniquely Japanese qualities, contributed to the normalization of the
act of dying for the nation. For those who participated in the acts, ritual played
an important role. For instance, labor contributions (*kinrō hōshi*) typically
involved reciting the participants' devotion to the Emperor, shouting "*Banzai!*" (a celebration of the longevity of the Emperor), and singing the national
anthem. Likewise, classroom education revolved around rites of emperor worship. Together, such smaller acts of sacrifice, aestheticized through uniquely
Japanese qualities, readied the nation for death at war.

    The modern practice of urban strolling constitutes an intimate engagement
with the affective dimensions of urban space. It signifies no immediate goal,
no destination that must be reached. Free from the routines of modern life,
including its preoccupation with financial gain, the urban stroller can wander
through the city's forgotten and overlooked places. Urban strolling—"the
greatest unpriced pleasure there is" and "a mild form of bracketing the burden
of identity," as one cultural critic puts it[8]—can resist the precise temporal
framework of urban existence imposed by modernity, within which all of
the activities and reciprocal relationships of metropolitan life are organized
and coordinated in the most punctual way.[9] A potentially subversive and
emancipatory legacy of modernity, urban strolling is capable of restoring
the subjective elements lost because of such a firmly fixed framework to a
metropolis such as Tokyo in the 1910s, a city whose rhythms had become
increasingly regulated with its Meiji-era transformation into an imperial
capital. From August 1914 to June 1915, Kafū Nagai (1879–1959) composed
a series of essays for the journal *Mita bungaku* 三田文学, documenting his
strolls through the city of Tokyo. Collected and published as *Fair-Weather
Geta* (*Hiyori geta* 日和下駄), these writings demonstrate an acute sensitivity
to the affective dimensions of urban space. Chapter 14, Timothy Unverzagt
Goddard's "Nagai Kafū and the Aesthetics of Urban Strolling," considers
Kafū's aesthetic vision as a critical response to the modernization of Tokyo,
foregrounding the stroll (*sansaku* 散策; *sanpo* 散歩) as a reflective mode
of spatial negotiation. Tracing a selective itinerary of the city, Kafū avoids
the cacophony of the modern metropolis as well as the more conspicuous
markers of its past, venturing instead into back alleys, vacant lots, and other
neglected corners of the capital. His navigation of these spaces delineates a
city rich in sensibility, places where vestiges of Edo (present-day Tokyo) still
linger. Yet it is Kafū's modern cosmopolitan perspective that enables him to
discover these remnants of the past. His descriptions of Tokyo are grounded
in eclectic references to foreign cities and French literature, *ukiyo-e* (pictures
of the floating world), and Edo popular fiction. These diverse sensibilities
come together in Kafū's *flânerie*, a leisurely wandering through urban space
that discloses a hybrid aesthetic vision of modern Tokyo. From a close examination of *Fair-Weather Geta*, this chapter extends theoretical consideration to

policies of urban renewal, emergent aesthetic discourse on the city, and the enduring image of Kafū's highly stylized persona as a refined man of leisure (*sanjin* 散人).

At the turn of the millennium, international youth culture is dominated by two types of aesthetics: the African-American cool and the Japanese *kawaii*. Propelled by hip-hop music, the former has become the world's favorite youth culture. Disseminated by Japan's powerful anime (animation) and manga (comics) industry, the latter is a "culture of cute" that not only affects every aspect of Japanese life but also enjoys a global reach and influence.[10] Cool and *kawaii* are antidotes to stereotypes of their respective homogeneous "official" societies, namely, the blandness of a plain, barren, vague, and featureless white American monoculture, and the uniformity of postwar Japanese group-oriented society determined by the corporate worker's lifestyle, entrance examination prep schools, and the domestic boredom of housewives. It is in these modern environments that cool and *kawaii* endeavor to establish personal identities. Cornel West sees "[t]he black-based hip-hop culture of youth around the world" as a grand example of "the shattering of male, WASP, cultural homogeneity."[11] *Kawaii* culture engages in a similar fight against an "official" modernity, attempting to replace it with a mode of what West calls 'New World Modernity.'[12] In a more global context, cool and *kawaii* are linked as they combat, each in its own way, the American "uncool" (and notoriously sexist) aesthetics of Disney by asserting and exemplifying the values of community, heritage, and history. Chapter 15, Thorsten Botz-Bornstein's "Cool-Kawaii Aesthetics and New World Modernity," defines a dialectics of cool and *kawaii* and demonstrates that on a deeper level this dialectics leads to the development of New World Modernity. African-American coolness is part of the modern aesthetic project, particularly in the context of the ethics and aesthetics of alienation. New World Modernity is cool because it depends on acts of delay, displacement, oblique representation, and stylization. The same holds true for *kawaii*. Cool and *kawaii* overcome a passive techno-future determined by coldness and automation. They overcome a world in which human-guided sensation is replaced with automated productions and where even art evolves toward automation and encoded techniques of production. As modern values, cool and *kawaii* embrace antagonistic terms such as 'liberation,' 'fragmentation,' and 'alienation.' According to Botz-Bornstein, both jazz and contemporary Japanese popular culture have found a type of cool that he dubs 'the anti-sarcastic cool.' Both African-American culture and Japanese anime and manga go against the grain of binary moralism and introduce features that transcend the bitter irony of mainstream white coolness. New World Modernism rises above "the binary opposition of machine-nature, civilized-primitive, ruler-ruled, Apollonian-Dionysian, male-female, white-black [and other peoples of color]," says West.[13]

In New World Modernity, be it the African-American cool instantiation or the *kawaii* counterpart located in futuristic postcolonial Japan, culture is "timed" in an eccentric fashion; it unfollows the "popular realism" of mainstream white Europeans or Americans. The expansion of cool and *kawaii* culture is thus an attribute of New World Modernism.

JAPANESE AESTHETICS AND LITERATURE

In a pair of essays on the Japanese language and poetry, Nishida Kitarō makes the following four observations.[14] First, life experience can be grasped subjectively and objectively, that is, from within and from without. Second, tanka, a type of Japanese poem consisting of 5 lines and 31 syllables following the 5–7–5–7–7 pattern, enables the poet to capture life in its moment of "pure experience," that is, life experience from the inside or its subjective character. Third, haiku, a type of Japanese poem consisting of 3 lines and 17 syllables following the 5–7–5 pattern, enables the poet to capture the "timeless" in the midst of daily life, that is, the timeless elements of our daily existence. Fourth, the function of prose is to provide objective descriptions of life experience. Guided by these observations, chapter 16, Michiko Yusa's "Bashō and the Art of Eternal Now," the first in a series of three chapters on the legacy of Matsuo Bashō (1644–1694) in this book (see also chapters 17 and 20), analyzes his masterpiece *Oku no hosomichi* (*The Narrow Road to the North*). In this work, Bashō experimented with weaving prose and poetry to capture both the historical perspective "then" and the present moment "now." Yusa's working hypothesis is that haiku retains the moment of the "present" and preserves something of a timeless quality while the prose narrates the background of the specific moment represented in the haiku. Bashō wove these two ways of grasping life experience while honing his artistic sensitivity to capture the "eternal" quality in the "now." His work thus contains the two modes of grasping temporal experience that Nishida investigates. According to Bashō, the ideal of art embodies the qualities of "the timeless and the temporal" (*fueki ryūkō*); art must respond to the ever-changing taste of the day (*ryūkō*) while seeking to endow it with a lasting quality (*fueki*). The only way to achieve this end, he discovered, was to become one with the "object" of his artistic thought, in particular his literary imagination. Bashō's aesthetic principles were developed under the influence of his Zen practice and experience of enlightenment (*satori*), which opened his eyes to the importance of being faithful to the moment of subject-object unity. In such a moment, we form oneness with the "object" of our thought and this "object" ceases to be an "object" but reveals its vivid living reality to us. It is out of such moments that the ideal poetic sentiment arises.

'Bunjin'文人 (literatus) is a term that has come to describe a literary aesthetic that flourished in seventeenth- and eighteenth-century Japan. Derived from the Chinese word 'wenren,' 'bunjin' refers to people of taste and discernment, especially those who excelled in calligraphy, painting, poetry, music, tea, chess, the Chinese classics, and other refinements of Chinese culture and civilization. More broadly, the term has been used to designate a wide variety of writers and thinkers active in a much longer period, and reference the work of intellectuals in the early modern, Meiji, and modern eras. Chapter 17, Cheryl Crowley's "Knowing Elegance: The Ideals of the *Bunjin* (Literatus) in Early Modern Haikai," the second in a series of three chapters on the legacy of Matsuo Bashō in this book (see also chapters 16 and 20), uses the term as a starting point from which to explore a set of concepts that have developed in the context of haikai. An informal type of Japanese linked-verse poetry in which two or more people provide alternating sections of a poem, haikai is one of the poetic genres most closely associated with what has come to be known as 'the *bunjin* aesthetic.' Crowley focuses on the work of two of the genre's most celebrated figures, Bashō and Yosa Buson (1716–1783). An unrivaled poet and theorist of the genre, Bashō took haikai beyond the level of pastime by demonstrating the depth and subtlety that it was able to achieve. Likewise, Buson resisted an early-eighteenth-century trend toward commercialization and called for a revival of Bashō's principles that was more about innovation than about return. Central to those principles was a set of loosely defined and interrelated concepts, all closely linked to the ideals of the *bunjin*: poetry created by transforming ordinary life and experience into something elegant and elevated. Drawing from poetic treatises of the Bashō School (*Shōfū*) and its successors, Crowley analyzes a number of critical concepts advanced by Bashō and Buson such as *fūryū* (taste), *fūga* (elegant sensibility), and *rizoku* (transcending the mundane). She shows how these concepts and the associated vocabulary have their origins in the Chinese classics, but come to be reinterpreted in early modern Japan in a way that was consistent with the social ambitions of urban and rural commoners. These interrelated ideas provide the foundation for a range of practices in the fields of literary and visual culture whose proponents sought to make art a way of life and life a way of art.

Chapter 18, Meera Viswanathan's "The Measure of Comparison: Correspondence and Collision in Japanese Aesthetics," investigates the nature and value of *mitate* and *nazorae*, two forms of aesthetic comparison, in the Edo period (1600–1868). During the Edo period, *mitate* (literally, "one thing standing in place of another" commonly understood as substitution, metaphor, or simile) and *nazorae* (illustrations involving parodic imitation) represented for *chōnin* (townsmen) culture an opportunity for reframing and reconstituting, in ways that ranged from the absurd to the subversive, the traditions of high culture from which they were precluded. Unlike earlier courtly Heian (794–1185) notions of convergence, stability, and insularity engendered by closed tropes of similitude that reinforced existing norms, in the Edo period, comparison as the juxtaposition of unlike things (*mitate* and *nazorae*) itself called into question the problem of value. The violent coupling of past and present, of *ga* (high culture) and *zoku* (low culture), of sacred and profane, ends entropically in a question mark, leaving the observer to make sense of the strained juxtaposition by moving beyond its confines rather than simply reencoding the *status quo ante*. As if recollecting the archaic myth of Ama no Uzume's legendary dance before the cave to lure the Sun Goddess Amaterasu no Omikoto out through mimicry, the anthropologist Masao Yamaguchi (1931–2013) asserts, "*Mitate*, in its original sense, was an exposition presented to the gods."[15] This exposition, which invokes representation and (dis)similitude, inevitably raises the question about "to what we might compare this world" in the words of the eighth-century Japanese poet Sami Mansei.[16] Comparison, in the guise of Edo-period *mitate*, raises the specter of new possibilities, the delimiting of existing boundaries, and finally the exploding of the sacrosanct status of existing categories. Rather than reinforcing traditional norms and hierarchies as in the Heian period, comparison in the Edo period forces us to rethink the utility of those categories and their ultimate value. For the Edo period, however, it is less a questioning of the past than a radical reconsideration of the present. We can never quite return to where we began.

Since World War II, Japanese artists have taken two seemingly contradictory approaches. On the one hand, many are radically innovative, furiously experimenting with ideas and forms and bringing them into the international *avant-garde*. On the other hand, many remain conscientious purists, resisting any new artistic developments and their wider social ramifications and persisting instead in the traditional way of art. More intriguing are those artists who combined the above two approaches, especially in a single work of art, to explore the emerging themes of the post-nuclear age. Grappling with World War II and its aftermath, three narrative works of different genres and media crafted for different purposes and audiences exemplify this third approach: *The Sound of the Mountain* (1949–1954), a novel by Yasunari Kawabata (1899–1972); *Thread Hell* (1984), a play by Rio Kishida (1946–2003); and *Barefoot Gen* (1983), a film directed by Mori Masaki (1941–), written by Keiji Nakazawa (1939–2012), and based on Nakazawa's manga (comics) series of the same name. Chapter 19, Mara Miller's "On Kawabata, Kishida, and *Barefoot Gen*: Agency, Identity, and Aesthetic Experience in Post-atomic Japanese Narrative," discusses the implications of the postwar utilization of traditional or classical aesthetics in these narrative works. Set in the 1930s textile industry that enabled the war (*Thread Hell*), during the waning days of the war when Hiroshima was obliterated (*Barefoot Gen*), and during the postwar American occupation of Japan (*The Sound of the Mountain*), all three works probe the horrific effects of the war, including the psychic numbing of the Japanese citizenry. A diminished capacity to feel and to sense reality, psychic numbing is at the heart of the traumatic syndrome and of the overall human struggle with pain.[17] Closely related to "death-linked images of denial ('If I feel nothing, then death is not taking place') and interruption of identification ('I see you dying, but I am not related to you or to your death')," psychic numbing (especially its acute form, psychic closing-off) impairs not only a person's capacity to feel and to sense reality but also her conception of herself as an agent.[18] Why do Kawabata, Kishida, and the duo of Masaki and Nakazawa return to traditional aesthetics to wrestle with psychic numbing, denial, severance of human bonds, and other horrors of the post-atomic era? The return to tradition results from many factors, the most important of which, Miller contends, include the desperation of the Japanese after World War II and their recognition of new demands placed on the individual, and the capacity of aesthetic experience for healing and for consolidating the individual's self-conception or self-understanding. Kawabata, Kishida, and the duo of Masaki and Nakazawa utilize classical aesthetics to provide aesthetic experiences: first, to their characters to demonstrate the role of positive aesthetic experience in making life worth living; and, second, to their audience to facilitate the experience of an artwork that deals with painful subjects. By providing us with meaningful and pleasurable experiences that connect us to our collective past, art establishes a foundation for a renewed sense of identity and agency in a self that was traumatically shattered.

In the immediate aftermath of the March 2011 Tōhoku triple disaster of earthquake, tsunami, and nuclear meltdown, the most impressive literary response to the disaster was a massive outpouring of poetry widely diffused through social media such as Facebook and Twitter. Some of the poems were in modern free-verse form (*shi*), but among the most effective were poems written in the traditional short-form genres of tanka and haiku. Chapter 20, Roy Starrs's "Japanese Poetry and the Aesthetics of Disaster," the third in a series of three chapters on the legacy of Matsuo Bashō in this book (see also chapters 16 and 17), attempts to analyze the aesthetic and ethical implications of this new poetic renaissance and answer some of the controversial questions that it raises about the appropriate literary response to major disasters—in particular, about whether traditional genres of Japanese poetry, highly aesthetic miniatures, are adequate to the challenge of dealing with human tragedy on such an immense scale and the overwhelming natural forces that produce them. Central to Starrs's argument is the distinction that he draws between the aristocratic aesthetic refinement in the Confucian-influenced tradition of court poetry after the *Kokinshū* (the first anthology of Japanese poetry compiled upon imperial order in 905) and the *wabi-sabi* aesthetic in the later Buddhist-influenced tradition. Guided by Confucian ideals of order and harmony, the aristocratic aesthetic confines itself to an aestheticized representation of a romanticized vision of nature. Nature is thus all cherry blossoms, Mount Fuji, and fireflies on a summer's night; it does not include much of nature in the raw as embodied in earthquakes and tsunamis and the death and destruction that they cause. By contrast, inspired by the Buddhist conception of reality as transient or impermanent, according to which neither nature nor human life has a fixed or enduring identity, the *wabi-sabi* aesthetic combines aristocratic elegance and playfulness with a darker view of existence. Originating in the late Middle Ages and exquisitely realized in the haiku of Bashō, "*wabi-sabi* is the Japanese art of finding beauty in imperfection and profundity in nature, of accepting the natural cycle of growth, decay, and death."[19] This chapter argues that, despite their brevity, Bashō's haiku, while maintaining the aesthetic restraint of classical court poetry, are also able to evoke the full power of a primal and impersonal nature, a nature that can inflict devastating damage on human society.

JAPANESE AESTHETICS AND THE VISUAL ARTS

Art theory and criticism developed slowly in Japan. Beginning in the fourteenth century, Japanese painters eagerly learned from Chinese painting treatises but did not then attempt to formulate their own theories of art. After the seventeenth century, however, artists affiliated with various schools of painting documented their own schools' philosophies, creating the heyday of painting treatises in Japan. While these painters often sought to legitimize their own style, they tended to repeat or adopt the key concepts in Chinese classic texts. Professional art critics emerged in the late nineteenth century, but artists continued to be in demand as commentators on art. Kishida Ryūsei (1891–1929), best known today for his meticulously detailed still lifes and portraits, was one such artist. During the 1910s and 1920s, when fauvism and expressionism reigned in Japan, Kishida turned his back on mainstream modern art and crafted not only such paintings but also numerous essays to elucidate his own interpretation of realism. Kishida's view of realism (*shajitsu*) owed much to the traditional concepts of realism in East Asian art, which emphasized the external appearance of the object as well as its intangible essence. Contrary to what one might assume from his paintings, his ultimate aspiration was to go beyond the precise recreation of visual reality and convey what he called "inner beauty [*uchinaru bi*]" by combining realism with abstraction and idealization.

Kishida's theoretical inspiration was the traditional East Asian concept of *shasei*. *Shasei* (Chinese: *xiesheng*, "capturing life") usually meant a close study of the object that aimed to portray its formal likeness. Depicting this sort of likeness was not the ultimate goal, however; it was expected to assist the painter in accomplishing *shai* (Chinese: *xieyi*, "capturing the ambiance or meaning") or expressing the intangible essence of the object. *Shasei* in premodern East Asian art was, therefore, a rather broad concept that encompassed both direct observation of the object and attention to its spiritual energy. Kishida asserted that the artist could accomplish the most profound beauty by restraining his pursuit of optic reality, an idea he adopted from traditional Chinese painting treatises. Chapter 21, Mikiko Hirayama's "Inner Beauty: Kishida Ryūsei's Concept of Realism and Premodern Asian Aesthetics," begins with an overview of the dynamics of formal likeness and spirituality in premodern East Asian painting treatises that inspired his theory of realism. Hirayama then explicates the pivotal concepts in Kishida's writings—that is, inner beauty, beauty without shape, the spiritual realm, and the lack of realism—and how these concepts hang together, locating his artistic ideals in the Chinese paintings of the Song (960–1279) and Yuan (1279–1368) Dynasties. Hirayama concludes her study with a consideration of how Kishida's seemingly anti-modern approach to art-making in fact concealed a strong interest in modernism.

Kachō fūgetsu—literally, "flowers, birds, wind, and the moon" or, more generically, "the beauties of nature"—is a thematic corpus of usually nature-based subject matter that also includes the rituals and ceremonies of everyday life performed in accord with the changing seasons. While constituted differently across great spans of time, the corpus of seasonal materials has been largely accretive. In the East Asian tradition, according to some scholars, the genre is paramount to religious and landscape painting though these occasionally overlap. The thematic corpus has its origins in China. Through *waka* (Japanese court poetry) in the Heian period (794–1185) and later poetic genres, the beauties of nature as a category of aesthetic subject matter was transmitted to painting. As Haruo Shirane points out, this resulted in a variety of "Heian-period four-season paintings, twelve-month paintings, and famous-place paintings—not to mention the scroll paintings (*emaki*) that depict Heian court tales."[20] These themes and formats continue to be propagated in the present to varying degree. While scholarly discussion in Japanese aesthetics has frequently concerned the articulation of the reverence for nature in various Japanese art forms, far less attention has been given to the beauties of nature as a thematic concept in modern Japanese-style painting (*nihonga*). Less attention yet has been turned to the renunciation of this nature-based pictorial vocabulary in the modern period—a gap in the literature that chapter 22, Matthew Larking's "The Pan Real Art Association's Revolt against 'the Beauties of Nature,'" attempts to fill. In the aftermath of World War II, The Pan Real Art Association (*Pan Riaru Bijutsu Kyōkai*) led a revolt against the beauties of nature. Self-styled as the *avant-garde* of *nihonga*, this Kyoto-based reformist group sought a rapprochement with Western modernism. Announcing its thematic renunciation, Pan Real eschewed the prescriptive tradition of transmission sanctioned by art institutions, such as the one disseminated in the group members' art education and celebrated in museum exhibitions and catalogues, for an emphasis on the artist's responsibility to develop his own individual aesthetics. In breaking with the traditional expectations of thematic continuity and stressing the modern need for individual artistic expression, Pan Real strove to demonstrate that Japanese-style painting would be able to flourish in the postwar period. This remains a crucial issue for *nihonga* and *nihonga*-affiliated artists today.

There is something paradoxical about the very idea of an aesthetic of emptiness. Introduced into the philosophical lexicon by Alexander Gottlieb Baumgarten (1714–1762) during the eighteenth century, the term 'aesthetics,' from the Greek 'aistetike,' has been used to designate, among other things, the world perceptible by the senses—that is, the entire field of sensory experience—and the rational and systematic inquiry into what is beautiful in this world and what makes beautiful things beautiful. Emptiness (Sanskrit: *śūnyatā*) is a central Buddhist doctrine that all beings, all phenomenal forms, are empty of permanent and independent existence. Asserting the lack of self-subsistent and substantial forms, the doctrine of emptiness teaches us the folly of attaching ourselves to forms, beautiful or otherwise, as if they were abiding realities. If all things are empty of substantial form, as the Buddhist teaching goes, how can there be any appreciation of aesthetic forms? What sense would it make to speak of poetic and visual art practices as expressions of emptiness? Chapter 23, John C. Maraldo's "The Aesthetics of Emptiness in Japanese Calligraphy and Abstract Expressionism," sketches an answer to these questions through the perspective of Nishitani Keiji (1900–1990), one of the most prominent members of the Kyoto School of Philosophy, who found certain Chinese and Japanese poetic forms to manifest emptiness in the emotive space that they create. Nishitani's insights, Maraldo contends, apply equally well to some visual arts in both Asian and Western traditions, specifically Japanese *avant-garde* calligraphic art and American abstract expressionist painting that influenced it and in turn was influenced by it. Some artworks make manifest the space within which things occur and the interplay between such space and things exemplifies the relation between emptiness and form. The calligrapher Morita Shiryū (1912–1998) created space to allow objects or events to appear in a particular place. Similarly, painters like Mark Tobey (1890–1976), Mark Rothko (1903–1970), and Franz Kline

(1910–1962) enabled us to sense the forms of emptiness and the place where the cocreation of artist and painting is at work. Maraldo sets the discussion in the context of the geocultural space of artists at work and the varieties of nationalism and Orientalism (Western stereotyping of Asian artists) that they might invoke. He suggests a way that not only avoids Orientalism but also preserves the possibility of finding expressions of emptiness in artistic forms at the crossroads of East and West.

In "Aus einem Gespräch von der Sprache zwischen einem Japaner und einem Fragenden," Martin Heidegger (1889–1976) and his Japanese interlocutor discuss *Rashōmon*, the 1950 film that first brought Akira Kurosawa (1910–1998) international recognition, as a "fitting" example of "how the Europeanization of the human and the earth is dissipating everything essential at its source."[21] Claiming that some of its scenes were too "realistic," the interlocutor disagrees that *Rashōmon* introduced something distinctively Japanese about the film aesthetic. He goes on to make a more sweeping statement: namely, it is film as such that distorts the Japanese aesthetic; with film as such "the overall Japanese world is imprisoned in the object-oriented character [*das Gegenständliche*] of photography and is specifically posited in its terms."[22] Apparently, the interlocutor insists that (1) film is just a form of photography; (2) as such, it is objectifying; and (3) the idea of a Japanese film is oxymoronic: either there is the nonobjectifying Japanese aesthetic tradition or there is photographic image, moving or otherwise, that captures ("imprisons") the world in the form of an object. Are the Japanese world and the technical-aesthetic product of filmmaking not compatible with each other, as seems to be suggested? Chapter 24, Jason M. Wirth's "On Not Disturbing Still Water: Ozu Yasujirō and the Technical-Aesthetic Product," seeks another way to think about the possibilities of Japanese cinema by turning to *Tokyo Story* (*Tōkyō monogatari*), a 1953 film by Yasujirō Ozu (1903–1963) about family life and generational conflict. Wirth frames his discussion around a remarkable analysis of Ozu that Gilles Deleuze (1925–1995) develops in *Cinema 2: The Time-Image*. In a key passage, Deleuze argues that Ozu, unlike either Kurosawa or Kenji Mizoguchi (1898–1956)— the three are often regarded as Japan's most important filmmakers—is a master of the time-image (*l'image-temps*) and, as such, a cinematic thinker of time from a Zen perspective. "Time is the full, that is, the unalterable form filled by change," writes Deleuze. "Time is 'the visual reserve of events in their appropriateness.'"[23] Coming from *Shōbōgenzō* (*Treasury of the True Dharma Eye*) by Dōgen Zenji (1200–1253), the embedded quotation constitutes an integral part of the Zen master's conception of time. Wirth attempts to make sense of Deleuze's claim and explore the prospects for a radically Japanese Zen cinema aesthetic. At the heart of Ozu's cinema and its images are not ideas about Zen practice but rather a Zen perception of suchness or things just as they are (*tathatā*). This is not because one finds in Ozu's cinema the superficial stylization of traditional Japanese gestures, Zen or otherwise. It is because Ozu in practice attempted to rethink the possibilities of cinema beyond their technological degradation into "the object-oriented character of photography." Playing on the meaning of Dōgen's *Shōbōgenzō*, Wirth submits that Ozu shows us a way to open the true cinematic eye and, in so doing, displays not Zen themes or Zen references but rather a Zen cinematic sensibility.

THE LEGACY OF KUKI SHŪZŌ

The last three chapters address the legacy of Kuki Shūzō (1888–1941), whose slim treatise *The Structure of* Iki (*Iki no kōzō*) is widely heralded as the most seminal and important work in Japanese aesthetics from the twentieth century.[24] Focusing on *iki* and other closely related concepts through a cross-cultural lens, this trio investigates the phenomenological richness and cultural embeddedness of *iki*, the similarities and differences between *iki* and glamour (and between the corresponding conceptions of selfhood), and olfactory aesthetics in Kuki and Immanuel Kant (1724–1804). Chapter 25, David Bell's "Finding *Iki*: *Iki* and the Floating World," begins with an account of these two concepts. The term 'iki' was used during the Tokugawa period (1600–1868), also called the Edo period, a time of peace and stability under the shogunate founded by Tokugawa Ieyasu (1543–1616), to describe elegant and sophisticated experiences within the floating world (*ukiyo*) of Edo, the city later renamed 'Tokyo' and made the official capital of Japan. The term 'ukiyo' refers to the world of artistic and sensual enjoyment in the licensed pleasure quarters of large Japanese cities during this period, a world that contained Kabuki theaters, Bunraku (puppet) theaters, restaurants, sake shops, tea houses, gambling houses, bath houses, and brothels frequented by members of Japan's growing middle class. 'Ukiyo' signifies habits, attitudes, values, tastes, standards, and other aspects of lifestyle that inform and constitute diverse engagements within this world. Originating in a particular cultural context and rich in meaning, 'iki' is untranslatable due to its cultural embeddedness like the French 'esprit' and the German 'Sehnsucht.'[25] 'Iki' conveys a sense of urbane sophistication manifested in provocative relations between the opposite sexes. Kuki submits that the closest Western equivalents may be found in the French terms 'coquette,' 'raffiné,' and, especially, 'chic.' *Iki* exists in opposition to what is conventional, boorish (*yabo*), or unrefined (*gehin*). Suggestive of stylishness, fashionableness, and tastefulness, and hostile to loudness, showiness, and demonstrativeness, *iki* finds subtly provocative expression in attitudes of countenance or posture, lightness of bearing, and self-contained urbanity. Seeing in *iki* qualities of cool elegance, subtle flirtatiousness, spontaneity, and suggestiveness, Hiroshi Nara describes it as "urbane, plucky stylishness," characterized by "the ability to resign oneself quickly to inescapable destiny, an embodiment of *iki*, and a type of spiritual tension called *hari*."[26] As Bell notes, *The Structure of "Iki"* has attracted diverse critiques.[27] Most recognize one persistent issue: *iki* sensibility was a specific cultural and historical phenomenon integral to the floating world of the Edo period. Kuki draws on this Edo-period context to illustrate his elucidation of *iki* with examples from popular Kabuki theater, couture, and *ukiyo-e* (woodblock prints depicting scenes of the pleasure quarters). Like Kuki, Nishiyama Matsunosuke articulates *iki* in terms of the everyday habits, sensibilities, and aesthetic engagements of the floating world.[28] Following Nishiyama, Bell explores the correspondence between Kuki-style expressions of *iki* and the sensibilities and practices of this world. He locates his explanation of *iki* both in recent accounts of it and within the social, artistic, and literary engagements of the floating world. Bell finds in these engagements recurrent themes of urbanity (*tsū*), stylishness (*fūryū*), lightness and play (*asobi*), detachment, and resigned acceptance of fate—all constituting a thematic amalgam that blends Edo-period understandings of *iki* and *ukiyo* with earlier Buddhist appreciations of an ephemeral and melancholic floating world. Examining four characteristic "moments" of floating-world engagements, he identifies and probes the currency of *iki* consciousness in examples of the tension-infused constructions of the theater, the strategic vulgarity of popular fiction, the stylish detachment of the pleasure quarters, and the provocative themes and "flavors" of the pictorial arts of the era. Bell confirms that the refined and elusive consciousness of *iki* style, *iki* gesture, and *iki* taste enjoyed a pervasive presence in popular and cultivated engagements of the period.

Chapter 26, Carol Steinberg Gould's "*Iki* and Glamour as Aesthetic Properties of Persons: Reflections in a Cross-Cultural Mirror," the second in a series of three chapters on the legacy of Kuki Shūzō in this book (see also chapters 25 and 27), continues the discussion of *iki*, analyzing Kuki's now canonical work on the subject, *The Structure of "Iki."* According to Gould, Kuki demonstrates the Japanese appreciation for what she calls "the aesthetic properties of the person *qua* person." As Kuki has it, the intensional features constituting the meaning of 'iki' include coquetry and seductiveness (*bitai*), honor and pride (*ikiji*), and resignation and acceptance (*akirame*). At first glance, it seems odd to conjoin coquetry with samurai-like courage and Buddhist resignation. Kuki insightfully points out, however, that erotic interaction requires a certain *bushidō* quality, a sense of pride that will not allow a person to give herself to someone whom she finds boorish. Honorable and not desperate for erotic alliances, a person of *iki* keeps her own counsel, has a sense of her

own worth, and maintains, says Kuki, "a rather aggressive range of sentiments directed toward the opposite sex, showing a bit of resistance."²⁹ *Iki* also
requires an element of clarity, serenity, and acceptance that erotic connections
change once consummated. This relates to *iki*'s origin in the floating world,
which is transitory and ultimately meaningless. A resignation accompanies
this insight, lightening the significance of the erotic connection and leading
to a kind of weightlessness that Kuki, in Gould's view, conflates with stylishness. With coquetry connoting mystery and bewitchment, the acceptance of
flux would make one appreciate the refined style, with which some identify
iki.³⁰ In elucidating Kuki's concept of *iki,* Gould uses glamour as an illustra-
tive example. Glamour is like *iki* in having both authentic and contrived forms
as well as erotic connotations. Seeing the similarities between the two enables
us to understand how *iki* is an aesthetic property of a person, whereas seeing
their differences enables us to appreciate how each embodies the aesthetic and
philosophical sensibilities of the culture from which it emerged. This does
not mean that Japanese culture is unique and superior, that Kuki privileges it
over others, or that his concept of *iki* betrays a fascist orientation or any other
insidious form of nationalist ideology, as some scholars charge,³¹ but rather
that *iki* exemplifies the Japanese aesthetic, whose primary principles Donald
Keene identifies as suggestion, irregularity, simplicity, and perishability.³² In
addition, *iki* reflects the Japanese relational conception of selfhood, whereas
glamour reflects its Western subjective counterpart. *Iki* is relational in that it
consists in one's relation to a member of the opposite sex; an eroticized *iki*
self exists only in relation to another—it emerges from "we-ness." Glamour,
in contrast, bestows mystery on its possessor, who inhabits an unknown or
unknowable world, thus encapsulating the Western conception of selfhood as
a unique and private subjectivity, an atomic self. Despite the Japanese character of *iki*, Kuki's treatment of it would have been markedly different had he
not spent his formative years in France under the tutelage of Henri Bergson
(1859–1941). The tradition of subjectivity in French intellectual life is close
to the Japanese emphasis on the experience of the phenomenal world. Moreover, Bergson's notion of intuition is close to the Zen concept of understanding a person or an artwork by intuitively becoming that entity or experiencing
the world in the way one intuits its vantage point.

A persistent problem in the study of Japanese aesthetics is its high cultural specificity and manifestation in uniquely Japanese practices such as nō
theater and the tea ceremony (*chanoyu*). Kuki claims, for instance, that "the
study of *iki* can only be constituted as the hermeneutics of ethnic being,"
that is, as an interpretation aimed at clarifying the Japanese character of this
concept.³³ It would be quite wrong, however, to think of Kuki as culturally
insular. His unique traverse of Japanese and European ideas in fact reveals a
phenomenological aspect of Japanese aesthetics with unparalleled originality

and cross-cultural breadth. Chapter 27, Peter Leech's "Scents and Sensibility: Kuki Shūzō and Olfactory Aesthetics," the third in a series of three chapters on the legacy of Kuki Shūzō in this book (see also chapters 25 and 26), examines two features of Kuki's thought, offering yet another set of "reflections in a cross-cultural mirror" (to use Carol Steinberg Gould's phrase), which evidences both Kuki's and Leech's cross-cultural engagements with Japanese and Western aesthetics. The first feature is Kuki's unusual focus on the olfactory, prompted in part by his encounter with the perfumes of Paris in the 1920s. Upon his arrival in Paris in 1924, he began to sprinkle his vest with the legendary Guerlain perfume, *Bouquet de Faunes*. The second feature is Kuki's immersion in the philosophy of Immanuel Kant, cemented by his studies in Germany during the same decade. His interest in Kant traces back to 1909 when, as an undergraduate at Tokyo Imperial University, he first encountered the work of Kant through the German-Russian aesthetician Raphael von Koeber (1848–1923). The first section of the chapter, "The Scents of Kuki," explores his aesthetic fascination with smell. Leech's contention is not that Japanese culture gives greater aesthetic prominence to the sense of smell than Western cultures; actually, in his view, the reverse is often true. But the peculiar nature of smell, he argues, acts as a conceptual fulcrum in determining deep-lying issues of aesthetics in general and Japanese aesthetics in particular. In the second section, "Kuki, Kant, *Iki*," Kant's derogations of smell (both aesthetically and epistemically) are examined closely, for they seem to entail a direct philosophical collision with Kuki. Kuki is prepared aesthetically to contemplate olfactory sensations, whereas for Kant smell is an inferior sense that is identified only as a modality of the agreeable (or, more often, the disagreeable) and thus cannot figure in any construction of aesthetic delight involving both sensation and cognition. Indeed, Kant claims, "we cannot describe smell" since it lacks "appellations" in contrast with, say, color names.[34] As noted above, what is remarkable about Kuki's thought is that it so readily traverses cultural and philosophical diversity. Drawn to aesthetic delicacies (equally Japanese and French), Kuki is also simultaneously drawn to a strict aesthetic architectonic (equally Japanese and German). It is the latter that Leech seeks to emphasize, for Kuki's thought consistently turns around Kant's. In the final section, "The Contingent and the Aesthetic," Leech contends that Kuki and Kant are actually exercised by the very same—and very deep—cross-cultural aesthetic problem. That problem is the degree to which aesthetic experience can be construed as contingent ("free") or structured ("rule-governed"). Our sense of smell can assume prominence because, among the senses, the evident peculiarity of smell is its contingent and uncontrolled nature. Leech concludes that Kuki's focus on the olfactory offers an enriched way of understanding not only Japanese aesthetics but also Western aesthetics.

NOTES

1. Donald Richie, *A Tractate on Japanese Aesthetics* (Berkeley, CA: Stone Bridge Press, 2007), 27.

2. John Armitage, Ryan Bishop, and Douglas Kellner, "Introducing *Cultural Politics*," *Cultural Politics* 1, no. 1 (2005): 1.

3. Peter Jackson, "The Cultural Politics of Masculinity: Towards a Social Geography," *Transactions of the Institute of British Geographers* 16, no. 2 (1991): 200.

4. Ibid.

5. *Encyclopædia Britannica Online*, s. v. "Ainu," accessed August 31, 2014, http://www.britannica.com/EBchecked/topic/10567/Ainu.

6. Arnold Berleant, *The Aesthetics of Environment* (Philadelphia: Temple University Press, 1995), 26.

7. Yukio Yashiro, *2000 Years of Japanese Art*, ed. Peter C. Swann (New York: Harry N. Abrams, 1958), 17.

8. Mark Kingwell, "Bright Stroll, Big City," *The Chronicle Review*, June 2, 2014, B12.

9. Georg Simmel, "The Metropolis and Mental Life," in *On Individuality and Social Forms*, ed. Donald N. Levine (Chicago: University of Chicago Press, 1971), 328.

10. Manami Okazaki and Geoff Johnson, *Kawaii!: Japan's Culture of Cute* (Munich, BY: Prestel Publishing, 2013).

11. Cornel West, *Keeping Faith: Philosophy and Race in America* (New York: Routledge, 1993), 13, 33.

12. Ibid., xii.

13. Ibid., 45.

14. Nishida Kitarō, "Tanka ni tsuite" ("On Tanka") (1933), in *Nishida Kitarō zenshū* (new edition) (Tokyo: Iwanami Shoten, 2005), 11:163; (old edition) NKZ-O (1979), 13:131. Nishida Kitarō, "Kokugo no jizaisei" ("The Flexibility of the Japanese Language") (1936), in NKZ-O, 12:152–53.

15. Masao Yamaguchi, "The Poetics of Exhibition in Japanese Culture," in *Exhibiting Cultures: The Poetics and Politics of Museum Display*, ed. Ivan Karp and Steven D. Levine (Washington, DC: Smithsonian Institution Press, 1990), 64.

16. *Man'yōshū* (*The Anthology of Ten Thousand Leaves*), ed. Takagi Ichinosuke, Gomi Tomohide, and Ōno Susumu, *Nihon koten bungaku taikei*, vols. 4–7 (Tokyo: Iwanami Shoten, 1957–1960), #352. English translation is Meera Viswanathan's own.

17. Robert Jay Lifton, *The Broken Connection: On Death and the Continuity of Life* (Washington, DC: American Psychiatric Press, 1979), 173.

18. Ibid.

19. Tadao Ando, "What Is *Wabi-Sabi*?," accessed August 31, 2014, http://noble-harbor.com/tea/chado/WhatIsWabi-Sabi.htm.

20. Haruo Shirane, *Japan and the Culture of the Four Seasons: Nature, Literature, and the Arts* (New York: Columbia University Press, 2012), 57.

21. Martin Heidegger, *Unterwegs zur Sprache* (Pfullingen, BW: Neske, 1959), 104. All translations are Jason M. Wirth's own.

22. Ibid., 105.

23. Gilles Deleuze, *Cinema 2: The Time-Image*, trans. Hugh Tomlinson and Robert Galeta (Minneapolis, MN: University of Minnesota Press, 1989), 17. Gilles Deleuze, *Cinéma 2: L'image-temps* (Paris: Les Éditions de Minuit, 1985), 28.

24. Steve Odin, *The Social Self in Zen and American Pragmatism* (Albany, NY: State University of New York Press, 1996), 79. Graham Parkes, "Japanese Aesthetics," in *The Stanford Encyclopedia of Philosophy*, Winter 2011 Edition, ed. Edward N. Zalta, accessed August 31, 2014, http://plato.stanford.edu/archives/win2011/entries/japanese-aesthetics/.

25. Parkes, "Japanese Aesthetics."

26. Hiroshi Nara, *The Structure of Detachment: The Aesthetic Vision of Kuki Shūzō, with a Translation of* Iki no kōzō (Honolulu: University of Hawai'i Press, 2004), 1.

27. Thorsten Botz-Bornstein, "'Iki,' Style, Trace: Shūzō Kuki and the Spirit of Hermeneutics," *Philosophy East and West* 47, no. 4 (1997): 554–80; John Clark, "Sovereign Domains: *The Structure of 'Iki,'*" *Japan Forum* 10, no. 2 (1998): 197–209; Hans Ulrich Gumbrecht, "Martin Heidegger and His Japanese Interlocutors: About a Limit of Western Metaphysics," *Diacritics* 30, no. 4 (2000): 83–101; Nara, *The Structure of Detachment*; and Leslie Pincus, *Authenticating Culture in Imperial Japan: Kuki Shūzō and the Rise of National Aesthetics* (Berkeley, CA: University of California Press, 1996).

28. Nishiyama Matsunosuke, *Edo Culture: Daily Life and Diversions in Urban Japan, 1600–1868* (Honolulu: University of Hawai'i Press, 1997).

29. Nara, 20.

30. Parkes, "Japanese Aesthetics."

31. Pincus, *Culture in Imperial Japan*.

32. Donald Keene, "Japanese Aesthetics," in *Japanese Aesthetics and Culture: A Reader*, ed. Nancy G. Hume (Albany, NY: State University of New York Press, 1995), 27–41.

33. Kuki Shūzō, *Reflections on Japanese Taste: The Structure of* Iki, trans. John Clark (Sydney: Power Publications, 1997), 118.

34. Immanuel Kant, "Reflexionen zur Anthropologie," cited in Winfried Menninghaus, *Disgust: The Theory and History of a Strong Sensation*, trans. Howard Eiland and Joel Golb (Albany, NY: State University of New York Press, 2003), 111. For further commentary on Kant on smell, see Christopher Turner, "Leftovers / Dinner with Kant: The Taste of Disgust," *Cabinet* 33 (2009), accessed August 31, 2014, http://www.cabinetmagazine.org/issues/33/turner.php.

Part I

JAPANESE AESTHETICS
AND PHILOSOPHY

Chapter 1

A Philosophic Grounding for Japanese Aesthetics

Robert E. Carter

The many "Japanese arts" such as the ways of tea and flower arranging blossomed from the fifteenth to the seventeenth centuries, and "though in decline thereafter, the roots of this cultural complex still remain alive today."[1] These cultural forms were brought to Japan from China, where they had already flourished for centuries, but the Japanese adapted and refined these forms so that they resulted in a pure and simple aesthetic that was different from what was found in China.[2] Hisamatsu Shin'ichi contends that the source of the "complex of cultural forms" that are distinctly Japanese is "nothing but Zen."[3] He further maintains that these aesthetic forms "possess an artistic quality that ordinarily cannot be seen," for something "beyond art is involved, something toward which art should aim as its goal."[4] It is this something more that is "prior to form."[5] In his essay on the German writer Johann Wolfgang von Goethe (1749–1832), Nishida Kitarō (1870–1945) suggests that Eastern art expresses both *form* and the *formless*, whereas Western art focuses on *form* alone.[6] It is the formless as the "something more" that Zen contributes to Japanese aesthetics.

Whether in *haiku* poetry, *Nō* drama, flower arranging, the serving of tea, the making of pottery, calligraphy, or *sumi-e* painting, the Zen influence is usually present if not dominant. The impact of Zen extends far beyond the meditation halls in Japan, for it envelops the entire culture in one way or another. Not that most Japanese know very much about Zen, but that Japanese artistic forms, even now, are predominantly expressions of Zen. It used to be the case, a generation ago, that most Japanese were schooled in one or more of the arts, and while considerably fewer still walk the "ways" of the Japanese arts, sensitivity to the *beautiful* remains a central feature of Japanese culture. As Charles A. Moore states:

> So important is the aesthetic in Japanese culture that it has been accepted by many students of Japan as the outstanding positive characteristic of Japanese

3

culture as a whole—as of the very essence of Japanese life. In comparison with other cultures, the aesthetic has been considered to be the essentially unique expression of spirituality in Japan.[7]

Moore goes on to say that "[t]heir love of beauty; their extreme and seemingly universal love of Nature; [and] their attempt to express beauty in all aspects of life (the tea ceremony, flower arrangement, gardens, etc.)" are generally accepted to be the essence of Japanese culture.

Scholars of Japanese aesthetics regularly list those characteristics that serve to describe the Japanese sense of beauty, and Hisamatsu is no exception.[8] However, such lists, while important, do little to explain the origin of such qualities except to point to Zen as the source. Yet it remains to be explained why it is that these aesthetic qualities became part of the Zen tradition. The answer lies, I think, in the nature of enlightenment (*satori*) itself, which is so emphasized in Zen. Enlightenment is a spiritual awakening, an alteration in and an expansion of consciousness. It is a direct experience of reality unfiltered by the ego and its desires, emotions, assumptions, and habits of understanding. It is the realization that one is not a separate entity, for it becomes clear that there is no longer any separation between the self and the entire cosmos. Enlightenment stands as the highest human achievement for the Japanese and, despite its rarity, for centuries virtually all Japanese embarked on at least one of the pathways to enlightenment: the *dō* (ways) ranging from poetry to the martial arts. To walk a pathway offers no assurance that a desired destination will be reached, but it unceasingly reminds one of the importance accorded to enlightenment all along the way. These Japanese arts all teach that the self-cultivation they engender point straight to enlightenment, however long the path may be and whether or not it is actually achieved by an individual. While the path is never-ending, all along the way one may experience bursts of insight that are transformative of oneself and of the way one experiences the world and others. The aesthetic qualities attributed to Zen insight are all grounded in the remarkable transformations in perception that enlightenment brings about.

YANAGI SŌETSU

An essential characteristic of enlightenment is leaving the everyday ego behind. A fine introduction to Zen and its influence on the Japanese arts can be found in the writings of the philosopher and aesthetician Yanagi Sōetsu (1889–1961), the founder of the Japanese Folkcraft Movement (called 'the *Mingei* Movement') and the Korean and Japanese Folkcraft Museums. He argues, in his *The Unknown Craftsman: A Japanese Insight into Beauty*, that

Zen Buddhist and Buddhist ideas in general are the foundation of Japanese aesthetics. "Beauty," he tells us, "is a kind of mystery, which is why it cannot be grasped adequately through the intellect."[9] He distinguishes between "seeing" and "knowing," maintaining that "to 'see' is to go directly to the core" of a thing, while "to know the facts about an object of beauty is to go around the periphery."[10] The "seeing" that he most admires is "intuition," "for it takes in the whole, whereas the intellect only takes in a part."[11] Intuition (referring to direct, immediate perception) demands developing the habit of "just looking," of not treating an object as an object for the intellect, and of setting the "mind [free] of all intellectualization, like a clear mirror that simply reflects."[12]

A common theme among the Japanese philosophers included in this study is the notion that knowledge of things arises from "becoming the thing itself." Yanagi writes that true knowledge of a thing arises when one is in the Zen state of *mushin* ("no mind," "the mind without mind," or "the flowing mind"), and while this "may seem to represent a negative attitude, … from it springs the true ability to contact things directly and positively."[13] Thus, unless we can become "egoless" by forgetting the ego-self, we inescapably continue to wear spectacles which impose the "color called ego" on whatever we see.[14] Therefore, "in order to give free play to intuition, one must not permit anything to intervene between oneself and the object."[15] Then, with the ego-self out of the way, "the opposition between that which sees and that which is seen [is] dissipated."[16] Hence, "[t]rue beauty exists in the realm where there is no distinction between the beautiful and the ugly, … a state where 'beauty and ugliness are as yet unseparated.'"[17] For the artist, it is a return to what Nishitani Keiji (1900–1990), to be discussed shortly, referred to as our 'home-ground,' our 'old home of non-duality.'[18] Thus, it is through no-minded intuition that the artist becomes the flower or the mountain and there is no separation between the painter and the painted, the landscape gardener and the rocks and plants, or the tea master and the tea ceremony. With the forgetting of the self, the seeing of and the acting on an object have become one, unseparated: "When an artist creates a work, he and the work are two different things. Only when he becomes the work itself … does true work become possible."[19] So, it is the work itself, and not the artist that now cries out that it exists as it is, but only because the artist and the art are now one.

Yanagi defines enlightenment as 'the state of being free of all duality,'[20] resulting in a oneness that he terms 'non-dual entirety' in order to block the tendency to contrast oneness as the opposite of duality, which leaves one still within a dualism. Shades of enlightenment, he teaches, may be discovered in the creativity of the spontaneous, simple, unidentified laborers and craftsmen of old, whose creations were unsigned, unpretentious objects intended for everyday use. The heart of the craftsman is expressed in the creations of an artist as the ego recedes and a oneness with the craft-object advances. The notion of enlightenment always includes this abandoning of the everyday ego, the loss of a sense of self and other, and a blossoming of a non-dual entirety.

NISHIDA KITARŌ AND NISHITANI KEIJI

As with Yanagi, Nishida emphasizes the importance of non-dual awareness. Nishida sees clearly that one of the characteristic aspects of the Japanese mind is the desire to become selfless in order to "become one with" an object of perception; to see things as they are in themselves: It is "negating the self and becoming the thing itself. ... To empty the self and see things, for the self to be immersed in things, 'no-mindedness' (*mushin*) [in Zen Buddhism] or effortless acceptance of the grace of Amida (*jinen-hōni*) [in Pure Land Buddhism]—these, I believe, are the states we Japanese strongly yearn for."[21]

In his first major work, *An Inquiry into the Good*, Nishida stresses the point that knowing is a kind of becoming: "To say that we know a thing simply means that the self unites with it. When one sees a flower, the self has become the flower."[22] This requires that one "discard all of the self's subjective conjectures and thereby unite with the basic nature of the flower. ... Those without a self—those who have extinguished the self—are the greatest."[23] Emphasis should be placed on the phrase 'the basic nature of the flower.'

Returning to Nishida's *Inquiry*, in chapter 32, "Knowledge and Love," Nishida argues that they are fundamentally the same activity: "This activity is the union of subject and object; it is the activity in which the self unites with things."[24] He adds that "to love a flower is to unite with the flower, and to love the moon is to unite with the moon."[25] Moreover, when we are absorbed in something we love, "we forget the self, and at this point an incomprehensible power beyond the self functions alone in all of its majesty; there is neither subject nor object, but only the true union of subject and object."[26] Nishida concludes that "love is the deepest knowledge of things," and that "analytical, inferential knowledge is a superficial knowledge, and it cannot grasp reality."[27] It is in this sense that "love is the culmination of knowledge."[28] These are provocative claims, to say the least, but what is not clear is exactly what "knowledge" arises from love. What precisely do we come to know when we love deeply? How is it possible for us, as individuals, to unite with things? Is "to unite with something" merely a metaphor?

In his final essay, "Nothingness and the Religious Worldview," Nishida again affirms that "*we think by becoming things, and we act by becoming things.*"[29] In this same essay, Nishida borrows an expression from Martin Buber through which he explains that "the world grounded in absolute love" is one of mutual love and respect "through the I and Thou becoming one."[30]

In "A Preface to Metaphysics," in *Fundamental Problems of Philosophy*, Nishida elaborates as to what he means by this 'I-Thou' relationship.[31] It is not a "mere opposition between individuals," for the I-Thou relationship demands that the self be absolutely negated. What results from this is that "everything which stands opposed to the self—even the mountains, rivers, trees, and stones—is a Thou. In such a sense, the concrete world becomes a metaphysical society."[32] Furthermore, "that which stands in opposition to the I must possess expression. In fact, the mountains and rivers must also be expressive."[33] Moreover, "the true personal self exists when the absolute other is seen in the self and the self in the absolute other."[34] Writing of an earlier philosopher who held that plants had souls, Nishida reminds us that while plants may not have souls, they must have a "kind of unconscious consciousness," or else living things would be thought of as mere complexes or "material forces."[35] Nishida appears to expand on this belief to include inanimate things such as rivers and stones as entities that have some form of awareness.

Nishitani Keiji spoke directly to whether one can somehow communicate with the vast variety of things in the world, and here, too, borrowing Martin Buber's analysis of second- and third-person attribution (the "you" and "it" in communication), Nishitani writes:

> Ordinarily, a second-person way of thinking is applied to the relationship between human beings. But we relate ourselves to inorganic and non-living things other than humans in a third-person fashion, in the form of "it."... I am sure ... [that a second-person way of thinking] holds true not only of human beings, but also, for example, of animals. There is, in fact, a way of thinking among those who have a dog or a cat, whereby these animals are addressed as "you" or "thou," just as a farmer who may relate to cows or horses by giving them respectively proper names. I hold the view that this is true not only of animals but also of trees, grass, stones or even such a thing as a desk. ... With regard to stones, we Eastern people have long had a special love for them. ... While a person loves a stone, there takes place an exchange of communication between them. To speak to a stone might sound like a metaphor. But truthfully ... the question of whether speaking to a stone or to a plant is to be regarded as a mere metaphor is something worthy of deep consideration.[36]

Nishitani then attempts to provide a solution to how it is possible to communicate with the seemingly nonsentient by turning to an examination of the roots of language. The Greek *logos*, or 'word,' comes from *legein*, which means "to gather." He relates this gathering sense to the Japanese *morotomo*, which means to be "together with." *Morotomo* is a relational indicator, indicating "that one thing and the other are together with each other. If this relationship is spoken of in reference to the '*I-Thou*' relation, it is described in terms of *tomo*... [which] also means 'a friend.' What is at issue here is the

friendly relationship between one thing and another."[37] Applying this sense
of relationship to communication with a stone, he concludes that "a human
being and a stone are together, they stand face to face with each other. It is not
the case here that these two things stand side by side in complete isolation.
Instead, at a place where a relation between one thing and the other obtains, a
deep connection is somewhere established."[38] He suggests that there is always
something that cannot be exhaustively expressed in language, and it is this
depth beyond and beneath language out of which language itself comes. This
depth or place beneath language is described in detail in his major work,
Religion and Nothingness.

Readers of Nishitani will know that his attempt to articulate "the standpoint
of *śūnyatā*" (nothingness or emptiness) constitutes the focal center of his
work. This is his attempt to provide a viable alternative to the all too common
standpoint of nihilism, the initial assumption of much of the rest of the world
(nihilism is the view that all values are baseless, resulting in a complete lack
of any footing from which to derive genuine meaning). *Śūnyatā*—nothingness, emptiness, or Nishida's idea of "place"—is more like a *field* in which
events occur, and not any kind of "thing." The late Jan van Bragt, Nishitani's
friend and translator, wrote that "'place' is not a mere nonexistent 'nothing'
and yet neither is it an existent 'something.' It is more in the nature of what
[Karl] Jaspers [(1883–1969)] calls an 'encompassing' (*Umgreifendes*) that
allows things to exist where they are: each on its own, and yet all together in
a sort of oneness."[39] It is on this field of *śūnyatā* that we can grasp the reality
of things as they truly are, in their depths.

Nishitani describes what is involved in existing in this field of *śūnyatā* with
the Japanese phrase *egoteki sōnyū*, which Van Bragt translates as 'circuminsessional interpenetration,' a phrase often employed to depict the interconnection that exists among the parts of the Christian Trinity. My former student
and colleague, Bradley Douglas Park, suggested several alternative English
renderings, opting for 'convergent interpenetration' as possibly the best, and
added that while he does not like the "ring" of any of the translations, "nothing could be much worse than 'circuminsessional interpenetration.'"[40] He
prefers the term 'convergent interpenetration' because 'convergent' suggests
a sense of distinctness in the coming together rather than a resultant monistic
porridge. It also emphasizes a dynamic process rather than a static state of
relational being. And like the Jewel Net of Indra, each and every thing inter-
penetrates each and every other thing so that any one thing is supported and
sustained by everything else.[41] Van Bragt refers to this place of interpenetration as 'being in one's home-ground,' while at the same time everything is in
its home-ground as well as in the home-ground of everything else. Park also
suggests that 'originating situation' or 'root' might be a better translation than
'home-ground,' but the point is this: things are not separated by an absolute

breach, as is the case with the field of nihility "on which the desolate and bottomless abyss distances even the most intimate of persons or things from one another."[42] On the field of *śūnyatā*, there is "a most intimate encounter with everything that exists."[43] Nishitani uses the analogy of a white light that "breaks up into rays of various colors when it passes through a prism, so we have here an absolute self-identity in which the one and the other are yet truly themselves, at once absolutely broken apart and absolutely joined together. They are an absolute *two* and at the same time an absolute *one*."[44]

In this same way, this radical interconnectedness on the field of *śūnyatā* is the source of home-ground familiarity that allows us to communicate intimately with all "others." We are, at base, kinfolk. Each and every thing holds up the being of every other thing. This is the "natural light" of origi- nary awareness, independent of ego and yet the true source of the self. The natural light is not reason for Nishitani, but an enlightened awareness of the interconnectedness and oneness of all that exists. He quotes Musō Kokushi (1275–1351), who wrote that "hills and rivers, the earth, plants and trees, tiles and stones, all of these are the self's own original part."[45] As Watsuji Tetsurō (1889–1960) might have put it, had he commented on Nishitani's viewpoint on interconnection: we come into the world already connected to the things in the world, and we meet in the space ("betweenness") between each and every thing. However, the point of using the term 'circuminsessional inter- penetration' must include the understanding that while all is one within the field of nothingness, at the same time rivers are rivers, flowers are flowers, and the self is the self, only now seen as though for the first time as standing out against the background of nothingness. These three are one, and yet they are evidently also utterly distinct. Rivers, flowers, and the self are, at the same time, rivers, flowers, and the self by not being rivers, flowers, and the self. That is to say, at the deepest point, they are not rivers, not flowers, and not the self, but rather they are now at the level of intimacy and interconnected- ness on the field of nothingness. Nishitani insists that "the interpenetration of all things ... is the most essential of all relationships, one that is closer to the ground of things than any relationship ever conceived on the fields of sensa- tion and reason by science, myth, or philosophy."[46]

Language cannot put into words all that is felt and this is true even with respect to ordinary love between human beings. We look for various ways to express our love, and yet the expression is never complete, never completely adequate. What we feel is a connectedness, a deep kinship, which makes third-person attribution inappropriate. At this deep level, all things become "thous." But this can occur only on the field of *śūnyatā*, where every individ- ual thing is also the whole, and the whole manifests as every individual thing. No doubt this is what Nishida is referring to when he writes that everything is lined with nothingness. Like a fine kimono that hangs just right because of the unseen lining so deftly tailored, the unseen nothingness in which things exist, and to which they eventually return, is sensed by one who is in love with the world. This awareness is the deepest knowledge possible, and it is a knowing as nonknowing, that is, it is not known in the ordinary sense of knowing.[47] The self, at its depth, is a nonself, a "protensive" knowing, and never an object but always a pure subjectivity.[48] It is that which is at our base and that which cannot be known directly through sense experience or reason, but is rather that which makes these possible. It is, in effect, a kind of selfless self that knows it is not a discrete self but a temporary result of an originating situation: the self is empty, yet at the same time, it is also filled with the entire universe. It is nothing, and yet it is everything. Such "not-knowing constitutes the essential possibility of knowing."[49]

MASUNO SHUNMYO'S LANDSCAPE ARCHITECTURE

An example of the transformative power of an art-practice is provided by the Sōtō Zen priest and landscape architect Masuno Shunmyo (1953–), head priest of Kenko-ji Temple in Yokohama, who creates in accordance with traditional Zen Buddhist landscape design principles. Masuno always meditates before beginning work on a garden, for he urges that it is meditation that enables the conscious mind to find its way into the unconscious world: "*Zazen* or *Zen* meditation trains our consciousness and is the best way of reaching down to the boundary between the conscious and unconscious mind."[50] He maintains that a dialogue between gardener and garden can take place only when the mind is focused and tranquil: "When I encounter a stone or a tree, I communicate with it; I ask it where it wants to be planted or placed."[51]

Furthermore, "[e]verything that exists has *kokoro* [heart, mind, spirit, essence]: there is rock *kokoro*, and there is tree *kokoro*. In whatever form it exists, *kokoro* is to be respected." Masuno stresses that "the most important thing in executing a design is to talk to the plants and stones and hear what they themselves have to say about how they want to be laid out. In other words, I engage in a kind of dialogue with them."[52] Masuno describes the care that he takes in the initial selection of rocks: "Even when I am looking for suitable stones and other materials for a garden, I go up into the mountains and make numerous sketches in order to find stones and plants with the right degree of empathy." It is "empathy" that allows the correct position of each rock and plant to be discerned and recognized as unique, important, and possessed of immense value, and to say all of this is already to be in an intimate relationship with them, thus creating a "Thou" response rather than an "It" response (to use Martin Buber's schema). Even the garden site itself is important:

It is not acceptable to move in the earth-moving machines to fit some economic or leveling demand. The site and its history must be itself engaged as a part of the whole garden which is in the making. When I am on site, I don't simply arrange stones and things like waterfalls or cascades to suit the forms of the remaining concrete. Instead, what I try to do is to make the landscaping and such things as retaining concrete walls fit in with the waterfalls, cascades, and other features that have been formed by the temporarily set out groups of stones, themselves arranged as a result of their dialogue with me.

This elaboration is indicative of the importance that the oneness of things has for him. He writes, "I wonder just what kind of spirit a certain stone has and how it would prefer to be set out. This is also true of plants and I always consider how I think the plants would like to be displayed. I always feel at one with the plants, when I am planting them, and with the stones, when I am arranging them."[53] Masuno believes that for a truly Zen person, "the mind, hands, body, time, and materials merge into one [and] then an unconscious mind, which goes beyond the bounds of consciousness, is responsible for creating things."[54] For Masuno, it is Zen that leads many artists to realize who they really are, for *kensho* (seeing into one's true, deeper nature; used interchangeably with *satori*, although sometimes *satori* is used to imply a deeper enlightenment experience) is a seeing of that which is not ordinarily available to consciousness. Japanese artists who have gone beyond the surface-ego strive to give expression to this deep, perceptually invisible self. Indeed, a landscape garden or any other artistic expression, for Masuno, is to be thought of as an attempt to make visible the invisible, and while the invisible cannot itself be made visible, a visible creation can point the viewer toward the invisible. He adds a philosophical reflection on gardening, reminding us that to be in the moment is not to be reflecting on gardening but to be in the garden. One is then free to be oneself, in one's depth, unreachable through reason or language, but attainable only through experience that is immediate rather than mediated. Ordinary experience is mediated by our concepts, categories, assumptions, prejudices, and habits, whereas a not-self self receives such information directly, undistorted by the workings of the everyday self.

People come to a Zen garden to at least glimpse the landscape gardener's depiction of his *satori* experience. This taste of enlightenment can then be carried over to their own everyday life. A monk at Kyoto's moss garden (Saihō-ji) told me that a Zen garden is a "place removed from the everyday, and yet what it teaches is how one is to live every day." Indeed, Nishitani Keiji told me, on one of my visits to his home in Kyoto, that a garden is an expression of the artist's *satori* experience. He looked me in the eye and gently insisted that the rock garden at Ryōan-ji, a Zen temple located in northwest Kyoto from which I had just come, had, in fact, been my teacher: "You were *in* the garden," he told me, and therefore in the midst of a *satori* experience. "Did you hear the garden roar?" he asked. "The garden is a Zen master, your very own Zen master." For one who can hear the roar of the inaudible or see the invisible, each and every Japanese art is a personal invitation to experience the "something more" provided by the great masters of the past and the present.

CONCLUSION

The impact of all of this for Japanese aesthetics is that, with the awareness that is enlightenment, the entire world and everything in it comes alive with meaning and beauty. One then sees clearly that things have inherent value and are to be treated as such. Each thing is then seen as a manifestation of the creative oneness (or nothingness) from which it emerged and to which it will return. One is then intimate with the "other," with the result that it becomes clear that the other deserves our respect and compassion. Moreover, the entire world now bursts forth in vivid color, in its suchness, revealing its heretofore hidden beauty. Even black and white becomes enriched and breathtaking, as is evidenced by the black and white of some *sumi-e* paintings. Furthermore, the utter simplicity of the tiny tea hut of the great tea master Sen no Rikyū (1522–1591) now shines with an extraordinary vividness. It is not necessary to "dress up" a plain tea bowl or an old wooden gate. An ancient, earthy quality is magnificent just as it is, while the attempt to dress it up is to verge on turning the profound into mere kitsch. The beauty is in the ancient and rustic gate just as it is, in its natural, pure, unadulterated simplicity.

One's awareness is now akin to the ninth ox-herding picture's depiction of a world seen anew, fresh and vibrant, beautiful and wondrous beyond words.[55] If one superimposes the eighth picture of the empty circle upon the ninth, one is able to see that everything is as it is in all its glory, and that each and every thing rests on the "nothingness" as originating force and sustainer of things. It would not be too much of a stretch to say that the entire cosmos is now experienced as "sacred." One cannot help but be awestruck, as when seeing the starry sky in its clear brightness, or when a dew drop on a rose petal strikes one speechless. From the infinite array of stars to the tiniest dew drop, or an old rowboat partially submerged in a pond, the awesome beauty of the world is now apparent when seen from the standpoint of *śūnyatā*. The everyday is no longer ordinary but is simply incredible to behold. Every thing, every person, is now seen as though for the first time. And this is what the Japanese arts are pathways toward. The bubbling kettle in the tea room, the flower arrangement for the *tokonoma* alcove, the kimono displaying a magnificent bamboo pattern, the moss garden of green-on-green splendor, the frog jumping into the pond, the inked rendition of a simple circle representing nothingness. These are all instances of transformed seeing made possible by a transformation of self.

Seeing in this sense is always and everywhere seeing anew. Just such insight is revealed in *haiku* poetry, in Japanese landscape gardens, in flower arranging, and in the serving of tea. These are all "ways" of saying and teaching that each and every snapshot of our experience is overflowing with beauty and profundity. We see the world, and it sees us, from the standpoint of *śūnyatā*. For now the world is no longer separate from our egolessness, since the seer and the seen have become one and the same. This magic arises because of the serious practice of self-cultivation. Self-cultivation by means of the Japanese arts is transformative. It can yield enlightened seeing and enlightened being. All along the "way" one has come to see, with increasing clarity, the beauty that has been underfoot from the beginning, including the heretofore unseen "something more" that always has been unseen, yet quietly present as the sustaining undergarment of reality: the formless nothingness of Zen.

NOTES

1. Hisamatsu Shin'ichi, *Zen and the Fine Arts*, trans. Gishin Tokiwa (Tokyo: Kodansha International, 1971), 7.

2. Ibid. Hisamatsu reminds us that "a unique complex of cultural forms arose in China at the beginning of the sixth century, and flourished for nine centuries until the fifteenth century." These "cultural forms" were introduced into Japan in the thirteenth century and flourished "through the fifteenth, sixteenth, and seventeenth centuries" (ibid.).

3. Ibid.

4. Ibid., 12.

5. Ibid.

6. Nishida Kitarō, *Intelligibility and the Philosophy of Nothingness: Three Philosophical Essays*, trans. Robert Schinzinger (Westport, CT: Greenwood Press, 1973), 146.

7. Charles A. Moore, ed., *The Japanese Mind: Essentials of Japanese Philosophy and Culture* (Honolulu: University of Hawai'i Press, 1967), 296.

8. Hisamatsu's list of seven characteristics of the Japanese sense of beauty includes asymmetry, simplicity, austere sublimity or lofty dryness, naturalness, subtle profundity or deep reserve, freedom from attachment, and tranquility. Within these categories, such qualities as *wabi*, *sabi*, and *yūgen* are discussed.

9. Yanagi Sōetsu, *The Unknown Craftsman: A Japanese Insight into Beauty*, adapt. Bernard Leach (Tokyo: Kodansha International, 1972), 110.

10. Ibid.

11. Ibid., 114.

12. Ibid., 112.

13. Ibid.

14. Ibid., 153.

15. Ibid., 154.

16. Ibid.

17. Ibid., 130.

18. Ibid., 139.

19. Ibid., 146.

20. Ibid., 127.

21. Ryusaku Tsunoda, Wm. Theodore de Bary, and Donald Keene, eds., *Sources of Japanese Tradition* (New York: Columbia University Press, 1964), 2:362.

22. Nishida Kitarō, *An Inquiry into the Good*, trans. Masao Abe and Christopher Ives (New Haven, CT: Yale University Press, 1990), 77.

23. Ibid.

24. Ibid., 173.

25. Ibid., 174.

26. Ibid., 174–75.

27. Ibid., 175.

28. Ibid.

29. Nishida Kitarō, *Last Writings: Nothingness and the Religious Worldview*, trans. David A. Dilworth (Honolulu: University of Hawai'i Press, 1987), 55.

30. Ibid., 101.

31. Nishida Kitarō, *Fundamental Problems of Philosophy*, trans. David A. Dilworth (Tokyo: Sophia University Press, 1970), 24–31.

32. Ibid., 29.

33. Ibid., 35.

34. Ibid., 37.

35. Ibid., 59.

36. Nishitani Keiji, *Religion and Modernism: Essays and Lectures by Nishitani Keiji*, trans. Jonathan Augustine and Yamamoto Seisaku (in preparation), 66–67.

37. Ibid., 69.

38. Ibid., 69–70.

39. Nishitani Keiji, *Religion and Nothingness*, trans. Jan van Bragt (Berkeley, CA: University of California Press, 1982), xxxi.

40. Bradley Douglas Park, associate professor of philosophy, St. Mary's College of Maryland, email message to author, September 10, 2008.

41. A metaphor of a giant spider web that is covered with jewels or dew drops at each and every intersection of the strands where each jewel reflects all the other jewels so that every dew drop contains the reflections of all the other dew drops.

42. Nishitani, *Religion and Nothingness*, 102.

43. Ibid.

44. Ibid.

45. Ibid., 164.

46. Ibid., 150.

47. Nishida, *An Inquiry into the Good*, 154. Nishida writes that "to love something is to cast away the self and unite with that other. When self and other join with no gap

between them, true feelings of love first arise. ... The more we discard the self and become purely objective or selfless, the greater and deeper our love becomes" (174).

48. Nishitani, *Religion and Nothingness*, 154. Nishitani describes "protensive" as follows: "[T]he intuitive knowledge or intellectual intuition that are ordinarily set up in opposition to reflective knowledge leave in their wake a duality of seer and seen, and to that extent still show traces of 'reflection.' I call this self-awareness 'a knowing of non-knowing' because it is a knowing that comes about not as a *refraction* of the self bent into the self but only on a position that is, as it were, absolutely straightforward or *protensive*. This is so because it is a knowing that originates in the 'middle.' It is an absolutely non-objective knowing of the absolutely non-objective self in itself; it is a completely non-reflective knowing" (154–55). Such knowing is of a self that is empty and that "posits itself" as it is in itself and, of course, on the field of *śūnyatā*. What Nishitani is saying is that when not on the field of *śūnyatā*, the self does reflect on itself in an impossible attempt to grasp itself, yielding only an ever receding self (i.e., as not reflected). The everyday self can never be caught as pure subjectivity but only as the objective self.

49. Ibid., 156.

50. Masuno Shunmyo, "Landscapes in the Spirit of Zen: A Collection of the Work of Shunmyo Masuno," *Process Architecture* Special Issue 7 (1995): 8.

51. From an interview that I conducted with Masuno Shunmyo at his Sōtō Zen Temple in Yokohama, Japan in September to October 2003. Readers should be aware that passages in quotation marks or block quotations but without endnote numbers are from interviews that I conducted with various Japanese artists. The context makes it clear who it is that spoke these words. A more extensive account of these and other interviews can be found in my book *The Japanese Arts and Self-Cultivation* (Albany, NY: State University of New York Press, 2008).

52. Masuno, 6.

53. Ibid., 10.

54. Ibid., 8.

55. The ten Ox-Herding pictures are from a twelfth-century Chinese Zen text, depicting the student from an initial search for the Ox (actually his deep-self) to his eventual non-dual enlightenment experience. The eighth drawing is that of an empty circle; both the ego-self and the deep-self have vanished into nothingness. But the ninth drawing is that of a world restored with greater vividness and clarity. It may be that an enlightened person would see drawings eight and nine simultaneously: everything disappears into nothingness, and yet everything is now seen against the background of nothingness, or in Nishida's words, everything is now "lined with nothingness."

Chapter 2

Cloud, Mist, Shadow, *Shakuhachi*

The Aesthetics of the Indistinct

David E. Cooper

THE INDISTINCT

Here are some well-known remarks, spanning eight centuries, from the writings of three famous Japanese authors:

> [W]hen one gazes upon the autumn hills half-concealed by a curtain of mist, what one sees is veiled yet profoundly beautiful; such a shadowy scene, which permits free exercise of the imagination in picturing how lovely the whole panoply of scarlet leaves must be, is far better than to see them spread with dazzling clarity before our eyes.[1]

> Are we to look at ... the moon only when it is cloudless?[2]

> [W]e do prefer a pensive luster to a shallow brilliance, a murky light that ... bespeaks a sheen of antiquity.... . [W]e find beauty not in the thing itself but in the patterns of shadows.[3]

The remarks attest to a distinctive Japanese appreciation of mists, clouds, shadows, and related phenomena—smoke, dusk, haze, and soft moonlight, for example. It is a sensibility evident in Japanese poetry. Matsuo Bashō, for instance, writes of "a distant moon and a line of smoke" glimpsed as he rides his horse,[4] and of "nameless hills ... decorated with thin films of morning mist."[5] And in scores of Kobayashi Issa's verses, the themes are those of darkness or shadow, smoke or steam, mist or moonlight—often in combination, as when he tells, in an 1822 poem on mist, how "the river's mist helps out the haze [on a] moonlit night."[6]

How might one usefully label the taste or sensibility indicated by such remarks and verses, one manifested moreover by many Japanese arts and "ways," including gardening and music? One commentator speaks of a Japanese preference for "the hidden and the obscured" over "the fully exposed."[7] Others refer to a preference for "the rough" and "the indeterminate." These terms help to characterize the taste in question, but they are insufficiently general. I propose that we speak of a taste for "the indistinct." This is intended as something of a term of art, so I need to explain my use of it.

There are three modes of the indistinct, three ways for something to be an indistinct object of experience. To begin with, there are phenomena that are themselves indistinct, in that they lack clear contours, precise location, or stable, determinate form. Examples would include wispy clouds, mists, and the "dark, smoky patina" on the surface of Tanizaki's unpolished silver kettle.[8] Next, something may be indistinct because it is occluded, partly hidden by something else: Kenkō's moon half-hidden behind a cloud, perhaps,[9] or Buson's temple that is glimpsed, when "cherry blossoms are falling ... between the trees."[10] Finally, something may be rendered indistinct by, as it were, being "dimmed down"—as when looked at through a veil or in a murky light. One thinks, say, of Fujiwara no Teika's famous "bayside reed hovel" viewed "in the autumn dusk,"[11] or of a tree, in a novel by Natsume Sōseki, whose "black silhouette" is given a "smoky look" by the "bluish light of the moon."[12]

My illustrations have so far been taken from the realm of visual experience, but sensitivity to the indistinct is not confined to this. There are parallels in other realms of experience. The scent of a flower, for instance, may be all the more alluring because it is partly masked by another smell. More importantly, sounds may be indistinct for reasons similar to the three I distinguished in connection with visible things. Like the chiming of muffled bells, a sound may itself be indistinct and blurred. Like "the call of a teal" in a haiku by Bashō, a sound may be partly hidden—by the sound of the sea in this case. Or, as in another Bashō poem, a sound—this time a temple's bell—may be dimmed down, since it is audible only through a mist.[13]

A taste for the indistinct is apparent in Japanese music. One of the main traditional instruments, the *shakuhachi*, would surely provide a fitting soundtrack to a film about the indistinct. Breathy, fuzzy, smoky, sliding and gliding between notes, it is unsurprising that the *shakuhachi* is often used to evoke such indistinct phenomena of nature as a sighing wind or the distant call of a deer. Nor is it a surprise to find a modern Japanese composer who is indebted to his country's musical tradition comparing one of his pieces to water "wending its way through the scenery of night," its barely separable motifs "dispersing, disappearing, and recurring."[14]

In this chapter, I consider how to explain the taste for the indistinct that is attested to in the remarks I have cited. I take it that this sensibility does indeed call for explanation. Yuriko Saito has pointed out that for Yoshida Kenkō and Motoori Norinaga among others, it is more "natural" to admire or "long for clarity [and] perfection" than for the occluded, blurred, rough, or otherwise indistinct.[15] It is not obvious, perhaps, how one might validate their claim, but Kenkō, Norinaga, and indeed Saito herself are surely right to think that there is nothing innate or routine in a taste for the indistinct. Explanation, therefore, is invited. But before addressing this question, a few more preliminary remarks that will serve both to avert misunderstanding and to elaborate on my characterization of the indistinct.

A JAPANESE SENSIBILITY?

Questions about the ubiquitous nature of an aesthetic sensibility are not of interest solely to anthropologists and cultural historians, since answers to these questions shape the kind of explanation that is sought. If, contrary to what I have been suggesting, there were nothing distinctive in the Japanese taste for the indistinct, one might look for an explanation in terms of a general human inclination. If, at the other extreme, the taste were confined to Japan, explanation would be sought in the specifics of, say, Japanese religion, history, or climate even. But this is indeed an extreme view, albeit one that remarks by Tanizaki and D. T. Suzuki, among others, appear to endorse.

When Tanizaki writes that "we [Japanese] find it hard to be really at home with things that shine and glitter," and that "this propensity to seek beauty in darkness [is] strong only in Orientals," he implies that the taste for the indistinct among Japanese or East Asian people is exclusive, and in a double sense.[16] Their taste is only for the indistinct and they alone share this taste. Suzuki hints at something similar in stating that the Japanese are "generally averse" to the bright and that they are "singularly attracted" to "bluish" moonlight, "semi-darkness," and other aspects of the indistinct.[17]

If this is their view, it is an exaggerated one, redolent of an era in which many writers were trying to identify a uniquely Japanese aesthetic mentality. For a start, it is clear that appreciation of the indistinct is not confined to East Asia. It was an English poet (John Keats) who lauded the mists of autumn, with its "barréd clouds [that] bloom the soft-dying day."[18] It was an Italian artist (Leonardo da Vinci) who invented the *sfumato* (smoky) style of painting and described as "despicable" any artist who "avoids shadows."[19] It was a French artist (Claude Monet) whose vague and hazy picture of the Port of Le Havre, "Impressions," gave its name to a movement committed to rendering experiences of the indistinct—a commitment echoed by a French composer (Claude Debussy) whose impressionistic works evoked fogs, gardens in the rain, and waves. It has been jazz saxophonists, as well as *shakuhachi* players, who have cultivated breathiness of tone, glissandos, and sinuous bends.

Nor, of course, does appreciation of the indistinct exhaust the aesthetic sensibility of the Japanese and exclude other forms of appreciation. There

is nothing *sfumato* or otherwise indistinct, for example, in the *ukiyo-e* art of
Kitagawa Utamaro and Utagawa Hiroshige. While many poems by Bashō
express his appreciation of the indistinct, he is also able to behold "with awe ...
fresh green leaves, bright in the sun."[20] There have, moreover, been Japanese
thinkers—most famously, Motoori Norinaga—who rejected the "Buddhist"
taste for the indistinct associated with an enthusiasm for the qualities of
wabi and *sabi*. An aesthetic more faithful to the Shinto tradition, Norinaga
maintains, is one of "cherry blossoms in the morning sun" and of attention to
"order, clarity, ... brightness."[21]

Should we conclude, then, that there is no distinctive Japanese aesthetic
of the indistinct—that, in Japanese and most other traditions, different tastes
simply rub shoulders with one another? Such, perhaps, is the pluralist spirit
of a *waka* by Yamaoka Tesshū: Mount Fuji is "fine against a brilliant sky,
fine when wrapped in clouds."[22] But that would be too quick a conclusion.
To begin with, one wonders how many American or European tourists would
regard it as fine if a famous mountain they had gone to view was wrapped in
clouds or obscured by mist. Second, while we encounter examples of enthusiasm for the indistinct among Western poets, painters, and musicians, the scale
is modest in comparison to the widespread and pronounced preference for the
indistinct attested to in Japanese literature, art, and aesthetic theory. Finally,
and conversely, while Japanese men and women may, of course, admire
order, clarity, and brightness, these qualities have not in Japan enjoyed the
status that they enjoyed in Europe as prominent ideals of beauty and art. For
Thomas Aquinas, *claritas* (splendor, radiance) was one of the "three conditions of beauty"—a view that at once influenced and reflected "the predilection of the medieval mind [for] luminous brightness." During the century
when Kenkō and Zeami were articulating an aesthetic of the suggestive and
the subdued, French writers like Jean Froissart and Eustache Deschamps
were trumpeting "the beauty of light and splendor," of "all that glitters."[23]

The contrasts here may be seen as ones over the importance of *form* in
aesthetic appreciation. For Aristotle and Aquinas, beauty is beauty of form,
and *claritas* is a condition of beauty because, as Umberto Eco explains, it is
"the radioactivity of the form of things," that which enables forms to manifest
themselves.[24] Nishida Kitarō was surely right to remark that nothing in the
East Asian aesthetic tradition corresponds to this emphasis on exposing and
communicating the forms of things—not least, as we'll see later, because of
doubts about the very idea of an intrinsic form as that which makes something
what it is. Instead of seeking, like the Greek artist, to create "perfection of
form and boundaries," the Japanese artist, Nishida writes, is concerned to
make something "reverberating without form and without bounds."[25]

The many poets who wrote in praise of experiences of the indistinct
would endorse Nishida's remark—as would the composer Toru Takemitsu.

"Thinking of musical form," he wrote, "I think of liquid form," and he compared the forms in his own music with "the shapes of dreams" and of waves.[26] Plenty of contemporary Western musicians, to be sure, also eschew clarity of formal structure in their compositions or improvisations. But then I am struck by the frequent similarity between the products of this recent development in Western music and the repertoire of traditional *shakuhachi* music in Japan.

While disclaiming, then, any pretense to identify the essence or uniqueness of Japanese aesthetic sensibility, there is in my judgment something sufficiently pronounced and distinctive in the Japanese appreciation of the indistinct to invite explanation.

THE INDISTINCT IN JAPANESE AESTHETICS

Explanations seek to make what is puzzling less so. Those who offer what might be called 'vertical explanations' of the taste for the indistinct would seek to ground it in something more fundamental, a worldview perhaps, of which it is seen to be an understandable consequence. (I turn to such explanations in the next section.) A horizontal explanation, by contrast, would locate this taste in an already familiar conceptual landscape, integrating it with what we are used to. In this section, I want to locate appreciation of the indistinct in relation to some familiar aspects of Japanese aesthetics.

Among the concepts highlighted in surveys of Japanese aesthetics are the following: *yūgen, wabi, sabi,* and *shibui.* The importance of these concepts in the Japanese tradition attests to a sensitivity toward the mysterious and the recessive, the simple and the humble, the stark and the weathered, the rough and the austere. These glosses are not intended as translations of the Japanese terms—a fruitless ambition, perhaps, given that the individual contributions of the terms to Japanese aesthetic discourse are not precise. They form something of a cluster, combining and conspiring to oppose an aesthetic of "the showy, gaudy, boastful and vulgar."[27]

The indistinct, I propose, is adjacent or auxiliary to the cluster of properties indicated by the familiar concepts—and in two ways. First, perceptions of the indistinct are apt for enhancing people's experience of these properties. Second, a taste for properties in the cluster invites appreciation of the indistinct.

The affinity between the indistinct and this cluster has been noted by several writers. The tea master Takeno Jōō thought that the atmosphere of *wabi* was perfectly conveyed in the Fujiwara no Teika poem, cited earlier, about a "bayside reed hovel."[28] The aspect of *wabi* it evokes is a "tranquil, austere beauty" very different from the "vivid beauty" of, say, a bright spring morning. And it evokes this precisely through drawing attention to the indistinctness of the hovel, viewed as it is "in the autumn dusk."[29] As a pioneering master of *chanoyu*, moreover, Jōō was aware how an already established appreciation for this tranquil, austere beauty would encourage mindfulness of the muted light in the tea hut, the rough and irregular contours of the path leading to it, and other indistinct phenomena.

When a poet quoted by Kenkō remarks that "it is only after the silk wrapper has frayed at top and bottom that a scroll looks beautiful," the affinity is between the indistinct and the quality of *sabi*. The poet displays his "excellent taste" for the "withered" or "desolate" beauty usually associated with *sabi* through his admiration for a scroll whose edges are no longer sharp or defined.[30]

But it is, perhaps unsurprisingly, with the appreciation of *yūgen* that a taste for the indistinct is most congruent. Unsurprisingly, since etymologically the very term signifies what is dim, dark, and shadowy. It would be eccentric, if not impossible, to be sensitive to the suggestion of mystery associated with *yūgen* while being utterly insensitive to the indistinct. Certainly, the two sensitivities are often linked and mutually enhancing. When Chōmei wants to illustrate the experience of *yūgen*, of "mystery and depth," his example is an autumn evening in which "there is no color in the sky, nor any sound," and "though we can give no definite reason for it, we are moved to tears."[31] For Tanizaki, nothing conjures "an inexpressible aura of depth and mystery" more effectively than the indistinct sheen of gold-flecked lacquerware that, "set out in the night, reflects the wavering candlelight."[32]

If appreciation of the indistinct comfortably combines with concepts like *yūgen* and *wabi*, it is related as well to two frequently emphasized aspects of Japanese aesthetic sensibility. The first of these is a preference for "allusiveness over explicitness and completeness,"[33] the second an openness to "the special pleasure of impermanence."[34] It is not difficult to discern how appreciation of the indistinct integrates with and, indeed, promotes each of these aspects.

From Chōmei and the fifteenth-century poets Shōtetsu and Shinkei to twentieth-century theorists like Kusanagi Masao, Japanese authors have advocated the practice by poets and artists of *yojō*—"overtones" or the communication of an atmosphere that is not made verbally or pictorially explicit. "Good is the artist," declared a seventeenth-century painter, "who detests painting anything without leaving a sufficient amount unsaid."[35] While not everything that intimates rather than asserts, or that alludes rather than makes explicit, is indistinct, it is not an accident that indistinctness is often the vehicle for conveying overtones. For Chōmei, those autumn hills glimpsed through the mist exemplify not only *yūgen*, but the value of *yojō* as well: for "this shadowy scene ... permits free exercise of the imagination in picturing ... the scarlet leaves," and this, he adds, is something "far better than to see them spread with dazzling clarity before our eyes."[36] In a similar vein, the architect of the Nō drama, Zeami Motokiyo, urges that the consummate actor "does nothing"—nothing, at any rate, that obviously or "directly" manifests his "inner state" to the audience. He communicates instead through subtle, indistinct gestures whose intimations only connoisseurs of the drama are able, through the use of their educated imagination, to recognize.[37] And surely the *shakuhachi*'s aptness for intimating rather than imitating the call of a deer or the soughing of a wind is due to the indistinctness of its tones and dynamics.

In short, an indistinct object of experience—the misty hill, the Nō actor's slight gesture, the *shakuhachi* melody—is typically one that, precisely in virtue of its indistinctness, does not explicitly refer the perceiver to anything, but instead provides scope for the imagination to conjure something up. In virtue of their indistinctness, too, objects of experience are apt for inviting a sense of impermanence. This occurs for different reasons. Many indistinct phenomena are themselves paradigmatically transient or ephemeral: patches of mist or plumes of smoke that form and then dissipate as one watches them, for example, or waves that rise from the water only to fall back and disappear. More stable, less impermanent objects—even if, in reality, they are "slowly unfolding events"[38]—tend to have definite forms and outlines; hence, they are less suited as symbols of what Buddhists view as the universal impermanence of things. Second, things are often indistinct—like Kenkō's frayed scroll, Tanizaki's dark smoky patina, or a mossy rock in a garden—because they are, or belong to, what is old. Or, better, because they announce their age and "bespeak" their antiquity—their subjection to weathering, long usage, natural cycles, decay, or some other agent of change. This is why the pleasure of impermanence often coincides with the pleasure of ruins, especially those whose original forms have become indefinite, occluded perhaps by vegetation and with their towers or pillars crumbling.

In this section, I have offered some explanation of the taste for the indistinct—a horizontal one—by placing it in relation to features already familiar from the discourse of Japanese aesthetics: first, to a number of well-known aesthetic categories, such as *yūgen*, and second, to appreciation of the allusive and the ephemeral. But explanation of this kind has its limits: for the puzzlement at the taste for the indistinct that it addressed may now simply be redirected at the larger sensibility in which this taste is at home. So I now turn to the possibility of a vertical explanation: of identifying a ground for the taste for the indistinct, one that may also help to explain the related tastes—for the allusive, say, or the weathered—just discussed.

INTERFUSION AND EMERGENCE

Some readers may think that this ground has already been identified. For isn't the taste for the indistinct, through its association with experiences of ephemerality, rooted in a Buddhist and Daoist vision of the impermanence of things, of reality as an unceasing process? The Japanese celebration of and pleasure in the experience of transience, some authors have proposed, is due to its confirmation that "things are proceeding as they must," to its "corroboration of this great and natural law of change."[39] Certainly, impermanence is an essential aspect of the world according to several East Asian visions, but it is an aspect best regarded, in my view, as a consequence of the fundamental way of things. And it is this fundamental way that I want now to articulate and to propose as the ground for appreciation of the indistinct.

Here are two remarks suggestive of the position I shall articulate. D. T. Suzuki speculates that the Japanese love of moonlight displays an aversion to anything that, "glaringly bright," is "too distinctive in its individuality." In gentle moonlight, "objects … appear not too strongly individualized."[40] The phenomenologist Erazim Kohák makes a similar point about things perceived indistinctly in subdued light when explaining his preference for dusk over daylight. Daylight has an "individuating brightness," in which "the beings of this world stand out in insistent individuality." At dusk, by contrast, "the failing light mutes the insistent individuality of the day."[41]

The aesthetic aversion expressed by these remarks—to what is too glaring, distinctive, bright, and insistent—reflects a metaphysical aversion. The world, as these authors see it, is not one of strongly individualized objects, of things that possess their own "insistent individuality." To experience them as such, in the glare of bright daylight, therefore encourages a false perception of the way of things. A more authentic experience would instill a sense—emphasized, for example, in Tendai Buddhism—of "the boundlessness of the interpenetration of phenomena with one another."[42] Just as a word is the one it is only because of its relationship to other words in a whole language, so it is only in virtue of a thing's interfusion with other things in a whole network that it is the thing it is.

There is a further, though closely connected, reason why, when beings stand out for us in insistent individuality, our experience is unfaithful to the reality of the world. When we experience something in this way, we are inclined to think of it as "just there," a ready-made ingredient of the world independent of and awaiting our perception of it. But belief in the existence of things as independent substances is an "illusion," a failure to realize that something is "'itself' only in relation to a set of conditions."[43] These conditions include, crucially, those that allow something to figure for us at all—to be experienced as this, that, or the other. For things to be experienced—to stand out at all for us—they must emerge for us from a background. This emergence is the condition for a being to be anything, a process that belies the illusion of unconditioned, objective existence that is encouraged by the perception of strongly individualized objects.

Our question is how appreciation of the indistinct might relate to recognition of the interfusion and emergence of things. The answer is that they reinforce each other. Mindful, reflective appreciation of the indistinct promotes a sense for interfusion and emergence, while this in turn promotes a discernment of the indistinct as an epiphany or a symbol of the way of things.

Each of the three modes of the indistinct identified in my opening section is able to cultivate a feel for the interfusion of things. Phenomena that are in themselves indistinct—for instance, wisps of cloud, puffs of smoke, and soft shadows—are not clearly demarcated from one another: they may merge, separate, and merge again. The same, we noted, was true of indistinct sounds and musical structures or flows. Indistinctness of borders is a device used by Japanese garden designers to convey a sense of union between human artifact and the natural order.

When objects of vision are rendered indistinct through occlusion—the hill or the moon half-hidden by a cloud, the temple obscured by falling blossoms—the effect is again to cultivate a sense of interfusion. The temple is not perceived standing in proud isolation, but only in relation to the blossoms that partly conceal it—blossoms that are themselves experienced, as they fall from branch to earth, as relating things to one another. Occlusion should remind us, too, that our experience of the world is always mediated and dependent on conditions. Staring at a mountain on a bright day with a clear line of vision, we tend to forget this dependence. It may require a painter of genius—a Turner or Monet—to make us mindful of the different qualities of light and atmosphere that shape our perception of things. Things are always occluded in the sense that our experience of them is inevitably mediated in a web of relationships to which they and we belong.

As for things rendered indistinct through being dimmed down, this is the very kind of indistinctness alleged by Kohák to promote a sense of "an intimate unity [or fusion]" of things. At dusk and in soft moonlight, the appearance of things is more faithful to their reality than under the noonday sun. Many Western philosophers have held that it is how something looks under "normal" conditions of clear daylight that is the criterion for its real look. Kohák proposes, in contrast, that "dusk is the time of philosophy"—for it is then that the illusion of the insistent individuality of things dissolves and they are seen to "fuse" together.[44]

The indistinct, then, is well equipped in its various modes to suggest, enhance, or reinforce a sense of, or a feel for, the interfusion of things. For this reason, the indistinct is an epiphany—an apt symbol, cipher, or metaphor—of this aspect of the way of things. And so it is of the other, related aspect that I labeled 'emergence.' To be more exact, it is a certain type of experience of the indistinct that evokes and illustrates the truth of emergence. This is the type recorded in two poems of Bashō's cited earlier, in which the call of a teal comes through the sound of the sea and the muffled tone of a bell emerges through the mist. These poems represent a very common theme of Japanese poetry. Shūōshi, for instance, writes of a reed warbler's song piercing the grey morning mist,[45] while throughout his poetry Issa displays what is almost an obsession with the emergence of sounds through an opaque medium—those of geese, skylarks, dogs, dung haulers, harps, and flutes, for example, coming through mist or rain.

Nor is it only sounds that the poets describe as penetrating through some medium to reach us. In verses by Bashō and Issa, it is a "gold chapel glowing through the sombre shade"[46] and the moon through a paper mosquito screen,[47] respectively, that overcome opacity so as to become objects of experience. And here is Tanizaki writing of the impression made on him after entering the "mouldy darkness" of an old house in Osaka:

> And yet there was in it something too of the quiet, mysterious gloom of a temple, something of the dark radiance that a Buddha's halo sends out from the depth of its niche ... . [I]t was a low, burnished radiance, easy to miss, pulsing out from beneath the overlays of the centuries.[48]

The Zen master Dōgen described the manifesting of Buddha-nature—of "suchness" and "emptiness"—as "something ineffable coming like this," an "advancing by all things" as they crystallize into objects of experience.[49] Reality is a process of the emergence of a world from a background that is not yet a structured realm of objects and forms. It is a sense of, or feel for, this conception of reality and experience that is promoted by mindful attention to faint sounds or sights emerging or "pulsing out," with growing distinctness, from the muffled, the dark, or the turbid. This is why the coming toward us of such sights and sounds is an apt metaphor for the "coming like this ... [of] all things" that, for Dōgen, is the coming to be of a world for us.

As a world of experience, this world is, of course, conditioned by ourselves: or, better, the "coming like this of all things" is a coming to be, not just of objects, but of us too. The role of the indistinct in evoking this intimacy or fusion between us and the world is recognized by many Japanese artists. Takemitsu, for example, observes that sounds are not simply heard, they "penetrate" us, while being dependent on us for their "freedom to breathe." This is why he is "assured of being in the sounds, becoming one with them"—an assurance he communicates in works that, precisely through their indistinct and fluid forms, reenact the gradual emergence of structure from an "original material" that preceded form.[50]

Here, then, is a proposal for a vertical explanation of the taste for the indistinct. It is an appreciation, a pleasure, grounded in an implicit recognition of reality as the emergence or coming to presence in experience of interfused, interpenetrating beings, ourselves included, that are devoid of insistent individuality. In the perception of the indistinct—of what is without this individuality—there is an intimation of the way of things. Taken in conjunction with a horizontal explanation that locates the indistinct within the larger matrix of Japanese sensibility, the proposal reduces, I hope, the puzzlement of Yoshida Kenkō and Motoori Norinaga at this "unnatural" taste.

NOTES

1. Kamo no Chōmei in Wm. Theodore de Bary, Donald Keene, George Tanabe, and Paul Varley, eds., *Sources of Japanese Tradition*, vol. 1, *From Earliest Times to 1600*, 2nd ed. (New York: Columbia University Press, 2002), 387.

2. Yoshida Kenkō, *Essays in Idleness: The Tsurezuregusa of Kenkō*, trans. Donald Keene (New York: Columbia University Press, 1998), 115.

3. Jun'ichirō Tanizaki, *In Praise of Shadows*, trans. Thomas J. Harper and Edward G. Seidensticker (London: Vintage, 2001), 20, 46.

4. Matsuo Bashō, *The Narrow Road to the Deep North and Other Travel Sketches*, trans. Nobuyuki Yuasa (London: Penguin, 1966), 53.

5. Ibid., 61.

6. David G. Lanoue, "Haiku of Kobayashi Issa," HaikuGuy.com, accessed June 11, 2015, http://haikuguy.com/issa/index.html.

7. Yuriko Saito, "Japanese Aesthetics: Historical Overview," in *Encyclopedia of Aesthetics*, vol. 2, ed. Michael Kelly (New York: Oxford University Press, 1998), 548.

8. Tanizaki, *In Praise of Shadows*, 18.

9. Kenkō, *Essays in Idleness*, 115.

10. Robin D. Gill, *Cherry Blossom Epiphany: The Poetry and Philosophy of a Flowering Tree* (Key Biscayne, FL: Paraverse Press, 2006), 583.

11. As quoted in De Bary et al., *Sources of Japanese Tradition*, 390.

12. Natsume Sōseki, *Sanshiro*, trans. Jay Rubin (London: Penguin, 2009), 64.

13. Geoffrey Bownas and Anthony Thwaite, trans. and eds., *The Penguin Book of Japanese Verse* (London: Penguin, 1964), 111.

14. Toru Takemitsu, *Confronting Silence: Selected Writings*, trans. and ed. Yoshiko Kakudo and Glenn Glasow (Berkeley, CA: Fallen Leaf Press, 1995), 6.

15. Saito, "Japanese Aesthetics," 549.

16. Tanizaki, *In Praise of Shadows*, 18, 47.

17. Daisetz T. Suzuki, *Zen and Japanese Culture* (Princeton, NJ: Princeton University Press, 1973), 393.

18. John Keats, "To Autumn," in *The Oxford Book of English Verse, 1250–1918*, ed. Arthur Thomas Quiller-Couch (Oxford: Oxford University Press, 1939), 749.

19. Leonardo da Vinci, *A Treatise on Painting*, trans. John Francis Rigaud (New York: Dover, 2005), 68.

20. Bashō, *The Narrow Road*, 100.

21. Richard B. Pilgrim, *Buddhism and the Arts of Japan* (Chambersburg, PA: Anima Books, 1993), 10.

22. As quoted in Kōshirō Haga, "The *Wabi* Aesthetic through the Ages," in *Japanese Aesthetics and Culture: A Reader*, ed. Nancy G. Hume (Albany, NY: State University of New York Press, 1995), 274.

23. Johan Huizinga, *The Waning of the Middle Ages* (London: Penguin, 2001), 257–58.

24. Umberto Eco, *Art and Beauty in the Middle Ages*, trans. Hugh Bredin (New Haven, CT: Yale University Press, 1986), 81.

25. As quoted in James W. Heisig, *Philosophers of Nothingness: An Essay on the Kyoto School* (Honolulu: University of Hawai'i Press, 2001), 58.

26. Takemitsu, *Confronting Silence*, 40.

27. Sōetsu Yanagi, *The Unknown Craftsman: A Japanese Insight into Beauty*, adapt. Bernard Leach (Tokyo: Kodansha International, 1989), 148.

28. As quoted in De Bary et al., *Sources of Japanese Tradition*, 390.

29. As quoted in Haga, "*Wabi* Aesthetic," 249.

30. Kenkō, *Essays in Idleness*, 70.

31. De Bary et al., *Sources of Japanese Tradition*, 387.

32. Tanizaki, *In Praise of Shadows*, 24.

33. Graham Parkes, "Japanese Aesthetics," in *The Stanford Encyclopedia of Philosophy*, Winter 2011 Edition, ed. Edward N. Zalta, accessed June 11, 2015, http://plato.stanford.edu/archives/win2011/entries/japanese-aesthetics/, 4.

34. Donald Keene, "Japanese Aesthetics," in *Japanese Aesthetics and Culture: A Reader*, ed. Nancy G. Hume (Albany, NY: State University of New York Press, 1995), 39.

35. As quoted in Masao Kusanagi, "The Logic of Passional Surplus," in *Modern Japanese Aesthetics: A Reader*, trans. and ed. Michele Marra (Honolulu: University of Hawai'i Press, 1999), 153.

36. De Bary et al., *Sources of Japanese Tradition*, 387.

37. Ibid., 371.

38. Crispin Sartwell, *Six Names of Beauty* (London: Routledge, 2004), 128.

39. Donald Richie, *A Tractate on Japanese Aesthetics* (Berkeley, CA: Stone Bridge, 2007), 37–38.

40. Suzuki, *Zen and Japanese Culture*, 393.

41. Erazim Kohák, *The Embers and the Stars: A Philosophical Inquiry into the Moral Sense of Nature* (Chicago: University of Chicago Press, 1984), 32.

42. William R. LaFleur, *The Karma of Words: Buddhism and the Literary Arts in Medieval Japan* (Berkeley, CA: University of California Press, 1983), 106.

43. Graham Parkes, "Ways of Japanese Thinking," in *Japanese Aesthetics and Culture: A Reader*, ed. Nancy G. Hume (Albany, NY: State University of New York Press, 1995), 85.

44. Kohák, *The Embers and the Stars*, 32.

45. Bownas and Thwaite, *Japanese Verse*, 170.

46. Bashō, *The Narrow Road*, 119.

47. Lanoue, "Haiku of Kobayashi Issa."

48. Jun'ichirō Tanizaki, *Some Prefer Nettles*, trans. Edward G. Seidensticker (London: Vintage, 2001), 34.

49. Dōgen, *Master Dōgen's Shōbōgenzō, Book 2*, trans. Gudo Nishijima and Chodo Cross (London: Windbell Publications, 1996), ch. 3.

50. Toru Takemitsu, "Nature and Music," in *The Book of Music and Nature: An Anthology of Sounds, Words, Thoughts*, ed. David Rothenberg and Marta Ulvaeus (Middletown, CT: Wesleyan University Press, 2001), 184, 189; as quoted in Oliver Knussen, "Toru Takemitsu," liner notes to *Takemitsu: Quotation of Dream*, London Sinfonietta, with Paul Crossley and Peter Serkin, cond. Oliver Knussen, Deutsche Grammophon ♭453 495–2, 1998, CD, 6.

Chapter 3

Authority in Taste

Richard Bullen

HUME'S STANDARD OF TASTE

In his *A Tractate on Japanese Aesthetics*, Donald Richie writes:

> A Western justification of taste was voiced by the philosopher David Hume (1711–1776), who held that [the] authorization of the beautiful was the result of experience and education. Men of taste were in a position to assess worth and beauty. They could set a universal standard. Hume's thesis inspired its direct contrast in Kant's view that the worth and beauty lay in the art work itself and not in any evaluation of it. The Japanese definition of worth and beauty is much closer to Hume's than to Kant's.[1]

Richie's suggestion that Hume's treatise on taste provides a way for understanding Japanese aesthetic thinking is intriguing and, as far as I am aware, unique. In this chapter, I first outline an aspect of Hume's aesthetic philosophy: his notion of the standard of taste, manifested in the imaginary figure of the "good judge." Following Richie's prompt, I then explain Hume's theory as finding concrete parallels in Japanese traditions. I provide the specific examples of two towering figures in Japanese cultural history, Sen no Rikyū (1522–1591) and Kobori Enshū (1579–1647), and explore the institutional and aesthetic systems that perpetuate and define their tastes. The chapter concludes with some thoughts on correspondence between aesthetic and moral philosophy in Hume's work and in traditional Japanese systems.

To begin with, a clarification regarding Kant's aesthetic theory is explored. Richie's assertion that, according to Kant, "the worth and beauty lay in the art work itself and not in any evaluation of it" is misleading. In the very first section of his third critique, *The Critique of Judgment*, Kant unequivocally establishes that the judgment of taste centers on the experiencing subject, *not* the external object, as Richie implies. Richie is correct, however, that Hume's ideas may be contrasted with Kant's, but not because Kant understands beauty to reside in the object. In fact, in Hume's essay "Of the Standard of Taste," dedicated exclusively to aesthetics, he advocates something of a middle ground: beauty is the pleasure felt in the presence of certain objects. Although he is adamant that beauty and deformity "are not qualities in objects," things we call 'beautiful' are "naturally fitted to excite agreeable sentiments" or "naturally calculated to give pleasure." This idea is central to his scheme: sentiment or feeling derives from the qualities of the object judged.[2]

A general problem Hume identifies is that, very often, people fail to recognize these qualities because of personal defects or imperfect conditions. Thus arise disputes about the objectivity of aesthetic value, so that the proverb "Beauty is in the eye of the beholder," based on our experience, may *seem* to hold true. However, Hume claims, "It is natural for us to seek a *Standard of Taste*; a rule, by which the various sentiments of men may be reconciled; at least, a decision, afforded, confirming one sentiment, and condemning another." We feel that some judgments of taste are correct and others are not, but how are we to know which?

Hume's method to achieve this standard manifests in the authority of what he calls 'good judges,' people of supreme taste, whose judgments about art can be trusted and followed, and hold true over time. These arbiters of taste, or ideal critics, he describes as possessing five qualities, from which their authority derives. The qualities are as follows: sound faculties of reason and good sense; an innate sensitivity to perceive the smallest detail; freedom from prejudice and openness to different cultures; plenty of practice in their particular chosen field of art; and individual judgments perfected by opportunities for comparison. The culmination of these virtues results in the expert, whose knowledge enables him to assess and compare individual objects in his field.

In summary, Hume claims, taste requires innate talent, refined through experience and practice. The good judges hone their natural skills by engagement and study. Others may learn to sharpen their own tastes by recognizing and emulating this standard, that is, by aligning their skills and behavior with Hume's true judges. "It is sufficient for our present purpose," Hume writes,

> if we have proved, that the taste of all individuals is not upon an equal footing, and that some men in general, however difficult to be particularly pitched upon, will be acknowledged by universal sentiment to have a preference above others.

Aesthetic education implies acknowledging the true judges' authority as to which works of art set standards. These judges express the universal standard, and thus their assessments pass the "test of time." Great works of art are attended with the "durable admiration" of men of taste, and "have survived all the caprices of mode and fashion, all the mistakes of ignorance and envy."

Unsurprisingly, given his model of the judge who embodies the standard of taste, Hume does not identify those whom he sees as fulfilling the role. When we look for good judges in (Western) history, we find figures who tend to define beauty in their *own* age, such as Denis Diderot (1713–1784), John Ruskin (1819–1900), and Roger Fry (1866–1934), as opposed to universal beauty across the ages. I suspect the thought that prompted Richie was that, by contrast, something like Hume's good judges *are* recognized in Japanese culture, and the standards of taste identified with them retain power well after their deaths. Although Richie is not explicit in identifying who set the standards, the aesthetic assessments and theories of poetry by Fujiwara no Teika (1162–1241), of *Nō* by Zeami Motokiyo (c. 1363–1443), and of tea practice by Sen no Rikyū are discussed elsewhere in his *Tractate* and would serve as examples of this idea. These figures exerted authority on questions of taste and embody universal standards that have passed the test of time. I turn now to examine two tea masters, Rikyū and Enshū, whose cultural authority and aesthetic standards continue to be recognized to the present day.

STANDARDS OF THE MASTERS

The breadth of influence that tea masters have had on Japanese culture generally can be attributed to a number of factors. First and foremost, since the second half of the sixteenth century, the tea ceremony (*chanoyu*) has been practiced by many with power, or those close to power. *Chanoyu* was, in Kendall Brown's words, "virtually a required avocation for any man who sought access to the highest levels of Momoyama society."[3] It continued to be central to Japanese aesthetic culture until the nineteenth century, practiced by those with wealth or political influence. *Chanoyu* is still considered a refined art, particularly for women, and the number of people practicing today is in the millions.

From the sixteenth century, *chanoyu* has also attracted and absorbed some of Japan's finest aesthetic minds, who have shaped the artistic canon and tastes of the Japanese people. Eminent figures such as Honami Kōetsu (1558–1637), Shōkadō Shōjō (1584–1639), Emperor Gomizunoo (1596–1680), Ogata Kōrin (1658–1716), and Matsudaira Fumai (1751–1818) were tea practitioners, and their understanding of tea culture informed their art-making and connoisseurship.

The nature of *chanoyu* practice demands a wide range of expertise and skills. The practitioner trains in far more than the apparently simple preparation and offering of a bowl of tea—for example, the ways to walk, sit, open and close a door, bow, and handle and clean utensils are all subject to rules and conventions. The forms learned are naturally carried outside the tea-room, and in many cases they define everyday Japanese standards of behavior. In addition, students study the history and connoisseurship of the diverse cultural products used in tea practice, including ceramics, painting, calligraphy, cooking, gardening, architecture, and flower arranging. Again, the standards and rules are recognized across Japanese culture. *Kaiseki* cuisine, the style of food served at a *chanoyu* gathering, for instance, is among gastronomists' most highly valued modes of cooking. As Richie notes, "it was the bureaucracy of the *chanoyu* that defined many aspects of Japanese aesthetics."[4]

Sen no Rikyū and Kobori Enshū, who lived in the Momoyama and early Edo periods, were masters of *chanoyu* and held positions of influence close to the rulers of the day. Rikyū acted as tea master to Oda Nobunaga (1534–1582) and, following Nobunaga's death, as tea and general aesthetic advisor to Toyotomi Hideyoshi (1536–1598). Rikyū has been called 'the Thomas More of Japan'; both he and his student Furuta Oribe (1544–1615) wielded significant power and were ordered to commit suicide by their respective political masters.[5] Enshū held a number of official government roles, as well as acting as tea master to Tokugawa Iemitsu (1604–1651). From their positions of influence, Rikyū and Enshū were able to direct changes in culture.

Many of the forms and conventions of *chanoyu* remaining in practice today were codified at this time. The masters' authority was institutionalized and embedded in culture following their deaths through schools based around the forms of practice created by them. In the case of Rikyū, three schools were founded by three great-grandsons (today these are large schools known as 'the *San-Senke*'), and smaller schools dedicated to the styles of tea of Oribe and Enshū also exist to this day.[6]

In the mid-eighteenth century, the *iemoto* system, by which most traditional arts are organized, was established in the practice of *chanoyu*. Previously, tea masters had passed knowledge and authority to a single student (as Rikyū had done to Oribe). The new system evolved by the school head (*oiemoto-sama*, or grand master) delegating his authority to a number of others to teach the art on his behalf. This system continues into the present day and is found in various arts, including flower arranging (*kadō*), calligraphy (*shodō*), and incense appreciation (*kōdō*). The *iemoto* system perpetuates the cultural authority of the founding master, and his taste as interpreted by succeeding grand masters is the standard others follow.[7]

Under the *iemoto* system, the grand master is generally a hereditary position. Urasenke, the largest tea school, claims the present grand master to be the sixteenth-generation head in line from Rikyū. It is interesting by comparison that Hume considered aesthetic sensitivity an inborn skill, refined through training and practice. In the story from *Don Quixote* that he recounts in "Of the Standard of Taste," to illustrate the level of sensitivity necessary for a good judge, Sancho explains his skill in judging wine as "a quality hereditary in our family." The *iemoto* system, likewise, is grounded in the idea that authority and skill will succeed from parent to child.[8]

The grand master's authority is exercised across a number of areas. Within the world of *chanoyu*, the grand master holds the sole authority to create or alter rules of practice. One obvious way this authority manifests is in designing new methods (*temae*) for host and guests to act in *chanoyu* (in some ways analogous to a choreographer composing a dance). The grand master is also the ultimate authority on the traditions of the school, some of which issued from the school's founding master.

Tea masters make, design, and commission objects used in *chanoyu*, for example, tea bowls, paintings, calligraphy, vases, buildings, and gardens. In the case of *oiemoto-sama* and masters with established reputations, they are regarded as exemplary: paraphrased, copied, or inspiring others' artistic creativity. These roles were carried out by early masters such as Rikyū and Enshū. A master's favored sources are recognized for being so admired and remain identified with the master's taste, as in the so-called "seven kilns of Enshū" (*Enshūnana-gama*), from which Enshū commissioned utensils for tea. Commissioning works for use in the school sets standards of taste that, through *chanoyu* practice, reach a wide audience.

The connoisseurship of masters has directed tastes (and collecting habits) for 400 years. A way of achieving this has been through the selection of "masterpieces." Three categories of masterpieces were recognized and refined in the eighteenth century by members of the Matsudaira family: those from before the time of Rikyū (*ōmeibutsu*); those from the time of Rikyū (*meibutsu*); and those selected by Enshū (*chūkō meibutsu*, or "rediscovered masterpieces"). These categories remain recognized and used today. Grand masters also hold a great deal of power in matters of taste and connoisseurship, through their authority in assessing utensils and verifying the authenticity of objects used in tea. Such assessments are often attested through certificates issued by the master. Another method of authenticating an object is through inscribing the box in which it is held. Morgan Pitelka explains:

> It was widely assumed that the *iemoto* was the leading connoisseur of tea utensils, making his written description of an object's provenance equivalent to a pledge of quality. The *iemoto* could also use box inscriptions to construct hierarchies of connoisseurship. His decision to accept or reject a request for a box inscription, and his choice of words, could create standards of taste within the school.[9]

The aesthetic authority of the masters such as Rikyū and Enshū, then, was passed on to and mediated through the schools' subsequent grand masters. *Oiemoto-sama* dictated "the aesthetic beliefs and consumption habits" of tea practitioners in their schools by imposing, as Pitelka puts it, the "*iemoto gaze*." The *iemoto* system, in the words of Pitelka again, "fundamentally transformed culture in Japan by creating a monopoly on the definition and regulation of meaning in key fields of cultural production such as tea."[10]

KONOMI AND STANDARDS

There is a specific Japanese aesthetic term that describes the mechanism of an institutionalized taste as issuing from some masters: *konomi* (*gonomi*). Used as a suffix to a name (*k* changes to *g* for euphonic purposes), it means "according to the taste of ___," or "in the style preferred by ___," where '___' is a placeholder for a specific master. As well as describing specific charac-teristics of the object, it carries qualitative value. An object so described may have been commissioned or even designed or made by the master—such as a tea scoop (*chashaku*), garden, or teahouse—at the time of the master or some time later. Hence, a contemporary bowl can be described as Rikyū-*gonomi*, meaning it exhibits characteristics that align with Rikyū's taste and within that aesthetic system carries value. Although *konomi* classifies an object according to the master's taste, it may remove the power of judgment on the object from the master himself.

The identification of an object as a master's *konomi* classifies the object through the taste of the master—as the guiding principle in its manufacture, in the principles through which it is assessed to hold aesthetic value, or both—as distinct from identifying it exclusively through the person responsible for its manufacture. Instructive instances in this regard are imported Dutch ceram-ics used in tea gatherings, as favored by Enshū.[11] A well-known example of Enshū-*gonomi* is the Katsura Palace, which today is generally accepted as not having been designed by Enshū.

Konomi may be seen as a class within the wider Japanese aesthetic system known as 'categorical aesthetics,' including principles such as *shibui* or *iki*. As with *konomi*, these standards have directed the establishment of the Japa-nese canon through centuries of usage. In line also with these terms, *konomi* exhibits the quality of universality; there would never be any measure of disagreement about whether an object was an instance of a master's *konomi*. Like the more well-known aesthetic categories, *konomi* carries qualitative and referential meanings.

Enshū-*gonomi* and Rikyū-*gonomi* are understood through other principles. The Enshū-*gonomi* aesthetic is explained through the epithet *kirei-sabi*.[12] *Sabi* referred to Enshū's engagement with ancient (largely Heian period) aesthetic culture. *Kirei* was a conception of beauty held by those people surrounding the Kanei Imperial Court (1624–1644), in which Enshū played a leading role.[13] In modern Japanese language, *kirei* is an everyday word expressing pleasure in a beautiful object, as well as cleanness and neatness, and suggests a close connection between Enshū's taste and a broadly held Japanese sense of taste. Susumu Ōno writes:

> As can be seen from the following example used in Japan, '*zashiki wo kirei ni shite*' (Clean up the [*tatami*] room), '*kirei*' conveys a meaning of purity or cleanness. On top of this, it is also used to mean that absolutely nothing remains as in the phrase, '*kirei ni tabete shimatta*' (I ate every last bit).[14]

Spareness, neatness, and cleanness are qualities immediately identified with Enshū-*gonomi*, such as the Katsura Palace or the Mittan-seki tearoom at the Ryōkōin sub-temple of Daitokuji (designed by Enshū). In his canonical essay "Japanese Aesthetics," Donald Keene described an aspect of the modern tea ceremony—"the expense of a great deal of money to achieve a look of bare simplicity"—as "entirely in keeping with Japanese tradition." Simplicity, "[t]he use of the most economical means to obtain the desired effect," Keene claimed, is one of four concepts that "point to the most typical forms of Japanese aesthetic expression."[15] Enshū's taste sanctioned aesthetic cleanness and simplicity within the aesthetic system of tea and, through tea, within Japanese culture generally.

Rikyū-*gonomi* is understood through *wabi*, which refers to a different kind of simplicity or economy than Enshū's. Whereas Enshū-*gonomi* evidences a simplicity that is clean or sharp, the simplicity of *wabi* is to be identified more in deliberate artlessness or plainness. The quality of *wabi* is the antithesis of showy, overt, or ostentatious, and hence the *wabi* object is seemingly ordinary. *Wabi* was used as an aesthetic term before Rikyū, primarily in poetry, but its meaning was adopted into *chanoyu* culture and altered by his taste.[16] Perhaps the most obvious instance of Rikyū-*gonomi* is a style of black *raku* tea bowl. It is believed that around 1588 Rikyū commissioned the ceramic tile-maker Tanaka Chōjirō (1516–1592) to make tea bowls from local Kyoto clay, modeled by hand. Following Rikyū's selection, Chōjirō's bowls became highly favored, and his descendants continue to make *raku* ware for tea practitioners, including Sen family masters. *Raku-yaki* are now some of the most internationally recognizable objects associated with Japanese aesthetic taste.

In the culture of *chanoyu*, categorizing objects as in line with a *konomi* is a clear way by which assessments of aesthetic value are institutionalized and become standards for others to recognize and follow. In the case of Rikyū and Enshū, they became, in Arata Isozaki's words, "enduring aesthetic styles." In fact, although he rightly admits to overemphasizing the case, Isozaki claims that "the concept of *Enshugonomi* subsumes all of what is called Japanese taste, sensibility, and design."[17]

Through the structure of *konomi*, standards of taste are immediately recognizable to those acting in the culture. The idea that communally accepted
aesthetic values direct and train the individual has a long history in Japanese
aesthetic understanding: what is beautiful, as Richie notes, depends on social
consensus.[18] The *iemoto* system, "with its strict emphasis on aesthetic value
as a product of authority,"[19] and a *konomi* effectively institutionalizes and
stabilizes taste in the area it dominates. Hume's suggestion that sentiment
be refined through practice by aligning one's taste with the good judges' is
instantiated in the Japanese aesthetic tradition, where aesthetic pleasures are
trained to conform to standards established by masters. Following on from
this idea, in the final section, I suggest a further point of comparison between
Hume's and traditional Japanese aesthetic philosophy.

MORAL AND AESTHETIC STANDARDS

Masters' *konomi* are unusual as aesthetic categories in the Japanese sphere
in that they evidence no explicit moral dimension. Describing an object as
a master's *konomi* identifies it as of the form or style that the master would
make, that is, as aligned with his "system of methods" in art-making.[20] Other
aesthetic categories I have discussed have clear moral dimensions. Most
obvious is *wabi*, which evidences strong moral values, and for most commentators these cannot be separated from its aesthetic meanings. An authoritative
and straightforward description of *wabi*'s moral dimension is that given in the
eighteenth-century *chanoyu* text, the *Zencharoku*:

> [W]abi means that even in straitened circumstances no thought of hardship
> arises. Even amid insufficiency, you are moved by no feeling of want. Even
> when faced with failure, you do not brood over injustice. If you find being in
> straitened circumstances to be confining, if you lament insufficiency as priva-
> tion, if you complain that things have been ill-disposed—this is not *wabi*. Then
> you are indeed destitute.[21]

Wabi sets as an ideal ridding of desires and acceptance of one's lot in the world.
The *wabi* aesthetic is conventionally understood as enmeshed with this aspiration, as rejecting luxury in favor of the humble and the ordinary. Art-related
activity is an aspect of the person's moral being, and aesthetic philosophy is
concerned with the construction of the moral being. In conflating the moral and
the aesthetic, such thinking diverges from the Western philosophical tradition
following Kant, which distinguishes the source of aesthetic pleasure from the
domain of morality. In judging the goodness of an object, the subject refers to a
concept (of the good), whereas in judging an object's beauty, the subject refers

to an indeterminate cognitive free play that he feels as pleasurable. The structures of these types of judgment are distinct, and much of Western aesthetics since Kant has recognized the nature of aesthetic pleasure as distinct from moral feeling.[22] By contrast, for Hume, moral judgment is described as akin to aesthetic assessment, and it issues from the same source as the aesthetic, that is, from sentiment, not reason. The judgment of taste, as Hume describes it, shares its structure with moral judgment. He writes:

> To have the sense of virtue, is nothing but to *feel* a satisfaction of a particular kind from the contemplation of a character. The very *feeling* constitutes our praise or admiration. ... The case is the same as in our judgements concerning all kinds of beauty, and tastes, and sensations. Our approbation is imply'd in the immediate pleasure they convey to us.[23]

The identification of the sources of the aesthetic and the moral is evident in early Japanese history. In the culture of the Heian period, to display good taste was a moral imperative.[24] The Buddhist priest Kūkai (774–835) was the first to write theoretically about the arts in Japan, and he proposed art of various kinds as being central to religious education. When he wrote that "[a]rt is what reveals to us the state of perfection," his meaning was epistemological, as well as aesthetic and moral.[25]

In China, by the Song Dynasty, the idea had developed that nobility in painting was a reflection of the nobility of the man. The most immediate model for painters was calligraphy, where it was established prior to Song that the calligraphic line manifested the spirit of he who penned it, and that the reader of the written character retraced the movements of the master's brush and sensed his goodness. The art of painting later adopted this idea.[26] For Song thinkers, such as Guo Ruoxu (fl. third-quarter of the eleventh century), if moral goodness is a quality of the artist, it will show in the painting he produces: a painting, in Guo Ruoxu's terms, is a "mind print."[27] Thus, the Yuan poet and calligrapher Yang Weizhen (1296–1370) was able to reason that "a painting's excellence or inferiority lies in the loftiness or baseness of an artist's character."[28]

For the viewer of pictorial art, tracing the lines of the master's brush is in itself a moral act. James Cahill describes the representation of moral goodness in art thus:

> If the manifold facets of the mind, the character, the exemplary qualities, of the superior man can be communicated in a work of art, then those qualities may be perceived by others and implanted in them.[29]

The connoisseur retraces in imagination the movements of the master's brush and senses an affinity with him. In surveying the painting of the good man, we evidence and in a way inherit his goodness. As Cahill explains, past masters set moral/artistic standards that, when followed by others, create a group's identity.

> The scholar who comes to understand his predecessors by reading their literary works or savoring their calligraphy and painting comes also to feel a kinship with them; another dimension, an extension into the past, is added to his sense of communion with men of like mind.[30]

The notion that aesthetic and moral community standards are created by artists and inherited by those who, following past masters, practice that art became part of the understanding of art that the Medieval Japanese inherited from the continent. *Chanoyu* evolved from aspects of Zen tea-making rituals, *renga* (linked verse poetry), and profane tea-drinking practices. From the sixteenth century, it had strong aesthetic associations with a wide range of arts, including painting, calligraphy, and incense appreciation. All of these arts evidence a moral role in helping foster the individual's growth through studying the methods of past masters and the teacher-student relationship.

The wider moral dimension of *chanoyu* practice in particular is obvious— the entire procedure is directed toward hosting a guest or guests for refreshments.[31] The tea ceremony, in Yuriko Saito's words, is "usually credited for setting the model for civilized behavior and rules of etiquette that are still alive and well in Japan today." This model of refinement is represented by the schools of *chanoyu* founded by masters such as Rikyū and Enshū and carried on by subsequent masters and *oiemoto-sama*. In this, they instantiate what Timothy M. Costelloe describes as Hume's true judge, "a model of perfection that shows how one ought to behave if one wishes to become a person of taste."[32] The universally recognized high level of aesthetic culture Japan has produced for over a millennium is attributable, in no small measure, to the models that masters such as Rikyū and Enshū have provided to those seeking to refine their taste.

NOTES

1. Donald Richie, *A Tractate on Japanese Aesthetics* (Berkeley, CA: Stone Bridge Press, 2007), 27. The passage finishes: "It is still believed that, although the elements found common to beauty are perhaps universal, it is their reception (the universal standard) that creates the excellence of the art." Peter Leech considered parallels between Kant's aesthetic philosophy and Japanese aesthetic philosophy in "Freedom and Formula: An Inter-Cultural Problem of Western and Japanese Aesthetics," in *The Pursuit of Comparative Aesthetics: An Interface Between East and West*, ed. Mazhar Hussain and Robert Wilkinson (Aldershot, UK: Ashgate, 2006), 233–47.

2. David Hume, "Of the Standard of Taste" (1757), in *The Philosophy of Art: Readings Ancient and Modern*, ed. Alex Neill and Aaron Ridley (New York: McGraw-Hill, 1995). Because the essay is short and is reprinted widely in collections and anthologies, I have not footnoted quotations.

3. Kendall H. Brown, *The Politics of Reclusion: Painting and Power in Momoyama Japan* (Honolulu: University of Hawai'i Press, 1997), 59.

4. Richie, 30–31. A further reason that might be cited for the strength of influence *chanoyu* has over Japanese aesthetic culture is the length of its history—*chanoyu* lore has Murata Jukō (c. 1423–1502) introducing his tea-making procedure to Ashikaga Yoshimasa (1435–1490) at the Silver Pavilion in the 1480s. As Richie writes, "In Japan as elsewhere, the longer this standard prevails, the more legitimate becomes the canon of taste itself" (25).

5. Eiko Ikegami notes that "the grand masters who could claim descent from Sen no Rikyū elevated the master's tragic death to the level of aesthetic martyrdom and emphasized his authority as the embodiment of the true spirit of the tea ceremony." Ikegami, *Bonds of Civility: Aesthetic Networks and the Political Origins of Japanese Culture* (New York: Cambridge University Press, 2005), 167. Historians have recognized a number of possible causes for Rikyū's falling into disfavor with Hideyoshi, provoking Hideyoshi to order his death. One explanation is that Rikyū used his authority to manipulate the pottery market to his advantage.

6. Other influential *chanoyu* masters were Murata Jukō, Takeno Jōō (1502–1555, Rikyū's teacher), and Katagiri Sekishū (1605–1673). According to Paul Varley, Rikyū's disciples "established Murata Shukō, Takeno Jōō, and Rikyū as a trinity of gods of *chanoyu* whose achievements would remain the highest models for all tea masters who followed them." Varley, "*Chanoyu*: From the Genroku Epoch to Modern Times," in *Tea in Japan: Essays on the History of* Chanoyu, ed. Paul Varley and Kumakura Isao (Honolulu: University of Hawai'i Press, 1989), 161.

7. The *iemoto* system may go back to the Muromachi period (although not under that name). The system as it developed to regulate arts in the Edo period has been criticized, most notably by Matsunosuke Nishiyama, for stifling creativity and freedom in the arts. Donald Keene reports that the *iemoto* system in *Nō* "has increasingly become a target not only of criticism but [also] of scorn." Keene, "The *Iemoto* System (*Nō* and *Kyōgen*)," in *The Blue-Eyed Tarōkaja: A Donald Keene Anthology*, ed. J. Thomas Rimer (New York: Columbia University Press, 1996), 237. In my experience, although it occasionally is a source of frustration, *chanoyu* practitioners do not routinely or severely criticize the *iemoto* system.

8. See Patrick G. O'Neill, "Organization and Authority in the Traditional Arts," *Modern Asian Studies* 18, no. 4 (1984): 635.

9. Morgan Pitelka, *Handmade Culture: Raku Potters, Patrons, and Tea Practitioners* (Honolulu: University of Hawai'i Press, 2005), 101.

10. Ibid., 90.

11. On Enshū's collection of art, including tea utensils, see Sokei Kobori, *The Enshū Way of Tea* (Leiden: Rijksmuseum voor Volkenkunde, 1980).

12. On *kirei-sabi* and *wabi*, see Richard Bullen, "Refining the Past," *British Journal of Aesthetics* 30, no. 3 (2010): 249–53. *Sabi* is sometimes conjoined with *wabi*, as *wabi-sabi*, but their qualities are different. Under the entry for *sabi*, *Genshoku*

chadō daijiten, ed. Iguchi Kaisen et al. (Kyoto: Tankosha, 1975), has the following: "*Wabi* also is a foundation for the spirit of *chanoyu*, and the two are conjoined easily. However, at about the time of the *Shin kokinshu* [c. 1205] something like a conflict in aesthetic consciousness occurred. 'Wabi' means 'miserable,' 'to be worried about,' 'a sad and troubled state of mind'; as a state of affairs, terms such as 'omoi wabi' and 'urami wabi' imply dislike or loathsomeness. On the other hand, *sabi* ... is desirable or agreeable."

13. See Hidetoshi Saitō, *Katsura Rikyū* (Tokyo: Shōgakukan, 1982), 166.

14. Susumu Ōno, "Biishiki no hattatsu to Nihongo," *Risō* 483 (1973): 27–40, 39.

15. Donald Keene, "Japanese Aesthetics," in *Appreciations of Japanese Culture* (Tokyo: Kodansha International, 1990), 20, 13.

16. Takeno Jōō was probably the first tea practitioner to use the term *wabi*, to describe the "cold and withered" taste Murata Jukō had adopted from *renga* and *waka*.

17. Arata Isozaki, "The Diagonal Strategy: Katsura as Envisioned by 'Enshu's Taste,'" in *Katsura Imperial Villa*, ed. Virginia Ponciroli (Milan: Electa Architecture, 2005), 36. Richie makes a similar claim for Rikyū, that he created "many of the subtle, understated, aesthetic standards we now associate with traditional Japanese art" (30).

18. Richie, 28.

19. Pitelka, 104.

20. See Isozaki, 33.

21. This translation from Denis Hirota, "The Practice of Tea 5—*The Zen Tea Record*: A Statement of *Chanoyu* as Buddhist Practice," *Chanoyu Quarterly* 54 (1988): 50. *Kirei* also manifests a moral dimension. On cleanliness as an aesthetic/moral idea, see Kitamura Tomoyuki, "Clean, Clear Mind and Love for Nature," *Literature and Aesthetics* 15, no. 1 (2005), accessed June 25, 2015, http://openjournals.library.usyd.edu.au/index.php/LA/article/view/5080/5785. The aspect of *Kirei* I distinguish in Enshū's taste is identified with "cleanness," as of a line, as opposed to "cleanliness," as in hygiene.

22. A well-reasoned example of this is Stuart Hampshire, "Logic and Appreciation," in *Æsthetics and Language*, ed. William Elton (Oxford: Basil Blackwell, 1954), 161–69.

23. David Hume, *A Treatise of Human Nature*, ed. L. A. Selby-Bigge, 2nd ed. (Oxford: Oxford University Press, 1978), 471.

24. See Ivan Morris, *The World of the Shining Prince: Court Life in Ancient Japan* (Tokyo, New York, and London: Kodansha International, 1994), especially "The Cult of Beauty," 170–98.

25. Cited in *Sources of Japanese Tradition*, ed. Ryusaku Tsunoda, Wm. Theodore de Bary, and Donald Keene (New York: Columbia University Press, 1964), 138. A good example of the conflation of moral and aesthetic issues is found in Yasunari Kawabata, *Japan, the Beautiful, and Myself: The 1968 Nobel Prize Acceptance Speech*, trans. Edward G. Seidensticker (Tokyo: Kodansha International, 1969).

26. Expressed, for example, by Yang Weizhen: "Calligraphy and painting are one and the same. Scholar-officials who are skilled in painting must be proficient

in calligraphy, since the techniques of painting are already there in the methods of calligraphy." Susan Bush and Hsio-Yen Shih, eds., *Early Chinese Texts on Painting* (Cambridge, MA: Harvard University Press, 1985), 245.

27. Ibid., 96.

28. Ibid., 246.

29. James F. Cahill, "Confucian Elements in the Theory of Painting," in *The Confucian Persuasion*, ed. Arthur F. Wright (Stanford, CA: Stanford University Press, 1960), 124.

30. Ibid., 125.

31. This point and the following quote from Yuriko Saito, *Everyday Aesthetics* (Oxford: Oxford University Press, 2007), 7, 236.

32. Timothy M. Costelloe, *Aesthetics and Morals in the Philosophy of David Hume* (New York: Routledge, 2007), 23.

Chapter 4

Beauty as Ecstasy in the Aesthetics of Nishida and Schopenhauer

Steve Odin

INTRODUCTION

In this chapter, I develop the Zen-colored aesthetic ideal of beauty as *muga* (無我) in its meaning as self-effacement or ecstasy articulated by Nishida Kitarō (西田幾多郎, 1870–1945), the founder of the Kyoto School of Modern Japanese Philosophy.[1] Moreover, I endeavor to show how Nishida's initial concept of beauty has been influenced by Arthur Schopenhauer (1788–1860) in post-Kantian German aesthetics. It is further shown how like Nishida in Japan, the modern Chinese philosopher Wang Guowei has forged a synthesis of Zen/Chan Buddhism and the neo-Kantian aesthetics of Schopenhauer, thus to arrive at a notion of beauty as *wu-wo* (無我) or ecstasy. Wolfgang Schirmacher points out that due to the many profound insights Schopenhauer had discovered in common with the early Indian philosophy of Buddhism, he became known as 'the Buddha of Frankfurt.'[2] He adds: "Increasingly ... we understand that behind the mask of a pessimist Schopenhauer was a Zen master and arguably the greatest mystic of the nineteenth century."[3] It is here clarified that like Schopenhauer, the modern Zen philosophy of Nishida comprehends beauty as a self-forgetting, an act of *losing oneself* in an aesthetic experience of art and nature. It is thus my contention that both Nishida and Schopenhauer develop an aesthetics of beauty as a function of selflessness or ecstasy. For Nishida, as for Schopenhauer, the realms of art, morality, and religion are all modes of ecstasy as loss of self. Yet for Nishida, as well as for Schopenhauer, the aesthetic experience of beauty is an ecstasy of the moment, while religious salvation culminates in an eternal ecstasy.

45

NISHIDA'S EARLY CONCEPT OF BEAUTY

Nishida Kitarō wrote "Bi no setsumei" (1900, 美の説明), "An Explanation of Beauty," in 1900, eleven years before publishing his first major work, *Zen no kenkyū* (1911, 善の研究), *An Inquiry into the Good*. As one of his earliest philosophical essays, Nishida's "Bi no setsumei" outlines an initial formulation of themes characteristic of what has come to be known as *Nishida tetsugaku* 西田哲学、or 'Nishida philosophy.' I have previously published a fully annotated translation of Nishida's "Bi no setsumei."[4] All references to Nishida's essay will therefore be to my own translation.

Nishida's "Bi no setsumei" is an original essay on the Japanese sense of beauty that synthesizes elements from both Eastern and Western aesthetics. Nishida begins the essay with an effort to formulate an adequate definition of 'beauty,' or *bi* (美). First, he directs his critical remarks against the identification of the "sense of beauty" (*bikan* 美感) with a merely hedonistic kind of "pleasure" (*kairaku* 快楽), arguing that there are many sensuous pleasures that cannot be described as beautiful or aesthetic. He then considers a more sophisticated theory of beauty as pleasure elaborated by the American psychologist Henry Rutgers Marshall.[5] For Marshall, as Nishida points out, the differentia of aesthetic experience lies in the relative permanence of pleasure both in impression and in memory. According to this criterion of beauty, sense pleasures elicited merely by gratification of appetite are not aesthetic, since they quickly pass over into satiety when the physiological conditions of appetite are removed. In contrast, the beauty of art produces a relatively permanent or stable pleasure that does not pass over into satiety and is not diminished as it is gratified. The beautiful artwork always yields pleasure in impression, or contemplative revival. For this reason, Marshall argues that "stable pleasure" is the special pleasure provided by art and is known to us as 'beauty.'

Although Nishida agrees that there is at least a partial truth to Marshall's hedonistic definition of beauty as stable pleasure, he cannot accept it as a complete explanation of the aesthetic experience. He now asks: what is the special kind of pleasure characterizing the experience of beauty? At this point, he turns to the explanation developed by the tradition of German aesthetics inspired by Kant's *Critique of Judgment* (1790), wherein the sense of beauty was defined as consisting in a "disinterested pleasure":

> Then what are the characteristics of the type of pleasure that makes up the sense of beauty?… According to the explanation of German Idealism since Kant, the sense of beauty is pleasure detached from the ego. It is a pleasure of the moment, when one forgets one's own interest such as advantage and

disadvantage, gain and loss. Only this *muga* is the essential element of beauty.[6]

Nishida here defines the disinterested pleasure of beauty as losing oneself in aesthetic experience, "a pleasure of the moment, when one forgets one's own interest such as advantage and disadvantage, gain and loss" (*isshin no rigai tokushitsu o wasuretaru toki no kairaku* 一身の利害得失を忘れたる時の快楽). He continues:

> A great man who is not only aloof from external matters but is also completely divorced from any thought of self-interest, reaches the point where everything in life gives a sense of beauty … . Therefore, if you want to obtain an authentic sense of beauty, you must confront things in the state of pure *muga*.[7]

It is significant how in the above passage Nishida reformulates the Kantian sense of beauty as a disinterested pleasure, or an artistic detachment from egoistic desires, in terms of a key philosophical notion of Zen Buddhism in Japan: namely, *muga* 無我 (Sanskrit: *anātman*), which can be translated as 'no-self,' 'nonego,' 'self-effacement,' or 'ecstasy.'[8] To repeat Nishida's words: "Only this *muga* is the essential element of beauty."[9] This Zen-colored notion of beauty as *muga* or ecstasy is at once simple, elegant, and profound. In the context of Japanese aesthetics, it is vital that the Zen concept of *muga* is not conceived only in negative terms as no-self, thus to suggest nihilism, but also in positive terms as ecstasy, thus to elicit the intoxicating rapture of an aesthetic experience of beauty in art, nature, or everyday life. As we know from Nishida's journals and correspondence, "Bi no setsumei" was written during that period of his early years, extending from around 1896 to 1902, when he was most actively engaged in the intensive practice of Zen meditation.[10] Although he makes no direct reference to Zen in this brief essay, his use of the signature Zen term *muga* is nonetheless laden with traditional Zen associations.

Nishida's early notion of beauty as *muga* designating no-self or ecstasy itself corresponds to his associate Daisetz T. Suzuki's position expressed in *Zen and Japanese Culture,* whereby the traditional Japanese arts of ink wash painting, calligraphy, flower arrangement, haiku poetry, the tea ceremony, and samurai martial arts are all alike based on the realization of Zen *satori* (悟り) or sudden enlightenment rooted in *mushin* (無心) or "no-mind."[11] Suzuki further holds that *wabi* (侘び) or rustic poverty, *sabi* (寂び) or impersonal loneliness, *yūgen* (幽玄) or profound mystery, *shibumi* (渋み) or graceful understatement, *fūryū* (風流) or windblown elegance, and other Japanese poetic ideals of beauty that emerged under the influence of Zen aestheticism are also rooted in *mushin* or no-mind.

SCHOPENHAUER'S INFLUENCE ON NISHIDA

Nishida's essay on beauty is at once reminiscent of Schopenhauer's aesthetics as well as his philosophy of art, morality, and religion. Nishida does not make reference to Schopenhauer in "Bi no setsumei." Nevertheless, one can see the influence of Schopenhauer's aesthetics on Nishida's early concept of beauty.

In her intellectual biography of Nishida titled *Zen and Philosophy*, Michiko Yusa reports that Nishida studied Schopenhauer during his early student years at Tokyo University under the tutelage of Raphael von Koeber, who had come to Japan from Germany in 1893, noting: "[Von] Koeber's seminar on Schopenhauer's *Parerga and Paralipomena* ... elevated Nishida's interest in Schopenhauer."[12] Moreover, in what she titles 'Nishida's Letter to D. T. Suzuki Concerning Zen Practice,' dated October 28, 1902, Yusa translates Nishida's correspondence describing his intensive meditation practice of Rinzai Zen *kōans* under Setsumon Rōshi.[13] In the same letter to his friend D. T. Suzuki, Nishida conveys his enthusiasm for Schopenhauer's voluntaristic idea of ultimate reality as absolute will over Hegel's rationalistic notion of absolute mind. In Nishida's words, "I think Schopenhauer's theory of *reine Anschauung* [pure intuition] (which takes the will as its foundation) more interesting than Hegel's theory, which has the *Intellekt* as its core."[14]

James Heisig emphasizes that in Nishida's early voluntarism, the absolute as "will" (*ishi* 意志) beyond the subject-object distinction is influenced especially by Schopenhauer. While discussing Nishida's early voluntarism in such works as *Intuition and Reflection in Self-Consciousness*, Heisig thus writes:

> The idea of absolute will as extending beyond conscious subjective ends to cover all of reality as a fundamental principle is Schopenhauer's. Nishida does not cite him in the work, but he was moved by his ideas during his undergraduate years, and he had read his life and dipped into his writings during the years preceding the publication of *An Inquiry into the Good*. A 1902 letter alludes to his preference for grounding the absolute in will with Schopenhauer rather than in intellect with Hegel (NKZ 18:61). Much of his interest in artistic expression also bears the mark of Schopenhauer's thinking though again it is not cited.[15]

As Heisig points out, Schopenhauer's influence on Nishida's early voluntaristic thought based on primacy of the will is especially seen in the latter's philosophy of art. In *Intuition and Reflection in Self-Consciousness,* for instance, Schopenhauer's influence can be seen when Nishida asserts that "[t]he primary world of the immediate objects of absolute will, which eludes reflection, is the world of art and religion."[16]

Nishida's initial formulation of beauty in terms of *muga* as self-effacement or ecstasy anticipates his Zen-like Jamesian notion of an egoless "pure experience" (*junsui keiken* 純粋経験) devoid of subject-object distinction as articulated in *An Inquiry into the Good*, as well as his more explicit Zen concept of ultimate reality as the "field of nothingness" (*mu no basho* 無の場所), conceived as the locus of *muga* or no-self. In *An Inquiry into the Good*, Nishida makes reference to Schopenhauer's "pure intuition without will" (*ishi naki junsui chokkaku* 意志なき純粋直覚) in relation to his own idea of "intellectual intuition" (*chiteki chokkan* 知的直観; German: *intellektuelle Anschauung*).[17] Intellectual intuition, which "deepens and enlarges our state of pure experience," is best exemplified by the "aesthetic spirit."[18] He illustrates intellectual intuition as the unifying power of pure experience through the aesthetic spirit exemplified by the artistic genius of Wolfgang Amadeus Mozart, who could discern a whole musical symphony while composing each single note.[19] Nishida's illustration of intellectual intuition by reference to the aesthetic spirit of Mozart is significant, in that according to Schopenhauer's hierarchy of the arts, it is above all others the supreme art of music that reveals the innermost metaphysical nature of ultimate reality as the blind force of will.[20]

NISHIDA, SCHOPENHAUER, AND WANG GUOWEI ON BEAUTY

I would like to briefly consider a parallel between Nishida's concept of beauty as *muga* and the modern Chinese aesthetics of Wang Guowei (王国維、1877–1927). Wang developed a poetic ideal of beauty influenced by both the Chan Buddhist/Daoist traditions of Chinese aesthetics and the post-Kantian German aesthetics of Schopenhauer. In his 1910 treatise *Jen-chien Tz'u-hua* (Poetic Reflections in the Human World), Wang asserts that there are two aesthetic worlds: the "world of self" (*yu-wo chih ching* 有我之境) and the "world of no-self" (*wu-wo chih ching* 無我之境).[21] According to Wang, the traditional Chinese sense of 'the beautiful' (*yu-mei* 優美) is to be understood as manifesting *wu-wo chih ching* (無我之境), the transpersonal state of ecstasy as no-self, nonego, or self-effacement.

Here I would like to point out that just as in modern Japanese aesthetics Nishida defines beauty as *muga* (無我), so in modern Chinese aesthetics Wang defines beauty as *wu-wo* (無我), both conceived as a momentary aesthetic experience of selflessness or ecstasy. In the commentary to her English translation of Wang's treatise on Chinese aesthetics, Adele Rickett emphasizes how Wang's Chan Buddhist/Daoist notion of the beautiful as *wu-wo* (無我) is on the Western side especially influenced by Schopenhauer's theory of artistic detachment, wherein beauty is momentarily enjoyed through a selfless and will-less attitude of disinterested aesthetic contemplation.[22] Likewise, Nishida's Japanese aesthetics is based on a Zen/Chan notion of beauty as *muga* (無我) or ecstasy, while on the Western side he is influenced by the German aesthetics of Schopenhauer. Both Wang and Nishida have thereby arrived at a philosophy of art based on an East-West synthesis of Zen/Chan Buddhism and the post-Kantian tradition of Schopenhauer. They have thus arrived at an aesthetics of beauty as ecstasy.

NISHIDA ON ART, MORALITY, AND RELIGION AS DEGREES OF ECSTASY

While Nishida's "Bi no setsumei" begins with an effort to define beauty, it ends by attempting to clarify the interrelationships among art (*bijutsu* 美術), religion (*shūkyō* 宗教), and morality (*dōtoku* 道徳). Nishida argues that since beauty is rooted in the experience of *muga* as no-self or ecstasy, it is ulti-mately of the same kind as religion, differing only in degree. He then asserts that morality also ultimately derives from the experience of *muga*. This fol-lows since another definition of *muga* is 'altruism,' which is the moral impli-cation of the term as selflessness. Here I will quote the concluding paragraph of Nishida's essay:

> If I may summarize what has been said above, the feeling of beauty is the feeling of *muga*. Beauty that evokes this feeling of *muga* is intuitive truth that transcends intellectual discrimination. This is why beauty is sublime. As regards this point, beauty can be explained as the discarding of the world of discrimina-tion and the being one with the Great Way of *muga*; it therefore is really of the same kind as religion. They only differ in the sense of deep and shallow, great and small. The *muga* of beauty is the *muga* of the moment, whereas the *muga* of religion is eternal *muga*. Although morality also originally derives from the Great Way of *muga,* it still belongs to the world of discrimination, because the idea of duty that is the essential condition of morality is built on the distinction between self and other, good and evil. It does not yet reach the sublime realms of religion and art. However, ... when morality advances and enters into reli-gion, there is no difference between morality and religion.[23]

The basic insight of Nishida's "Bi no setsumei" is that while the standpoints of art, morality, and religion differ in degrees of shallowness and depth, thereby establishing a hierarchy of values, they all ultimately originate from the same fundamental experience of *muga* as self-effacement or ecstasy. Yet for Nishida, both art and morality culminate in the supreme ecstasy of religion.

According to Valdo H. Viglielmo, "Bi no setsumei" is a blueprint for Nishida's later writings on aesthetics: "For in it he treats the aesthetic sense as one of a self-effacement, or ecstasy (*muga*) ... which, at its deepest level, is one with the religious Spirit."[24] He adds:

> This brief study can also be seen as a very rough sketch of his mature, detailed work *Geijutsu to dōtoku* (*Art and Morality,* 1923). Here we have clear proof of the logical course of development from Nishida's ideas in "Bi no setsumei," for once again ... he sees religion and intuition and ecstatic rapture of the saint, as the ultimate state toward which both art and morality tend.[25]

In Nishida's aesthetics, the value spheres of art, morality, and religion are each a function of *muga* or ecstasy. Yet as Viglielmo asserts, the beauty of art and the good of morality both move toward the divine ecstasy of saints at the level of religion.

NISHIDA AND SCHOPENHAUER ON
ECSTASY IN ART AND RELIGION

At this point, I would like to elucidate the key distinction Nishida posits between art and religion in "Bi no setsumei":

> 美の無我は一時の無我にして、宗教の無我は永久の無我なるなり。(*Bi no muga wa ichiji no muga ni shite, shūkyō no muga wa eikyū no muga naru nari.*).[26]

> The *muga* of beauty is the *muga* of the moment, whereas the *muga* of religion is eternal *muga*.[27]

Both art and religion are based on the impersonal feeling of *muga* as self-lessness or ecstasy. However, while the impersonal feeling of ecstasy arising from the beauty of art is "the *muga* of the moment" (*ichiji no muga* 一時の無我), the divine ecstasy of religion is "eternal *muga*" (*eikyū no muga* 永久の無我). In a few words, Nishida thus conveys Schopenhauer's aesthetic vision whereby there is a transition from the momentary release from suffering through delight in the beauty of art, to eternal salvation at the level of religion achieved by the resignation of the saints.

In his magnum opus, *The World as Will and Representation* (1818), Schopenhauer holds that the best candidate for the *summum bonum* or highest good in life is "the complete self-effacement and denial of the will, true will-lessness, which alone stills and silences forever the craving of the will."[28] It is through self-effacement by denial of will that one penetrates the Hindu "veil of Maya" as the *principium individuationis* or principle of individuation. Moreover, Schopenhauer explicitly states that what philosophy can express only negatively as "denial of the will" can also be expressed positively as "rapture" or "ecstasy."[29] Elsewhere in the text he proclaims: "The mystics of all religions ultimately arrive at a kind of *ecstasy.*"[30] Moreover, there are two ways to achieve blissful repose in ecstasy as denial of the will:

1. *Temporary ecstasy* through an occasional moment of will-less and selfless disinterested aesthetic contemplation of the beautiful in art and nature.
2. *Eternal ecstasy* through complete negation of the individual will by asceticism: first through a moral transition from egoism to altruism as egoless compassion; and ultimately through resignation in an exalted state of holiness as achieved by saints in the great world religions such as Hinduism, Buddhism, and Christianity.

Schopenhauer's philosophy can be visualized as an ascending journey toward liberation from the suffering of transitory existence, marked by a series of *transitions* from stage to stage. There is an initial transition from ordinary experience of particular objects to the aesthetic experience of beauty in art and nature, whereupon an artist briefly silences the will, thus to cognize the universal in the particular as a Platonic Idea. Schopenhauer, like Nishida, here conceives of this transition to an aesthetic experience of beauty as a losing of oneself or a forgetting of one's individuality so as to become completely absorbed in the aesthetic object: "We *lose* ourselves entirely in this object ... ; in other words, we forget our individuality."[31] Likewise, Nishida writes that beauty perceived by the intuition of poets is that wherein one has "separated from the self and become one with things" (*onore o hanare yoku mono to itchishite* 己を離れ能く物と一致して).[32] For both Schopenhauer and Nishida, this act of forgetting oneself to become one with an object of aesthetic experience is in negative terms a loss of self, and in positive terms a state of ecstasy.

In Schopenhauer's pessimism, the suffering of transitory existence arises through the blind striving of the individual will, and release from suffering comes when we lose ourselves in aesthetic contemplation, moral compassion, and ascetic renunciation. Yet in Schopenhauer's account of salvation, there is a transition whereby both the beauty of art and the virtue of morality lead to the holiness of saints at the standpoint of religion. In the realm of art this transition from disinterested aesthetic contemplation to spiritual resignation is especially facilitated by tragedy, wherein the misery and suffering of temporal existence is revealed. According to Schopenhauer's hierarchy of the representational arts, there is an ascension from architecture to painting to sculpture to poetry, which then mounts upward to the sublimity of tragic drama:

Tragedy is to be regarded, and is recognized, as the summit of poetic art, ... The unspeakable pain, the wretchedness and misery of mankind, the triumph of wickedness, the scornful mastery of chance, and the irretrievable fall of the just and the innocent are all here presented to us.[33]

He adds: "We see in tragedy the noblest men, after a long conflict and suffering, finally renounce for ever all the pleasures of life … and willingly give up life itself."[34] The feeling of "the sublime" elicited by tragedy discloses the terrible side of life arising through the awesome destructive force of blind will, thereby bringing the tragic hero or the spectator of tragic drama to the threshold of salvation in a state of resigned exaltation: "Thus the summons to turn away the will from life remains the true tendency of tragedy, the ultimate purpose of the intentional presentation of the sufferings of mankind."[35] The misery of ephemeral existence as revealed by the spectacle of tragic art thus operates as an impetus to turn away from the individual will and achieve the ecstatic resignation of the saints, mystics, and ascetics.

Schopenhauer, like Nishida, agrees with Kant's view that an aesthetic experience of beauty is a disinterested pleasure.[36] Following Kant, Schopenhauer holds that disinterested aesthetic contemplation of beauty is characterized by an objective attitude of detachment from selfish desires:

> For the beauty with which those objects present themselves rests precisely on the pure objectivity, i.e., disinterestedness, of their perception, … . Everything is beautiful only so long as it does not concern us. (Here it is not a case of the passion of love, but of aesthetic enjoyment.)[37]

While for Kant the disinterested contemplation of beauty in art is restricted to the autonomous sphere of aesthetic experience, for Schopenhauer it becomes a transitional step toward release from misery through the resignation of ascetics as typified by the Buddhist renunciation of selfhood in nirvana. For a permanent liberation from suffering one must therefore shift from the temporary ecstasy of art to the lasting ecstasy of religious salvation, thereby to achieve complete denial of will through the selfless resignation of mystics: "Resignation … frees its owner from all care and anxiety forever."[38] Likewise, for Nishida, as for Schopenhauer, the aesthetic ecstasy of the artist moves toward the deeper spiritual ecstasy of the saint at the standpoint of religion.

Schopenhauer holds that disinterested aesthetic contemplation of beauty in art provides temporary relief from suffering in a state of tranquility by suspension of will as the correlate to objective knowledge of truth as perception of a (Platonic) Idea. The delight arising through disinterested aesthetic contemplation of beauty is in some cases due to cognition of the universal in the particular as a Platonic Idea, and in others due to the peace and bliss attained by a temporary silencing of the will.[39] Yet for Schopenhauer, disinterested aesthetic contemplation of beauty in art results only in a momentary calming of the will in an egoless state of blissful repose: "[T]he momentary silencing of all willing, which comes about whenever as pure will-less subject of knowing, the correlative of the Idea, we are devoted to aesthetic contemplation, is a principal element of pleasure in the beautiful."[40]

Here we find a significant difference between the aesthetics of Schopenhauer and Nishida. Both Schopenhauer and Nishida disagree with Kant's view that the judgment of taste based on a disinterested delight in the beautiful is only an aesthetic feeling of the subject devoid of any objective truth.[41] Schopenhauer holds that through disinterested aesthetic contemplation of beauty the artist loses his individuality so as to become a pure will-less subject that cognizes the universal in the particular as a Platonic Idea. Nishida also affirms that there is truth as well as beauty in the work of art. For Nishida, however, the truth of beauty is not a cognition of ideas or universals. After defining the sense of beauty as *muga* or ecstasy, Nishida then argues that beauty is identical with truth. He further emphasizes that beauty as *muga* is identical only with "intuitive truth" (*chokkakuteki no shinri* 直覚的の真理).[42] Indeed, Nishida identifies this intuitive truth of beauty as ecstasy with the "open secret" or "open mystery" (*offenes Geheimnis*) of nature revealed through the poet as described by Goethe.[43] Nishida here anticipates the position of Heidegger articulated in "The Origin of the Work of Art" (1977), wherein the beauty of art is not identical with the conceptual truth of Platonism, but with the ancient Greek notion of primordial truth as *aletheia* or "openness." For Heidegger, the function of beauty in art and poetry is to disclose phenomena so that they radiate into primordial truth as openness or unconcealment. Heidegger's notion of poetic truth as openness thus approximates Nishida's view that the intuitive truth of beauty as grasped by poets functions to disclose events as an "open mystery."

Schopenhauer goes on to argue that morality, like art, is a *transitional* activity that moves toward its consummation in the selfless ecstasy of mystical resignation.[44] He rejects Kant's rationalistic ethics of duty for a virtue ethics based on sympathy or compassion. For Schopenhauer, the two cardinal virtues are "justice," as prevention of harm to others, and "loving-kindness," as altruistic concern for the welfare of others. Moreover, these two moral virtues are rooted in "compassion" (*Mitleid*) as the sole ground of morality:

> It is simply and solely this compassion that is the real basis of all voluntary justice and genuine loving-kindness. Only insofar as an action has sprung from compassion does it have moral value.[45]

For Schopenhauer, as for Buddhism, the moral response to suffering is compassion. The virtue of loving-kindness based on compassion for all sentient beings tends toward complete denial of the will realized through the self-renunciation of asceticism.[46] Explaining the transition from the selfless compassion of morality to the total resignation of asceticism, he writes: "The moral virtues are not really the ultimate end but only a step towards it."[47] The ultimate end is not the practice of moral virtue, but final salvation achieved by "denial of the will," understood in Hinduism as "moksha, i.e., reunion with

Brahma," and in Buddhism as "nirvana."[48] Just as the momentary suspension of will in aesthetic contemplation requires a transition to ascetic self-renunciation, so in moral compassion the will must turn and pass beyond itself to the level of mystical resignation, thereby to achieve permanent liberation from suffering through complete nullification of will in the holiness of empty nothingness. Thus for Schopenhauer, as for Nishida, both art and morality tend toward the eternal ecstasy of the saint at the standpoint of religion.

Like Nishida, Schopenhauer has been deeply influenced by Buddhist thought. Schopenhauer cites with approval the four noble truths of Buddhism: (1) suffering, (2) origin of suffering in desire, (3) cessation of suffering in nirvana, and (4) the middle path.[49] As Schopenhauer explains, his concept of salvation as an egoless state of resignation achieved by denial of will is in agreement with the Buddhist concept of liberation from suffering in nirvana realized by total renunciation of selfhood and its insatiable desires. He explicitly identifies denial of will with Buddhist nirvana.[50] For Schopenhauer, affirmation of will results in the suffering of *samsara*, whereas negation of will is salvation and equivalent to Buddhist nirvana.[51] Schopenhauer elsewhere describes this final transition to the holiness of spiritual resignation achieved by denial of will as "a transition into empty nothingness."[52] Moreover, he identifies nothingness with Buddhist nirvana.[53] Aesthetic contemplation of beauty, however, offers a brief intimation of nirvana.

According to Schopenhauer, the artistic genius has an ability to sustain an ecstatic state of disinterested will-less aesthetic contemplation of beauty in art and nature for a longer duration than normal. Yet even for an artistic genius, the ecstatic contemplation of beauty is only a "moment of rapture or exaltation."[54] An eternal deliverance from suffering in a state of everlasting peace requires a transition to the complete spiritual resignation attained by saints. Describing the limitations of an artist who stops with delight in the beauty of art and goes no further, Schopenhauer propounds:

> Therefore it [art] does not become for him a quieter of the will, as … in the case of the saint who has attained resignation; it does not deliver him from life for ever, but only for a few moments … . The St. Cecilia of Raphael can be regarded as the symbol of this transition.[55]

Again, Schopenhauer clearly explicates the transition from momentary ecstasy through disinterested aesthetic contemplation of beauty achieved by artists to the eternal ecstasy achieved through mystical resignation of the saints:

> [A]esthetic pleasure in the beautiful consists to a large extent, in the fact that, when we enter the state of pure contemplation, we are raised for the moment above all willing, above all desires and cares; we are, so to speak, rid of ourselves. We are

no longer the individual that knows in the interest of its constant willing, ...
From this we can infer how blessed must be the life of a man whose will is
silenced not for a few moments, as in the enjoyment of the beautiful, but forever.[56]

The momentary aesthetic contemplation of beauty in art thus functions to provide a foretaste of eternal salvation through the denial of the will as attained
by saints, mystics, and ascetics.

ECSTASY OF ART, MORALITY, AND RELIGION
AS "BETTER CONSCIOUSNESS"

In his early *Manuscript Remains,* the youthful Schopenhauer's initial reflections on aesthetics, ethics, mysticism, and value were expressed in terms of
his notion of a "better consciousness" (*bessere Bewusstsein*) as recorded in
his notebooks of 1812–1814.[57] In contrast to the suffering that arises through
will in ordinary empirical consciousness, the better consciousness is characterized as "bliss" and "the supreme happiness," as well as "light, repose,
joy."[58] As noted by Cross, Schopenhauer discontinues the use of his phrase
better consciousness and replaces it with *denial of will* in his published
works.[59] Cross suggests that although the term 'better consciousness' does
not appear in the work published during Schopenhauer's lifetime, it nevertheless functions as the "hidden compass" that navigates his later writings.[60]
The better consciousness is the hidden source of art, morality, and holiness,
as well as the aesthetic experience of beauty: "In ... the *Manuscript Remains*
it is said that the better consciousness, when 'very vivid,' reveals itself as the
beautiful or the sublime, or it finds expression as saintly behavior."[61] Janaway
writes that although Schopenhauer abandoned the term 'better consciousness'
in his published works, the core of this vision remains throughout, especially
in terms of a theory of aesthetic experience as enjoyment of beauty through
a temporary silencing of will.[62] Safranski clarifies how in Schopenhauer's
philosophical diaries he uses the notion of "better consciousness" to designate states of ecstasy, including "the ecstasy of art, especially music."[63] He
continues, "Undoubtedly the 'better consciousness' is a kind of ecstasy, a
crystalline ecstasy of clarity and immobility, a euphoria."[64] Hence, just as for
Nishida, art, morality, and religion are rooted in *muga* or ecstasy, for Schopenhauer, the beauty of art, the virtue of morality, and the holiness of religion
have their source in the ecstasy of better consciousness.

Nietzsche criticizes what he regards to be Schopenhauer's Apollonian idea
of disinterested aesthetic contemplation through denial of will as amount-
ing to nihilism. Safranski, however, argues that Schopenhauer's notion of
beauty cannot be reduced to Nietzsche's Apollonian-Dionysian aesthetic
categories. Against Nietzsche's charge of nihilism, Safranski points out that

although Schopenhauer's "better consciousness" as the ecstasy of art seems Apollonian with its disinterested contemplative attitude of calmness, indifference, and clarity, "the inspirations of the 'better consciousness,' from which his philosophy stemmed, were also boundary-transcendent, ego-dissolving, and therefore not Apollonian."[65] Further clarifying Schopenhauer's view of beauty as the ecstasy of art, in contrast to Nietzsche's passionate, sensuous, and embodied Dionysian aesthetics of intoxicating rapture, Safranski writes:

> *This* [Schopenhauer's] ecstasy stands at the exact opposite pole from that which has always been associated with the name of Dionysus: the plunge into a flood of desire carried away by the body, self-dissolution in orgiastic sensuality. … From the heights of such ecstasy Schopenhauer hurled his anti-Dionysian thunderbolts, invectives against the temptations of the body.[66]

Schopenhauer's "better consciousness" as the ecstasy of self-effacement includes both the temporary ecstasy of art and its consummation in the eternal ecstasy of religion. Yet as explained in Safranski's biographical account, in his own life, Schopenhauer the connoisseur enjoyed only the temporary ecstasy provided by aesthetic contemplation of beauty in art, especially music, while avoiding the permanent ecstasy attained through the resignation of the saints: "Before greedy Arthur consumes his opulent midday meal at the restaurant he plays his flute for an hour: Rossini's 'celestial music.' Schopenhauer's 'better consciousness' knows only a time-restricted ecstasy. Holiness and prolonged ecstasy are things he shuns."[67]

SCHOPENHAUER'S AESTHETIC ECSTASY AND BUDDHIST MEDITATION

According to Dauer, Schopenhauer's disinterested aesthetic contemplation establishes a parallel to Buddhist meditation as a technique for release from suffering in a state of ecstasy. Dauer asserts that while Buddhist yoga practice touches nirvana through the "psychological ecstasy of meditation," for Schopenhauer, one approximates this egoless state of resignation through the "aesthetic ecstasy" of art.[68] She continues:

> The *aesthetic ecstasy* [of Schopenhauer] which makes the admirer forget the torments of life, consists of the fact that the intellect … liberates itself temporarily from the will … . And in this sense, it presents a parallel to the yoga which was a psychological technique of creating an ecstatic feeling of union with the absolute. Buddhism incorporated this yoga in the form of meditation, in which the monks believed to have intuitively enjoyed the foretaste of nirvana.[69]

According to Dauer, then, the aesthetic ecstasy of art and the psychological ecstasy of Buddhist meditation are both alike temporary reprieves from suffering, and thus provide a foretaste of nirvana.

CONCLUSION

In this chapter, I have endeavored to clarify Nishida's initial concept of beauty as *muga* (無我) in its Zen meaning as selflessness or ecstasy. Moreover, I have examined how Nishida's early concept of beauty as ecstasy has been influenced by Schopenhauer's aesthetics. I have further discussed the view that Schopenhauer's aesthetic contemplation of beauty in art coincides with early Indian Buddhist meditation as a technique for the production of ecstasy, thereby providing an intimation of nirvana. The correlation between the ecstasy of Schopenhauer's disinterested aesthetic contemplation and that of traditional Zen practice in Japan is even more explicit, insofar as Zen aestheticism seeks enlightenment through meditation on the ephemeral beauty of art, nature, and everyday life. The core of Schopenhauer's pessimistic vision is that release from the suffering of existence as the tyranny of blind will is realized by losing one's individuality in aesthetic experience, moral compassion, and ascetic renunciation. It has been seen how in the modern Zen philosophy of Nishida, the value domains of art, morality, and religion are rooted in *muga* or ecstasy, just as for the youthful Schopenhauer, they have their source in the ecstasy of better consciousness. Also, for Nishida and Schopenhauer, both art and morality are transitional stages that achieve their consummation in the ecstatic rapture of saints at the standpoint of religion. For Nishida, as for Schopenhauer, the aesthetic experience of beauty in art is an ecstasy of the moment, while religion attains to an eternal ecstasy. In such a manner, then, Nishida illuminates Schopenhauer's insight that ecstasy realized by disinterested aesthetic contemplation of the beautiful in art is a temporary glimpse of nirvana, while the supreme ecstasy of religion culminates with the exalted resignation of the saints as a permanent renunciation of selfhood in the eternal peace and bliss of nirvana.

NOTES

1. An earlier version of this chapter was delivered as the keynote address at the 26th Japan Schopenhauer Society Conference held at Rissho University in Tokyo on November 30, 2013.

2. Wolfgang Schirmacher, ed., *The Essential Schopenhauer: Key Selections from* The World as Will and Representation *and Other Writings* (New York: Harper Perennial, 2010), x.

3. Ibid., vii.

4. Steve Odin and Nishida Kitarō, "An Explanation of Beauty: Nishida Kitarō's *Bi no Setsumei*," *Monumenta Nipponica* 42, no. 2 (1987): 211–17. "Bi no setsumei" 美の説明 is also found in *Nishida Kitarō zenshū* 西田幾多郎全集、(*The Complete Works of Nishida Kitarō*), ed. Shimomura Toratarō et al., 19 vols., 2nd edition (Tokyo: Iwanami Shoten, 1965), 13:78–80. The essay originally appeared in *Hokushinkai zasshi* 北辰会雑誌、26 (March 5, 1900), 1–3. Also, *Shinpan Nishida Kitarō zenshū* (*The Complete Works of Nishida Kitarō: New Edition*), ed. Takeda Atsushi et al., 24 vols. (Tokyo: Iwanami Shoten, 2005), 11:58–60.

5. See Henry Rutgers Marshall, *Pain, Pleasure, and Aesthetics: An Essay Concerning the Psychology of Pain and Pleasure, with Special Reference to Aesthetics* (London: Macmillan, 1895); and *Aesthetic Principles* (London: Macmillan, 1895).

6. Ibid., 216.

7. Ibid.

8. Ibid.

9. Ibid.

10. For a detailed account of Nishida's practice of Zen meditation from about 1896 to 1902 as recorded in his diary and correspondence, see Valdo H. Viglielmo, "Nishida Kitarō: The Early Years," in *Tradition and Modernization in Japanese Culture*, ed. Donald H. Shively (Princeton, NJ: Princeton University Press, 1971), 507–62.

11. Daisetz T. Suzuki, *Zen and Japanese Culture* (Tokyo: Tuttle, 1988), 94.

12. Michiko Yusa, *Zen and Philosophy: An Intellectual Biography of Nishida Kitarō* (Honolulu: University of Hawai'i Press, 2002), 38–39.

13. Ibid., 73. See Nishida, *Nishida Kitarō zenshū*, 18:61.

14. Cited in Yusa, 74.

15. James W. Heisig, *Philosophers of Nothingness: An Essay on the Kyoto School* (Honolulu: University of Hawai'i Press, 2007), 292.

16. Odin and Nishida, 167.

17. Nishida Kitarō, *An Inquiry into the Good*, trans. Masao Abe and Christopher Ives (New Haven, CT: Yale University Press, 1990), 32.

18. Ibid.

19. Ibid., 31.

20. Arthur Schopenhauer, *The World as Will and Representation*, trans. E. F. J. Payne, 2 vols. (New York: Dover Publications, 1969), 2:448.

21. Adele Austin Rickett, trans., *Wang Kuo-Wei's Jen-Chien Tz'u-Hua: A Study in Chinese Literary Criticism* (Hong Kong: Hong Kong University Press, 1977), 14–15, 26, 40–41.

22. Ibid., 13.

23. Odin and Nishida, 217.

24. Viglielmo, 555.

25. Ibid., 556.

26. Nishida, *Nishida Kitarō zenshū*, 13:80.

27. Odin and Nishida, 217.

28. Schopenhauer, *The World as Will*, 1:362.

29. Ibid., 1:410.

30. Ibid., 2:611.

31. Ibid., 1:178.

32. Odin and Nishida, 213.

33. Schopenhauer, *The World as Will*, 1:253.

34. Ibid.

35. Ibid., 2:435.

36. Immanuel Kant, *Critique of Judgment*, trans. James Creed Meredith (Oxford: Clarendon Press, 1952), 42.

37. Schopenhauer, *The World as Will*, 1:374.

38. Ibid., 1:336.

39. Ibid., 1:212.

40. Ibid., 1:363.

41. Kant, 141.

42. Odin and Nishida, 217.

43. Ibid.

44. Schopenhauer, *The World as Will*, 1:380.

45. Arthur Schopenhauer, *On the Basis of Morality,* trans. E. F. J. Payne (Oxford: Berhahn Books, 1995), 144.

46. Schopenhauer, *The World as Will*, 1:380.

47. Ibid., 2:608.

48. Ibid., 2:608–09.

49. Ibid., 2:623.

50. Ibid., 2:508, 2:560.

51. Ibid., 2:609.

52. Ibid.,1:408–09. For a comparative study on "nothingness" as negation of will in Nishida and Schopenhauer, see Yujin Itabashi, "'Nichtigkeit' of Nihilism: Schopenhauer and Nishida," *Jahrbuch der Schopenhauer-Gesellschaft* 93 (2012): 127–40.

53. Schopenhauer, *The World as Will*, 2:508, 2:608.

54. Ibid., 2:380.

55. Ibid., 1:267.

56. Ibid., 1:390.

57. Arthur Schopenhauer, *Manuscript Remains*, ed. Arthur Hübscher, trans. E. F. J. Payne, vol. 1, *Early Manuscripts (1804–1818)* (Oxford: Berg, 1988).

58. Ibid., 182, 58.

59. Stephen Cross, *Schopenhauer's Encounter with Indian Thought* (Honolulu: University of Hawai'i Press, 2013), 193.

60. Ibid., 211.

61. Ibid., 194.

62. Christopher Janaway, "Schopenhauer's Philosophy of Value," in *Better Consciousness: Schopenhauer's Philosophy of Value*, ed. Alex Neill and Christopher Janaway (Malden, MA: Wiley-Blackwell, 2009), 2.

63. Rüdiger Safranski, *Schopenhauer and the Wild Years of Philosophy*, trans. Ewald Osers (Cambridge, MA: Harvard University Press, 1989), 132.

64. Ibid., 134.

65. Ibid., 135.

66. Ibid., 134.

67. Ibid., 237.

68. Dorothea W. Dauer, *Schopenhauer as Transmitter of Buddhist Ideas* (Bern, Switzerland: Herbert Lang, 1969), 23.

69. Ibid., 23, italics added.

Chapter 5

Bodily Aesthetics and the Cultivation of Moral Virtues

Yuriko Saito

AESTHETICS AND MORAL VIRTUES

How do we act respectfully toward others? At the very minimum, we should not violate the rights of others by injuring them or their property, restricting their freedoms, or slandering their reputation. Carrying out these negative duties toward others is necessary, but not sufficient, for respecting them. Sometimes we should fulfill positive duties toward others, such as helping them when they are in dire need. Although ignoring their pleas for help may not violate their negative rights, it will be a sign of our disrespect, particularly when helping others does not place an unreasonably heavy burden on us.

The ethics of care places emphasis on this latter kind of action. The virtues of care and consideration for others are manifested in things we do for others, rather than or in addition to simply refraining from certain actions. In fact, for many of us, our everyday moral concerns seem to be directed more toward such acts as caring for a sick neighbor and bailing out a friend from a bad situation than toward refraining from acts of violence such as murder, rape, assault, and theft. A person who never goes beyond not violating others' rights is certainly better than a murderer or rapist, but such a person still seems morally deficient. Similarly, in a society where no egregiously immoral acts occur but where human interactions expressive of care and respect are also absent, we wouldn't have to fear for our safety, but neither would our lives there be satisfying or fulfilling.[1]

What does not get sufficient attention, however, is the fact that the moral character of an action motivated by care and respect is largely determined by the *manner* or the *way* in which it is carried out. For example, Nel Noddings observes that "I cannot claim to care for my relative if my caretaking is perfunctory or grudging."[2] Similarly, citing Seneca, Nancy Sherman remarks that "we spoil kindness ... if our reluctance is betrayed in inappropriate 'furrowed brows' and 'grudging words'" and concludes that "[p]laying the role of the good person ... has to do with socially sensitive behavior—how we convey to others interest, empathy, respect, and gratitude through the emotional expressions we wear on our face (or exhibit through our body language and voice)."[3] Even if I accomplish the goal of kindness and caring, say, by taking a relative to the doctor, the way in which I carry out the action changes the nature of the act: I can do so kindly and gently, or spitefully and grudgingly.

The manner in which one carries out an action is often considered a matter of etiquette, civility, and courtesy. Compared to the matters of justice and rights, which have grave social consequences, they are considered superficial and trivial, not worthy of the same kind of attention. Furthermore, manners and etiquette often raise the "questions of social hierarchy and identity politics."[4] These seemingly trivial aspects of our daily lives, however, go a long way toward determining the quality of our lives and society. As Karen Stohr observes, "the rules of polite behavior play a far more important role in helping us live out our moral commitments than most people realize" and "the study of morality is incomplete unless we attend to its manifestation in ordinary human interactions."[5] This is because, as Sherman notes, courteous interactions in our everyday lives are "the ways [in which] we acknowledge others as worthy of respect" and "[t]he communication of those appearances is a part of the glue of human fellowship."[6]

What is relevant to my discussion is that the way in which we interact with others consists of *aesthetic* factors: handling of objects, tone of voice, facial expression, and body movement. I am here using the term 'aesthetic' not in the usual honorific sense often identified with beauty or artistic excellence. Rather, I am referring to sensory perception in the original Greek sense and in Alexander Gottlieb Baumgarten's use of the term in *Aesthetica.*[7] The list of what constitutes the "aesthetic of character" or the "aesthetic of morals," according to Sherman, includes "how we appear to others as conveyed through formal manners and decorum, as well as manner in the wider sense of personal bearing and outward attitude," specifically "voices, faces, and gestures."[8] Sarah Buss also asks us to "think of the significance we attribute to the subtlest gestures (the curl of the lip, the raised eyebrows), the slightest differences in vocal tone."[9] The specifics of what bodily gestures express courtesy or rudeness of course vary from situation to situation and, more importantly, from culture to culture, giving rise to the all-too-familiar cases of cultural *faux pas.*[10] The most important point for my current purpose, however, is that the *aesthetic* dimension of the way in which an action is carried out can determine its *moral* character.

But how do we cultivate the aesthetic expression of other-regarding virtues such as respect, care, civility, consideration, and thoughtfulness? I suggest that an aesthetic practice involving bodily engagement is one effective means of cultivating these virtues. Furthermore, I suggest that the Japanese aesthetic tradition offers a rich legacy of this kind of moral education. The role of aesthetics in the Japanese cultural tradition goes beyond a diverse array of objects and art forms. Numerous classical writings on art-making all emphasize that a successful artistic achievement is a by-product of the more important aspect of art practice, which includes self-discipline, cultivation of virtues, and enlightenment. In his discussion of the role of Japanese arts in self-cultivation, Robert E. Carter observes that "respect and helpfulness are culturally transmitted from the earliest years on up, and the *arts* are major purveyors of these attitudinal values."[11] I would further argue that traditional Japanese artistic pedagogy has influenced the aesthetic dimension of people's everyday lives, which in turn has affected their moral lives. In what follows, I will explore this aspect of Japanese aesthetics.

JAPANESE AESTHETICS AND CULTIVATION OF MORAL VIRTUES

Friedrich Nietzsche characterized Western aesthetics as "receiver" or "spectator" aesthetics.[12] As such, the relationship between the aesthetic and the moral usually concerns the spectator's judgment regarding the aesthetic relevance or irrelevance of the moral content of a work of art such as a novel or a film. In comparison, the Japanese aesthetic tradition is dominated by accounts given by practitioners of the arts. The practitioners have to cultivate a certain way of living through rigorous training, which, it is believed, will lead to artistic excellence. It is true that various rules regarding art-making need to be observed in training, but the purpose of those rules is for each practitioner not only to achieve artistic excellence but also, more importantly, to become a certain kind of person by developing moral virtues, such as respect, care, thoughtfulness, and humility.

Both Shintoism and Zen Buddhism provided a spiritual foundation for the Japanese artistic tradition. According to these spiritual traditions, a virtuous person is one who can form a sympathetic relationship with the other, whether the other be human beings or natural creatures and objects, by transcending self and respecting the other. Specifically, Zen enlightenment is possible only when one succeeds in "forgetting" oneself and letting "the other" guide one's experience. A thirteenth-century Zen priest, Dōgen, states that "acting on and witnessing myriad things *with the burden of oneself* is 'delusion'" and "acting on and witnessing oneself *in the advent of myriad things* is enlightenment."[13]

As such, according to him, "studying the Buddha Way is studying oneself. Studying oneself is *forgetting oneself*. Forgetting oneself is *being enlightened by all things*."[14]

Classical art treatises apply this transcendence of ego to specific art mediums by encouraging respect for the natural materials and subject matters: "following the request" of the stones and trees to make a garden appear natural; "letting the flowers lead" to render their arrangement alive; making oneself "slender" and "enter[ing] into" the bamboo or pine tree so that a haiku about it "becomes" rather than being "composed"; and capturing "the spirit of bamboo" such that its ambience naturally emerges in a painting.[15] That this process of artistic training is still alive and well is documented in Robert E. Carter's interviews with today's masters in various arts.[16]

Dōgen urges the same attitude of respecting materials when cooking as a form of Zen training. He admonishes the unenlightened mind that discriminates between fine and humble ingredients: "Do not arouse disdainful mind when you prepare a broth of wild grasses; do not arouse joyful mind when you prepare a fine cream soup."[17] In short, he teaches that "[w]hen you prepare food, do not see with ordinary eyes and do not think with ordinary mind." The native characteristics of a humble ingredient are as worthy of respect as those of a fine ingredient.

Respect for materials is expressed not only in the end product but also in the process of working with them. For example, Carter points out that "landscape gardening brings about a *gentleness* in the designer, the builders, and the caretakers."[18] The gentle attitude is reflected in the treatment of materials through certain body movements, as illustrated in the construction of a garden for the Canadian Museum of Civilization in Ottawa by a contemporary master gardener, Masuno Shunmyo. Carter reports that "the Japanese crew entered and left the actual site by walking in the footsteps of a single pathway, which had already been established in the mud on the site, rather than tracking mud all over the newly placed sand, or on or around the rocks, keeping tracking and foreign markings to a minimum" and concludes that "[i]t was a degree of *caring and concern* for the state and cleanliness of the site that was itself quite foreign to the Canadians on hand."[19]

A similarly respectful attitude informs the art of flower arrangement. "[T]he *tender* way in which the materials for flower arrangements are handled"[20] includes carefully unwrapping the bundle of flowers to be used, gently bending and twisting when shaping the branches and stems, and neatly arranging unused remnants of flowers for disposal. Ultimately, the aim of flower arrangement is "not just to teach techniques and basic skills, but [also] to convey attitudes which would apply both to flower arranging and to living one's life generally."[21]

These expressions of care and gentleness toward inanimate objects, such as rocks and flowers, may strike one versed in mainstream Western ethical tradition as falling outside of moral discourse, because these objects don't have a "good of their own" that gets damaged by soiling or rough handling. Simon James argues, however, that such an attitude *is* morally relevant in the sense that "part of what makes someone morally good or virtuous is the fact that she will tend to exhibit … a 'delicacy' towards her surroundings, taking care not to damage the things with which she deals, even when those things are neither sentient nor alive."[22]

The Japanese practice of respecting "the other" is not limited to the ways of handling natural objects and materials. It also concerns other human beings by encouraging one to transcend one's self-regarding attitude and desire and to extend consideration, care, and thoughtfulness through aesthetic means. Most of us are familiar with unpleasant experiences such as when someone slams the door shut or places an object in front of us in a wanton and rough manner. In one sense, the tasks get accomplished: the door is closed and the item is placed before us. Yet how different would our experiences be if these tasks were executed in a gentle and careful manner without making a racket? The aesthetic difference made by a particular body movement and the resultant sound communicates a different moral attitude: one of respect and consideration in one case and their absence or neglect in the other.

This phenomenon, all-too-familiar to us today, was already observed by an eleventh-century Heian court lady, Sei Shōnagon, in her *The Pillow Book*.[23] Reflecting what Ivan Morris calls 'the cult of beauty,'[24] the Heian aristocrats' lives revolved around cultivating aesthetic sensibility and judging the worth of a person based upon his aesthetic sensibility. Their courtship ritual was almost entirely based upon aesthetics. A "good" person worthy of one's interest and pursuit was somebody who displayed impeccable artistic skills in poetry, calligraphy, letter writing, clothing, and the like, as well as a capacity to appreciate the delicacy and ephemerality of natural beauty and other people's expressions of aesthetic sensibility. Sei Shōnagon thus contrasts two gentlemen's leave-taking from their female partners after a night of lovemaking. A hateful behavior is described as "flurried," producing "a great rattle" and "terrible noise" by banging into things because he is preoccupied with getting ready to leave for his work.[25] This commotion-filled departure is contrasted with an elegant one expressive of his reluctance to leave the lady and tenderness toward her by "whisper[ing] whatever was left unsaid during the night" and "linger[ing], vaguely pretending to be fastening his sash" before slipping away.[26]

Though far removed from our lives both historically and culturally, I suspect that her comparison rings a bell for most of us. One's body movement accompanied by a loud noise and a hurried and fidgety motion communicates thoughtlessness or indifference, whereas a gentle and elegant body movement implies a caring and respectful attitude. The virtues of care and thoughtfulness or the lack thereof is expressed aesthetically through bodily actions and the sensory impressions they create. Focusing on the sound created by one's movement, Sei Shōnagon states that "even a head-blind does not make any noise if one lifts it up *gently* on entering and leaving the room; the same applies to sliding-doors," while "if one's movements are *rough*, even a paper door will bend and resonate when opened; but, if one lifts the door a little while pushing it, there need be no sound."[27]

Similar other-regarding considerations expressed by specific bodily gestures underlie the training practices of Zen priests for eating. In addition to instructions on how to cook, Dōgen left extensive rules regarding the manner of eating required of Zen trainees, which include maintaining correct posture, holding the bowl and using chopsticks in the right way, when to begin eating, and taking time to carefully pick up each morsel to savor its taste and texture rather than devouring and gulping down the food.[28] These painstakingly detailed rules are all guided by being mindful and showing respect for the food itself, the cooks, and fellow priests who are eating companions.

The tea ceremony established in the sixteenth century crystallizes the attention to other-regarding aesthetics. Its founder, Sen no Rikyū, himself characterizes the art of tea as very simple: "Know that the essence of the art of tea is simply to boil water, make tea, and drink tea."[29] This characterization is misleading, however, as participants are required to observe detailed aesthetic rules regarding every aspect of the event. Some aesthetic decisions are directed at the choice and placement of the various objects used in the ceremony, whereas other aesthetic considerations guide the body movements of both the host and the guest with almost excruciating specificities.

For example, the host opens the sliding door slowly and carefully to allow enough time to indicate his entrance without causing alarm or commotion. The host also handles implements for making tea in a gentle and elegant manner. The guest cradles the tea bowl with both hands to honor the bowl and the tea inside. Through beautifully and economically choreographed actions, both the host and the guest practice conveying a respectful, considerate, gentle, caring, and pleasant impression to each other. This mutual respect should linger even after the tea ceremony is over as the guest leaves the tea hut through the garden path. The guest should not converse loudly with other guests but rather turn around to see the host, who in turn sees them off until they are out of sight before returning to the tea hut for cleanup.[30]

All these rules are motivated by a desire to cultivate a morally sensitive way of carrying out an action. One nineteenth-century tea practitioner who is also a noted statesman remarks, "The host should attend to every detail to express his consideration and kindness so that there will not be any mishaps, and the guest in turn should recognize that the occasion is one time only and show sincere appreciation for the thorough hospitality given by the host."[31] A contemporary Japanese sociologist also states: "The host's care and consideration is expressed through artistry of motion and gesture. ... The guests were expected to reciprocate through their unspoken appreciation of the host's hospitality and concern for their comfort."[32] Ultimately, "the deepest human communication took place through silent *aesthetic* communion."[33]

The aesthetic communication of consideration and respect for others nurtured by Zen training and practice of the tea ceremony permeates today's Japanese daily life. For example, in food preparation, cooks cut the materials in a certain way not only to provide a visually pleasing impression but also to facilitate easy eating.[34] The guests are discouraged from digging items out from the bottom of an arrangement as a sign of respect for the cook who took care in preparing a beautiful presentation. Similarly, after picking the meat off a whole fish, the bone, head, and skin should be neatly collected on the plate to avoid an unsightly visual impression of debris. Also, the used chopsticks should be put back into the paper envelope to hide the soiled end.[35]

Another example of the bodily expression of respect regards the handling of packaging. Carter describes how a master potter, Hamada Shoji, unwraps and rewraps a pottery piece slowly and carefully "as a sign of respect and appreciation."[36] Here the emphasis is not upon what gets accomplished— unwrapping and rewrapping the item—but rather upon the manner in which the task is accomplished. If this is the case with receiving and opening a gift, which is part of daily life in a gift-giving culture such as Japan, consider what different attitude would get expressed if the receiver were to take the same care in opening the gift as opposed to ripping apart the beautiful packaging in order to get to the item quickly. Even if unintended, the latter act cannot help but convey a failure to recognize and appreciate the thoughtful and considerate preparation by the giver, particularly because Japanese packaging is known for embodying a "deep respect for material and process, and *respect* too for the intended user" as well as "care for the object inside, and therefore *care* for the recipient of the object."[37] The action and its unsightly aftermath of the ripped-up packaging material inevitably indicate a deficiency in both aesthetic and moral sensibilities. What people experience in daily life becomes a powerful, though subtle, vehicle for moral education, and it is practiced through bodily engagement with its aesthetic expression.

It is instructive that the written character for social discipline or cultivation of manners, *shitsuke* (躾), is a Japanese invention that combines two Chinese characters: body (身) and beauty (美).[38] A significant part of learning proper behavior concerns body movements of daily activities such as opening and closing a door, holding a cup, serving a drink, giving and receiving a name card, opening a gift, and bowing, to name just a few. *Shitsuke* training requires that we practice engaging in these acts gently, carefully, respectfully, and mindfully. If we act carelessly, roughly, and without regard to how the appearance and sound affect others, our actions will appear not only inelegant but also disrespectful, even if it is unintended and despite the fact that the task gets accomplished.[39]

AESTHETIC CULTIVATION OF VIRTUES AND GOOD SOCIETY

Is this aesthetic cultivation of moral virtues something peculiar and limited to the Japanese tradition? I believe that the value of expressing and cultivating moral virtues aesthetically transcends historical and cultural contexts. Consider Karen Stohr's discussion of "virtuous hospitality" as it applies to contemporary American life. Despite the usual connotation of 'hospitality' as entertaining, Stohr points out that its morally oriented basis honors "the welfare, comfort, and dignity of the guest" by creating a certain environment and acting in a certain way.[40] Furthermore, just as in the tea ceremony, "virtuous hospitality" must be responded to or reciprocated by "receiving hospitality virtuously," which "requires unflagging cheerfulness, consideration, and cooperation, regardless of how difficult that is to manage."[41]

One may claim that performing such an outward aesthetic expression is simply putting on an act, not necessarily indicative of a person's virtuous character. I could be a very callous person indifferent to my friend's plight or my guest's discomfort while acting *as if* I cared with a respectful and gentle demeanor. It is possible, for example, that "[a]s a 'pretense, or semblance' of respect and goodwill, civility makes despicable individuals appear likable, and it conceals uninterested, unflattering, and even contemptuous appraisals of others."[42] We can even imagine a cruel person acting with graceful manners.[43] In addition, as Carter admits, even within the Japanese tradition, "[i]t may well be true [in some instances] that this caring for others is less heartfelt and more an uneasiness about being seen not to care."[44]

There are several responses to this challenge. First, while these objections reveal that outward appearance of respect and care is not sufficient for a virtuous character, they do not refute the necessity of such an appearance. Respect and care for my neighbor cannot be conveyed by merely accomplishing a certain task like taking her to the doctor, although this is better than refusing to do so at all. The kindness of my action is compromised or even nullified if I act in a grudging or spiteful way, even if I insist that I did show my care by taking her to the doctor. As Cheshire Calhoun states, "the function of civility ... is to *communicate* basic moral attitudes of respect, tolerance, and considerateness. We can successfully communicate these basic moral attitudes to others only by following socially conventional rules for the expression of respect, tolerance, and considerateness." In short, "civility always involves a *display* of respect, tolerance, or considerateness."[45]

Even if it is true that my gentle demeanor can disguise my callous and uncaring attitude, such a possibility does not make the practice of cultivating virtues through engaging in specific bodily training inane or ineffective. We cannot develop or acquire virtues simply by studying virtues; we have to keep practicing and exercising the bodily manifestations of respect and care in our daily lives. As Megan Laverty states, "civility is a learned behavior—individuals develop civility by habitually practicing civil interactions."[46] We practice engaging in these interactions by submitting to generally accepted social norms and foregoing whatever personal desires we may have (such as acting contrary to social expectations) so that the other-regarding attitudes get displayed and communicated. As Calhoun states, "civility requires obedience to social norms not for their own sake but for the sake of one important moral aim: the communication of moral attitudes to fellow inhabitants of our moral world."[47]

Furthermore, citing results of empirical research, Nancy Sherman concludes that "emotional change can sometimes work from the outside in" and that "we nurse a change from the outside in," because "outward emotional demeanor can sometimes move inward and effect deeper changes of attitude."[48] In fact, testimonies of Japanese art practitioners and those who had a proper *shitsuke* discipline sufficiently demonstrate that, through repeated bodily engagement and practice, artistic skills and respectful conduct *tend to* become internalized so that one becomes a certain kind of person who, at the masterful stage, will "naturally" exhibit virtuous qualities. One may not achieve a perfectly virtuous self, but that does not nullify the *ideal* of cultivating moral virtues through bodily engagement both within and outside of artistic training.[49]

The training of geisha best illustrates this process of internalizing outward bodily training. Literally meaning a person accomplished in the arts, a geisha practices classical music, dance, and the art of entertaining guests. The arduous physical regimen of all of these activities, a trainee reports, is "as much a discipline of the self as the technical mastery of an art form" and "if art is life for a geisha, then her life must also become art." Accordingly, "a geisha's professional ideal is to become so permeated with her art that everything she does is informed by it, down to the way she walks, sits, and speaks."[50]

A good society is one that promotes everyone's well-being, consisting of civil rights, health, education, economic security, and political participation. Another important ingredient is what Yrjö Sepänmaa calls 'aesthetic welfare,'[51] wherein we can experience a sensuous manifestation of the way in which our lived experience is attended and responded to with care.

We need a sensuous verification that our experience matters, both in the physical environment and in the social interactions that take place within it. As Arnold Berleant reminds us in his proposal for "social aesthetics,"[52] human relationships constitute an important dimension of our environment. Care and thoughtfulness expressed through the kinds of object created and arranged and the kinds of action executed in a certain manner define the nature of the environment that surrounds us. The character of our environment cannot but affect the quality of our lives and society.

If our environment is responsive to our need for aesthetic welfare in all these senses, we are motivated to pay it forward, so to speak, by encouraging ourselves to engage in caring actions for others, whether human or nonhuman. In contrast, if we have no indication that our experience is honored, we tend to become indifferent to others' experience; as Sarah Buss notes, "when people treat one another rudely, they are less likely to accommodate their actions to others, or even to believe that they ought to."[53] Such a reaction is not conducive to developing civic virtues or moral sensibility.

The aesthetic dimension of our lives is thus not a frivolous triviality or decorativeness. It has an often unrecognized role to play in cultivating moral sensibility, which in turn contributes to defining the quality of our lives and society. I maintain that, whether we recognize or not, as humans we are all implicated in the collective and cumulative project of world-making. Not all of us are professional world-makers like architects, designers, manufacturers, and politicians. But nonprofessionals among us do participate in the world-making project as consumers with our purchasing decisions, as residents with our management of environments, and as citizens with our support for public policies and projects. Together we are creating the world for ourselves and our fellow citizens, as well as for our descendants. Good life and good society certainly require a welcoming, comfortable, nurturing, as well as stimulating and engaging physical environment, but it is not sufficient if human relationships are cold, impersonal, disrespectful, and alienating.

The world-making project thus must include nurturing, courteous, civil, and respectful human interactions. I hope I have demonstrated that aesthetics has a crucial role to play in facilitating such human interactions, and that the Japanese aesthetic tradition provides one example of promoting such a practice.

NOTES

1. Sarah Buss urges us to imagine what it is like to live in such a society in "Appearing Respectful: The Moral Significance of Manners," *Ethics* 109, no. 4 (1999): 799, 804.

2. Nel Noddings, "An Ethics of Care," in *Introduction to Ethics: Personal and Social Responsibility in a Diverse World*, ed. Gary J. Percesepe (Englewood Cliffs, NJ: Prentice Hall, 1995), 176.

3. Nancy Sherman, "Of Manners and Morals," *British Journal of Educational Studies* 53, no. 3 (2005): 285.

4. Megan Laverty, "Civility, Tact, and the Joy of Communication," *Philosophy of Education* (2009): 229.

5. Karen Stohr, *On Manners* (New York: Routledge, 2012), 166, 167.

6. Sherman, 273, 282. In addition to what have already been cited, see Cheshire Calhoun, "The Virtue of Civility," *Philosophy & Public Affairs* 29, no. 3 (2000): 251–75.

7. Alexander Gottlieb Baumgarten, *Aesthetica/Ästhetik*, ed. Dagmar Mirbach, 2 vols. (Hamburg: Felix Meiner Verlag, 2007).

8. Sherman, 272, 281, 272, 281.

9. Buss, 814.

10. In what follows, my discussion of communicating care and respect through a particular body movement is based upon what I take to be an ordinary context in which taking time and acting gently in opening a door, bidding farewell, eating food, or opening a package do not cause a problem. In certain contexts, however, extenuating circumstances may require accomplishing these tasks as swiftly as possible, and in such cases, the most thoughtful way of acting will have to be adjusted and modified.

11. Robert E. Carter, *The Japanese Arts and Self-Cultivation* (Albany, NY: State University of New York Press, 2008), 143, emphasis added.

12. "Our aesthetics have hitherto been women's aesthetics, inasmuch as they have only formulated the experiences of what is beautiful, from the point of view of the *receivers* in art. In the whole of philosophy hitherto the artist has been lacking." Friedrich Nietzsche, *The Will to Power*, trans. Walter Kaufmann and R. J. Hollingdale, ed. Walter Kaufmann (New York: Vintage Books, 1968), 429, emphasis added. "Kant, like all philosophers, instead of envisaging the aesthetic problem from the point of view of the artist (the creator), considered art and the beautiful purely from that of the '*spectator.*'" Friedrich Nietzsche, *On the Genealogy of Morals*, in *Basic Writings of Nietzsche*, trans. and ed. Walter Kaufmann (New York: Modern Library, 1968), 539, emphasis added.

13. Dōgen, *Shōbōgenzō: Zen Essays by Dōgen*, trans. Thomas Cleary (Honolulu: University of Hawai'i Press, 1986), 32, emphasis added.

14. Ibid., emphasis added.

15. I give a detailed account of each in "Representing the Essence of Objects: Art in the Japanese Aesthetic Tradition," in *Art and Essence*, ed. Stephen Davies and Ananta Ch. Sukla (Westport, CT: Praeger Publishers, 2003), 125–41; and in "The Moral Dimension of Japanese Aesthetics," *Journal of Aesthetics and Art Criticism* 65, no. 1 (2007): 85–97.

16. Carter, *The Japanese Arts and Self-Cultivation*.

17. Dōgen, *Tenzo kyōkun (Instructions for the Cook)*, in *Cooking, Eating, Thinking: Transformative Philosophies of Food*, ed. Deane W. Curtin and Lisa M. Heldke

(Bloomington, IN: Indiana University Press, 1992), 282. The next passage is also from 282.

18. Carter, 70, emphasis added.

19. Ibid., 61, emphasis added.

20. Ibid., 102, emphasis added.

21. Ibid., 108–09.

22. Simon P. James, "For the Sake of a Stone? Inanimate Things and the Demands of Morality," *Inquiry* 54, no. 4 (2011): 392.

23. Sei Shōnagon, *The Pillow Book of Sei Shōnagon*, trans. and ed. Ivan Morris (Harmondsworth: Penguin Books, 1982).

24. Ivan Morris, "The Cult of Beauty," in *The World of the Shining Prince: Court Life in Ancient Japan* (New York: Kodansha International, 1994), 170–98.

25. Sei Shōnagon, 49–50.

26. Ibid., 49.

27. Ibid., 46, emphasis added.

28. Dōgen, *Fushuku-hampō* (*Meal-Time Regulations*), in *Cooking, Eating, Thinking: Transformative Philosophies of Food*, ed. Deane W. Curtin and Lisa M. Heldke (Bloomington, IN: Indiana University Press, 1992), 153–63.

29. Yasuhiko Murai, *Cha no bunkashi* (*A Cultural History of Tea*) (Tokyo: Iwanami Shinsho, 1979), 192. My translation.

30. Ii Naosuke, *Sayu ikkaishū* (*Collection of Tea Meetings*), finished in 1858, cited by Murai, 169. Details of required body movement can also be found in Sen Sōshitsu, *Shoho no sadō* (*Introductory Way of Tea*) (Kyoto: Tankōsha, 1965).

31. Ii, *Sayu ikkaishū*, cited by Murai, 169. My translation.

32. Eiko Ikegami, *Bonds of Civility: Aesthetic Networks and the Political Origins of Japanese Culture* (Cambridge: Cambridge University Press, 2005), 226.

33. Ibid., 227, emphasis added. It is instructive that meals and snacks prepared and served by the host are sometimes referred to as *furumai* (振舞), which also means dance-like movement, *chisō* (馳走), or *gochisō* (御馳走), which literally means running around (to prepare food with the utmost consideration). See Murai, 165.

34. For example, a piece of filleted squid receives a mesh-like cut to make for an easier eating of otherwise slippery and chewy texture; it also looks decorative like the surface of a pine cone.

35. These specifics are culled from Yaeko Shiotsuki, *Washoku no itadakikata: oishiku, tanoshiku, utsukushiku* (*How to Eat Japanese Cuisine: Deliciously, Enjoyably, Beautifully*) (Tokyo: Shinchōsha, 1983).

36. Carter, 124.

37. Joy Hendry, *Wrapping Culture: Politeness, Presentation, and Power in Japan and Other Societies* (Oxford: Clarendon Press, 1993), 63, emphasis added.

38. I owe this point regarding the Japanese character to Kazuo Inumaru. Ikegami also discusses this character and further points out that the same term is also used for "basting" in sewing, which is a preliminary rough sewing to put the fabric's shaping and folding in place to prepare it for the *bona fide* sewing. This process may be compared to "training" a material such as a plant material to create a desired shape and the analogy extends to the training of the body so that it expresses moral virtues (Ikegami, 344).

39. During the Edo period, various rules of etiquette involving body movements were established, sometimes formally written as manuals and sometimes as towns-people's cumulative wisdom referred to as *Edo shigusa* ('Edo Way of Acting'). For various written documents, see Ikegami's chapter on "Hierarchical Civility and Beauty: Etiquette and Manners in Tokugawa Manuals," 324–59. For *Edo shigusa*, specific body movements are discussed in Harutake Iikura, *Nihonjin reigi sahou no shikitari* (*Japanese Custom of Etiquette and Manners*) (Tokyo: Seishun Shuppansha, 2008).

40. Stohr, 148–49.

41. Ibid., 164.

42. Laverty, 228.

43. Indeed there is a Japanese term for this: 慇懃無礼 (*ingin burei*).

44. Carter, 138.

45. Calhoun, 259, 255.

46. Laverty, 235.

47. Calhoun, 273.

48. Sherman, 277, 277, 278.

49. The point here is similar to Aldo Leopold's discussion of land ethic. "We shall never achieve harmony with land, any more than we shall achieve absolute justice or liberty for people. In these higher aspirations the important thing is not to achieve, but to strive." *A Sand County Almanac* (New York: Ballantine Books, 1977), 210.

50. Liza Crihfield Dalby, "The Art of the Geisha," *Natural History* 92, no. 2 (1983): 51. Geisha training of body and mind is analogous to the artistic training of medieval performing arts. Ikegami points out that "the distinctive characteristic of medieval performing arts was their emphasis on the relationship between a careful aesthetic training of the corporeal body and personal and internal cultivation. It was through the repeated training of body movements in the performing arts that unity of body and mind might be actualized" (Ikegami, 345).

51. Yrjö Sepänmaa, "Aesthetics in Practice: Prolegomenon," in *Practical Aesthetics in Practice and in Theory*, ed. Martti Honkanen (Helsinki: University of Helsinki, Lahti Research and Training Centre, 1997), 15.

52. "Social aesthetics may ... *be* a kind of environmental aesthetics, for it is both needless and false to restrict environment to its physical aspects." Arnold Berleant, *Aesthetics and Environment: Variations on a Theme* (Hants: Ashgate, 2005), 154. Berleant's notion of social aesthetics is developed in *Aesthetics and Environment*, chap. 14, "Getting along Beautifully: Ideas for a Social Aesthetics," and in "Ideas for a Social Aesthetic," in *The Aesthetics of Everyday Life,* ed. Andrew W. Light and Jonathan M. Smith (New York: Columbia University Press, 2005), 23–38.

53. Buss, 803.

Part II

JAPANESE AESTHETICS
AND CULTURE

Chapter 6

Beyond Zeami

Innovating Mise en Scène *in Contemporary Nō Theatre Performance*

C. Michael Rich

INTRODUCTION

This chapter discusses the performance ideas and innovations of several professional nō performers (*nōgakushi*) based in Kyoto under whom I have studied nō performance.[1] Katayama Shingo, Tamoi Hiromichi, and Ōe Nobuyuki are professional Kanze-ryū main role performers (*Kanze-ryū shitekata nōgakushi*) whom I met in a Traditional Theatre Training Workshop at the Kyoto Art Center in 2004, which I repeated in 2008. This three-week-long workshop, organized by Dr. Jonah Salz, Professor of Theatre at Ryukoku University, has been training artists from around the world in nō, *kyōgen*, and *nihon buyō* for over twenty years. During both workshops, I also took lessons in the shoulder drum (*kotsuzumi*) from Hisada Shunichirō, Hisada Yasuko, and Takahashi Naoko.

The richness of this experience encouraged me to invite some of my teachers to offer nō workshops in the United States. In 2005, Tamoi and Ōe came to the State University of New York at Albany to give a weeklong workshop in nō; and, in 2007, Katayama, Tamoi, and Ōe led another weeklong workshop at Georgetown College in Georgetown, Kentucky. The three instructors were joined by Kawamura Haruhisa, also a *Kanze-ryū shitekata nōgakushi*, in 2009 for another workshop at Georgetown College. Some months later, Tamoi introduced me to *Kanze-ryū shitekata nōgakushi* Asano Atsuyoshi. Asano said that he wanted to teach nō in the United States, so I arranged for Asano to be invited to perform and teach in California and Kentucky. In addition to his training in nō performance under Sugiura Motozaburō, Asano is one of the few people in Japan who make nō stage properties (*kodōgu*). He also carves nō masks, having apprenticed under one of the most respected modern nō mask carvers, Hori Yasuemon. A sabbatical year (AY 2011–2012) spent in Shiga Prefecture enabled me to continue studying under Asano, Tamoi, and also Kanze-ryū main role performer Hashimoto Kōzaburō and Ishii-ryū hip drummer (*Ishii-ryū ōtsuzumikata nōgakushi*) Taniguchi Masatoshi, and to participate in amateur performances. Moreover, I was able to see a great variety of nō performances, both professional and amateur, that expanded my understanding of what Tamoi calls 'the cosmic number of performance variations available to the nō performer.'[2]

TRADITIONAL DEPLOYMENT OF *MISE EN SCÈNE* IN NŌ THEATRE

Mise en scène refers to the deployment of all aspects of the production that are intentionally shown to the audience. Although not traditionally used as a critical term for nō theatre, it can be helpful in explaining the scope of choices available to nō performers in organizing and staging a performance, and in foregrounding their aesthetic preferences.

No alludes to a wide spectrum of artistic modes that can be performed independently or in various combinations. A performance can be staged by male-only professional performers (at the top of this hierarchy would be a performance featuring the *sōke*), mixed gender all-professional performers, mixed amateur and professional performers, and, occasionally, all-amateur performers. Performances can be staged by family lineages and their associated students (*teikinō*), by members of the Kyoto Kanze Kai (*reikai*), or by prominent *nōgakushi* to commemorate important events (*bekkai*). Advanced amateurs may perform at the regularly scheduled performances staged by their teacher's family (*teikinō*). Amateurs perform at student recitals arranged by their teachers. University nō clubs also stage performances, which can include alumni and professionals. No can be performed on a specialized nō stage or a temporarily erected stage in a venue such as a temple, shrine, park, community center, art gallery, or spacious home. A nō performance can consist of short dances (*shimai*) backed up by a chorus, solo or ensemble performances of the instruments used in nō (*ikkan, itchō, dokko, renchō*), singing without instrumental or dance accompaniment (*su-utai, rengin, dokugin*), dance to chorus and instruments (*maibayashi*), performance of the second half of a play in full costume (*han-nō*), or performance of the entire play in full costume (*nō*). Other venues for nō performance may be in films as varied as *Banshun* (*Late Spring*, Japan, 1949), *Kagemusha* (Japan, 1980), and *Songjia Huangchao* (*The Soong Sisters*, Hong Kong, 1997), and in *taiga* historical drama series broadcast by Nippon Hoso Kyokai (NHK), Japan's national public broadcasting corporation. Alternatively, a performance may take place in an art gallery displaying nō masks, or even in a jazz bar or laboratory theatre in collaboration with Western and non-Western theatrical and musical traditions and artists. Thus, nō artists deploy an almost infinite variety of *mise en scène* in order to expand their audiences, cultivate student-teacher relationships, and respond to criticisms that see nō as a museum piece irrelevant to contemporary culture.

Yokomichi Mario writes,

> Nō, as a classical artistic tradition that has been transmitted through centuries, has the image of being completely immutable, but it is actually not so fixed. The range to which a performer can intentionally make changes is quite wide. Through this freedom the performer's individuality is made viable and the audience's interest attracted. This is why nō has been able to survive for so many centuries.[3]

Nō performers—musicians (*hayashikata*), chorus (*ji*), stage manager (*kōken*), main role actor (*shitekata*), supporting role actor (*wakikata*), comedian and villager (*kyōgenkata*)—explore an almost limitless scope of possible variations for activating their individual artistic visions within the supporting musical and artistic structures of nō theatre.

Nō productions traditionally fall into different categories. Regular performances (*teikinō*) are staged by teaching lineages, usually six per year, and, in the case of the *Kyōkanze*, are scheduled a year ahead of time at the Kanze Kaikan in Kyoto. Katayama, Hayashi, Inoue, Sugiura, and Urata are some of the Kyoto-based family teaching lineages that schedule regular performances at the Kanze Kaikan, while Kawamura and Ōe perform their regularly scheduled nō performances at their own theatres in Kyoto. Also scheduled at least a year in advance are the Kyoto Kanze Kai's ten monthly performances (*getsureikai*—no performances in July or October). *Teikinō* and *getsureikai* promote solidarity among Kyoto Kanze performers and help all active Kyoto Kanze Kai members gain valuable stage opportunities. A *getsureikai* performance usually consists of three full nō plays, interspersed with *shimai* and an independent *kyōgen* play (*kyōgenkata* also perform the *ai* role in a full nō play). The performances are ordered according to the five categories (*gobandate*) of God-Warrior-Woman-Deranged-Demonic (*shin-nan-nyo-kyō-ki*), and the second play is often performed by the most senior actor in the program, sometimes even the *sōke* or a member of one of the *sōke* branch families from Tokyo.

Additionally, the Kyoto Kanze Kai sponsors a number of seasonally or regionally themed productions, fall and summer *su-utai* and *shimai* recitals, charity performances for disaster-struck regions, and other initiatives such as the Young Performers Recital (*wakate nō*) and the Interesting Museum of Nō (*omoshiro nōgakkan*, an exhibition of nō to introduce audiences to nō and expand its audience), in addition to special performances and workshops for schoolchildren.

Teikinō, since they represent a family teaching lineage, can seem a bit more casual and familiar than the monthly performances, which represent the entire Kanze School. Advanced amateur students of the teaching lineage are sometimes included in the program. Since many members of the audience study under the performers featured in the program, the atmosphere in the lobby can seem like a class reunion. *Teikinō* tend to offer more opportunities for individual interpretation and they use alternate performance options, called '*kogaki*,' which can range from using a white wig instead of the usual black wig (aging the character), to incorporating more dance sections, or even changing the gender of the main character.[4] Tickets for *teikinō* are typically purchased by the students and supporters of the performers, yet these programs rarely break even.

Bekkai are special nō performances with various functions and offer the widest latitude for self-expression on the part of the organizer and sponsor of the performance. Examples include performances commemorating professional debuts (*hiraki*). These are often plays that are noted for their difficulty, such as *Dōjōji*, and that require permission from the *sōke* to perform. Memorial nō (*tsuizen nō*) may be performed in designated years following a prominent artist's death to make a statement about the deceased artist's artistic vision and legacy. Other occasions for *bekkai* include the tenth anniversary of a performer's debut, 60th birthday (*kanreki*), and 77th birthday (*kijū*). Sponsors for these performances usually pull out all the stops by inviting high-ranking performers and charging triple the amount of a typical *teiki* or *reikai* performance. *Bekkai* are thus opportunities to stage personal favorites, difficult plays that may require more than the customary single rehearsal, and to express gratitude to fellow performers and teachers. Revival productions (*fukkyoku-nō*) of plays that were removed from the canon in 1765 cost a great deal more money to stage since the performers require multiple rehearsals in order to learn the piece, so additional payment for their time is required.[5]

The most over-the-top form of *bekkai* must be *ran-nō*, in which *nōgakushi* perform roles that are outside their areas of expertise. At the *ran-nō* performance celebrating Hayashi Kiemon's 70th birthday in 2011, every role was performed by someone who did not specialize in that role. In other words, the chorus was performed by *kyōgenkata*, drums and flute by *shitekata*, main role by *kotsuzumikata*, and so on. Adding to the festive atmosphere, alcohol and snacks were served in the lobby and behind stage in the green room (*gakuya*). Two *kyogenkata* put a sign on the usually near-sacred stage saying "Hayashi Sensei is a handsome man," and Hayashi wore a red sash over his costume proclaiming the celebration of his birthday. He seemed to blush in embarrassment when he first entered the stage. Despite the atmosphere of frivolity and celebration, the performers still approached their roles with intense concentration. More than a month earlier, I had seen four *shitekata nōgakushi* backstage of an amateur recital practicing their drum parts for their performance of *Okina* in the upcoming *ran-nō* program. This seriousness contrasted with how they hurriedly glanced over their librettos seconds before going on stage to sing for the student recital.

Since Tamoi had apprenticed under Hayashi, I asked him about the atmosphere in the *gakuya* during a *ran-nō* performance. Tamoi said that while alcohol was served, the function of *ran-nō* was to deepen mutual understanding of the various roles performed by *nōgakushi,* regardless of specialization.[6] Since cross-training in the arts of drum, flute, song, and dance is an important aspect of the education of a young actor, *ran-nō* strengthens artistic bonds among specializations.[7] Because performers' livelihoods are based on being asked by organizers (usually *shitekata*) to perform, performance in *bekkai* reaffirms artistic interdependence and stimulates the economy of debt and repayment among performers.

Patrick Galbraith, the discussant for a panel at which portions of this chapter were presented, asked if this party-like nō performance in the end did not serve to reinforce the stability of original role specializations, referring to Mikhail Bakhtin's articulation of the "carnivalesque."[8] Since the relations among nō role specializations are often fraught with conflict, perhaps *ran-nō,* which by definition overturns performative norms, may serve to resolve long-standing artistic tensions. One of the most "carnivalesque" moments in the Hayashi *ran-nō* program occurred when the drummer performing the *sambasō* role in *Okina* (a *kyōgenkata* specialty) made several mistakes, whereupon a *kyōgenkata* (playing the *shitekata* role of *kōken,* or stage manager) gave the drummer impromptu lessons right in the middle of the performance. That this "blasphemy" occurred during *Okina,* a ritualistic play among the "heaviest" in the nō repertoire indeed, perhaps telegraphs a final return to traditional order.

Performances sponsored by shrines, such as Itsukushima Jinja, Taga Taisha, and Kasuga Taisha, often with long histories behind them, also qualify as a form of *bekkai.* These performances tend to foreground nō's ritual function over artistic expression.[9] The discovery of an *Okina*-type mask named 'matara' at Tanzan Jinja recently occasioned the creation of a new "tradition" of nō performance at this remote shrine nestled deep in the mountains of Nara Prefecture.

In its more restricted sense, *mise en scène* refers not only to the artistic intention of a dramatic presentation in the choice of venue, performers, and theme, but also to the costuming and staging of a presentation. In a typical *teikinō* or *getsureikai* performance, the *shitekata* plays the main role in determining *mise en scène.* However, musicians (*hayashikata*) and *kyōgenkata* are also active in sponsoring performances, and may be even more *avant-garde* in their approaches, for instance, by incorporating Western-trained dancers or musicians into their performances.

The *shitekata*'s choice of mask(s) demonstrates the long tradition of varying *mise en scène* in a nō performance. During the Muromachi period (1337–1573), masks were created in three modes: *setsu-getsu-ka* (snow-moon-flower). Since nō was performed on a variety of stages and types of surfaces during the Muromachi period, the *shitekata* would choose a mask that best showed the audience the character's emotions according to the actor's position on the stage at that moment. The mask, like the human face, is not perfectly symmetrical; one half is carved to convey suffering, and the other half, enlightenment. With most nō stages constructed with the *hashiga-kari*, or bridge, on stage right, the moon (*getsu* or *tsuki*) mask best conveys the character's suffering at the beginning of the play and enlightenment at the conclusion of the play. When performed on a *kagura*-style stage in shrines where the *hashigakari* comes from the middle of backstage, flower (*ka* or *hana*) would be more appropriate with its more symmetrical design. The snow (*setsu*) mask shows the suffering aspect on the left side of the face, and may be suitable if the climactic moment occurs near the flute position (*fue-za*) on stage.

According to Asano, a *shitekata* will decide what segment of the play best expresses the main character's climactic moment.[10] Although the "climax" (*kiri*) is predetermined by the script and occurs at the end of the play, the *shitekata* enjoys the latitude to highlight sections of the play that he feels best depict his interpretation of the play's dramatic essence. The *shitekata* will then choose the mask and costume to best convey those scenes.

Masks, even within a generic designation such as *ko-omote* or *fukai*, demonstrate almost infinite varieties of expression and mood depending upon their maker. Thus, the choice of mask (often done in consultation with one's teacher if the performer is not of *shokubun* status) bears greatly on the dramatic effects of the performance. Masks may be borrowed from one's teacher or purchased. The best masks, according to Asano and his teacher, Hori, are those copied from Muromachi-period masks. Since most of the masks made during the Muromachi period were stored in private collections and not available for Edo-period mask carvers to copy, most of the better masks being used today, other than the few Muromachi originals owned by the major nō families, are copies of masks that only became known post-1945 when these families sent them to Hori for repair.[11]

Costumes too, being very expensive, are often borrowed from the teacher under whom one has apprenticed. The *shitekata* often chooses his costume in a customary meeting after the rehearsal in consultation with the other performers. Although the *shitekata* may have aesthetic preferences for a certain costume (to a certain extent the costumes used for each role are pre-determined), the teacher's relationship with the student may determine how extraordinary a costume he may lend him. Even after one's debut and formal declaration of independence as an artist, *nōgakushi* return to their teachers for continued training, permission to perform plays classified as "difficult" (*narai*), and to borrow costumes and masks.[12]

Kodōgu and *tsukurimono* are props held or used by actors or set on stage to represent things that help to visually concentrate on an aspect of a play's theme. Asano says that an overriding nō aesthetic is to avoid their use as much as possible, since the actor wishes the song and dance to communicate the essentials of the play. *Tsukurimono* are supposed to be constructed by the *shitekata* (although in fact are often built by a stage technician), and are usually intended to be temporary (except for the bell used in *Dōjōji*). Some examples include a tomb (*Sumidagawa*), a boat (*Funa Benkei*), a drum on a stand (*Tenko*), a well (*Izutsu*), or a flowering tree (*Yoshino Tennin*). Examples of *kodōgu* include a representation of a piece of ice (*Himuro*), a flower basket (*Hanagatami*), a demon mallet (*Aoi no Ue*), or a mirror (*Nomori*). Like the graphic designs on the fans and the patterns in the clothing, these conform to preset designs, and are meant to evoke something about the character in a visually symbolic manner. When I asked Asano how he made the slab of ice for the play *Himuro*, he answered, "It is a copy, of course." The principle of copying a classic form, *utsushi*, whether in mask carving or in the construction of *kodōgu* and *tsukurimono*, remains one of the invariables of deployment of *mise en scène* in nō theatre. The idea of *utsushi* also applies to dancing and singing. Asano says, "My goal as an actor is to reproduce what my teacher taught me and to change it as little as possible."

The way in which a *shitekata* selects his cast of course bears heavily upon the overall aesthetic effects of the play. As soon as the venue is confirmed and the title of the play determined, he tries, often by cell phone while travelling between lessons, performances, and rehearsals, to line up performers for the date. But because *nōgakushi* are often booked up to two years in advance, it can be difficult to gather one's ideal cast. Personality conflicts between performers occur, and some performers will try to avoid performing with another performer with whom they do not get along, for artistic reasons or otherwise. The aesthetic vision of the *shitekata* may also be further infringed upon if particular performers, perhaps more senior, take the lead in setting the tempo of the song or dance. The *shitekata*, like a symphony conductor, is supposed to lead all performers to cocreate his personal artistic vision, but if another performer, particularly an instrumentalist (*hayashikata*) or chorus head (*jigashira*), perceives a wide enough gap in hierarchy, he may attempt to lead the *shitekata*. As Tamoi has said, for the *shitekata*, the play may not so much resemble a collaboration as it does a fight.

There are limitations on artistic freedom and individualism imposed by traditional modes of production and adherence to what Yokomochi calls 'kimari,' or certain aspects of production that cannot be changed by the availability of certain masks and costumes, by the use of *utsushi* or copies of canonical stage properties, or by hierarchical structures in the world of nō among the performers themselves. The tension between these limitations and the actor's desire not only to interpret the play but also to recontextualize it for a modern audience forms the creative space in which nō is now performed. As Thomas Hare notes, "the weight of tradition is not a new problem to noh. It is a problem that has persisted since the fifteenth century when noh became noh."[13]

Experimentation with *mise en scène* provides the primary mode for creative recombination of the traditional artistic elements transmitted in nō theatre training and practice. In the following section, I discuss some of the ways current nō performers deploy their own visions of nō production while developing and expanding an audience that will appreciate their efforts.

INTERPENETRATION WITH OTHER MEDIA AND ARTISTIC TRADITIONS

Experimentation with *mise en scène* by professional nō performers beginning with the Meiji period is prompted by a sense of crisis as well as a desire for artistic innovation. While teaching amateurs has provided a solid economic footing for many nō performers, they struggle to maintain relevance among the exploding variety of cultural offerings available today. In the past, if the president of a company practiced nō, many of his employees might feel compelled to do so as well. Today, golf is more popular in the corporate world than nō. Asano mentioned that many of his students in the rural areas of Shiga Prefecture used to take lessons in preparation for singing a celebratory wedding song from the play *Takasago*. At weddings today, celebratory songs are more likely to be J-pop standards or perhaps a piano solo. Western music is more familiar to most Japanese today than traditional forms of Japanese music.

One way nō performers have sought to make nō relevant to contemporary Japanese has been to set up tours to locales where nō plays are set. Place names, *uta makura*, are one of the most important principles of Japanese poetry,[14] and thoroughly exploited in nō librettos. Taking the audience out of the theatre and into the streets or mountains deconstructs the very concept of *mise en scène*. Following the 2011 Great East Japan Earthquake and Tsunami, nō plays set in northeast Japan (Tōhoku) have been staged more frequently, including the revival of *The Pine of Akoya* (*Akoyanomatsu*). Japan's literary and cultural history is imprinted on its geography, which is reassembled in the nō text. Incorporating the sense of place into the production can happen in different ways. Hisada Yasuko leads her students to places where the stories in nō plays occurred, such as the Shōsei-en Garden in Kyoto, purportedly the site of the garden and salt kiln in the play *Tōru*. Tamoi creates detailed pamphlets to accompany his productions with photographs of the places where the plays took place, and details his journeys to these historic spots. He also regularly posts pictures of these visits on Facebook.

As opposed to visiting actual sites, *mise en scène* may also be deployed internally to assist the actor in his performance. One of Katayama Keijirō's students told me that when another of his students was preparing to perform *Hachinoki*, Keijirō's advice was for the student to simply go find the snowiest place he could find and contemplate it until he had internalized the image.

Just as Western academics seek to increase student enrollment in Japanese studies by offering courses in Japanese popular culture, nō actors have also sought to (re)appropriate popular culture in order to reach a younger audience. One of these interpenetrations has been through "*taiga*" historical drama series, months-long television series based on Japanese historical figures and produced by NHK. The broadcast of a *taiga* drama series that features a period or people treated in nō plays, such as *Yoshitsune* in 2005 or *Kiyomori* in 2012, offers the potential for tie-in promotion and enhances the perception of the art form. The massive torchlight nō festival (*takiginō*) at the Heian Shrine in Kyoto in July 2012, put on jointly by the Kanze and Kongō groups, featured *Futari Shizuka*, about Yoshitsune's lover and renowned dancer Shizuka Gozen, and *Ikarizuki,* about Tomomori's legendary suicide by tying an anchor to his feet and leaping into the sea at the Battle of Dan no Ura. Both plays portrayed scenes that had been recapitulated in recent *taiga* drama series.

Tamoi has collaborated with the Kyoto Art Center to produce a series of *su-utai* concerts with his yearlong series *Yoshitsune wo utau* (*Singing Yoshitsune*) and *Heike wo utau* (*Singing Heike*) that coincided with the television broadcasts of the *taiga* drama series *Yoshitsune* and *Kiyomori*. Other well-marketed historical events such as the 1000th anniversary of the writing of *Tale of Genji* in 2008 occasioned a number of nō plays that year based on this classic work of fiction.

During the Edo period, the Kyokanze specialized in *su-utai*, or unaccompanied singing. Performances would often be held in traditional Kyoto homes in a large room in which the singers would sit behind a screen. The audience would focus on the aural effects without visual distractions. In Tamoi's performances at the Kyoto Art Center, the performers sit directly in front of the audience in a slightly darkened room. Performers and audience sit at the same level on the tatami-matted floor. Only a bolt of red felt divides the space between audience and performers. Tamoi often uses these performances as an opportunity to showcase one of Kyoto's teaching lineages, such as Inoue, Hashimoto, Katayama, or Sugiura, and thus to demonstrate the diversity of singing styles among these Kanze families.

A performer at one of these *su-utai* concerts told me before the performance how uncomfortable and nervous singing in this venue made him feel. *Su-utai* performed on a nō stage can seem dull because of the formality and distance between audience and performers. A *nōgakushi* once wanted me to see her son perform in a play, but told me that the day's program began with *su-utai*. She added, "You can arrive late so that you miss the *su-utai*," summing up how *su-utai* is viewed today as a perhaps necessary but tedious practice done mainly for the benefit of students or to generate fees to support teachers. Yet during the numerous *su-utai* performances that I saw at the Kyoto Art Center, the audience listened with rapt attention. The chorus, usually separated from the audience by stage and theatre-type seating, sat on tatami only a few feet away from the first row of the audience. The performer's effort and concentration, made palpable by the close proximity, heightened the tension and interest of the performance. Because of the tatami seating, the audience could not slump into their seats during the concert. As Hashimoto Kōzaburō once told me, "we are performing within an inch of our lives; it wouldn't do for the audience to be too comfortable."[15] Tamoi has thus reinvigorated a traditional Kyoto practice in a unique space (the Kyoto Art Center is a gorgeous old elementary school originally built for the children of wealthy textile and clothing merchants and recently remodeled into studio and performance space).

With the ranks of retirees growing every day and the influence of mask carver Hori Yasuemon and his students, nō mask carving has grown in popularity in Japan, supporting a whole subindustry of suppliers such as Kind Lake (www.kindlake.co.jp). While nō performers interact with mask carvers at a variety of levels in selecting and ordering masks for their performances, Tamoi has interacted with the masks in an innovative way—by performing with them in full costume at a gallery showing of nō masks in Kyoto, something he has done for several years. The show I saw in November 2011 involved changing costumes and masks through five characters, starting with the *hatsukamari* mask used in the play *Fujito* and ending with the *kasshiki* mask of the boy hero of *Kagetsu*.

The previous night, Tamoi had been drinking with some of his students, and at around 2 a.m., Tamoi called a *shitekata* friend of his and discovered that he was still up talking with a hip drummer visiting from Kyushu. We took a taxi to the hotel where they were staying, and through the plate glass doors of the hotel we saw the two men chatting in the lobby. Tamoi escorted them to the waiting taxis and we departed together to a nearby bar for an hour or two of conversation. The next day at the mask exhibition, as Tamoi put on his final mask and costume for *Kagetsu*, I saw to my surprise the hip drummer with whom we had been drinking about twelve hours earlier emerge formally dressed in *montsuki* and *hakama* holding his drum. Tamoi, who had never met this drummer previous to our 2 a.m. get-together, had spontaneously recruited him for the gallery performance that afternoon. This testifies to how Tamoi constantly seeks opportunities to present nō in new ways and, in this case, to respond to the last-minute request of the gallery owner to use five particular masks in his performance. The collaboration between Tamoi and the drummer also demonstrated how traditional nō training enables impromptu performance. The two, who had never before practiced together, were able to pull off a flawless performance of a section of the play *Kagetsu*. Given the time frame and the nature of their meeting, the drummer undoubtedly had no opportunity to rehearse or refresh his memory of the piece. Tamoi often jokes during such nontraditional performances that he will get into trouble if his teacher finds out about them, and he asks the audience not to post any video on YouTube or Facebook. I am never sure how seriously to take him, but I tend to feel that there is at least tolerance of his unconventional methods as long as he is successful at growing the audience for nō.

This performance not only provided a venue to showcase nō theatre to an audience that might not otherwise have seen a nō play, but it also gave prominence to the carvers whose masks were used in the performance. Among the many active nō mask carvers in Japan, only a handful produce masks *shitekata* deemed worthy of use on the stage.

Katayama Shingo's nō company, *Kashūjuku*, has taken novel approaches to expand nō's contact with other arts. Because of the unique role of the Katayama family as head of the Kanze School in Kyoto, and its connection through marriage with the headmaster of the Inoue School of Japanese Dance, Shingo feels a special connection with a variety of Kyoto traditional arts. He hosts the *Tsumugi no Kai*, which organizes events that feature discussions, interviews, and coperformances with makers of traditional Kyoto sweets, sake brewers, kabuki performers, kimono dyers, and so on. Two particularly memorable collaborations come to mind. Both were held at the Kyoto Art Center. The first was in July 2008, when the kabuki star Nakamura Shibajaku was doing a series of evening performances at Mt. Hiei, and Katayama invited him to the Kyoto Art Center one afternoon to discuss kabuki dance. Shibajaku, dressed in informal *yukata* and *hakama*, performed a graceful and intricate female dance role that demonstrated the mutual appreciation possible between two artists of vastly different disciplines. The second was when Shingo invited a young master of Japanese dance, Onoe Kikunojō, to a *Tsumugi no Kai* presentation at the Kyoto Art Center. The two performed an excerpt from *Shakkyō* (an auspicious lion dance) together: Shingo according to nō choreography and Onoe according to the style of the Onoe School of Japanese Dance (*Onoe ryū nihonbuyō*). The contrast of Onoe's playful eroticism with Shingo's grim ferocity conveyed the elements of each artistic style more than either could have done on its own. The audience's palpable exhilaration and delight with the unique performance permeated the intimate, tatami-matted hall on the second floor of the Kyoto Art Center.

One of the oldest nō stages remaining in Kyoto, the Ōe Nohgakudo, has become a favorite venue for artists seeking to combine the unique atmosphere of a patinaed nō stage and tatami viewing area (*kenjo*) with elements of modern drama and dance. The building's sweeping tiled roof and understated Kyoto-style entryway fits well with the current retro boom in Kyoto that seeks to preserve and repurpose traditional Kyoto architecture. *Nōgakushi* stage events there ranging from student recitals and candlelit nō to demonstrations and workshops for schoolchildren. One particularly memorable performance that I saw there was sponsored by Living National Treasure shoulder drummer Sowa Hiroshi, and featured an adaptation by a male dancer trained in modern dance of the pillow scene (*makura no dan*) of *Aoi no U*e, in which Lady Rokujō's spirit attacks the prostrate figure of the wife of her fickle lover, Genji. Sowa and the dancer had rearranged the traditional chorus and instrumentation to support the dancer's focused interpretation of Lady Rokujō's torment, anger, and jealousy. Other performances included solo rearrangements of the traditional drum pieces that accompany the play. After the play, Ōe Nobuyuki Sensei asked me how I enjoyed it, and I answered that while I was impressed by the dancer's tension and control, the nō elements such as the dancer's modified *hakama* forced me to compare it with a traditional nō performance. Perhaps if he had worn an entirely Western costume, it would have made it easier to view the dance independently from the expectations generated by dancing such a famous piece. Ōe responded, "Well, that just shows you how good nō is." I interpreted his statement to mean that nō performance has undergone so many centuries of study, practice, and refinement that it is hard to do something in a nō "style" without inviting an unfavorable comparison. Further evidence of the difficulty of drawing a line between adapting nō might be seen in Ōe's comment that, "I at least tried to convince him [the dancer] to put a robe in front of the stage." A robe (*kosode*) is traditionally placed on the front of the stage during a performance of *Aoi no Ue* to suggest the presence of Lady Aoi, the victim of Lady Rokujō's anger.[16]

CONCLUSION

Visiting a bourbon distillery is de rigueur on the itinerary for nō performers when they come to Kentucky. Buffalo Trace Distillery has even sponsored two nō workshops in Kentucky. But it wasn't until Mark Brown, the company's president and CEO, complained that bourbon distillers had to produce a product for which they had no idea what the market would be when it was ready to be packaged and sold that I realized the connection between bourbon and nō.

In August 2012, Hashimoto Kōzaburō came to Kentucky with a troupe of eleven nō performers for a production of a *han-nō* performance of *Tamura* and a full nō performance of *Izutsu*. As we were touring a distillery, Kōzaburō's nephew, Hashimoto Kōji, began cajoling his uncle, "Why don't you take a rest and let me play the *shite* role in *Izutsu* tonight?" (Kōji is about twenty years younger than Kōzaburō.) The two joked back and forth, but in the end, the performance opportunity, organized by Asano, had been intended as a gift from Asano to Kōzaburō, and of course Kōzaburō was too excited about this opportunity to give it up to someone else. When I told Asano about the exchange and expressed my surprise that Kōji would try to take the lead role, he seemed amazed at my ignorance. "Of course, *nōgakushi* are always looking for opportunities to perform."

Nōgakushi spend decades learning the skills and memorizing the texts and music necessary to perform and teach. Almost by necessity, they begin this learning process as small children before they have any idea whether or not they want to perform nō professionally. Just as a bourbon distiller has no idea whether or not bourbon will still be popular eight years after he makes his product, neither can a *nōgakushi* predict that an audience will be there for him when he enters the stage as a full-fledged professional performer. Even though nō music and texts have changed over the centuries, audiences will still continue to grow more distant from their language, melodies, and rhythms. Octavio Paz writes, somewhat hopefully, that

> we can long for the past—which is thought to be better than the present—but we know that the past will not return. Our "good" time dies the same death as every time: it is succession. On the other hand, the mythical date does not die: it is repeated, incarnated. And so, what distinguishes the mythical time from every other representation of time is that it is an archetype. A past always susceptible to being today, the myth is a floating reality, always ready to be incarnated and to be again. The function of rhythm now becomes clearer: by the action of the rhythmic repetition the myth returns.[17]

Nō theatre is more than a theatrical form; it comprises part of the myth that forms the foundation of Japanese identity and aesthetic sensibility.[18] But in this world of immediate gratification, nō becomes more and more emotionally distant and incomprehensible to Japanese and foreigners alike. For some, that aura of impenetrability may constitute some of its attraction. Nonetheless, nō must train its audience as well as its performers in order for the art to remain aesthetically viable. Nō continues to attract students willing to undergo mentally and physically grueling training, not only to learn how to perform but also to learn how to appreciate a professional performance. Innovations in deploying *mise en scène* will expand the possibilities for exploiting the artistic training immanent in the world of nō theatre and increase its interconnectedness with a diversity of artistic forms. Perhaps nō's future success will lie in its taking greater risks by departing from the formalistic style of the Edo period and regaining some of the spontaneity and freedom it enjoyed in the early days of its creation. Thus, variation and innovation will remain the primary aesthetic impetuses in performing nō.

NOTES

1. The writing of this chapter was made possible in part through a sabbatical year in Japan funded by Georgetown College. I am also grateful to my teachers—Asano Atsuyoshi, Hashimoto Kōzaburō, Hisada Yasuko, Katayama Shingo, Ōe Nobuyuki, Takahashi Naoko, Tamoi Hiromichi, and Taniguchi Masatoshi—and the staff of the Kyoto Art Center for their generosity, patience, and dedication. I would like to thank my teachers' students for their friendship, support, and encouragement. Also thanks to the many individuals, families, foundations, and corporations who made the nō workshops in New York and Kentucky possible. Chris Rich, Patricia Pringle, Erik Liddell, and Arie May provided invaluable assistance in rewriting the drafts of this chapter. Patrick Galbraith's insightful comments gave me a much better understanding of the significance of what I had experienced at nō performances in Japan. Special thanks to A. Minh Nguyen for attending a performance of *Takasago* at Georgetown College, which led to his inviting me to contribute to this book. Finally, thanks to my family for accompanying me from place to place in pursuit of learning, and for putting up with my long absences during workshops, practices, and performances.

2. Public lecture, Albany, NY, February 3, 2005.

3. Yokomichi Mario, *Nō ni mo enshutsu ga aru* (Tokyo: Hinoki Shoten, 2007), 30.

4. Ibid., 36.

5. Yokomichi says that the custom of practicing only once before a performance limits the degree to which performers can depart from traditional performance norms (ibid., 8). Also see Eric C. Rath, *The Ethos of Noh: Actors and Their Art* (Cambridge, MA: Harvard University Asia Center, 2004), 195, for a description of the construction of the present nō repertoire.

6. This and following statements from conversation with author, Kyoto, November 14, 2011. Permission received for publication of statements about nō.

7. *This Is Noh*, VHS, dir. Takao Toshioka (Kyoto: Kyoto Branch, Noh Theatre Association, and Kyoto Noh Association, 2000).

8. C. Michael Rich, "Performers, Artwork, and Audiences" (paper presented at the 53rd Annual Meeting of the Southeast Conference of the Association for Asian Studies, Duke University, Durham, NC, January 17–19, 2014).

9. Rath, 237–38.

10. This and following statements from conversation with author, Georgetown, Kentucky, May 15, 2013. Permission received for publication of statements about nō.

11. Hori Yasuemon, *Nōmen wo utsu* (Kyoto: Tankosha, 2008).

12. Rath, 176.

13. Thomas Blenman Hare, *Zeami's Style* (Stanford, CA: Stanford University Press, 1986), 226.

14. Edward Kamens, *Utamakura, Allusion, and Intertextuality in Traditional Japanese Poetry* (New Haven, CT: Yale University Press, 1997).

15. Conversation with author, Kyoto, February 20, 2012. Permission received for publication of statements about nō.

16. Conversation with author, Kyoto, October 8, 2011. Permission received for publication of statements about nō.

17. Octavio Paz, *The Bow and the Lyre: The Poem, the Poetic Revelation, Poetry and History,* trans. Ruth L. C. Simms (Austin, TX: University of Texas Press, 1974), 51.

18. Nakanishi Susumu, *Nihonjin no wasuremono* (Tokyo: Wedge, 2001), 17.

Chapter 7

The Appreciative Paradox of Japanese Gardens

Allen Carlson

INTRODUCTION

I begin this chapter by stressing some of Yuriko Saito's insights into the nature of Japanese aesthetics.[1] In "Representing the Essence of Objects: Art in the Japanese Aesthetic Tradition," Saito observes that it is "both difficult and unwise" to generalize about Japanese art and aesthetics, noting that it ranges from "the minimalist aesthetics of haiku" to, on the one hand, "the opulence and flamboyance of … Kabuki theater," and, on the other, "the *wabi* aesthetics, often described as the aesthetics of impoverishment."[2] Nonetheless, she points out that there is a "common thread" in Japanese art and aesthetics in that regardless of "the medium or historical period, Japanese art-making emphasizes grasping the essence of an object or a material … . that art is a representation of reality, understood not as empirical reality but rather as essence."[3] In this chapter, I utilize Saito's observations about this "common thread" to address what I call 'the appreciative paradox of Japanese gardens.'[4] However, mindful of Saito's warning of the dangers of generalizing about Japanese art and aesthetics, I recognize that there are different kinds of Japanese gardens with different features, styles, and designs that, accordingly, may present different issues concerning aesthetic appreciation. Consequently, I focus primarily on certain types of gardens, called 'tea and stroll gardens.' Although other kinds may do so as well, I think these types of gardens clearly pose the appreciative paradox of Japanese gardens.[5]

What is the appreciative paradox of Japanese gardens? I shall introduce it with my own experience: I usually find Japanese gardens of the relevant kind easy to appreciate aesthetically. Within such a garden, I find myself effortlessly slipping into a state of calm and serene contemplation, with feelings of quiet joy and well-being. This in itself is not paradoxical; in fact, it is hardly worthy of remark. Japanese gardens are well-known, widely acclaimed, and, by many accounts, explicitly designed precisely for this feature; they frequently bring about this kind of aesthetic experience. What is remarkable and yields a touch of paradox is that Japanese gardens are in many ways the kinds of things that are frequently found to be somewhat difficult to appreciate aesthetically.

DIFFICULT APPRECIATION AND DIALECTICAL RELATIONSHIPS

In general, both pristine nature and pure art are relatively easy to appreciate aesthetically. As a rule, neither causes much appreciative difficulty or confusion. The relevance of this to Japanese gardens is that they, although also typically easy to appreciate, are neither pristine nature nor pure art. Rather they are classic examples of things "between" art and nature, paradigm cases of the meeting and mixing of the artificial and the natural. However, such cases of interactions between artifact and nature are typically somewhat difficult to appreciate aesthetically. This is frequently true of nonartistic cases. For example, many individuals have some aesthetic difficulty appreciating the results of large-scale agriculture, mining, resource extraction, urban sprawl, and other kinds of human intrusions into natural landscapes.[6] Sometimes, such intrusions are simply regarded as eyesores, but in many cases, particularly if the resultant landscapes are not especially unpleasant to the eye, the difficulty in appreciation is more a matter of something like aesthetic uneasiness—aesthetic confusion rather than condemnation.[7]

More to the point, however, are instances of the meeting and mixing of the artificial and the natural in which the artificial component is clearly artistic, for Japanese gardens are anything but simple human intrusions into natural landscapes. We might think that more artistic cases would pose fewer problems for aesthetic appreciation, but this is not necessarily so. In "Nature and Art: Some Dialectical Relationships," Donald Crawford distinguishes traditional harmonious relationships between art and nature from what he calls 'dialectical relationships.'[8] In harmonious relationships, art and nature serve as models for each other and in a sense reinforce each other, but do not *interact* with each other. In dialectical relationships, by contrast, art and nature are two distinct and frequently conflicting elements whose "interaction is a determining factor in the constitution of the object of appreciation."[9] Crawford suggests that certain kinds of environmental artworks exemplify such dialectical relationships between art and nature, in particular some of the earthworks of Robert Smithson and the placement pieces of Christo (Vladimirov Javacheff). Many such environmental artworks are controversial.

As Crawford notes, they are attacked on environmental and ethical grounds as well as posing appreciative problems.[10] And, as with nonartistic cases, the appreciative difficulty seems to involve uneasiness and confusion rather than simply a negative reaction. Thus, such environmental artworks exemplify the problem of difficult aesthetic appreciation.

Gardens, especially Japanese gardens, are not earthworks or placement pieces, of course. Do gardens exemplify dialectical relationships between art and nature or rather just more traditional harmonious relationships? As noted, Crawford characterizes harmonious relationships as ones in which art and nature serve as models for each other. Within the Western gardening tradition, there are clear examples of such harmonious relationships. On the one hand, in "French-style" formal gardens, as at Versailles, harmonious relationships are achieved by art serving as a model for nature. On the other, in "English-style" natural gardens, as at Stourhead, harmonious relationships are achieved by the opposite means, with nature serving as a model for art.[11] However, in the Western tradition there are also topiary gardens. In such cases, as in environmental artworks, clear dialectical relationships exist between art and nature. In topiary gardens, nature and art are distinct and in a sense conflicting forces, and the interaction between the natural and the artificial is constitutive of the object of aesthetic appreciation. And, as with some environmental artworks, topiary gardens are frequently difficult and confusing objects of aesthetic appreciation. For example, in their philosophical study of topiary, although initially focusing on ethical concerns, Isis Brook and Emily Brady call attention to "the uneasiness some appreciators might feel when experiencing topiary as a manipulation or contortion of natural processes."[12]

JAPANESE GARDENS AS DIALECTICAL RELATIONSHIPS

What about Japanese gardens? Do they, like earthworks, placement pieces, and topiary gardens, but unlike formal gardens and natural gardens, involve dialectical relationships between art and nature? A number of considerations suggest this possibility. For instance, Japanese gardens sometimes include topiary. However, as Josiah Conder notes in his classic study of Japanese gardens, "the clipping and carving of trees and bushes into shapes such as mountains, water-falls, boats, and buildings" is "kept within the bounds of moderation."[13] In fact, topiary is increasingly uncommon in Japanese gardens. Nonetheless, dialectical interactions between the natural and the artificial are yet manifest in what Conder calls 'a sort of surgical treatment.'[14] This treatment, described by another authority as the necessity for "pruning, clipping, shearing, pinching, or plucking," is an essential aspect of Japanese gardens.[15] Japanese garden scholar Teiji Ito even notes that if one asks "a Japanese gardener the secret of gardening, ... he will hold up his pruning shears."[16] Thus, although they do not serve the representational ends of topiary gardens, the shrubs and trees of Japanese gardens are yet highly artifactualized. And it is not just a little casual pruning. The vegetation of Japanese gardens is carefully formed and shaped to realize distinctive styles such as the "ball treatment" and the "fraying treatment."[17] In addition, Japanese gardeners frequently utilize complex systems of bending, binding, bracing, and weighting to achieve certain desired effects. Occasionally, chemical retardants are used to control the shape of trees or entire trees are thinned by hand—one needle at a time![18]

Dialectical interactions between the natural and the artificial in Japanese gardens are evident not only in the vegetation, but also in the entire landscapes, which are themselves highly artifactualized. For example, Conder notes that in designing gardens, "the hillocks should first be arranged, and then the water channels; the principal rocks and stones are next distributed, and lastly the trees and shrubs are planted."[19] And, as with the vegetation, there are distinctive styles and means of forming, shaping, and positioning hills, rocks and stones, and water. The control of water is especially striking. A popular Western account of Japanese gardens from the turn of the last century notes that Westerners "cannot understand how water, which, like the wind, goes where it wills, has had its bed of white stones built for it, and has been trained, as pet dogs are, to run and tumble and lie down at the will of the master."[20]

Another obvious way in which Japanese gardens manifest dialectical interactions between the natural and the artificial is, as with many environmental artworks, by the careful placement of the artificial within the context of the natural. An essential aspect of the landscapes of Japanese gardens is a scattering of artifacts throughout. These include the paradigmatic lanterns, bridges, and teahouses, as well as pagodas, shrines, wells, arbors, and occasional statuary. One Western introductory work on the appreciation of Japanese gardens notes that superficial contact might unfortunately leave the impression of "a quaint, tinkling medley of little arched bridges, carp ponds, paper lanterns, oddly pruned trees, bamboo blinds, grotesquely jutting rocks, and perhaps a dainty geisha."[21]

THE APPRECIATIVE PARADOX OF JAPANESE GARDENS

It is now possible to state succinctly the appreciative paradox of Japanese gardens. On the one hand, such gardens lend themselves to easy aesthetic appreciation not unlike each of pure art and pristine nature. But, on the other, they are neither pure art nor pristine nature, and, moreover, not even examples of harmonious relationships between art and nature, such as formal gardens and natural gardens. Rather, they, like earthworks, placement pieces, and topiary gardens, involve dialectical relationships between the natural and the artificial, and thus they should be similarly difficult and confusing objects of aesthetic appreciation. Consequently, the questions posed by Japanese gardens are: First, why are they not difficult to appreciate aesthetically? Second, how do they manage to solve so successfully and completely the problem of difficult aesthetic appreciation? In short, what is the resolution of the appreciative paradox of Japanese gardens?[22]

Addressing these questions requires pursuing beyond the intuitive level the theoretical question of why objects that involve dialectical relationships between art and nature pose the problem of difficult appreciation. This is not simply because dialectical relationships involve conflicting forces. When conflicting forces are present in either pure art or pristine nature, they typically give the aesthetic object a dynamic, dramatic quality that makes it an easy, natural focus of appreciation. Rather, the answer lies not in the conflict between the natural and the artificial, but simply in the differences in their respective natures. Because of their different natures, each of the natural and the artificial lends itself to different kinds of appreciation. Moreover, given that in dialectical relationships, as Crawford puts it, "both forces retain their identity as separately identifiable components of the completed work," the resultant object of appreciation is difficult to appreciate.[23] Aesthetic appreciation is difficult because both the natural and the artificial are independently present, each requires different kinds of appreciation, and thus together they force the appreciator to perform various kinds of appreciative gymnastics. For example, the appreciator may attempt to force either the natural or the artificial component into the appreciative modes of the other or may attempt to achieve some blend of the different kinds of appreciation. However, such appreciative maneuvers are often difficult and cause aesthetic uneasiness and confusion.

APPRECIATION OF THE NATURAL AND THE ARTIFICIAL

What is the difference between the kinds of appreciation to which the natural and the artificial each lends itself? Part of the answer is suggested by aesthetician Francis Coleman. In delineating what he calls 'the critical point of view,' Coleman comments:

> Suppose we are in the country. We might ask someone who is with us to look at the hills and valleys aesthetically, but never critically … . Only if man's efforts

are mingled with the products of nature do we speak of criticism or judging or judges ... . [T]he critic supposes that the object could have been otherwise and that it is as it is because someone designed it to be so. The design rests upon the artist's judgment, and his judgment can be good or bad, faulty or sure.[24]

If Coleman is correct about the differences between appreciating nature and appreciating art, then a significant component of appreciation appropriate for the artificial is some dimension of judgment, which is appropriate because the object of appreciation, since it is seen as designed, is seen as something that could have been otherwise. In contrast, the natural is not seen as designed by an artist whose judgment might have been less than perfect, and thus it is not seen as something that, in the relevant sense, could have been otherwise. Consequently, aesthetic appreciation appropriate for the natural takes the object of appreciation as given and thus to be, as it were, beyond judgment.[25] Thus, one aspect of the appreciative difficulty involved in appreciating objects constituted by dialectical relationships between the artificial and the natural is the question of the proper role, if any, of, as Coleman puts it, "criticism or judging or judges" in such appreciation. This is the appreciative problem of whether to judge, how to judge, and to what extent to judge.

If the problem of the proper role of judgment is, therefore, part of the difficulty in appreciating objects such as earthworks, placement pieces, and topiary gardens, then the question about Japanese gardens can be put as the question of how they manage so successfully to solve or evade this appreciative problem. Objects of appreciation constituted by dialectical relationships between art and nature may solve the problem in many different ways, but two general lines of approach immediately suggest themselves. They are by following either the lead of art or the lead of nature. For example, to the extent that they successfully deal with the problem, many famous environmental artworks, such as those by Smithson and Christo, do so by following the lead of art in the sense of making the artificial component of the work so dramatic that there is little doubt about the appropriateness of judgment. By contrast, other lesser-known environmental works, such as some by Michael Singer and Alan Sonfist, follow the lead of nature in the sense of making the artificial component so unobtrusive that, as with pristine nature, the tendency to judge does not arise.[26] Likewise, Japanese gardens successfully solve the problem by following the lead of nature rather than that of art. However, they do so not by making the artificial unobtrusive, but rather by making the natural appear in such a way that the tendency to judge is again averted. In short, Japanese gardens solve the problem of the proper role of judgment by rising above judgment in a way somewhat similar to the way in which nature itself does.

A LOOK OF INEVITABILITY

Consider the aesthetic appreciation of nature. In such appreciation, we are not confronted by the problem of the proper role of judgment because, according to Coleman's account, nature rises above judgment by virtue of appearing as something that could not have been otherwise. This, however, is not to say that any particular bit of nature appears as if it could not have turned out differently from how it, in fact, has. Rather, it is to say that nature in general has a certain kind of look, a look of inevitability—indeed, what is often called a 'natural' look. I suggest that Japanese gardens solve the problem of judgment because they, as nature, are seen as having this kind of look of natural inevitability. This is a common theme in the literature. For example, even after becoming completely acquainted with the design and construction of Japanese gardens, one Western commentator describes her intuitive reaction as follows:

> What luck, what wonderful luck, these people have! They do not need to make their gardens: Nature has done it for them. It is not that they are so artistic in composing, but only so wise in not changing a single stone or tree from the place in which it was found.[27]

She continues:

> And so one feels that the garden *had* to be arranged as it was, ... that the lake and the trickling stream and the cascade must have been set there by the Divine Landscape Gardener Himself, and that the beautiful old trees had grown to that precision of shape and loveliness by the help of Nature alone.[28]

As she notes, the general impression is that the garden *had* to be as it is, that is, it could not have been otherwise. It is thus beyond judgment. Who, after all, would attempt to judge the work of the "Divine Landscape Gardener Himself"?

This does not mean, however, that Japanese gardens *look just like nature*. This is because, first, in many ways they do not, in fact, look just like nature. And, second, because if they did, they would not exemplify dialectical relationships between art and nature, but rather simply harmonious relationships such as natural gardens. Natural gardens are more or less copies of nature and often look, if not just like, then at least quite a lot like nature. In Japanese gardens, by contrast, a certain kind of look—a look of natural inevitability—is achieved and in the realization of this kind of look such gardens solve the problem of judgment. But the look is not achieved by the creation of a copy of nature. Rather, it results from a process of isolating and revealing the essential—the creation of an idealization of nature that attempts to uncover what are taken to be its essential qualities. The idea is in accord with Saito's insight noted at the outset of this chapter: that a "common thread" of Japanese aesthetics is that it "emphasizes grasping the essence of an object or a material."[29] Japanese garden scholar Ito echoes this insight, characterizing Japanese gardens as "the continuous endeavor to extract the essence of a stone, a tree, a view" that results in "a celebration of the elementals."[30] Likewise, the guidebook for a well-known North American Japanese-style garden puts the point simply by saying that the garden is "intended to demonstrate the *essence* of nature."[31]

The idea that Japanese gardens articulate the essential features of nature puts the artificial side of the dialectical relationships between art and nature in a new light. The artifactualization in Japanese gardens, although a separate identifiable aspect of such gardens, is yet completely subservient to the aim of revealing the essence of nature. Therefore, this artifactualization, instead of prompting judgment as it seemingly does in many environmental artworks, rather contributes to seeing Japanese gardens as something that could not have been otherwise and thus as beyond judgment. Consider again the pruning and shaping of vegetation. This is aimed at what Conder calls 'natural prototypes,' ideal forms that display the essential qualities of each species—the pine, the maple, and the willow, for example.[32] One authority says that the "Japanese gardener can emphasize these qualities, eliminate distracting elements, simplify [a plant's] lines, and thus reveal its true nature to the world."[33] Saito makes a similar point, noting that the Japanese gardener must "discern and articulate the essential features of the particular material by eliminating adventitious, inessential, and irrelevant parts."[34] Ito describes this as "a glimpse of nature bare," which is achieved as follows:

> There is pruning and placing but this results in the revealing of a line which nature itself created and then obscured in its own plenitude ... . [T]his pruning ... allows a more natural and, at the same time, more ideal beauty to emerge ... [that] is there from the first. It is not created, it is merely allowed to express itself in a louder voice and in plainer terms.[35]

In a similar fashion, the presence of artifacts within Japanese gardens also aims at the accentuation of the natural. First, consider the character of many of the artifacts themselves. Items such as bridges, shrines, wells, and arbors are the kinds of artifacts that do not seem out of place in a more or less natural landscape. Moreover, they are typically made of natural materials and designed to have a natural, somewhat rustic look. Second, and perhaps more important, the artifacts are carefully placed within the landscape, as Conder puts it, "so as to look as accidental and natural as the landscape itself."[36]

Third, the artifacts contribute to the aim of accentuating nature in that by subtle contrast they, as Ito sums up the total effect, "create within the viewer that feeling of nature heightened which is the salient quality of the Japanese garden."[37]

It is now possible to summarize how Japanese gardens, although exemplifying dialectical relationships between the artificial and the natural, yet successfully deal with the problem of difficult and confusing aesthetic appreciation that frequently accompanies such relationships. The idea is that they do so by following the lead of nature in the sense of making the artificial subservient to the natural. They employ the artificial in the creation of an idealized version of nature that emphasizes the essential. They thereby achieve a look of inevitability—the appearance of something that could not have been otherwise—and in achieving this look, they, as pristine nature itself, rise above judgment. Japanese gardens do not generate difficult and confusing aesthetic appreciation because the question of judgment does not arise. Thus, since they are reasonably pleasant in other ways, Japanese gardens lend themselves to easy aesthetic appreciation in spite of involving dialectical interactions between art and nature.

A PROBLEM WITH JUDGMENT

Does this line of thought fully resolve the appreciative paradox of Japanese gardens? The heart of the paradox is that such gardens lend themselves to easy aesthetic appreciation not unlike each of pure art and pristine nature even though they are neither art nor nature nor even examples of harmonious relationships between art and nature, as are formal gardens and natural gardens. Rather, they involve dialectical relationships between the natural and the artificial and thus should be difficult and confusing objects of aesthetic appreciation. The line of thought developed so far addresses this paradox by arguing that Japanese gardens achieve a certain appearance, a look of inevitability, and thus, like pristine nature, rise above judgment. However, there is a problem here in that nature, if it is beyond judgment, is so not simply because it has a look of inevitability, but also because it is not seen as designed by an artist whose judgment might have been less than perfect, and therefore it is not seen as something that could have been otherwise. Recall that Coleman notes that to "speak of criticism or judging or judges ... supposes that the object could have been otherwise and that it is as it is because someone designed it to be so. The design rests upon the artist's judgment, and his judgment can be good or bad, faulty or sure."[38]

Consequently, the paradox is seemingly resolved by this line of thought only if one of three alternatives obtains. First, appreciators believe that

Japanese gardens are not, in fact, designed by artists, that, as it is put by the Western commentator quoted above, the Japanese "do not need to make their gardens" for "Nature has done it for them"; they are not "so artistic in composing, but only so wise in not changing a single stone or tree from the place in which it was found."[39] Second, whatever appreciators believe or know about Japanese gardens is irrelevant to their aesthetic appreciation; in this case, appreciation is properly focused only on appearances. Third, although Japanese gardens are in some cases proper objects of judgment, they somehow, at least in some instances, rise above being judged. The first two alternatives are clearly untenable. The belief that Japanese gardens are not designed is not only false but also, given the nature of such gardens, difficult to sustain. Moreover, someone who held such a belief would not take Japanese gardens to involve dialectical relationships between art and nature and thus not find them to be difficult and confusing objects of aesthetic appreciation. In short, for such an appreciator, the case is not that the paradox would not be resolved, but rather that it would never arise in the first place. The second alternative fares no better. It would amount to adopting some version of aesthetic formalism for Japanese gardens, and, again, this would not resolve the paradox, but only prevent it from arising. Moreover, since aesthetic formalism is currently widely rejected for both art and nature, adopting it for objects that involve dialectical relationships between the two would be implausible and even more implausible for only one case of such objects, Japanese gardens.[40]

This leaves the third alternative, that, although Japanese gardens are in some cases proper objects of judgment, they somehow, at least in some instances, rise above being judged. This alternative is the most promising, not only because of the problems with the other two, but also simply because the most counterintuitive aspect of this attempt to resolve the appreciative paradox of Japanese gardens is the claim that Japanese gardens are never proper objects of judgment. Upon a moment's reflection, it seems obvious that Japanese gardens can be and frequently are objects of judgment. For example, in an endnote to this chapter—see n. 31—I observe that a certain North American Japanese-style garden is judged to be one of the most authentic outside of Japan. This is certainly a judgment about the garden. However, it might be argued that this is not the relevant kind of judgment, for all that is necessary to resolve the paradox is that Japanese gardens rise above *aesthetic* judgment. Be that as it may, I also report in the same endnote that the McFadden guidebook to Oriental gardens in America judges the same garden as "surely ... one of the most beautiful."[41] This is clearly an aesthetic judgment. Consequently, to pursue this alternative, it is necessary to consider different cases of aesthetic judgment, asking in which cases—if any—Japanese gardens rise above judgment, and, if so, whether escaping such judgment is sufficient to resolve the appreciative paradox of Japanese gardens.

To distinguish different cases of aesthetic judgment, it is useful to return to the examples of harmonious relationships between art and nature, formal gardens and natural gardens. Recall that harmonious relationships are ones in which art and nature serve as models for each other. In formal gardens, harmonious relationships are achieved by art serving as a model for nature, while in natural gardens by nature serving as a model for art. What is important concerning distinguishing different cases of aesthetic judgment is that for these gardens there are seemingly two different kinds of judgments that can be made. Judgments can be made about the model that is followed and also about the success of the garden in question in following that model. For example, in formal gardens in which art serves as a model for nature, aesthetic judgments can be made about the particular artistic model that is employed in designing the garden and about the success that has been achieved by the garden in following that model. Moreover, to the extent that a particular garden is more successful in following the model, aesthetic judgments typically focus more on the model rather than on the particular garden. In the limiting case in which a formal garden is perfectly successful in following its model, aesthetic judgment will be appropriate only of the model itself. In such a case, we might say that the garden is beyond aesthetic judgment about its success in following the model.

Now consider natural gardens in which nature serves as a model for art. Again, two kinds of aesthetic judgments initially seem possible: first, about the particular model employed in designing a garden; and, second, about the success that has been achieved by the garden in following that model. However, since the model in question is pristine nature, if we follow Coleman's assumption, as we have done throughout this discussion, we do not judge this model, for, as he puts it, "Only if man's efforts are mingled with the products of nature do we speak of criticism or judging or judges."[42] Consequently, the only kind of aesthetic judgments that are possible are judgments about the success of the garden in following the model. Moreover, as with formal gardens, to the extent that a particular garden is more successful in following its model, aesthetic judgments typically focus more on the model than on the garden itself. However, in natural gardens, where nature is the model, judgments of the model are simply not appropriate. Thus, in the limiting case in which a particular garden is perfectly successful in following the model and in which, therefore, only judgment of the model itself would be appropriate, in fact, no judgments whatsoever are appropriate. In such a case, the particular garden rises above judgment.

CONCLUSION

In conclusion, I apply these observations about different cases of aesthetic judgment and the appreciation of natural gardens to the aesthetic appreciation of Japanese gardens. Since, like natural gardens, Japanese gardens follow the lead of nature, in the limiting case in which a specific Japanese garden is perfectly successful in capturing the essence of nature and in which, therefore, only judgment of nature itself would be appropriate, it follows that no judgments whatsoever are appropriate. Thus, when a Japanese garden is perfectly successful, we can say that it is beyond judgment.[43] And in such cases, the appreciative paradox of Japanese gardens is resolved. This line of thought also explains the nature of the aesthetic experience sometimes felt in Japanese gardens. As described at the outset, when experiencing such gardens, I sometimes find myself slipping into a calm, serene contemplative state. Such an aesthetic experience is exactly what is to be expected in a reasonably pleasant environment that seems as if it could not have been otherwise. Moreover, it is an aesthetic experience that quite naturally follows from the suspension of judgment. However, what is now clear is that this is an aesthetic experience that can typically be expected only in those Japanese gardens that approach perfection in achieving their aim of capturing the essence of nature—and thereby move Zen-like beyond being judged as such.

NOTES

1. I am especially indebted to Yuriko Saito for comments and suggestions concerning this chapter. Some of its ideas were initially presented at a symposium on Japanese gardens at the Annual Meeting of the Pacific Division of the American Philosophical Association in Portland, Oregon in March 1992. I thank my copresenters Donald Crawford and Yuriko Saito, as well as Arnold Berleant, Arlene Kwasniak, Soili Petajaniemi, and Joni Petruskevich, for helpful comments. My contribution to the symposium, "On the Aesthetic Appreciation of Japanese Gardens," appeared in the *British Journal of Aesthetics* 37, no. 1 (1997): 47–56.

2. Yuriko Saito, "Representing the Essence of Objects: Art in the Japanese Aesthetic Tradition," in *Art and Essence*, ed. Stephen Davies and Ananta Ch. Sukla (Westport, CT: Praeger, 2003), 125.

3. Ibid.

4. In "The Moral Dimension of Japanese Aesthetics," *Journal of Aesthetics and Art Criticism* 65, no. 1 (2007): 85–97, Yuriko Saito describes this "common thread" as a "sensitivity to, respect for, and appreciation of the quintessential character of an object," adding that the "attitude gives rise to a guiding principle of design that articulates the essence of an object, material, or subject matter, regardless of whether it is considered artistic" (85–86). The confirmation that the guiding principle applies

beyond the realm of the artistic is important given my application of it to Japanese gardens, which some may not consider paradigm works of art.

5. A classic Western introduction to the different kinds of Japanese gardens and their different features, styles, and designs is Josiah Conder, *Landscape Gardening in Japan* (New York: Dover, 1964). The oldest source on these matters appears to be an eleventh-century manuscript, *Memoranda on Garden Making*. It is attributed to a Fujiwara nobleman, Tachibana-no-Toshitsuna, and now published as *Sakuteiki: The Book of Garden, Being a Full Translation of the Japanese Eleventh Century Manuscript: Memoranda on Garden Making Attributed to the Writing of Tachibana-no-Toshitsuna,* trans. Shigemaru Shimoyama (Tokyo: Town and City Planners, Inc., 1985).

6. I discuss some of the aesthetic difficulties involved in appreciating agricultural landscapes in "On Appreciating Agricultural Landscapes," *Journal of Aesthetics and Art Criticism* 43, no. 3 (1985): 301–12, and in "Aesthetic Appreciation and the Agricultural Landscape," chapter 6 in *Nature and Landscape: An Introduction to Environmental Aesthetics* (New York: Columbia University Press, 2009).

7. That the difficulty in appreciation is due to the actual meeting and mixing of the artificial and the natural is evidenced by the fact that when the results of such intrusions are captured in art, such as landscape photography, especially if the works of art are pleasant to the eye, the aesthetic uneasiness and confusion are greatly diminished, if not completely overcome. For such photographs of the results of mining and resource extraction, for example, see Edward Burtynsky, *Oil* (Göttingen: Steidle/Corcoran, 2009), as well as the documentary film *Manufactured Landscapes,* dir. Jennifer Baichwal (Montreal: National Film Board of Canada, 2007).

8. Donald Crawford, "Nature and Art: Some Dialectical Relationships," *Journal of Aesthetics and Art Criticism* 42, no. 1 (1983): 49–58.

9. Ibid., 49.

10. I discuss closely related issues in "Is Environmental Art an Aesthetic Affront to Nature?" *Canadian Journal of Philosophy* 16, no. 4 (1986): 635–50.

11. For consideration of these distinctions, as well as some different aspects of Japanese gardens, see Mara Miller, *The Garden as an Art* (Albany, NY: State University of New York Press, 1993). On philosophy and gardens more generally, see Stephanie Ross, *What Gardens Mean* (Chicago: University of Chicago Press, 1998); David Cooper, *A Philosophy of Gardens* (Oxford: Oxford University Press, 2006); and Glenn Parsons, "Nature in the Garden," chap. 8 in *Aesthetics and Nature* (London: Continuum Press, 2008). Issues involving comparisons of gardens and environmental artworks are pursued in Stephanie Ross, "Gardens, Earthworks, and Environmental Art," in *Landscape, Natural Beauty, and the Arts,* ed. Salim Kemal and Ivan Gaskell (Cambridge: Cambridge University Press, 1993), 158–82, and in Thomas Heyd, "Understanding Japanese Gardens and Earthworks on the Way to Understanding Nature Restoration," *Æ: Canadian Aesthetics Journal / Revue canadienne d'esthétique* 6 (2001), accessed July 30, 2015, http://www.uqtr.ca/AE/Vol_6/Manon/Heyd.html.

12. Isis Brook and Emily Brady, "Topiary: Ethics and Aesthetics," *Ethics & the Environment* 8, no. 1 (2003): 127. Brook and Brady develop ideas concerning aesthetic appreciation of topiary that have relevance to what I argue in this chapter.

13. Conder, 7.

14. Ibid., 108.

15. David H. Engel, *Japanese Gardens for Today* (Tokyo: Charles E. Tuttle, 1959), 46.

16. Teiji Ito, *The Japanese Garden: An Approach to Nature,* trans. Donald Richie (New Haven, CT: Yale University Press, 1972), 140. Ito's volume is especially illuminating concerning the central ideas of this chapter.

17. Conder, 109.

18. Mitchell Bring and Josse Wayembergh, *Japanese Gardens: Design and Meaning* (New York: McGraw-Hill, 1981), 203. See also Saito, "The Moral Dimension of Japanese Aesthetics," 95n6.

19. Conder, 132.

20. Mrs. Basil Taylor (Harriet Osgood), *Japanese Gardens* (New York: Dodd, Mead and Co., 1912), 7.

21. Engel, 5.

22. It could be argued that the appreciative paradox of Japanese gardens would not arise (and thus would not require resolution) within Japanese aesthetic appreciation, for such appreciation presupposes a unity of humanity and nature, of the artificial and the natural, and not the separation of the two that characterizes Western aesthetic appreciation. If so, the paradox is perhaps an example of a quandary generated at least in part by "cross-cultural" aesthetic appreciation. For an account of how Japanese aesthetics presupposes a "unity and co-identity between man and nature," see Yuriko Saito, "The Japanese Appreciation of Nature," *British Journal of Aesthetics* 25, no. 3 (1985): 239–51. Yet, in other essays, Saito herself expresses some doubt about the extent to which Japanese gardens exemplify a harmonious unity of humanity and nature. See Yuriko Saito, "The Japanese Love of Nature: A Paradox," *Landscape* 31, no. 2 (1992): 1–8; and "Japanese Gardens: The Art of Improving Nature," *Chanoyu Quarterly: Tea and the Arts of Japan* 83 (1996): 40–61.

23. Crawford, 57.

24. Francis J. Coleman, "What Is the Aesthetic Point of View?" in *Contemporary Studies in Aesthetics*, ed. Francis J. Coleman (New York: McGraw-Hill, 1968), 7.

25. I discuss a related position known as 'positive aesthetics,' which holds that pristine nature is open to only positive aesthetic judgment, in "Nature and Positive Aesthetics," *Environmental Ethics* 6, no. 1 (1984): 5–34, and in "Appreciating Art and Appreciating Nature," in *Landscape, Natural Beauty, and the Arts*, ed. Kemal and Gaskell, 199–227. The aesthetic appreciation of nature is discussed more generally in my *Aesthetics and the Environment: The Appreciation of Nature, Art and Architecture* (London: Routledge, 2000).

26. For an introduction to environmental art, and especially to somewhat lesser-known artists, such as Alan Sonfist and Michael Singer, see *Art in the Land: A Critical Anthology of Environmental Art*, ed. Alan Sonfist (New York: Dutton, 1983). Ross, "Gardens, Earthworks, and Environmental Art," provides a useful taxonomy of environmental art, sorting works into seven different categories. Various philosophical issues concerning environmental art are discussed in a special issue of the journal *Ethics, Place and Environment: A Journal of Philosophy and Geography* 10, no. 3

(2007), titled 'Environmental and Land Art.' The issue has an introduction by guest editor Emily Brady, as well as articles by Brady, Sheila Lintott, John Andrew Fisher, Jason Boaz Simus, Isis Brook, Jim Toub, Jonathan Maskit, Thomas Heyd, and Allison Hagerman. Brady's article "Aesthetic Regard for Nature in Environmental and Land Art," 287–300, is especially relevant to some of the topics discussed here. Also pertinent is Parsons, "Art in Nature," chapter 9 in *Aesthetics and Nature*.

27. Taylor, 6.

28. Ibid., 6–7.

29. Saito, "Representing the Essence," 125.

30. Ito, 197, 139.

31. Anonymous, *The Japanese Garden, Portland, Oregon, United States* (Portland, OR: Japanese Garden Society, nd), 1. The Portland garden is widely judged to be one of the most authentic Japanese-style gardens outside of Japan. Moreover, it is described in the McFadden guidebook as "surely … one of the most beautiful." See Dorothy Loa McFadden, *Oriental Gardens in America: A Visitor's Guide* (Los Angeles: Douglas West, 1976), 198.

32. Conder, 108.

33. Engel, 46.

34. Saito, "Representing the Essence," 126.

35. Ito, 197, 139–40. The idea of Japanese gardens revealing the essence of nature has deep roots. In "The Japanese Appreciation of Nature," Saito relates the idea to Zen Buddhism, suggesting that by presenting "an idealization of nature," Japanese gardens give us "a glimpse of this world as it appears to a Zen-enlightened sensibility." She finds a source in the notion of *kowan ni shitagau*. Literally meaning "following the request," this is the central design principle of the eleventh-century *Sakuteiki* manuscript. Originally, it was a principle of stone placement, recommending that a gardener follow the request of the mind (essence, true nature) of an initial stone in the placement of others. However, it was subsequently employed in the placing, designing, shaping, and pruning of other elements of the garden, in each case "following the request" indicated by the true nature of the object in question. Similarly, Donald Keene relates the idea of Japanese gardens revealing the essence of nature to one of the four themes in terms of which he analyzes Japanese aesthetics, which he labels 'simplicity' and traces to the Zen preoccupation with the "use of the most economical means to obtain the desired effect." See Donald Keene, "Japanese Aesthetics," *Philosophy East and West* 19, no. 3 (1969): 293–306; reprinted in *Japanese Aesthetics and Culture: A Reader*, ed. Nancy G. Hume (Albany, NY: State University of New York Press, 1995), 27–41.

36. Conder, 11.

37. Ito, 187.

38. Coleman, 7.

39. Taylor, 6.

40. Although aesthetic formalism has not been widely accepted recently, Nick Zangwill yet defends moderate aesthetic formalism for both art and organic nature and extreme aesthetic formalism for inorganic nature. See Nick Zangwill, "Formal Natural Beauty," *Proceedings of the Aristotelian Society* 101 (2001): 209–24; and

The Metaphysics of Beauty (Ithaca, NY: Cornell University Press, 2001). For criticisms of aesthetic formalism as well as for the development of a cognitively focused alternative position, see Carlson, *Aesthetics and the Environment*, as well as Glenn Parsons and Allen Carlson, "New Formalism and the Aesthetic Appreciation of Nature," *Journal of Aesthetics and Art Criticism* 62, no. 4 (2004): 363–76.

41. McFadden, 198.

42. Coleman, 7.

43. There are interesting questions about the nature of the aesthetic judgments that are appropriate when a Japanese garden is less than perfectly successful. Saito's discussion of the "art of artlessness" as a general principle of Japanese aesthetics is relevant to these issues. Concerning gardens, she again refers to the eleventh-century *Sakuteiki* manuscript that "cautions against obvious signs of artifice and intentionality in garden making," recommending that gardens should be made without any "touch of artificiality" and that "garden makers should cultivate their art in such a way that their carefully considered design would appear as if it were not so intended." Failures to achieve "artlessness" in this sense would be grounds for criticism of a garden. See Saito, "Representing the Essence," 133–35.

Chapter 8

Savoring Tastes

Appreciating Food in Japan

Graham Parkes

When a friend of mine saw the phrase 'savoring tastes,' he said it was pleonastic, suggesting that 'savor' already means to taste and 'taste' implies to savor. He was right, of course, but perhaps he has lived in Japan for too long, since in the United States these days, to judge from the prevalence of fast food and "preprepared meals" (another pleonasm), not so many people seem interested in tasting what they eat, let alone savoring it. This in spite of the fact that eating is one of the central, because indispensable, activities we engage in, one that any culture worthy of the name endows with ritual significance as a primary mode of social intercourse. While there are, of course, gourmets in all cultures, the artistry of Japanese cuisine provides especially rich grounds for aesthetic reflection.

The notion of taste in the wider sense is central to Western aesthetics: think of Kant's concern with "judgments of taste" in the third *Critique*. And for some thinkers, taste is germane to the project of philosophy as a whole. In one of his early, unpublished works, Nietzsche wrote that "the Greek word for 'wise' is linked etymologically with [the Latin] *sapio*, I taste, and *sapiens*, the taster"—so that the "peculiar art of the philosopher," or lover of wisdom, consists in discerning taste and tasteful discrimination.[1] Nietzsche's popularity in Japan stems at least in part from his rejection of Western religions and metaphysics that ignore the body in favor of the soul, and his counterclaims that among "the things in life that deserve to be taken seriously [are] questions of food, accommodation, [and] spiritual diet," and that "the salvation of humanity" lies more than anything in "the question of *nutrition*."[2]

For a long time it was thought that there were four "basic tastes": sweet, sour, salty, and bitter. It was only at the beginning of the twentieth century that a fifth basic taste, *umami*, was discovered—by a professor of chemistry at Tokyo Imperial University. Typical examples of *umami* are the flavors of the broths made from *kombu* (a kind of kelp), *katsuobushi* (dried bonito), or dried *shiitake* mushrooms that serve as the basis of many dishes in Japanese cuisine.

TASTEFUL COMBINATIONS

Let's begin with the kind of meal that you find in a typical family-run eatery in Japan. The first thing you notice is how good the meal usually *looks*. Japanese cuisine is usually as much a feast for the eyes as it is a treat for the palate; even in modest eating establishments, far from the metropolis, care is taken as a matter of course concerning the aesthetic appearance of the meal. Even when the food is simple and inexpensive, the tableware is generally elegant (except where they've introduced the abomination of disposable chopsticks), as is the way the items of food are arranged on dishes of various shapes and sizes. Insofar as the ensemble of the meal provides satisfaction for the senses of sight and touch as well as smell and taste, you may find yourself eating less than usual before feeling sated. The particular sense of satisfaction experienced after a good Japanese dinner is rarely accompanied by a feeling of overfullness—perhaps because a savoring of the visual and tactile pleasures also inclines one to eat more slowly. As Roland Barthes remarks, in a slight overstatement, steamed rice is "the only element of weight in all of Japanese alimentation (antinomic to the Chinese); it is what sinks, in opposition to what floats."[3]

Whereas the standard Western meal is a mostly linear affair, served in three or more courses, in the Japanese case several smaller dishes are served at once, which affords the eater freedom to compose an aesthetic experience of greater complexity. The main course in Western cuisine (usually consisting of meat, a starch, vegetables, etc.) does offer some opportunity for enjoying differing taste sensations by combining the components in different ways, but the range of combinations is far greater in Japanese cuisine.

The first items to arrive are typically a few small dishes of pickled vegetables and some miso soup in a lacquer bowl. You drink the soup by lifting the bowl to your lips with both hands. The pleasure that ensues has been well celebrated by the novelist Tanizaki Jun'ichirō.

I know few greater pleasures than holding a lacquer soup bowl in my hands, feeling upon my palms the weight of the liquid and its mild warmth ... . With lacquerware there is a beauty in that moment between removing the lid and lifting the bowl to the mouth when one gazes at the still, silent liquid in the dark depths of the bowl, its color hardly differing from that of the bowl itself. What lies within the darkness one cannot distinguish, but the palm senses the gentle movements of the liquid, vapor rises from within forming droplets on the rim, and the fragrance carried upon the vapor brings a delicate anticipation.[4]

Tanizaki must have been blessed with hypersensitive palms, but even just to watch the "gentle movements of the liquid" is a joy unavailable to observers of Western soups. Miso soup when hot looks like the primeval chaos preparing to give birth to "the ten thousand things," and the continual welling up of convection currents (visible thanks to the minuscule suspended solids of soybean paste) adds a distinctive dynamism to the aesthetics of soup drinking.

Westerners used to eating meals in courses do well to resist finishing the pickles and drinking the soup right away, since they provide greater enjoyment when consumed gradually in the course of the meal. The pickles taste good alone, as the first item on the palate, and as the last, when the meal is over—and moreover, they contain probiotics that aid digestion. When eaten together with single items of the main meal they enhance the flavor, especially in combination with rice. The exhortation "Drink your soup before it gets cold," while well meant by mothers in the West, deprives us of the experience of the soup's changing taste with temperature. If you consume the soup Japanese-style, slowly and intermittently, you can not only savor a range of different tastes as it cools, but also orchestrate the combinations of these changing tastes with the flavors of the other dishes. The meal can then be appreciated as a multilayered experience offering a vast variety of tastes.

At the next level of sophistication (and price), the options become more numerous and the visual appearance more aesthetically pleasing. Barthes compares the large tray on which the pricier Japanese restaurants serve dinner with a painting, a frame containing numerous small containers and dishes. But the beautiful order of the presented work is destined to be disrupted by the act of eating.

> What was a motionless tableau at the start becomes a work-bench or chessboard, the space not of seeing but of doing—of praxis or play; the painting was actually only a palette (a work surface), with which you are going to play in the course of your meal, taking up here a pinch of vegetables, there of rice, and over there of condiment, here a sip of soup, according to a free alternation.[5]

Whatever may be lost in the disturbance of the perfection of the presentation is more than compensated for by the pleasure to be gained from dealing with the various components through the medium of hands and chopsticks.

The care with which the food has been prepared and presented invites corresponding care and attention in the handling and eating of it. Since the ingredients have already been cut down to a manageable size, there is no need to set upon the food with anything as weapon-like as a knife or fork. What is called for is simply selection, then transfer from dish to mouth—tasks for which chopsticks are the perfect implement. In spite of their long and pointed shape, Barthes sees in "the gesture of chopsticks ... something maternal, the same precisely measured care taken in moving a child." Western languages appear to lack an appropriate term for the action of picking up and holding items of food with chopsticks. Barthes remarks that 'pinch' is too aggressive. 'Grasp,' 'grab,' 'seize,' 'grip,' 'clutch' are all too forceful, and 'caress' or 'embrace' too soft. By contrast with the knife and fork, chopsticks are, according to Barthes,

> the alimentary instrument which refuses to cut, to pierce, to mutilate ... They never violate the foodstuff: either they gradually unravel it (in the case of vegetables) or else prod it into separate pieces (in the case of fish, eels), thereby rediscovering the natural fissures of the substance.[6]

The discovery of "natural fissures" is just right: the ancient paragon here is the famous cook in the Daoist classic *Zhuangzi*, who dismembers ox carcasses with such finely attuned precision that he never has to sharpen his knife. But such discovery comes less from any kind of "prodding" with the chopsticks than from practicing the reverse of the pincers movement: an insertion of the joined points of the chopsticks at just the right place, followed by a separating that divides the item in two parts. This operation takes a fair amount of practice and requires paying careful attention until you get the knack. Then the point would be to hold that careful attention and expand it to the rest of the eating.[7]

The slender chopsticks used in Japan don't work well with rice from China or other Asian countries (where the chopsticks are thicker), but they are perfect for Japanese rice, which is short-grained and slightly glutinous. Once again Barthes finds *les mots justes* when he describes it as somehow "a contradiction of substance":

> It is at once cohesive and detachable; its substantial destination is the fragment, the clump, the volatile conglomerate; ... it constitutes in the picture a compact whiteness, granular (contrary to that of our bread) and yet friable: what comes to the table, dense and stuck together, comes undone at a touch of the chopsticks, though without ever scattering, as if division occurred only to produce still another irreducible cohesion.[8]

In a more lyrical vein, after a lament over the way excessive illumination spoils the visual effect of most Japanese foods, Tanizaki writes of how the whiteness of rice shines forth in a shadowy dining room.

> A glistening black lacquer rice cask set off in a dark corner is both beautiful to behold and a powerful stimulus to the appetite. Then the lid is briskly lifted, and

this pure white freshly boiled food, heaped in its black container, each and every grain gleaming like a pearl, sends forth billows of warm steam—here is a sight no Japanese can fail to be moved by.[9]

The philosopher Nishitani Keiji amplifies this point in an essay titled 'The Experience of Having Eaten Rice,' invoking the Buddhist notion of "the non-duality of soil and body." He writes of the joy of eating Japanese rice again after being in Europe for several years, and suggests this is because constituents of the soil pass into the rice and thence into the body. He also notes the archaic aspect to this process, insofar as it has been going on for millennia, such that the body one inherits from one's ancestors is already configured by certain elements from the soil. This doesn't mean that you can't move to a different country and establish a relation with the soil there by eating locally grown food, but it does explain the special relationship people feel with land that their forebears have farmed for ages.[10]

Tanizaki and Nishitani have been criticized for making such politically incorrect remarks—bad examples of *Nihonjinron* discourse or "theory of Japanese uniqueness." Indeed, many people have suggested that Japan ought to defer to American exceptionalism and the dictates of free trade, and acknowledge that strains of Japanese rice grown in California are every bit as good as rice grown in Japan, quite apart from their being much cheaper even when imported. So why do the Japanese insist on continuing to grow their own, even though it's more expensive and still can't fully meet domestic demand? Well, because it tastes better—and what's wrong with that?[11]

The high point of Japanese cuisine is *kaiseki ryōri*, which is said to derive from the kind of food originally served with the tea ceremony. It is certainly a consummate example of the Zen aesthetic in its least ascetic aspect. *Kaiseki* consists of a beautifully arranged and carefully orchestrated series of a dozen or so small dishes, chosen according to the season and presented with ultimate attention to the meal's visual appearance: a magnificent feast for the eyes, as well as the nose and the palate. It is usually served at a pace that allows for the successive overlapping of several dishes at a time, so that one can play with combinations of flavors, textures, and temperatures. Traditional *kaiseki* is unfortunately expensive, but well worth the price. For one thing, it can inspire some Zen-style experimentation at home.

PRACTICAL APPLICATIONS

From the Zen perspective as explicated by Dōgen Zenji, arguably the most profound thinker in the tradition, the distinction between *haute cuisine* and simple cooking with fresh, natural ingredients is merely conventional.

|He advises the head cook in the monastery not to "arouse disdainful mind when you prepare a broth of wild grasses" or "arouse joyful mind when you prepare a fine cream soup."[12] The preparation and eating of both kinds of food equally are an opportunity for enlightened practice. Nor does it make sense to separate the eating of food from the purchasing of it—nor, ultimately, from everything else we do in our lives. We enact such a separation by imposing a means-end structure on our activities: by treating the buying and cooking of the ingredients as a means to the end of eating and enjoying the meal. But this attitude condemns us to drudgery by turning the shopping and preparing into a series of chores that have to be discharged before we can get down to the main business of eating.

Dōgen recounts how he learned this life lesson from the head cook in a monastery in China, who had visited a ship he was staying on in order to buy some mushrooms from Japan. Dōgen asked the old man why he didn't delegate the buying of mushrooms to a younger subordinate so that he, as head cook, could concentrate on his zazen practice. It was only later that Dōgen came to realize the import of the cook's reply: that the buying of mushrooms, and everything else connected with eating, is itself, like zazen, a practice that can be profoundly enlightening.[13]

Dōgen thus recommends paying close attention, as well as respect, to everything that we use in preparing the meal: not only the ingredients, but also the utensils and other pieces of tableware. We need to ensure that everything in the kitchen is in its appropriate place and is kept clean, and that we "select chopsticks, spoons, and other utensils with equal care, examine them with sincerity, and handle them skillfully." He invokes the Buddhist idea of "kind" or "parental mind," which naturally gives rise to a concern for the welfare of others: "You should look after water and grains with compassionate care, as though tending your own children."[14]

What is crucial here, from the Zen perspective, is that we *pay attention* to what we're doing, that we *tend* those people and things with whom and with which we interact. If we say nowadays that it's good to pay attention to what we eat, we're recommending a healthy diet and warning against consuming too much junk food. But it can also be an encouragement to become more aware of the actual act of eating, so that we taste more fully what we're ingesting and thereby enjoy it more—with the happy consequence that we don't need to eat as much. There is, however, a problem here, which is that eating is not only a necessity of life but also a social activity that's imbued with cultural values. To the extent that we enjoy eating with others, and because meals are an occasion for convivial intercourse with family, friends, and acquaintances, we tend to be less aware of how the food actually tastes. If we are guests in someone's home, or at a restaurant, we'll want to pay attention to the taste of the food so that we can say sincerely to our hosts that it's delicious; but the more interesting the conversation around the table, the less likely we are to fully enjoy the food.

Since eating habits tend to reduce our attention, it's good to have them disrupted by travel—unless you prefer to resist the opportunities for exploring different cuisines. (Japanese tour groups are notorious for trundling around with them suitcases packed with instant ramen.) Traditional Japanese food is as healthy as it is tasty, which is no doubt a major factor behind the long life expectancy in Japan. But even for a foreigner who loves the food, what to eat for breakfast can be problematic. While the traditional Japanese breakfast is delicious—miso soup, pickles, rice, dried seaweed—it's very similar to Japanese lunch and dinner. This poses a difficulty for those looking to start the day with something different, especially since it's hard to find good bread in Japan, and most foodstuffs that Japanese marketers imagine as "Western" breakfast are oversweetened with sugar. But if we think of how Dōgen's broth of wild grasses might taste, we can find a solution that's applicable in any place where fresh ingredients are available.

Fruit in Japan is generally excellent, because it's sold and eaten according to the season. Imagine, then, a breakfast in winter, where one could begin with a satsuma tangerine, which is native to Japan and plentiful there. The color: orange—indeed, the perfect example of orange color—like the rising or setting sun in the cold season. A blessing, at this darker time of year with its abundance of root vegetables and their generally muted colors, to enjoy a burst of bright orange as a reminder of sunnier times. The texture is smooth to the touch and malleable, caressable like soft flesh. The fragrance somehow sweet, but indefinable—except by the word 'tangerine.' It's a good idea to sit down and relax, for if you eat the satsuma "on the run," or while preparing some other items of breakfast, you're likely to miss the richness of the experience.

The tangerine is easier to peel than an orange, since the skin lies more loosely on the flesh. A shallow bite with the incisors is a good way to start, and provides an appetizing foretaste that's slightly bitter, thanks to the flavor of the rind. The sound of the rind tearing and coming away from the flesh inside is a unique delight: a subdued crackling as the inner spheroid is gradually revealed, sometimes accompanied by a puff of fragrant mist. There are twelve segments typically, easily pulled apart. The teeth sink gently through the skin and into the succulent flesh, releasing a soft burst of juice and flavor, a little on the tart side but also somehow sweet. The taste turns slightly tarter as you swallow the flesh and chew the remaining skin and pith: the balance in taste between the sweeter flesh and tarter pith reflects the way something in the pith counteracts the acid of the juice.[15]

Now for a piece of toast (a necessary expedient if the bread is mediocre) and, to go with it, an apple and a dried persimmon. When cutting crisp fruit like an apple, the sharper the knife, the more enjoyable the experience—and the more likely one will pay careful attention to the activity. Traditional craftsmen sometimes talk of "becoming friends" with their tools, and this is an especially sensible idea in the case of a well-sharpened knife. A keen blade is unforgiving to the tender flesh of those who handle it carelessly. Once you learn the basics of safe chopping with a sharp knife, you can enjoy paying attention to the interplay between holding-hand and chopping-hand. With increasing expertise, certain rhythms begin to inform the interactions, and the eye-hands coordination becomes a kind of dance, in which eight fingers and two thumbs twirl and flip the segments of fruit. You can see a similar dance with certain professional chefs, who in Japan often work right behind the counters where the food is served. Not those *teppanyaki* operations like Benihana of Tokyo, with their Las Vegas-style showmanship, but rather the modest display of spectacular dexterity that can be enjoyed in the humblest of eating places in Japan.

A freshly toasted slice of bread affords a special textural pleasure when you apply a little butter while it's still hot. Again there's a characteristic and unmistakable sound to the preliminary, rather like an amplified version of the tearing of the tangerine skin, as the knife scrapes the melting butter lightly over the crisply toasted surface. As with many foods, much depends on the contrast between outer and inner, and on the different levels of resistance as one's incisors slice though the crust to the increasingly yielding interior.

In the chewing phase, the dance that the tongue performs in distributing the food to the molars for crushing is an amazing operation, but we usually don't notice. The coordination between chomping molars and undulating tongue and inner cheek surface is extremely complex, which makes it all the more amazing that it hardly ever goes wrong. You only rarely bite your tongue while chewing, even though you perform innumerable chomps in the course of a lifetime. And listen to the mastication! The sounds gradually change from crunching the crisp surface to softer thudding and crushing as the contents of the mouth are progressively ground and liquefied. Since they're amplified through the jaws on their way to the ears from the inside, these sounds can easily be enjoyed in the privacy of one's own skull without disturbing those around us. Attention to these aesthetic dimensions of chewing affords greater enjoyment of the activity, and so tends to prolong it—with obvious benefits for digestive health.

The modest combination of toast, sliced apple and dried persimmon clearly displays the pleasure that can be derived from chewing. Start with a bite of apple to clear the palate, followed by a bite of toast to be savored on its own. Then some toast accompanied by a piece of sliced apple: the juice of the apple immediately transforms the experience of chewing the toast, as the different levels of crispness contrast and the flavors intermingle. Now introduce the dried persimmon, which is softer than dried fig, but with a pleasing contrast between chewy skin and succulent interior. A bite of toast together with a bite of persimmon offers a novel blend of flavors and less contrast between textures than with a bite of apple.

Next, you can play with the timing, by partially chewing a piece of toast *before* biting the apple—an interestingly different experience from biting the apple first and then the toast. Introducing similar delays between biting toast and persimmon, and vice versa, gives rise to a whole different range of tastes. Both the toast and the fruits will be finished before you can embark on the many other combinations that are possible when varying the timing between the ingestion of toast and apple *and* persimmon.[16] And if boredom should threaten, you can substitute pear for apple, or banana for persimmon, or whatever is locally available and in season. Rich and diverse enjoyment of innumerable taste combinations can be had for a very modest price indeed. Such an enjoyable breakfast is possible because seasonable fruit in Japan is generally tasty: in spite of a high level of industrialization, the country is fortunate to have a good deal of small-scale agriculture around towns and near urban centers, so that fruits and vegetables can be eaten fresh and close to the source.

If you add to the routine a cup of tea or coffee, this multiplies the taste combinations immeasurably. Green tea requires a little more care to prepare than black tea, since the water needs to be boiled then allowed to cool a little before the infusing, but the elegance of the taste and the beauty of the color make it well worth the extra effort. The flavor of a hot beverage like tea or coffee changes as it cools down—think of the difference between coffee hot from the pot and at room temperature, or iced. A mouthful of tea or coffee tastes different if you've eaten something just before taking it, and likewise a bite of food tastes different if you've just drunk tea or coffee. So, intersperse sips of tea or coffee—gradually changing in flavor as it cools down—between the bites of toast, apple, and persimmon, and you greatly amplify the delight.

If you're ever meant to savor a taste, it's in the Japanese tea ceremony. As the host serves the tea, or the guest admires the bowl, these activities express an awareness that here are two human beings who have come together under the heavens and on a particular piece of the earth, and in the context of a unique configuration of the elements of fire and water, wood and metal, in order to partake of a delicious and vitalizing beverage. Sipping the tea in this context, you can really savor the taste. Just as in Zen, the awareness that accompanies sitting meditation (zazen) is to be extended throughout one's waking life, so the atmosphere of the tea ceremony optimally comes to pervade the practitioner's entire being, so that every meal and all other waking activities may become occasions for experiencing the ultimate context of emptiness that is the womb of all human possibilities.

There is an echo of this sensibility in the relatively prosaic custom operative in the drinking of beer or *sake*, whether with an exquisite *kaiseki* dinner or an ordinary meal. In a public place or a private home, you may find the host proffering a bottle, the neck tilted forward. The appropriate response is to lift your glass a little off the table so that the other person can fill it. The roles are often reversed on the second round. Of course, we clink glasses in the West and thank someone who pours a drink for us; but in Japan, where the bottle is shared, there's something special about the physical act of lifting one's glass, or sake cup, in response to a sign from the pourer. The custom may allude to the tea ceremony in its function of bringing to awareness the uniqueness of the human situation in which the participants find themselves. You and I, here together for the first and last time—if we were here before, or will be here again, it's a different situation and we will have changed as people—drinking something that we can never drink again.

So, here's to the flourishing of the field of Japanese aesthetics!

NOTES

1. My translation from Friedrich Nietzsche, *Die Philosophie im tragischen Zeitalter der Griechen*, §3 (Berlin: CreateSpace Independent Publishing Platform, 2013), accessed July 24, 2015, http://www.zeno.org/Lesesaal/N/9781484049655?page=12.

2. Friedrich Nietzsche, *Ecce Homo: How to Become What You Are*, trans. Duncan Large (Oxford: Oxford University Press, 2007), 95, 19. Nietzsche actually felt a special affinity with Japan; he once wrote to his sister, "I would like, simply in order to attain greater serenity, to emigrate to *Japan*." Friedrich Nietzsche to Elisabeth Förster-Nietzsche, Nice, France, December 20, 1885, in *Friedrich Nietzsche, Sämtliche Briefe: Kritische Studienausgabe*, ed. Giorgio Colli and Mazzino Montinari, 8 vols. (Munich, BY: Deutscher Taschenbuch Verlag, 1986), 7:127. English translation is my own.

3. Roland Barthes, *Empire of Signs*, trans. Richard Howard (New York: Hill and Wang, 1982), 12.

4. Jun'ichirō Tanizaki, *In Praise of Shadows* (New Haven, CT: Leete's Island Books, 1977), 14–15.

5. Barthes, 11.

6. Ibid., 16, 18.

7. For the central role of attentive practice in Chinese and Japanese philosophy and aesthetics, see my essay "Awe and Humility in the Face of Things: Somatic Practice in East-Asian Philosophies," *European Journal for Philosophy of Religion* 4, no. 3 (2012): 69–88.

8. Barthes, 12, 14.

9. Tanizaki, 16–17.

10. *Nishitani Keiji chosakushū (Collected Writings of Nishitani Keiji)* (Tokyo: Sōbunsha, 1990), 20:202.

11. For a comprehensive discussion of the Japanese love of their own rice, see Emiko Ohnuki-Tierney, *Rice as Self: Japanese Identities through Time* (Princeton, NJ: Princeton University Press, 1994).

12. Dōgen, "Instruction for the Tenzo," in *Moon in a Dewdrop: Writings of Zen Master Dōgen*, ed., Kazuaki Tanahashi (New York: North Point Press, 1985), 56.

13. Ibid., 59–60.

14. Ibid., 55, 65.

15. One's enjoyment of this noble fruit may be enhanced by knowledge of the wealth of nutrients and other healthful substances it contains: various vitamins and acids and enzymes and fiber, and above all "nobiletin," a phytochemical that's been found to have antioxidant, anticancer, anti-inflammatory, and cholesterol-lowering properties, to reduce obesity, counteract memory loss and dementia, and help prevent heart disease, diabetes, and stroke. How wonderful that something that good for you should also taste so delicious.

16. Admirers of Samuel Beckett's *Molloy* will appreciate how much simpler this method is than the stone-sucking of that notorious complicator.

Chapter 9

Art of War, Art of Self

Aesthetic Cultivation in Japanese Martial Arts

James McRae

INTRODUCTION

The Japanese word *bugei* (武芸) literally means "martial art," a term that has become common parlance in the Western world. But why do we refer to these combative systems as *arts*? The purpose of this chapter is to explore the aesthetic value of martial arts training. The first section examines John Dewey's aesthetic of experience to provide a coherent, systematic framework upon which an investigation of Japanese arts can be built. The second section investigates Takuan Sōhō's concept of *fudōshin* and contemporary psychological research into flow states and hyperpraxia to explain how Dewey's aesthetic of experience can apply to self-cultivation in Japanese martial arts. The final section examines particular Japanese aesthetic paradigms evident in the martial arts. *Bugei* is an art form because it not only contributes to the self-development of its practitioners as living works of art but also provides a medium through which martial artists can express themselves through performance.

JOHN DEWEY'S AESTHETIC OF EXPERIENCE

John Dewey's aesthetic focuses on the quality of the individual's experience rather than the nature of art objects. He argues that while the aesthetic reaches its highest intensification in fine art, it is ultimately an aspect of all human experience.[1] Because one can find aesthetic experience in every aspect of daily life, one can view life as a work of art to be crafted and appreciated in every moment.[2] Western art often obscures this notion by isolating what it considers to be "fine art" from all other modes of experience.[3] Though every experience has the potential to be aesthetic, some are "maximally unified" in the sense that they are "set apart, bounded, whole, complete" and represent an interactive relationship between the viewer and the object.[4] Dewey calls this a 'consummatory experience' or '*an* experience.'[5] *An* experience is maximally unified to the extent that the subject fully participates in the artwork. Thus, for art to be considered aesthetically good, it must be capable of regularly producing *an* experience in the sense of a maximally unified relationship between the viewer and the object.[6]

Although great works of art tend to produce the richest, most enduring aesthetic experiences, Dewey believes that anything can produce *an* experience, even those things that we might consider ordinary and nonartistic.[7] In order for any act to qualify as an aesthetic experience for Dewey, it must ultimately contribute to the development of one's self. He states, "It is this degree of completeness of living in the experience of making and of perceiving that makes the difference between what is fine or esthetic in art and what is not."[8] Seemingly insignificant acts, if performed with the proper attention to aesthetic detail, might provide opportunities for one to deepen one's understanding of oneself (e.g., the act of making tea in the Japanese art of *sadō* 茶道).[9] Everyday acts might not have the expressive power that is possessed by more deliberate artworks, but they nonetheless have potential aesthetic value.

For Dewey, art is a means of expressing natural life emotions. Every life has the potential to be a work of art and one's emotions are the raw material out of which this work is constructed.[10] All good art is based upon the real life emotions of the artist who creates it:[11] "Without emotion, there may be craftsmanship, but not art; it may be present and be intense, but if it is directly manifested the result is also not art."[12] The insincere artist will create an artifact that fails to exhibit the natural life emotions of its creator. However, it is not the case that every expression of emotion in one's life constitutes a work of art. In order for such emotional expression to be artistic, one must focus these emotions into a performance that is an expression of one's self. Eliot Deutsch argues, "Emotion in art is thus a kind of performance, so that the artwork itself may be said to be creative of the emotion that is presented and not simply expressive of an identifiable kind of life emotion."[13] One must truly imbue one's work with emotional content in order for that work to rise above mere emotional exhibition to the level of expression. An expressive work of art is inseparable from the natural emotions of the artist, which are grounded in the interrelation of the artist, the work, and the audience. Without this relationship, the work ceases to be a work of art and becomes only an object.[14]

For Dewey, the aesthetic is the process of self-cultivation and self-expression that can potentially take place at any moment of a person's life. The following section explores how aesthetic cultivation is pursued in the martial arts. If Dewey is correct that one's life can be a work of art, the martial arts promote the kind of psychophysical training that is necessary for optimal aesthetic experience.

THE CULTIVATION OF AESTHETIC EXPERIENCE IN JAPANESE MARTIAL ARTS

Zen is an essential component of both Japanese aesthetics and martial arts training. Neuroscientist and Zen practitioner James Austin states, "The Zen trainee's graceful behavior goes on to find its twofold expression: first in the overlooked art of workaday living; and second in those other activities usually designated as arts, including the martial arts."[15] Zen has been so influential upon Japanese culture that its values are "apparent in every aspect of the lives of the people of modern Japan."[16] It was studied extensively by the samurai class, who were interested in maximizing their performance both on and off the battlefield.[17] Zen master Takuan Sōhō has been particularly influential in the philosophy of the martial arts. He was a close friend of Yagyū Munenori, the legendary sword master of two Tokugawa shoguns. It is in a letter to Yagyū that Takan develops the idea of *fudōshin*, or "the immovable mind," in an attempt to "unify the spirit of Zen with the spirit of the sword."[18]

According to Takuan, the least effective mindset for a warrior to be in is "the affliction of abiding in ignorance," which he relates to an "absence of enlightenment." 'Abiding' refers to the action of stopping the mind by becoming attached to an opponent's attack and focusing upon it to the exclusion of other phenomena: "if you think of meeting that sword just as it is, your mind will stop at the sword in just that position, your own movements will be undone, and you will be cut down by your opponent."[19] Takuan argues that the afflicted mind attaches itself to particular objects in the environment. This myopic intentionality leads to a kind of tunnel vision in which one misses the whole of one's reality due to the restricted scope of one's awareness.[20]

This phenomenon of "stopping the mind" can be best understood by contrasting it with Nishida Kitarō's analysis of enlightenment as a type of "pure experience" (*junsui keiken* 純粋経験) of the world:

> To experience means to know facts just as they are, to know in accordance with facts by completely relinquishing one's own fabrications. What we usually refer to as experience is adulterated with some sort of thought, so by *pure* I am referring to the state of experience just as it is without the least addition of deliberative discrimination. The moment of seeing a color or hearing a sound, for example, is prior not only to the thought that the color or sound is the activity of an external object or that one is sensing it, but also to the judgment of what the color or sound might be. In this regard, pure experience is identical with direct experience. When one directly experiences one's own state of consciousness,

there is not yet a subject or an object, and knowing and its object are completely unified. This is the most refined type of experience.[21]

According to Nishida, ordinary, unenlightened experience involves three things:

1. *Subject-Object Distinction*: One distinguishes between oneself as the experiencing subject and the object that is experienced. One does not consider oneself a part of the world one experiences, but rather draws a line between the "world out there" and the "world in here."[22]
2. *Intentionality*: One seeks out specific objects in the environment to experience rather than experiencing the environment as a whole. I, as the subject, have chosen a *specific* object to experience; other empirical data become mere "background noise."
3. *Deliberative Discrimination*: When one reflects upon one's experience in an attempt to understand it, one is thinking about the experience rather than simply having the experience. Carter states that, for Nishida, "[a]s soon as we are able to talk about pure experience, to conceptualize and 'language' it, it thereby becomes a mixture of perceptual and conceptual awareness."[23] By processing the experience in this way, one can sometimes make errors of judgment about the nature of the experience. One mulls over it and interprets it in a certain way, which informs further experience by defining the way in which one intentionally chooses to interpret it.

For Nishida, when one has a pure experience of the world, one is intuiting directly from the environment without intentionality, subject-object distinction, or deliberative discrimination. One can only experience reality as it is by "completely relinquishing one's own fabrications."[24]

T. P. Kasulis and David Shaner offer a phenomenological interpretation of enlightenment experience that elucidates Takuan's distinction between *fudōshin* and abiding in ignorance. There are three states of consciousness that a martial artist might exhibit during a fight:

1. *Thinking (Shiryō 思量)—"The Affliction of Abiding in Ignorance"*: According to Kasulis, *shiryō* is the state of mind in which one is "considering with the intent of weighing ideas."[25] In this state, the mind is intentionally objectifying its environment and processing this information according to rational thought. This process corresponds to the everyday experience that Takuan calls 'the affliction of abiding in ignorance.' In Figure 9.1, the samurai on the left is the experiencing subject, or "noesis" in phenomenological terms. The samurai on the right represents the

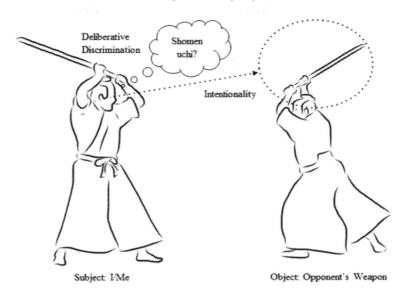

Figure 9.1 **James McRae, *Thinking*.** 2016. Digital image, 6.13 in. × 5 in.

experienced object, or "noema."[26] The arrow represents the noetic vector, or strand of intentionality, from the samurai to his opponent's sword. This samurai has stopped his mind on his opponent's weapon by completely focusing his intentionality upon it, by distinguishing himself from his opponent as a separate object, and by pausing to think about the incoming strike. All three features of Nishida's everyday mind are present: intentionality, subject-object distinction, and deliberative discrimination. Shaner argues that in this state, the individual's body and mind are uncoordinated: multiple parts of consciousness simultaneously try to focus on different objects within the world.[27]

2. *Not-Thinking (Fushiryō 不思量)—"Unsentient like Wood or Stone"*: *Fushiryō* is a cognitive state in which the individual is not thinking at all. There is no subject-object distinction (since the experience is purely subjective), no intentionality (since there is no experience of the outside world), and no deliberative discrimination (since the mind is empty). Unfortunately, it is impossible to actually do anything in this state, which means it is of little use for combat. Takuan argues that the "immovable" quality of *fudōshin* is not immobile. He states, "Although wisdom is called immovable, this does not signify any insentient thing, like wood or stone. It moves as the mind is wont to move … and the mind that does not stop

at all is called *immovable wisdom*."[28] Kasulis describes not-thinking as the "negation or denial of *shiryō* [thinking]."[29] Unlike *shiryō*, where the mind is both affirming and negating objects in the world, with *fushiryō,* the mind is only negating, with thinking as the object of its negative noematic focus. Here, the mind (noesis) is not connected to the environment (noema) via a noetic vector. Although no objectification is taking place, the mind is separate from its environment, and thus not-thinking cannot signify enlightenment.

3. *Without-Thinking (Hishiryō* 非思量*)—"Fudōshin"*: Takuan's *fudōshin* represents mindfulness, which is the middle ground between mindlessness (not thinking) and abiding (a mind that is stuck on a particular object of focus). This mindfulness is a state in which one is not thinking of anything *in particular.*[30] Takuan says, "The function of the intellect disappears, and one ends in a state of No-Mind-No-Thought."[31] There is no intentionality, but rather a hyperawareness of all of one's surroundings. There is no subject-object distinction; the martial artist feels one with the opponent. There is no deliberative discrimination; one is not thinking about anything in particular. Takuan states, "Glancing at something and not stopping the mind is called *immovable*."[32] He cautions his readers to avoid creating

Figure 9.2   James McRae, Not-Thinking. 2016. Digital image, 6.13 in. × 5 in.

a "one-sided mind" by placing one's awareness in a particular location. Rather, one must strive to keep "No Mind" or "the Right Mind" that "stretches throughout the entire body and self."[33] One must "engender the mind with no place to abide."[34] Kasulis argues that *hishiryō* "goes 'beyond thinking and not-thinking'… merely accepting the presence of ideation without either affirmation or denial."[35] With *hishiryō*, things are simply "presenc[ed] as they are" (*sono mama de*).[36] This, Shaner argues, is the phenomenal state of the enlightened consciousness in which body and mind are completely unified.[37]

Fudōshin is desirable for the martial artist because it promotes a type of hyperpraxia in which there is no hesitation between thought and action. Takuan states, "To be called, to respond without interval, is the wisdom of all Buddhas." In any sport, response time is one of the primary factors in a successful performance. Austin articulates the advantages that a Zen-trained athlete has over his opponents, describing enlightened behavior as:

1. without initial hesitation;
2. quick in execution;
3. simple but efficient;

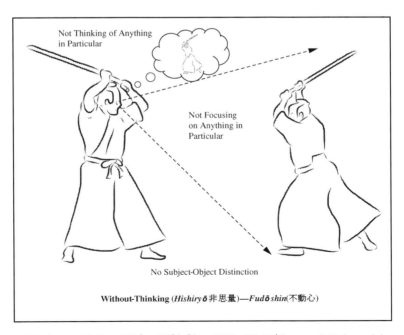

Figure 9.3 James McRae, *Without-Thinking*. 2016. Digital image, 6.13 in. × 5 in.

4. highly creative, improvisational, yet capable of both resolving the immediate situation and addressing the big picture as well;
5. expressed from a foundation of poise;
6. liberated from word-thoughts and personal concerns.[38]

Austin argues, "One result of Zen training is to encourage faster links
between attention, implying the readiness to perceive, and activation, the
readiness to act." He notes that in empirical studies on reaction time, subjects
with proactive training in Zen methodologies were able to respond to stimuli
approximately 500 to 800 milliseconds before they were consciously aware
of the act.[39] In Takuan's terms, it seems they are acting with "no mind."

According to Austin, "a person's normal ability to perform skilled
movements is called *praxis*," but in Zen, "a kind of 'hyperpraxia' prevails": "Motor skills are now unbound, unsuppressed. A mere hint suffices
to initiate complex motor sequences. Enhanced behaviors flow perfectly
and effortlessly."[40] The practice of the martial arts is a dynamic, interre-
lative process through which an individual becomes harmonized with the
environment. The hyperpraxia indicated by Takuan's notion of *fudōshin*
closely parallels the concept of flow states articulated by contemporary
psychologist Mihaly Csikszentmihalyi. The flow state is a type of "optimal
experience" in which an individual is completely engrossed by a particular
activity.[41] Csikszentmihalyi takes a phenomenological approach that understands consciousness as "intentionally ordered information." The typical
human mind suffers from "psychic entropy," a state in which it is trying to
simultaneously pay attention to a variety of disparate stimuli. Even though
the human brain is capable of processing 126 bits of information per second, most people fall below this peak capacity because the way they pay
attention to the environment is distracted and disordered.[42] This leads to a
suboptimal experience of the world that can produce a profound sense of
unsatisfactoriness.[43] However, because the self is completely defined by
consciousness, it can be fundamentally reshaped by changing the way that
one experiences the world.[44] As with *shiryō* or the "afflicted" mind that
Takuan describes, martial artists who attempt to perform in this state will
do so at a suboptimal level.

The opposite of psychic entropy is the flow state: an "optimal state of inner
experience ... in which there is order in consciousness."[45] In a flow experience, a person's consciousness is completely invested in the task at hand
with 100 percent of available brainpower actively processing environmental
stimuli.[46] This produces a state of "negentropy" in which the distractions of
a chaotic mind fall away and one's performance is optimized.[47] In flow, one
ceases to be self-conscious and distracted; one's actions become spontaneous, effortless, and harmonious.[48] Flow states are "autotelic" experiences

because they are intrinsically rewarding and promote self-cultivation.[49] Even when engaging in activities that entail a serious risk—such as the combative arts—one is filled with a sense of inner peace and happiness. In fact, those individuals who lead the happiest lives are the ones who spend the most time in flow states.[50]

Csikszentmihalyi explicitly identifies flow states with Zen Buddhism, though he insists that flow can be brought about by a variety of different activities, including the experience of art.[51] He argues that Dewey was the first to articulate the notion that the aesthetic refers to those "experiences that are relatively more clear and focused than everyday life."[52] Csikszentmihalyi argues that flow states represent this kind of aesthetic experience: "When the viewer focuses attention on the object, there follows a sense of concentration, of freedom, clarity, control, wholeness, and sometimes transcendence of ego boundaries, a condition so rewarding as to be sought out for its own sake."[53] Flow involves a "Zen-like encounter" with the art object in which psychic entropy is replaced by optimal experience.[54] This is not just limited to works of fine art; the practice of the martial arts can also be a medium for aesthetic experience:

> The warrior strives to reach the point where he can act with lightning speed against opponents, without having to think or reason about the best defensive or offensive moves to make. Those who can perform it well claim that fighting becomes a joyous artistic performance, during which the everyday experience of duality between mind and body is transformed into a harmonious one-point-edness of mind. Here again, it seems appropriate to think of the martial arts as a specific form of flow.[55]

Organized, goal-oriented activities have the highest chance of producing flow. The martial arts not only encourage this kind of discipline, but also provide a medium through which one may achieve optimal experience, be it *randori* (乱取り free-sparring), *kata* (方 forms), or *shiai* (試合 competition). Takuan's *fudōshin*, which embodies the Zen notion of *hishiryō*, is this type of flow state in which not only is one's performance optimized, but one's character is also cultivated. The martial arts are a kind of moving meditation (*dō chū no sei* 動中の静) that allows a person to transform the experience into what Dewey would call '*an* experience.'

JAPANESE MARTIAL ARTS AS PERFORMANCE ART

Japanese martial arts capture Dewey's notion that every moment of a person's existence can be viewed as an aesthetic experience, an opportunity for cultivating oneself as a living work of art. Dewey suggests that everyday experience can have aesthetic value, and Japanese arts have traditionally included activities that might be considered crafts or trades by Western standards, which nonetheless promote aesthetic experience.[56] Just as Dewey argues that the aesthetic reaches its apogee in the fine arts, Japanese arts (including the martial arts) create opportunities for both practitioners and observers to have *an* experience.

The type of artistic cultivation that takes place in the martial arts, or *budō* (武道), parallels the self-actualization that occurs in the fine arts, or *geidō* (芸道). The artist's character is cultivated through the practice of the art and revealed to the audience through performance to the extent that the "artwork becomes, to the audience, an image of the artist."[57] The aesthetic experience in Japanese art is one that involves "cosubjectivity": the practitioner and the audience both participate in the artwork to the extent that "the work of art is not achieved by the artist alone, but in company with the audience."[58] In the martial arts, this coparticipatory process takes place in multiple types of performance: solo *kata* practice, group training, sparring, competitions, rank testing, and public demonstrations. In every case, martial artists cultivate themselves through their interrelation with other human beings (even in solo *kata* practice, the martial artist visualizes an opponent).[59] The martial arts emphasize a respect for others, both in terms of etiquette and ethics, and this profound sense of respect is considered to be a core moral virtue that promotes a heightened aesthetic sensitivity to the experiencing agents with whom the artist participates in the performance.[60]

Art and philosophy are fundamentally interrelated in Japanese culture: all forms of art are considered to be methods of self-cultivation that ultimately pursue the same goal.[61] A universal aesthetic (*bigaku* 美学) is manifested in all of the *dō* (道) or ways of self-cultivation.[62] The term *dō* literally means "the way" and refers to an area of study that had been elevated beyond its original practical purpose to become a form of self-development and self-expression.[63] The Dō are thus a form of *seishin tanren* (精神鍛錬), or "spirit forging," in which the individual is cultivated through the disciplined study of a particular art.[64] Core aesthetic and ethical paradigms are taught and practiced through these *dō*, including the martial arts,[65] which emphasize the transcendence of the self through the mastery of an artistic discipline.[66] This is reflected in the Japanese practice of designating the masters of traditional art forms as *Ningen Kokuhō* (人間国宝 "Living National Treasures") whose ability to promote aesthetic and ethical cultivation is considered essential to the welfare of the country.[67] What follows is an analysis of how some of the universal aesthetic paradigms promoted by the Japanese Dō are specifically embodied by the practice of the martial arts.

UNDERSTANDING SPACE: *MA* (間) AND *MA-AI* (間合)

The concept of *ma* is derived from the Zen notions of impermanence and emptiness and is pervasive in Japanese art and philosophy: the best art and the most graceful human motions all exhibit *ma*.[68] *Ma* can be defined as the spatiotemporal interval that is continually created between two or more persons or things by their interaction and through which those persons or things interrelate.[69] The term *ma-ai* (間合) refers to the space-time through which persons or things become unified. When specifically applied to combat, *ma-ai* is the timing and the distance between the defender and the attacker.[70] Whoever is able to dominate this *ma-ai* will be able to dominate the confrontation.

The importance of space and time can be found in Dewey's aesthetics as well. He states, "Works of art express space as opportunity for movement and action."[71] Seemingly empty space, for Dewey, is actually pregnant with potential acts of artistic expression. This space must also be incorporated into a work of art via the space-time interrelations of the individual objects that make up the art (this is found in the negative space in an artwork). For Dewey, life is an ongoing opportunity for aesthetic experience, so *ma* is the medium of all artistic expression through which one can shape one's life as a work of art.

Interacting with other persons in daily life necessitates a command of *ma*. Richard Pilgrim states that all human relations are "a matter of negotiating the *ma* (*ma no torikata*) between/among human beings."[72] Thus, to train oneself in the nature of *ma* is to train oneself in the basis of human association. Because the mastery of a martial art requires the mastery of *ma*, one who has seriously trained oneself in the martial arts can be said to be "at peace with himself and in harmony with his social as well as his natural environment."[73] The Zen notion of interrelationality is reflected in the Japanese term for human being, 人間 *ningen*, which contains the character for *ma* and literally means "person in-between" or "person as a field."[74] Cultivated people positively interact with their environment and the people within that environment and this goal of developing the social self is consistent throughout Japanese martial arts. It is by developing this sensitivity to one's environment that one can realize the fundamental interrelation between the self and the environment that defines the self. The martial arts practitioner is a human being as defined by his or her spatiotemporal context, and it is through this "creative" space (*ma* or the measure) that he or she is able to imaginatively develop himself or herself in light of his or her environment and exert a positive influence upon that environment.[75]

For Dewey, expression always occurs through the medium of nature.[76] Furthermore, in aesthetic expression, the emphasis is always upon the interrelation of the artist and the environment. Dewey states that the aesthetic is characterized by "the constant rhythm that marks the interaction of the live creature with his surroundings."[77] The environment inspires the artist with the emotions that become expressed in the art: "In other words, art is not nature, but is nature transformed by entering into new relationships where it evokes a new emotional response."[78] The aesthetic is not something that is simply characteristic of nature itself. Rather, it is the product of the positive interrelation of the artist and his or her context. The artist must become one with the natural world and, by doing so, simultaneously find both the source of inspiration and the medium of aesthetic expression.

Because the artist is inspired by and expresses himself through the medium of his natural environment as shown above, simple acts of interpersonal relation become opportunities for aesthetic expression. Dewey states, "When the natural and the cultivated blend in one, acts of social intercourse are works of art."[79] The "natural" of which Dewey speaks is one's natural environment, and the "cultivated" represents the developed aesthetic awareness of the artist. The study of *ma-ai* in the martial arts provides the basis for the development of the social self. By coordinating the mind with the body, the context, and the other persons within that context, martial artists begin to view other persons as extensions of themselves. They become sensitive to the *ma*, the space *between* themselves and others, but this space is not empty; because of their training in body-mind coordination, they view this space as an extension of their minds, and thus the persons encompassed by this space are likewise within the scope of their minds.

UNDERSTANDING TIME: *MUJŌ* (無常), *MONO NO AWARE* (物の哀れ), AND *WABI-SABI* (侘寂)

The Buddhist concept of *mujō* (無常 impermanence) has permeated Japanese culture to the extent that it is the predominant metaphysical paradigm. Japanese art reflects this worldview in its focus upon the transient nature of all things and the beauty of the present moment.[80] *Mono no aware* (物の哀れ) refers to "the pathos of things" or "the tragic beauty of impermanent things." It is epitomized by cherry blossoms, which are made intensely more beautiful by the fact that they bloom for only a few days before being scattered by the breeze. Like Dewey's aesthetic of experience, *aware* is highly subjective: beauty is found in the way the experiencer responds to an object, not in some inherent quality in the object itself.[81] This is particularly acute in the martial arts because *bushidō* (武士道 the samurai ethical tradition) emphasizes the ephemeral nature of a warrior's existence. Warriors may be called upon at any time to die for their lords, so they must find beauty in the intrinsic value of each moment of existence.[82] The philosophy of *ichi go, ichi e* (一期一会 "one encounter, one opportunity") reminds the martial artist that each moment is a unique, invaluable opportunity for self-cultivation and aesthetic experience.[83]

The beauty of transience is reflected in the aesthetic paradigm of *wabi-sabi*. As a compound term, *wabi-sabi* celebrates a minimalist aesthetic that emphasizes the beauty of simplicity and impermanence.[84] The concept has its origins in medieval Japanese Buddhism, which rejected the artificial beauty and affluence of courtly life.[85] *Wabi* (侘), the first part of the compound, refers to the idea that beauty is found in simplicity. Understatement is always more powerful than overstatement, which is evident in the subtlety of color and lines and in the use of empty space in Japanese art and architecture. Minor imperfections actually make an object more beautiful than a flawless specimen.[86] In the martial arts, *sabi* is evident in the reserved aesthetic of the *dōjō* (道場 training hall) and *keikogi* (稽古着 uniform) and the simple, efficient movements of the practitioners. Martial arts training is a process of removing unnecessary artifice so that each motion can be maximally efficient with minimum effort.[87] *Sabi* includes the aesthetic of desolation (particularly in landscapes) and an aged, worn appearance in handcrafted objects. Objects with a patina are considered to be ripe with wisdom and experience.[88] Over time, the martial artist's equipment begins to epitomize *sabi*: for example, the *obi* (帯 belt) becomes soft and worn so that the inner white core shows through the outer black wrapping, symbolically representing a return to *shoshin* (初心 beginner's mind).[89] The martial artist's body itself takes on an aesthetic of *sabi*—lean, scarred, and calloused from countless hours of training. Because it stresses the beauty of imperfection, *wabi-sabi* serves as a reminder that while martial artists should take their training seriously, they should not become perfectionists in their quest for self-cultivation. As Zen teaches, they must accept the imperfection and impermanence of all things.

CONCLUSION

The martial arts help cultivate *fudōshin*, a state of mind in which any activity becomes a hyperpraxic flow state that optimizes performance and maximizes happiness by creating *an* experience for the practitioner. This enlightened consciousness is particularly reflected in aesthetic paradigms such as *ma, mono no aware,* and *wabi-sabi*, which promote aesthetic cultivation through a realization of the interdependence and impermanence of all things. Thus, the martial arts are a form of artistic expression possessing an aesthetic as rich and rewarding as any other accepted form of art, and the primary value of this aesthetic lies in its ability to shape oneself and one's relationships with other people as an artist shapes a work of art.

NOTES

1. John Dewey, *Art as Experience* (New York: Minton, Balch and Company, 1934), 5.

2. Ibid., 3.

3. Ibid., 10.

4. David E. W. Fenner, *Introducing Aesthetics* (Westport, CT: Praeger, 2003), 11, 124.

5. Thomas M. Alexander, "John Dewey," in *A Companion to Aesthetics,* 2nd ed., ed. Stephen Davies et al. (Malden, MA: Wiley-Blackwell, 2009), 245.

6. Fenner, 11.

7. Dewey, 187. See also Fenner, 125.

8. Dewey, 26.

9. Ibid., 26, 15.

10. Ibid., 70.

11. Ibid., 41.

12. Ibid., 69.

13. Eliot Deutsch, *Essays on the Nature of Art* (Albany, NY: State University of New York Press, 1996), 19.

14. Ibid., 29.

15. James H. Austin, *Zen and the Brain* (Cambridge, MA: MIT Press, 1998), 668–69.

16. Roger J. Davies and Osamu Ikeno, *The Japanese Mind: Understanding Contemporary Japanese Culture* (North Clarendon, VT: Tuttle Publishing, 2002), 73.

17. Ibid., 73.

18. William Scott Wilson, introduction to *The Unfettered Mind: Writings from a Zen Master to a Master Swordsman,* by Takuan Sōhō, trans. William Scott Wilson (New York: Kodansha, 1986), xi–xv.

19. Takuan Sōhō, *The Unfettered Mind: Writings from a Zen Master to a Master Swordsman,* trans. William Scott Wilson (New York: Kodansha, 1986), 19.

20. Ibid., 22.

21. Nishida Kitarō, *An Inquiry into the Good,* trans. Masao Abe and Christopher Ives (New Haven, CT: Yale University Press, 1990), 3–4.

22. David Edward Shaner, *The Bodymind Experience in Japanese Buddhism: A Phenomenological Study of Kūkai and Dōgen* (Albany, NY: State University of New York Press, 1985), 15.

23. Robert E. Carter, *The Nothingness Beyond God: An Introduction to the Philosophy of Nishida Kitarō* (St. Paul, MN: Paragon House Publishers, 1997), 8.

24. Nishida, 3.

25. T. P. Kasulis, *Zen Action, Zen Person* (Honolulu: University of Hawai'i Press, 1981), 72.

26. Ibid., 73. See also Shaner, 48–54.

27. Shaner, 48.

28. Takuan, 20.

29. Kasulis, 72.

30. Takuan, 39.

31. Ibid., 23–24.

32. Ibid., 21.

33. Ibid., 30–33.

34. Ibid., 35.

35. Kasulis, 72.

36. Ibid., 73. Kasulis bases his discussion of *hishiryō* (without-thinking) on a key passage from the beginning of the *"Zazenshin"* fascicle of Dōgen's *Shōbōgenzō.* See Kasulis, 71–77.

37. Shaner, 48.

38. This list is quoted directly from Austin, 668.

39. Ibid., 673.

40. Ibid., 674–75.

41. Mihaly Csikszentmihalyi, "Happiness Revisited," chapter 1 in *Flow: The Psychology of Optimal Experience* (New York: HarperCollins, 2008), Kindle edition.

42. Csikszentmihalyi, "Anatomy of Consciousness," chapter 2 in *Flow.*

43. Csikszentmihalyi, "Happiness Revisited."

44. Csikszentmihalyi, "Anatomy of Consciousness."

45. Csikszentmihalyi, "Happiness Revisited."

46. Csikszentmihalyi, "Enjoyment and the Quality of Life," chapter 3 in *Flow.*

47. Csikszentmihalyi, "Anatomy of Consciousness."

48. Csikszentmihalyi, "Enjoyment and the Quality of Life."

49. Csikszentmihalyi, "Happiness Revisited."

50. Csikszentmihalyi, "Happiness Revisited" and "Enjoyment and the Quality of Life."

51. Csikszentmihalyi, "Happiness Revisited."

52. Csikszentmihalyi, *Flow*, 9.

53. Mihaly Csikszentmihalyi and Rick E. Robinson, *The Art of Seeing: An Interpretation of the Aesthetic Encounter* (Los Angeles: Getty Publications, 1990), 18–19.

54. Csikszentmihalyi, "The Body in Flow," chapter 5 in *Flow.*

55. Ibid.

56. Yuriko Saito, "Japanese Aesthetics," in *A Companion to Aesthetics,* 2nd ed., ed. Stephen Davies et al. (Malden, MA: Wiley-Blackwell, 2009), 386.

57. Mara Miller, "Japanese Aesthetics and Philosophy of Art," in *The Oxford Handbook of World Philosophy*, ed. Jay L. Garfield and William Edelglass (Oxford: Oxford University Press, 2011), 327.

58. Ibid., 329.

59. Deborah Klens-Bigman, "Toward a Theory of Martial Arts as Performance Art," *Journal of Asian Martial Arts* 8, no. 2 (1999): 9.

60. Saito, 385–86.

61. Robert E. Carter, introduction to *The Japanese Arts and Self-Cultivation* (Albany, NY: State University of New York Press, 2008), Kindle edition.

62. H. E. Davey, "Aesthetics of the Way," chapter 2 in *The Japanese Way of the Artist* (Berkeley, CA: Stone Bridge Press, 2007), Kindle edition.

63. Davey, preface to *The Japanese Way of the Artist.*
64. Davey, "The Spirit of the Way," chapter 3 in *The Japanese Way of the Artist.*
65. Carter, introduction to *The Japanese Arts and Self-Cultivation.*
66. Saito, 385.
67. Carter, introduction to *The Japanese Arts and Self-Cultivation.*
68. Louis Frederic, *A Dictionary of the Martial Arts*, ed. and trans. Paul Crompton (Boston: Charles E. Tuttle Company, 1994), 151.
69. Steve Odin, *The Social Self in Zen and American Pragmatism* (Albany, NY: State University of New York Press, 1996), 58–59.
70. Frederic, 151.
71. Dewey, 209.
72. Richard B. Pilgrim, "Intervals (*Ma*) in Space and Time: Foundations for a Religio-Aesthetic Paradigm in Japan," in *Japan: In Tradition and Postmodern Perspectives*, ed. Charles Wei-Hsun Fu and Steve Heine (Albany, NY: State University of New York Press, 1995), 67.
73. Oscar Ratti and Adele Westbrook, *Secrets of the Samurai: A Survey of the Martial Arts of Feudal Japan* (North Clarendon, VT: Tuttle Publishing, 1973).
74. Graham Parkes, "Japanese Aesthetics," in *The Stanford Encyclopedia of Philosophy*, Winter 2011 Edition, ed. Edward N. Zalta, accessed August 31, 2014, http://plato.stanford.edu/archives/win2011/entries/japanese-aesthetics/. See also Odin, 19; and Watsuji Tetsurō, *Watsuji Tetsurō's Rinrigaku: Ethics in Japan,* trans. Yamamoto Seisaku and Robert E. Carter (Albany, NY: State University of New York Press, 1996), 18–19.
75. Pilgrim, 58–61.
76. Dewey, 64.
77. Ibid., 15.
78. Ibid., 79.
79. Ibid., 63.
80. Parkes, "Japanese Aesthetics."
81. Ibid.
82. Yamamoto Tsunetomo, *Hagakure: The Book of the Samurai*, trans. William Scott Wilson (New York: Kodansha, 1983). See also Roger T. Ames, "*Bushidō*: Mode or Ethic?," in *Japanese Aesthetics and Culture: A Reader*, ed. Nancy G. Hume (Albany, NY: State University of New York Press, 1995), 279–94; and Mishima Yukio, *The Way of the Samurai: Yukio Mishima on Hagakure in Modern Life*, trans. Kathryn Sparling (New York: Basic Books, 1977).
83. Davey, "Aesthetics of the Way."
84. Saito, 386.
85. Davies and Ikeno, 223–25.
86. Parkes, "Japanese Aesthetics." See also Davey, "Aesthetics of the Way."
87. This is reflected in one of the mottos of *jūdo, seiryoku zenyō* (精力善用), which is often translated as 'maximum efficiency with minimum effort.'
88. Parkes, "Japanese Aesthetics." See also Davey, "Aesthetics of the Way."
89. For a detailed discussion of *shoshin*, see Davey, "Aesthetics of the Way."

Part III

JAPANESE AESTHETICS AND CULTURAL POLITICS

Chapter 10

Ainu Aesthetics and Philosophy of Art

Replication, Remembering, Recovery

Koji Yamasaki and Mara Miller

PROLOGUE: THE RELATIONSHIP BETWEEN AINU AND JAPANESE AESTHETICS

The question of in what sense or senses Ainu aesthetics is Japanese is surely pertinent in a book on Japanese aesthetics.[1] As citizens of Japan, the Ainu people are legally and geographically Japanese. But, politically, the Ainu have been subject to Japanese rule only since the Meiji period (1868–1912).[2] Since then, Ainu identity has been compromised by the forced adoption of non-Ainu names, discouragement of the use of the Ainu language during the Meiji period, and other measures (Advisory Council for Future Ainu Policy 2009, 9). In addition to the differences attendant on agricultural versus hunting-gathering societies (for the Ainu, supplemented by small farming), the Ainu and the Japanese are not ethnically related, nor are their languages. Historically, the two groups were entirely distinct culturally. It comes as no surprise, then, that their arts and aesthetics also diverge sharply.

More specifically in terms of aesthetics, Ainu traditional culture did not include many of the features that have shaped Japanese aesthetics; such Japanese influences as there were were reinterpreted or reshaped in the context of Ainu culture. There has been no courtly culture, no close ties to hegemonic China or Korea (within the past millennium or prior to the Meiji era), no Buddhism or Confucianism with their elaborate aesthetics and philosophies of art, and no written language—and consequently no calligraphic tradition (with its deep imprint on East Asian mind, spirit, and art)—all forces that have deeply shaped Japanese arts. At the same time, there are a number of interesting parallels between Ainu and Japanese aesthetics, particularly in the twenty-first century, and particularly seen in the fascination of contemporary artists with arts of earlier, even Neolithic, times and with "traditional" arts.

139

INTRODUCTION

Ainu arts (Kindaichi and Sugiyama 1993) fit well into both anthropologist Richard L. Anderson's cross-cultural definition of art, expounded in *Calliope's Sisters* (1990), as "culturally significant meaning, skillfully encoded in an affecting, sensuous medium" (Anderson 1990, 234) and philosopher Denis Dutton's list of twelve characteristics of art (Dutton 2009, 52–59; Miller 2014, A52–A57). The present chapter, possibly the first to study Ainu aesthetics as opposed to Ainu arts, is based upon an extraordinary experiment by artists, scholars, and museum professionals to open up the renowned collection of Ainu art and handcrafts held at Hokkaido University's Natural History Museum in the Botanic Garden[3] (MBG) to Ainu artists[4] and craftspeople so that they could make replicas of the objects they selected. The project, sponsored by MBG, the Hokkaido University Center for Ainu and Indigenous Studies (CAIS), and the Hokkaido University Museum (HUM), had three unusual purposes: first, since the full experience of physical objects is not exhausted by touch alone, to allow tactile and *kinesthetic* contact; then, to enable the artists to make replicas of works they had selected; and, finally, to facilitate their discussion with one another and to record their observations, both about the objects and about their processes of discovery as they selected, examined, and replicated the works. An explicit principle was that Ainu individuals should be involved in the planning from the beginning.[5] The project resulted in a 2009 themed exhibition, *Teetasinrit Tekrukoci: The Handprints of Our Ancestors: Ainu Artifacts Housed at Hokkaido University—Inherited Techniques*, and a catalogue by that name (Yamasaki, Kato, and Amano 2012).[6] (All subsequent page numbers are to this book unless otherwise noted.) The exhibition had two concepts: to encourage more people, particularly the Ainu, to make use of the MBG specimens in the Ainu ethnological collection, and to explore their present-day significance through their utilization (Yamasaki 2012, 93).[7] The exhibition implemented this plan by three means: (1) "the unambiguous presentation of replicas as the central concept of the exhibition with accompanying introductions to the production processes and tools/memos used during the replica-making work," with the original models being exhibited "only when they had some specific relation to the replicas," when they "were placed in parallel with [the replicas] so viewers could understand the connection"; (2) integrated video; and (3) respect for both Ainu communiqués and CAIS's educational and research values (Yamasaki 2012, 93–94).

Because conversations among participants and the discoveries of the artists were among the primary goals of both the exhibition process and the catalogue, the exhibition included videos of the artists working and explaining their work and process, and the catalogue contained interviews with the artists providing entirely new material that carried important implications for the study of not only Ainu but also other indigenous cultures and for the aesthetics of everyday life in general, as well as for theory. This chapter, therefore, focuses on these artists' observations.

Ainu aesthetics[8] challenges and changes our understanding of aesthetics and the philosophy of art on at least four levels: descriptive aesthetics, categorical aesthetics, implications of these aesthetics for a variety of human activities such as museum practice and daily life, and the implications of these three for our broader understanding of aesthetics and the philosophy of art.[9]

DESCRIPTIVE AESTHETICS

Although there are similarities with those of other indigenous small-scale societies in terms of their reliance on locally available natural materials (with the exception of metal), their use of preindustrial-age and even Neolithic tools, and the sacrality of objects, Ainu aesthetics are distinctive and immediately recognizable.

Materials and Techniques

While also changing depending on the times, Ainu traditional culture seems to have remained true to their hunter-gatherer lifestyle even after adopting more sedentary lives.[10] Traditionally, they avoided pottery and metal forging, and used back-strap rather than floor looms.[11] They traded for Japanese plain weave (tabby) dyed cotton and silk fabric and Chinese silk and iron pots. Metal, usually tin or brass, was used as decoration rather than as the substance of objects.

The Ainu use the hides of bear, deer, fox, seal, dog, and other animals, as well as fish skin (salmon and trout), bird skin, and seagull feathers, as material for their art and artifacts. Deer horn was used for harpoon tips, deer foot bones for arrow shafts, and bird bones for needle cases. Animal tusks and bear claws were attached to plaited knife cords to increase their spiritual power and were used in the making of effigies for altars. Fiber made from nettle and the endodermis of elm and other tree barks were used for clothing; textile techniques include tabby weave, *appliqué*, and embroidery. Bark, twigs, and woods of local trees such as dogwood, elder, elm, maple, linden, and willow were used for other purposes. Wood carving is typically low relief. They hollowed out log interiors for quivers. A special wood-shaving technique was used in the crowns (*sapanpe*) that men wore in important ceremonies and also for the end of the ritual wooden wands offered to the gods (http://www.ainu-museum.or.jp/). Wood artist Masashi Kawakami describes the complexity of this process:

> I visited the Botanic Garden and held the materials in my hands. At first glance, the *cehorkakep inaw* from Biratori seemed smaller than its counterpart from Nibutani and it looked thinner. The greatest difference was that the tip of the *inaw kike* (the wood shaving of the *inaw*) was wide, and I had no idea how *inawke* (wood shaving) had been done to make it so. When I use the *inawke* technique, I usually use a *makiri* (knife) with a curved point. This might just be me, but whenever I shaved wood, I ended up with a narrow-tipped *inaw* and tightly curled shavings. I puzzled over how I could produce loosely curled shavings resembling waves as seen in this *inaw* from Biratori. Maybe it was that I didn't dry the willow enough, or that I dried it too much. Or perhaps the angle of the knife blade against the willow was wrong.
>
> I asked my seniors what I was doing wrong, including the above musings, and as a result I found a way to produce *inaw* like the one from Biratori. First, the *makiri* blade needs to be carefully sharpened on a medium whetstone and then on a finishing whetstone. After barking the willow, it needs to be dried in the shade for about six days to create perfect conditions. The most important part is how the knife blade is placed against the willow. First, it should be set crosswise on the wood and pulled, then gradually tilted diagonally until the wood surface is shaved off all at once. This produces a loosely curled, wavy *inaw kike* with a wide point. (38)

Textiles for clothing, the best-known of Ainu work, are visually stunning, employing *appliqué*, patchwork, and embroidery (in indigo, white, or colored thread) on tabby-woven hemp or (imported) cotton. Garments' nomenclature depends on the basic fiber and decorative technique (84). The overall cut (untailored, with straight panels stitched together), collar, and lapel resemble those of a kimono, although with significant differences in proportions, being shorter and broader, and with sleeves cut at a diagonal. *Appliqué* patterns are distinctive, with powerful overall impact. The visual language of Ainu arts is unique. Although outsiders may not recognize them as representational, many designs, highly stylized motifs inspired by geometrically rendered plant life, represent nature.

Ainu artistic materials are of special interest because so many of the artists mention the differences in technique, knowledge, understanding, skill, and perceptual sensitivity imposed by the materials themselves. As Yasuko Uetake explains, "The texture of the materials and sewing methods determine the overall feel of the garment" (50). Although the native materials impose limits, they also pushed the artists not only to expand their techniques, but also to recognize the spirit either in the work itself, in the original maker, or in a tool (such as needles, which are considered divine)—which can be an important aesthetic consideration, according to Anderson. It certainly seemed to be so for the Ainu artists who mentioned it. Ainu artists saw an overlap between current techniques, attitudes, and approaches and those imposed by the original materials, describing discrepancies variously as "my individuality," deliberate innovation, originality, and even failure, though ultimately the judgment of failure was rejected (Yamasaki 2012, 95).

LEARNING FROM LANGUAGE, THE BODY, AND OBJECTS

'Categorical aesthetics' is the term Mara Miller coined for the categories of aesthetic experience and evaluation used by a given culture (Miller 2011). In any study of aesthetics, it behooves us to acknowledge the terms in which a culture understands its own work and values, although philosophers sometimes assume such values are universal, and indeed one's own terms can nearly always be applied to works, experiences, and judgments regardless of the other culture's own descriptors, provided that one overlooks essential distinctions.

Ainu categorical aesthetics are independent and must be understood on their own terms. What are the aesthetic categories by which Ainu understand, value, and judge experiences, environments, activities, aspects of nature, and works of art? What did the artists learn from their study, and what can we learn from their commentary? What principles do we need to follow?

We cannot just assume that people are ready to explicate their aesthetic values. In some cases, the language might not exist (or at least not for a given person); in others, articulation might be possible but undesirable for psychological, emotional, political, or social reasons. (Do parents who roll their eyes at a child's garb really want to take time or effort to explain why they find it aesthetically offensive?) There are additional difficulties during conditions of change, such as modernization and colonization, when meanings, techniques, materials, and aesthetic and other values are changing rapidly, and all of these carry social and political implications. The problem is confounded for the Ainu by the fact that under the forced relinquishment of their language, and especially given the absence of a written Ainu language, many of the terms that would historically have been used to describe desirable or undesirable characteristics have undoubtedly been lost. Questions arise regarding whether Japanese concepts influenced not only the words but also the underlying concepts through which the artists express their approval, delight, and frustration regarding their own replications, the original works on which they based their replicas, and perhaps even the perception of the older works.

Loss of language is not always the case, however. Terms for Ainu clothing, for instance, preserve their reference to the color of the fiber used, suggesting

that color was fundamental to their ways of thinking about ceremonial clothing, in some way that may have been different than merely giving aesthetic
pleasure.[12] Whether linguistic study of Ainu aesthetic terms can help us
reconstruct an Ainu categorical aesthetics remains to be seen.

The project described above advances the cause of understanding Ainu
categorical aesthetics in three ways. First of all, although the aesthetic categories of ancient, and even nineteenth-century, Ainu may be lost forever,
some of the terms for understanding and appraisal used by contemporary
Ainu artists emerged in the artists' statements in this catalogue. Terms related
to "delicately balanced beauty" and "delicacy" (Toru Kaizawa, 27), beauty
and goodness, and "harmony" occur repeatedly, as do more general terms
expressing delight, such as 'wonderful.' We must be careful in our interpretations, of course: the Ainu term *pirka* is defined as 'both beautiful and
good.' Secondly, there is much to be discovered from the selection process
itself. Finally, unfamiliar and even unsuspected aesthetic values seem to have
emerged for the artists from their visual, tactile, and spiritual encounters with
the objects and from their bodily efforts to replicate them. The interviews and
hopefully others in the future thus warrant further analysis.

Men and women used slightly different criteria for selecting objects to
replicate. Women based their selection on "the beauty of their design, such
as elements of the embroidery and colors," while men mentioned an additional criterion: the genres they were good at, had experience with, or used
themselves in hunting (Yamasaki 2012). Criteria related only tangentially to
aesthetics (by Western definitions) were "the desire to restore lost techniques,
the will to make replicas of poorly preserved specimens for the future, the reasoning that the originals were from their hometowns, the desire to help revive
aspects of local traditional culture, and the will to use their replica-making
experience to create modern works" (Yamasaki 2012, 94). Although historical accuracy has been jeopardized through the loss of the Ainu language, the
"authenticity" of such terms is unquestionable in the sense that these are the
terms used *today* by Ainu and by individuals of non-Ainu descent who work
in the Ainu traditions.

In addition to caution regarding our interpretation of interpreted and
sometimes translated language, we add a second principle, regarding the
questions that interviewers ask and the definition of the task at hand. Among
the undoubtedly modern concepts used by these artists to describe their processes and results are *accuracy* and *individuality*—the first a quality inherent
in the task of "replication," the second both a modern term of approval and a
justification for deviating from strict replication. Whether these terms would
have been so salient had the artists not been asked about them is open to question. For the artists, accuracy of replication was highly desirable ("When I
produce a replica, I try to make it as close to the original works as possible";

Tahachi Urakawa, 15). Several expressed frustration when they were unable to achieve this accuracy, which both constituted an end in itself and led them to other realizations about aesthetic value, even as it also sometimes led them to judge their attempts as "failures."

Individuality appears in many guises: the inevitable connection between maker and her object ("Deer calls have different shapes and skins depending on who made them"; Tahachi Urakawa, 15), "self-expression," the result of decisions the artist makes about materials and methods for achieving desired effects (not having been taught how to do the work), and what seems to be an almost Leibnizian understanding of the inevitable idiosyncrasy of the work of any person given her unique position in space and time. Individuality appears in the methods of investigation too: "They reflected the personality of each artisan—some were written with an artistic touch, others were written in great detail with measurements, and others were just rough sketches. Some artisans noted their measurements directly onto the photos we gave them as preparatory materials to help them select their targets" (Yamasaki 2012, 94).

Satoru Kawakami's search for accuracy leads to admiration of the object's beauty, but this beauty is on a par with the efficacy of the weapon:

> I produced the *kite* harpoon with accurate reproduction in mind while picturing which animals (marine creatures) the tool would have been used to hunt. Although we have many and various tools nowadays, only a limited range was available to the Ainu at that time. Despite this, they produced a tool as rational as this, featuring both artistic beauty and the power to kill its prey; this level of technical capability surprised me. (33)

We might hope that further study could reveal whether such efficacy and rationality are *intrinsic* to certain kinds of beauty for the Ainu.

Recovering Indigenous Aesthetics by Means of Replication

Is there any way to recover the categorical aesthetics of Ainu before their society was overwhelmed by modernization, Japanization, and Westernization? Aside from questions related to language, there is the extremely interesting question of whether values original to the makers and early "audience" can be recovered now (and in circumstances that have become so different)—and if so, by whom and on what basis?

Several of the artists suggested this might be possible, mentioning the "free" quality of the earlier work (in contrast to their expectations): "[P]eople in the old days may have carved freely, regardless of formalities. Through it, we can feel the sensitivity and sharpness of our ancestors toward nature" (Toru Kaizawa, 27). Several described their impressions as the result not of looking, but of feeling, in all its manifestations: touching, feeling the weight, and so on. In Yamasaki's summary: "[T]he specimens were also photographed, but the sketches and photos played only a supplementary role; ... the artisans unanimously said that it was more important for their hands to remember the thickness and feel of the specimens. The same conclusions were reached in relation to garments, since the texture of cloth plays a key role in replica making" (Yamasaki 2012, 94).

Others found something discernible through the process of struggling to replicate the work, especially when it required techniques that were foreign to them. This points out the importance of the process of replication itself:

> According to Ms. Kayoko Nishida, when she replicates embroidery work, she has to start over many times until she gets the knack of it. By starting over repeatedly, she acquires the hand movements and habits of the person who produced the original. After that, even if she comes to an unknown branching point ... her hands are guided naturally toward the right or left line, and she can proceed without thinking. She finds that such choices are true to the original when she later checks. (Yamasaki 2012, 94)

These changes in perception and understanding thus took place in two ways—by holding objects and by trying to reproduce them—and led iteratively to further changes in perception and understanding.

Ainu Aesthetics

There are a number of interesting points about what these artists learned. Many artists talked about the relationships between the works and nature even when there is no handy aesthetic term for them. Koji Kaizawa, for instance, cites the "the carving of the curves that make the flowers look alive" in a tray (21). In some cases, an enhanced relationship with nature is due to the artists' own activities, as Urakawa's comments regarding his replication of deer calls show:

> Playing a deer call in a mountain environment causes any male deer that hears it to believe that an intruder is on their turf; this puts them within the hunter's sights because they come to try to expel the intruder. Elders told me to watch my back when I blow on it, because the sound brings out the deer-hunting bears as well as deer themselves. (15)

Satoru Kawakami echoes this motivation: "I selected pieces that I hadn't produced often before. Since I go hunting myself, I am interested in the tools used by the Ainu in days gone by for hunting and fishing; I therefore selected the *kite* (harpoon, No. 09691)" (33). Artists' choice of objects to replicate based on their birthplace or current home and the origin of the work is another aspect of this connection to the *local* natural environment.

Second, some artists report that the processes of trying to replicate the effects in the works enabled them to understand the mind of the works' makers in ways that merely viewing did not. Yasuko Uetake says of this process, "When I make a replica, I consider what the producer of the original might have been feeling while creating it, and I try not to compromise that sentiment. That is, I try to avoid doing it my way or choosing the easy way" (50). Koji Kaizawa reports something similar: "While I was carving the tray's floral design, I wondered what its producer, Shitaehori, was feeling and thinking while creating his work. I imagined him carving peacefully in a place surrounded by flowers" (21). Similarly, Nishida's passage above continues, "As she continues her needlework, she can sometimes understand the emotional vacillation of those who produced the originals"—something she could not have recognized from just visual inspection (Yamasaki 2012, 94).

Third, for some artists, this sense of contact with a living presence was extended to a sense of the work itself as alive and able to communicate with them. Masashi Kawakami says that "I believe the Ainu specimens will be pleased if many people see the Ainu materials at the [MBG] and many opportunities are created for people to learn these ancestral techniques" (38). Nishida describes her process in detail:

Whenever I make a replica garment, I say to the original, "I'm going to make a replica of you. I'm not very skilled yet, but I'll do my best, so please help me." However, this garment was reluctant to cooperate until I began enjoying the work, and then I felt it become willing to help me complete the task at hand. After that, whenever I wondered how to proceed at a certain point in the embroidery, I felt my hands being guided naturally and was able to proceed without thinking. This may be because whenever I create a replica, I try to understand what the producer was feeling while making it. (68)

She continues, extending this to the ideas themselves:

The ideas [our ancestors] wove into the garments do not want to be buried in museum warehouses hidden from view. I think they want to be seen more and more so that they can convey the ideas of their producers to people. Originals in museums are constrained in order to ensure their preservation. (68)

Her last comment leads to our fourth point, namely, that the sense of the importance of the works as a means of communication extends to new generations. Nishida iterates this feeling as follows: "I hope my work will help the wonderful designs made by our ancestors to be passed on into the future" (68).

IMPLICATIONS OF THESE AESTHETICS
FOR LIFE AND MUSEUM PRACTICE

From descriptive and categorical aesthetics we now move on to implications for daily life, identity, and museum practice—implications that remain preliminary at our present level of investigation.

Daily Life, Ethnic and Personal Identity

The existence of distinctive categories of aesthetics carries implications for a variety of human activities. Anderson speaks of the threats to indigenous aesthetics under the onslaught of modern commercial culture and tourism (Anderson 1990, 236–37). But the present study suggests that even in the absence of direct contact with elders who can teach, and without texts explaining techniques, craftspeople can, (1) recover lost techniques, (2) develop an awareness of unfamiliar styles and aesthetic values, (3) find themselves in contact with the individuals who made the earlier works, (4) discover a sense of spiritual connection with the works themselves (as spirits, as was common in the precontact world), and thus (5) revivify their spiritual connection with their people and extend their own sense of connection into the future for new generations.

All of this suggests that works such as these—both the originals and their replicas, individually and in concert, either as components of exhibitions carrying the prestige of hegemonic institutions or as constituents of entire domestic and social environments—hold enormous capabilities for the reconstruction of collective memory and thus for the preservation and/or reconstitution of partially destroyed communities.

The observations of the artists suggest that objects and their replication can play vital roles in the rediscovery, confirmation, and elaboration of personal and group identity.

Artistic Practice

Artists stated that the experience would affect their own work in the future:

- "While producing these replicas, I was surprised by our ancestors' skill, wisdom, and eagerness for production. I would like to use the lessons I have learned from these reproductions in my own work in the future" (Koji Kaizawa, 21).
- "The techniques used for their replication can be employed in present-day Ainu craftwork and gave me many new ideas" (Toru Kaizawa, 27).

It will be interesting to see what follows this process.

Museum Practice

Museum practice in the West has largely relied on an evolving set of characteristics derived from philosophical categorical aesthetics (the beautiful, the sublime, and later, the interesting, kitsch, camp, etc.) and from art-historical terms of Western art history. Although there have been increasing efforts to understand and present non-Western objects along lines derived from their own culture, these remain haphazard and partial. Western preferences in museums and the discipline of art history have also often stressed the monumental: unique works, often large-scale and designed to be permanent; the ephemeral has been difficult to accommodate, as has been the tiny (except in cases where it is "jewel-like" and/or fabulously expensive). Although these preferences are increasingly superseded, they remain largely in place.

The Ainu, the indigenous people of Hawai'i, and the indigenous people of other parts of the world are taking the initiative to revive their traditional cultures, and it seems these movements are picking up steam, as the exhibit discussed here attests. The success of this project, the wealth of new material it produced, and the implications it carries for several branches of theory and several disciplines, suggest that projects of this sort should if possible be replicated and studied further, for they promise important implications for a number of disciplines as well as for museum practice.

This study of Ainu aesthetics suggests six major challenges to Western museum practice:

1. Following Cameron (1971), changing the model of the art museum from "temple" to "forum," facilitating interactions of different kinds among a variety of people, materials (objects and environments), and information.
2. Offering opportunities for using the museum's materials, including handling and replication.
3. Creating replicas of museum works.
4. Studying the social situation around the materials.
5. Transforming museums into places of hands-on learning of many kinds.
6. Recognizing new sources of information and changing the direction of transmission from scholars-and-museums-to-the-public to (certain members of) the-public-to-scholars-and-museums.

Such a model differs from the conventional ways of conceiving museum relationships to knowledge in that it is not just the transmission of existing knowledge—typically from curators to the public and from museum objects to scholars—but also the discovery of *new* knowledge by the public and the transmission of knowledge from objects themselves to outsiders (artists, the public) and from them back to the curators and the database.

CONCLUSION: THEORETICAL IMPLICATIONS

Ainu aesthetics and this new way of studying it carry important implications for our broader understanding of aesthetics and the philosophy of art as well as for other disciplines and bodies of theory. Dovetailing with Richard L. Anderson's theory, they challenge a common assumption that where there is no body of written aesthetic theory, there can be no philosophy of art. They also offer alternatives to the "authentic" versus "forgery" dichotomy so usefully studied by Denis Dutton (1983, 2009). Ainu artists showed interest not only in objects themselves, but also in the ways they link human beings to the world and "sew that world together," making a harmonious whole of people, place, activities, earning a living, animals, plants, and spirits. This finding warrants further study in light of Alfred Gell's theory of art as agency (Gell 1998), in which artworks are seen as effective in their own right and in some cases as alive. It might additionally provide "thing" theory with an alternative foundation for examining the significance of things outside the confines of either Heideggerian, postmodernist, or critical theory. As noted in the catalogue, the reliance of the artists on social networks created by these activities also suggests the need for study in terms of the actor-agent theory (Yamasaki 2012).

Recent studies of collective memory, especially those derived from the founding theoretical contributions of Maurice Halbwachs (1992), suggest not only that collective memory exists and is essential to group cohesion, group functioning, and the creation of meaning, but also that it is a necessary condition of individual memory, inhering not solely in cognition—in the brain and in texts—but in environments and objects as well. Collective memory, however, is often defined logocentrically: in terms of linguistic cognition and written texts.[13] The work of these Ainu artists shows the inadequacy (if not falsity) of such conceptions. As studies of muscle memory and many forms of art suggest, information is stored not only in the brain and in language but also in objects. Theorists of the body will be intrigued by findings regarding information, changes in perception, and impressions that artists recovered from objects by means of the body.

In summary, this experiment of Ainu replication strongly suggests the importance of an aesthetics that is made literally tangible, and it shows that there is a great deal to learn about thinking about art through feeling and making and from the objects themselves.

NOTES

1. We would like to extend our sincere appreciation to the Ainu master hands, our friends, Hokkaido University's Natural History Museum in the Botanic Garden, the Hokkaido University Museum, Dr. Michael Schuster and the East-West

Center (Honolulu, Hawai'i), and all those who provided us with guidance and cooperation.

2. "[T]he Ainu ... were attacked and forced north on the mainland [Honshu] since the Yamato era [250–710 C.E.]. They were eventually driven out of the mainland and compelled to settle in Hokkaido [which has a much harsher climate]. In the Tokugawa period, a northern feudal lord extended his authority into Hokkaido and deprived the Ainu of their economic rights, reducing them to semi-slavery status. The Meiji government brought Hokkaido under its administrative control and deprived the Ainu of their land and fishing and hunting rights. Then to Japanize the Ainu, the government banned traditional Ainu practices and compelled Ainu children to learn Japanese and forsake their native language" (Hane 2001, 439–40). While Hane cites a (total Ainu) population of 50,000 people, the Survey on the Hokkaido Ainu Living Conditions conducted in 2006 by the Hokkaido Government gives the population in Hokkaido as 23,782 (Ainu Association of Hokkaido 2010).

3. The full name is 'Botanic Garden, Field Science Center for Northern Biosphere at Hokkaido University.'

4. This chapter uses the term 'artists' rather than 'artisans' as in the catalogue because here we follow Denis Dutton's cluster criteria for art (Dutton 2009) and Richard L. Anderson's cross-cultural definition of art (Anderson 1990, 238, 251, 262). For a full discussion of how the thinking of the individuals cited here illustrate Dutton's points, see Miller 2014.

5. An additional objective was to help rectify the dissatisfaction often expressed by Ainu people about being kept passive and/or ignorant regarding the kinds of studies that are done of them and their culture, an objective in keeping with those of CAIS, whose three major characteristics are interdisciplinarity, an emphasis on education, and collaboration with the Ainu. The CAIS Steering Committee is the first at Hokkaido University to have Ainu individuals as members. CAIS has also "put in place a research structure that is ... open to the Ainu to ensure that they can become deeply involved in the Center's activities and ... in studies on their rights and culture" (Tsunemoto 2007, 18–19).

6. A version of this exhibit was subsequently shown at the East-West Center Gallery in Honolulu, Hawai'i under the direction of Dr. Michael Schuster and Koji Yamasaki.

7. This project—close to unprecedented in the museum world—was strongly influenced by three earlier exhibits: "A Scottish Physician's View: Craft and Spirit of the Ainu from the N.G. Munro Collection" (Foundation for Research and Promotion of Ainu Culture 2002); "Message from the Ainu: Craft and Spirit (2003–2004)" (Foundation for Research and Promotion of Ainu Culture 2003, Yoshida 2003); and "Handiwork in the North—*Tekekarpe Nukar Wa Unkore Yan*—(See Our Works)" (Historical Museum of Hokkaido 2007).

8. In this chapter, we use 'aesthetics' as a singular noun to refer to the field and to a range of human experience and judgment, and as a plural noun to stress the different types and categories of such ranges.

9. Although dance, music, and storytelling are also salient in Ainu life, here we examine visual and tactile aesthetics.

10. Some information on materials in this section is taken from the webpage of the Ainu Museum Poroto Kotan, in Shiraoi-gun, Hokkaido, http://www.ainu-museum. or.jp/ (accessed June 30, 2015), in addition to the catalogue.

11. The ancestors of the Ainu historically produced earthenware pottery until about the thirteenth to fourteenth century, when iron pots came to be used instead; why they abandoned earthenware is unclear.

12. In spite of the relative lack of attention by recent philosophers of art, color has been shown to be extremely important both to cultures of all kinds today and to Paleolithic and Neolithic people (Anderson 1990; Desdemaines-Hugon 2010).

13. Jack Goody (2011) contends, for example, that, "Basically, information is stored in the memory, in the mind. Without writing there is virtually no storage of information outside the human brain and hence no distance communication over space and time" (321). Many cultures with strong visual narrative art traditions have used the visual arts to convey information and knowledge, as in medieval Christian stained glass windows telling stories from the Bible. East Asia has particularly rich traditions of this type, as with Buddhist scrolls and mandalas. See *Painting with Pictures* and Victor Mair's study of how storytelling using painting originated in India a thousand years ago, and its influence on performance and literary traditions around the world (Mair 2009).

REFERENCES

Advisory Council for Future Ainu Policy. 2009. *Final Report of the Advisory Council for Future Ainu Policy*. Provisional translation by the Comprehensive Ainu Policy Office, Cabinet Secretariat, Government of Japan. Accessed June 30, 2015. http://www.kantei.go.jp/jp/singi/ainu/dai10/siryou1_en.pdf.

Ainu Association of Hokkaido. 2010. *Brochure on the Ainu People*. Sapporo, Japan: Ainu Association of Hokkaido. Accessed June 30, 2015. http://www.ainu-assn.or.jp/english/eabout03.html.

Anderson, Richard L. 1990. *Calliope's Sisters: A Comparative Study of Philosophies of Art*. Englewood Cliffs, NJ: Prentice Hall.

Cameron, Duncan F. 1971. "The Museum, a Temple or the Forum."*Curator: The Museum Journal* 14, no. 1: 11–24.

Desdemaines-Hugon, Christine. 2010. *Stepping-Stones: A Journey through the Ice Age Caves of the Dordogne*. New Haven, CT: Yale University Press.

Dutton, Denis. 1983. *The Forger's Art: Forgery and the Philosophy of Art*. Berkeley, CA: University of California Press.

———. 2009. *The Art Instinct: Beauty, Pleasure, and Human Evolution*. New York: Bloomsbury Press.

Fitzhugh, William W. and Chisato O. Dubreuil, eds. 1999. *Ainu: Spirit of a Northern People*. Seattle, WA: University of Washington Press.

Foundation for Research and Promotion of Ainu Culture, ed. 2002. *A Scottish Physician's View: Craft and Spirit of the Ainu from the N. G. Munro Collection*. Sapporo, Japan: Foundation for Research and Promotion of Ainu Culture.

———, ed. 2003. *Message from the Ainu: Craft and Spirit*. Tokushima, Japan: Association of Tokushima Prefectural Museum.

Gell, Alfred. 1998. *Art and Agency: An Anthropological Theory*. Oxford: Clarendon.

Goody, Jack. 2011. "From 'Memory in Oral and Literate Traditions.'" In *The Collective Memory Reader*, edited by Jeffrey K. Olick, Vered Vinitzky-Seroussi, and Daniel Levy, 321–24. Oxford: Oxford University Press.

Halbwachs, Maurice. 1992. *On Collective Memory*. Edited, translated, and with an introduction by Lewis A. Coser. Chicago: University of Chicago Press.

Hane, Mikiso. 2001. *Modern Japan: A Historical Survey*. Third edition. Boulder, CO: Westview Press.

Historical Museum of Hokkaido, ed. 2007. *Handiwork in the North—Tekekarpe Nukar Wa Unkore Yan—(See Our Works)*. Sapporo, Japan: Historical Museum of Hokkaido.

Kindaichi, Kyōsuke and Sueo Sugiyama. 1993. *Ainu geijutsu (Ainu Art)*. Sapporo, Japan: Hokkaido Publication Project Center.

Kodama, Sakuzaemon. 1971. *Meijizen Nihon jinruigaku senshigakushi: Ainu minzokushi no kenkyū (Early Meiji Japanese Anthropological Studies of Prehistory: Research on the History of Ainu Culture)*. Tokyo: Nihon Gakujutsu Shinkokai.

Mair, Victor. 2009. *Painting and Performance: Chinese Picture Recitation and Its Indian Genesis*. Warren, CT: Floating World Editions.

Miller, Mara. 2011. "Japanese Aesthetics and Philosophy of Art." In *Oxford Handbook of World Philosophy*, edited by Jay L. Garfield and William Edelglass, 317–33. Oxford: Oxford University Press.

———. 2014. "Denis Dutton's *The Art Instinct* and the Recovery of Ainu Aesthetics." *Philosophy and Literature* 38, no. 1A (*Evolutionary Aesthetics: A Special Issue in Memory of Denis Dutton*): A48–A59.

Miller, Mara and Koji Yamasaki. 2017, online 2014. "Japanese and Ainu Aesthetics and Philosophy of Art." In *Oxford Handbook of Japanese Philosophy*, edited by Bret W. Davis. Oxford: Oxford University Press.

Preaching from Pictures: A Japanese Mandala. 2006. DVD. Directed by David W. Plath. Urbana, IL: Asian Educational Media Service, University of Illinois at Urbana-Champaign.

Tsunemoto, Teruki. 2007. "Formation of a Center for Ainu and Indigenous Studies." *Monbu kagaku kyōiku tsūshin (Ministry of Education Educational Correspondence)* 183: 18–19.

Yamasaki, Koji. 2012. "Indigenous Peoples and Museum Materials—Lessons from Preparing for the Ainu Cultural Exhibition." In *Teetasinrit Tekrukoci: The Handprints of Our Ancestors: Ainu Artifacts Housed at Hokkaido University—Inherited Techniques*, edited by Koji Yamasaki, Masaru Kato, and Tetsuya Amano, 92–96. Sapporo, Japan: Hokkaido University Museum / Hokkaido University Center for Ainu and Indigenous Studies.

Yamasaki, Koji, Masaru Kato, and Tetsuya Amano, eds. 2012. *Teetasinrit Tekrukoci: The Handprints of Our Ancestors: Ainu Artifacts Housed at Hokkaido University—Inherited Techniques*. Sapporo, Japan: Hokkaido University Museum / Hokkaido University Center for Ainu and Indigenous Studies.

Yoshida, Kenji. 2003. "Aboriginal Peoples and Museums—New Attempts to Realize Self-Representation in the 'Message from the Ainu' Exhibition." In *Message from the Ainu: Craft and Spirit*, edited by Foundation for Research and Promotion of Ainu Culture, 146–55. Tokushima, Japan: Association of Tokushima Prefectural Museum.

Chapter 11

The Idea of Greece in Modern Japan's Cultural Dreams

Hiroshi Nara

INTRODUCTION

In 2003, the Tokyo National Museum held an exhibition entitled 'Alexander the Great: East-West Cultural Contacts from Greece to Japan' featuring museum artifacts from around the world. This exhibition used artifacts to demonstrate that Hellenism reached Japan via the Silk Road during early Japan. When did such awareness or fantasy, as the case may be, take root? What significance did this supposed connection serve in Japan's modernization? For an answer, we may go back at least to the Meiji period (1868–1912). During this time, the government was voracious in absorbing the best technologies and frameworks from the Western powers (e.g., civil engineering, manufacturing, military, and legal systems) that were most useful to suit Japan's needs. It was a period of rapid flux in the arts, when artists, writers, and institutions were mesmerized by new ideas from the West and began to chart their own artistic paths. This situation was ripe for Japanese intellectuals to evaluate Japan's cultural place in world civilization, a question that had not been contemplated in earnest before Meiji. During the period of varied orientation in the Meiji (1868–1912) and Taishō (1912–1926) eras, it is curious to observe that some Japanese thinkers became palpably drawn to the idea of Greece. It is not immediately clear why Greece garnered such an interest, since the country at that time was not a colonial power and its international influence was limited. Exploring this phenomenon will provide us with new insight into inchoate Japanese cultural identity and self-consciousness about Japan's own place in the world, as well as a clue to the discourse in aesthetic experience.

A FASCINATION WITH GREECE

A fascination with the idea of Greece may have begun with the art historian Ernest Fenollosa (1853–1908), a hired foreign expert at Tokyo Imperial University. When Fenollosa arrived in Japan from the United States in 1878, most Buddhist temples were dilapidated owing to iconoclasm and the loss of adequate support bases. He thought that traditional Japanese art was on the verge of extinction. Although Fenollosa was initially interested in promoting Western-style painting (*yōga*), he soon began calling policymakers' attention to the high quality of Japanese traditional art and eventually made a plea for its protection and resurrection.[1] The government agreed. In 1884, Fenollosa made a trip to Kansai to catalogue artworks held at temples and shrines, where he encountered the Kuze Kannon, which had stood in Hōryūji's Golden Hall shrouded in dusty cloth, unseen for more than two centuries. When the statue was finally revealed, Fenollosa was astonished by what he saw. He compared the bodhisattva's facial expression to that of a Greek sculpture, writing, "But it was the aesthetic wonders of this work that attracted us most. From the front the figure is not quite so noble, but seen in profile it seemed to rise to the height of archaic Greek art."[2] Eventually, he conjectured that Japan received Greek influence in the following way: Alexander the Great planted the seed of Greek art in western Asia and left a Greek state (Bactria), which transmitted its art to Gandhara, where it mixed with Buddhist art. This Greco-Indian art then traveled to China during the Han (206 BC–220 AD) and Tang (618–907) periods and finally reached Japan. As evidence for the easterly progression of Hellenism, Fenollosa cited a number of design and iconographic similarities to Japanese Buddhist sculpture, such as facial modeling, the shell-like openings of downward falling drapery, corkscrew curves on a Buddha's head, and circular grass pattern (*karakusa*), which he contended could not be explained as independent artistic developments.[3] Unproven conjecture though it was, by merely mentioning Japanese art alongside Greek art and mainstream European civilization, his proposal for the Greece-Japan connection immediately raised the stature of Japanese art. This highly influential foreign authority's legitimization was useful to policymakers and intellectuals in their effort to place Japanese art in relation to the art of other world civilizations in the West for the first time. Now, world-class art had been discovered in Japan. Within a few years after his arrival, Fenollosa became one of the most knowledgeable and respected connoisseurs of Japanese art and an expert on art policies. He raised Japanese art's reputation even higher when he stated that Japanese painting was able to express *myōsō* (artistic ideas) with more freedom and ease than Western painting.[4] Thus, the idea of Greece changed from comparative iconography in art history to one of ideological utility.

Okakura Kakuzō (1862–1913), an influential art historian and former assistant to Fenollosa, took a position similar to that of Fenollosa.[5] With regard to Fenollosa's version of the easterly progression of Hellenism, Okakura was resistant to Fenollosa's Eurocentrism, and although he believed that the Greek influence was considerably diluted by the time it reached Japan after having traveled vast distances over a thousand years, he stated that Japan's Suiko (604–628) and Tenpyō (724–794) period art received some influence from Hellenism.[6] Fenollosa himself was not able to offer proof of his theory. He wrote, "A full account of its slow passage north-eastward across the continent of Asia will, some day, fill a most romantic chapter in Art History."[7]

Itō Chūta (1867–1954), a prominent architect and architectural historian, apparently picked up on this idea of Japan's connection to Greece, or perhaps he arrived at it independently. In an 1893 talk at an architectural society meeting, Itō claimed that the entasis in the pillars of Hōryūji's Second Gate (Chūmon) provided direct evidence of Greek influence. He recounted the easterly progression much like Fenollosa, saying that although the Greco-Indian influence had very much disappeared now along its transmission route, Hōryūji retained its Hellenistic heritage in the shape of the pillars and overall proportion of the architecture.[8] This talk titillated the imagination of the Japanese, for it seemed that Fenollosa's idea might not be off the mark after all.

Art historians' curiosity about the Hellenistic influence should be understood in a larger sociopolitical discourse in which intellectuals pondered self-consciously about the place of Japan as it was caught in the crease of modernity and tradition. Was the Hōryūji complex design derived from a Chinese design or was it Japan's adaptation? Where did the Japanese race originate? What features does Japan have in comparison to the West? Questions abounded. Some of the answers to these questions were outlandish. Shiga Shigetaka (1863–1927), a geographer and nationalistic writer, suggested that Japan had an affinity with Europe (especially Italy) by pointing out assiduously that Western civilization arose from a volcanic country (e.g., Italy) and that Japan, a volcanic country itself, should likewise become the fountainhead of Eastern civilization.[9] In a similar vein, a progressive Christian thinker, Uchimura Kanzō (1861–1930), argued, along the line of the geographical determinism promoted by the Swiss-American geologist and geographer Arnold Guyot (1807–1884), that Japan and Greece shared the same geographical characteristics and similar national characters, as well as roles in the international arena. Uchimura wrote, "Japan is a Greece in Asia. They are both situated in the eastern end of a continent. They play the role of protecting the gate to the east."[10] The sudden interest in geography during this time is intriguing—Shiga and Uchimura acknowledged Japanese interest in nature and helped transform the idea of scenic beauty to one that was based more on actual geographical features, replacing the traditional, stereotypical celebrated views of Japan, such as the *Nihon Sankei* (Three Views of Japan). More importantly, Shiga and Uchimura expressed great interest in discussing Japan's natural beauty in relation to the West (but not to other parts of Asia) and the physical characteristics that would shape Japan's international role.

In this effervescent, self-conscious assessment of Japan, two rhetorical directions in the general political and intellectual atmosphere developed. One was the assertion that, as the leading nation of Asia, Japan had the mandate to stand up to stop Western nations' colonization in the absence of other Asian nations' ability to do so.[11] This position required intellectuals to provide evidence that Japan was more particularly endowed than other Asian nations, such as in cultural heritage, with various characteristics that licensed Japan to resist colonialism more effectively. The second direction was that intellectuals tried to demonstrate that Japan shared many commonalities with Western nations, in terms of physical features, genealogy of the populace, cultural heritage, and its role in Asia and the world, so much so that Japan was practically a Western nation.[12] The idea of Greece served both of these purposes. Okakura, the most influential art historian cum politician around the turn of the twentieth century, was most successful in promoting these two fronts to the West. For example, his book *The Ideals of the East* (1903) attempted to symbolize Japan's leadership role in solidarity with all of Asia (India, China, and Japan), stating that "Asia is one." Then in 1904, in *The Awakening of Japan,* Okakura asserted that Japan was not only morally obliged to stop the colonial advance of the West, but it was also uniquely qualified, both technologically and spiritually.

Around the time of the Russo-Japanese War in 1904, the Yellow Peril encapsulated Western nations' disquiet about the colonial role of Japan and immigrants from Japan and China in the West. In this anti-Japanese and anti-Chinese climate, the same bifurcated argument prevailed. The most typical argument was to connect Japan more broadly to the West in general. As a rebuttal to the Yellow Peril, historian and economist Taguchi Ukichi (1855–1905) argued that the skin complexion of ruling Japanese was not actually yellow but pale and that the Japanese language was in the same family as Sanskrit and Persian.[13] Historian and statesman Takekoshi Yosaburō (1865–1950) proposed the idea that the Japanese race might be partly Phoenician on the basis that the Phoenicians were good seafarers, who could have traveled to the Indian subcontinent, Indonesia, and Japan during prehistory. He stated the Chinese did not share the same racial origins as the Japanese.[14] In the same vein, journalist, writer, and translator Kuroiwa Ruikō (1862–1920) wrote an essay claiming that the Heian poet Ono no Komachi was an Indo-Aryan.[15] These ideas based on race and language genealogy were meant to discredit the Yellow Peril and to set the Japanese alongside Westerners. It may be difficult to assess how influential these writers were, but they were ebullient promoters of Japanese identity.

GREECE IN THE SERVICE OF AESTHETIC EXPERIENCE

The idea of Greece continued to stimulate people's imaginations in the Taishō (1912–1926) and Shōwa (1926–1989) eras. This was particularly true of writers who looked to Greek culture to enrich their personal inner selves. Celebrated cultural historian Watsuji Tetsurō (1889–1960) was one of the first intellectuals who wrote on the issue of Japan's cultural roots in a world context, and his commitment to things Greek ran deeper than most.[16] In *Koji junrei* (1919), a rumination upon his pilgrimages to temples in the city of Nara, he gave strong support to the theme of the easterly progression of Hellenism. Availing himself of Marc Aurel Stein's and Albert von Le Coq's reports of archeological excavations along the Silk Road in Central Asia, Watsuji argued for the plausibility of the progression. Watsuji's other examples included not only entasis at Tōshōdaiji and Hōryūji, but also *gigaku* masks, wall paintings at Hōryūji, folds of Buddhist statues, and body modeling.[17] His expressed love for ancient Buddhist statues could not have been any more effusive than his encounter with the Yakushi Nyorai in Hōryūji's Golden Hall. After showering it with superlatives, he compared the statue to the ideal of beauty for Greek art:

> This beauty is different from the beauty of the human body that we feel from Greek sculpture. Greek sculpture no doubt expresses ideal beauty as a reflection of a pinnacle of human desire, but in this Buddhist statue, we see something else, that is, a transcendent being in human form, which reflects our desire for reaching the 'Other Shore.'[18]

In a later writing, *Itaria koji junrei* (1950), a record of his trip to Italy in 1927–1928, an Italian version of *Koji junrei* in spirit, Watsuji observed how the Greek spirit was embodied in Roman art and architecture with various degrees of success. Similarly, in *Fūdo*, he remarked that Japanese gardens were painstakingly maintained to look natural and represented idealized forms of nature that captured its essence, just as a Greek sculpture embodied the essence of man.[19] Watsuji was also excited to find that Greco-Roman temples there exuded the same dignity as Tōshōdaiji, and concluded that the Greeks were geniuses in art.[20] Watsuji's leaning to classicism was influenced, by his own admission, by the works of Goethe and Schiller, which looked to Italy and Greece for inspiration. Moreover, Watsuji considered himself a student of Goethe.[21] Watsuji may well have composed *Koji junrei* and *Itaria koji junrei* in the same spirit as Goethe's *Italian Journey* (1786–1788), written 130 years earlier during Goethe's sojourn to his spiritual home in Italy. Watsuji was accordingly very much attracted to Greece and its cultural descendent Italy.

The writer Hori Tatsuo (1904–1953) and the poet Aizu Yaichi (1881–1956), both contemporaries of Watsuji, also testified to the privileged place Greece held in their hearts. Hori wrote intensely self-conscious *zuihitsu* accounts of a trip to Nara in a diary style in 1943, which were compiled with other essays and published as *Yamatoji Shinanoji*. In this book, he makes numerous references to Greece—he tried to find inspirations from Nara sceneries and Greek tragedies, for example. He described the Miroku bodhisattva of Chūgūji as having an "archaic smile." Later in the same trip, he visited Tōshōdaiji and wrote:

> Now, the autumn sun is shining brightly on the Golden Hall and the Lecture Hall. Pine trees cast their shadows crisply on the tile roofs and the round pillars, of which their vermillion paint had faded gray. The trees sway in the breeze; it is the perfection of bracing freshness. This place is our *Greece*—That's right, if you ever tire of worrying about little things in the world, come to this place, anytime, even for a half a day.[22]

He acknowledged that Nara was Japan's Greece, that is, Nara is the origin of Japanese culture. Then he trekked to Tōshōdaiji and remarked:

> I thought I had enough for today and it was time to leave. But, feeling that perhaps I'd be allowed the last, little capriciousness, I approached a round pillar. I ran my hand over the pillar trying to get a good feel of the entasis in the mid-section of the pillar. I stopped my hand and pressed it hard against the pillar. Curiously my heart thumped. When I felt it with the hand, the pillar was still warm, warmer than the cool of the ending day. Faintly warm. It seemed that the warmth of the sun that seeped into the depth of the pillar must not have disappeared.[23]

The palpitations he felt were the sense of comfort in coming home by way of Greece. In both places, the phrases 'archaic smile' and 'entasis' clue us in to the degree to which the idea of Greece had precipitated in his mind.

The writer-poet Aizu Yaichi created poems about the faraway past, which were not only about his beloved ancient Nara, but also about the land of Greece. Aizu was born in Niigata, a prefecture that faces the Japan Sea and is known for gray skies and heavy snow in winter. These characteristics made him long for a warmer, sunnier place, like Nara, where oranges could grow.[24] Aizu's predilection for ancient Japan and Greece began early. He took a class from Lafcadio Hearn (1850–1904), who had a leaning toward Greece, and wrote a thesis on John Keats, who professed love for Greece, to graduate from Waseda University. Aizu, too, held an unabashed admiration for Goethe; in a letter he wrote to a friend, he remarked, "Goethe! The greatest soul that ever existed!" In another letter, he told the same friend about a small plaster bust of

Goethe he had placed on a rotating bookcase and lamented how infrequent it became to read names like Goethe, Homer, and Dante in literature.[25] This admiration was based on what Goethe meant to Aizu: the love of humanistic learning in Greece. In 1920, Aizu founded the *Nihon Girisha Gakkai* (Japan Greece Association) and became its inaugural president. He dissolved the group three years later to establish an association to study Nara, an event which brought the Greece-Nara connection in his mind to the fore. During his many trips to Nara, he composed a number of *Man'yōshū*-inspired *waka*, which became a major part of *Rokumeishū* (1940), where Aizu clearly juxtaposes Japanese Greek imagery.[26] One of the best-known *waka* written during his trip to Nara is:

Ōtera no	The round pillars of this great Tōshōdaiji
maroki hashira no tsukikage o	cast a shadow in the moonlight
tsuchi ni fumitsutsu	I think of the faraway past
mono o koso omoe	as I walk treading on the shadows

Here the poetic imagery of Tōshōdaiji is set side by side with that of the Parthenon in Athens.[27] The parallelism Aizu draws between Japan and Greece emerges clearly in the comparison of the dilapidated ancient temple and Greek ruins, the entasis, the synonymy of Nara to ancient Greece, and the long shadows of columns that surely reminded him of Goethe's stroll in Rome in the moonlight.[28] When stepping back from this poem and examining Aizu's entire poetic output in broad perspective, one cannot help but be struck by the prominence of Greek culture in it.

In Japanese intellectuals' quest for Japan's rightful place in world civilization, a spiritual underpinning was important to legitimatize Japan in the world. In addition to comfortable modern living conditions and benefiting from technology on par with the West, these intellectuals felt the need for ideological bedrock on which to build the nation—love of knowledge and broad humanistic learning, which are professed clearly in their admiration of Greek culture.[29] The idea of Greece, initially a curious idea about Japan's early Buddhist art, turned out to serve nationalism. Then in the Taishō and Shōwa eras, it nourished the souls of intellectuals.

THE NATURE OF AESTHETIC EXPERIENCE

This discourse on Greece can be seen as enhancing Japan's prestige but it may not be clear what role it played in the service of aesthetic experience. How did it affect the enjoyment of art? Recent scholarship on the nature of aesthetic experience seems to be divided into two main strains of thought: externalism and internalism. Externalism holds that objects possess independent, external properties that give rise to aesthetic experience in us, along the line of artistic formalism. But this idea requires that external properties somehow be "correctly" perceived to invoke aesthetic experience, and it is not clear how a property is correctly perceived. The competing idea is that aesthetic experience is phenomenologically linked to the external properties of the object. This line of thought accounts for the possibility that two perceivers have distinct aesthetic experiences of the same work of art. The aesthetician Monroe Beardsley contended that the common features of all aesthetic experiences could be teased out so that an aesthetic experience could be, in a way, quantified, but such a proposal, if true, would make it possible for two different experiences to result in an identical aesthetic experience, clearly an unsavory consequence.[30]

Which is a better account? Neither proposal is easily determinable, but we can say this: for anyone to recognize anything—whether the source exists independently of our perception or not—he must do so through perception. Thus, instead of asking what aesthetic experience is, we can perhaps be more productive if we ask how it behaves.

It seems plausible that an object is more meaningful to the viewer if he perceives it as possessing meaningful, important attributes, and that the quality and quantity of such attributes determine the impact of the object. Attributes may consist of formal characteristics, such as line, color, and composition, but they can also include the perceiver's knowledge of an object's historical context, rarity, and provenance, as well as his physical and social surroundings. Indeed, an object's connection to Hellenism is part of these attributes. For example, a collector would be unlikely to drool over a box of pencils in an estate sale until he finds out they were once held in the hands of Frank Lloyd Wright. The pencils' association with the architect adds value to them. We also know that an accidental occurrence, such as a burn pattern on a piece of toast, can become intensely meaningful if seen as an image of Jesus Christ. Aesthetic pleasure arises from these attributes. In other words, the object's meaningfulness, including aesthetic pleasure, is proportionate to the intensity of experience or the amount of importance associated with the object.[31] The aesthetic analogue to pareidolia is to say that the evocation and intensity of aesthetic experience is association-based, personal, and outside of the realm of reason. The intensity increases depending on the amount of favorable, associated meaningfulness the perceiver holds. The aesthetic impact of a Buddhist statue increases if it invokes in the viewer a great deal of favorable associations, whether they be about the maker, the time period of production, its role in society, the stories associated with it, the curative power when prayed to, and, indeed, the idea that it might even embody Greek influence.[32]

In conclusion, we may say that comparing early Japan to Greece served to strengthen Japan's cultural place in world civilization by arguing that the nascent nation and Greece were cut from the same spiritual cloth. In relation to aesthetic experience, the ruminations of Watsuji, Hori, Aizu, and others on the Japanese race, geography, cultural origin, Hellenism, and Nara added deep, meaningful associations to works of art. In all these discourses, these authors, and vicariously their readers, can be said to have derived heightened aesthetic enjoyment from art objects by being engaged in this collective act of imagination.

NOTES

1. Kanbayashi Tsunemichi, *Bigaku kotohajime* (Tokyo: Keisō shobō, 2002), 12, 29.

2. Ernest Fenollosa, *Epochs of Chinese and Japanese Art* (New York: ICG Muse, 1912), 51.

3. Ibid., 73–94.

4. Ernest Fenollosa, "Bijutsu shinsetsu," in *Fenorōsa bijutsu ronshū*, ed. Yamaguchi Seiichi (Tokyo: Chūōkōronshuppan, 1988), 27.

5. Okakura Kakuzō, "Nara bijutsu kenkyū no hitsuyō," in *Okakura Tenshin zenshū* (*OTZ*) (Tokyo: Heibonsha, 1979), 3:320.

6. Okakura Kakuzō, "Chūgoku Nihon bijutsubu no genjō to shōrai," in *OTZ*, 2:252. See also "Nihon bijutsushi," in *OTZ*, 3:168–78. The idea of an easterly progression of Greek art also made its way into some Westerners' understanding of Japanese art. Writing in 1905 after he had traveled to Japan, the influential American architect Ralph Adams Cram (1863–1942) praised Japanese architecture and strongly supported the Greek idea. See *Impressions of Japanese Architecture and the Allied Arts* (New York: Baker & Taylor, 1906), 79, 81, 136. In a similar vein, the English designer Christopher Dresser (1834–1904) made numerous comparisons of Japanese craft to those in other parts of the world, including Greece, but his effort was not to situate Japan as the eastern terminus of Hellenism. He noted that some objects in the Shōsōin at Tōdaiji appeared to have come from Persia. See Dresser, *Japan: Its Architecture, Art, and Art Manufactures* (London: Longmans, Green, & Co., 1882).

7. Fenollosa, *Epochs*, 73.

8. Itō Chūta, "Hōryūji kenchikuron," *Kenchikugaku zasshi* 83 (1893): 317–50. The transcript of the question and answer session immediately after Itō's talk shows that his theory was received with some skepticism.

9. Shiga Shigetaka, *Nihon fūkeiron* (Tokyo: Seikyōsha, 1895), 112–13. A geographer and statesman, Shiga was very influential in Meiji Japan. In fact, this book was reissued thirteen times in the span of eight years and had the largest number of books printed, second only to Fukuzawa Yukichi's writing. See Irokawa Daikichi, ed., *Okakura Tenshin, Shiga Shigetaka*, vol. 39 of *Nihon no meicho* (Tokyo: Chūō kōronsha, 1970), 57. In addition, Shiga's geography textbook, *Chirigakukōgi* (*Lectures in Geography*), was adopted as an official middle school textbook. By 1894, six editions had been issued.

10. Uchimura Kanzō, *Chijinron* (Tokyo: Keiseisha, 1897), 226. Shiga and Uchimura contributed to the prevailing wave of interest in Japan's geography. For example, an influential writer Kojima Usui (1873–1948), hailed as Japan's father of mountaineering along with Walter Weston (1861–1940), encouraged readers to look at the physical features of Japanese mountains and introduced many famous mountains around the world, although he never made references to Greece.

11. "Datsuaron," an 1885 *Jijishinpō* article attributed to the Meiji statesman Fukuzawa Yukichi (1835–1901), is an early example of such a view. This line of thinking continued in many permutations through the years leading to World War II.

12. Along this line, historian Kume Kunitake (1839–1931) speculated that Prince Shōtoku might have a similar birth myth as Jesus, in that the prince was conceived miraculously and was born in a horse stable. See *Jōgū Taishi jitsuroku* (Tokyo: Seiretsudō, 1905). Educator and Christian minister Oyabe Zen'ichirō (1868–1941) proposed in 1924 that Genghis Khan was the same person as Minamoto no Yoshitsune and that the Japanese (not to mention the Imperial Family) and the Jews shared the same ethnic roots (the Japanese were one of the ten lost tribes of Israel). The proposals were published in *Nippon oyobi Nippon kokumin no kigen* (Tokyo: Kōseikaku, 1929), which became a bestseller. Oyabe was not the originator of the Genghis Khan theory; in one theory, the Confucian scholar Hayashi Razan (1583–1657), and in another, the German geographer Philipp Franz von Siebold (1796–1866), was responsible for this idea. Historian Kimura Takatarō (1870–1931) claimed that Japan was the source of all world civilizations in *Kaiyō torai Nihon shi* (Tokyo: Hakubunkan, 1911–1912), reprinted in 1981 by Sheru shuppan, Tokyo. These scholars may have been considered to be outside of the mainstream but their works spoke to the amount of effort that went into making the Japanese more Western.

13. Taguchi Ukichi, *Ha-Ōkaron* (Tokyo: Keizaizasshisha, 1903), 2.

14. Takekoshi Yosaburō, *Nisen gohyakunen-shi* (Tokyo: Keiseisha shoten, 1896), 1–4.

15. Kuroiwa Ruikō, "Ono no Komachi ron," in *Kuroiwa Ruikō-shū* (Tokyo: Chikuma shobō, 1971), 255. Originally published in 1913.

16. Watsuji's interest in Greece was much more than skin-deep; in collaboration with classicist Tanaka Hidenaka (1886–1974), Watsuji translated Samuel H. Butcher's *Some Aspects of the Greek Genius* (London: McMillan, 1891) into Japanese in 1923. This work might have been instrumental in introducing Greek humanism to the Japanese people.

17. Watsuji Tetsurō, *Koji junrei* (Tokyo: Iwanami Shoten, 1919). The original is now available from Aozora Bunko at http://www.aozora.gr.jp/. See the English translation in *Pilgrimages to the Ancient Temples in Nara*, trans. Hiroshi Nara (Portland, ME: MerwinAsia, 2012).

18. Watsuji, *Koji junrei*, 114. Art historian Yashiro Yukio (1890–1975) questioned the wisdom of comparing Japanese Buddhist statues to Greek sculptures, stating that Greek sculptures were idealized human forms, whereas Japanese Buddhist statues were idols for worshiping. In his 1978 book, Yashiro reflected on the process of Japanese becoming interested in viewing Buddhist sculptures as objects of appreciation starting in the 1920s and this attitude's relation to the idea of Greece. He recalled

that Kojima Kikuo (1887–1950), Watsuji Tetsurō, Hara Zen'ichirō (1892–1937), and others adored Greek art and became excited about starting a "Japanese renaissance" like the Italian Renaissance. Such an episode characterizes the effervescent intellectual scene during Taishō and the interest in Greek culture. See Yashiro Yukio, *Nihon bijutsu no saikentō* (Tokyo: Shinchōsha, 1978), *inter alia* 55–71. Reprinted in 1994 by Perikansha, Tokyo.

19. Watsuji Tetsurō, *Fūdo*, in *Watsuji Tetsurō zenshū* (Tokyo: Iwanami Shoten, 1961), 8:184–96.

20. Watsuji, *Koji junrei*, 144, 158.

21. In *Koji junrei*, Watsuji was very clear about how he felt about Johann Wolfgang von Goethe. He wrote, "Think of Goethe, who was extremely endowed with talent, I thought to myself. Even he regretted the fact that, when he traveled to Italy, he felt that he had not spent the necessary time to perfect his craft and that he hadn't taken the time to acquire the necessary skills for it" (31). Watsuji owned a number of Goethe's books as well as those by Gotthold Ephraim Lessing and Johann Joachim Winckelmann in his personal library.

22. Hori Tatsuo, *Yamatoji Shinanoji* (Tokyo: Shinchō bunko, 1955), 343.

23. Ibid., 351.

24. See Hasegawa Masaharu and Izumi Hisako, *Umi yama no aida: Rokumeishū* (Tokyo: Meiji shoin, 2005). Aizu found the same longing for a warmer sunny country in Goethe's poem about Mignon in *Wilhelm Meister's Apprenticeship*.

25. Hasegawa and Izumi, 328–29.

26. For an English translation and commentaries on *Rokumeishū*, see Michael F. Marra, *A Poetic Guide to an Ancient Capital: Aizu Yaichi and the City of Nara* (Baltimore, MD: Modern English Tanka Press, 2009).

27. Aizu himself confesses to this connection in *Konsai zuihitsu*. See Marra, 102.

28. See Johann Wolfgang von Goethe, *Italian Journey: 1786–1788,* trans. W. H. Auden and Elizabeth Mayer (New York: Schoken Books, 1968), 156–57. Clearly conscious of Goethe, Watsuji recorded a similar experience when he walked through the South Gate of Tōdaiji in *The Pilgrimages to the Ancient Temples in Nara* (157).

29. Many intellectuals of the day thought that the intellectual orientations of England and the United States were too pragmatic and felt more kinship to German and French ideas. Related to this idea, the incalculable influence that Raphael von Koeber (1848–1923) exerted should be mentioned. Von Koeber came as a foreign expert in 1893 and remained on the philosophy faculty of Tokyo Imperial University until 1914. During this time, he educated many future leaders of Japan, who then defined the Japanese intellectual life in late Meiji and Taishō eras. Von Koeber encouraged classical languages and cultivated in his students a love for wide humanistic studies. "He was most like a Greek philosopher," wrote Watsuji Tetsurō of Von Koeber, summarizing his impact. See "Professor Koeber," in *Watsuji Tetsurō zenshū*, 6:1–39.

30. Monroe Beardsley, *Aesthetics* (Indianapolis, IN: Hackett, 1958).

31. See John Dewey, *Art and Experience* (New York: Putnam, 1934) and Beardsley, *Aesthetics* for such an attempt to give a philosophical precision to the distinction between aesthetic and nonaesthetic experience.

32. This position can also answer the question about the role of culture in aesthetic experience. We may say that a common or similar aesthetic experience can occur across a society in which the people possess more or less a shared set of aesthetic standards (e.g., associations), acquired implicitly or explicitly. Many Japanese today find beauty in "deformed, rough-edged ceramic bowls" or in other daily, utilitarian objects, while Americans generally do not. The Japanese seem, therefore, culturally more accustomed to attaching aesthetic meaningfulness to a wider range of objects, while a typical American would more often limit it to the fine arts. See also Donald Keene, "Japanese Aesthetics," *Philosophy East and West* 19, no. 3 (1969): 293–306; reprinted in *Japanese Aesthetics and Culture: A Reader*, ed. Nancy G. Hume (Albany, NY: State University of New York Press, 1995), 27–41.

Chapter 12

Yashiro Yukio and the Aesthetics of Japanese Art History

J. Thomas Rimer

The creative life experience, scholarship, and museum work of Yashiro Yukio (1890–1975) remain central to any historical account of the development of the field of art history in twentieth-century Japan.[1] In addition to his important research and writings on both Western and Asian art, two institutions in Japan owe their present importance to his early leadership: the Tokyo National Institute of Cultural Properties, founded in 1930 under a slightly different name, and the Yamato Bunkakan, an important museum for the traditional Japanese arts founded in 1960.

Yashiro began his professional career as a student and scholar of Western art history. When he returned to Japan after the Tokyo earthquake in 1923, much of his subsequent research came to involve the study of Japanese and Chinese art. Yashiro's ability to address art-historical issues related to both Europe and Japan made him a unique figure during his time. In this chapter, I would like to examine how certain of his views on what might be termed 'the aesthetics of art history' came to influence the attitudes expressed in his important *2000 Years of Japanese Art*, published in 1958.

A number of Yashiro's cosmopolitan attitudes came about because of his upbringing and early training, which are described in some detail in his revealing and entertaining memoir, *Watakushi no bijutsu henreki* (*My Artistic Pilgrimage*), written when he was 73. In this account, he articulates with some wit and insight his intellectual and artistic adventures as he discovers the ways in which one set of cultural values can fruitfully engage with another.

Born in Yokohama, Yashiro had the opportunity to study and speak English as a child. This gave him what he calls 'an overwhelming sense of curiosity about the world.' "My attitudes about the universality of art are thus normal, as I look back on Japan from a world view."[2] He then compares his views to those of his occasional mentor, the famous art scholar Okakura Tenshin (1862–1913), who also came from a similarly cosmopolitan atmosphere in Yokohama.[3]

These early experiences and his skills in the English language helped put him in touch with Hara Sankei (1868–1941), a wealthy Yokohama industrialist whose villa, the Sankeien, housed an impressive collection of Japanese art, including modern *nihonga* paintings by such highly appreciated artists as Yokohama Taikan, Maeda Seison, and Imamura Shikō. Hara's collection attracted a series of important foreign dignitaries as well. Charles Lang Freer, the American industrialist, was an early visitor, and Yashiro was chosen to spend the summer at the villa in 1916 in order to serve as an interpreter for the famous Indian poet Rabindranath Tagore during his visit to Japan. Yashiro's contacts with Hara remained important until Hara's death in 1939. All of these events are well described in the early chapters of Yashiro's memoir.

Yashiro had some interest in becoming an artist himself, experimenting with watercolor and other media. He might well have chosen to become an artist, and his early understanding of the process by which art is created helped to form his thinking about art throughout his subsequent career. He soon made the decision, however, to enter the field of Western art history.

After Yashiro's eventual appointment as a professor at the Tokyo School of Fine Arts, the young professor was able to make his first trip to Europe in 1921, first to London, then to Florence, where he worked with Bernard Berenson (1865–1959), the well-known American scholar of Renaissance art. This important encounter is well described in chapter 7 of Yashiro's memoir. Yashiro's research with his mentor led to the publication of his first major work, *Sandro Botticelli*, written in English and published in London by the Medici Society in 1925. The study is still considered an important piece of research on the work of this Renaissance painter.

Certain attitudes toward the relationship between art and spectator emerge in this first English-language work of Yashiro, and they were to continue to remain important to him throughout his life. A brief articulation of those convictions can be most easily found in his retrospective account of his early encounter with Renaissance art in his 1952 article "The 'Oriental' Character in Italian Tre- and Quattrocento Paintings."[4] Looking back on his first encounter with Italian art, he writes:

> [A]t that time, coming from the distant seas in the East as a young art student and wandering into the Uffizi Gallery, I was almost taken aback by the art of Botticelli and others, which immediately went deep into my heart and which seemed so near to my sense of beauty, that it seemed as if these paintings were painted for me, and for no one else.[5]

In reflecting on this early experience, he asks how this identification came about. "According to my idea, that is because in the Early Renaissance Painting there is something which causes an irrepressible resonance in my inmost heart. In other words, because there is what I may call an 'Oriental' character contained in it."[6] The article continues on to take up a number of topics, including possible attitudes and cultural similarities between Italy and Japan, but the point I would like to call attention to here is Yashiro's firm conviction that, for him, the authentic study of any work of art must stem from a strong sense of identification with the work of art by the viewer (in this case, the scholar or critic). This conception has a lengthy pedigree in Japan, as we will see. Yashiro's convictions were to give his own art-historical investigations an unusual dimension, and one quite different from the kind of exceptionalist views many Japanese during this period adopted in their attempt to define the nature of their culture within (or against) the larger context of the modern world. Hiroshi Nara discusses some of these same issues in chapter 11, "The Idea of Greece in Modern Japan's Cultural Dreams," in his contribution to this book.

Perhaps the most accessible place for English-speaking readers to encounter Yashiro's mature ideas can be found in his *2000 Years of Japanese Art*, published in 1958 by Thames and Hudson in London and H. N. Abrams in New York. The book may well have grown out of the contributions he made to an important exhibition of Japanese painting and sculpture that toured the United States in 1953, an effort, Yashiro wrote in his memoir, that he had hoped would help heal the scars of war by showing some of the historical accomplishments of traditional Japanese sculpture. Yashiro is listed in the catalogue as one of the sponsors, and some points raised in the brief text (which lists no author) suggest his perspective.

While the manuscript was being completed, Yashiro was apparently ill and so some of the editing fell to Peter Swann, the British art scholar, who remarks in his brief Editor's Foreword that "in editing Professor Yashiro's text, I have tried to remain as faithful as possible to his original meanings. His assistance and his most kind confidence in my discretion have greatly eased what is always difficult and can be a dangerous task." Whatever editing strategies were employed, Yashiro's convictions and predilections come across with clarity.

Yashiro dedicates his study to Bernard Berenson, "who in my youth guided me through my Italian studies, opening for me the door to Western art, and whose inspiration has illuminated and enriched my work in Eastern fields." Even in this brief dedication, Yashiro looks both ways. Yashiro's book is arguably the first large-scale historical treatment of its kind since the publication in 1900 (originally in French, later in Japanese and English) of *L'Histoire de l'art du Japon*, supervised by Okakura Tenshin and prepared in connection with the works shown in the Japanese pavilion at the Paris World Exposition of 1900.[7]

Examining Yashiro's own Introduction, entitled 'Japanese Art as Art,' one readily sees a number of his guiding intellectual principles. First, the art of Japan is part of world art and should not be viewed as exceptional or idiosyncratic. Thus, Yashiro stresses parallels and similarities between Japanese and Western art and, occasionally, between Japanese and Chinese art, rather than emphasizing differences. Second, making use of imaginative comparisons among works of art from Japan, the West, and China is a legitimate intellectual undertaking. Third, the assertion of basic aesthetic categories such as lyricism and realism can be applied with equal validity when examining artworks, whatever their cultural provenance. He writes eloquently of his conviction that

> inquiries into the historical and linguistic backgrounds are only means to an end—which is the true knowledge of art. We must realize that, if we base our appreciation of all art on an assessment of its fundamental quality of beauty, then there should be no difference between East and West.[8]

Yashiro then reminds his readers that

> [u]nfortunately, Japanese art has shared the custom of being regarded as the exclusive domain of specialists. In all fairness, it must be admitted that Japanese scholars themselves have encouraged this misconception by stressing what is unusual in our art, i.e. the peculiarities resulting from our historical background.

Yashiro takes particular exception to the Western fascination with woodblock prints, which for him represent "an abnormal manifestation of Japanese art and to dwell exclusively on it can give a false idea of the centuries of art which lie behind it."[9]

Ultimately, for Yashiro, based on his early experience with Botticelli, the proper study of art history must arise from a personal encounter between a given work of art and the viewer, who is genuinely moved by what he or she observes:

> In its essence the study of art ought to be based on the direct impression a work creates and the enthusiasms it arouses … . Long years of study have taught me how precious are the moments of first impression and how vital it is to try to keep them alive in the absorbing intellectual interests which research into the background of works of art provides … . Works of art were not made for art historians—they were created for the enjoyment, and sometimes for the salvation, of ordinary people. The vital quality required of a lover of art is that he possesses sensibility and an awareness and love of beauty.[10]

A close reading of Yashiro's text reveals the particulars of these strategies at work. Throughout, his conviction remains strong that Japan's art is, in the end, simply one particular cultural example of the larger goals of authentic artistic expression around the world. Not surprisingly, on the last page of his book, he writes:

> As modern communications shrink the world and modern forms of industrial-ization bring the Japanese closer to the West, so our architecture, clothes, and even the food we eat become more Western. The Japanese approach to art is being internationalized, whether we like it or not.[11]

In one sense, therefore, he is extending backwards in time this sense of Japan's present existence within a worldwide artistic milieu in order to show that Japanese art has always, in some fashion or other, belonged to that larger world. And it is perhaps for similar reasons that he has chosen to discuss neither woodblock prints nor modern oil paintings (*yōga*), two areas, ironically, to which Western sensibilities can most quickly relate. Rather, he seeks to reveal certain unexpected affinities that lay further afield from more familiar Western traditions.

In adopting this general strategy, Yashiro often makes comparisons between Japanese and Western art in the course of his analysis of the arts of Japan of various periods. (He also makes a number of cogent comments about the artistic connections between Chinese and Japanese art, but these are more directly historical and thus not so unusual.) These comparisons with Western art may sometimes strike the reader as surprising, even naïve or fanciful. Still, it is well to remember that among Japanese scholars of art history during this period, Yashiro was virtually unique because of his training in the history of both Asian and Western art and because of his high level of connoisseurship. His comparisons seem both to be based on immediate and intuitive responses to the works of art that he is in the process of observing and directly to express his enthusiasms and affinities.

Here are some examples, chosen more or less at random. In discussing an early work of bronze sculpture, an Asuka-period Buddhist Miroku figure in the collection in the Tokyo National Museum that he dates to 606 CE (plate 10), Yashiro writes of such images thus:

> In their concern for purity and holiness of spirit ... [i]n type and expression they may recall to Western readers the goddesses and maidens from the Acropolis in Athens which date to the sixth century B.C. They also remind one of some products of the Romanesque and Early Gothic periods, in particular the tall figures of saints at the entrance to Chartres Cathedral. (37)

Yashiro categorizes Shintō images of worship such as the Goddess Nakatsuhime at the Yakushiji in Nara (plate 36) as "a type of portraiture," and he continues on to indicate that, in his view, "in all Japanese portraits, either in painting or sculpture, there is certainly some desire for realistic representation, which, of course, is indispensable, but Japanese artists always felt the need for idealistic or symbolic forms." "Buddhist images," he elaborates, "produced many fine portraits representing the saints and founders of the various sects. The impulse to create images for religious purposes must have been similar to those which produced the figures of St. Peter or St. Francis in Catholic art. However, the tendency towards idealization was much stronger in the Japanese images than in Western religious art" (134).

Some of Yashiro's comparisons skip lightly over time and space. In discussing medieval picture scrolls (*emakimono*), for example, he reminds his readers that this art form "depends for its success on an art of fluid movement and it requires that the spectator shall be prepared to participate actively in his viewing of it," remarking that these qualities have brought critics "to see in them the forerunner of the technique of the cinema" (161).

In discussing *nanban* painting of the late 1500s, created during the period in which Christian Catholic missionaries were active in Japan, Yashiro's remarks reveal his bold penchant for making active comparisons in the comparative history of art.

> The first Western nation to have important relations with Japan was Spain and Spanish Baroque art of the sixteenth century with its vivid colours and strong contrasts of tone, was the first European influence to reach these shores. The Baroque spirit met with a welcome response in the heroic atmosphere of the Momoyama and strengthened the grandiose character of the art of the age. (209)

What Yashiro terms the 'overwhelming brilliance and vast scale' of the castle art of the powerful feudal lords, in his view, owes much to direct European inspiration.

In the art of the Tokugawa period, *ukiyo* painting brings comparison with Henri de Toulouse-Lautrec, and in the work of Maruyama Ōkyo, Yashiro singles out important influences both from realistic imported Chinese painting styles and from European copperplate engravings and medical books. Ike no Taiga's eighteenth-century ink paintings suggest nineteenth-century European *pointillism* techniques, and Taiga's technique of piling up of cube-like areas of ink are "reminiscent of Cézanne."

Yashiro is one of the first authors writing in English to deal with the new varieties of Japanese art created since the beginning of the Meiji period in 1868. As I remarked earlier, he does not take up the subject of *yōga* (modern Western-style oil paintings), although he does indicate his belief that "modern Japan has fully assimilated oil painting, recognizing it to be one of the most suitable vehicles for the expression of native ideas" (261), and he does discuss in some detail *nihonga* (modern Japanese-style paintings) including black-and-white and color plates of works by such iconic artists as Hishida Shunsō, Kano Hōgai, Shimomura Kanzan, Yokoyama Taikan, Takeuchi Seihō, and Tomioka Tessai, many of whom were admired by Yashiro's early patron, Hara Sankei. And Yashiro is quick to mention the fact that Rabindranath Tagore, for whom he served as interpreter and whom he very much admired, was so impressed with a work by Kanzan that he had a copy made to take back with him to India.

In the end, Yashiro's highly personal and intuitive approach to Japanese art history may strike contemporary readers as idiosyncratic and "unscientific." It might be said, by the same token, that his privileging of the primacy of a personal authentic response reflects one important component that parallels attitudes important in traditional Japanese aesthetics. I would go so far as to say that such historical precedents, although to my knowledge never explicitly articulated or discussed by Yashiro, form one basis for his method of making his artistic judgments.

These traditional aesthetic principles have been applied over the centuries to a variety of art forms, including, of course, the visual arts, but the clearest statements concerning the development and continuing prevalence of these attitudes occur in the area of traditional poetics.

Perhaps the earliest statement of these principles, at least in nascent form, and one of the most famous, can be found in the celebrated Preface to the *Kokinshū (Collection of Old and Modern Poetry)*, the first court anthology of *waka* (31-syllable poems) compiled about 920 CE. Here, the author of the Preface, Ki no Tsurayuki (871?–945?), attempts to define and justify the art of Japanese poetry (in contradistinction to Chinese poetry, widely read and studied at the time). Whole aesthetic theories were later constructed on the basis of his opening sentences:

> Japanese poetry has the human heart as seed and myriads of words as leaves.
> It comes into being when men use the seen and heard to give voice to feelings
> aroused by the innumerable events in their lives.[12]

The basic mechanism suggested here posits the artist (poet, painter, musician) responding to the environment (usually nature, but occasionally a work of art) that surrounds him or her through the creation of a new work of art based on his or her most personal level of response. The primacy of such an intuitive response thus makes a distinction between the techniques necessary for the composition of poetry in Chinese (somewhat analogous to the use of Latin in medieval Europe), which privileges learning over spontaneity. The personal emotional response of the artist thus becomes the direct conduit from what is observed to what is created. Such a process is deemed to be authentic precisely *because* it is uniquely personal. Thus, many of those early Japanese writings we now often categorize as dealing with "aesthetics" are in fact manuals created to increase both the sensitivity of the putative artist and his or her skill in creating an artistic product (poem, painting, musical composition) that can best render that moment of authentic response.

The majority of the early treatises that survive concern the art of poetry. In the great Heian prose narrative of the Heian period, the *Genji monogatari* (*The Tale of Genji*), however, the author, Murasaki Shikibu, includes a lengthy section thought to capture with effectiveness both the creative and social functions of the visual arts during the period. The passage is far too long to cite here; briefly, it concerns a friendly "contest" between two groups of amateur painters. Genji, the protagonist of the tale, has been in exile, where he painted a number of scrolls of the wild scenic spots he witnessed during this period. He has now returned to the court in triumph. At the end of the contest, with the winner still undecided, he now submits these works and so easily wins the day. In response to his victory, he explains himself as follows:

> Then there was painting. I was the merest dabbler, and yet there were times when I felt a strange urge to do something really good. Then came my years in the provinces and leisure to examine that remarkable seacoast. All that was wanting was the power to express what I saw and felt, and that is why I kept my inadequate efforts from you until now.[13]

The aesthetic mechanism suggested here is an elaboration of the same one expressed in the Preface to the *Kokinshū*. The artist responds to an external stimulus (in both these cases directly from nature) and as a result creates a work of art to which the spectator, whose sensitivities are equally well defined and developed, is thus able to respond in an authentic fashion.

It is important to note the unspoken assumption that both artist and spectator must possess refined and sophisticated tastes. The aesthetics of the art of the Heian period set the tone for the arts in Japan all the way down to the Tokugawa period, the period between 1603 and 1868 in the history of Japan. After 1600, the newly-moneyed merchant class, in their desire to partake in the older and more aristocratic traditions of Japanese culture, began an attempt to participate as well by learning at least simplified versions of the products of high culture. Thus, a simpler form of the traditional 31-syllable *waka* poetry, the 17-syllable *haiku*, developed, the somewhat flamboyant *kabuki* theatre challenged the austere medieval *nō,* and such plebian art forms as the woodblock print (distained by Yashiro) came into prominence. Nevertheless, the same attitudes continued. For example, the great master of *haiku*, Matsuo Bashō (1644–1694), indicated to his disciples his thoughts on the composition of poetry. Among the most striking is the following, taken down by one of his students:

When the Master said "As for the pine, learn from the pine; as for the bamboo, learn from the bamboo," he meant casting aside personal desire or intention. Those who interpret this "learning" in their own way end up never learning. The phrase 'learn' means to enter into the object, to be emotionally moved by the essence that emerges from that object, and for that movement to become verse. Even if one clearly expresses the object, if the emotion does not emerge from the object naturally, the object and the self will be divided, and the emotion will not achieve poetic truth. The effect will be the verbal artifice that results from personal desire.[14]

To reduce a thousand years of aesthetic tradition to a few pages, as I have attempted to do here, can only result in a crude parody of a long and complex tradition. Nevertheless, I do believe that the mechanism of transfer to the spectator of the depth of the artist's original response to his material does remain a constant aesthetic mechanism from one period to the next. And Yashiro, who insists that "the study of art ought to be based on the direct impression a work creates and the enthusiasm it arouses,"[15] indeed seems to reaffirm these classical aesthetic proclivities when he privileges his own intuitive responses to both Western and Asian works of art as he makes them the basis for scholarly analysis. In his case, the response is to art rather than to nature, but the principles involved are virtually the same.

Within the framework of traditional Japanese aesthetics, this kind of sup- posedly "intuitive response" is created or channeled within certain boundar- ies of both taste and knowledge. The opening section of the Preface to the *Kokinshū*, for example, continues on after the opening statement quoted above to suggest the kinds of emotional transfer that art (poetry, in this case) can evoke: "It is song that moves heaven and earth without effort, stirs emo- tions in the invisible spirits and gods, brings harmony to the relations between men and women, and calms the hearts of fierce warriors."[16] As these artistic traditions developed, such emotional responses began to be characterized as those which can create in the reader or viewer a sense of what came to be called *mono no aware*, literally, the "ahness of things," a sense of wonder and pathos, or, as Donald Keene paraphrases the term, "the moving quali- ties of the sights and experiences of the world."[17] The term took on a lasting importance as an ideal; artists, writers, and musicians sought to create works capable of arousing these feelings in their respective audiences. Perhaps the most explicit and detailed statement that sets out to explain the term can be found in an essay by the great Tokugawa scholar Motoori Norinaga (1730– 1801) concerning *The Tale of Genji,* which was often criticized by Confucian scholars as immoral. For Motoori, a sense of *aware* was created in the readers of *Genji*. He points out with great eloquence that the text dwells not on any moral judgments but "only upon the goodness of those who are aware of the sorrow of human existence." Many of the characters in the *Genji* narrative are portrayed as imperfect, yet "sympathetically kind and ... aware of the sorrow of human existence." Thus, *Genji* "holds these feelings to be the basis of the good man."[18] Such an interpretation therefore suggests that such a genuinely sympathetic response can reveal connections to a deeper truth.

Yashiro's response to art reveals many of the same methods of approach. As cited above, when he wrote that, when visiting the Uffizi Gallery, he was taken aback by the art he witnessed, "which immediately went deep into my heart and which seemed so near to my sense of beauty, that it seemed as if these paintings were painted for me, and for no one else," he is, consciously or unconsciously, employing the same mechanisms of transfer, by which a work of art can stir in the spectator feelings related to the intentions of the artist.

One observes immediately a crucial difference, however: despite his unconscious privileging of this traditional aesthetic mechanism, Yashiro was living in a very different time. The kind of aristocratic attitudes important to Japanese artistic practice through the centuries was considerably dissipated after the inroads made into Japanese culture by the coming of Western artistic and cultural values during and after the Meiji period; indeed, by the time Yashiro took up his studies, it had become possible in Japan to earn an academic degree in Western literature and art. Nevertheless, even in this much more heterogeneous environment, Yashiro's stance suggests his lingering affinities for these older techniques of appreciation.

As I suggested above, the traditional elements of aesthetic appreciation were based on a code of emotional response that was certainly genuine, yet limited by proprieties and precedents determined both by social status and by poetic and other artistic traditions absorbed from one generation to the next. By now these cultural models had more or less disappeared. Yashiro replaced them, it seems to me, by creating for himself a form of personal elitism based both on his own developing sense of taste and on the taste and acumen of mentors such as Hara Sankei, as well as other collectors and artists, both in Japan and in the West, whom he came to respect. Through these experiences, Yashiro came to have gained a sure sense of confidence in his own artistic judgments. With the maturing of his personal taste, and the confidence this engendered in him, he was able to approach individual works of art and feel comfortable with what he took to be his instinctive reaction to them. Yet in fact, these reactions were based on his well-developed sense of artistic propriety, which, while much broader, was not entirely different from that possessed by artists and spectators in preceding periods.

Certainly, on the basis of Yashiro's methods as revealed in the text he composed for *2000 Years of Japanese Art*, his approach seems at a considerable remove from the kind of scholarly writings on art being composed and published in our day. His written style is suggestive, intuitive, and open-ended;

he invites his readers to speculate and ponder on their own affinities with the works he has chosen to discuss. Some might be tempted to dismiss his writing as high-level journalism, more an effort at consciousness-raising than the kind of deductive "scientific scholarship" now often considered important. Nevertheless, when his work is read with sympathy, one cannot help but enjoy being led through the history of Japanese art by a person of such dedication, distinction, and refinement. Yashiro makes the journey a very stimulating one, particularly as he implicitly invites his readers to make their own comparisons with the Japanese artworks he discusses, just as he has done himself. In this offer, there is, in fact, a kind of democratic gesture. Become an enthusiast, he seems to be telling his readers, and see, on the basis of your own experience, what you can make of what you see. In the end, I believe the invitation is an attractive one. At a minimum, Yashiro's writing can serve as a corrective to the kind of art history that is overladen with theory, ideology, or technical detail. He attempts to make connoisseurs out of his readers. Yashiro's scholarship was his art.

NOTES

1. For a concise and useful account of Yashiro's career, see Akira Takagishi, "A Twentieth-Century Dream with a Twenty-First-Century Outlook: Yashiro Yukio, a Japanese Historian of Western Art, and His Conception of Institutions for the Study of East Asian Art," in *Asian Art History in the Twenty-First Century*, ed. Vishakha N. Desai (Williamstown, MA: Sterling and Francine Clark Art Institute, 2007), 138–48.

2. Yashiro Yukio, *Watakushi no bijutsu henreki* (Tokyo: Iwanami Shoten, 1971), 97–98.

3. Okakura Tenshin, the author of *The Book of Tea* (Rutland, VT: Charles E. Tuttle Company, 1956) and other well-known works, had a controversial and colorful career, finishing up as the first Head of the Asian Art Division of the Boston Museum of Fine Arts. Like Yashiro, he often wrote directly in English. His career has been widely discussed in a number of books and articles, too many to list here.

4. Yashiro Yukio, "The 'Oriental' Character in Italian Tre- and Quattrocento Paintings," *East and West* 3, no. 2 (1952): 81–87.

5. Ibid., 81–82.

6. Ibid., 82.

7. For trenchant details about the exhibition and Okakura, see Ellen Conant, ed., *Challenging Past and Present: The Metamorphosis of Nineteenth-Century Japanese Art* (Honolulu: University of Hawai'i Press, 2006), 18. The first comprehensive treatment of the history of Japanese art by a Western scholar was doubtless Robert Treat Paine and Alexander Coburn Soper, *The Art and Architecture of Japan* (Baltimore, MD: Penguin Books, 1955).

8. Yashiro Yukio, *2000 Years of Japanese Art*, ed. Peter C. Swann (New York: Harry N. Abrams, 1958), 17.

9. Ibid., 19.

10. Ibid., 20–21.

11. Ibid, 261.

12. Helen Craig McCullough, trans., *Kokin Wakashū: The First Imperial Anthology of Japanese Poetry* (Stanford, CA: Stanford University Press, 1985), 3.

13. For the entire section on the painting competition, see Murasaki Shikibu, *The Tale of Genji*, trans. Edward G. Seidensticker (New York: Knopf, 1976), 310–16.

14. See Haruo Shirane, *Traces of Dreams: Landscape, Cultural Memory, and the Poetry of Bashō* (New York: Columbia University Press, 1998), 276.

15. Yashiro, *2000 Years*, 20.

16. *Kokin Wakashū*, 3.

17. See various entries in *Anthology of Japanese Literature: From the Earliest Era to the Mid-Nineteenth Century*, ed. Donald Keene (New York: Grove Press, 1955).

18. Ryusaku Tsunoda, Wm. Theodore de Bary, and Donald Keene, eds., *Sources of Japanese Tradition* (New York: Columbia University Press, 1958), 533–34.

Chapter 13

Aestheticizing Sacrifice

Ritual, Education, and Media during the Asia-Pacific War

Akiko Takenaka

On March 26, 1942, 144 fifth and sixth graders from elementary schools throughout Fukushima Prefecture embarked on a seven-hour train ride to Tokyo.[1] A common loss brought these children together: their fathers had all lost their lives while serving in the Japanese military in the Asia-Pacific War.[2] Their purpose was to visit Yasukuni Shrine, the military memorial where it was understood that the spirits of their fathers had been collectively transformed into a god to protect Japan.[3] Upon their return home after four days in Tokyo, the children each wrote about their experiences in the capital city. In their essays, words such as 'excitement' and 'happiness' abound to describe their emotions while "visiting" their fathers.[4] They also wrote of the overwhelming gratitude upon seeing Prime Minister Tōjō Hideki and Emperor Hirohito. But useful for the purpose of this chapter are the expressions of appreciation the children had for their fathers, as well as the goals and aspirations with which many concluded their essays. For example, one boy wrote: "I could not wait to tell [Father] that, because of his achievements, even someone like myself was able to receive such a prize."[5] Another promised to "become as fine a soldier as [his] father," and resolved to "demonstrate [his] devotion to the Emperor."[6] One girl lamented: "Had I been born a male, I could have become a soldier and made as fine an achievement as my father."[7] 'Achievement' in these cases means death at war; to 'become as fine a soldier as [one's] father' implies future war death for the children. Beginning in the summer of 1939, many children who had similarly lost their fathers at war made such government-subsidized trips to Tokyo. Most composed similar essays upon their return home.

This chapter explores the culture of wartime Japan in which children came to express in writing their willingness to die for the nation. I examine rituals practiced in schools and elsewhere, textbooks and other guidebooks

179

instructing teachers and pupils on appropriate behavior, and mass-media representations of such activities. In particular, I examine how the concept of sacrifice was aestheticized through this process. One key strategy prevalent at the time is what I call 'the manufacturing of desire': the process through which mandates enforced from above (i.e., the Japanese state) were repackaged and aestheticized into objects of desire, to be dispensed in response to "requests" that typically included evidence that the requesting entity (whether an individual or an institution) was worthy of receipt. Such requests at the outset of this process were for more or less concrete items such as copies of the imperial portrait, blueprints for local war memorials, or letters of permission to attend events associated with the Imperial Family. But the steps toward proving worthiness and then placing the requests were meant to condition those involved to later desire the ultimate prize: death at war for the sake of the Emperor.

The politicization of aesthetics during the Asia-Pacific War is a topic that has already received scholarly attention. Perhaps the most well-known example is the use of the cherry blossom symbolism to aestheticize war death.[8] Others have pointed out similarities between certain particularities of wartime Japanese culture and broader characteristics of fascist aesthetics.[9] I examine the process through which ritual played a key role in promoting the idea of an honorable military death. By 'ritual,' I mean a variety of repetitive group activities such as recitations of the *banzai* chorus and the *kimigayo* anthem, labor contributions (*kinrō hōshi*), and, to some extent, activities such as composing particular kinds of essays and letters and reading mass-media reports commending sacrifices by imperial subjects. Conceptually, ritual and the unified movements involved constructed a kind of "timeless uniformity" often ascribed to fascist aesthetics.[10]

By 'politicized aesthetics,' I do not mean visual or stylistic qualities in cultural products that have often been discussed in relation to Italy and Germany.[11] Visually or stylistically, an identifiable coherence did not exist in wartime Japan.[12] But in the process of beautifying imperial warfare as a national moral crusade, Japanese society was gradually restructured to fit with certain aestheticizing concepts—those that presented a beautiful nation where people worked in agreement and in unison for a higher cause, where acts of sacrifice including death were considered necessary to achieve this cause, and where people would willingly dedicate their lives for the sake of the nation. The result was what might be called 'a beautiful rationalization of war death.'[13] These sacrifices, which in and of themselves were framed as beautiful, simultaneously provided the crucial labor and resources for the war effort. Ritual produced unity in the sacrificial activities and, at the same time, reinforced positive ideals in the people's minds. The repetitive actions transformed some into believers of the nationally sanctioned narrative, and others into self-censors, capable of performing as loyal imperial subjects.[14] Furthermore, the kinds of visual qualities available through the use of ritual were especially well suited for reproduction through mass media.

KŌKYOMAE HIROBA: RITUAL AND BEAUTIFUL LABOR

Much of the constructed beauty in wartime activities involved group movements in which participants acted in unison. But the visual component is only secondary in importance to the psychological effect of such acts on the participants. Group activities that incorporate simple repetitions allow for easy participation, transforming all involved into active agents of the national effort. Acting in unison reinforces in each individual the idea that they are merely a small, unexceptional part of a larger order. In fact, the *banzai* chorus—the celebration of the longevity of the Emperor—had been invented precisely for this purpose.[15] Spectacles that comprised unified rituals were held for a variety of occasions from war victory celebrations to ceremonies to send off troops to the battlefront, and even funeral rites.

Unified rituals also took place as part of war-related labor contributions (*kinrō hōshi*). As a case in point, consider this example. November 1940 saw a momentous event that brought the entire empire together in celebration: the 2,600th anniversary of the enthronement of the mythical first emperor Jimmu.[16] In Tokyo, a formal ceremony was planned at the Palace Plaza (Kōkyomae Hiroba), the open space in front of the Imperial Palace. Preparation for this event relied heavily on contribution of labor and resources; for the 12.5 million yen project, as much as 1.5 million yen was to come from private organizations and 1.3 million yen from Tokyo households.[17] In December 1938, major newspapers began to print articles soliciting volunteers and donations for the Plaza improvement project.[18] According to *Shisei shūhō*, the official wartime bulletin of Tokyo City, an average of 1,400 people volunteered labor every day, and by early 1940 donations totaled over 1.85 million yen in cash and 450,000 yen in materials.[19] *Shisei shūhō* kept readers informed of the Plaza improvement starting with its second issue (April 15, 1939) and continuing until the termination of the project in 1943. Major newspapers also updated readers on the progress of the project, typically featuring the labor and resources offered by the imperial subjects as examples of exemplary acts of patriotism.

Strict rituals dictated volunteer work at the Plaza, as the labor contributions had an objective beyond improvement of the site: they were to serve as an opportunity for the regimentation and patriotic education of the participants. The groundbreaking ceremony on November 19, 1939 started with the singing of the *kimigayo* anthem and the paying of tribute to the

palace and concluded with a *banzai* chorus.[20] The daily labor provided by
the members of the newly founded Service Troops for Nation Founding
(Kenkoku Hōkōtai) was also structured around similar activities to promote
nationalism, which included the recitation of readings honoring Emperors
Jinmu and Meiji. Students and other volunteers also engaged in similar rituals
before and after their service.

In each case, the media applauded the contributions as beautiful acts of
patriotism, but these services were not necessarily voluntary. A close reading
of newspaper articles of the time reveals that employers, schools, and local
associations had organized most of the activities. For example, *Tokyo Asahi*
newspaper featured seventy-four members of the Patriotic Youth Brigade,
who were in training near Tokyo before relocating to Manchuria when they
participated in the project on December 9, 1939.[21] The Wakayama edition of
the *Asahi* newspaper reported that the industrial labor union planned to send
25 members to serve at the Plaza.[22] *Kanagawa* newspaper noted in an article
that 216 students from Hiratsuka Engineering High School would be participating in the "volunteer" activities at the Palace Plaza.[23] Employees, students,
and members of organized groups typically had no choice but to participate,
yet the activities were always acknowledged as voluntary, willing acts of
patriotism and sacrifice for the national cause.

The aestheticization of "volunteer" work at the Palace Plaza is more or
less a straightforward case. The work was not for the destruction associated
with war (which was ongoing in the background), but rather for a national
celebration. Further, the labor and donated resources yielded concrete, positive
results. On November 10, 1940, some 500,000 people gathered at the Plaza for
a ceremony that was broadcast on live radio throughout the empire, followed
by another celebration the next day.[24] All the events were reproduced and disseminated via media outlets (including news reels) throughout the empire. The
participants were rewarded with a tangible outcome: their sacrifice resulted in
what was considered at the time as the largest national celebration in history.
In the final years of the war, however, sacrifice did not lead to positive results,
but rather produced countless deaths and widespread destruction. In the next
section, I examine the role of elementary school education and the associated
rituals that readied young imperial subjects to sacrifice for the nation.

KOKUMIN GAKKŌ: EDUCATION AND THE
MANUFACTURING OF DESIRE

Nowhere were the aestheticizing rituals incorporated with more rigor than
in elementary schools. Rituals promoting patriotism gradually increased in
the elementary school curriculum during the fifteen-year war. Following the

April 1941 reorganization of elementary schools into national schools (*koku-min gakkō*), collective practices associated with the nation and the military became an integral part of students' education. In the case of Naka Daini Kokumin Gakkō in Gifu Prefecture, as many as 85 out of the 133 school rituals that took place in the school year from April 1941 to March 1942 were associated with the celebration of the nation or the military.[25] Celebratory rituals took place on birthdays of key members of the Imperial Family, the National Foundation Day, and commemoration of other key historical figures. Military tributes were conducted on dates on which a key conflict commenced (such as September 18, the date of the Manchurian Incident) and Yasukuni Shrine festival days.[26] The rituals typically included the *banzai* chorus, the singing of the anthem, and the paying of tribute to a key national site (the Imperial Palace, Yasukuni Shrine, Ise Shrine, etc.). During the more prominent events, such as celebrations of the Four Grand National Holidays,[27] the entire school assembled in the auditorium in front of the imperial portrait, where the school principal recited the Imperial Rescript on Education and gave a speech on a related theme.

Although these rituals took place separately in each school, a national uniformity existed in the ways that they were conducted and how children behaved during these rituals. Several instruction booklets published around 1941 by the Ministry of Education and associated institutions detailed the proceedings for the ceremonies and the appropriate behavior of the attendees. *The Imperial Edict on the National Elementary School and Regulations for Implementation* presented instructions not only on the daily operations of the national schools but also on the rituals including the proceedings to be followed on the Four Grand National Holidays.[28] Booklets such as *Points on Etiquette*, published as the national standard of appropriate manners, provided detailed instructions on the specificities of behavior in situations that involved emperor worship.[29] Further, texts such as *General Common Sense for Imperial Children* instructed readers not only on how to behave but also on how to feel.[30] As an example, in the section entitled 'Emotions While Singing the National Anthem,' the children were instructed on exactly how they are supposed to feel: to "preserve [within themselves] a sense of peaceful joy within austere gravity."[31] Together, such instructional texts contributed to the cre¬ation of obedient subjects and at the same time ensured that while conducted in separate spaces, the movements (and emotions) of the participants would be identical.

Writing exercises in the classrooms can also be considered a ritualized behavior. Wartime lessons were often replaced by sessions for writing "comfort letters (*imon bun*)" to the soldiers. At the aforementioned Naka Daini Kokumin Gakkō, students wrote letters to soldiers nine times a year.[32] In these letters to soldiers that they had never met, children expressed their gratitude to the troops and wrote of the small ways that they themselves were contributing to the war effort. There were many other opportunities for composing patriotic essays as teachers mandated class diaries and picture diaries as assignments. As an example, in their class diary from 1944, fifth graders of Seta Kokumin Gakkō in Shiga Prefecture often equated their schoolwork with the ongoing war. Sentences such as the following appear in the diary: 'Our hard work in the classroom will lead to victory in the Greater East Asia War,' and 'We are engaged in both study and war. We must win them both.' In their writing, the children often vowed to contribute as much to the nation as the soldiers.[33] These compositions reflect thorough indoctrination on the value of serving the nation as a soldier. The group contribution to the class diary also functioned as an opportunity for everyone involved not only to write, but also to read and confirm the patriotism of their classmates. Each activity was designed for the children to reaffirm their role in the beautiful nation built on willing sacrifices of patriotic subjects.

Group activities to promote patriotism were not limited to the classroom. In the last years of the war, with more men drafted to the battlefronts, school children were often mobilized to help the community with labor. These labor service periods became opportunities for ritual, as they often involved activities such as bowing to the members of the household that they were helping and paying tribute to the Imperial Palace. Children often worked in groups and sang patriotic songs during their labor. These activities also instructed the children in proper ways to think as a patriotic imperial subject. The families that they were helping had sacrificed male members to the national cause; the children, not yet old enough to go off to war, were contributing their labor to the honorable households. Through a combination of unified ritual, sacrificial labor, and an opportunity for positive reflection on one's deed, their experience was beautified as a contribution to the larger, national war effort, allowing the participants to feel like an integral member of the society.

Before going onto the next section, I want to expand upon one aspect of the school rituals mentioned above: the imperial portrait that always made an appearance on the Four Grand National Holidays. These portraits had been distributed to schools and other public institutions throughout the nation in a calculated process that resulted in what I call 'the manufacturing of desire and gratitude.' Although the state mandated schools to receive and carefully maintain the photographs, the task was presented as something that each school was to aspire to and be grateful to be able to achieve. In order to receive the portrait, which all public schools and municipal institutions were required to own, each institution had to make a formal request to the government. Distribution of the portrait was first limited in scope. In the case of schools, the first to receive were the normal schools for teacher training, after which it expanded to include high schools, and finally, elementary schools.

Even within elementary schools, distribution began with so-called schools of excellence.[34] This method of distribution turned the portrait into a valued commodity and in many schools created a strong desire to receive the portrait. Schoolmasters eagerly sent their requests as soon as their schools became eligible. Through this calculated distribution, the state fabricated the impression that the portrait was not imposed, but was a result of their request, and should thus be received with gratification and honor.

The imperial portrait was not the only object of desire. A similar manufacturing of desire was put to use in 1939 for the nationwide effort to construct memorials for the local war dead in every city, town, and village throughout the empire. In this case, the municipalities needed to gather enough resources and secure an appropriate site in order to prove that they were worthy of receiving permission to construct these memorials.[35] These practices were meant to create a feeling of gratitude in every imperial subject for the receipt of an object associated with the Emperor or the ongoing war. The goal of this practice was to normalize in the popular mind the ultimate "object" of desire: death at war.

YASUKUNI SHRINE: MEDIA AND THE DESIRE FOR WAR DEATH

In the classrooms, Yasukuni Shrine and the Emperor were key in indoctrinating the students with the concept of honorable war death. While many of the rituals I introduced above began after the start of the national school system in April 1941, the presence in the textbooks of Yasukuni Shrine and the associated concept of war death had a much longer history.[36] The 1904 edition of the fifth grade Japanese language reader gave a detailed historical as well as descriptive account of the shrine, including its history, details of those enshrined, and key structures on the grounds.[37] The idea of following in the footsteps of the war dead—the point made in many of the children's essays I started with—was already firmly established in the 1910 edition. The fourth grade ethics reader introduces Yasukuni Shrine as follows:

Yasukuni Shrine is located on top of the Kudan Hill. Enshrined here are those people who lost their lives fighting for this country. An imperial messenger visits the spring and fall festivals, and the Emperor and the Empress themselves sometimes visit the annual special festivals (*rinji taisai*). These loyal warriors have come to be memorialized with special care through these ceremonies due to the Emperor's kind intentions. We must remember the depth of the Emperor's blessings, and devote ourselves for our country following the people who are enshrined here.[38]

That is, already in 1910, children were instructed that enshrinement in Yasukuni Shrine was the highest honor they could achieve; one that merited personal visits by the Emperor. The third and fourth sentences of the passage explain that those who demonstrated their loyalty by dying at war would be rewarded by the Emperor's visits, an honor only obtained through death. The last sentence of the passage instructs children to "follow the people who are enshrined here"—in other words, honor associated with war death was already being used to instill into the minds of elementary school children the myth and symbolism of Yasukuni Shrine.

Chapters on the shrine were included in almost all editions of the state-authored ethics and language readers, usually as the third or fourth chapter, so that the lesson on Yasukuni would coincide with the shrine's spring festival, which took place in late April. The textbooks, then, provided the foundation for all the activities involving the Emperor and the shrine. Alongside lessons on Yasukuni Shrine, children read in their history textbooks accounts of the ongoing war in Asia and the Pacific, updated with each new edition to reflect Japan's changing fortunes. Music lessons often comprised songs closely associated with the patriotic topics covered in other classes. In grades one through three, children learned songs that created a sense of admiration toward soldiers. In later years, they sung lyrics that covered specific aspects of the military life such as "Enlistment (Nyūei)," "A Young Tank-man (Shōnen senshahei)," "Special Attack Forces (Tokubetsu kōgekitai)," and accounts of war death and "heroic silent return."[39] Yasukuni Shrine also appeared regularly in music lessons. Here again, the act of singing and repeating the lyrics was designed to reinforce a sense of admiration for the military and utmost respect for war death.

I return here to the children's visits to Yasukuni Shrine with which I started this chapter. These trips to reunite the "war orphans"[40] with their fathers were an annual event sponsored by the Soldiers' Relief Association (Gunjin Engokai) that started in August 1939.[41] The visits were officially recorded as photo albums. According to the 1939 album, 1,301 sixth graders representing every prefecture as well as Korea and Sakhalin, gathered in Tokyo for three days in August. During their stay in Tokyo, the orphans received gifts from the Empress at the Military Hall and visited Yasukuni Shrine, Yūshūkan, National Defense Hall, Navy Hall, Meiji Shrine and its Treasure Hall, and the National Picture Gallery. At Yasukuni Shrine, the children paid tribute to their fathers while standing in the gravel courtyard between the inner shrine and the worship hall, as two orphan representatives entered into the main shrine to present an offering. Also at the Military Hall, various military officials made speeches, assuring the children that their fathers had become the protector-god for the nation, regardless of their social status or military rank at the time of death.[42]

Of course, it was not only the children who regularly received patriotic messages and participated in activities and rituals as imperial subjects honoring the national cause, as Yasukuni Shrine also played a central role in the patriotic education of adults. While the generations that had completed their schooling before the introduction of the national school system did not receive as rigorous an education on patriotism as students, there were ample opportunities for them to receive similar messages through mass media and organized activities. Adults were granted similar visits to Yasukuni Shrine upon the loss of a family member. They were also invited to attend the enshrinement rituals that preceded the spring and fall festivals. Similar to the children's visits, the families paid tribute at the shrine and visited various sites in Tokyo. And their visits were also recorded as photographs and compiled into albums. Newspapers and mass-market magazines carried stories on related topics twice a year in the weeks leading up to the festival.

Media representation of war-related topics functioned in a similar way to classroom education in that they instructed the readers on ways to perform patriotism as members of the home front. During festival days, newspapers featured personalized stories picked up from among the bereaved attendees. During the April 1942 festival, for example, the *Asahi* newspaper featured three visitors to Yasukuni as representative cases of "faithful devotion to the *eirei* (*eirei ni sasagu sekisei*)"[43]: a father of a fallen soldier who became ill during his trip from Fukuoka and died upon his arrival (his wife vowed to pay tribute for both of them); a wealthy widow who donated 50 yen for every festival in keeping with her fallen husband's wishes; and a younger brother of a fallen soldier who collected money from his classmates as donation to the shrine.[44] Mothers and wives of the deceased also provided good material for newspaper articles. For example, a mother interviewed at the fall 1941 event was quoted as feeling grateful and honored to be invited to the ceremony for the second time—the year before for her eldest son and this time for her third son.[45]

Mass-market magazines featured stories for targeted audiences. *Shufu no tomo (The Housewife's Companion)*, the most popular women's magazine of the time, regularly featured articles on Yasukuni intended to capture the attention of women. Rare cases of female enshrinement at Yasukuni were always covered in detail. In May 1938, the magazine published an article on three nurses who were enshrined in Yasukuni, detailing the heroic death of each.[46] The May 1939 issue of *Shufu no tomo* featured a discussion among five young mothers whose husbands had died before the births of their children. In the interview, a young widow responds to a sympathetic comment about the loss of her husband: "It cannot be helped as it is for the nation, for Japan. I am happy that my husband has died for the Emperor." Another recalls her husband telling her not to worry since his spirit will live on at Yasukuni after his body dies.[47] In the following issue (June 1939) was a discussion among elderly widows who had lost their only child at war. The women, who were now alone without family, expressed awe and gratitude in response to their experiences using such words as, 'I am just so grateful that folks like us were given children that could serve the Emperor.'[48] Just as the children were grateful for their fathers, who, in their minds, allowed them to visit Yasukuni Shrine through war death, so too did these women express gratitude to their lost husbands and sons. While war death was a result of the Japanese state's foreign policy—something imposed from above—it ultimately became an experience that many thought they desired.

CONCLUSION

A perusal through documents and visual records produced during the Asia-Pacific War presents an impression of an entire nation indoctrinated in the idea of aestheticized sacrifice. But this image, of course, is somewhat deceiving. The sentences composed by the Fukushima children, or the words uttered by the women who had lost their loved ones, may not always be a true indication of how they actually felt. Teachers typically vetted children's essays to eliminate inappropriate expressions. Bereaved families that were interviewed most likely chose appropriate words for their responses. It is also likely that the newspaper and magazine editors made interventions in the wording of their stories. But the ritual that was created through the repetition of acts of patriotism, the repeated recitation and writing of expressions of gratitude for the military dead, and the frequent reading and witnessing of such voices can be believed to have reinforced the state-sanctioned appropriate behavior and emotions into the participants, witnesses, and readers, and sometimes rendered them true in the minds of some. Alternatively, the repetitive practice conditioned many to act and feel in ways considered appropriate and consciously or unconsciously to censor themselves. Rituals that aestheticized sacrifice in wartime Japan thus played a crucial role in the transformation of imperial subjects into obedient participants in the creation of an ideal society founded upon beautiful sacrifices.

NOTES

1. I thank A. Minh Nguyen for inviting me to contribute this chapter, and Doug Slaymaker and two anonymous copy editors for their extremely helpful comments and suggestions. This project was funded by a long-term research fellowship from the Japan Foundation.

2. Japan's military conflict spanning the fifteen years from 1931 to 1945 has been variously named over the years including 'Pacific War (Taiheiyō Sensō)' and 'Fifteen-Year War (Jūgonen Sensō).' Most Japan scholars now favor the term 'Asia-Pacific War (Ajia Taiheiyō Sensō)' to represent Japan's wars both in Asia and the Pacific. The term initially covered only the years 1941 to 1945, but has since taken on a wider coverage sometimes from 1937 and at others, from 1931. On the naming of the Asia-Pacific War, see Kisaka Jun'ichirō, "Ajia Taiheiyō Sensō no koshō to seikaku," *Ryūkoku hōgaku* 25, no. 4 (1993): 386–434.

3. For the history and analysis of Yasukuni Shrine in English, see John Breen, ed., *Yasukuni, the War Dead, and the Struggle for Japan's Past* (New York: Columbia University Press, 2008); and Akiko Takenaka, *Yasukuni Shrine: History, Memory, and Japan's Unending Postwar* (Honolulu: University of Hawai'i Press, 2015).

4. The essays have been compiled as Gunjin Engokai, ed., *Yasukuni Jinja ni sanpai shite: iji no kansō bunshū* (Fukushima: Gunjin Engokai Fukushima Shibu, 1943).

5. Ibid., 130.

6. Ibid., 11.

7. Ibid., 179.

8. Emiko Ohnuki-Tierney, *Kamikaze, Cherry Blossoms, and Nationalisms: The Militarization of Aesthetics in Japanese History* (Chicago: University of Chicago Press, 2002).

9. See essays in *The Culture of Japanese Fascism*, ed. Alan Tansman (Durham, NC: Duke University Press, 2009).

10. Tansman, introduction to *The Culture of Japanese Fascism*, 4.

11. See, for example, Susan Sontag, "Fascinating Fascism," in *Under the Sign of Saturn: Essays* (New York: Picador, 1980), 73–108; and Simonetta Falasca-Zamponi, *Fascist Spectacle: The Aesthetics of Power in Mussolini's Italy* (Berkeley, CA: University of California Press, 1997).

12. See Tansman, introduction to *The Culture of Japanese Fascism*; and Akiko Takenaka, *The Aesthetics of Mass-Persuasion: War and Architectural Sites in Tokyo, 1868–1945* (PhD diss., Yale University, 2004).

13. This term takes inspiration from the phrase 'beautiful rationalization of factory labor' in Kim Brandt, "The Beauty of Labor: Imagining Factory Girls in Japan's New Order," in *The Culture of Japanese Fascism*, 115–37.

14. Self-censorship was indeed the goal of wartime censors. See Jonathan Abel, *Redacted: The Archives of Censorship in Transwar Japan* (Berkeley, CA: University of California Press, 2012), 16.

15. In 1889, Minister of Education Mori Arinori invented the custom of shouting *banzai* for celebrations as a way to discipline the crowds observing imperial parades. See Makihara Norio, *Kyakubun to kokumin no aida: Kindai Nihon no seiji ishiki* (Tokyo: Yoshikawa Kōbunkan, 1998), 159–72.

16. See Kenneth Ruoff, *Imperial Japan at Its Zenith: The Wartime Celebration of the Empire's 2,600th Anniversary* (Ithaca, NY: Cornell University Press, 2010).

17. *Shisei shūhō*, no. 44 (February 10, 1940): 9–13.

18. *Tokyo Asahi shinbun*, December 13, 1938.

19. *Shisei shūhō*, no. 44: 9–13.

20. The ceremony was reported in *Tokyo Asahi shinbun*, November 15, 1939, and *Shisei shūhō*, no. 34 (November 25, 1939): 20–24.

21. *Tokyo Asahi shinbun*, December 10, 1939.

22. *Asahi shinbun*, Wakayama edition, February 9, 1940.

23. *Kanagawa shinbun*, January 31, 1943.

24. Live radio played a key role in bringing the nation together in uniform ritual during wartime Japan through what historian Hara Takeshi refers to as 'control through time.' See Hara Takeshi, "Senchūki no jikan shihai," *Misuzu* 46, no. 9 (2004): 28–44.

25. Tsubouchi Hirokiyo, *Kokumin gakkō no kodomotachi* (Tokyo: Sairyūsha, 2003), 67.

26. A list of all rituals is included in Tsubouchi, 68–71.

27. The Four Grand National Holidays (Shidaisetsu) are New Year's Day, Empire Day, the Emperor's Birthday, and Emperor Meiji's Birthday.

28. Monbushō Futsū Gakumubu, ed., *Kokumin gakkōrei oyobi kokumin gakkōrei shikō kisoku* (Tokyo: Naikaku Insatsukyoku, 1941), 29.

29. *Reihō yōkō* (Tokyo: Monbushō, 1941).

30. Instruction covers a wide range of items from home and school life, including how to pay tribute to the Imperial Palace, how to listen to the school principal's speech, recommended activities for Sundays, appropriate hobbies, and how to avoid illnesses. See Kiyama Jun'ichi, *Kōkokumin no rensei, jidō seikatsu no kakujū, shōkokumin no ippan jōshiki* (Osaka: Juken Kenkyūsha, 1940).

31. Ibid., 31.

32. Each national school was assigned units to which to send letters. See Tsubouchi, 81.

33. Yoshimura Fumishige, "Sensō no jidai no kodomotachi: Seta Kokumin Gakkō 'gakkyū nisshi' o yomitoku," *Ryūkoku Daigaku kokusai bunka kenkyū*, no. 13 (2009): 105–25.

34. Taki Kōji, *Ten'nō no shōzō* (Tokyo: Iwanami Shoten, 2002).

35. Akiko Takenaka, "Architecture for Mass-Mobilization: The Chūreitō Memorial Construction Movement, 1939–1945," in *The Culture of Japanese Fascism*, 235–53.

36. The national textbook system began streamlining classroom instruction in 1904.

37. Most textbooks published in modern Japan, including all government-produced textbooks in every subject published between 1904 and 1941, are reprinted in their entirety in the 27-volume *Nihon kyōkasho taikei* edited by Kaigo Tokiomi.

38. *Jinjō shōgaku shūshinsho* 4, 2nd ed., chapter 4 in *Nihon kyōkasho taikei*, vol. 3, 86.

39. Imada Kyōko and Murai Sachiko, "Kokumin gakkō geinōka ongaku no kashō kyōzai ni miru kokumin keisei no ichisokumen," *Seishin Joshi Daigaku ronsō* 121 (2013): 265–36.

40. While most of these children were not technically orphans since their mothers were still alive, such children were broadly publicized as "war orphans (*sensō iji*)."

41. Those eligible that year included children up to sixth grade who lost their fathers in either Manchuria or China. Yasukuni Jinja, *Yasukuni Jinja ryakunenpyō* (Tokyo: Yasukuni Jinja Shamusho, 1973), 134.

42. The description of the orphans' visit is from the first photo album of the annual visits. *Yasukuni Jinja sanpai kinen shashinchō* (Military Relief Association, 1939).

43. *Eirei*, literally translated as 'heroic spirits,' was a term that came to refer to the war dead at Yasukuni Shrine from the Russo-Japanese War era. See Tanakamaru Katsuhiko, *Samayoeru eirei tachi: kuni no mitama, ie no hotoke* (Tokyo: Kashiwa Shobō, 2002).

44. *Tokyo Asahi shinbun*, April 24, 1942.

45. *Tokyo Asahi shinbun*, October 15, 1941. This report parallels a chapter of the third-grade ethics reader (5th edition) that describes a conversation between a younger brother (presumably the same age as the reader) and his brother, his mother, and his eldest brother who came home wounded in a battle. The mother tells the younger brothers that it is now their turn to become soldiers. The two younger brothers smile at each other upon hearing their mother's comment. The textbook demonstrates the honorable mindset of a mother who is proud and honored to send her sons to the battlefield regardless of the danger. See *Nihon kyōkasho taikei*, vol. 3, 398–99.

46. *Shufu no tomo* 22, no. 5 (1938): 488–96.

47. *Shufu no tomo* 23, no. 5 (1939): 66–74.

48. *Shufu no tomo* 23, no. 6 (1939): 98–105.

Chapter 14

Nagai Kafū and the Aesthetics of Urban Strolling

Timothy Unverzagt Goddard

INTRODUCTION

Nagai Kafū's 永井荷風 (1879–1959) self-conscious declaration of his stylized appearance recurs throughout his collection of essays on Tokyo entitled *Fair-Weather Geta* (*Hiyori geta* 日和下駄, 1915), drawing attention to the modern practice of urban strolling. The stroll (*sansaku* 散策; *sanpo* 散歩) constitutes an intimate engagement with the affective dimensions of urban space. It signifies no immediate goal, no destination that must be reached. Free from the routines of modern life—most notably, its preoccupation with financial gain—Kafū can wander through the city's overlooked and forgotten places. His strolling resists the precise temporal framework of urban existence imposed by capitalist modernity, described by the German sociologist Georg Simmel in his 1903 essay "The Metropolis and Mental Life": "The technique of metropolitan life in general is not conceivable without all of its activities and reciprocal relationships being organized and coordinated in the most punctual way into a firmly fixed framework of time which transcends all subjective elements."[1] It is precisely these "subjective elements" that Kafū endeavors to restore to Tokyo, a city whose rhythms had become increasingly regulated with its Meiji-era transformation into a modern imperial capital (*teito* 帝都).

Through the act of strolling in the city (*shichū no sanpo* 市中の散歩), Kafū criticizes the regimentation and superficiality of Tokyo's modernity while also revealing alternative temporal and spatial possibilities latent in the urban landscape. Tracing a selective itinerary of the city, Kafū avoids the cacophony of the modern metropolis as well as the more conspicuous markers of its past, venturing instead into back alleys, vacant lots, and other neglected corners of the capital. His navigation of these spaces delineates a city rich in feeling, places where vestiges of Edo still linger. Yet it is precisely Kafū's modern, cosmopolitan perspective that allows him to discover these remnants of the past. His descriptions of Tokyo are grounded in eclectic references to foreign cities and French literature, *ukiyo-e* and Edo popular fiction. These diverse sensibilities come together in Kafū's *flânerie*, a leisurely wandering through urban space that discloses his aesthetic vision of modern Tokyo.

Fair-Weather Geta consists of eleven essays, nine of which first appeared in the journal *Mita bungaku* between August 1914 and June 1915. The collected essays were published in a single volume by Momiyama Shoten in November 1915. Each essay takes a different feature of the city as its subject: water, trees, temples, local shrines, maps, alleys, hills, cliffs, vacant lots, and sunsets. The origins of this sustained aesthetic contemplation of urban space can be traced to Kafū's literary output following his return to Japan in 1908 after five years abroad in the United States and France. Works such as "A Song of Fukagawa" (*Fukagawa no uta* 深川の唄, 1909) and "Diary of a Returnee" (*Kichōsha no nikki* 帰朝者の日記, 1909) display Kafū's sensitivity to the unevenness of the city and to the crudeness of its rampant modernization.[2] Kafū's trenchant criticism of modern Tokyo does not mean, however, that a return to premodern Edo is possible. Even as he encounters traces of the old capital, Kafū retains his position as a modern observer. In this regard, the narrator's lament at the end of "A Song of Fukagawa" is emblematic. Having endured an arduous streetcar ride through the city, crossing over Eitai Bridge to Fukagawa, he longs to stay and savor the archaic mood that prevails on the east bank of the Sumida River. Yet he knows that such a life is impossible for him: "Ah, but instead I must go back. That is my destiny."[3] This ineluctable return to the *yamanote* 山手 from the *shitamachi* 下町, much like the return to Japan from the West, is a fundamental condition of Kafū's aesthetic understanding of Tokyo.

Kafū navigates Tokyo by accessing different modes of urban experience and representation, whether the deliberate anachronisms of his *sanjin* pose or the evocative depictions of the old city in art and literature.[4] From 1913 to 1914, immediately prior to starting work on *Fair-Weather Geta*, Kafū published two series of essays that later appeared in the collections *Tidings from Ōkubo* (*Ōkubo dayori* 大窪だより, 1916) and *On the Arts of Edo* (*Edo geijutsu ron* 江戸芸術論, 1920). In the former, Kafū documents his daily life in Tokyo and the changing of the seasons in a series of brief, dated entries written in the epistolary style (*sōrōbun* 候文). *Fair-Weather Geta* draws upon this conceptualization of the city as subjective experience, but departs from the chronological structure of *Tidings from Ōkubo*; instead, the topographical organization of *Fair-Weather Geta* foregrounds specific sites and physical features in Tokyo. *On the Arts of Edo*, meanwhile, establishes a direct connection between Kafū's affinity for *ukiyo-e* and his aesthetic vision of the city.

"An Appreciation of *Ukiyo-e*" (*Ukiyo-e no kanshō* 浮世絵の鑑賞, 1913), the first essay in the collection, begins with a lamentation of Tokyo's aesthetic decline. Kafū deplores the "public works project known as 'municipal reform' [*shiku kaisei* 市区改正]" that resulted in the destruction of an old palace gate and the removal of the pine trees that once grew in abundance around it.[5] In the aftermath of this physical erasure, images of the city preserved in works of art and literature take on particular importance. "To dream of the past," Kafū writes, "I have no choice but to rely on the power of the literature and the art that still remain from the past. Through the famous views of Edo in prints by Hiroshige and Hokusai, I yearn to glimpse the city and its environs."[6] This artistic mediation of the city transfigures the urban landscape, offering Kafū an alternate reality akin to a dream or fantasy. Representations of Edo in print collections such as Utagawa Hiroshige's 歌川広重 (1797–1858) *One Hundred Famous Views of Edo* (*Meisho Edo hyakkei* 名所江戸百景, 1856–1858) and Katsushika Hokusai's 葛飾北斎 (1760–1849) *Thirty-Six Views of Mount Fuji* (*Fugaku sanjūrokkei* 富嶽三十六景, ca. 1822–1831) present romantic visions of the city prior to the modernization of the Meiji period. Through the mediation of *ukiyo-e*, Edo appears as an object of aesthetic appreciation, its geography defined by views of famous places (*meisho* 名所). Kafū channels this mode of perception throughout his strolls in the Taishō-era capital, describing vistas that have been obscured or destroyed.

KAFŪ, *UKIYO-E*, AND THE CITY OF WATER

The modernization of Edo-Tokyo can be characterized as a transition from a city of water (*mizu no miyako* 水の都) to a city of land (*riku no miyako* 陸の都).[7] With this profound change to Edo-Tokyo's spatial and economic configuration came fundamental shifts in the perception and representation of the city. The *ukiyo-e* artist Kobayashi Kiyochika 小林清親 (1847–1915) documented the changing capital during the early Meiji period in a print series entitled *Famous Views of Tokyo* (*Tōkyō meisho zu* 東京名所図, 1876–1881). Kiyochika's vision of Tokyo is suffused with the aesthetics of the water-based city, even in his depictions of modern buildings and other sights.[8] The rediscovery of Kiyochika in the early Taishō period signaled a renewed sensitivity to the changing capital. The poet Kinoshita Mokutarō 木下杢太郎 (1885–1945) returned the artist to prominence with a brief 1913 essay in which he writes, "to appreciate Kiyochika's paintings is, I think, to appreciate the poetic realm of the common people."[9] For Kinoshita, Kiyochika is more than an artist who merely portrays external phenomena. Instead, he captures the sensibility of an era in which ordinary citizens are continually confronted by new and awe-inspiring sights. Kafū, too, expresses his admiration for Kiyochika's ability to embed these cultural conditions in his documentation of early Meiji Tokyo. In "Vacant Lots" (*Akichi* 空地), the eighth essay in *Fair-Weather Geta*, Kafū describes an empty space adjacent to the Imperial Palace where barracks were constructed in the early Meiji period. Kiyochika depicts these barracks in "Distant View of Soto Sakurada" (*Soto Sakurada enkei* 外桜田遠景), a print from his *Famous Views of Tokyo*. The barracks are seen from afar, through by a grove of trees. For Kafū, the interplay between the modern subject matter and the archaic technology of printmaking signals the artist's simultaneous engagement with the city's two temporal registers. Maeda Ai articulates a similar tension in his analysis of light and shadow in Kiyochika's prints, with the modern gas lamps of Tokyo set against the darkness of Edo.[10] Yet by the early Taishō period, Kiyochika's Tokyo, too, was vanishing. "During my comical strolls in fair-weather geta in search of the vestiges of Edo," writes Kafū, "I often strive to seek out this Tokyo of early Meiji. Yet with the development of a new, second Tokyo in the mere twenty or thirty years that have passed, the Tokyo that Kobayashi depicted in woodblock prints is gradually disappearing without a trace."[11] Rather than a simple dichotomy of Edo and Tokyo, Kafū's observations suggest an urban palimpsest that is inscribed successively, as even the barracks that were once so new and unfamiliar are left in ruins. From this perspective, strolling becomes an effort to uncover multiple layers of the same city. While the *ukiyo-e* of Hiroshige and Hokusai offer glimpses of premodern Edo, Kiyochika's *ukiyo-e* evoke the capital's spatiotemporal heterogeneity at the moment of its transition from Edo to Meiji. By channeling these disparate visions of the city through his ambulatory explorations, Kafū performs an aesthetic reimagining of the imperial capital.

In navigating the land-based city that Tokyo had become by the early Taishō period, Kafū willfully has to seek out vestiges of the city of water. Kafū references the French writer Émile Magne (1877–1953), who devotes an entire chapter of *The Aesthetics of Cities* (*L'Esthétique des villes*, 1908) to water as a key characteristic of urban space.[12] The rhythms associated with Tokyo's waterways inspire Kafū's affection for ferries, an outdated form of transportation that he poses in opposition to the city's modern conveyances. Unlike automobiles and streetcars, "ferries provide a great respite to those who trudge through the city carrying heavy bundles on their backs, and cause those of us who walk about at leisure to feel a sense of relaxation that cannot be experienced in modern life."[13] The ferries hold both a simple physical appeal for the city's workers as well as an elevated aesthetic attraction for the leisurely man about town. Kafū describes these sensations as "respite" (*kyūsoku* 休息) and "relaxation" (*ian* 慰安), respectively, words that indicate a temporary departure from the harried rhythms of urban modernity. During the Edo period, rivers served the dual function of transportation and recreation, as vital to the city's economic livelihood as they were to residents' well-being. "But today," Kafū observes, "the waterways of Tokyo are used strictly for transportation, and have completely lost their inherited aesthetic value."[14] Boarding the ferry, Kafū accesses an alternate temporality still present in modern Tokyo, and achieves a fleeting return to the aesthetics of the water-based city.

THE CITY REMEMBERED AND REIMAGINED

In one sense, Kafū's wandering through Tokyo's streets is a wandering through personal memories, a journey that leads him back to his childhood days in Koishikawa and the surrounding areas. As he writes in the opening essay of *Fair-Weather Geta*,

> [F]or me, walking in the city of Tokyo these days is just like following a path of my life's memories, from the time of my birth down to the present. And as the famous places and historic remnants of the past are destroyed day after day, the vicissitudes of the present era tinge my strolls in the city with the lonely poetry of the sadness of impermanence.[15]

Kafū apprehends the destruction of the urban landscape in aesthetic terms, describing the accompanying feeling of pathos as *mujō hiai* 無常悲哀. Kafū's mode of urban experience hinges on his recognition of the city's decay, his attunement to the vanishing traces of the past. By inscribing memory and emotion into the places that he visits, Nagai Kafū organizes the city of Tokyo into an interwoven collection of narratives. In their spatial and temporal specificity, these itineraries mark out the trajectory of his own life. In one passage, Kafū thinks back to when he was thirteen or fourteen years old, after his family relocated temporarily to Nagatachō. He describes the daily route that took him from his family's home around the Imperial Palace to his private English-language school in Kanda-Nishikichō. There were no streetcars at the time, so the young Kafū would cover the entire distance on foot, entering the Hanzōmon and following the road behind the Fukiage Garden through the old pine trees of Daikanchō. Gazing at the tall stone walls and the deep moat of the palace's outer fortifications as he passed by, he would cross Takebashi and head toward the castle gate at the Hirakawamon. Continuing on past the Ōtsukiya, an Edo-period storehouse where the Ministry of Education was later built, he would finally come out to Hitotsubashi, and from there proceed to his school nearby.[16] "I didn't think that the distance was particularly far," he writes, "and early on I was quite delighted by the curious sights."[17] The abundance of place names in the passage locates Kafū's childhood walking within a distinct geography of Tokyo. The path, however, is Kafū's own; his steps move him from place to place, connecting his residence in Nagatachō to his school in Nishikichō by way of a long, winding itinerary. Temporal references—the absence of streetcars, the archaic names of buildings—situate the account in the past, in a world now sustained only by memory. Kafū's act of recollection hints at the multiple temporal registers that the city contains. Juxtaposing past and present urban visions produces a double image of Tokyo in the early Meiji period (the time of Kafū's childhood) and Tokyo in the Taishō period (the time of Kafū's writing of *Fair-Weather Geta*). Kafū's oscillation between these two moments gestures to an enduring instability in the city's composition, as instances of rupture continually elicit nostalgic recollection. While Kafū can draw upon personal memory to call forth these visions of early Meiji Tokyo, the city of Edo remains beyond the scope of his lived experience.

For Kafū, born in the twelfth year of Meiji, Edo can be glimpsed only through imagination and representation. He must rely on material artifacts from the old city to superimpose a fantastic Edo onto the present-day city. Carrying a pictorial map (*ezu* 絵図) from the Kaei 嘉永 era (1848–1854) as he wanders through Taishō-era Tokyo, Kafū engages in "comparison and contrast" (*hikaku taishō* 比較対照) of the city at different moments in time.[18] Through this activity, he illustrates a key difference between past and present modes of topographical representation:

> Generally speaking, for a map of Tokyo that is precise and accurate, nothing is better than a map from the Land Survey Department. Looking at this map, however, does not provoke any kind of interest, nor does it enable one to imagine the actual landscape. On the contrary, the map's accuracy and precision—from the topographical lines that look like a centipede's feet to the scale measuring one ten-thousandth or something—lack improvisational freedom and inspire only annoyance in the viewer. Look at the inaccurate Edo map: it has liberal drawings of cherry blossoms in places like Ueno where cherry trees bloom, and sketches of willow branches in places like Yanagiwara where willow trees abound. And where the mountains of Nikkō and Tsukuba, more distant than Mount Asuka, happen to be visible, they are depicted just beyond the clouds. By employing ad hoc these techniques that completely contradict standard cartographic methods, the map conveys essential details in a simple and very interesting manner. On this point, the inaccurate Edo pictorial map is far more intuitive and impressive than the accurate new map of Tokyo.[19]

The official map published by the Land Survey Department is deficient in that it fails to acknowledge the emotional connection between the reader and the map, and, by extension, between the reader and the city. While it is undoubtedly "precise and accurate" (*seimitsu seikaku naru* 精密正確なる), the official map's lack of "improvisational freedom" (*tōi sokumyō no jiyū* 当意即妙の自由) and strict adherence to scale obfuscate the reader, who has no way of knowing which areas of the city are interesting. The subjective, affective qualities of the Edo pictorial map bridge this gap in their very departure from cartographic convention. The result is a representation of the city that is far more "intuitive" (*chokkanteki* 直感的) and "impressive" (*inshōteki* 印象的), qualities that are, in turn, intrinsic to Kafū's navigation of urban space. Just as personal remembrance awakens the particularity of the city as dynamic, lived experience, so too does the pictorial map express an idea of the city as an open, readable text.

"LET'S WALK THE BACKSTREETS, LET'S STROLL THE SIDE STREETS"

In his efforts to uncover alternative spaces and temporalities within Tokyo, Nagai Kafū responds to the reordering of the capital that proceeded apace from the third decade of the Meiji period. With the passage of the Tokyo Municipal Reform Act (*Tōkyō shiku kaisei jōrei* 東京市区改正条例) in 1888, the Japanese government codified a comprehensive plan for urban renewal. Remaining in place until 1919, the resulting policies addressed the commercial and political needs of the metropolis through broad infrastructural changes.[20] These changes—including the development of the city's water supply, improvements to the sewer system, and the building and widening of roads—shaped the modern capital. Hibiya Park was created in 1903, adjacent to the Imperial Palace, and governmental buildings were clustered in nearby Kasumigaseki. In this transformation of urban space, the forces of modernization advanced against the dark, dirty regions of Tokyo, enacting a logic that Maeda Ai terms a 'mythology of the negative.'[21]

In his 1917 memoir, *Thirty Years in Tokyo* (*Tōkyō no sanjūnen* 東京の三十年), the author Tayama Katai 田山花袋 (1872–1930) recalls the effects of these policies as the Japanese government sought to remake Tokyo as "the capital of the new Japanese Empire" (*atarashii Nippon teikoku no shufu* 新しい日本帝国の首府):

> The main streets, too, have lost almost all traces of Edo. For a time, the flurry of demolition and construction produced a strange and disharmonious spectacle, but now things seem to have settled down—albeit in a state of disharmony. Hibiya Park, the processional route, and Tokyo Station have all changed completely, when one thinks about it.[22]

Katai's observations describe the tumultuous spatial upheaval that characterized Tokyo's transformation into an imperial capital. The most dramatic effects of this urban renewal can be seen on the main streets, where the combination of open space and monumental architecture signals the progress of capitalist modernity and Japan's burgeoning imperial power.

Rather than a fully realized modern metropolis, however, the resulting condition of this development is an unresolved "state of disharmony" (*futōitsu no mama* 不統一のまま). For Kafū, the city's incongruities are all too readily apparent. In *Fair-Weather Geta*, he characterizes the unevenness of the imperial capital through a series of oppositions—steel bridges and ferries, official maps and pictorial maps, main streets and back alleys—that contrast the aesthetic qualities of the city's variegated spaces. Again and again, Kafū ventures away from the main streets to seek out the traces (*omokage* 面影) of Edo. Ishizaka Mikimasa employs the concept of the labyrinth (*meiro* 迷路) to describe this search, which guides Kafū's seemingly purposeless wanderings through overlooked corners of the modern city.[23] Excavating an order subsumed in the city's progress, Kafū critiques the careless pattern of development that has disrupted that order:

> Nowadays, it goes without saying that Tokyo's main streets—Nihonbashidōri in Ginza, of course, as well as Ueno's Hirokōji and Asakusa's Komagatadōri—have lost the tranquil beauty that the order of the Edo streets had preserved. Everywhere there are faux Western buildings, painted signs, and rows of thin, scraggly trees. On top of that, telephone poles stick up shamelessly in indiscriminate locations, and there is a bewildering tangle of electrical wires. These streets, moreover, do not yet possess the rhythmic, lively beauty of Western cities. Faced with this half-baked city, it is impossible to summon any sort of artistic feeling whatsoever, aside from that which accompanies natural changes like the wind and snow, the rain, and the setting sun. The sensation of displeasure and revulsion that I always feel while walking along the main streets is the biggest reason why I am so interested in the spectacle of those alleys hidden in the shadows.[24]

This "half-baked city" (*chūto hanpa no shigai* 中途半端の市街) is rife with the brazen, the superficial, and the inauthentic. Tokyo lacks the "tranquil beauty" (*seijaku no bi* 静寂の美) of Edo as well as the "rhythmic, lively beauty" (*onritsuteki naru katsudō no bi* 音律的なる活動の美) of Western cities. While Kobayashi Kiyochika could bring together heterogeneous elements in his depictions of the city in the early Meiji period, by early Taishō there exists only a confused jumble of telephone poles and electrical wires on the city's main streets. For Kafū, seeking a respite from this vulgar disorder, alleys hold a powerful aesthetic appeal. Dark and hidden spaces, they possess a physical intimacy that enables an intermingling of the public and private realms. Perambulation is essential to the exploration of alleys, which are inaccessible to the modes of transportation that predominate in the modern city.

As Kafū writes, "there is nothing better than meandering down the side streets where cars cannot pass, or walking along the old roads that have escaped the destruction of urban renewal."[25] Here, too, temporal and technological oppositions define the spatial dynamics of the city. Kawamoto Saburō identifies this "discovery of the alley" as a Taishō-era phenomenon, linking Kafū's *Fair-Weather Geta* to other writings of the period that seek to recuperate the alley as a symbolic site of premodern Edo.[26] The alley becomes an alternative space, to be experienced in a manner that might be termed 'aesthetic voyeurism.' In its distinct spatial qualities, the alley evokes a sensation of depth that is absent in the bright, open spaces of Tokyo's main streets.

In this sense, Kafū's navigation of Tokyo constitutes a movement from the shallow and superficial to the deep and profound. The architect Maki Fumihiko describes inner depth (*oku* 奥) as a key quality in Japanese conceptions of space, noting that "the use of the term with respect to space is invariably premised on the idea of *okuyuki* [奥行き], signifying relative distance or the sense of distance within a given space."[27] Kafū's strolls take him into the hidden depths of the city's alleys, revealing glimpses of the humble lives that unfold there in dark anonymity: "Just as one sees in *ukiyo-e*, alleys are the dwelling places of the common people, unchanged from the past to the present. They hide all kinds of lives that cannot be seen from the bright main streets."[28] Suffused with the richness of human experience, the alley encapsulates what Kafū terms 'a whole world of artistic harmony' (*konzen taru geijutsuteki chōwa no sekai* 渾然たる芸術的調和の世界).[29] Kafū's aesthetic fascination with the deprivation of Tokyo's backstreets discloses an ambiguous coexistence of poverty and peacefulness, spaces that are at once abject and alluring.

KAFŪ'S *FLÂNERIE*

As Kafū's navigation of the alleys makes plain, the act of strolling is inseparable from his aesthetic vision of the city. *Fair-Weather Geta*'s alternative title, 'An Account of Strolls in Tokyo' (*Tōkyō sansakuki* 東京散策記), foregrounds the author's agency in the exploration of urban space. And while Kafū summons elegiac visions of the declining old city, his urban strolling is a distinctly modern phenomenon. "In old Tokyo (the *shitamachi*)," reveals Kawamoto Saburō, "the concepts of 'stroll' [*sanpo* 散歩] and 'city walking' [*machi aruki* 町歩き] did not exist. It can be said that Kafū's city walking—a person of the *yamanote* going out for a walk in the *shitamachi*—was a new form of behavior at the time."[30] This separation between the *yamanote* and the *shitamachi* is a requisite condition of Kafū's walking, imposing an aesthetic distance that enables him to perceive and reflect on the urban landscape. Only once in his life did Kafū actually dwell in the *shitamachi*, when he moved to Tsukiji in 1917. His dissatisfaction with life there led him to move back to the *yamanote* in May 1920, to his so-called Eccentricity House (*Henkikan* 偏奇館) in Azabu.

Kafū's subjective, self-conscious movement through the city of Tokyo is inherently stylized. Kafū describes his walking as a "leisurely strolling" (*burabura sanpo* ぶらぶら散歩), a spatial practice in perfect accord with his *sanjin* pose.[31] Kafū acts the part of an individual who has turned his back on society and is guided solely by his own whims, completely indifferent to the exigencies of modern life. Kawamoto notes that Kafū's adopted literary persona of an old, sickly recluse is deeply at odds with his actual state of health in the early Taishō period, when Kafū was in his mid-thirties and was quite vigorous in his ambulatory exploration of the city.[32] This disjuncture did not escape Edward Seidensticker, either, who in his analysis of *Fair-Weather Geta* remarks that "the frequent complaints of ill-health make so much walking seem a touch unlikely."[33]

The performative nature of Kafū's strolling casts a critical perspective on urban space under capitalist modernity. Writing a little more than twenty years after the publication of *Fair-Weather Geta*, Walter Benjamin applies similar scrutiny to the dynamics of the modern city in describing the figure of the *flâneur* in the Paris of Charles Baudelaire (1821–1867). In contrast to the pedestrians who allowed themselves to be jostled by the crowd, the *flâneur* "demanded elbow room and was unwilling to forego the life of a gentleman of leisure. He goes his leisurely way as a personality; in this manner he protests against the division of labor which makes people into specialists. He protests no less against their industriousness."[34] The *flâneur*'s mannered stance against the harried rhythms and commodity fetishism of the modern metropolis articulates an oppositional subjectivity in the negotiation of urban space.

As a vernacular spatial practice, *flânerie* opposes the panoptic vision of the city as seen from above. Centralized Meiji-era development brought about the transformation of Tokyo into a modern, imperial capital, but also provoked moments of tension and rupture within the patterns of everyday life. Michel de Certeau describes walking as "a space of enunciation," an expressive mode that improvises on the geography of the city and resists the hierarchical impositions of a centralized power.[35] Concurrent to the spatial transformation of Tokyo, new and faster forms of transportation altered the phenomenal experience of the city. On foot, one is free to wander, to deviate from the tracks, lines, and major thoroughfares to which other forms of transportation are obliged to adhere. Walking also affords space for contemplation; impressions are not rushed or scattered, but rather focused and prolonged. These qualities are echoed in the literary structure of *Fair-Weather Geta*, with each essay focused on a particular characteristic of Tokyo. Through the practice of urban strolling, Kafū articulates an aesthetic critique of Tokyo's superficial and insensitive modernization while developing an alternative historical and cultural geography of the city.

CONCLUSION

Nagai Kafū's leisurely negotiation of Tokyo reveals the many spatiotemporal layers concealed in the modern imperial capital. His writings demonstrate an acute sensitivity to the affective qualities of urban space, and insofar as they condemn Tokyo's modernization, they do so because modernization has obscured those qualities of the city most necessary to a rich and meaningful life within it. Kafū's invocation of the past does not constitute a naïve advocacy of a return to it, but rather illuminates alternative ways of imagining the present-day city. While I have endeavored to contextualize *Fair-Weather Geta* among other representations of urban space in Kafū's literature prior to 1914, the collection of essays also foreshadows his subsequent efforts to reimagine the Japanese capital. In fictional works such as *Rivalry* (*Udekurabe* 腕くらべ, 1917) and *A Strange Tale from East of the River* (*Bokutō kidan* 濹東綺譚, 1937), Kafū combines formal experimentation with richly evocative descriptions of the city's vanishing past.[36] By highlighting Tokyo's potential as subjective, lived space, Kafū suggests the possibility of different rhythms, different sensibilities. In his modern, self-conscious practice of urban strolling, Kafū shows a keen affinity for the city as a repository of cultural life and aesthetic experience. Umbrella in hand, he strolls along in his fair-weather geta, meandering through the uneven spaces of Taishō Tokyo.

NOTES

1. Georg Simmel, "The Metropolis and Mental Life," in *On Individuality and Social Forms*, ed. Donald L. Levine (Chicago: University of Chicago Press, 1971), 328.

2. For a sustained analysis of these and other writings by Kafū published between 1909 and 1910, see Rachael Hutchinson, *Nagai Kafū's Occidentalism: Defining the Japanese Self* (Albany, NY: State University of New York Press, 2011),133–71.

3. Nagai Kafū, "Fukagawa no uta," in *Kafū zenshū*, vol. 6 (Tokyo: Iwanami Shoten, 1992), 118. All translations, unless otherwise indicated, are my own.

4. The *sanjin* 散人, or refined man of leisure, is an enduring figure in Kafū's writings. See Edward Seidensticker, *Kafū the Scribbler* (Stanford, CA: Stanford University Press, 1965), 152; and Stephen Snyder, *Fictions of Desire: Narrative Form in the Novels of Nagai Kafū* (Honolulu: University of Hawai'i Press, 2000), 1–7, 116–18.

5. Nagai Kafū, *Edo geijutsu ron*, in *Kafū zenshū*, vol. 10 (Tokyo: Iwanami Shoten, 1992), 145.

6. Ibid., 146.

7. See Jinnai Hidenobu, *Tokyo: A Spatial Anthropology* (Berkeley, CA: University of California Press, 1995), 66–118; and Kawamoto Saburō, *Taishō gen'ei* (Tokyo: Iwanami Gendai Bunko, 2008), 151–71.

8. Maeda Ai, "Panorama of Enlightenment," trans. Henry D. Smith II, in *Text and the City: Essays on Japanese Modernity*, ed. James A. Fujii (Durham, NC: Duke University Press, 2004), 70–72.

9. Kinoshita Mokutarō, "Kobayashi Kiyochika ga Tōkyō meisho zue," in *Kinoshita Mokutarō zenshū*, vol. 8 (Tokyo: Iwanami Shoten, 1981), 146.

10. Maeda Ai, "Kiyochika no hikari to yami," in *Toshi kūkan no naka no bungaku* (Tokyo: Chikuma Shobō, 1992), 145–54.

11. Kafū, *Hiyori geta*, in *Kafū zenshū*, vol. 11 (Tokyo: Iwanami Shoten, 1993), 159.

12. Émile Magne, *L'Esthétique des villes* (Paris: Mercure de France, 1908), 210–69. Kafū also alludes to Magne's work in *Ōkubo dayori*. See Nagai Kafū, *Ōkubo dayori*, in *Kafū zenshū*, vol. 11 (Tokyo: Iwanami Shoten, 1993), 266.

13. Kafū, *Hiyori geta*, 151.

14. Ibid., 140.

15. Ibid., 113.

16. Today, the Palace Side Building occupies this site (Chiyoda Ward, Hitotsubashi 1-1-1).

17. Ibid., 112.

18. Ibid., 128.

19. Ibid., 128–29.

20. André Sorensen, *The Making of Urban Japan* (London: Routledge, 2002), 71–74.

21. Maeda Ai, "Utopia of the Prisonhouse: A Reading of *In Darkest Tokyo*," trans. Seiji M. Lippit and James A. Fujii, in *Text and the City: Essays on Japanese Modernity*, ed. James A. Fujii (Durham, NC: Duke University Press, 2004), 45.

22. Tayama Katai, *Literary Life in Tōkyō, 1885–1915*, trans. Kenneth G. Henshall (Leiden: Brill, 1987), 230. Translation modified. See also Tayama Katai, *Tōkyō no sanjūnen* (Tokyo: Iwanami Bunko, 1981), 262.

23. Ishizaka Mikimasa, *Toshi no meiro* (Kyoto: Hakujisha, 1994), 19.

24. Kafū, *Hiyori geta*, 152–53.

25. Ibid., 115–16.

26. Kawamoto Saburō, *Taishō gen'ei* (Tokyo: Iwanami Gendai Bunko), 84–86.

27. Maki Fumihiko, "The Japanese City and Inner Space," in *Nurturing Dreams: Collected Essays on Architecture and the City* (Cambridge, MA: MIT Press, 2008), 153.

28. Kafū, *Hiyori geta*, 152.

29. Ibid., 137–38.

30. Kawamoto Saburō, *Kafū to Tōkyō*, vol. 1 (Tokyo: Iwanami Gendai Bunko, 2009), 40.

31. Kafū, *Hiyori geta*, 116.

32. Kawamoto, *Kafū to Tōkyō*, vol. 1, 12.

33. Seidensticker, 68.

34. Walter Benjamin, "The Paris of the Second Empire in Baudelaire," trans. Harry Zohn, in *Walter Benjamin: Selected Writings*, ed. Howard Eiland and Michael W. Jennings, vol. 4, *1938–1940* (Cambridge, MA: Harvard University Press, 2003), 30–31.

35. Michel de Certeau, *The Practice of Everyday Life*, trans. Steven Rendall (Berkeley, CA: University of California Press, 1984), 98.

36. See Snyder, 54–91, 115–53.

Chapter 15

Cool-Kawaii Aesthetics and New World Modernity

Thorsten Botz-Bornstein

According to the *National Geographic World Music* website, the new millennium has been characterized by an international youth culture dominated by two types of aesthetics: the Afro-American cool, which, propelled by hip-hop music, has become "the world's favorite youth culture," and the Japanese aesthetics of *kawaii*, or cute, distributed internationally by Japan's powerful anime and manga industry.[1] Since around 2006, Japanese contemporary popular culture has become fashionable worldwide. Meanwhile, hip-hop has become "the center of a mega music and fashion industry around the world"[2] and "the Black aesthetic," whose stylistic, cognitive, and behavioral outfits are to a large extent based on cool, has arguably become "the only distinctive American artistic creation."[3] Japan is no longer a faceless economic superpower, but has managed to mass export cool products. Sixty percent of the world's cartoon series are made in Japan and Japanese games running on PlayStation 2 and Nintendo are just as popular.[4] Since the release of Ōtomo Katsuhiro's popular animation film *Akira* (1999), "Japanimation" continues to invade the world. Asian cartoons are bought by Hollywood producers and, in general, Hollywood borrows liberally from past anime and manga. In 2008, Steven Spielberg adopted the manga/anime *Ghost in a Shell* (*Kōkaku kidōtai*, 1995) and the Wachowski brothers adopted the 1960 Japanese anime series *Speed Racer* in the same year. New schemes, like that of hit-producing music stars exclusively known as animated characters such as Gorillaz, have become acceptable in the American mainstream. Super Mario is now a better-known character among American children than Mickey Mouse.[5] The world is impressed by what Roland Kelts has called the 'third wave of Japanophilia.'[6] In 2013, Christine Yano coined the term 'Pink Globalization' to describe the process through which cute items from Japan are introduced into all parts of the industrialized world.[7] The key word is *kawaii*, which is, as this

207

chapter will argue, a particular mixture of cute and cool. Kawaii continues to attract academics who have been producing research on this phenomenon since the late 1980s. Recently, in her book *Our Aesthetic Categories: Zany, Cute, Interesting*, Sianne Ngai considers aesthetic categories that go beyond traditional terms such as 'beautiful' and 'sublime,' and that extend to 'cute' and 'kawaii.'[8]

The African-American philosopher Cornel West sees "black-based hip-hop culture of youth around the world" as a grand example of the "shattering of male, WASP [White Anglo-Saxon Protestant] cultural homogeneity."[9] It is possible to say that kawaii culture engages in a similar fight against an "official" modernity and replaces it with a subtler mode of what West calls 'New World Modernity.'[10] This chapter attempts to define a certain dialectics of cool and kawaii, as well as models of convergence or commutation that are characteristic of a contemporary aesthetics of which popular culture merely represents the surface. It also shows that, on a deeper level, this dialectics leads toward the development of a New World Modernity. An analysis of cool and kawaii, especially when they are used as intercultural concepts, reveals patterns that are obvious, going back to Marshal McLuhan's reflections in *Understanding Media: The Extensions of Man* on the hot and the cool in the 1960s,[11] but that have most recently been reinforced through globalization as well as through the "cool" technology of the Internet. Let me first provide the basic definitions of 'cool' and 'kawaii.'

COOL

The aesthetics of cool developed in the form of a behavioral attitude practiced by black men in the United States at the time of slavery. During this time, residential segregation made necessary the cultivation of special defense mechanisms, which employed emotional detachment as well as irony. A cool attitude helped slaves and former slaves to cope with exploitation or simply made it possible for them to walk the streets at night. In most basic terms, to be cool means to remain calm even under stress. Of course, the definition of 'cool' is more complex. The above definition, harking back to the historical origins of the term, seems to clash with more contemporary forms of "commodified cool" or "mainstream consumer cool."[12] The latter does not heroically speak up against dominating powers, but seeks integration into a consumer game in an apparently uncritical fashion. Yano even believes that the "overly defiant aspect of cool may get lost in Japan, where cool is more likely to devolve into a consumer choice label as mere style."[13] It is thus necessary to distinguish at least two kinds of cool: the "I want to be different from others" cool and the "I want to be like the others" cool.

On the other hand, even if such distinct types exist, they are always interdependent. Furthermore, as a recent study has shown, both types begin to overlap. In 2014, the trend-forecasting agency K-Hole released a report on youth culture arguing that today's truly cool people attempt to master *sameness* because "the act of fitting in with the mainstream is the ultimate camouflage." The reason is the growth of a more and more perfect surveillance system that has made the "disappearance" of the individual almost impossible, and to do the impossible is always cool. At the moment, the act of blending in gives people a particular kind of power, and "when standing out means being put on the no-fly list for 10 years,"[14] the idea of disappearing has become cool.

KAWAII

The word 'kawaii' is defined in English as 'cute,' 'childlike,' 'sweet,' 'innocent,' 'pure,' 'gentle,' and 'weak.' It can be written with the Chinese characters 可爱, meaning roughly "which can be loved." This word appears for the first time in the eleventh century in Murasaki Shikibu's *Genji monogatari* as the root word *kawai*. The phonological resemblance to the Chinese pronunciation of 可愛 (*ke'ai*) seems to be merely coincidental. In Japan, the popular aesthetic appeal of kawaii is of national importance. The aesthetics of kawaii has developed especially in Japan since the 1980s. In the late 1990s, it turned into an explicit culture of which Pokémon animals and Hello Kitty are the most famous symbols. Kawaii culture is more than an aesthetic style, but can appear as a full-fledged way of articulating a subjective attitude that can become manifest in design, language, bodily behavior, gender relations, and perceptions of the self. Even though kawaii may appear outside contexts that are properly aesthetic, it always remains—as Ngai also contends[15]—a statement of taste, and it is thus basically aesthetic.

COOL AND KAWAII

At first glance, cool and kawaii do not have much in common. One is masculine and preoccupied with the dissimulation of emotion; the other is feminine and engaged in the ostentatious display of sentimentality. Cool produces an aesthetic of the emotionally restrained and the detached, while kawaii excels in attachment to creations with childhood resonances. Cool appears as an aesthetic used by the leader of the gang, while kawaii seems to remain the option of women who have decided to remain children. This does not mean that cool and kawaii are gendered, but they are most typically associated with gendered behavior.

In spite of these external oppositions and in spite of their different origins, these phenomena have important conceptual structures in common: both are social expressions that invite interaction and involve the spectator's imagination; both engage in a consistent aestheticization of sexuality in which the repressed parts will not necessarily reappear in a sublimated Freudian form; both "hold back," are *potentially* sexually fecund, and operate within the realm of possibilities rather than appearing as openly threatening and aggressive behaviors; both undertake a subversive liquefaction of values up to the point that even gender identities get dissolved though they are at the same time reinstated; and both contribute to the construction of a personal identity.

Apart from that, both cool and kawaii are also antidotes to stereotypes of their respective homogeneous "official" societies, which are the blandness of a plain, barren, vague, and featureless white American monoculture, and the uniformity of post-war Japanese group–oriented society determined by the corporate worker's lifestyle, entrance examination prep schools, and the domestic boredom of housewives. It is in these modern environments that cool and kawaii, successfully or unsuccessfully, attempt to establish personal identities. In a more global context, cool and kawaii are even linked, as they combat, each in its own way, the American "uncool" (and notoriously sexist) aesthetics of Disney by introducing values of communities, cultural heritages, and histories.

The "shared areas" in which cool and kawaii most commonly meet are the following:

1. *Control.* Both cool and kawaii require a considerable amount of control in order to be functional as styles. They are most effective as performing arts or poses.
2. *Ethnicity.* Both cool and kawaii are nonwhite cultural phenomena and are ethnic in the largest sense of the word. Though a tradition of the "white cool" (principally the male loner) is firmly established in American culture, the African-American cool dominates the field at present, since cool has been brought back into the black community through hip-hop culture.
3. *Subjective Demands.* Expressions of cool and kawaii appear to follow motivations the logic of which is dependent on concrete persons and thus difficult to establish in terms of neutral objectivity. Often the motivations are unconscious and therefore deeply personal. This is the reason why they are often opposed to the detached character of proceedings dominated by the official cultural norms of their respective spheres (white American society and male Japanese society, respectively).
4. *Commercial.* If we were to replace cool with hip, the parallelism would suffer. As a matter of fact, both cool and kawaii (at least in their more developed states) are at odds with puritan traditions, but are constantly

ready to shelve a large part of their rebellious status in order to become the dominant ethic of late consumer capitalism.

5. *Attempts to Soften.* Both cool and kawaii are nonconfrontational social techniques that attempt to absorb stress symptoms related to problematic power relations and acts of violence produced in an overly hierarchical society.

6. *Search for Security.* Both cool and kawaii provide security. Japanese who surround themselves with Hello Kitty pictures "suffuse their lives with a sense of security,"[16] and in its more original forms, coolness offers a similar quality to the black man.

7. *Narcissism.* There is a certain self-referentiality in cool and kawaii culture. The *shōjo*, the typically kawaii girl, has been said to have a narcissistically invested self-image.[17] The same can be said about the cool male whose cool posing may expose a potential emptiness of signification.

8. *Group Identity.* Cool and kawaii function as established social values and can do so only because they are able to express a certain group identity through style. Kawaii characters, for example, are appropriate as symbols for identity,[18] which, in return, quickly consolidate their definition through the group. Group-based social schemes that are typical for Japan accelerate these developments. Also, the African-American "I am because we are" attitude[19] that Cornel West crystallizes as a manifestation of African-American criticism toward Cartesian philosophical worldviews[20] has been essential for the establishment of cool as a social phenomenon.

9. *Elasticity.* The elasticity of both cool and kawaii is intrinsic to their most original meanings: cool and kawaii can cover such large fields of aesthetic expression because they reunite contradictory elements.

10. *Indirect Empowerment.* Paradoxically, both cool and kawaii empower their bearers because they have decided to partially *give away* power. For coolness, this strategy is part of its intrinsic concept: to accumulate power is never cool. Kawaii as a play with apparent weakness follows similar lines.

SIMILAR SOCIAL CONDITIONS

What Richard Majors and Janet Mancini Billson say about the formation of cool also concerns that of kawaii: "When a society is in a state of rapid change, the old rules no longer have sufficient power to inspire conformity. At the same time, new rules that emerge may not receive full commitment from all members of the society."[21] The social situation within which the aesthetics of cool arose is a case in point. Cool and kawaii insert themselves in the gap between old rules and new rules and "catch society off-guard," as Terry Williams states about cool.[22] Cool and kawaii do not encounter "evil" societies that need to be combated, as did, for example, Marxists in nineteenth-century industrialized Europe. The societies that the protagonists of cool and kawaii encounter are rather "sick," because they are threatened by imminent disillusionment. Cool developed at a time when the Confederate system of the Southern states disintegrated and structures were loose and less defined than before. Though the Civil War and the Emancipation Proclamation might have convinced many black leaders that the world was progressing morally, ironically, as pointed out by Wilson Jeremiah Moses, "the power of abolitionist moral preachments had resulted in a great military struggle, in which freedom had been proclaimed by fiat and imposed at gunpoint."[23] The result was a crisis of values.

Modernization within the nations of East Asia produced a similar vacuum of rules as they were exposed to social change brought about by both industrialization and westernization, linking a moral crisis caused by materialism to a crisis of national identity. The anomie examined by Émile Durkheim in nineteenth-century industrializing Europe is not comparable to that of East Asia. In Europe, industrialization had a one-dimensional impact. In modern East Asia, however, the twofold social change has brought about the "extreme opportunism and escapism, together with greed and selfish individualism" that still characterizes contemporary culture.[24] All this shows that cool and kawaii attempt to establish values within crisis-ridden situations by creating inimitable styles while existing as expressions of the crisis.

ALIENATION

In value-oriented descriptions of cool, the term is still conceived of as a desperate masculine attempt at gaining respect from a hostile society through willful alienation *from* the society. The aim of this alienation has been for the individual to stay calm and dignified. This was a difficult task as "one could not," writes W. E. B. Du Bois, "be a calm, cool, and detached scientist while Negroes were lynched, murdered, and starved."[25] Though this makes sense, it overlays the idea of alienation with a strange connotation, because African-Americans were *already* alienated even without any aspirations toward coolness. As Cornel West observes, "With no legal status, social standing or public worth—indeed, no foothold in the human family—black people were natally alienated."[26] West names the first chapter of his early *Prophesy Deliverance!: An Afro-American Revolutionary Christianity* 'American Africans in Conflict: Alienation in an Insecure Culture.'[27] Alienation is a central concept in African-American thought. Most generally speaking, it is related to the teachings of Marxism. Karl Marx pondered in his early writings about the alienating effects of life under capitalism as well as the essential inhumanity of the social relations produced by the economic changes of the early Industrial Revolution. The concept of alienation or estrangement (*Entfremdung* in German) in a modern context was born here.

NEW WORLD MODERNITY

"We are, all of us, *moderns*, whether we like it or not," said the African-American writer Amiri Baraka.[28] From the preceding explanations, it follows that African-American coolness is part of the modern aesthetic project, particularly in the context of the ethics and aesthetics of alienation. New World Modernity is cool because it depends on willful acts of alienation. It depends on acts of delay, displacement, oblique representation, and stylization. This is the reason why cool is a futurist vision and a catalyst of modern aesthetics.

There are similar things to say about kawaii, which achieves a sort of New World Modernity by relying, just like cool, on similar acts. Both cool and kawaii overcome a passive techno-future determined by coldness and automation. They challenge the automatized world criticized by Paul Virilio in which human-guided sensation is replaced with automated productions and where even art evolves toward automation and encoded techniques of production. Virilio believes that "automation of postindustrial production is coupled with the *automation of perception* and then with this attended conception favored by the marketplace of systems analysis while future developments are sought in cybernetics."[29] Perception and even thinking will no longer be individual but mechanical. According to Virilio, there is already "machine for *seeing*, machine for *hearing*, once upon a time; machine for *thinking* [will be there] very shortly with the boom in all things *digital* and the programmed abandonment of the *analogue*."[30]

Here we understand the importance of cool and kawaii as value-oriented concepts. The active cool-kawaii values of New World Modernity can help one to move around in the contemporary world in a more authentic and less alienated fashion. This "authenticity" has nothing to do with ethnicization, because neither cool nor kawaii is a *purely* ethnic notion. Kawaii images are used, for example, for the personalization of new technologies or for customizing cyberspace. From the beginning, kawaii was supposed to *humanize* the modern Japanese world in which life had become too formalized and static. Kawaii thus stands in opposition to industrial alienation and affirms naturalness, intimacy, innocence, and simplicity—all of which are very positive attributes. I see this as an act of disautomatization. Kawaii objects can be touched; they provide an authenticity that is getting lost in industrial societies. Kawaii effectuates, for example, a familiarization of impersonal, mass-produced items like cell phones.

There is a similarity with cool. In general, cool as a stylistic expression deals with the unexpected, that is, it follows nonlinear structures most often flourishing in the realm of ephemerality, fragmentation, and discontinuity. A *Verfremdungseffekt* pertains to New World Modernity. An aesthetic term coined by Berthold Brecht, *Verfremdungseffekt* is usually translated as 'distancing effect' but occasionally also as 'alienation effect' or 'estrangement effect.' It is related to the above *Entfremdung* popularized by Karl Marx. Coolness depends to a large extent on such an alienation effect. It overlaps with the intertextual devices that Henry Louis Gates, Jr. recuperates from Ralph Ellison's works and that he calls 'critical signification,' 'pastiche,' 'critical parody,' or 'troping.'[31] In his formalist study of African-American literature, Gates crystallizes devices such as repetition and play of language that form a certain "way of seeing" as well as a "new manner of representation and its relation to the concept of presence" proper, for example, to Ellison.[32]

In a similar way, kawaii alters modern expressions without being *against* modernity. Paradoxically, though softening the effects of modernity, kawaii also functions as a catalyst of modernity, which represents a further parallel with cool. In the 1970s when self-centered consumption was seen as an escape from traditional Japanese culture, kawaiiness signified freedom from tradition and thus modernity. "The cute look that dominated young Japanese's fashion in the late 1970s was adopted explicitly as a rejection of a typically Japanese style," reports Lise Skov.[33] Kawaii does not mean to go back to Japaneseness but is rather partly foreign in its origin.[34] It does not at all refer to traditional Japanese cultural patterns.

The conclusion is that both cool and kawaii must be perceived as modern values able to embrace antagonistic terms such as 'liberation,' 'fragmentation,' and 'alienation.' As Kelts points out, the world appreciates Japanese aesthetics not as a derivation of the traditional culture of an old civilization but rather, on the contrary, because of the eminently modern and futuristic ambiance it offers.[35] For many Westerners, the "eccentricities, spastic zaniness, [and] libertarian fearlessness"[36] of contemporary Japanese popular culture represent "a vision of the future, a fresh way of telling stories and of reproducing the world."[37] The futuristic vision of a postcolonial Japan that develops an autonomous culture able to invade a world whose culture it had once been supposed to passively consume and imitate is indeed reminiscent of West's definition of African-Americans as "New World African Moderns" who "constitute a homebound quest in offbeat temporality."[38]

TOWARD A COOL-KAWAII MODERNITY

Cool and kawaii do not refer back to a premodern ethnic past. Just like the cool African-American man has almost no relationship with traditional African ideas about masculinity, the kawaii *shōjo* is not the personification of the traditional Japanese ideal of the feminine, but signifies an ideological institution of women based on Japanese modernity in the Meiji period, that is, a feminine image based on westernization.[39] However, cool and kawaii do not transport us into a futuristic, impersonal world of hypermodernity based on assumptions of constant modernization, either. This means that cool and kawaii stand for another type of modernity, which is not the technocratic one but the one closely related to the search for human dignity and liberation. In West's words, New World Modernity attempts to "time" modern civilization in an eccentric fashion. Cool and kawaii are modern inasmuch as to be modern means to have "the courage to use one's critical intelligence to question and challenge the prevailing authorities, powers and hierarchies of the world."[40] This is indeed a very particular concept of modernity, because it is able to act against both traditionalism and antitraditionalist modernism. New World Modernity embraces this spirit.

There is an ambiguity at work in this concept of modernity and this ambiguity is also part and parcel of the definitions of both cool and kawaii. Apart from that, both cool and kawaii are bound to this ambiguity through the cultural situation in which they are imbedded. A statement from Kenzaburō Ōe on ambiguity makes this obvious. Ōe has designed for himself a "habit of being" that he wishes to illustrate with the help of a poem by W. H. Auden ("The Novelist," lines 11–14). "[A]mong the Just," Auden writes, one must "[b]e just, among the Filthy filthy too." "And in [one's] own weak person, if [one] can," continues Auden, one "[m]ust suffer dully all the wrongs of Man."[41]

This poem captures a lot of the qualities of cool that have been described above. Ōe feels a deep concern about the ambiguity to which he is submitted as a Japanese writer in a modernized Japan (which he considers to be a "disaster") and announces that for him the highest ideal of a life in an alienated world is to remain "decent."[42] He wants the word 'decent' to be understood in the sense of 'humanist.' Obviously, he is referring to a sort of alienating "coolness" that is necessary when attempting to maintain human dignity in a modern world.

How can one stay "decent" and cool in Japanese society? The situation is complicated because an undercurrent of identity problems is at work when it comes to establishing a "habit of being." Ōe's insistence on "ambiguity" in several of his writings shows that his striving for humanist "decency" has much to do with Japan's ambiguous status as a country able to articulate two

identities. In this sense, Japanese modern culture is not "linear." Instead, its
national identity is determined by a duality, or even a "triality" composed of
Asia, the West, and Japan. Koichi Iwabuchi explains that "Japan is unequivocally located in a geographical area called 'Asia,' but it no less exists outside
a cultural imaginary of 'Asia' in Japanese mental maps."[43] To a large extent,
Ōe's "ambiguity" overlaps with the double consciousness of the African-
American philosopher W. E. B. Du Bois, which is "a peculiar sensation, ...
this sense of always looking at one's self through the eyes of others, of mea-
suring one's soul by the tape of a world that looks on in amused contempt
and pity."[44]

Contemporary Japanese culture is not "linear" and that's what makes it
cool. A further nonlinear input is produced by Japan's relationship with
modernity. Though Japan has responded very quickly to the challenges posed
by the prior development of science and technology in the Western world,
Japanese culture still has a "curious quasi-Third World status."[45] Ōe recognizes that "the modernization of Japan was oriented toward learning from and
imitating the West, yet the country is situated in Asia and has firmly maintained its traditional culture."[46] As a consequence, Japanese culture embraces
both first-worldliness and third-worldliness. Expressions of kawaii need to be
understood within this nonlinear context. Like cool, they *can* be ambiguous
forms of resistance only within a world that is profoundly ambiguous, or, to
put it in a formula, they are forms of cool resistance. This is why they so often
overlap with African-American cool procedures.

It is interesting to compare this "coolness resulting from nonlinearity" with
another cultural expression of New World Modernity: jazz. As a nonwhite
American music, jazz adopts "fluid and flexible positions toward reality
[and is] suspicious of 'either/or' viewpoints, dogmatic pronouncements, or
supremacist ideologies."[47] Still, jazz can be seen as part of real American
culture because "culturally, America is a backward country; Americans are
backward. But jazz is American reality—total reality."[48]

Both jazz and contemporary Japanese popular culture have found a type
of cool that can be called the 'anti-sarcastic cool.' Both African-American
culture and Japanese anime and manga brush against the grain of binary mor-
alisms and introduce features that transcend the bitter irony of white mainstream coolness. "White cool" thrived together with republican and puritan
virtues such as rational thinking and self-control, which could be crystallized
in the Protestant work ethic. It highlights the tough loner and his fight for
justice, identity, and cultural superiority.[49] According to Kelts, among the
more complex aspects of anime are "the acceptability of the illogical and
the ambiguous, the hero's sense of duty above all else, the concepts of child
as hero and of unending quest, the undependability of a happy ending, and
the fact that no individual episode ever satisfactorily ties up the various and

addictive narrative threads."[50] Other scholars have argued that the aesthetic of kawaii can be considered to have a relationship with Daisetz T. Suzuki's notion of "non-discrimination" (*mufunbetsu no funbetu*), which overcomes typical Western duality concepts such as subjectivity versus objectivity, object versus mind, existence versus nothingness, God versus human beings, good versus bad, and sacred versus profane.[51]

Similar to Kelts, Cornel West opposes his New World Modernity not only to optimistic futurism but also to "pessimistic" postmodernism. Interestingly, he uses the work of the Swiss-French architect Le Corbusier as an example for a modernism able to overcome the "the binary opposition of machine-nature, civilized-primitive, ruler-ruled, Apollonian-Dionysian, male-female, white-black [and other peoples of color]."[52] According to West, Le Corbusier integrates female and Third World elements into his overall modern expressions, which makes his architecture emblematic for the African-American New World Modernity that West attempts to formulate. West quotes Charles Jencks, who points out that Le Corbusier found in American Negro music and in the hot jazz of Louis Armstrong "equilibrium on a tightrope" and "a lyrical 'contemporary' mass so invincible that I could see the foundation of a new sentiment of music capable of being the expression of the new epoch and also capable of classifying its European origins as stone age—just as has happened with the new architecture."[53]

West's intuition that links Le Corbusier's architecture to the general situation of African-American culture is visionary. In the 1970s, when Jencks published his book, Le Corbusier's critical evaluations of modernism had for the most part escaped notice. In a chapter entitled 'At War with Reaction 1928–1945,' Jencks analyzes an explicit change in the architect's work that began to consciously introduce "objects invoking a poetic reaction" into his paintings and buildings.[54] It is in this context that Le Corbusier produces a vision of African-American culture as a humanist New World Modernism bearing an uncanny resemblance to Kelts's futuristic Japan. Le Corbusier describes Josephine Baker—of whom he made realistic portraits when traveling in the United States, bringing out her artistry and vitality in a "kawaii" fashion—as "a small child pure, simple, and limpid. She glides over the roughness of life. She has a good little heart."[55]

CONCLUSION

Essentializations of culture in terms of exoticism or the "Other" always happen by referring to some "natural," traditional, historic truth. New World Modernism, on the other hand, is able to overcome the aforementioned binary oppositions (machine-nature, civilized-primitive, ruler-ruled, male-female, whites-peoples of color, etc.). This is why in New World Modernism—be it the African-American cool one or the kawaii one located in futuristic post-colonial Japan—culture is "timed" in an eccentric fashion. In principle, this means that this culture does not follow the "popular realism" of mainstream white Europeans or Americans. The expansion of cool and kawaii culture is thus an attribute of this New World Modernism.

NOTES

1. Tom Pryor, "Hip-Hop," *National Geographic*, accessed June 29, 2015, http://worldmusic.nationalgeographic.com/worldmusic/view/page.basic/genre/content.genre/hip_hop_730.
2. Carol Walker, "Hip-Hop Culture Crosses Social Barriers: Musical Artists Tell America's Story in Rap," US Department of State, last modified May 13, 2006, http://iipdigital.usembassy.gov/st/english/article/2006/05/20060508165055bcreklaw0.4616358.html#axzz3eQlu45N3.
3. Joseph L. White and James H. Cones III, *Black Man Emerging: Facing the Past and Seizing a Future in America* (London: Routledge, 1999), 60.
4. Natalie Avella, *Graphic Japan: From Woodblock and Zen to Manga and Kawaii* (Mies, Switzerland: RotoVision, 2004), 218.
5. Koichi Iwabuchi, *Recentering Globalization: Popular Culture and Japanese Transnationalism* (Durham, NC: Duke University Press, 2002), 30.
6. Roland Kelts, *Japanamerica: How Japanese Pop Culture Has Invaded the U.S.* (New York: Palgrave Macmillan, 2006), 5.
7. Christine R. Yano, *Pink Globalization: Hello Kitty's Trek across the Pacific* (Durham, NC: Duke University Press, 2013).
8. Sianne Ngai, *Our Aesthetic Categories: Zany, Cute, Interesting* (Cambridge, MA: Harvard University Press, 2012).
9. Cornel West, *The Cornel West Reader* (New York: Basic Civitas Books, 1999), 13.
10. Ibid., xiii.
11. Marshall McLuhan, *Understanding Media: The Extensions of Man* (New York: Prentice Hall, 1964).
12. Cf. Alan Liu, *The Laws of Cool: Knowledge Work and the Culture of Information* (Chicago: University of Chicago Press, 2004), 77.
13. Yano, *Pink Globalization*, 27.
14. Kate Crawford, "The Anxieties of Big Data," *New Inquiry*, May 30, 2014, accessed June 27, 2015, http://thenewinquiry.com/essays/the-anxieties-of-big-data/.
15. Ngai, *Aesthetic Categories*.
16. Anne Allison, "The Cultural Politics of Pokémon Capitalism" (paper presented at the Media in Transition 2: Globalization and Convergence Conference, Massachusetts Institute of Technology, Cambridge, MA, May 10–12, 2002), 5.
17. John Whittier Treat, "Yoshimoto Banana Writes Home: The *Shōjo* in Japanese Popular Culture," in *Contemporary Japan and Popular Culture*, ed. John Whittier Treat (Honolulu: University of Hawai'i Press, 1996), 298.

18. Cf. Anne Allison, "Cuteness as Japan's Millennial Product," in *Pikachu's Global Adventure: The Rise and Fall of Pokémon*, ed. Joseph Tobin (Durham, NC: Duke University Press, 2004), 40.

19. Fred Lee Hord (AKA Mzee Lasana Okpara) and Jonathan Scott Lee, eds., *I Am Because We Are: Readings in Black Philosophy* (Amherst, MA: University of Massachusetts Press, 1995).

20. Cornel West, "Philosophy and the Afro-American Experience," in *A Companion to African-American Philosophy*, ed. Tommy L. Lott and John P. Pittman (Oxford: Blackwell, 2003), 7.

21. Richard Majors and Janet Mancini Billson, *Cool Pose: The Dilemmas of Black Manhood in America* (New York: Lexington Books, 1992), 5.

22. Terry Williams, foreword to *What Is Cool?: Understanding Black Manhood in America*, by Marlene K. Connor (New York: Crown, 1994), xii.

23. Wilson Jeremiah Moses, *Creative Conflict in African-American Thought: Frederick Douglass, Alexander Crummell, Booker T. Washington, W. E. B. Du Bois, and Marcus Garvey* (Cambridge: Cambridge University Press, 2004), 4.

24. Byong-Je Jon, "Republic of Korea," in *Youth in Asia: Viewpoints for the Future*, ed. Association of Asian Social Science Research Councils (New Delhi: New Statesman, 1988), 139.

25. Paul Gilroy, *The Black Atlantic: Modernity and Double-Consciousness* (Cambridge, MA: Harvard University Press, 1993), 118.

26. West, *Cornel West Reader*, 51.

27. Cornel West, *Prophesy Deliverance!: An Afro-American Revolutionary Christianity* (Louisville, KY: Westminster John Knox Press, 1982), 27.

28. Amiri Baraka (AKA LeRoi Jones), *Black Music* (New York: Morrow, 1967), 70.

29. Paul Virilio, "The Third Interval: A Critical Transition," in *Rethinking Technologies*, ed. Verena Andermatt Conley (Minneapolis, MN: University of Minnesota Press, 1993), 10, emphasis added.

30. Paul Virilio, "Silence on Trial," in *The Virilio Reader*, ed. James Der Derian (Malden, MA: Blackwell, 1998), 230.

31. Henry Louis Gates, Jr., *The Signifying Monkey: A Theory of African-American Literary Criticism* (Oxford: Oxford University Press, 1989), 106.

32. Ibid., 107.

33. Lise Skov, "Fashion Trends, Japonisme and Postmodernism: Or 'What Is So Japanese about *Comme des Garcons*?'" in *Contemporary Japan and Popular Culture*, ed. John Whittier Treat (Honolulu: University of Hawai'i Press, 1996), 145.

34. Sharon Kinsella, "Cuties in Japan," in *Women, Media, and Consumption in Japan*, ed. Lise Skov and Brian Moeran (Honolulu: University of Hawai'i Press, 1995), 226.

35. Kelts, *Japanamerica*.

36. Ibid., 6.

37. Ibid., 7.

38. Cornel West, *Keeping Faith: Philosophy and Race in America* (New York: Routledge, 1993), xiii.

39. Cf. Fusami Ōgi, "Gender Insubordination in Japanese Comics (*Manga*) for Girls," in *Illustrating Asia: Comics, Humor Magazines, and Picture Books*, ed. John A. Lent (Honolulu: University of Hawai'i Press, 2001), 171.

40. West, *Cornel West Reader*, xvii.

41. W. H. Auden, "The Novelist," in W. H. Auden, *Collected Poems*, ed. Edward Mendelson (New York: Modern Library, 2007), 180.

42. Kenzaburō Ōe, *Japan, the Ambiguous, and Myself* (Tokyo: Kodansha International, 1995), 122.

43. Iwabuchi, *Recentering Globalization*, 7.

44. W. E. B. Du Bois, *The Souls of Black Folk* (Boston: Bedford, 1997), 3.

45. Iwabuchi, *Recentering Globalization*, 2.

46. Ōe, *Japan*, 117.

47. Cornel West, *Race Matters* (New York: Vintage Books, 2001), 150.

48. Baraka, *Black Music*, 155.

49. Cf. Peter N. Stearns, *American Cool: Constructing a Twentieth-Century Emotional Style* (New York: New York University Press, 1994).

50. Kelts, *Japanamerica*, 91.

51. Keith Vincent, "Nihon-teki miseijuku no keifu" ("The Genealogy of Japanese Immaturity"), in *Nihon-tekisōzōryoku no mirai: Kūru japonorojii no kanōsei (The Future of the Japanese Imagination: The Potential of Cool Japanology)*, ed. Azuma Hiroki (Tokyo: NHK Books, 2010), 19. Cited in Kyoko Koma, "Kawaii as Represented in Scientific Research: The Possibilities of Kawaii Cultural Studies," *Hemispheres* 28 (2013): 13.

52. West, *Keeping Faith*, 45.

53. Charles Jencks, *Le Corbusier and the Tragic View of Architecture* (Cambridge, MA: Harvard University Press, 1973), 102.

54. Ibid., 99.

55. Ibid., 102.

Part IV

JAPANESE AESTHETICS
AND LITERATURE

Chapter 16

Bashō and the Art of Eternal Now

Michiko Yusa

INTRODUCTION

Nishida Kitarō (1870–1945) in his essay on the feature of Japanese short poetry observed that life experience can be either grasped at its very tip of scintillating sparks or viewed objectively, as if one were standing on the side of the environment. The former is to grasp life in its "pure experience," and the latter to apprehend it objectively. Nishida's point was that the Japanese short poetic form known as 'tanka' enabled the poets of all ages to capture the former.[1] In another essay, he commented on an even shorter seventeen-syllable poetic form of *haiku* in relation to the Japanese penchant for grasping the "timeless" in the midst of daily life.

Taking these observations as a guide, we shall analyze Matsuo Bashō's masterpiece *Oku no hosomichi* (completed in the year of his death, 1694), which remains enormously popular to this day. In this work, Bashō (1644–1694) experimented with weaving prose and verse, capturing both the moment "now" and the historical perspective "then." He had already been combining haiku verse and free-flowing prose in his earlier works, but it was in the *Oku no hosomichi* that he finally came to strike the ideal balance he wanted to achieve between the two. My working hypothesis is that haiku retains the moment of the "present" and preserves something of the timeless element, while the prose narrates the background or context of the specific moment expressed in the haiku. Bashō interwove these two ways of grasping life experience, while honing his artistic sensitivity to capture the "eternal" quality in the "now."

Accompanied by his travel companion Sora, Bashō set out on a six-month journey (which may be dubbed a 'poetic pilgrimage') in 1689 to the north-eastern region of Japan known as 'Michinoku.' This travel resulted in *Oku no*

hosomichi (*The Narrow Road to the North*).[2] It was during this journey that
Bashō came to talk about the ideal of art as embodying the qualities of "the
timeless and the temporal" (*fueki ryūkō*),[3] by which he meant that art must
respond to the ever-changing taste of the day (*ryūkō*), while seeking also to
endow it with a lasting quality (*fueki*) that transcends the passage of time. He
found the only way to achieve this end was to pursue his art by becoming
truly one with the "object" of his poetizing, sustained by the mental-spiritual
posture of sincerity (*makoto*). At the same time, his inner gaze was focused
on the question of art and temporality. It is by no coincidence therefore that
he began this work with the imagery of time as eternal travelers:

> Months and days are passing guests of the hundreds of generations. The years
> that come and go are also travelers. Those who float away their lives on boats
> or who grow old leading horses are forever travelling, and their homes are
> wherever those travels take them. Many a poet of old, too, died on his journey.[4]

Nature is in constant motion and human lives are short, but art may capture
and preserve the fleeting moments so that they may live on beyond the life
and times of the artist.[5] Art, unlike nature, is the keeper of timeless human
experience. That Bashō's work still possesses the power to appeal to today's
readers not only among the Japanese but also across cultural boundaries
already seems to give us the answer to our inquiry—that he indeed succeeded
in embodying his ideal of *fueki ryūkō* in his art by paying attention to how to
incorporate both modes of temporality.

NEW YET ENDURING QUALITIES OF A POPULAR ART

Bashō was an artist and not a scholar, and did not leave any written treatises
on haiku composition. Fortunately, however, his able disciples recorded their
master's precious words of teaching. One such distinguished disciple was
Hattori Tohō (1657–1730), whose *Sanzōshi* (*Three Notebooks*) has been considered the invaluable record of his master's aesthetic theories.[6] Tohō began
his "Red Notebook"—the three notebooks were differentiated by their black,
white, and red covers—with the statement that the idea of *fueki ryūkō* was at
the heart of his master's art:

> In Master's art, there was something timeless and eternally changeless. Also
> there was something that responded to the changing times. His art ultimately
> boiled down to these two aspects of the changeless and the change, which,
> moreover, stemmed from one and the same source—his *sincere* pursuit
> of art.[7]

Tohō continues:

> If we do not know the "changeless," we really don't know art in the real sense of
> the word. What is meant by "changeless" [*fueki*] is the appearance of the poem
> that can stand on its own in its truthfulness, regardless of whether it is new or
> old, independent of the fashion and the taste of the day [*ryūkō*]. As we study the
> works of the successive poets of the past, we recognize that each generation is
> colored by the taste of the day. Regardless of how ancient or modern, however,
> what the poets saw and expressed in their poems still possesses the power to
> move and evoke deep feelings within us. *This* is what is meant by "changeless."[8]

Bashō was fully aware that poems of different times necessarily reflected the
respective tastes of those times, and that time moves on. When he was residing in Edo (today's Tokyo) from 1672 to 1694, the city was full of vibrant,
youthful energy, as it was emerging as the new cultural center to be reckoned
with by the old cultural arbiters of the Kyoto and Osaka region.[9] He thrived
in the open spirit of burgeoning Edo, where his bold artistic experiments were
eagerly sought and embraced by his likeminded fellow haiku poets as opening
a new frontier. Moreover, his verses had a popular appeal. Not to move on
with time for him meant to render his art obsolete. Tohō speaks of this fact:

> What the late Master was constantly after was the "scent" of freshness. He took
> delight in those who understood this quality, and pursued it himself and encour-
> aged others to do the same. Even if we relentlessly pursue our art to push the
> frontier, if our poems do not catch the fancy of the people of the day, it must be
> so because freshness is lacking. Freshness is a quality that emerges out of the
> poetic soul, as we take a new step in our constant artistic endeavor.
>   The Master's poem, "Under the bright moon, a cloud-like mist covering
> the foothills hovers over the rice paddies" [*Meigetsu ni fumoto no kiri ya ta
> no kumori*], emphasizes the quality of *fueki*, the timeless quality; whereas the
> other verse of his, "Under the bright moon, is the field abloom? So the cotton
> fields appear" [*Meigetsu no hana ka to miete watabatake*],[10] is imbued with the
> sensitivity of freshness.[11]

Although Bashō recognized that innovations were part of the poetic tradition,
he also wished to add "classical" depth to his verses, which would render
them timeless. Even a popular poem can harbor a universal dimension of
human experience. Bashō understood that while the "fresh" and "timely"
elements responded to the milieu of the time, this did not preclude the introduction of the "timeless" quality. In this context, his words of advice to his
beloved student Kyoroku—"Do not seek to follow in the footsteps of the
ancients; seek what they sought"—make clearer sense.[12]

ZEN PRACTICE AND BASHŌ'S
MEDITATION ON TEMPORALITY

It is curious that biographies and commentaries on Bashō often remain silent about the fact that he was an adept practitioner of Zen Buddhism.[13] In fact, it was his *satori* experience that nurtured his existential posture and his worldview, and informed his aesthetic principle. Zen practice also opened Bashō's eyes to the significance of "temporality and experience" in close connection with his literary activities. What is thought-provoking here is that many thinkers who dig deeply into the mode of existence seem to arrive at an inquiry into the nature of time (take, for instance, Bergson, Heidegger, Nishida, and Dōgen, the last of whom wrote about his meditation on time[14]).

Bashō's lifestyle also underwent a change as his *satori* experience fermented within him. He became progressively attracted to a minimalist lifestyle in the spirit of detachment and freedom from the yoke of worldly possessions. His desire for journey appears to be the expression of his yearning for spiritual freedom, which, moreover, took him into close contact with nature. He spent the last years of his life in a semi-continuous journey, traveling from one famous site celebrated by the ancient itinerant poets to another. To combine in one's life spiritual-religious practice with aesthetic pursuit was by no means new but was a time-honored tradition lived by many artistically minded figures of the past such as Priest Nōin (988–1051?) and Saigyō Hōshi (1118–1190). Bashō's exposure to Zen literature also augmented his appreciation of Chinese poets, notably Li Bo, Du Fu, Su Shi, and Huang Shangu.[15] In addition, he dearly cherished and savored a close affinity with the Daoist philosophy of the *Zhuangzi*.

Kinsei zenrin sōhōden, a collection of concise biographies of notable Zen masters and lay practitioners of the recent past, contains an entry on Matsuo Tōsei—'Tōsei' being an earlier penname before he adopted 'Bashō.' According to this biographical information, Bashō took up Zen practice under the Rinzai Zen master, Bucchō Kanan (1642–1715),[16] and received an *inka* (master's approval) as an enlightened lay practitioner (*koji*).[17] Bucchō, the abbot of Konponji in Kashima, was stationed in Edo from 1674 to 1682, representing his temple's landholding rights at a prolonged legal hearing. Rinsenji Temple, where he was residing, was in the vicinity of Bashō'an, the abode of the poet.

Around 1680, Bashō came to know Bucchō and began his *sanzen* practice.[18] He was then in his mid-thirties, and the Zen master was only two years his senior. The Japanese Zen literati have traditionally associated Bashō's famous "frog" verse—"Oh, old pond! A frog jumps in, the sound of water" (*furuikeya kawazu tobikomu mizu no oto*)—with his Zen awakening experience, as the following exchange illustrates their claim:

On one spring day Bucchō called on Bashō, whose *kōan* practice was nicely progressing ... . Bucchō walked into the garden, saw Bashō, and asked: "What is up these days?" Bashō answered: "After the rain, the moss is greener than ever." Bucchō asked: "What was it like before the moss had yet come into being and the spring rain had yet to fall?" At that time, a frog jumped into a nearby pond. Bashō happened to see this, and these words issued spontaneously: "A frog jumps in, the sound of water!"[19] Bucchō nodded his head in approval.[20]

This stylized exchange is *not* to be taken as something that actually took place, but as a later reconstruction by the compiler of the various known elements associated with Bashō. We notice, moreover, that their "conversation" is steeped in the Mahayana Buddhist worldview, namely, that animate and inanimate things have their "buddha nature"—be it the moss in the garden, the rain, the frog, not to mention human beings, and that the world comes into being at the moment of the arising of one's consciousness. Bucchō was satisfied with his student's response, "a frog jumps in, the sound of water," which revealed to him that Bashō had broken through the barrier of the ordinary mental confines of subject-object dichotomy. Bashō's answer shot out of his direct experience of oneness with the frog, which indicated to the master that Bashō now stood in the *realm of freedom beyond concepts*—he was one with the very heartbeat of the cosmos.

According to the *Kinsei zenrin sōhōden*, after Bucchō left Edo in 1682, Bashō visited him at Konponji in Kashima to further his practice, and later at Unganji in Nasu, where his *satori* breakthrough was acknowledged by Bucchō. The content of his *satori* experience appears to have consisted of the recognition of the "utter emptiness of all things including the self" (*honbun musō*) and "the oneness of the mind and the dharma realm" (*isshin hokkai, hokkai isshin*), or the oneness of consciousness and the cosmos.[21] There is no record of when Bashō actually attained his *satori*, but it may be conjectured to have been sometime around 1683, when he still had the time to devote himself to Zen practice. We know that even after the completion of his formal Zen practice, Bashō maintained contact with Bucchō and made a trip to Kashima to call on him in the fall (August of the lunar calendar, present-day September) of 1687.[22] Later, he paid homage for the last time when he visited the master's former hermitage at Unganji in the early summer of 1689 on his way to Michinoku. Bucchō appeared to have resided elsewhere by then, for the hut was unoccupied. Bashō found the master's hut shaded by the tall trees thick with summer leaves, and undamaged by the woodpeckers notorious for demolishing temple buildings. He composed the following verse:

Kitsutsuki mo   Even the woodpeckers
io wa yaburazu   Stay away from the thatched hut
natsu kodachi.[23]   Intact under the trees with thick summer leaves.

His heart must have been filled with the memory of the days of his *sanzen* practice under Bucchō, who was a kind master.

NISHIDA ON THE SHORT POETIC FORM

As mentioned at the outset, the most suggestive reflection on "temporality and poetry" comes from Nishida's essay "Tanka ni tsuite" ("On *Tanka*"),[24] wherein we find the following passage:

> To grasp our life experience by way of short poetic form [*tanshi*] is to grasp it from the very midst of the present moment. It is to view life from the very point of the moment of experience. Life, for sure, is one whole unity, but in grasping this concrete and vibrant life, it is one thing to look at it from the environment; it is another to grasp it at the very tip of vividly pulsating life. Depending on from which angle we approach it, life presents itself differently, and we live a different significance of life.[25]

Here, Nishida distinguishes two different ways of grasping life experience: from within, at the "very tip" of vivid life experience, and from without, from the side of the environment, objectively. To grasp life at its very tip is tantamount to approximating a "pure experience." Because Nishida began this essay on *tanka* by mentioning Henri Bergson, it is reasonable to presume that the objective way of grasping life refers to the Bergsonian philosophical approach. Nishida, on his part, observed that the short poetic form, and specifically *tanka*, has the unique capacity to express deep emotions. He wrote: "I believe that by *tanka* the innermost experiences can be expressed, for *tanka* is ultimately lyrical as that which expresses the rhythm of our emotion and feelings."[26] We may take a step further and propose here that the way to approximate the direct experience is to *express* it, whereas the way to capture it from the environment is to *describe* it. Short poems contain and "express" our life experience, whereas prose "describes" it at length and in detail.

Haiku, having evolved out of the first three lines of *tanka*, consists of only seventeen syllables and is thus even shorter than *tanka*. In another essay, Nishida makes the following observation concerning haiku:

> Just as it is said that the Greek language is suited for philosophy and Latin for law, is there something that the Japanese language is uniquely suited for? I would think *haiku*, for instance, is something that is hardly translatable into any other language. It contains beauty that would only be possible in the Japanese language. To put it on a grander scale of things, *haiku* expresses the unique characteristics of the Japanese people's way of viewing life and the world. The characteristics of the Japanese way of thinking and viewing life and the world

consist in apprehending the infinite within the realities of daily life [*genjitsu no naka ni mugen o tsukamu*].[27]

Here, Nishida stops short of analyzing what features of the Japanese language render the art of haiku so unique. Certainly, this is a fascinating linguistic question to be revisited some other time. Here, we simply note that Nishida saw haiku to have developed out of the penchant of the Japanese mentality that seeks to capture the "timeless" reality in the midst of daily experience.

Since this is not the place to carry out a full-fledged discussion of Nishida's view of time, we only delineate some main points that are relevant to our present purpose. He, like Augustine, maintained that the three modes of time—the past, the present, and the future—are copresent in the mind, but for Nishida, Augustine's view did not explain how time moves on.[28] Although agreeing with the view that the present and the future are present in "at the present moment," Nishida regarded the present as *coming into being at each moment and disappearing in the next*. The succession of discrete moments coming into being at one moment and disappearing in the next (*hirenzoku no renzoku*) explains how time moves on.[29] Instead of considering time simply to "flow" from the past to the future, Nishida pondered the fact that when we become self-conscious, it is always "at the present moment." This radically "present" nature of self-consciousness led him to formulate his view that the present moment arises as the "self-determination of the absolute present," and this absolute present he called the 'eternal now.' Moreover, each moment has a spatial dimension, that is, it has its expanse and length. Interestingly, Aristotle and other ancient Greek thinkers did give a special attention to the "now" (νῦν, the moment, the present) as "outside" time, but they did not further pursue their reflection on the nature of time, and maintained it as "a stretch with a beginning and an end."[30]

IMPERMANENCE, "FRESH" MOMENTS, AND BEAUTY

The recognition that all things must pass and nothing is forever (*anitya* in Sanskrit, *mujō* in Japanese) is the hallmark of the Buddha's teaching, which profoundly colored the Japanese worldview. Japanese authors of the Nara and Heian periods regarded impermanence, accentuated by the "fleeting youth and beauty," with a melancholic sigh, but by the fourteenth century, they came to affirm impermanence as the very source of marvel and beauty. Yoshida Kenkō (1283–1350), for instance, famously stated that "precisely because this human world is marked by uncertainty, it is so fantastic" (*yo wa sadame naki koso imiji kere*).[31] Positively understood as momentariness,

230 Michiko Yusa

impermanence also found its aesthetic expression in Zeami Motokiyo (1363–1443?), who compared the secret of a splendid Noh performance to a flower—flowers bloom on all sorts of trees, but they do so only at certain times of the year. Thus, when they bloom, they strike the viewer as "fresh" and "delightful."[32] In short, the understanding of all things as impermanent gave rise to the appreciation of fleeting moments as unique and beautiful. This widely shared perception is at the core of medieval and modern Japanese aesthetics. Tohō, speaking of Bashō's search for the "freshness," dubbed it as 'the flower of the art of haiku' (*atarashimi wa haikai no hana nari*),[33] and Bashō himself mentioned the imagery of the flower in his travel journal *Oi no kobumi* (*A Small Bundle of Writings in a Rucksack*):

> If artists find no "flower" in the appearance of things, they are no longer human beings but brutes. If they perceive no "flower" in their heart, they are no different from wild birds and beasts. Artists must leave barbarity behind, draw a line between themselves and wild birds and beasts, listen to nature, and return to nature's bosom.[34]

EXPRESSION IN A VERSE: THE MOMENT OF PURE EXPERIENCE

Poetic inspirations came to Bashō in his experience of forming oneness with the "object" of poetizing. In the moment of subject-object unity, this "object" in fact ceases to be an "object" but reveals its vivid living reality to the poet.[35] In conveying this insight, Bashō famously taught to "go to a pine tree to learn about a pine tree, and go to a bamboo to learn about a bamboo." Tohō, while noting these words of the master, added his understanding that by 'to learn,' Bashō was referring to the essential importance of getting rid of one's preconceptions, which after all were the products of willfulness (*shii*). When a poet has duly discarded willfulness and emptied her mind, she resides in an utterly receptive mood, merges into the thing, and sees the thing giving out a sort of "light" that forms an impression in the poet's mind. This important passage by Tohō merits close attention:

> "About a pine tree, learn from a pine tree; about a bamboo, learn from a bamboo." What the Master wanted to say by these words was that when we compose poetry, we must leave our preconceptions behind … . When we enter the object and glimpse its hidden spark, a poetic sentiment arises within us. However nicely phrased our verse may be, if it is not sustained by the sentiment that spontaneously flows out of the "thing," the thing and the poet remain two separate entities, and the poet's sentiment falls short of truthfulness. A verse that

is composed out of the separation of the thing and the poet is but an artificial product of the arbitrary will.[36]

In the unity of subject and object, the poet intuits the "light" that emanates from the object and gives rise to the poetic emotion. Bashō reassures that when the poet follows this "glimmer" of the thing, a verse will form of itself.

Moreover, for a poet to see the glimmer of a thing is to seize the moment. A poet must "capture" the sight and the sound in the fleeting moment. It is like taking a *mental snapshot* of the scene. Tohō writes:

> The Master said that the incessant mutation of nature is the seed of art. In repose, it reveals the appearance of the unchanging aspects of reality; in motion, it reveals the appearance of that which is in dynamic mutation. Unless we "arrest" [or "retain" or "capture"] the appearance of things in time, nothing remains. 'To apprehend' means to put it in words in terms of sight and sound. Even the wonderful scattering of spring flowers or autumnal leaves cannot be captured unless we commit them to our memory in terms of sight and sound; for it is the nature of all living things to disappear without a trace.
>
> Concerning verse composition, the Master said to commit our impressions in words while the light of the thing is still flickering in our mind. He also said that there was a technique to focus on the most vivid image of a thing, obtainable by entering its innermost realm. While the impression of the thing is still fresh, we ought to put it in words, and later rework the verse to refine it.[37]

Bashō basically taught his students to keep written notes (and sketches) to remember the fleeting yet memorable moments. (In fact, Bashō took delight in producing occasional sketches of the places he visited.)

DESCRIPTION IN A PROSE: CAPTURING THE EXPERIENCE FROM OUTSIDE

If the life of haiku consists in the moment that is captured by words, Bashō made full use of *prose* to narrate in his *Oku no hosomichi* such things as the circumstances of his visit, geographical features of the place, historical events and anecdotes associated with the place, and his personal impressions. Moreover, what make Bashō's prose alive are his personal feelings. Prose does not have to be cut-and-dried or "prosaic." He carefully crafted his prose with certain cadence and rhythm, and deftly incorporated numerous poetic allusions and imageries.

It is not surprising, then, that whenever he came into the presence of the legacy of the past, he was often quite moved, for such came to him as the enduring affirmation of the timeless aspect of human experience. In *Oku no hosomichi*, these moments abound. Here, we quote a segment from his visit to the ancient fortress of Tagajō,[38] where he encountered a stone monument with a barely legible inscription dated from the sixth year of Tenpyō Hōji (i.e., 762 C.E.), which corresponded to the time shortly after the reign of Emperor Shōmu (724–749). Emperor Shōmu is known, among many other achievements, for having commissioned the casting of the great Buddha image at Tōdaiji in Nara. Bashō could not help but be moved to tears by this encounter with the monument forgotten in the remote countryside:

> Many place names celebrated in the old *waka* poems have survived to our time, but mountains crumble, rivers change their course, new roads replace the old, stones get buried under the earth, and trees grow old and give way to new growth. Time passes, the generations change, and often we are no longer certain of what remains of the past. And yet lo! Here right before my eyes is the monument, a memory of the ancient people of one thousand years ago, standing before me as if it were my privilege to "pry" into the hearts of the ancients. If this is not the reward of the peregrination and the joy of having lived as long as I have, what is? I forgot the weariness of my travel, and tears streamed down on my face.[39]

Unlike, say, the Eternal City of Rome, where one readily encounters the remains of the ancient past, in Japan, where wood and paper were the major building materials, coming across ancient monuments is a much rarer occasion. Thus, for Bashō, whenever he had such an encounter, it augmented his conviction that some things do endure even against the tide of impermanence.

TEXT READING AND APPRECIATION: *OKU NO HOSOMICHI*

We shall now read a brief section on Hiraizumi from the *Oku no hosomichi* to try out our working hypothesis, namely, that while the prose section *describes* pertinent facts and sets the scene for us, the haiku *captures and retains* something of the timeless quality of the poet's impression and experience. The intended effect of haiku is to bring the scene set by the prose to the present moment. Interestingly, Bashō's prose is predominantly written in the present tense.

The two travelers, Bashō and Sora, reached Hiraizumi on May 13 (of the old lunar calendar, today's mid-June), 1689. The opening passage of this section contains the historical information concerning the events that led up to the year 1189—going back exactly five hundred years to date from the time of their visit:

The glory of the three generations of the Fujiwaras vanished in the space of a dream; the ruins of the great castle portal and other major buildings are a few miles behind where we stand, and the site where Hidehira's palatial mansion stood has turned into farm lands and fields, and only [the manmade] Golden Cockerel Hill remains as in former days. We first climbed up Takadachi Hill, from where we could see Kitakami, the large river that flows from the northern region of Nanbu to the south. Koromo River skirts around the former residence of Izumi, and falls and merges into the great river Kitakami under the former fortress. Yasuhira's mansion across the Koromo Barrier appears to have been placed there to cut off access from the north to protect the city from the invasion of the Ezo tribesmen. Here loyal retainers [of Yoshitsune] fiercely fought for their master, but the site of their bravery has long turned into the grass.

> *A country fell, but rivers and mountains remain.*
> *When spring comes around to the ruined city wall,*
> *the grass is green again.*[40]

These lines crossed my mind as I sat on my bamboo hat spread on the ground. There I sat in tears, unaware of the passage of time.

> *Ah, summer grass!*
> *brave warriors'*
> *site of dreams.*[41]

This should give us enough text to work with.

Here, 'the three generations of the Fujiwaras' refers to the Ōshū Fujiwara Clan of the Northern Province. In the twelfth century, the leader of the clan, Fujiwara no Kiyohira (1086–1128) established a splendid cultural center in the heart of northern Honshū (in today's Iwate Prefecture) with Hiraizumi as its capital city.[42] The Ōshū Fujiwaras made their fortune on the gold mines discovered in their province, which enabled them to engage in lucrative overseas trade. Hiraizumi was strategically located as it was connected to the sea route by way of Kitakami River that flowed out into Shiogama Bay. With the huge fortune they amassed, elaborate exquisite gold-gilded temples, splendid mansions, and elegant gardens were constructed in the capital city during the reigns of Kiyohira, Motohira, and Hidehira—the three generations of the Fujiwaras.

The "brave warriors" alluded to in the haiku are the retainers and supporters of Minamoto no Yoshitsune (1159–1189), the charismatic General of the Minamoto (or Genji) Clan who led his army to victory over the Heike Clan at the decisive battle of Dan'no-ura in 1185 that decimated the once-mighty Heike Clan.[43] Yoshitsune was the younger brother of Minamoto no Yoritomo, the founder of the Kamakura Shogunate. Following the conclusion of his successful military campaign, however, Yoshitsune had to flee for his life from the jealousy of his elder brother and take refuge in Hiraizumi. In fact, Yoritomo turned against his younger brother, fearing that Yoshitsune's immense popularity would be an obstacle for him to solidify his power base. Yoshitsune's patron-protector, Fujiwara no Hidehira (1122?–1187), on his part, harbored high ambitions for his own clan with Yoshitsune at the helm to stand against Yoritomo's new government. Several months after Hidehira had offered refuge to Yoshitsune, however, this ailing patriarch died, signaling the beginning of the end for the Ōshū Fujiwara Clan. Yoritomo in Kamakura pressured Hidehira's son, Yasuhira, into slaying Yoshitsune. Yasuhira eventually obliged and carried out a surprise attack on Yoshitsune at the mansion on Takadachi Hill on June 15, 1189. Knowing that his end was near, Yoshitsune chose to commit suicide rather than suffer the humiliation of being captured and killed. His brave vassals, outnumbered by the army of Yasuhira, all perished in this surprise attack. In October of the same year, Yoritomo marched in person with his army from Kamakura to vanquish Yasuhira, who set the city of Hiraizumi on fire before fleeing. Yasuhira met a gruesome end at the hand of his own man, and the glory of the Ōshū Fujiwaras and the city of Hiraizumi came to an abrupt end on October 14, 1189, only four months after the demise of Yoshitsune.

Now, with this historical information in mind, which forms the background of the haiku, let us read Bashō's text once again. The haiku, "Ah, summer grass! / brave warriors' / site of dreams," speaks more directly to us now, as we may recall a comparable story or incident, or examples in our respective historical and narrative traditions. Meanwhile, the prose section gains life now that we know enough details about the historical background and the tragic incident to which Bashō referred. The poet's sympathy for the fallen hero Yoshitsune and his loyal supporters expressed in the haiku seems to flow into the prose to bring it back to the present moment—as if we were standing on Takadachi Hill where Yoshitsune had met his end and Bashō once stood. Meanwhile, the haiku, "Ah, summer grass! / brave warriors' / site of dreams," gains further vividness and evokes multiple layers of meaning and imagery over against the historical backdrop, while the prose wraps around the haiku. Once we are in the possession of the historical background information, a creative hermeneutical circle is set in motion, between the text and the reader, and between the prose and the haiku.

CONCLUSION

In the above, I have provided a glimpse into how Bashō masterfully interwove haiku and prose in his *Oku no hosomichi* to achieve a literary style that retains the element of eternity in temporality. Even without the conscious knowledge of the temporal properties of the "present moment" captured and preserved in a haiku and the "passage of time" retained in the prose, the reader nonetheless responds accordingly to Bashō's poetic prose. His haiku, containing a timeless universal human experience, requires very little explanation for it to resonate in the reader's mind, unlike the prose section, which narrates factual information and therefore requires a certain amount of historical knowledge. Bashō combined these different qualities of time in his work to heighten the impact of his art. In this harmonious tapestry woven out of the "eternal now" and the "at one time," we may have unlocked the secret of the lasting appeal of *Oku no hosomichi* and other works by Bashō. To conclude, we see that indeed Bashō's insight into *fueki ryūkō*—the timeless and the temporal—served as a guide in his creative activities. In closing, let us recall that Bashō was convinced that an artistic pursuit, in its objective faithfulness sustained by personal openness, elevated humanity from the crude mindset of beasts and savages and made humanity the friends of nature as well as the custodians of beauty and loftiness of the spirit.

NOTES

1. It is made up of thirty-one Japanese syllables, in the cluster of 5, 7, 5, 7, 7.

2. This title is translated into English variously. See, for instance, *The Narrow Road to Oku*, trans. Donald Keene (Tokyo: Kodansha, 1996); and *The Narrow Road to the Deep North and Other Travel Sketches*, trans. Nobuyuki Yuasa (Baltimore, MD: Penguin, 1966). It is clearly a play on the word *Michi-n[o]-oku*. The Japanese text for *Oku no hosomichi* is Matsuo Bashō, *Oku no hosomichi, ta yonpen* (*The Narrow Road to the North and Four Other Works*), modern Japanese trans. Asō Isoji (Tokyo: Ōbunsha, 1970). Unless otherwise indicated, all translations from Japanese are mine.

3. *Kyoraishō* (*Kyorai's Notes*), "Shugyō" ("Religio-Spiritual Training"), secs. 5–6, in *Rengaron-shū, Nōgakuron-shū, Hairon-shū*, modern Japanese trans. Ichiji Tetsuo, Omote Akira, and Kuriyama Riichi (Tokyo: Shōgakukan, 1973), 494–500.

4. Asō, 10.

5. There is a *prima facie* semblance to *ars longa vita brevis*, but in Bashō's case, it is the insight into the "brevity" of life that was at once the source of the longevity of art.

6. *Sanzōshi* was a treasure among Tohō's followers in Ueno, the birthplace of Bashō, and made public only in 1776, that is, 45 years after Tohō's death. The text of *Sanzōshi* is by Nose Asaji, *Sanzōshi hyōshaku* (*Three Notebooks of Hattori Tohō*) (Tokyo: Sanseidō, 1954).

7. Nose, 91.

8. Ibid.

9. The contact with the Chinese Continent and the Korean Peninsula remained even under the policy of the closure of the ports to "foreign lands." Exotic vegetables

and fruits were imported and available at a large market in Edo. The Chan master of the Ōbaku lineage, Ingen, came to Japan from Ming China and opened his monastery outside Kyoto in 1654, enlivening the Japanese Zen scenes.

10. These two verses were composed on August (today's September) 15, 1694.

11. Nose, 114–15.

12. From "Saimon no ji," in *Sources of Japanese Tradition*, ed. Ryusaku Tsunoda, Wm. Theodore de Bary, and Donald Keene (New York: Columbia University Press, 1964), 459.

13. The notable exception is Daisetz T. Suzuki, who mentions Bashō's Zen practice and refers to this frog verse in his *Zen and Japanese Culture* (Princeton, NJ: Princeton University Press, 1973), 239–44. Japanese scholars conversant with Bashō's Zen practice often remain within the traditional boundaries of Zen literature and do not venture out of their familiar turf to have an interdisciplinary conversation. Consequently, Bashō's Zen practice largely remains confined within the field of Zen literature.

14. Dōgen saw each person and each thing (*u*) to be time (*ji*); time also has the aspect of "passage" (*kyōryaku*) on account of which the past and the future are dynamically connected. For Dōgen, this radical temporality enabled the practitioner of later periods to access and attain the original enlightenment of the Buddha. "Uji," in *Gendaigo-yaku Shōbōgenzō*, vol. 1, modern Japanese trans. Masutani Fumio (Tokyo: Kadokawa Shoten, 1973), 193–213.

15. For detailed discussion, see Takizawa Seiichirō, *Bashō to Ryōkan* (*Bashō and Ryōkan*) (Tokyo: Daigaku Kyōikusha, 1986); also Satō Madoka, *Bashō to Zen* (*Bashō and Zen*) (Tokyo: Ōfūsha, 1973).

16. On Bucchō, see Obata Buntei, ed., *Kinsei zenrin sōhōden* (*Biographies of Treasured Recent Zen Monastics and Lays*) (Kyoto: Shibunkaku, 1973), 2:90–94.

17. "Matsuo Tōsei koji-den" ("Biography of Lay Practitioner Matsuo Tōsei"), in Obata, 2:520–23.

18. *Sanzen* means a form of Zen practice, in which the student has a regular audience with the master, who closely guides the student's spiritual progress by asking questions conducive to the student's achieving a "breakthrough."

19. See Suzuki, 239. Suzuki rightly points out that Bashō's answer did not have the first line, "the old pond," at that time but was added later to make it into a complete haiku. It appears that Suzuki consulted a different version of Bashō's biography. The completed frog verse was published years later in 1686.

20. Obata, 2:521.

21. Ibid.

22. On this trip, Bashō was accompanied by Sora and Sōha. The record of their visit and the verse composition were published as *Kashima mōde* or *Kashima kikō* (*A Visit to Kashima Shrine*).

23. Asō, 22. Bashō's verse is mentioned in relation to Bucchō's 31-syllable *waka* poem, which reads: "How annoying it is to have to build a simple hut of five-foot square. I would not have done it if not for the rain!" The idea is that the Zen master preferred to live in the open air, which of course is not possible for most human beings.

24. *Tanka* is another word for a short *waka*, the traditional 31-syllable form of Japanese poetry.

25. Nishida Kitarō, "Tanka ni tsuite" ("On *Tanka*") (1933), in *Nishida Kitarō zenshū* (new edition) (Tokyo: Iwanami Shoten, 2005), 11:163; (original edition) NKZ-O (1979), 13:131.

26. Ibid.

27. Nishida Kitarō, "Kokugo no jizaisei" ("The Flexibility of the Japanese Language") (1936), in NKZ-O, 12:152–53.

28. Augustine, *Confessions*, bk. 11, chap. 20: "[T]here are three periods of time: the present of things past, the present of things present, and the present of things future. For these three are in the soul and I do not see them elsewhere: the present of things past is memory; the present of things present is immediate vision; the present of future things is expectation." Nishida first referred to this passage in "Chokusetsu ni ataerareru mono" ("That Which Is Given Directly") (1923), in NKZ-O, 4:31. See Augustine, *St. Augustine's Confessions*, vol. 2, bks. 9–13, trans. William Watts (Cambridge, MA: Harvard University Press, 1912), 252–53.

29. Nishida came up with the phrase 'the continuation of the discontinuous' (*hirenzoku no renzoku*) out of his observation of this mode of time.

30. Aristotle, *Physics*, trans. R. P. Hardie and R. K. Gaye (Oxford: Clarendon Press, 1930), bk. 4, pt. 13, accessed June 27, 2015, http://classics.mit.edu/Aristotle/physics.4.iv.html.

31. Yoshida Kenkō, *Essays in Idleness: The Tsurezuregusa of Kenkō*, trans. Donald Keene (New York: Columbia University Press, 1967), sec. 7.

32. Zeami, *Fūshi kaden*, in *Zeami-shū*, ed. Konishi Jin'ichi (Tokyo: Chikuma Shobō, 1970), 99.

33. Nose, 114.

34. Asō, 126–27.

35. It is as if the "it" turned into a "thou" in that moment.

36. Nose, 97–98.

37. Ibid., 115.

38. Tagajō is located about 15 kilometers northeast of the city of Sendai. Its foundation was originally laid in 724 C.E., the first year of Jingi.

39. Asō, 38–40.

40. Bashō is alluding to a poem by Du Fu (712–770) entitled 'The Spring Vista.' Du Fu's original reads: "There are mountains and rivers in the country in ruins. Within the city wall, grasses and trees are growing robustly. I shed tears as I see flowers and think of what happened to this country. My mind, in remorse, is still startled by the flying birds." See Asō, 48–49 n13.

41. Asō, 48. I consulted Donald Keene's English translation in *Anthology of Japanese Literature: From the Earliest Era to the Mid-Nineteenth Century*, comp. and ed. Donald Keene (New York: Grove Press, 1955), 369.

42. Hiraizumi in the twelfth century was said to be a large city with the population of 100,000, comparable to the city of Kyoto in those days.

43. For the episodes dealing with this battle and the background leading up to it, see *The Tale of the Heike* (*Heike monogatari*), trans. Burton Watson, ed. Haruo Shirane (New York: Columbia University Press, 2008).

Chapter 17

Knowing Elegance

The Ideals of the Bunjin *(Literatus) in Early Modern Haikai*

Cheryl Crowley

'Bunjin' (literatus) 文人 is a term that has come to describe a literary aesthetic that flourished in seventeenth- and eighteenth-century Japan. Derived from the Chinese word *wenren, bunjin* is associated with intellectuals and people of taste, especially those who excelled in calligraphy, painting, and Chinese learning. More broadly understood, however, it includes writers and thinkers active in a much longer period of time, and has been used to reference the work of people as varied as Ueda Akinari 上田秋成 (1734–1809), Hiraga Gennai 平賀源内 (1728–1779), Natsume Sōseki 夏目漱石 (1867–1916), Mori Ōgai 森鷗外 (1862–1922), Murō Saisei 室生犀星 (1889–1962), and Dazai Osamu 太宰治 (1909–1948).[1] Indeed, application of the term is often so flexible as to make its meaning opaque; nevertheless, the frequency with which it is used by scholars makes it a compelling subject of discussion.

This chapter uses the term as a starting point from which to explore a set of concepts that have developed in the context of haikai, one of the poetic genres most closely associated with what has come to be called 'the *bunjin* aesthetic.' I focus on the work of two of the genre's most prominent figures, Matsuo Bashō 松尾芭蕉 (1644–1694) and Yosa Buson 与謝蕪村 (1716–1783). In particular, I consider the terms *fūryū* 風流 (taste), *fūga* 風雅 (elegant sensibility), and *rizoku* 離俗 (transcending the mundane). These interrelated ideas are the foundation for a range of practices in the fields of literary and visual culture whose proponents sought to make art a way of life and life a way of art.

I have found Michel de Certeau's writing about the "practice of everyday life" useful in devising a way to think about the haikai of early modern *bunjin.* De Certeau discusses the strategies of marginalized groups of "poaching" on elite traditions, thereby creating a culture of making, rather than one of

239

passive consumption. Speaking of the members of the disempowered groups
who become the users of the elite culture, De Certeau argues:

> The presence and circulation of a representation (taught by preachers, educators,
> and popularizers as the key to socioeconomic advancement) tells us nothing
> about what it is for its users. We must first analyze its manipulation by users
> who are not its makers. Only then can we gauge the difference or similarity
> between the production of the image and the secondary production hidden in
> the process of its utilization.[2]

The consumers of early modern haikai were also its producers; they
included both those of elite status, like the samurai Bashō, as well as non-
elites, like Buson, who was born in a farming village. However, as haikai
was a commoners' genre, many of its most idealistic poets were continually
occupied with the process of making their genre into serious literature even
as they were composing and consuming work that belonged to that genre.
Emphasizing the correspondences between haikai's aesthetics and those that
were associated with the Chinese literati was one means by which they tried
to accomplish this goal.

Haikai's social status underwent a number of changes throughout its history. Unlike waka and renga, haikai permitted the use of common, everyday
(*zoku* 俗) language and imagery; although it originally grew out of courtly
renga, the majority of the people who composed and read haikai were people
of relatively little social prestige. Furthermore, throughout the early modern
period, the *haidan* 俳壇 (haikai community) tended to be dominated by fac-
tions that promoted one style over another, and often the members of most
popular haikai schools, such as the Danrin 談林, aspired to little more than
proficiency in creating witty word puzzles to amuse and impress their friends.

In the late seventeenth century, however, Bashō took the genre beyond the
level of pastime by demonstrating the subtlety and depth that it was possible
to achieve. Buson was involved in much the same process fifty years later, as
he resisted a trend toward commercialization that characterized the haikai of
the early eighteenth century, and called for a "revival" of Bashō's principles
that was more about innovation than return. Central to those principles were a
set of loosely defined, interrelated concepts, all of which can be closely linked
to ideals associated with *bunjin*: poetry created by transforming ordinary life
and experience into something elegant and elevated.

These ideals originate with the aesthetic of the Chinese literati, one
historically admired by Japanese writers and artists, but outside the elite/
nonelite, *ga/zoku* 雅俗 dualities that were so much a part of the Japanese
literary tradition. For that reason, as Chinese *wenren* culture underwent a
resurgence of interest among the members of Sinophile intellectual circles

of the early modern period, their associates in the *haidan* found in the Chinese *wenren* a model for achieving many of their literary, and sometimes social, ambitions.

While it is perhaps clear that intellectuals interested in Chinese learning might reasonably be drawn to the ideals of the *bunjin*, the strong connection between the *bunjin* aesthetic and haikai, a native Japanese literary genre, might benefit from greater exploration. The same might be said of the ways that this connection can be compared to De Certeau's notion of the practice of everyday life, which was formulated to discuss aspects of modernity. The writings of Matsuo Bashō and Yosa Buson, who composed very different haikai but offered similar arguments about the nature of haikai, offer a place to start such an exploration. I will begin by briefly tracing through the development of Japanese reception of the image of the Chinese literati as an ideal and a model, and then move to consider aspects of its effect on the work of Bashō and Buson.

HAIKAI LITERATI

Wenren refers to a category of culturally influential but politically marginalized people. Disaffected members of the scholar-official class during the Song (960–1279) and Ming (1368–1644) periods, *wenren* withdrew from worldly affairs to share interests in calligraphy, painting, and poetry with similarly disengaged peers. *Wenren* distinguished themselves from commercial artisans by embracing a cult of amateurism, and concerned themselves not with deriving an income from their art, but with the high-minded pursuit of virtue. Justification from this came from many sources in the Confucian classics, such as the much venerated statement from the *Analects* (*Lunyu* 論語), "Set your intention on the Way, hold firmly to virtue, put your reliance on benevolence, amuse yourself with the arts."[3] In this way of thinking, artistic practice (藝) was not to be admired for its own sake, but rather as a tool of self-cultivation.

Japan never developed a scholar-official class analogous to that of premodern China, but for a number of reasons the ideal of the Chinese literatus was a compelling one among many Japanese, particularly in the early modern period. While Japan had a long history of literary and artistic recluses, from the seventeenth century onward, support from the Tokugawa government affirmed the value of the Confucian classics as the basis of learning. At the same time, access to education, once limited to elites, spread to larger numbers of commoners along with a slow but steady rise in economic prosperity.

There were other developments in the scholarly communities of the day that gradually yet significantly contributed to the establishment of a relatively large population of educated people who could both read and compose poetry. For instance, the middle of the seventeenth century saw the emergence of popularizers of literature like Matsunaga Teitoku 松永貞徳 (1571–1654), an immensely erudite scholar of waka and renga who gave public lectures on Japanese poetry. In the early eighteenth century, Ogyū Sorai 荻生徂徠 (1666–1728) was at the forefront of promoting the composition of poetry (i.e., *kanshi* 漢詩, poetry in Chinese) for its own sake, rather than as a mere supplement to the study of Chinese classics.

The manner in which *wenren* identified themselves as amateurs was very attractive for early modern Japanese commoner poets and artists. The social status of commoners precluded participation in the political sphere as much as did the avowed scruples of their continental predecessors. On the other hand, the commoner status of would-be *bunjin* did not prevent them from acquiring the financial means by which they paid for the knowledge and leisure that was a prerequisite for participation in literary circles. In other words, economic, social, and intellectual changes during the seventeenth and eighteenth centuries created a constituency of educated commoners who had personal ambitions to create and read poetry, yet not to use it as a source of income, and they found the example of the *wenren* offered a useful narrative to frame their activities.

Despite the convenience of the term *bunjin*, it is important to note that while many eminent literary scholars and art historians employ it, others have questioned it, especially in recent years. Influential twentieth-century expositions of the term and its application in literature include Kuriyama Riichi's 栗山理一 *Bunjinron* 文人論 (*Theories of the Bunjin*, 1939) and Nakamura Yukihiko's 中村幸彦 *Bunjin ishiki no seiritsu* 文人意識の成立 (*Development of the Bunjin Consciousness*, 1959). Both of these trace the history of the term in Japan, although they differ in the sense that most of Kuriyama's emphasis is on the literature of the early modern period while Nakamura extends the discussion into the Meiji period. A newer work on Japanese literati culture from the early modern period onward is Ibi Takashi's 揖斐高 *Edo no bunjin saron: Chishikijin to geijitsukatachi* 江戸文人サロン— 知識人と芸術家たち (*Edo Literati Salons: Intellectuals and Artists*, 2009), whose thoughtful exploration of the interrelationship among intellectuals as diverse as *kyōka* (comic waka) poets, *rangaku* (Western learning) specialists, and calligraphers indicates that the notion of the *bunjin* continues to have great resonance even in the twenty-first century.[4]

On the other hand, there are critics. Its title notwithstanding, Lawrence Marceau's *Takebe Ayatari: A Bunjin Bohemian in Early Modern Japan* (2004) employs the term with caution and some skepticism. Anna Beerens's *Friends, Acquaintances, Pupils and Patrons—Japanese Intellectual Life in the Late Eighteenth Century: A Prosopographical Approach* (2006) expresses serious concerns about existing research on *bunjin*, arguing that it implies a cohesive sense of identity and common purpose that did not necessarily exist at the time.[5]

Though it has weaknesses, I use the word *bunjin* here because it helps foreground commonalities within the work of two very different poets, work that in turn had great influence on the development of one of the major genres of Japanese literature. The principles that Bashō and Buson put forth in their discussions of *fūryū*, *fūga*, and *rizoku* are at once distinct yet difficult to separate, and their closeness derives from their shared origin in theories pertaining to the Chinese classics that were common in the discourse of the day.

FŪRYŪ: A RESOLUTION

Bashō is credited with almost singlehandedly inventing haikai, and his reputation both as a poet and as a theorist of the genre has remained unrivalled since his death. His deft sense of how to balance immediacy with spare elegance of expression in linked verse, hokku, and prose alike was matched by broad erudition in both Japanese and Chinese texts. Furthermore, while he embraced a lifestyle of simplicity as a recluse and an itinerant, he was also enormously adept at attracting large numbers of loyal disciples who developed his school, the Shōfū 蕉風, into the most influential of all in haikai history.

Fūryū is a term that appears often in haikai treatises that were produced by his school, but its meaning varies. 'Fūryū' appears in a frequently cited passage that explains the basic elements of haikai from Bashō's disciple Kagami Shikō's 各務支考 (1665–1731) *Zoku Go ron* 続五論 (*Sequel to Five Theses*, 1698):

華月の風流は風雅の躰也[6]
The changing glamour of the seasons [literally, blossoms and the moon] is the foundation of poetic style.

Here, *fūryū* suggests the drama of seasonal variation; its meaning draws on the literal sense of the graphs, "winds and rivers," with which it is written. In other contexts, however, *fūryū* appears to be synonymous with haikai itself. A famous example is a *hokku* 発句(seventeen-syllable verse) from Bashō's most well-known travel journal, *Oku no hosomichi* 奥の細道 (*Narrow Road to the Interior*):

風流の初やおくの田植うた
fūryū no hajime ya Oku no taue uta[7]
the origin of *fūryū*
rice planting songs
of Oku

This verse appears early on in *Oku no hosomichi* as a conclusion to Bashō's description of his visit to the home of the poet Tōkyū 等窮 in Sukagawa. To compliment his host, Bashō compares the work songs of local farmers to the elegance of sophisticated poetry, that is to say, haikai. What, then, is the relationship of *fūryū* and haikai?

Like 'bunjin' itself, the term originates in Chinese literature in a slightly different context than it acquired in Japan. Kuriyama Riichi, mentioned above as a theorist of the term *bunjin*, presents a history of *fūryū* in his comprehensive study *Fūryūron* (*Theories of Fūryū*, 1939). He first explains that the Chinese *fengliu* meant "good deportment" or "good manners," in other words, the opposite of vulgar or popular. *Fūryū* was associated with the elegant tastes of the Heian courtiers, and its meaning was extended to things as well as people, referring to things that were refined or tasteful, including objects that were ornately decorated; behaviors or things that were not rustic or provincial. In the medieval period, Kuriyama argues, *fūryū* was associated with the lifestyles and practices of an elite community of connoisseurs; it described the beauty of landscape gardens, rustic architecture, and nature poetry. In another medieval definition, however, it meant a more ostentatious, gaudy beauty, particularly in the context of the performing arts where it referred to various kinds of popular entertainment and folk dance.[8]

These two meanings survived in the early modern period. The popular aspect of *fūryū* was clearly evident in prose fiction like *ukiyo-zōshi*, which frequently included the word *fūryū* in their titles to suggest a sense of the up-to-date, fashionable, and erotic. *Fūryū* was close in meaning to *sui* 粋 and was used to describe urban sophisticates—people of fashion and fast living, particularly men who spent their lives in pursuit of pleasure. The second meaning of *fūryū* was related to medieval ideas of *suki*数寄, or cultivated taste.[9]

Haikai was situated in an intermediate, dynamic position between these related, yet contradictory, usages of *fūryū*. Indeed, *fūryū* was exactly the kind of beauty to which haikai poets aspired. That is to say, *fūryū* as fashionable and erotic is linked closely with *zoku* (low culture), and as cultivated taste, with *ga* (high culture).

As his *fūryū no hajime* verse shows, Bashō, who was extremely aware of the tension between these values, precisely expressed the ambiguous aspects of *fūryū*, which embraces both. In this verse, Bashō uses the tactic of identifying the work songs of farmers with a word that implies a sublime sophistication, improvising elite elegance on a landscape of ordinary commoners' lives.

BASHŌ'S *FŪGA*: THE VIRTUE OF POETRY

Related to *fūryū*, and perhaps even more common in Shōfū poetic treatises, is *fūga*. Like *fūryū*, it is often nearly synonymous with haikai, as we see in these two very well-known passages attributed to Bashō:

I. 西行の和歌における、宗祇の連歌における、雪舟の絵における、利休の茶における、その貫道するものは一つなり。しかも風雅におけるもの、造化にしたがひて四時を友とす。見るところ花にあらずといふことなし。思ふところ月にあらずといふことなし。[10]
Within Saigyō's waka, within Sōgi's renga, within Sesshū's painting, and within Rikyū's tea, is a single thing that runs through them all. Furthermore, what is within *fūga* is to be in accord with creation and as a friend to the seasons. There is nowhere to look that is not in bloom. There is nothing to be thought that is not brilliant as with moonlight.

II. 東海道の一筋しらぬ人、風雅に覚束なし。[11]
People who know nothing of the Tōkaidō have no understanding of *fūga*.

The first example (I) is included in Bashō's travel journal *Oi no kobumi* 笈の小文 (*Knapsack Notebook*, 1709); the second (II) in *Sanzōshi* 三冊子 (*Three Notebooks*, 1776), edited by Bashō's disciple Hattori Dohō 服部土芳 (1657–1730). In both cases, commentators often gloss 'fūga' as 'haikai'—the first is read as a declaration of haikai's equality with other prestigious arts; the second as asserting the importance of travel in haikai. Implicit in both passages is 'poaching,' as De Certeau would term it, making new classics by recombining elements of old ones in a contemporary context.

Fūga as Bashō uses it originates in *Shijing* 詩經 (*Book of Odes*), a collection of poems dating from the eleventh to seventh centuries BCE that is one of the major books of the Chinese literary canon. Its contents break down into *feng* 風 (airs), *xiaoya* 小雅 (lesser odes), *daya* 大雅 (grand odes), and *song* 頌 (hymns). 'Fūga' is derived from the first three types, *feng* and *ya*, and thus is more or less synonymous with 'poetry.' Japanese in the early modern period came to use *fūga* to refer to *shi* 詩 (in Chinese, a specific poetic genre), that is to say, *kanshi* 漢詩, and eventually to waka and haikai.[12]

Ibi Takashi has argued that early modern Japanese *kanshi* poets developed distinctive theories of the merits of their work, theories not entirely consistent with what one might expect from an orthodox neo-Confucian view of literature. He points out that Japanese Sinophiles were likely to find persuasive Hayashi Razan's claim in "Theories on 'Writing Poems on the Wind and Celebrating the Moon'" 「吟風弄月論」 that the great Confucian thinkers saw no contradiction between composing poetry and the more philosophical pursuits of "investigating things" (格物) and "comprehending principles" (窮理).[13] Rather, poetry and acquiring knowledge were both forms of self-cultivation that had the capacity to make a person more virtuous. In other words, the implications of *fūga* were not just related to aesthetic qualities of taste and beauty as in the case of *fūryū*, but also aligned with the theory that poetry is a means to self-improvement. Because of its association with *Shijing*, *fūga* describes poetry that is of the highest possible value in that it confers goodness on those who read and compose it, and so it is a worthy and respectable endeavor.

Keeping these strong moralistic connotations in mind, Bashō's frequent use of the word takes on another dimension. To claim, as he does in the first passage, that haikai shares an essential quality with the work of Saigyō, Sōgi, Sesshū, and Rikyū—some of the most estimable artists in Japanese history—is ambitious in itself. However, to identify it as *fūga* is to emphasize its power not just to amuse and entertain, but also to cultivate the self. Bashō's statement here, then, suggests that haikai is more than the game many of his contemporaries viewed it to be. Rather, it was a means of cultivating virtue every bit as venerable as the airs and the odes of the great Chinese poetic classic, *Shijing*.

As the second example reminds us, travel was another activity that Bashō emphasized as intrinsic to the development of an accomplished haikai poet, and it may seem that this element deviates somewhat from a straightforward linking of poetry and the acquisition of virtue implicit in the term *fūga*. On the other hand, Bashō's traveler persona identifies him with other itinerants, recluses, and exiles both in the Japanese past (such as Saigyō and Sōgi) and ultimately those of the Chinese literati tradition. Prominent disciples also took up this theme in treatises that purport to represent Bashō's own teachings.

旅は風雅の花、風雅は過客の魂。西行 宗祇の見残しは、皆俳諧の情なり。

Travel is the flowering of *fūga*, *fūga* is the spirit of the traveler. All that was overlooked by Saigyō and Sōgi serves as the emotional content of haikai.[14]

This phrase in *Infutagi* 韻塞 (1697), compiled by Morikawa Kyoriku 森川許六 (1656–1715), uses both 'fūga' and 'haikai.' Taken in the context of Bashō's views on the critical importance of travel in achieving an authentic understanding of *fūga*, and his own lifelong practice of living on the road, it seems clear that they both reference the same thing: haikai in its finest form. The allusion to famous literary travelers Saigyō and Sōgi supports this identification of travel with poetry. What is interesting, though, is the confidence with which this statement describes the work of the haikai poet: to pick up and possess those impressions and experiences that these great predecessors overlooked.

As these passages show, poets of the Bashō School looked both to their predecessors among Chinese literati and to the native tradition of poet-recluses to set the standards for elegance in writing and virtue in personal conduct. Travel, whether done firsthand or by reading accounts of journeys such as *Oku no hosomichi*, was a means by which haikai practitioners could withdraw (if only vicariously) from ordinary existence and take part in an authentic *bunjin* way of life. Finally, Bashō's doctrine of *fūga* allowed not only for the passive absorption of the great works of literary predecessors, but also for the making of new great works that extended the traditions of the past into the everyday contexts of the present.

BUSON'S *RIZOKU*: THE EVERYDAY, AT A DISTANCE

Fifty years after Bashō's death, the Shōfū was still very prominent, but Bashō's disciples differed on which of his teachings were the most important. Other schools, both older and newer than the Shōfū, also competed for students; infrastructure that supported haikai, such as publishers and booksellers, was more developed; and the number of haikai poets was greater than ever. Many of the leading haikai poets in the first five decades of the eighteenth century were content with the trends of the day, and became successful at making a living as haikai markers (*tenja* 点者). Eventually, though, a small but growing minority began to deplore the fact that so many of their colleagues seemed to have lost sight of the possibilities Bashō's example represented. In loosely connected networks that have since come to be called 'the Bashō Revival Movement,' they criticized their contemporaries who emphasized profit over aesthetics, and called for a "return" to Bashō's principles.

The most prominent among them was Yosa Buson. Equally skilled at painting and calligraphy as well as haikai, in many ways he was the quintessential *bunjin*. Unlike Bashō, he grew up in a farming village rather than in a samurai household; his education was haphazard, and he was largely self-taught. As an adult, he studied with and befriended many *kanshi* poets, including Ogyū Sorai's literary successor, Hattori Nankaku 服部南郭 (1683–1759), and Kuroyanagi Shōha 黒柳召波 (1727–1771), who became his haikai disciple. Their instruction, as well as his readings of Chinese painting manuals, convinced him of the connections between painting and haikai. Furthermore, as his haikai teacher Hayano Hajin 早野巴人 (1676–1742) had studied with one of Bashō's disciples, Buson's sympathies lay with the Shōfū, and from the time he established himself as a poet in Kyōto, his Yahantei School became the center of activities related to the Bashō Revival.

Buson was not a great haikai theorist. He did not write long treatises in the manner of Bashō or his disciples. He did, however, provide prefaces to a number of haikai collections, the most famous among them being the preface to *Shundei kushū*春泥句集 (*Shundei Verse Anthology*), which was dedicated to his *kanshi* poet friend Shōha:

> I went to visit Shundei-sha Shōha at his second house in the west of Kyoto. Shōha asked me a question about haikai. I answered, "Haikai is that which has as its ideal the use of *zokugo*, yet transcends *zoku*. To transcend *zoku* yet make use of *zoku*, the principle of *rizoku*, is most difficult. It is the thing that So-and-So Zen master spoke of: 'Listen to the sound of the Single Hand,' in other words haikai Zen, the principle of *rizoku*." Through this, Shōha understood immediately.
>
> He then continued his questions. "Although the essence of your teaching must be profound, is there not some method of thought that I could put into use, by which one might seek this by oneself? Indeed, is there not some shortcut, by which one might, without making a distinction between Other and Self, identify with nature and transcend *zoku*?" I answered, "Yes, the study of Chinese poetry. You have been studying Chinese poetry for years. Do not seek for another way." Doubtful, Shōha made so bold as to ask, "But Chinese poetry and haikai are different in tenor. Setting aside haikai, and studying Chinese poetry instead, is that not more like a detour?"
>
> I answered, "Painters have the theory of 'avoiding *zoku*': 'To avoid the *zoku* in painting, there is no other way but to read many texts, that is to say, both books and scrolls, which causes the *qi* to rise, as commercialism and vulgarity cause *qi* to fall. The student should be careful about this.' To avoid *zoku* in painting as well, they caused their students to put down the brush and read books. Less possible still is it to differentiate Chinese poetry and haikai." With that, Shōha understood.[15]

Scholars regard this text as Buson's most comprehensive statement of *rizoku*, or separating from the mundane, an ideal that seems to be the basis of many of his most imaginative, dreamlike verses. The preface's dialogic format recalls Buddhist texts, and Buson alludes somewhat superficially to Zen teachings, but its content is framed in terms that a *kanshi* poet like Shōha would find familiar.

The admonishment to carefully consider the interaction of *ga* and *zoku* was by no means an invention of Buson. One of the earliest statements about the difference between haikai and classical renga was by Matsue Shigeyori 松江重頼 (1602–1680), who said haikai was determined by the presence of a *haigon*俳言, or *zoku* word. Bashō argued that good haikai poets should "know the high, but return to *zoku*" (高く心を悟りて、俗に帰るべし).[16] One might expect, given the earnestness with which he expressed his admiration for Bashō, that Buson's views on the relationship between *ga* and *zoku* would be similar to those of his predecessor.

However, as the *Shundei kushū* preface shows, Buson drew not only on his haikai forebears for his poetic theory, but also on Chinese sources that were linked to the literati tradition. Most obvious here is the early Qing painting copybook *Mustard Seed Garden Manual of Painting* 芥子園畫傳 (*Jieziyuan huazhuan*). He quotes from it nearly exactly when he describes his statement to Shōha that it was necessary for painters to "read books and scrolls" in order to maintain high moral qualities in one's work, and that this was just the same for poets. Notable also is the way that his recommendation to improve one's haikai is to read Chinese verse. As we have seen, reading Chinese verse is good for everyone according to the logic of neo-Confucianism. However, here Buson does not just say that the study of Chinese poetry improves one's virtue, or even that it improves the Chinese poetry one might actually write. Since familiarity with Chinese poetry betters a person's character, it also distances a person from *zoku* (the ordinary world). Buson acknowledges that everyday language (*zokugo*) is essential to haikai. Nonetheless, he argues, a poet who has followed the *wenren* practice of improving his character through study of literature will be able to use everyday language to create haikai that transcends the everyday world.

The aesthetic created by the Chinese scholar-officials who called themselves *wenren*—and by the Japanese *bunjin* who identified with them—had a powerful effect on the development of haikai. The genre's most influential poets, Bashō and Buson, both argued that haikai was not only a means to literary self-expression but also a way to improve the character of those who wrote it. The capacity for reinventing the self through literature that haikai poets found so compelling was at the center of the *bunjin* ideal, and is in large part the reason that this ideal has continued to hold such powerful appeal throughout Japanese history.

NOTES

1. For example, see Kuriyama Riichi, "Bunjinron," in *Fūryūron* (Tokyo: Shibun Shobō, 1939), 70. For a listing of modern haiku poets associated with *bunjin*, see Komuro Yoshihiro, *Bunjin haiku no seikai* (Tokyo: Honami Shoten, 1997).

2. Michel de Certeau, *The Practice of Everyday Life*, trans. Steven Rendall (Berkeley, CA: University of California Press, 1984), xii.

3. Yoshida Kenkō, *Shinsho kanbun taikei*, vol. 1, *Rongo* (Tokyo: Meiji Shoin, 2002), 90.

4. Kuriyama, 67–122; Nakamura Yukihiko, *Iwanami kōza Nihon bungaku shi*, vol. 9, *Bunjin ishiki no seiritsu* (Tokyo: Iwanami Shoten, 1959); Ibi Takashi, *Edo no bunjin saron: Chishikijin to geijutsukatachi* (Tokyo: Yoshikawa Kōbunkan, 2009).

5. Lawrence E. Marceau, *Takebe Ayatari: A Bunjin Bohemian in Early Modern Japan* (Ann Arbor, MI: Center for Japanese Studies, University of Michigan, 2004); Anna Beerens, *Friends, Acquaintances, Pupils and Patrons—Japanese Intellectual Life in the Late Eighteenth Century: A Prosopographical Approach* (Leiden: Leiden University Press, 2006).

6. Horikiri Minoru, *Haisei Bashō to haima Shikō* (Tokyo: Kadokawa Gakugei Shuppan, 2006), 71.

7. Ōtani Tokuzō and Nakamura Shunjō, eds., *Bashō kushū*, vol. 45 of *Nihon koten bungaku taikei* (Tokyo: Iwanami Shoten, 1962), 86.

8. Kuriyama, 6–20.

9. Ibid., 20–33.

10. Sugiura Shōichirō, Miyamoto Saburō, and Ogino Kiyoshi, eds., *Bashō bunshū*, vol. 46 of *Nihon koten bungaku taikei* (Tokyo: Iwanami Shoten, 1959), 52.

11. Ebara Taizō, *Kyorai shō, Sanzōshi, Tabine ron* (Tokyo: Iwanami Shoten, 1991), 89.

12. Ibi Takashi, "Fūgaron," in *Haikai to kanbungaku*, ed. Wa-Kan Hikaku Bungakkai, vol. 16, *Wakan hikaku bungaku kenkyū no kōsō* (Tokyo: Kyūko Shoin, 1994), 30.

13. Ibid., 34–35.

14. Yamashita Kazumi, *Bashō hyaku meigen* (Tokyo: Kadokawa Bunko, 2010), 50.

15. Teraoka Yasutaka and Kawashima Tsuyu, eds., *Buson shū Issa shū*, vol. 58 of *Nihon koten bungaku taikei* (Tokyo: Iwanami Shoten, 1959), 290–92.

16. Ebara, 101.

Chapter 18

The Measure of Comparison

Correspondence and Collision in Japanese Aesthetics

Meera Viswanathan

Early in the *Man'yōshū* 万葉集, the eighth-century Japanese poet Sami Mansei 沙弥満誓 poses this aesthetic conundrum in his *waka*:

世間乎	よのなかを
何物尓将譬	なににたとへむ
旦開	あさびらき
榜去師船之	こぎいにしふねの
跡無如	あとなきごとし

this world of ours,
to what may we compare it?
like a boat
rowing out at the break of dawn
nothing left in its wake.[1]

Though seemingly so ready at hand, "This world of ours," Mansei suggests, remains elusive, ironically resisting our grasp. Furthermore, even comparisons, usually those heuristic stepping stones on our path to understanding, evade us. We are left instead with an image that is no image, a barely discernible trace, which itself leaves no trace, setting forth to limn the nebulous contours not only of this impalpable world, but also of the very problem of comparison itself. Comparison, that posited relation of similarity and difference, juxtaposing what is nearby or present with its more distant or absent counterpart, implies an assay, a test, a question. These assays are always strained, fibrillating tensely between the relations of similitude and dissimilitude, threatened on the one side by collapse into sameness and identity and on the other by a gaping divide, a discontinuity that cannot be bridged. And implicit in any comparison is not simply the question of similarity or difference, but the question of what it means to compare or put into relation. For the philosopher Watsuji Tetsurō 和辻哲郎,[2] it is relationship, or *aidagara* 間柄, that allows human beings, or *ningen* 人間, literally, the space between humans, to emerge. In other words, we only come into being in relationship to others. Comparison viewed from this perspective allows us to confront the question of identity and being through the constituting of relationship.

During the court-dominated Heian period (794–1185), the notions of *nazurae* 擬え (aesthetic comparison or intertextual imitation) and *awase* 合わせ (matching contests) become commonplace, in both *waka* (classical Japanese poetry) and other courtly pastimes functioning as shibboleths, thereby underscoring the importance of similitude, both aesthetically and politically. The act of juxtaposition or comparison of like objects in pursuit of similitude in this earlier period stands in contradistinction to the idea of *mitate* 見立 (substitution or metaphor) and *nazorae* in the urbanized and mercantilized era of the Edo period (1600–1868) and the first half of the Meiji period (1868–1900). In this later historical era, the Japanese conceits of *mitate* (literally, "one thing standing in place of another," commonly understood as simile/metaphor) and *nazorae* (illustrations involving parodic imitation) begin to straddle dissimilarity as they harness together disparate events, characters, texts, and ideals.

Significantly, the concept of *modoki*, written as 擬き and alternately translated as 'mimesis,' 'imitation,' or 'reversibility,' overarches this historical framework of comparison,[3] in the forms of *nazurae/nazorae,* both of which may be written with the same character as *modoki,* 擬え. Comparisons thus entail no mere static enumeration and groupings of similar or different attributes, but instead call forth dynamic and interactive relationships of resemblance and reference in which we may detect both *awase* 合わせ (correspondence) and *mitate* 見立 (substitution or parody). What these aesthetic concepts share is the notion of agonistic relational struggle between dualities, not necessarily in the service of a zero-sum game, but rather as a performance for its own sake, the eternal and inexorable interplay of identity and being.

MODOKI: FROM REENACTING TO REACTING TO RESISTING

Modoki in its many guises of sham, replica, counterfeit, mock, pseudo, quasi, ersatz, and "similar but different" has emerged in recent years, emblematic perhaps of our postmodern era, as one of the favored metaphorical constructs in fields as disparate as meteorology (viz., El Niño Modoki as coined by Professor Toshio Yamagata);[4] architecture (Arata Isozaki's *Shigen no modoki* [*The Origin of a Replica*]);[5] gastronomy (in the form of *ganmodoki* as a substitute for meat along the lines of mock turtle soup); and traditional theater where the *modoki* is the deuteragonist or auxiliary performer—the *waki* in Noh, for example, or simply a mode of performance, of what Bandō Kotoji has referred to as 'performing as if.'[6] Expressions like 'shibai modoki o sakeyō' ('Let's cut out the dramatics') attest to both the parodic and performative components of this modality.[7]

Though we have defined 'modoki' as 'imitation,' the verb 'modoku' in modern parlance means "to contradict." But this, according to the ethnologist, scholar of folklore, and poet Orikuchi Shinobu, may be understood to be a secondary or extended meaning. The earliest usage of *modoki* emerges as imitation or mimesis.

> Generally speaking, we think that the word "*modoku*" is used only to indicate "to offer opposition to," "to contradict," or "to reproach." But in the ancient use of this word it seems to have had a larger meaning. At least in the history of the performing arts, it is evident that it also meant "to counterfeit," "to explain," "to reinterpret in the name of someone," and "to tone down the explanations." For example, an expression such as "*hito no modoki ofu*" (to receive reproaches) originally meant "to be mocked by others while representing something of which you cannot help feeling ashamed." Thus the word seems to have always meant "to counterfeit" or "to imitate."[8]

Significantly, what all of these varied meanings invoke is relationship. In citing the passage above, the philosopher Sakabe Megumi notes that there are three principal meanings associated with *modoki*: as counterfeit, as reproach, and as the actor who embraces the role of the buffoon. It is in this last iteration, the embodiment of the ludicrous, that we witness the full range of *modoki*, a recapitulation of reenactment, reaction, and resistance.[9]

Zeami Motokiyo, the great fourteenth-century Noh playwright, identifies the Ur-moment of aesthetic mimesis in Japan, at least in the performing arts, in the oft-cited myth of *iwato-biraki* or the "Opening of the Cave."[10] Engaging on many levels, this narrative poses a number of interpretive challenges centering around the mocking reproach implicit in the notion of the counterfeit.

In the narrative described by the *Kojiki* (*The Chronicle of Things Past*), ca. 720 C.E.,[11] the supreme deity, the Sun Goddess Amaterasu no Omikami, offended by the transgressive behavior of her brother, sequesters herself in a cave, thereby leaving the world in perilous darkness. To remedy the situation, the other gods assemble and attempt various stratagems to coerce Amaterasu to emerge, but to no avail. Finally one of them, the goddess Ama no Uzume no Omikoto, performs what may be described as a primordial striptease, causing the gods to titter among themselves, temporarily distracted from the matter at hand. Baffled by the possibility of laughter in a world without light, the Sun Goddess opens the cave door a crack and queries the assembly about their laughter. The quick-witted Ama no Uzume retorts that the revelry and merriment revolve around the presence of an even greater divinity than the Sun Goddess.

Seizing the moment, one of the gods holds up a mirror to the gap in the door, thereby blinding Amaterasu with her own brilliant reflection and causing her to leave the cave to approach the unknown rival. In Zeami's account,[12] the faces of those gathered became illuminated by the shaft of light from the cave (*on omote shirokarikeri,* literally, "their faces grew white"), which ostensibly spawned the adjective *omoshiroshi,* a term that subsequently becomes a term of aesthetic approbation signifying beauty or charm during the classical period, and even today *omoshiroi* denotes something of interest. The aesthetic moment here literally bears witness to the notion of high mimetic tension in somatic terms.

Echoing Sakabe's delineation of the varied meanings of *modoki,* Ama no Uzume's comic clowning offers up a sham version of the Sun Goddess through her performance and her verbal repartee, which are underscored by the ruse of the actual mirror. Ultimately, it is her performance as a provisional act of aesthetic violence that functions to shift the balance of power, thereby reproaching the divinity and contriving her reappearance and presence. Sakabe speculates that the etymological origins of *modoki* are also cognate with the idea of *modoru* (to return) and *moto* (origin) and hence the story ends with the reemergence of Amaterasu and a return to the virtual *status quo ante.*[13]

This account has often been described as the originary instance of *modoki,* defined in common parlance as 'mimicry,' 'imitation,' 'parody,' or 'mimesis.' Just as the protagonist in the narrative, Amaterasu no Omikami, absents herself from the scene, leaving Ama no Uzume as a distorted mirror reflection of herself to hold forth, so too we can speculate that in the act of *modoki,* the disappearing originary, is always signified by a placeholder, an absent presence, a cave-like *aporia* concealing the possibility of illumination.

Hence we should not understand *modoki* as mimesis or imitation in which B apes the originary A, becoming an ersatz, quasi, or counterfeit A, but rather as the ongoing interplay between A and B, a kind of ludic competition. This interplay logically has the effect of imploding the very idea of the original, the authentic, leaving us only copies, just as the ritual renders us all ultimately numbered among the deities.[14]

As noted earlier, Orikuchi Shinobu presents the idea that it is precisely in this encounter that in fact *modoki* should be understood as a means "to explain, to oppose, to resist, and to make intelligible" as well as "to imitate" in its function of mediating the encounter between the *kami* world and the world of humans.[15] The literary critic Takahashi Tōru, in an essay on parody, understands the trope in Japan as exemplified in *modoki,* which he argues functions in a variety of ways, including "a 'translation' imitating an original, canonical text; a vulgarization of something sacred; criticism; and comic laughter."[16] *Modoki,* unlike *monomane,* which is simple imitation of a physical thing, entails relational and agonistic reciprocity, something that will be evident in its extended ideas of *nazurae* and *nazorae.*

HEIAN SIMILITUDE: *NAZURAE* AND *AWASE*

The *kanji* used to write *modoki*, as noted earlier, can also be read as the words *nazurae* or *nazorae*, which in the Heian period both meant "to compare" or "to imitate," somewhat more narrowly defined than the poly-valency implied by *modoki*. *Nazorae* though, which seems to appear less frequently than *nazurae*, seems still to carry with it overtones of 'to feign' implying intentional deception, suggesting a link to the earlier idea of parody.

One of the most frequently cited instances of *nazurae* is found in the Kana Preface to the *Kokin Wakashū*,[17] the first imperial anthology of Japanese poetry, where it functions as a translation of the Chinese f*eng*, or in Sino-Japanese, *hi*, meaning comparison. Here the primary architect of the anthology, Ki no Tsurayuki, introduces the *Rikugi* or "Six Styles of Poetry," a construct appropriated wholesale from the preface to the Chinese classic, the *Shijing* or *Book of Songs*, which describes various kinds of tropes, among which is the third principle, *nazuraeuta*, alternately translated as 'the figurative style' or 'comparison.' As the anonymous author of the interpolated note explains, "This style uses comparison: 'This resembles that.'" The basis for this style is similitude, a perceived resemblance between two things. In the preface, Tsurayuki offers this poem as an examplar:

kimi ya kesa	If on this morning
ashita no shimo no	you go your way and leave me
okite inaba	as frost leaves the sky
koishiki goto ni	will my spirit melt in grief
kie ya wataramu	each time I long to see you?[18]

Just as frost falls from the sky in the predawn hours, so too at precisely the same time does the lover, as in some medieval *aubade*, bid farewell to his lover. The chilling effect for the beloved as a result of both inexorable events parallels the subsequent melting of the frost during the day and the dissolution into tears of grief of the distraught woman.

As the prominent scholar Konishi Jin'ichi has argued,[19] the *Kokin Wakashū* betrays to an extraordinary degree the impact of the style of Six Dynasties poetry with its preoccupation with obliquity and hence a fascination with wit, conceits, and convoluted literary tropes. Konishi comments:

When the poet's 'clever judgments' operate in the area of comparisons, the result is the so-called *mitate*, or figure of speech, which, as we have seen, was much used in the Six Dynasties period, and which also figures prominently in early Heian Chinese poetry. The most obvious pattern is one in which the poet states unequivocally that a resemblance exists between two things.[20]

The typical instance poses the conundrum of whether the poet is seeing plum blossoms falling from the tree or snow, what Robert H. Brower and Earl Miner in their 1961 opus *Japanese Court Poetry* christened 'elegant confusion.'[21] Leaving aside the issue of "so-called *mitate*" as articulated by Konishi, to which we will return later in this chapter, let us consider an example of "elegant confusion." For example, in *Kokin Wakashū* 6, we find the following poem by Priest Sosei:

haru tateba	Now that spring has come,
hana to ya miramu	does he mistake them for flowers—
shirayuki no	the warbler singing
kakeru eda ni	among branches deep-laden
uguisu no naku	with mounds of snowy white flakes?[22]

We are presented with a poetic speculative rationalization for the singing of the bird assumed to be the harbinger of spring even while snow still remains piled on the branches of trees. Here, of course, we have the additional figurative technique employed of *gijinka* 擬人化, or personification. While an initial encounter with this kind of *nazurae* of comparison might strike us as novel and charming, upon even a superficial perusal of *waka* from the period, we realize that virtually all of these comparisons are conventionalized. Given the limited nativist poetic vocabulary enforced by poets from the Heian period onwards in the classical era (i.e., *yamatokotoba*), especially in the wake of the *Kokin Wakashū*, many of the comparisons such as one between maple leaves and brocade, or one between darkness and the human heart, are nearly as recognizable as the set pillow words, *makurakotoba* (e.g., *nubatama no* / *hisakata no* / *chihayaburu* / *ashibiki no*), or the formulaic epithets of Homer. These comparisons are not only based around resemblance, but in the course of poetic development they also overlap, becoming fused as a unit, a poetic trope.

If, as Konishi asserts, the hallmark of the poetry of the *Kokin Wakashū*, that standard-bearer of the Heian period, is indeed the witty, oblique conceit that compares two things based on some resemblance, the paradigmatic courtly pastime of the period might well be the practice of *monoawase*, or contests entailing the matching of objects from the literal matching of bivalve shells fitting together neatly, to the matching of iris roots, to kinds of incense and all manner of things. This playful and courtly game arises directly out of the elegant comparison of two things, as evidenced in the well-known seventh-century *chōka* poem of Princess Nukata, who speculates on the merits of spring versus autumn, thereby establishing her *bona fides* as a member of the court.[23] If we accept the idea that assumed conformity to idealized models of courtliness as constituted by the notion of decorum in the Heian period, not only in terms of social conduct, but in matters poetic and aesthetic as well, then the significance of *nazurae's* relationship to *awase* becomes apparent. *Nazurae* becomes the juxtaposition of two things in such a way that they become not only linked as similar to one another, but also linked specifically in a matched encounter (*shukkai* or *deai*) with each other. This encounter entails a dynamic mirroring back and forth, a matching of paired qualities, precisely what is entailed by the practice of *awase*. As suggested by the modern verb, *awasaru*, this dynamic mirroring ultimately implies a closing down or a shuttering of difference.

Much of the plot of the *locus classicus Genji Monogatari*, written in the early eleventh century, revolves around the idea of *nazurae*, comparing and evaluating. In "Umegae" ("A Branch of Plum"), for example, as Genji is preparing for his daughter by the Akashi Lady for her debut at court, we hear that, "he therefore had the storehouses at Nijō opened and Chinese things of all kinds brought to him. 'When it comes to brocades, twills, and so on,' he said as he compared them, 'the old ones are still the finest and the best.'"[24] Later in the same chapter, after Genji has exerted himself in compounding various incense blends, he invites Prince Hyobu, His Highness of War, for evaluation.

> "Please rank these. To whom else would I show them?" Genji said. He sent for a censer and insisted that His Highness test them. "It is not *I* who know!" His Highness modestly replied, but he established fine distinctions of quality between them, even ones of the same kind, and so managed after all to decide which was better than which.[25]

Here the issue of prowess has shifted from the original performance, that is, the blending of the incense, to the evaluation of the performance, so that now the evaluation or critique becomes the performance itself.

In chapter 17, entitled 'E-awase,' or 'Picture Contest,' which features a matching contest of paintings, we witness, for example, the lengths to which the two arch rivals and friends, Genji, by now the palace minister, and Tō no Chūjō, the acting counselor, go to procure and produce stunning masterpieces of painting for their respective ward and daughter in order to promote both their political prospects at court as well as their own personal rivalry. The author Murasaki Shikibu writes:

> The Acting Counselor redoubled his efforts when he learned that Genji was assembling his own paintings, and he was more attentive than ever to the excellence of rollers, covers, and cords … [Genji] began marshaling paintings in earnest. Both sides had a great many. Since illustrations of tales were the most attractive and engaging, the Ise Consort's Umetsubo party [i.e., that of Akikonomu, Genji's ward] had theirs done for all the great classics of the past,

while the Kokiden side favored tales that were the wonder and delight of their
own time, so that theirs were by far the more brilliantly modern. Those of his
Majesty's own gentlewomen who had anything to say for themselves spent their
time, too, rating this painting or that.[26]

Not unlike the earlier competition between Amaterasu and Ama no Uzume,
the vying between Genji and Tō no Chūjō is simultaneously playful and in
earnest, but with much less of the parodic buffoonery and overt mockery
that had charged the divine interaction. The two characters are compared in
nearly every chapter, and indeed afterwards their progeny, alleged progeny,
and progeny's progeny are juxtaposed as well. Ultimately, what serves to
demarcate the relative worth of these pairs is their ability to discriminate,
that shibboleth that determined courtly worth. What distinguishes this kind
of pairing or *awase* of characters from the kind of metaphorical wrestling of
the goddesses is the emphasis on evaluation as a central part of the performative struggle.

Evaluation becomes even more significant when it deals with textual matters. By the tenth century, *uta-awase* or poem-competitions had begun to
take place in which two sides, the Left and the Right, submitted poems on
set topics (*dai*) amidst a lavish and highly ornate ritualized court festivity
presided over by a *hanja* or judge, whose task it was to declare one of each
pairing to be a winner for such and such reasons or a tie, again with reasons
provided. Initially, the emphasis was as much on the gorgeous pageantry,
which often included musical concerts and the bestowal of sumptuous
gifts of clothing, as it was on the actual poetic competition. Konishi notes,
"Although 'waka match' signifies a variety of events, in all cases they were
based on striving for superiority over a rival."[27] Perhaps the best example
of this practice involves the medieval arch rivals in poetics, Minamoto
Toshiyori and Fujiwara Mototoshi.[28] They not only vied with each other
in the submission of *waka* at these gatherings, but also jousted with each
other in their withering comments as *omoibito*, those respective advocates
for the two sides whose critiques in the form of a debate served to assist the
judge in determining the winner of that round. At the *uta-awase* hosted by
Fujiwara Tadamichi in 1118, Toshiyori remarks at one point, "The syntax
seems askew. This is contrived, and since one cannot overlook the misuse
of an old poem, perhaps it should lose." Mototoshi assumes an even more
acidic tone:

> I have never before seen phrases like 'How regrettable!' used in poems for
> poetry matches. This is beneath contempt. As the people of old said, in compos-
> ing poetry both in Chinese and in Japanese, one puts the blossoms [*hana*] first,
> and the fruit [*mi*] second. Thus, such phrases are never used in any of the family
> collections or in poetry matches, let alone in an opening line.[29]

The idea of competition in Heian court poetry, as later generations sometimes deprecated, devolved around the degree of nondeviation from the practices of the past. Just as poems in these matches were evaluated on how well they hewed to the specified topic, the competition was one in which contestants vied to conform better to what already had been composed. When we super-impose comparative tropes like *nazurae* and institutionalized comparative practices like *awase* against the backdrop of the related construct of *modoki*, we realize that while in *modoki*, both the differences and the similarities are called into play during the contest, in the Heian period we tend to preclude difference. Instead, similitude is stressed and even idealized. Shells are seen to match and, by analogy, so too do other seemingly more disparate things if they signify membership within the court.

Comparison of like things (*awase*) serves to reinforce existing boundaries and categories and by extension privileges the sense of closed unity. Unlike the encounter between the goddesses noted in the *Kojiki*, this kind of com-petition is a zero-sum game in which both winners and losers remain within the known hermetically-sealed sphere with no waste, no overflow, no excess. Instead, the residue that results settles in the form of invidious judgment, a value that is recuperated to reinforce the existing order.

EDO DISSONANCE AND DISCORDANCE: *NAZORAE* AND *MITATE*

The roughly synonymous poetic tropes *nazurae* and *nazorae*, signifying imi-tation/comparison, never assume major importance as literary terms, unlike *awase*, despite the early reference in the *Kokin* preface. But increasingly in the medieval, post-Heian world, the term *nazurae* (which appears numerous times in *Genji Monogatari* as well as on occasion in *Ise Monogatari* and *Heike Monogatari*) in large measure disappears after the fourteenth century, yielding pride of place to *nazorae*. The latter term appears a number of times in the lengthy *gunki monogatari* (battle chronicle) account of the war between the Genji and Heike, in the *Genpei Seisuiki*, in other medieval texts such as *Hōjōki* (*An Account of My Hut*), and at various times in Edo-period litera-ture, including the works of Saikaku and Chikamatsu.[30] But its connotations increasingly assume the sense of something more than simple juxtaposition and similitude. We see this change foreshadowed, for example, in the afore-mentioned Minamoto Toshiyori's poetic treatise *Toshiyori Zuinō* (*The Poetic Essentials of Toshiyori*), ca. 1115, in which Toshiyori advocates a "new style" of poetic composition, deprecating the sterile use of convention, such as the traditional use of set comparisons, which he christens *nisemono* or 'counterfeit things.' *Nisemono* itself etymologically is cognate with *niru* (to resemble), *niseru* (to imitate), and *nise* (sham or counterfeit). He enumerates disparagingly canonical examples of the sort encountered in the *Kokin* Preface:

> To liken cherry flowers to white clouds; compare scattering flowers to snow; compare plum blossoms with the robe of one's love; doubt if deutzia flowers are really not the waves breaking on Hedge Island; analogize crimson leaves to a brocade.[31]

No longer are the conventional comparisons understood to be idealized moments of similitude and convergence in which past and present associations are matched to reinscribe the insular identity of the court; instead, pairings begin to fall apart with the idea of comparison as entailing deception and false identification.

The twentieth-century writer and erstwhile journalist Lafcadio Hearn (also known in Japan as 'Koizumi Yakumo' 小泉八雲), that lover of all things Japanese and traditional, elaborates on the idea of *nazoraeru* and its significance in one of his retellings of Japanese ghostly folk tales included in the anthology *Kwaidan*, using a narrative persona to interrupt the flow of plot to comment:

> Now there are queer old Japanese beliefs in the magical efficacy of a certain mental operation implied, though not described, by the verb *nazoraeru*. The word itself cannot be adequately rendered by any English word; for it is used in relation to many religious acts of faith. Common meanings of *nazoraeru*, according to dictionaries, are "to imitate," "to compare," "to liken"; but the esoteric meaning is *to substitute, in imagination, one object or action for another, so as to bring about some magical or miraculous result.*[32]

Here Hearn suggests a sense of *nazorae* that seems far removed from the exoteric formalist genre classifications of Heian poetics, something much more akin to the eighth-century (re)construction of the putatively primordial *modoki* with its deceitful pantomime of veiled illumination.

Hearn's explanation of *nazorae* sounds remarkably parallel to the anthropologist Masao Yamaguchi's understanding of *mitate* as articulated in his essay, "The Poetics of Exhibition in Japanese Culture."[33] Yamaguchi invites us to consider *mitate* as "in a sense, the art of citation," noting:

> *Mitate,* then, is the technique used to associate objects of ordinary life with mythological or classical images familiar to all literate people … . Japanese used *mitate* to extend the image of an object. By so doing they transcend the constraints of time.[34]

Further, he suggests:

> *Mitate* is something close to the idea of a simulacrum, a concept made popular by Jean Baudrillard. *Mitate* is always a pseudo-object. In Kabuki, everything is a simulacrum of what has been extant for a very long time. However, primordial things, in turn, are simulacra for what belongs to gods. It is understood that Japanese gods do not appreciate true things; they do not accept things that are not fabricated by means of a device (*shuko*). One must add something to that which already exists in order to present it to the gods.[35]

Suddenly, we are back in the world of *modoki* and the goddess in the cave. Here we move from the idea of converging dualities to counterfeit or ersatz objects, intended to deceive and/or lesser in quality or essence, to the fabricated as wondrous simulacrum.

Interestingly, the word *nazorae* assumes its greatest prominence in the mid-nineteenth century in its ekphrastic appearance in woodblock prints. It appears in the title of a number of prominent woodblock print series—the *Ogura Nazorae Hyakunin Isshu* (the *Ogura One Hundred Poets One Poem Each Anthology Parodied*), the *"Wakan Nazorae Genji"* (*Parodic Analogs from Japan and China for the Genji Chapters*), *Buyū Nazorae Genji* (*Heroic Parodies of the Genji Chapters*), *Imayō Nazorae Genji* (*Present-Day Parodies of the Genji Chapters*), and *Nazorae Gogyō* (*A Series of Analogs to the Five Cardinal Elements*), to name but a few. The parodic quality of these woodblock prints, as Joshua S. Mostow has illuminated wonderfully in his work,[36] emerges from a number of sources: from the often ludicrous rendering of hitherto sacrosanct iconic classical texts, such as Murasaki Shikibu's *Genji Monogatari* and Fujiwara Teika's *Hyakunin Isshu*; from the anachronistic repositioning of classical narratives into modern contexts; from the conjoining of "high culture," or *ga*, with "low or popular culture," or *zoku*; and, finally, from the generic media themselves, from the elegant manuscripts of Heian courtiers shared among themselves within the court to the mass-produced, mass-vended woodblock prints of the urban world of *chōnin* or townsmen.

Nazorae overlaps with its far more prominent aesthetic twin in the Edo period, *mitate*. Earlier, we encountered the use of the term *mitate* in the work of various modern literary critics, both Japanese and non-Japanese, as they evaluated classical poetry, especially in the Heian period. Yet as Suzuki Hiroyuki comments[37] in talking about the emergence of notions of similarity, *nazorae* is the term that began to be utilized in the Muromachi period, one that on the surface seems akin to *mitate*, but which lacks its playfulness. We move in the spectrum of comparison from the most conventional *nazurae* to *nisemono* to *nazorae* and finally to the most *outré* iteration of comparison, *mitate*.

Historically, *mitate* first appears as a distinct aesthetic trope in 1638 in the preface to Matsue Shigeyori's *Kefukigusa (The Down-Blown Grass)*,[38] a primer on Teimon *haikai* poetics, proffering a number of poetic tropes of which *mitate* is one. Others are *iitate* (the verbal equivalent of the visual *mitate*), *torinashi* ("recasting" the meaning of a line or link, usually involving homophonic reverberation), and *tatoe* (analogy). *Mitate* becomes associated with *omoigakenai deai*, that unexpected encounter between two things, rather than merely imitation, deception, or fabrication.[39] At the same time, it foreshadows Bashō in arguing for sincerity or integrity as the basis for poetry in its embracing of disparate polarities rather than conventionalized pairings.[40]

In virtually every field of the arts in Japan, from garden design to the art of incense, *mitate* occupies a prominent position. In the tea ceremony, *mitate* denotes a repurposing of quotidian objects as tea utensils as initiated by the great late-sixteenth-century tea master Sen no Rikyū. The Omotosenke School goes so far as to argue for it as the fundamental basis of the tea ceremony:

> In our enjoyment of the experience of *chanoyu* and the innovations that we make, this spirit of 'mitate' could be said to be the root of *chanoyu*. For example, while on a trip one might be looking at the traditional local craft works and wondering if something could be used as a lid rest or an incense container. Thinking about this while taking a walk is one of the pleasures of travelling and is also the pleasure of a life in *chanoyu*. The spirit of 'mitate' which is part of an exceptional aesthetic awareness, can also give life to traditional crafts and industries.[41]

In Kabuki theater as well, we see the major role played by *mitate* and *yatsushi* (dual identity).[42] Beginning in the early eighteenth century, playwrights of the Kabuki theater, a venue pejorated as one of the *akusho* or "bad places" of urban culture by the ruling shogunal ideology, were proscribed from employing certain contemporary events (*shinjū* or "love suicides") within their productions as well as occurrences among the ruling samurai families. *Mitate*, which offered a means of indirectly connecting present-day events, people, issues with their ostensible analogs from the past, allowed the dramatists a means of sidestepping the increasingly restrictive legal regulations on the content of the plays. A related stratagem was the idea of *yatsushi*, related to the verb 'to disguise' (*yatsusu*) or double identity, in which a character understood to be one individual would reveal himself to be in actuality (*jitsu wa*) someone else. The doyen of Japanese theater history, Gunji Masakatsu, notes:

> The type of "dual identity-double meaning" game represented by *yatsushi* and *mitate*, with all their elaborate ramifications, is one of the most characteristic features of the Kabuki.[43]

He further illuminates the connection between the arts commenting:

> The idea of *yatsushi*, which has much in common with the spirit of *haikai* (in the haiku style, that is, abbreviated and evocative) that established itself in the Edo period, is basically the attempt to 'modernize' everything, to translate it into terms of contemporary society, to 'parody' the old (though not necessarily in the grosser sense) by recreating it in terms of the present and familiar ... . The Kabuki itself, indeed, is no more than a *yatsushi* of No and Kyogen, in the same way that the haiku is a *yatsushi* of the classical *waka* verse form.[44]

Mitate, in the modern era, has been defined in myriad ways including 'courtly wit,' 'elegant confusion,' 'double vision,' 'to see and to construct,' 'parody,' 'the art of citation,' 'conceit,' and 'visual allusion,' to name just a handful. But often in an attempt to link *mitate* to Western concepts like metaphor and conceit, several distinctive elements are neglected. First, there is nothing transparent or preformed about *mitate*, unlike the *nisemono* decried by Toshiyori. Second, it invites a specific kind of conflation in which disparate realms, often in dualistic opposition, are brought together, inducing confusion or a sense of paradox. Finally, there is invariably a sense of the unexpected introduced, arousing surprise and a lack of clear closure in which the dissonance is never resolved. Hence, we need to question the use of *mitate* in limning classical poetry of the medieval periods, not simply on the grounds that it is anachronistic, but because to read *mitate* as simply metaphor, visual conceit, or even visual ambiguity obscures the subversive, indeterminate, and entropic element that defines it.

Masao Yamaguchi, reminding us of the concept of *modoki* once more, notes in his trenchant examination of exhibitions:

> All exhibitions suffer from the status of being fake. However, they acquire the status of being authentic when they are thrown into the theatrical context. The Japanese tradition and its art of representation seems to show this clearly.[45]

He goes on to define *mitate* as 'the art of citation,'[46] but this should not be understood as a transparent literary allusion. Instead, he stresses the role of fabrication in the very act of citation as imitation. The art historian Monta

Hayakawa, in his essay on *mitate*,[47] underscores Matsue's aligning of two unlike things in haiku cited in *Kebukigusa*: "kawa-gishi no hora wa hotaru no gato kana" ("fireflies in holes along the riverbank—like lanterns beneath the eaves [of a house]"). As Ian McCullough MacDonald notes in his brilliant dissertation on parody, satire, and *mitate* in seventeenth-century Japanese comic poetry, "In each case, a comparison is posited between two things in the physical world that are seemingly unrelated and unalike, producing a vivid, almost visual image."[48] He quotes Nakamura Yukihiko's book *Gesaku ron*:

> Simply stated, the subtlety of mitate relies on the discovery of similarities between things or between aspects [of things] which on the face of it are not similar, or are not generally thought to be similar. These similarities are discovered due to the acute sensibilities, the unusual powers of observation of the author, and must be accompanied by an appropriately refined mode of expression. As for the finished mitate, it is much more interesting to suppress skillfully the points of similarity; as long as some firm connection is maintained between the two, it is better to make them as different as possible.[49]

What is clear is that 'mitate' encompassed not merely comparison or metaphor, but also the deliberate bringing about of a collision between two seemingly unrelated things. This kind of *discordia concors*, as Samuel Johnson might have understood it, entailed "a combination of dissimilar images, or discovery of occult resemblances in things apparently unlike … . The most heterogeneous ideas are yoked by violence together; nature and art are ransacked for illustrations, comparisons, and allusions; their learning instructs, and their subtlety surprises."[50]

During the Edo period, *mitate* and *nazorae* represented for *chōnin* (townsmen) culture an opportunity for reframing and reconstituting the traditions of high culture from which they were precluded in ways that ranged from the absurd to the subversive. Unlike courtly Heian notions of convergence and stability engendered by closed tropes of similitude that reinforced existing norms, in the Edo period the juxtaposition of unlike things (*mitate* and *nazorae*) itself called into question the problem of value. The violent coupling of past and present, of *ga* and *zoku*, of sacred and profane, ends entropically in a question mark, forcing the observer to try to make sense of the strained juxtaposition. As if recollecting Ama no Uzume's dance before the cave, Yamaguchi asserts "*Mitate*, in its original sense, was an exposition presented to the gods"[51]—one, we might add, that inevitably raises the question about "to what we might compare this world," in the words of the poet Sami Mansei. Comparison, likewise in the guise of *mitate,* raises the specter of new possibilities, the delimiting of existing boundaries, and finally the exploding of the sacrosanct status of existing categories. And in so doing, comparison, rather than reinforcing existing boundaries and hierarchies as in the Heian period, forces us to rethink the utility of those categories and their ultimate value. But it is less a questioning of the past than a radical reconsideration of the present. We can never quite return to where we began.

NOTES

1. *Man'yōshū* (*The Anthology of Ten Thousand Leaves*), vols. 4–7 of *Nihon koten bungaku taikei*, ed. Takagi Ichinosuke, Gomi Tomohide, and Ōno Susumu (Tokyo: Iwanami Shoten, 1957–1962), no. 352. English translation is my own.

2. Watsuji Tetsurō, *Watsuji Tetsurō zenshū* (*Complete Works of Watsuji Tetsurō*), 27 vols., ed. Abe Yoshishigo et al. (Tokyo: Iwanami Shoten, 1992), 10:105.

3. Alternately written as 準える, 擬える, 准える.

4. Toshio Yamagata, K. Ashok, S. K. Behera, S. A. Rao, and H. Weng, "ENSO Modoki (Pseudo-ENSO) and Its Impact on the World Climate" (paper presented at the 3rd Annual APEC Climate Symposium, Busan, South Korea, September 14–16, 2006), accessed June 23, 2015, http://www.apcc21.org/eng/acts/pastsym/japcc0202_viw.jsp?symp_yy=2006.

5. Arata Isozaki, *Shigen no modoki: Japanesukizeshon* (Tokyo: Kajima Shuppankai, 1996).

6. "The spirit of Kabuki dance is always that of *modoki*, or 'performing as if.' It is not a matter of acting naturalistically, just like the action, but rather of acting so as to seem like that being imitated." Quoted in "Bandō Kotoji Dancing Sanbasō (三番叟)," Japanese Performing Arts Resource Center (JPARC), accessed June 23, 2015, http://www.glopad.org/jparc/?q=en/kabukidance/videos/sanbaso.

7. See Samuel Martin, *A Reference Grammar of Japanese* (Honolulu: University of Hawai'i Press, 2003), 120.

8. Orikuchi Shinobu, *Kodai kenkyū* (*Minzoku gakuhen 1*), vol. 2 of *Orikuchi Shinobu zenshū*(*Complete Works of Orikuchi Shinobu*) (Tokyo: Chūō Kōronsha, 1975), 409; quoted by Sakabe Megumi in "'*Modoki*'—Sur la Tradition Mimétique au Japan," *Acta Institutionis Philosophiae et Aestheticae* 3 (1985): 95–105; translated by Michele Marra in *Modern Japanese Aesthetics: A Reader*, trans. and ed. Michele Marra (Honolulu: University of Hawai'i Press, 1999), 254–55.

9. Sakabe, 253–54.

10. Fourth section of Zeami Motokiyo's *Kadensho*花伝書(*Treatise on the Transmission of the Flower*); *Zeami, Zenchiku*, vol. 24 of *Nihon shishō taikei*, ed. Omote Akira and Kato Shuichi (Tokyo: Iwanami Shoten, 1974).

11. *Kojiki* (*Chronicle of Ancient Matters*), vol. 1 of *Nihon koten bungaku taikei*, ed. Kurano Kenji and Takeda Yukichi (Tokyo: Iwanami Shoten, 1958).

12. Zeami, *Kadensho*.

13. Sakabe, 254.

14. Orikuchi, *Orikuchi Shinobu zenshū*, vol. 17, 348–50, quoted by Herbert E. Plutschow in *Chaos and Cosmos: Ritual in Early and Medieval Japanese Literature* (Leiden: Brill, 1990), 66.

15. Ibid., 64.

16. Takahashi Tōru, "Parodi," in Kokubungaku Henshubu, *Koten bungaku retorikku jiten* (*Dictionary of Classical Literary Rhetoric*) (Tokyo: Gakutosha, 1993), 56–57; quoted in Dean Anthony Brink, "At Wit's End: Satirical Verse Contra Formative Ideologies in Bakumatsu and Meiji Japan," *Early Modern Japan* 9, no. 1 (2001): 27.

17. *Kokin Wakashū* (*Anthology of Japanese Poetry, Ancient and Modern*), vol. 7 of *Nihon koten bungaku zenshū*, ed. Ozawa Masao (Tokyo: Shōgakkan, 1971), 51–53.

18. Ibid., 52.

19. Jin'ichi Konishi, "The Genesis of the *Kokinshū* Style," trans. Helen C. McCullough, *Harvard Journal of Asiatic Studies* 38, no. 1 (1971): 71.

20. Ibid., 134.

21. Robert H. Brower and Earl Miner, *Japanese Court Poetry* (Stanford, CA: Stanford University Press, 1961), 164.

22. *Kokin Wakashū*, 64.

23. *Man'yōshū*, I:16 in *Nihon koten bungaku taikei*, vol. 2, ed. Takagi Ichinosuke (Tokyo: Iwanami Shoten, 1962).

24. Murasaki Shikibu, *Genji Monogatari*, vols. 14–15 of *Nihon koten bungaku taikei*, ed. Yamagishi Tokuhei (Tokyo: Iwanami Shoten, 1958). Translation from *The Tale of Genji*, trans. Royall Tyler (New York: Penguin, 2001), 547.

25. Ibid., 549.

26. Ibid., 324.

27. Jin'ichi Konishi, *A History of Japanese Literature,* vol. 3, *The High Middle Ages,* ed. Earl Roy Miner, trans. Aileen Gatten and Nicholas Teele (Princeton, NJ: Princeton University Press, 1991), 198.

28. From the *Gen'ei Gannen Jūgatsu Futsuka Naidaijin Tadamichi Ie Uta-Awase, 1118,* excerpted and translated by Haruo Shirane in *Traditional Japanese Literature: An Anthology, Beginnings to 1600* (New York: Columbia University Press, 2007), 597–600.

29. Ibid., 599.

30. Ibid., 600.

31. See Kazutoshi Ueda, *Ueda's Daijiten: A Japanese Dictionary of Characters and Compounds* (Cambridge, MA: Harvard University Press, 1942).

32. Lafcadio Hearn, "Of a Mirror and a Bell," in *Kwaidan: Stories and Studies of Strange Things* (Ithaca, NY: Cornell University Press, 2009), 71.

33. Masao Yamaguchi, "The Poetics of Exhibition in Japanese Culture," in *Exhibiting Cultures: The Poetics and Politics of Museum Display*, ed. Ivan Karp and Steven D. Lavine (Washington, DC: Smithsonian Institution Scholarly Press, 1992), 57–67.

34. Ibid., 58.

35. Ibid., 64.

36. See, for example, "'Picturing' in *The Tale of Genji*," *Journal of the Association of Teachers of Japanese* 33, no. 1 (1999): 1–25; and *Pictures of the Heart: The Hyakunin Isshu in Word and Image* (Honolulu: University of Hawai'i Press, 1996), 99–115.

37. Hiroyoki Suzuki, "Ruiji no hakken: muromachi no nazorae, edo no mitate," *Nihon no bigaku* 24 (1996): 82–101. Quoted and translated in Ian McCullough

MacDonald, '*The Mock One Hundred Poets' in Word and Image: Parody, Satire, and Mitate in Seventeenth-Century Comic Poetry (Kyōka)* (Ph.D. diss., Stanford University, 2005).

38. 1647 is the date of the manual itself. Elaborate and exuberant wordplay become the hallmark of the Teimon School (that is associated with the poetic spirit and dicta of the Edo poet Matsunaga Teitoku).

39. Kazunobu Mitsuta, *Haikai to mitate: Bashō zing* (Kyoto: Kokusai Nihon Bunka Santa, 1990), 66.

40. Ueshima Onitsura, another prominent member of Teitoku's circle, flatly states in *Hitorigoto (Monologue)*, "makoto no hoka ni, haikai nashi" ("Without sincerity, there can be no haikai poetry"). Quoted in Cheryl Crowley, "Putting Makoto into Practice: Onitsura's *Hitorigoto*," *Monumenta Nipponica* 50, no. 1 (1995): 2.

41. *Japanese Tea Culture: The Omotesenke Tradition (Cha no yū: kokoro to bi)* (Kyoto: Omotesenke Fushin'an Foundation, 2005), 93.

42. Masakatsu Gunji, *Kabuki*, trans. John Bester (Tokyo: Kodansha, 1985), 15–16.

43. Ibid., 15.

44. Ibid., 16.

45. Yamaguchi, 67.

46. Ibid., 58.

47. Monta Hayakawa, "Mitate ni tsuite—'Mitate' no kōzō no imi," in *Bijutsu-shi no danmen*, ed. Takeda Tsuneo Sensei Koki Kinenkai (Osaka: Seibun-do Shuppan, 1995), 427–46.

48. MacDonald, 77.

49. Yukihiko Nakamura, *Gesaku ron (On Gesaku)*, vol. 8 of *Nakamura Yukihiko chojutsushū (Collected Writings of Nakamura Yukihiko)* (Tokyo: Chūō Kōronsha, 1982); quoted in MacDonald, 80.

50. Samuel Johnson, "The Life of Cowley," in *Lives of the Poets: Waller, Milton, Cowley* (Cambridge: Cambridge University Press, 2011), 92.

51. Yamaguchi, 64.

Chapter 19

On Kawabata, Kishida, and *Barefoot Gen*

Agency, Identity, and Aesthetic Experience in Post-Atomic Japanese Narrative

Mara Miller

INTRODUCTION

Since World War II,[1] Japanese artists have taken two seemingly contradictory approaches to their art.[2] On the one hand, many are radically innovative, experimenting wildly with all kinds of new artistic movements (Japanese, other Asian, Western, "nondenominational") and bringing them into the international *avant-garde*.[3] A few, such as the "Living National Treasures," remain purists, exploring traditional aesthetics, materials, themes, artistic methods, technologies, and approaches.

More intriguing are the cases where artists combine the two approaches in a single work. Countless examples could be given. This chapter, my eighth in an ongoing series on aesthetics and the arts after the atomic bombings,[4] explores those implications of the postwar utilization of traditional aesthetics in three narrative works dealing with the effects of World War II. These narratives are *The Sound of the Mountain* (*Yama no Oto*) (1949–1954), a novel by Yasunari Kawabata (1899–1972); *Thread Hell* (*Ito Jigoku*) (1984), a play by Rio Kishida (1946–2003), which won the Annual Kishida Prize for Drama in 1985 and which I saw in a recent production;[5] and *Barefoot Gen* (*Hadashi no Gen*) (1983), a film directed by Mori Masaki (1941–), written by Keiji Nakazawa (1939–2012), and based on Nakazawa's manga (comics) series of the same name. Although the three works examined here are narratives, my interest is less in their narrative and verbal dimensions than in why such narratives use other arts in the ways they do.

In spite of differences in medium, audience, date of composition, and genre (novel *vs. avant-garde* drama *vs.* anime film, fiction *vs.* memoir), plot takes a backseat in all three works: first, to scenes that present the individual consciousness with its sense of personal identity and agency (or lack thereof);

269

and, second, to three "levels" of aesthetic experiences—the characters' own aesthetic experiences with various arts in their lives, and those of the audience, who experience them both vicariously (through the characters) and directly as given by the work itself.

What can we make of this continued Japanese fascination with traditional aesthetics—especially in such horrific circumstances? Why do Kawabata, Kishida, and *Gen*'s filmmakers return to classical aesthetics to deal with the horrors of the nuclear age? The return to tradition in this paradoxical way can only be the result of the greatest self-consciousness and deliberation, and results from many factors. For our purposes, the five most important of these factors are the desperation of the Japanese position after World War II, their recognition of the new demands subsequently placed on individuals by the 'humanism' of the Occupation, the renewed demands of modernization itself, the usefulness of aesthetic experience for healing, and the capacity of aesthetic experience for consolidating the individual's experience of herself as an experiencing subject.

My contention is twofold. At the same time that these presentations of other arts within the texts offer their characters aesthetic experiences, they offer similar opportunities to their readers/viewers. Furthermore, these aesthetic experiences can play foundational roles in the constitution of one's sense of personal identity (the characters' and our own as readers/viewers), the reinvention of which is valuable and may even be necessary after trauma or mass disaster (Miller 2014a).

Such reinvention, while hardly unexplored, nonetheless still flies in the face of four common models of personal identity or self-identity. Many (Western) philosophers understand personal identity to be static. An alternative model would see the self as undergoing perpetual redefinition or revision, evolving continually and (for the most part) incrementally. A Buddhist model would see those two as equally illusory or delusional. Confucianists would find all three erroneous in overlooking the inherent relational aspects of every self, which is a combination of the various selves-in-relation. Whatever one's basic model, there are certainly circumstances and events—often traumatic but not necessarily so—that seem to participants (but not necessarily to outsiders) to call for radical redefinition of oneself. Psychic numbing is one such type of response.

The Sound of the Mountain, Thread Hell, and *Barefoot Gen* exemplify three separate varieties of psychic numbing, a phenomenon originally studied by Robert Jay Lifton in Hiroshima after the atomic bombings. It refers to the phenomenon wherein societies deny (in order to avoid) large-scale threats (Lifton 1968, 1982). Recently, the concept has been expanded to the level of individuals, especially those with Post-Traumatic Stress Disorder (PTSD), like Shingo (Kawabata's protagonist), Cocoon (Kishida's), and many of

Gen's compatriots (Feeny et al. 2000; Gregory 2003). Psychic numbing characterizes the social milieu of all three of our works. Finally, the diminished sensitivity to the value of life known as 'psychophysical numbing' (Slovic et al. 2013) is seen in the characters of the masters of the Thread House.

The postwar period, like the earlier onslaughts of modernization and Westernization during the Meiji (1868–1912) and Taishō (1912–1926) periods, and the war effort during the Shōwa period (1926–1989), brought ceaseless disruption, much of it unplanned and unanticipated, (further) alienation, and loss of comfort and stable roles. But after the war, the context was one of mass trauma that also affected personal cognition and emotional functioning.

Before we explore the connections between aesthetic experience and selfhood in our three works, let me introduce the works and note their differences.

THE DIFFERENCES AMONG THE THREE WORKS

There is little action in *The Sound of the Mountain* or *Thread Hell*, both of whose protagonists are psychically numbed. In the former, which is largely stream of consciousness, Shingo, the aging protagonist, becomes increasingly reflective and retrospective as he confronts a series of moral dilemmas supplied by family and friends toward the end of the American Occupation in the early 1950s. *Thread Hell* opens in 1939 with Cocoon, a young woman searching for her mother and her own identity in a place she does not recognize. She has no memory; Cocoon's loss of memory and identity presents like amnesia—commonly the result of trauma. Night guards tell her to go to Thread House, a textile factory by day and a brothel by night, whose women are supplied by their masters with fake life-stories to tell their clients. (Later, they tell their own stories, but no one can tell whether the stories are true or fictional.) Cocoon's (prewar) decisions are hers alone—until one of the women presents herself as Cocoon's mother and Cocoon tries to kill her.

Barefoot Gen's six-year-old Gen, by contrast, is exuberant, impulsive, still so new to the world he knows so little about that he is indefatigable; his buoyancy is unbounded. In spite of the difference in their ages and positions within the family, Shingo and Gen find that their postwar situations require them to make many decisions with life-and-death consequences for others, decisions that they realize they have no idea how to resolve. The chief difference between them is that this not knowing is normal for a six-year-old—it is the need to make such decisions that is abnormal. For Shingo, whose age should bring wisdom, the discovery that one does not know how to function in the postwar world is traumatizing in and of itself.

These three works all focus on the lives of ordinary people. The main characters of the three works are opposites. Kawabata's characters always seem to have unlimited resources, part of a cultural elite that takes for granted daily access to the most beautiful and moving works of art that Japan provides. Cocoon and the women of Thread House are entirely without resources—without money, memory, even without family or identity (social identity depended legally on required entry into the *koseki* or family registry). *Barefoot Gen* follows the individual consciousness of little Gen and his younger brothers—first his biological brother Shinji, who with their father and sister burns to death before Gen's eyes, and later the orphan, Ryūta, whom he finds among the rubble and whom Gen adopts because Ryūta resembles Shinji. Gen's family is barely staving off starvation, although the parents' love and the children's deep awareness of this love make theirs an enviable household. There are other riches, too—there is a sense of confidence in the parents' wisdom, which the kids find annoying but which proves to be reassuring when they recall it at the end of the film. Shingo's and Cocoon's situations have no such warmth and little humor.

The works' original audiences differed, too: adults exclusively for the novel and the play versus children and adolescents (and their parents) for the film. The audiences first encountered the stories seven, forty, and thirty-eight years after the war, respectively. Kawabata's first readers would have been familiar with the postwar period and its issues to the point of *ennui*—and exhausted from dealing with it. Most of Kishida's would have forgotten the near-slavery of women in textile factories on which Japan's prewar economy and indeed the war effort had been built—although the labor movement and strikes by female textile workers in Tokyo had been national news during the 1930s. Masaki's and Nakazawa's primary audience had never experienced the war directly (although they might have seen some of the lingering effects or heard about it from parents and grandparents); indeed the purpose was to supply knowledge in the absence of memory.

AESTHETIC DIFFERENCES REGARDING VAGUENESS

The Sound of the Mountain, Thread Hell, and *Barefoot Gen* differ in the directness with which they face the horrors of war and its results, the vast social machinery of the production of the war, and its aftermath. *The Sound of the Mountain* is deliberately vague, indefinite, and allusive—qualities that are adaptations of the tenth-century aesthetics of the Heian-era novel *The Tale of Genji* (1000–1014) by Murasaki Shikibu (c. 973–c. 1014).[6] *Thread Hell*, which like Murasaki's *Genji* addresses women's lives, is equally allusive in places. Its final section references the "Floating Bridge of Dreams" theme from the last section of *Genji*, although like a dream (a recurrent *Genji* motif) it also operates on a highly symbolic level. As part of the postwar *avant-garde* and "underground" theater called *angura, Thread Hell* radically reinvents theater, jettisoning Western-based realistic theater of the Meiji and Taishō periods for a return to the religious and magical origins of Japanese theater—while adopting various modernist aesthetics as well. (Set and setting, for instance, are minimalist, suggestive at most.) *Barefoot Gen*, by contrast, explicitly shows the effects of the atomic bombing on individuals in one of the most graphic sets of depictions to be found outside the atomic bombing museums. (Publishers and other filmmakers have been extremely reticent about showing such images, even in documentaries.[7]) In addition, *Gen*'s evocation of emotion is explicit: the children jump for joy, the little brother burning to death screams in terror, and enlarged tears of pain, fear, or exertion leap from the little boys' eyes.

Although *Gen, Thread Hell*, and *The Sound of the Mountain* adopt similar aesthetic strategies regarding tradition and innovation (see next section), returning to a variety of classical aesthetics in order to deal with the horrors of the war and nuclear age, these works weight tradition and innovation differently. Tradition predominates in Kawabata's novel. An *avant-garde* piece, *Thread Hell* is so radically new that it seems shocking—and puzzles audiences—even today, thirty years later. But because *angura* strove to return to classical Japanese theatrical precedents, it also embodies classical aesthetics.

AESTHETIC SIMILARITIES

More interesting are the similarities among the three works. Most obviously, they share the theme of the war's effects on ordinary people, including being habitually "out of one's depth"—needing to make life-and-death decisions (sometimes for others) in the absence of knowledge of what to do (in Cocoon's case, even of who one is). This theme is set within the context made familiar in fiction worldwide since the late nineteenth century: urbanization, industrialization, mechanization, alienation at work and in personal relations, anonymity in warfare and among social institutions, and the nature of individual consciousness and responsibility in such a context; only modernism's urgent pursuit of identity and the confrontation with alienation are missing (except in *Thread Hell*). (*Gen* is far more optimistic than either the novel or the play about the possibilities of triumph over such terrible adversity.) As in the West, in Japan the modern novel has played a special role in the construction of the modern self. In *The Dilemma of the Modern* (1995), Dennis C. Washburn discusses the importance of the "I-novel" and the theme of identity in literature written in the Meiji period (1868–1912) and up to World War II, a theme also discussed by Janet Walker (1979), Masao Miyoshi (1975), and others.[8] The theme of shattered personal identity that must be reforged by the individual, exemplified by *Thread Hell*, is directly in this vein. In contrast, the absence in *The Sound of the Mountain* and *Gen* of this preoccupation with identity and related issues such as alienation breaks with modernism and suggests a new era. Everyone in *The Sound of the Mountain* and *Barefoot Gen* knows exactly who they are. They just need to know what it means and how to survive.

Sound, Thread Hell, and *Gen* all employ modern, even cutting-edge media, genres, techniques, and aesthetics. Although the novel as a genre is a thousand years old in Japan, Kawabata's use of it derives from Japanese experiments of the late nineteenth and early twentieth centuries that were based on Western novels; he himself is regarded as a pioneer of modernist literary style. He relies heavily on stream of consciousness, a distinctively modernist technique, although in Japan it has precedents going back at least to *The Tale of Genji* (a fact of which Kawabata must have been aware, since he knew *Genji* well and even started a translation of it). He also explores the individual's consciousness of the unreliability of his own memory, a modern theme at the core of self-reflection and the awareness of the modern self, yet also found in *Genji*. At the same time, Kawabata's writing could almost be considered postmodern, insofar as there is deliberate borrowing from many other periods and juxtaposing what he deliberately borrows for his own purposes. *Thread Hell* similarly invents a new artistic language, necessitated by Kishida's decision to explore women's lives in urban factories. Because of both the medium and the premise, the ultra-new *seems to* prevail in the animated film—though with such a complex interplay of captivating cuteness and dead-serious dealing with the real issues of the atomic bombings that I doubt anyone has ever been either puzzled or put off.

SIMILARITIES REGARDING AGENCY

The three works share a dead-earnest cynicism regarding the possibility of any organized help. For Shingo, help is simply absent; everyone else is a fellow victim of a psychic numbness characterizing a traumatized Japan. For the women of *Thread Hell*, of course, there is no support other than the minimum needed to keep them alive as laborers and sex workers; *Thread Hell*'s men have long given up caring for fellow human beings who are female. Gen, however, cannot shed his childish belief that they should be there for him. Yet he is repeatedly turned away by adults and all government agencies.

Shingo continues to function as an adult, maintaining a household with an intact family and commuting to work every day, activities that provide the backdrop for his emerging moral and ethical decisions. The focus, though, is on his not knowing how to decide, his *lack* of agency in the face of requests for assistance from family and friends. *Thread Hell*'s women are all but incapable of action and memory; Cocoon lacks all knowledge and social context, while her new acquaintances have been cast out of traditional family roles and deprived of agency—they are slaves to the military-industrial complex. In spite of his youth and the fact that he lives in the midst of the greatest possible pain and disruption, Gen is surprisingly effective, first in securing carp's blood to sustain his pregnant mother, and later in helping his mother, finding food, and rescuing Ryūta; the two little boys even find a job and earn money by helping a bedridden depressed artist. Interpersonally, Gen is even more successful; twice he and his little brother persuade powerful, angry men to see things their way and give them what they want, in spite of their transgressions.

So in spite of the radically different capabilities of the protagonists and their situations prewar, immediately after the bombings and during the ongoing postwar life, all three works single out the individual moral agent and the qualities and conditions of agency in the absence of any support network by society or the government.

The works struggle to represent the new postwar awareness of the demands on individual conscience, demands that starkly differ from those in the society during the war, when collective action was celebrated above individual agency, and individual conscience received active discouragement and even harsh punishment.[9]

MODERNISM AND TRADITIONALISM
IN THE THREE WORKS

Aside from the beauty of the prose embodied in diction, sentence structure, and imagery, Kawabata utilizes traditional aesthetics in *The Sound of the Mountain* in three ways. First, he cites specific artworks—a Noh mask, a bonsai maple, an ink painting by the Sōtō Zen monk Ryōkan (1758–1831)[10]— that characters own, look at, or use, whose specific connotations carry weight psychologically, symbolically, and as cultural capital. Second, like complex textiles used for Noh robes, or illustrated handscrolls by Tawaraya Sōtatsu (act. 1600–1640) and Hon'ami Kōetsu (1558–1637), this novel is composed of different patterns built up in layers;[11] the intricacy, complexity, and subtlety of such visual works is demonstrably analogous to Kawabata's literary style in this novel. Third, the novel's aesthetics are clearly derived from classical sources. It borrows from Murasaki Shikibu such aesthetic values as elegance, the poignant awareness of things called *aware*, and allusion (in both senses: avoiding the explicit and as a way for *this* to conjure *that*), and others from various medieval (Kamakura-period) texts. (This integration is subtle and sophisticated, insofar as Heian and Kamakura aesthetics are largely antithetical.)

One of *angura*'s most definitive characteristics is the evocation of pre-modern theater, especially Noh, including the evocation of *kami* (local gods) and the forces of nature. The production I saw utilized techniques and staging from Kabuki and the Bunraku puppet theater as well—puppeteer-like manipulations of the women and masks with Kabuki-like make-up.

The play is poetic throughout, including the women's names ('Plum,' 'Cherry,' and 'Snow'—which are, however, common Japanese women's names) and the men's names ('Master,' 'Straw,' 'Fishing Gut,' 'Cord,' and 'Paper/String'—less lyrical, but metaphorically resonant and harsh, even ugly). There are segments where the flow of poetic narration among the women is reminiscent of medieval linked verse (*renga*).

Barefoot Gen's visual language derives from ancient and recent (anime) artistic forms. It includes techniques adapted from Heian-era illustrated scrolls, wherein the structured and physical environment embodies anxiety and insecurity for characters and viewers. Its use of graphic depictions of disease and war injuries stem from Kamakura-era painting (far more than from depictions in twentieth-century media, which avoided them). Seventeenth- and eighteenth-century woodblock prints also contribute: gradations of color, use of color that suits the emotion, and exploitation of emotional (rather than realistic) atmospheric qualities that are overwhelmingly beautiful. In addition, *Gen* employs unusual points of view taken from master nineteenth-century woodblock artists such as Hokusai (1760–1849)—for example, showing the landscape through the spokes of a wheel.[12] Like *Gen*'s widespread humor and playfulness, the enchanting beauty offers viewers much-needed respite from the infants suckling on dead mothers and the skin flayed from arms.[13]

The reliance on the beauty of nature and the grounding of narrative and art in the seasons, features that have pervaded the last fifteen hundred years of Japanese poetry and prose, are evident in all three works. In *Sound of the Mountain*, plants and insects provide constant visual "commentary" on—and occasionally symbolize—the ethical situations and choices Shingo confronts, although given the difficulty of those situations, Shingo rarely enjoys them. Rather, he uses them to understand or comment on the dilemmas. In *Thread Hell*, the women tell evocative stories of moon and cherry-blossom viewing; the unseen sea from which Cocoon has emerged provides one of the traditional categories of poetry subjects.

In *Gen*, such moments contribute to the sense of enjoyment of life and provide confidence in an underlying access to both nature and Japanese tradition that is unchanging in spite of temporary destruction. Poetic themes, such as the full moon and cherry-blossom viewing, are age-old sources of joy and aesthetic pleasure.[14] Their effect is to suggest that culture can be reinstated *even though* it has been destroyed—a destruction we now know to be temporary but that did not seem so in 1945. Gen's family is working class, so the primary aesthetic within the *mise en scène* (though not the film) is from the *mingei* (folk art) tradition, seen in the dishes and simple wooden houses. This *mingei* tradition is also one of the sources for the Zen-inspired aesthetics of the Urasenke and Omotesenka Schools of the Tea Ceremony, whence it entered the elite culture, a move that was subsequently reinforced by the twentieth-century *mingei* movement.

Yet *Gen* also demonstrates a sense of *aware*, keen appreciation of the poignant beauty of the moment in spite of its transience, a major aesthetic in Japan for at least a millennium that today is often associated with the elite class, celebrated as it was in *Genji* and other Heian works. Motoori Norinaga (1730–1801), however, one of the foremost commentators on *Genji* and a founder of the field of Japanese studies called *Kokugaku*, saw *aware* as a widespread indigenous aesthetic that was also deeply related to the ethical, grounding it in awareness of reality and in compassion:

> What sorts of thoughts and deeds, then, are considered good and evil in the novel? Generally speaking, those who know what it means to be moved by things [*mono no aware wo shin*], who have compassion [*sake arite*], and who are alive to the feelings of others [*yo no hito no kokoro ni kanaeru*] are regarded as good; whereas those who do not know what it means to be moved by things and are compassionless and insensitive to the feelings of others are regarded as bad.
>
> The main object of *Genji monogatari*, then, is the understanding of what it means to be moved by things. (Washburn 1995, 34; square brackets are Washburn's)

In this sense, the aesthetic sensibility found throughout *Barefoot Gen* may easily be seen as *aware*. Important as it is for understanding the aesthetic dimensions of *Gen*, however, it is equally crucial for our understanding of the connection to ethics that Motoori posits.[15] Ethics and aesthetics always coincide in *Gen*; no one is ever forced to choose between them.

Similar to *aware* is the Zen emphasis on the sensory experience of the moment, an aesthetic dimension that also appears at several points in *Gen*. Classic examples are the focus in the tea ceremony on the sound of water boiling or being poured; we hear and see Gen's and his brothers' reactions to a similar experience of water, and the sounds offer the viewer the same pleasurable respite they offer the characters. (As Carter 2008 points out, the connections of the tea ceremony with Zen are especially strong through the vision of its founder, Sen no Rikyū.)

Both Zen aesthetics and *aware* focus on the beauty of the moment, avoiding the brilliant, ostentatious, or symmetrical, within a larger Buddhist context of transience. They differ in that *aware* assumes actual beauty or elegance (of a subtle type, often natural), while with the Zen awareness, (1) emphasis is on the state of mind rather than the qualities of the object of perception, (2) that state of mind implies calm and serenity (though humor is certainly welcome), and (3) almost anything can be appreciated.

AESTHETICS, CONSCIOUSNESS, AND INDIVIDUAL AGENCY

Although a classic sense of beauty pervades Kawabata's prose, equally pervasive is his profound concern—revealed through art and aesthetics—with moral agency, the ability to act effectively on one's own behalf and on behalf of others, and to discern the right thing in a world that is far more incomprehensible than it was before the war. He seems especially interested in the limits of rather than the *limitations on* the person, the limits set internally rather than by external forces. Similarly, through its aesthetic beauty and the excitement of its narrative, *Barefoot Gen* addresses the importance of *individual agency* after the atomic bombing. At the same time, both works reveal the government, social institutions, and community groups to be useless in assisting individuals with their needs, at least in the context of mass disaster. In sharp contrast, Cocoon's lack of story (buttressed by the Thread House women's stories, fabricated for them by the bosses for the benefit of clients) places her in need of a novel as much as she needs a mother and an identity; her finding herself in an *avant-garde* play instead indicates the depth of the ostracism of women in prewar Japan.

It is generally acknowledged that the Japanese, rather more than some other groups, have a shared sense of self,[16] and are therefore more reliant upon social support than some other groups. But the end of the war (for some inhabitants before and during the war) saw social support decreasing sharply, just at the time when the need for individual agency was greater than ever before, for two reasons. First of all, after World War II, the Japanese were collectively and individually faced with the loss of many, in some cases all, of the actual bases for personal and national identity: families, friends, classmates, and colleagues had been killed; homes and neighborhoods, whole cities, and social institutions had been destroyed; their government was shown to have lied to and betrayed them; the Emperor, alleged during the war to have been the divine source of the Japanese polity, had declared himself to be human. Thus, collective identity was undermined to a degree that was historically unprecedented. And this undermining occurred at the very moment when support was most needed. Secondly, all this came at a time when the Japanese were called upon to undo all the training and education in obedience of the previous twenty years or more, to reverse their political and ethical understanding and behavior. During the build-up to the war and during it, they were expected to show absolute loyalty and obedience to political and military authority; disobedience could be punished harshly, with imprisonment or death. Now, under the Occupation, the ideology had shifted a hundred and eighty degrees. The new Constitution was written, installing democracy, representational government, women's rights, and expectations of individual moral autonomy and individual ethical agency. These demands upon the individual were unprecedented in Japan.

Postwar narrative works such as *The Sound of the Mountain, Thread Hell,* and *Barefoot Gen* illuminate individual consciousness and agency or the lack of them, because individual self-consciousness is required for political and ethical autonomy and agency.

But the roles of the arts in such circumstances are not limited to the illumination of the needs and consciousness of the individual as she develops necessary agency. The aesthetics of the various art forms—or, of course, of daily life, as these works show us—make two vital contributions to the individual at such junctures. First, aesthetic pleasure is able to intervene in the cycle of emotional and physical exhaustion. Individual self-consciousness plays a paradoxical role during difficult circumstances. It is the locus, if not the source, of the individual's pain, but also of her or his determination to do whatever may be necessary to stop the pain: to effect change, at whatever cost. Yet the awareness of pain—and often, in emergencies, our exertion even in the absence of pain (the heroic and often successful efforts to lift heavy objects, rescue comrades, etc.)—is also exhausting, countering willpower when it is most needed. Such internal forces, while useful, can also overwhelm us.

Aesthetic pleasure nourishes the *individual* consciousness—the same individual consciousness that must continue to rise to the occasion if she and others are to survive. This suggests a crucially important logical/psychological/phenomenological sequence: from aesthetic experience to the relief of the exhausted or traumatized person, her refreshment, and the reinstitution of the awareness of the possible joys of life. But second, beyond that ability to counter our negative feelings, aesthetic pleasure reminds us (or informs us) who we are, what it means to be "me." This ability to be oneself and to recognize oneself may be foundational, even essential, to ethical agency and autonomous selfhood. "*Sentio ergo sum.*" Or "*Sentio ergo ego sum.*"

In this context, traditional or classical aesthetics such as those exemplified in the arts discussed here reestablish the context of a larger community that shares values long predating the present-day disasters, and help to constitute new ethical agents in two ways: providing them with the community with which they can identify and providing them with (positive) experiences of being themselves that they can use as a basis for ethical agency.

NOTES

1. I would like to thank my intern Austin Rooks, University of Hawai'i at Mānoa '13, for his editorial help in the preparation of the final drafts of this manuscript, and Professor John Zuern, UH-M, for his sponsorship of the English Department's Internship Program.

2. Throughout this chapter, when I use the term 'arts' or 'art,' I am talking about the range of arts—visual, performing, literary.

3. Examples would be artists such as Yayoi Kusama, Minoru Kawabata, Toeko Tatsuo, Yoko Matsumoto (Munroe 1994, plates 90–93, 182, 183, and 184, respectively), Yoko Ono (Munroe and Hendricks 2000), and Yoshitomo Nara (Nara 2008), among many others. For twentieth-century Japanese, the family name (first in Japan) is given last, following Western usage.

4. The others examine (i) aesthetics and Japanese identity following the atomic bombings (Miller 2010, 73–82, special issue on Japan and identity after the atomic bombings); (ii) the relationships posited by stream of consciousness, aesthetic experience, and individual ethical agency after trauma in *The Sound of the Mountain* (Miller 2015); (iii) Kawabata's conclusion after the destruction of Hiroshima by the atomic bombing that "looking at old works of art is a matter of life and death" (Miller 2014a); (iv) the ways in which aesthetics and artistic decisions in two Japanese anime films about the bombings of civilians in cities, *Barefoot Gen* and *Grave of the Fireflies*, allow the films both to reach children (without traumatizing them) and to do justice to their subject matter (Miller under review a); (v) the role of war trauma in inspiring the work of two contemporary Japanese female artists, Tsuji Kei and Reiko Mochinaga Brandon (Miller 2014b, 7–31); (vi) the religious dimensions of beauty and the utilizations of historic and prehistoric aesthetics in post-atomic Japanese arts (Miller 2016); and (vii) the crucial roles that visual representational records and visual arts play in the construction, consolidation, iterative correction, preservation, and transmission (the "life cycle") of memory of the atomic bombings on both the personal and the collective levels (Miller forthcoming). A related article, "Visualizing the Past, Envisioning the Future: Unrecognized Religious Dimensions of the Atomic Bomb Memorials," is under review (Miller under review b).

5. The April 2013 production of *Thread Hell* I saw at the University of Hawai'i was directed by Colleen Lanki in an unpublished translation by Keiko Tsuneda and Colleen Lanki.

6. Murasaki's aesthetics have been widely used by twentieth-century Japanese writers, including Jun'ichiro Tanizaki in *Seven Japanese Tales* (Tanizaki 1981) and Fumiko Enchi in *Masks* (Enchi 1983). See Miller 2016 for more on the Japanese use of ancient aesthetics.

7. One three-hour documentary film on the atomic bombings, for instance, devoted a mere seven minutes to the victims' accounts and far less than that to images of injuries.

8. Washburn analyzes the complexity of Japanese novelists' integration of traditional Japanese, traditional Western, and evolving modern literary values and techniques. He sees the modern as having an inherently contradictory structure, defining the "dilemma of the modern" as follows:

By compelling a breaking and then remaking of traditional standards and practices, the modern suggests a process that is a source of literary renewal and of integration of the present into the cultural tradition. It represents a drive toward freedom from convention and is a necessary condition for the possibility of original literature. At the same time, the expression of the modern requires a sense of a discontinuity it cannot sustain, for in reinterpreting the concept of tradition, the present is reduced to a conventional form that destroys novelty and reasserts a sense of cultural continuity. This dilemma is ... expressed in Japanese narratives by a recurring pattern of irreconcilable polarities: descriptive pairs such as deep and shallow, constancy and mutability, intuitive and scientific, idealistic and realistic, orthodox and heterodox. The modern, however, is never defined by one or the other but lies instead in the ambiguous space whose boundaries are marked by these complementary extremes of language. (Washburn 1995, 12)

9. This is widely understood to be a general truth about Japanese society; my own view, however, is that both the role of the individual conscience and of individuality in the arts tend to be widely underestimated for early modern Japan and even earlier. For a study of individual ethics in *The Tale of Genji*, for instance, see Miller 2002.

10. Kawabata's fascination with Ryōkan's poetry and painting is documented in the catalogue of an exhibition of Kawabata's art collection focusing in part on Ryōkan's work (Mizuhara et al. 2008).

11. The analogy between the form of the novel and handscrolls was suggested by Donald Keene.

12. For a fuller analysis, see Miller under review.

13. A quick word about the use of humor in Japanese films about the atomic bombing: in *Barefoot Gen* and *Black Rain*, at least, such humor is never cruel and never used against anyone; it is usually made by the characters themselves, whose reliance on it to relieve their suffering is what allows viewers to enjoy the same relief—but only if they identify with the characters.

14. For a study of how cherry-blossom viewing can function in the lives of mid-twentieth-century people, see the Tanizaki novel *The Makioka Sisters* (Tanizaki 1957). For a glimpse into how it could work in the eleventh century, see the Sarashina diary *As I Crossed a Bridge of Dreams* (Sarashina 1989).

15. Although *aware* is often understood as originating in the Buddhist awareness of mutability or transience (which like *aware* also pervaded Heian culture more broadly and *The Tale of Genji* specifically), Motoori continues: "and hence it stands in opposition to the teachings of Confucianism and Buddhism." Washburn's quotation is from *Motoori Norinaga Shū* (Motoori 1969, 273); the translation is his (Washburn 1995, 34). Motoori is wrong about Confucianism, by the way; one can trace strong traditions of emphasis on the importance of basing one's actions on recognition of the feelings of others (to whom one is bound by the Five Relationships).

16. This is partly due to an inheritance from Confucianism, in which there is no such thing as an independent self. The self is inherently social and takes its definitions—which are several and various and change through time—from its participation in the Five Relationships (parent-child, husband-wife, older brother-younger brother,

friend-friend, ruler-subject). It is also shaped by Buddhist views of the self, namely, that the self is illusory. Equally important is an indigenous component based on various forms of Japanese sociality—shaped by socialization practices and by the arts. Given the decimated population, Japanese would have been severely impacted by the absence of loved ones, coworkers, and community leaders.

REFERENCES

Barefoot Gen. 1983. DVD. Directed by Mori Masaki. San Rafael, CA: Tara Releasing, 1993.

Carter, Robert E. 2008. *The Japanese Arts and Self-Cultivation.* Albany, NY: State University of New York Press.

Enchi, Fumiko. 1983. *Masks.* Translated by Juliet Winters Carpenter. New York: Random House.

Feeny, Norah C., Lori A. Zoellner, Lee A. Fitzgibbons, and Eden B. Foa. 2000. "Exploring the Roles of Emotional Numbing, Depression, and Dissociation in PTSD." *Journal of Traumatic Stress* 13, no. 3: 489–97.

Gregory, Robert J. 2003. "Venturing Past Psychic Numbing: Facing the Issues." *Journal for the Psychoanalysis of Culture and Society* 8, no. 2: 232–37.

Kawabata, Yasunari. 1970. *The Sound of the Mountain (Yama no oto, 1949–1954).* Translated by Edward M. Seidensticker. New York: Putnam.

Kishida Rio. 2002. *Thread Hell (Ito jigoku, 1984).* Translated by Carol Fisher Sorgenfrei and Tonooka Naomi. In *Half a Century of Japanese Theater IV: 1980s: Part 2,* edited by Japan Playwrights Association, 174–222. Honolulu: University of Hawai'i Press.

Lifton, Robert Jay. 1968. *Death in Life: Survivors of Hiroshima.* New York: Random House.

_____. 1982. "Beyond Psychic Numbing: A Call to Awareness." *American Journal of Orthopsychiatry* 52, no. 4: 619–29.

Maruki, Iri and Toshi Maruki. 1972. *The Hiroshima Panels.* Translated by Nancy Hunter and Yasuo Ishikawa. Saitama, Japan: Maruki Gallery for the Hiroshima Panels.

Miller, Mara. 2002. "Ethics in the Female Voice: Murasaki Shikibu and the Framing of Ethics for Japan." In *Varieties of Ethical Perspectives,* edited by Michael Barnhart, 175–202. Lanham, MD: Lexington Books.

_____. 2010. "Japanese Aesthetics and the Disruptions of Identity after the Atomic Bombings."*Kritische Berichte: Zeitschrift für Kunst- und Kulturwissenschaften* 38, no. 2: 73–82.

_____. 2014a. "'A Matter of Life and Death': Kawabata on the Value of Art after the Atomic Bombings."*Journal of Aesthetics and Art Criticism* 74, no. 2: 261–75.

_____. 2014b. "'I Let the Piece Sing Its Own Stories': Post-Modern Artistic Inspiration." *Sztuka i Filozofia (Art and Philosophy)* 45: 7–31.

_____. 2015. "Aesthetics as Investigation of Self, Subject, and Ethical Agency in Postwar Trauma in Kawabata's *The Sound of the Mountain.*"*Philosophy and Literature* 39, no. 1A: A122–A141.

_____. 2016. "Beauty, Religion, and Tradition in Post-Nuclear Japanese Arts and Aesthetics." In *Artistic Visions and the Promise of Beauty: Cross-Cultural Perspectives*, edited by Kathleen M. Higgins, Shakti Maira, and Sonia Sikka. Dordrecht: Springer.

_____. Forthcoming. "Re-Creating History and Memory of Hiroshima and Nagasaki: The Visual and Visceral Records." In *Hiroshima, Nagasaki, and Memory after the Atomic Bombings to Present*, edited by Kenya Davis-Hayes and Roger Chapman.

_____. Under review a. "Making Historic Terror Tolerable to Children: *Barefoot Gen and Grave of the Fireflies*." Preprint.

_____. Under review b. "Visualizing the Past, Envisioning the Future: Unrecognized Religious Dimensions of the Atomic Bomb Memorials." Preprint.

Miyoshi, Masao. 1975. *Accomplices of Silence: The Modern Japanese Novel*. Berkeley, CA: University of California Press.

Mizuhara, Sonohiro, Naoki Kaneko, Yasuo Kuwahara, Tomoko Matsuo, and Michiko Fukaya, eds. 2008. *Japan Is Beautiful: Kawabata Yasunari and Yasuda Yukihiko*. Translated by Rumiko Kanesaka, Brian Smallshaw, Fujisato Kitajima, Mark Frank, and Yoko Araki. Tokyo: Kyuryudo Art Publishing.

Motoori, Norinaga. 1969. *Motoori Norinaga shū (Collected Works of Motoori Norinaga)*. Edited by Kōjirō Yoshikawa. Vol. 15 of *Nihon no shisō (Thought in Japan)*. Tokyo: Chikuma Shobo.

Munroe, Alexandra. 1994. *Japanese Art After 1945: Scream Against the Sky*. New York: Harry N. Abrams.

Munroe, Alexandra and Jon Hendricks. 2000. *YES: Yoko Ono*. New York: Harry N. Abrams.

Nakazawa, Keiji. 1978. *Barefoot Gen*. Translated by Project Gen. Tokyo: Project Gen.

Nara, Yoshitomo. 2008. *Yoshitomo Nara: Nothing Ever Happens*. Edited by Larry Gilman. Cleveland, OH: Museum of Contemporary Art Cleveland.

Sarashina (AKA Takasue no Musume). 1989. *As I Crossed a Bridge of Dreams: Recollections of a Woman in Eleventh-Century Japan (Sarashina nikki, Sarashina Diary)*. Translated by Ivan Morris. New York: Penguin Classics.

Shikibu, Murasaki. 1976. *The Tale of Genji*. Translated by Edward G. Seidensticker. New York: Alfred A. Knopf.

Slovic, Paul, David Zionts, Andrew K. Woods, Ryan Goodman, and Derek Jinks. 2013. "Psychic Numbing and Mass Atrocity." In *The Behavioral Foundations of Public Policy*, edited by Eldar Shafir, 126–42. Princeton, NJ: Princeton University Press.

Tanizaki, Jun'ichiro. 1957. *The Makioka Sisters (Sasameyuki, 1943–1948)*. Translated by Edward G. Seidensticker. New York: Alfred A. Knopf.

_____. 1981. *Seven Japanese Tales*. Translated by Howard Hibbett. New York: Putnam.

Walker, Janet. 1979. *The Japanese Novel of the Meiji Period and the Ideal of Individualism*. Princeton, NJ: Princeton University Press.

Washburn, Dennis C. 1995. *The Dilemma of the Modern in Japanese Fiction*. New Haven, CT: Yale University Press.

Chapter 20

Japanese Poetry and the Aesthetics of Disaster

Roy Starrs

Art created in immediate response to disaster must confront certain ethical as well as aesthetic issues. Indeed, this is one clear case in which ethics and aesthetics seem inextricably linked—and, more than that, a case in which they often seem to conflict with each other. With time comes detachment, but in the immediate aftermath of a disaster writers and artists can feel themselves condemned to silence by the sheer overwhelming magnitude of human suffering that surrounds them. They are virtually compelled to ask fundamental questions about the value or appropriateness of their art in the face of such suffering. And they often tend, in the first instance, to be overcome by the debilitating sense that mere words or images cannot do justice to the enormity and tragic meaning of the disaster, or even that the making of "artistic capital" out of it is a kind of "disaster exploitation" on a par with the proverbial ambulance chasing of other professions. But such fainthearted hesitations or ambivalences also, almost inevitably, give rise to a creative counterreaction and new forms of "apologia" for the ultimate value of art. The creative energy of the artist overcomes initial ethical reservations and, especially in those most aware of this ethical/aesthetic conflict, a new and more powerful form of artistic expression may ultimately result.

Writers, for instance, must write, even if almost in spite of themselves, and their words can possess a mysterious healing power of their own. In the wake of "3/11" (as the March 11, 2011 "triple disaster" of earthquake, tsunami, and nuclear meltdown in northeastern Japan is now conventionally designated), Tanikawa Shuntarō, a senior figure in the Japanese poetic world, wrote a poem called 'Words,' which, as Roman Rosenbaum notes, poses "the question of how we can even write about things for which there are no words; yet 'Words put forth buds / From the earth beneath the rubble.'"[1]

This familiar pattern (in Japan as elsewhere)—an initial traumatized silence followed by a "defiant" outburst of creative productivity—may be seen among writers and artists after an earlier disaster such as the Great Kantō Earthquake of 1923. It may also be found in the literature and art produced, ultimately in great profusion, in the aftermath of 3/11. One significant new factor in the recent disaster, however, was the omnipresence of social media: Twitter, Facebook, and other communications progeny of the Internet. The immediacy, informality, and democratic ease of access of these new media (requiring no imprimatur from any literary or political establishment) seemed to make them the perfect "ethical" means for giving voice to the immediate responses of the victims themselves—and especially of those among them who possessed some literary talent.

From this point of view, it is perhaps no coincidence that the most notable literary response to the March 2011 disaster, at least in the short term, was a rich harvest of poetry. As Jeffrey Matthew Angles writes, "it is no exaggeration to say that in the midst of the crisis, it was the poetic world that asked some of the most incisive questions about the meaning of language, art, and truth—questions that continue to resonate even now."[2] Why poetry, one might ask? A poet, of course, can respond more quickly to an event than a novelist or even a short-story writer, because novels and short stories usually require some time to filter the experiences that they deal with. Poetry, after all, at least in its most common lyrical form, often involves the more or less spontaneous expression of an immediate personal response on the part of the poet—the fresher the better, one might say. Again, social media are obviously well suited to this purpose. For instance, one poet who came quickly to the fore after 3/11 was the Fukushima resident Wagō Ryōichi, who became an "overnight sensation" by using Twitter, a medium that seems ideally suited for haiku-like poetic one-liners, to broadcast to the world his minipoems and journal entries written in immediate response to his experiences as a resident of one of the worst affected areas. Since Wagō had been relatively unknown up to that point, his sudden prominence was a good example of what Angles notes: "At the same time that it shook poetry into the public eye, the earthquake leveled—at least temporarily—the hierarchical culture that had tended to keep established poets and relative newcomers apart."[3] This opening up, democratization, or mixing of the different Japanese poetic worlds in the wake of the disaster—as if, for one historical moment at least, the tsunami had washed away all barriers even in the literary world—is one of the unique features of the post-3/11 literary flowering. Even so, the issue of the tension between "ethics" and "aesthetics" in the artistic response to disaster was by no means decisively resolved. Although, as a victim broadcasting his spontaneous responses over the Internet, Wagō seemed above reproach ethically, questions were soon raised about the aesthetic value of his work. Wagō himself acknowledges that "other Japanese poets sometimes criticized his postearthquake work for being too direct and not 'poetic' enough."[4]

Thus, the issue of how best to "deal with disaster" becomes an aesthetic problem in itself: feelings of creative debility and disempowerment contend with an active creative struggle to find the right words or the right artistic style to do justice to the event—and its victims. This raises the interesting and perhaps unexpected question: is there actually an identifiable literary "style of disaster"? And the answer seems to be, somewhat surprisingly, yes—at least, in the short term. The general consensus among many writers, both in poetry and in prose, seems to be that the appropriate way to write about disaster, at least in its immediate aftermath, is in a simple, straightforward, sketch-like, "documentary" style of writing—a kind of "Hemingway style," a bare-bones minimalistic style which lets the experience speak for itself, without any unnecessary comment or elaboration from the writer. Indeed, Hemingway's own style was created in the first instance as a literary response to the devastating megadisaster of World War I, as a way of writing about the unspeakable shock and trauma of that war, and in explicit reaction against the high-flown empty rhetoric of all those patriotic "war leaders" who had led Hemingway's "lost generation" into that unprecedented and meaningless slaughter.[5] Wagō Ryōichi, for instance, as Angles notes, believes that "the events surrounding 3/11 revealed how self-isolating and even obscurantist the Japanese poetry world had been" and thus "his particular brand of down-to-earth language and powerful, relatively nonabstract expression represent one important direction that poetry seems to be taking in the post-3/11 poetic world."[6] Nonetheless, the fact remains, as we have seen, that his work was sometimes criticized for not being "poetic enough."

Indeed, these debates are universal: the widespread acceptance of a "simple, direct" or "documentary" style as the appropriate style for "disaster writing" is inevitably short term. The question soon arises: is such writing no more than a kind of "higher-level" literary journalism or reportage? In particular, is poetry written in this style "poetic" enough? No less a poet than W. B. Yeats became acrimoniously involved in just this debate when, as editor of *The Oxford Book of Modern Verse* in 1936, he chose to exclude all World War I combatant poets, explaining in his typically lofty, oracular way that

passive suffering is not a theme for poetry. In all the great tragedies, tragedy is a joy to the man who dies; in Greece the tragic chorus danced. When man has withdrawn into the quicksilver at the back of the mirror no great event becomes luminous in his mind; it is no longer possible to write *The Persians, Agincourt, Chevy Chase*: some blunderer has driven his car on to the wrong side of the road—that is all.[7]

In short, what Yeats seems to be saying is that the war poets did not have sufficient aesthetic distance from the disaster they had experienced to be able to turn it into significant poetry; the disaster overwhelmed their poetic gift, robbing them of that joyful, playful spirit that is a necessary element of poetic creation.

Japanese poets wrestled with this issue in the wake of the greatest natural disaster (in terms of loss of life) ever to have struck modern Japan, the Great Tokyo (or Kantō) Earthquake of 1923. One solution they discovered is, again, a familiar one: as Leith Morton puts it, they struggled to transform "documentary realism into art" through a "process of formalization."[8] Comparing their efforts to the "documentary realism" of some Holocaust poets, Morton writes of Mizutani Masaru's and Kawaji Ryūkō's work, for instance:

> The objectivity of representation is an interesting notion when applied to poetry. The variety of lyric poetry that Mizutani employs, by virtue of its lyricism, acts to distance the reader from the horror of the devastation caused by the earthquake but, at the same time, it also memorializes it in a way that transcends mere documentary journalism. Mizutani does this by utilizing a traditional figure and device of poetic art: anthropomorphizing the autumn wind; and, in exactly the same way, Kawaji anthropomorphizes Nature (which is why I capitalize it in translation) in his first poem. The transformation of documentary realism into art is one of the defining characteristics of significant poetry. In this sense, the memorialization of trauma/tragedy is the product of a process of formalization. The use of formal categories of poetic expression such as the dirge or elegy or lament transcend the reality of the present and point to a future where only memory—the memory of tragedy formally rendered into art—remains.[9]

But there are also poets who, while making good use of elements of the formal aesthetic tradition, undermine the comfortably "aesthetic" worldview implicit in that tradition as a way of expressing their outrage at the disaster that has befallen them. In other words, rather than by adopting the "simple documentary style" of a Wagō, they challenge the literary tradition which now seems inadequate to deal with disaster by the kind of postmodern parody that, so to speak, turns the tradition back against itself. An excellent example is the post-3/11 haiku by Seki Etsushi in which the poet describes Japan as being "crushed" and "soiled" by the "spring sea."[10]

Miniature though it is, this poem is brilliantly innovative in the way it uses the traditional haiku *ma* (a kind of suspenseful pause between images) to create a powerfully jolting tension between the traditionally lyrical poetic phrase 'haru no umi' ('spring sea') and the two brutal verbal phrases. This is one beautiful spring sea that has a very ugly impact: it demolishes and dirties Japan. In a few words, the poet has issued a devastating challenge to the thousand-year-plus tradition of Japanese nature lyricism. He calls for a radical reconfiguration of nature in the public imagination and challenges the sanitized, idealized, or aestheticized vision of nature that was prevalent in much of traditional Japanese poetry.

For, the fact is, the mainstream Japanese poetic tradition of court poetry, especially after the *Kokinshū* (905), excluded much of "nature in the raw" in the interests of an aristocratic aesthetic refinement—including, as Janice Brown has recently shown, much of the reality of the female half of humanity.[11] Thus, it could be argued, modern Japanese poets, in rebelling against this "exclusivity" or "hermeticism," especially after the experience of major disasters, are intent on showing that nature is not all cherry blossoms, Mount Fuji, and fireflies on a summer's night—it is also earthquakes and tsunami and the holocaust of indiscriminate death and destruction they can cause. What this implies, of course, is also that, although the Japanese have lived with major natural disasters since time immemorial, their mainstream classical poetic tradition has largely tended to ignore this fact. From this perspective, one might say that the traditional Japanese poetic vision of "nature" is every bit as idealized, aestheticized, or romanticized as, for instance, that of Wordsworth and the other English Romantic poets.

Japanese court poets, of course, had no inkling of the modern ideas of realism or naturalism, of "holding the mirror up to nature"; if anything, they wanted to "improve on nature," in the same manner as, say, a gardener who turns "natural trees" into bonsai by rigorous pruning. In a recent review of Haruo Shirane's *Japan and the Culture of the Four Seasons: Nature, Literature, and the Arts*, which posits the existence of a "secondary nature" in Japanese culture—that is, not "nature in the raw," but the highly aesthetic, artificial construct of Heian poets—Richard Bowring ventures some interesting speculations about the possible psychological origins of this cultural phenomenon:

> It emerged in the tenth century with an aristocracy coming to terms with having to live in one of the most violent and insecure environments on the planet. Hardly surprising that it sought to transform that environment into something it was not, to invent a "secondary" nature that brought comfort and beauty. The myth of a harmonious society living in a benign world was in this sense a fiction necessary to survival. So, are those such as Watsuji Tetsurō who followed in the footsteps of Johann Gottfried von Herder and argued that climate informs national character correct? Well, yes, but not quite in the way intended.[12]

Actually, there is an ethical choice involved here too, but the ethics implicit in classical Japanese poetry are exactly the opposite of the modern realist ethical imperative of "telling the whole truth about nature." As the very first article of Prince Shōtoku's Constitution of 604 AD announced, quoting Confucius directly: "Harmony is to be valued, and contentiousness avoided."[13] In ancient Japan, as in other Confucian-influenced cultures, "harmony" or *wa* was regarded as the supreme moral imperative or ethical value: harmony between man and man, man and nature, man and heaven, man and state. Thus, as with all other forms of culture in ancient Japan, poetry's primary purpose was to help achieve this harmony. And so its formal, restrictive, highly aestheticized character has an ethical and ideological, as well as aesthetic purpose.

As Haruo Shirane points out, nature in classical Japanese poetry is associated not only with beauty but also with harmony: union with nature brings harmony.[14] Indeed, the traditional word for Japanese poetry, *waka*, literally means "songs of the land of harmony." Thus, disharmonious elements or forces of nature were not considered appropriate for poetry. The great classical poet, Fujiwara no Teika (1162–1241), summarized court poetry aesthetics very tellingly as follows: "No matter how frightening a thing may be, when one writes about it in Japanese poetry, it must sound graceful and elegant."[15] Thus, as Shirane writes, classical *waka* tends to be "gentle and deeply moving" (*mono no aware*).[16] The stress is not on what nature necessarily is, but on what it should be: gentle and harmonious, graceful and elegant. This is a quintessentially aristocratic aesthetic. The famous Japanese "closeness to nature," argues Shirane, is really closeness to this refined "secondary nature" rather than to nature in the raw.[17] It is a nature that is not only highly aestheticized but also highly ethicized (in that it is made conducive to harmony). "Negative aspects" of nature such as "pestilence and natural disasters" were "not considered the proper subject matter for classical poetry," especially *waka* of the imperial anthologies, "which were intended to manifest the harmony of the state and the cosmos."[18] Thus, there was a political dimension, as well as an ethical dimension, to court poetry aesthetics. It was not only a highly aestheticized representation of nature and the four seasons but also an "ideological" one.

That is why, for instance, there was a "disjunction" between the actual climate (short spring and autumn, long and severe winter and summer) in Kyoto and Nara, the heartland of classical culture, and "the culture of the four seasons," which focused on spring and autumn as the main seasons.[19] The unpleasant or "difficult seasons," summer and winter, were either ignored or idealized. A gentle dusting of snow was appropriately poetic, but not a heavy snowfall; the pleasant cool of a summer evening was an acceptable topic, but not the unpleasant heat of a midsummer's day. Untamed or wild nature was similarly shunned; it was the realm of "violent gods" who could cause natural disasters, gods such as the river serpent in the *Kojiki* (712) who caused floods and was vanquished by the wind god Susano-ō.[20] For an agricultural people, wild nature and its violent gods were the enemy of civilization. (Significantly, the Japanese attitude to nature changed from mid to late Heian: the violent gods became harvest gods as the wilderness was tamed and cultivated.)

Nonetheless, it would be superficial and misleading to conclude from all of this that the Japanese poetic tradition, and its attendant aesthetics, is outmoded, irrelevant to the modern world, or incapable of an adequate response to the human experience of disaster. In fact, there is ample proof that quite the opposite is true: some of the most moving, powerful, and durable poetry written in response to 3/11, as to earlier disasters such as the 1923 earthquake, have been haiku and *tanka*. These traditional genres have proved, indeed, to be highly effective media for "disaster poems"—and by no means merely in parody form. Haiku and *tanka* seem to be uniquely suited to the task of representing the unrepresentable, if only in microcosmic form, of capturing the everyday human experience of an overwhelmingly vast catastrophe, of expressing a tragic pathos without sentimentality. Their minimalist aesthetic obviously helps here, their tradition of leaving much to the reader's imagination, of presenting the telling image and allowing it to speak for itself (especially in haiku). As the above-mentioned Seki Etsushi, one of the most highly regarded of the younger haiku poets today, has pointed out, haiku "focuses on small moments of revelation and is often written extemporaneously" and so is very effective at "documenting the small details of large events, thus bringing colossal events like 3/11 down to a manageable human scale."[21] Seki has published a number of his own haiku describing the earthquake and its aftermath, haiku that feature images of "twisted and fallen" gravestones, of exploding nuclear reactors, and even of the unfortunate children of Fukushima ironically writing the characters for "nuclear energy" as part of their calligraphy practice.[22]

Of course, 'nuclear reactor' and 'nuclear energy' are not among the "approved poetic words" of the classical poet's aesthetic lexicon.[23] Traditionalists would banish such words as unpoetic or anti-aesthetic. And, of course, one of the ways in which traditional art forms such as haiku, *tanka*—and also, in painting, *nihonga*—have adapted or "modernized" is precisely by opening up to "realistic" subject matter that all-too-obviously violates the aesthetic conventions of traditional Japanese poetry and art. But it is not as simple as that. There is actually a deeper issue at stake here, an issue that involves fundamental questions about the nature of poetry, its relation to reality, and the aesthetic implications of this relation. Before we reach any facile conclusions, I think we should probe a little deeper into these issues.

First of all, it should be acknowledged that what is happening here is simply the conflict between a modernist and a traditionalist form of poetics. The struggle over "subject matter" was, after all, a major part of the more general struggle of the "realist agenda" of modernism since the mid-nineteenth century: to encompass within poetry and the other arts aspects of life that were traditionally considered "unpoetic" or unmentionable in other ways, and also, stylistically, vulgar colloquial diction, slang, and even obscenities. If we think of a great modernist master such as James Joyce, for instance, we remember that he shocked his contemporaries not only with his explicit sex scenes but also with such narrative innovations as an account of his protagonist's thoughts while relieving himself on a toilet. Hardly a "poetic topic" as traditionally conceived! This struggle has long since been won, however, and the "realist" view has itself become a new orthodoxy. Looking back on the aesthetic values of classical poetic traditions such as the Japanese, it is all too easy for us today, from our present modernist perspective, to dismiss these as naïvely unrealistic or idealistic.

On the one hand, there is no denying that subject matter is important. On the other, we should also recognize that, from a purely aesthetic point of view, subject matter is not really of primary importance in any of the arts. As we have seen, the choice of subject matter involves ethical as well as aesthetic values, and these inevitably vary from culture to culture, age to age. Furthermore, it is also true that great art can be entirely "abstract" or "nonreferential"—that is, lacking any obvious "subject matter" apart from the artistic medium itself: line, color, structure, and so on, in the case of painting—as the modernists also discovered. And, in the art of poetry too, subject matter is certainly not of the essence. But, even more importantly, subject matter is also not really the equivalent of truth in art—although the two are often confused. What a poem is explicitly "about" does not define its implicit or ultimate "meaning" or its depth of "poetic understanding" of the world. A poem about ice cream may be simply a children's poem celebrating the delicious taste of ice cream or it may be Wallace Stevens's "The Emperor of Ice Cream," which is really about death. Symbolism and synecdoche are, after all, central to the poetic worldview and to poetic technique. Thus, a poem about disaster or the cruel indifference of nature does not have to explicitly refer to these subjects and certainly does not have to provide an exhaustively detailed description of all the tragic effects of a large-scale natural disaster. A single image might be just as effective or even more so. As William Blake wrote, "to see a World in a grain of sand" is the poet's ultimate mission and also modus operandi. Whether writing about the overwhelmingly destructive power of a natural disaster or about the gentle plop of a frog jumping into an old pond, it is the poet's insight that ultimately matters.

With this in mind, we might look again at traditional Japanese poetry and ask: What does it really tell us about nature? Or, more specifically, about man's relation to nature? One might question whether the poetry of Bashō, for instance, really does give us an "unrealistic," "idealistic," or "utopian" impression of nature. Yes, it tells us that nature is beautiful, but, as we shall see, even natural beauty in Bashō has a "bite," that astringent quality characterized by the key aesthetic terms, *wabi* and *sabi*. As we shall also see, the "lonely," "impersonal" atmosphere of the natural world in his poetry leaves us in no doubt that nature can be coldly and cruelly indifferent to individual human suffering—which is surely also the major theme of more "realistic" modernist disaster poetry. In fact, there is absolutely no conflict between "truth" and "beauty" in the poetry of Bashō; nature is seen or experienced exactly as it is. And, more generally too, one finds on closer observation that the worldview or religious/philosophic perspective implicit in traditional Japanese poetry, especially as found in the work of its greatest practitioners, was never really "untrue" to nature—even though its focus often seems "narrow" from a modern perspective. Consequently, to claim that classical poetry is somehow deficient in reality merely because it neglects to deal with certain subject matter not only is reductive but also betrays an ignorance of the true nature of poetry.

In considering this issue, it is important to recognize that the aristocratic influence was not the only one to shape traditional Japanese poetry. Another major influence was Buddhism, and this ultimately counteracted the tendency of classical Japanese poetry to become a kind of highly formalized game that served only an aristocratic ideal of beauty. With Buddhism, especially from the late Middle Ages onwards, a new moral imperative entered the world of poetry, one that to some extent was even in conflict with the Confucian imperative of harmony, at least as interpreted by the aristocracy. Enlightenment, rather than harmony, was the highest goal of Buddhism, and to achieve enlightenment, the Buddhist practitioner had first of all to recognize certain "negative" facts about nature and human life within nature: impermanence, transiency, death, "emptiness," and "nothingness," all key concepts of the Buddhist worldview.

With its central doctrines of accepting that life is transient and full of suffering and that it is therefore necessary to free oneself through enlightenment from the wheel of life and death, Buddhism provided a cogent and consoling worldview for a disaster-prone country. The Buddhist attitude is well expressed by the thirteenth-century hermit Kamo no Chōmei, who fled to the hills above Kyoto to escape a series of natural and man-made disasters. In his poetic diary, *An Account of My Hut* (*Hōjōki*, 1212), he admonishes that: "The flow of the river is ceaseless and its water is never the same. The bubbles that float in the pools, now vanishing, now forming, are not of long duration: so in the world are man and his dwellings."[24] (There are echoes here of Heraclitus.)

This sense of life as transient and fragile was elaborated into a more formal philosophy by Dōgen (1200–1253), the Thomas Aquinas of Zen Buddhism. Dōgen's philosophy is one of impermanence and emptiness, or nonessentialism: it is not only nature that has no fixed or permanent identity, neither does

man. "The thought of enlightenment ... is the mind which sees into impermanence."[25] Or, more poetically:

> How seems the world?
> Like moonlight caught
> In water droplets
> When a crane shakes its bill.[26]

Impermanence (*mujō*) became a central theme of Japanese art and literature,
and has permeated every other realm of the culture.

Based on these Buddhist insights, a new aesthetic arose in the late Middle
Ages, one that combined aristocratic elegance and playfulness with a darker
view of natural existence. This is what is now commonly referred to as 'the
wabi-sabi aesthetic.' As the leading architect Tadao Andō writes, "Pared
down to its barest essence, *wabi-sabi* is the Japanese art of finding beauty
in imperfection and profundity in nature, of accepting the natural cycle of
growth, decay, and death."[27]

Bashō's poetry may be legitimately regarded as the ultimate culmination
of this "Buddhist deepening" of the classical Japanese tradition. In his haiku,
we can see a fusion of aristocratic elegance with a Buddhistic profundity.
Indeed, some of his haiku are quite dark and would no doubt have shocked
the aesthetic conventions of the Heian aristocrats. But it is still, on the whole,
a poetry of small things, of seeing the world in a grain of sand rather than
of representing wholesale disasters, for instance. As Makoto Ueda points
out, many of the poems of Bashō's "peak years," 1686 to 1691, are unique
because of their "quality of *sabi*," which he defines as 'a primeval lonely feeling.'[28] A good example is the following haiku:

> *kareeda ni karasu no tomarikeri aki no kure*
> a crow alights
> on a withered branch—
> autumn dusk.[29]

The "desolate atmosphere" of this poem exemplifies what Ueda calls Bashō's
'admiration for harsh, austere natural beauty.'[30] This is very different to the
"tame," refined beauty admired by the court aristocrats; it is beauty with a
certain "bite," a certain astringency. Indeed, Bashō is traditionally said to
have attained maturity with this poem—that is, attained to a new level of
Buddhistic profundity, eschewing the merely formalistic, aesthetic wordplay
which, as a young poet, he had learned from the aristocratic tradition. There is
a new and darker tone and vision. And, most significantly, as Ueda points out,
the poem is "objective and impersonal"—the poet has "almost vanished."[31]

Under the influence of Zen, Bashō began to see poetry as a way to enlightenment, a *dō*. The poet would transcend his personal ego and achieve enlightenment by becoming one with nature, not the artificial "secondary" nature of the court aristocrats in their palace gardens at Kyoto, but the "lonely" wild nature of the Japanese countryside, the forests, rivers, moors, and mountains. As Ueda writes, Bashō wanted to "dissolve his ego" through *sabi*, to become one with "primitive nature," and to "submerge himself in the vegetable and mineral worlds."[32] In this respect, his *sabi* has a moral dimension, as well as an aesthetic dimension. It was a way human beings could rise above their sufferings and achieve a sense of detachment, even in the face of natural disasters.

Bashō's life was full of loss and sorrow, but he turned to nature to transform, or "refine," that sorrow into *sabi*. For him, poetic practice was an exercise in self-abnegation, rather like what John Keats called 'negative capability'—that state of egoless, nonjudgmental open-mindedness that enables the poet to be receptive to the mystery and beauty of the natural world. As Keats wrote, "with a great poet the sense of Beauty overcomes every other consideration, or rather obliterates all consideration."[33] As Ueda points out, Bashō often used the word *sabishii* ('lonely'). But he conceived of loneliness "as an impersonal atmosphere, in contrast with grief or sorrow, which is a personal emotion. The contrast cannot be overemphasized, because loneliness thus conceived lay at the bottom of Bashō's view of life, pointing toward a way in which his plea 'return to nature' can be fulfilled."[34] Sorrow, in other words, belongs to the human world, whereas loneliness belongs to the world of nature. Thus, human beings "can escape from sorrow only when they transform it into an impersonal atmosphere, loneliness."[35] This transformation is brought about by a deep communion with nature, as in the following haiku of Bashō:

uki ware wo sabishi garese yo kankodori
make my sad self
more deeply lonely,
oh cuckoo![36]

The poet, writes Ueda,

> as he set out to compose the poem, was still in the world of humanity, with a personal feeling like sorrow. The cuckoo, on the other hand, seemed to have already transcended sorrow, as it was closer to the heart of nature. Thereupon the poet wished that the bird's cry might enlighten his soul and eventually lead him into the realm of impersonal loneliness, where he would no longer feel sorrow … . Such a dissolution of personal emotion into an impersonal atmosphere constitutes the core of Bash 's attitude toward life.[37]

Significantly, at the very end of his life, Bashō chose to wander in the realm of a wild, primeval nature, far from the refined, artificial "secondary" nature of the Heian court aristocrats. His last poem, written just four days before his death, is one of his darkest:

> *tabi ni yande yume wa kareno o kakemeguru*
> falling sick mid-journey—
> my dreams go roaming
> over withered fields.[38]

The imagery here is as desolate and disturbing as in any more explicit "disaster poem"—although there is also a suggestion of transcendence in the dying old poet's "dreams." To the modern ear, Bashō's withered fields (*kareno*) inevitably carries echoes of T. S. Eliot's wasteland (*karechi*), an arch-modernist symbol (indeed, a major school of postwar Japanese poets, traumatized by their recent experience of the "disasters of war," called themselves the 'Wasteland School'). Like many great poems, this haiku functions on both a microcosmic and a macrocosmic level: Bashō's own personal disaster, his death as a lonely old traveler on a withered moor, is, at the same time, the disastrous fate of the whole of humanity. What could be a more poignant image of the "aloneness" of human beings existing in a vast world of impersonal, indifferent nature? Or, as so much better expressed by Bashō himself in an earlier poem:

> *sabishisa ya iwa ni shimikomu semi no koe*
> such loneliness—
> the cicadas' cries
> pierce through the rocks.[39]

Although these haiku are characterized by a highly refined aesthetic restraint, and indeed are worthy in this respect of the best traditions of classical court poetry, the view of nature they represent is by no means sentimental, romantic, or reductive. Their brevity does not impose a narrow focus on any courtly "secondary nature." On the contrary, we feel the full force of a "primary" or primal nature here: beautiful but also ruthlessly transient and impersonal. In this raw natural world, the death of the old poet in a bleak landscape amounts to nothing more than a cicada's cry.

Reading Bashō in the wake of 3/11, we see clearly that he, rather than the court poets, may be claimed as the true ancestor of present-day "postdisaster" poets such as Seki Etsushi. Like Bashō, Seki fearlessly confronts nature "in the raw," but, like Bashō too, he presents his vision in that most aesthetically restrained and minimalist of poetic genres, the haiku. Both poets prove that haiku of the highest quality can achieve that perfect union that, in John Keats's words, "dost tease us out of thought / As doth eternity" and that Keats found embodied in a Grecian urn: a perfect union between truth and beauty, ethics and aesthetics.[40]

NOTES

1. Roman Rosenbaum, "Post-3/11 Literature in Japan," in *When the Tsunami Came to Shore: Culture and Disaster in Japan*, ed. Roy Starrs (Leiden: Brill, 2014), 106.

2. Jeffrey Matthew Angles, "These Things Here and Now: Poetry in the Wake of 3/11," in *When the Tsunami Came to Shore*, ed. Roy Starrs, 114.

3. Ibid.

4. Ibid., 119.

5. For a more in-depth discussion of the ethics and aesthetics of Hemingway's style and its relation to Japanese aesthetics, see Roy Starrs, *An Artless Art—The Zen Aesthetic of Shiga Naoya: A Critical Study with Selected Translations* (London: Routledge, 1998), 75–83.

6. Angles, "These Things Here and Now," 136.

7. W. B. Yeats, preface to *The Oxford Book of Modern Verse: 1892–1935*, ed. W. B. Yeats (Oxford: Oxford University Press, 1936), xv.

8. Leith Morton, "The Great Tokyo Earthquake of 1923 and Poetry," in *When the Tsunami Came to Shore*, ed. Roy Starrs, 282.

9. Ibid.

10. Translated by Jeffrey Matthew Angles, in *When the Tsunami Came to Shore*, ed. Roy Starrs, 127.

11. Janice Brown, "The 'Silenced Nexus': Female Mediation in Modern Japanese Literature of Disaster," in *When the Tsunami Came to Shore*, ed. Roy Starrs, 318–44.

12. Richard Bowring, review of *Japan and the Culture of the Four Seasons: Nature, Literature, and the Arts*, by Haruo Shirane, *Journal of Japanese Studies* 39, no. 2 (2013): 427–30.

13. Quoted in *Sources of Japanese Tradition*, ed. Wm. Theodore de Bary, Donald Keene, George Tanabe, and Paul Varley, 2nd ed., vol. 1, *From Earliest Times to 1600* (New York: Columbia University Press, 2001), 51.

14. Haruo Shirane, *Japan and the Culture of the Four Seasons: Nature, Literature, and the Arts* (New York: Columbia University Press, 2012), 8.

15. Ibid.

16. Ibid.

17. Ibid., 8–9.

18. Ibid., 12.

19. Ibid., 11.

20. Ibid., 14.

21. As paraphrased by Jeffrey Matthew Angles, in *When the Tsunami Came to Shore*, ed. Roy Starrs, 126.

22. Quoted by Jeffrey Matthew Angles, in *When the Tsunami Came to Shore*, ed. Roy Starrs, 126–27.

23. For an index of the classical poetic lexicon, see Shirane, 271–87.

24. Translated by Donald Keene, in *Anthology of Japanese Literature: From the Earliest Era to the Mid-Nineteenth Century*, ed. Donald Keene (New York: Grove Press, 1955), 197.

25. Dōgen Kigen, "Guidelines for Studying the Way," trans. Ed Brown and Kazuaki Tanahashi, in *Moon in a Dewdrop: Writings of Zen Master Dōgen*, ed. Kazuaki Tanahashi (San Francisco: North Point Press, 1985), 31–43.

26. My translation.

27. Tadao Andō, "What Is *Wabi-Sabi*?," accessed July 27, 2015, http://nobleharbor.com/tea/chado/WhatIsWabi-Sabi.htm.

28. Makoto Ueda, *Matsuo Bashō: The Master Haiku Poet* (New York: Twayne Publishers, 1970), 50–51.

29. My translation.

30. Ueda, *Matsuo Bashō*, 156.

31. Ibid.

32. Ibid., 66.

33. John Keats, *The Complete Poetical Works and Letters of John Keats* (Boston: Houghton, Mifflin, and Company, 1899), 277.

34. Makoto Ueda, *Literary and Art Theories in Japan* (Cleveland, OH: Western Reserve University Press, 1967), 150.

35. Ibid.

36. My translation.

37. Ueda, *Literary and Art Theories in Japan*, 151.

38. My translation.

39. My translation.

40. John Keats, "Ode on a Grecian Urn," accessed July 27, 2015, http://www.bartleby.com/101/625.html.

Part V

JAPANESE AESTHETICS AND THE VISUAL ARTS

Chapter 21

Inner Beauty

Kishida Ryūsei's Concept of Realism and Premodern Asian Aesthetics

Mikiko Hirayama

Art theory and criticism developed slowly in Japan.[1] Since the fourteenth century, Japanese painters eagerly learned from Chinese painting treatises but did not then formulate their own theories of art.[2] But after the seventeenth century, artists affiliated with various schools of painting documented their own schools' philosophies, creating the heyday of painting treatises in Japan. While these painters often sought to legitimize their own style, they still tended to repeat or adopt the key concepts in classic Chinese texts. Professional art critics emerged in the late nineteenth century, but artists continued to be in demand as commentators on art.[3] Oil painter Kishida Ryūsei (1891–1929), best known today for his meticulously detailed still lifes and portraits, was one such artist (Figures 21.1–21.2). Throughout his relatively brief nineteen-year career, he published numerous essays in which he explicated his own interpretations of realism.[4]

Kishida's view of realism (*shajitsu*) owed much to the traditional concepts of realism in East Asian art, which emphasized not only the external appearance of the object but also its intangible essence. Contrary to what one might assume from his paintings, his ultimate aspiration was to go beyond the precise recreation of visual reality and to convey what he called 'Inner Beauty (*uchinaru bi*),' by combining realism with idealization and abstraction. His adaptation of traditional East Asian aesthetics reveals this important aspect of his art.

The concepts of *shasei* (Chinese: *xiesheng*, capturing life) and *shai* (Chinese: *xieyi*, capturing the ambiance or meaning) played a crucial role in Kishida's theory of realism.[5] These ideas address the complex dynamism between formal likeness and spirituality in both premodern Chinese and Japanese painting treatises. *Shai* usually signified an attempt to portray the

Figure 21.1   Kishida Ryūsei, *Three Red Apples, Teacup, Tin Can, and Spoon.* 1920.
Oil on canvas, 36.5 cm x 44.0 cm. Ōhara Museum of Art, Kurashiki, Japan. Photograph
courtesy of Ōhara Museum of Art.

intangible essence of an object rather than, or sometimes at the expense of, its
exact physical likeness. *Shasei*, on the other hand, frequently meant a close
study of the object that aimed to portray its formal likeness.[6] This likeness
was not the ultimate goal, however; it was expected to assist the painter in
accomplishing *shai*, or expressing the intangible essence of the object. Thus,
shasei in premodern East Asian art was a rather broad concept that embraced
both direct observation of an object and interest in its spiritual energy. This
relationship between *shasei* and *shai* will be addressed in more detail later.

   Kishida's usage of *shasei* and *shai* did not exactly conform to the traditional interpretation, but these concepts nevertheless helped him formulate
his own idea of realism. Furthermore, to discuss his own realism, he consistently chose the third term *shajitsu*, which by the early twentieth century had
become the standard translation for 'realism' both in the generic sense and
in the historical realism of nineteenth-century European art.[7] This implies
his sympathy with Western empirical naturalism. Kishida, however, often
described the ultimate goal of his art as the representation of "beauty beyond
shape and color"[8] and even recognized that such beauty had been addressed
in Sino-Japanese art theory as *shai*.[9] Thus, his idea of realism invoked the
traditional view of pictorial art in Japan and China, in which the expression
of spirituality was predicated on a certain degree of naturalism.

Figure 21.2 Kishida Ryūsei, *Landscape of Toranomon.* 1912. Oil on canvas, 23.0 cm x 32.0 cm. Seiji Tōgō Memorial Sompo Japan Nipponkoa Museum of Art, Tokyo. Photograph courtesy of Seiji Tōgō Memorial Sompo Japan Nipponkoa Museum of Art.

My investigation of Kishida Ryūsei's theories on realism will proceed in the following order. First, I will offer a brief overview of the dynamics of formal likeness and spirituality in premodern East Asian painting treatises that inspired his concept of realism. Second, I will summarize his explications of Inner Beauty and the Spiritual Realm, the pivotal concepts of his treatises. Third, I will discuss his "lack of realism" theory in his 1922 article "Shajitsu no ketsujo no kōsatsu" ("On the Lack of Realism"). Finally, my examination of his milestone essay from 1924 "Tōzai no bijutsu o ronjite Sōgen no shaseiga ni oyobu" ("A Discussion of Paintings in the East and West with Reference to the *Shasei* of the Song and Yuan Dynasties") will show that he recognized his artistic ideals in the paintings of the Northern (960–1127) and Southern (1127–1279) Song as well as Yuan (1279–1368) Dynasties of China.

BIOGRAPHY

During the nineteen years of his career, Kishida's painting went through three distinct stylistic changes: the Post-Impressionist phase, the Northern

Renaissance phase, and the Song-Yuan phase. When he debuted as a painter in 1910, he was heavily influenced by Post-Impressionists, especially Van Gogh and Cézanne, who enjoyed massive popularity in Japan at the time (Figure 21.2). These were some of the artists idolized by his close friends affiliated with the Shirakaba School, a group of aristocratic young writers who challenged the traditional Confucian ethics and endorsed individualism.[10] By 1913, however, he was beginning to outgrow this style and, in the manner of Northern Renaissance masters such as Albrecht Dürer and Jan van Eyck, to produce highly naturalistic paintings that meticulously depicted the texture of an object. Although this dramatic change in style seemed to contradict contemporary artistic trends, Kishida later claimed that his interest in the modernism and individualism of contemporary Western art kindled his quest for realism.

> The more I attempted to simplify, the more strongly I felt a desire for a fidelity to the realities of nature ... . I have been taught by them [Van Gogh and Cézanne] to see nature according to my own inner demands. ... By learning to feel within me the desire for an eternal beauty, I have come to realize that Post-Impressionists, too, were attempting to reveal that same verity.[11]

In the early 1920s, Kishida went through yet another significant stylistic change. This time, his sources of inspiration were bird and flower paintings from the Song and Yuan Dynasties in China, an example of which he had seen for the first time at a friend's house in 1919. His fascination with Chinese painting intensified to such an extent that he concentrated his efforts on Chinese- and Japanese-style paintings (Figure 21.3) instead of oils during 1925 and 1926. Formulated during this transitional phase, his theories about realism from the mid-1920s until his death in 1929 reflect his grappling with premodern East Asian artistic heritage.

"REALISM" IN PREMODERN CHINESE AND JAPANESE ART THEORY

The concept of "realism" in Japanese art largely derived from Chinese painting theories and left a lasting impact on the modern era, even after the influx of Western artistic principles. In the Sino-Japanese artistic tradition, the expression of the spirit, not the recreation of optical reality, was often considered the ultimate goal. Although technical mastery was highly regarded, excessive physical likeness was often scorned as an impediment to the expression of spirituality.

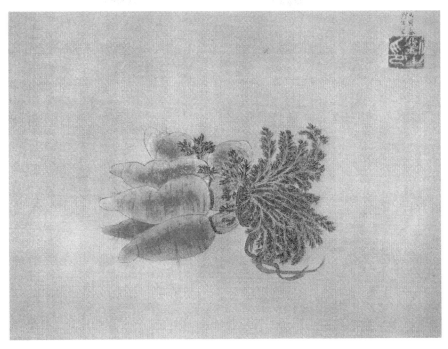

Figure 21.3   Kishida Ryūsei, *Carrots.* 1926. Ink and color on silk, 25.3 cm x 31.3 cm. National Museum of Modern Art, Tokyo. Photograph courtesy of National Museum of Modern Art, Tokyo.

The complex dynamism between the quest for visual accuracy and the urge to express the intangible spirit was one of the consistent themes of Chinese art theory. The earliest known painting treatise in China by Gu Kaizhi (ca. 344–406) addressed this issue. Gu believed the primary goal of formal accuracy was the transmission of the "spiritual essence (*shenqi*)" of the subject matter:[12] "In painting, human figures are the most difficult, then landscapes, then dogs and horses. Towers and pavilions are ... difficult to complete but easy to render well, and not dependent on a marvelous realization of the conveying of thought."[13] This passage implies that Gu was intent upon expressing the intangible spirit in the subject of his painting. At the same time, he also recognized significance in expressing the individual painter's spirit.[14] This view continued to be valued in traditional Chinese painting theories.[15]

The Six Laws of Painting (*liufa*), principles established by Xie He (active ca. 500–535?), also recognized that the expression of the spirit constituted the essence of painting.[16] The Six Laws are as follows: (1) spirit resonance, (2) structural method in the use of the brush, (3) fidelity to the object in portraying forms, (4) conformity to kind in applying colors, (5) proper planning in placing of elements, and (6) transmission of ancient masters by copying. The first law defines the expression of spirituality as the primary goal of pictorial art.[17] It subsequently became the single most important criterion for evaluating paintings in China. The other five laws address the technical skills necessary for the expression of spirit resonance.[18] Emphasis on accuracy and copying in the third, fourth, and sixth laws indicates that spirit resonance and formal likeness were not considered antithetical to each other; rather, the latter was believed to be crucial to the expression of the former.[19]

A significant change in art theory occurred during the Yuan Dynasty (1279–1368), when the expression of the artist's character became widely accepted as the most important criterion in evaluating paintings.[20] The scholar-gentlemen (*wenren*), or bureaucrats who left their positions to protest the takeover of the state by the Mongols, were responsible for this new approach. Their creative output, known as 'literati painting (*wenrenhua*),' became an independent category of art during the Yuan Dynasty. They intentionally adopted a naïve style to symbolize their resistance to the Mongols who favored the realistic style of professional academy painters. To them, spirit resonance meant reflections of a man's character and social condition and therefore stood as the determining factor for the quality of their painting.[21] They also considered the brushwork, not the subject matter, as the vehicle for the expression of the character.[22] These ideals were predicated on the painter's spiritual identification with his subject matter.[23]

When Wen Dong painted bamboo,
He saw bamboo and not himself.
Not simply unconscious of himself,
Trance-like, he left his body behind.
His body was transferred into bamboo,
Creating inexhaustible freshness.
Chuang Tzu is no longer in this world,
So who can understand such concentration?[24]

Through an extraordinary insight into the subject matter, the literati painter was expected to capture its essence and express it in his art, letting his own spirit emerge from his art. The continuing prominence of literati painting eventually altered the meanings of *shasei* and *shai* in painting treatises as well. Numerous texts of the Ming (1368–1644) and Qing (1644–1911) Dynasties addressed *shai* as the expression of the individual painter's character. *Shasei*, on the other hand, came to signify naturalistic representation based on direct observation of the object.[25] While the intricate relationship between spirit resonance and formal likeness thus remained one of the central topics in Chinese painting theories, it was ultimately the expression of the intangible spirit—whether that of the artist or of the subject matter—that determined the artistic quality of Chinese painting.

Japanese art treatises from the seventeenth century onwards often addressed the relationship between *shasei* and *shai*. Regardless of their stylistic affiliations, artists who wrote these texts tended to criticize excessive concern with formal likeness, which they felt diluted the expression of spirit resonance. As the head of the Kanō School, the official school of painters serving the feudal government, Kanō Yasunobu (1613–1685) expressed his disapproval of those painters who failed to portray the essence of an object: "Although these pictures portray the mind, they do not capture the spirit. They are therefore naturally devoid of force and look like burnt-out ashes."[26]

However, nobody elaborated on *shasei* and *shai* more than the Japanese literati painters of the late eighteenth and early nineteenth centuries. *Chikutō garon* (*Painting Theory by Chikutō*, 1802) by Nakabayashi Chikutō (1778–1853) is one example. Chikutō announced his support of *shasei*, or direct observation of nature, as follows: "Those who study painting must work on *shasei* by all means. There is no better way to study the vital force of things than study from Nature."[27] Nonetheless, he was also a harsh critic of *shōutsushi*, or the exact copying of optic reality through life drawing.[28] He argued that *shōutsushi* was very different from the *shasei* by classic Chinese master painters. In his view, contemporary painters practicing *shōutsushi* did not "portray the vitality and ambiance [of the subject matter]."[29] Thus, Japanese literati painters did not necessarily demand exact formal likeness, even though their views of *shasei* were predicated on some form of direct observation of nature. They gravitated toward the expression of intangible spiritual energy, which they learned from Chinese literati's painting theories. This caution against exact likeness resurfaced in Kishida Ryūsei's painting theory.

On the other hand, in the late eighteenth century, a number of Japanese painters began to pursue naturalistic representation and to question the supremacy of *shai*. The most prominent champion of this approach was Shiba Kōkan (1747–1818), who taught himself the principles of linear perspective and chiaroscuro.[30] A tireless advocate of Western-style painting, Kōkan wrote that the virtue of pictorial art lay in its ability to present a visually accurate image, not *shai*: "To paint reality is to paint all objects ... exactly as they appear."[31] Criticizing the traditional East Asian aesthetics, which valued expressive brushstrokes over formal likeness, he commented as follows: "The brush was originally nothing more than a tool for making paintings. Nevertheless, [now in Japanese and Chinese painting] only the feeling of the brushstroke is expressed."[32] In his view, Western painting methods were better suited than East Asian painting styles for creating "a spirit of reality":

"The technique employed in [Western art] produces a true representation of reality, greatly different from the style that is used in Japan."[33] His explicit elevation of *shasei* over *shai* heralded a fundamental change in nineteenth-century visuality.

Kōkan's primary successor in the modern period was the oil painter Takahashi Yuichi (1828–1894), whose view of realism represented a transitional stage in the history of Japanese art theory. Takahashi tirelessly lobbied for the superiority of oil painting, emphasizing its capacity for naturalistic representation. Much of his argument in fact derived from Kōkan's elevation of formal likeness over spirit resonance; however, he also recognized the significance of *shai*, which Kōkan had denied.

Direct observation was the key feature in Takahashi's view of *shasei*. *Shasei* strictly meant life drawing to him, as indicated by the following passage in which he posited it as the antithesis of Chinese-style spontaneous brushwork:

> I visited Yi Xian one day and discussed the strength of *shasei* at length. We talked about how Westerners these days tended to gravitate toward the Chinese-style fluid, spontaneous brushwork, whereas the Chinese were inclined to Western-style naturalistic *shasei*.[34]

But unlike Kōkan, Takahashi did not demonize *shai* nor completely separate it from *shasei*. He even recognized *shai* in masterpieces of Western art, as indicated by the following passage from an 1880 document: "Painting that is precise in brushwork but poor in *shai* is vulgar, whereas a painting that resonates with *shai* is graceful even if its brushwork is rough. The divine masterpieces in Western art are all like that."[35] Takahashi's ideas thus revived the traditional East Asian aesthetic concepts of *shasei* and *shai*, which were familiar to the educated lay audience at the time. Arguing that formal likeness alone would not make a masterpiece, he insisted that Western-style painting was capable of both formal likeness and spirituality and therefore superior to traditional Japanese painting.

KISHIDA RYŪSEI'S THEORY OF REALISM

Although Kishida Ryūsei never presented his theories on realism in a systematic fashion, the core concepts of his theory are present in the articles he published between 1918 and 1924, when his painting went through a transition from the Northern Renaissance phase to the Song-Yuan phase. The following analyses of important keywords, such as 'Inner Beauty,' 'Spiritual Realm,' and the 'lack of realism' theory, will reveal that his theory of realism explicitly appropriated the artistic ideal of *shai* even though he was a direct successor to the empirical approach endorsed by Shiba Kōkan and Takahashi Yuichi.

INNER BEAUTY AS THE BASIS OF ART

The concept of Inner Beauty was the pivotal point in all of Kishida Ryūsei's writings on art. He defined it as 'color without a hue, line without a shape.'[36] In his view, nature by itself was neither beautiful nor ugly unless the human mind recognized beauty or ugliness in it. "Natural beauty" is born when one's Inner Beauty, an "instinct and urge immanent in humans" to "make the world a happy, pleasant place," discovers a potential for beauty in nature.[37] A work of art, on the other hand, embodies a refined, condensed form of natural beauty.[38] The artist converts "natural form and [his] emotions" "into visually pleasant colors and lines" in his work.[39] The finished art object, therefore, reflects the Inner Beauty of the artist.

Kishida also believed that a work of art would truly represent Inner Beauty only when it reached the "Spiritual Realm (*yuishinteki ryōiki*)," a concept inspired by the idea of *shai*. According to Kishida, the Spiritual Realm was "the most profound domain of the visual arts."[40] Here, the object represented in a work of art would serve as a conduit for Inner Beauty, which would touch the viewer beyond the material realm.

> The essence of the visual arts ... transcends form. ... This is the Spiritual Realm, which deeply touches the viewer without relying on the visible ... it is the most profound beauty that is ever expressed in art.[41]

Works of art that have reached this realm would evoke "infinity, mystery, [and] solemnity" in the viewer.[42] In other words, he expected the viewer to perceive something other than sheer visual pleasure and representational content.

Although Kishida's aspirations for "beauty without shape" through his art may seem paradoxical, it was a perfectly valid idea in the East Asian artistic tradition. In fact, the concept of the Spiritual Realm overlapped that of *shai* in Kishida's mind: "I think that the concept of *shai*, which has been tradition-ally considered the opposite of *shasei*, in fact signifies this Spiritual Realm of beauty."[43] In a later essay, he added that his ultimate goal was "to practice *shai* in its absolute profundity ... to reach the Spiritual Realm and to pursue the deepest ... solemnity and mysticity."[44] He was indebted to traditional Chinese aesthetics, especially the empathetic relationship between the artist and his subject matter that the literati painters liked to emphasize.

[When working in the Spiritual Realm,] the artist's brush does not seek the shape of the subject matter itself. It seeks only the shape that is the most appropriate for the manifestation of the Spiritual Realm... . His mind ... pursues only the profound feelings that hover above the shape... . [Then he] projects his "heart" onto his brush.[45]

Thus, Kishida Ryūsei's statements on Inner Beauty and the Spiritual Realm reveal that his realism was by no means confined to superficial physical likeness. He strove to express something that was not readily perceivable to the eye, and traditional Chinese aesthetics played a crucial role in this endeavor.

THREE WAYS IN WHICH INNER BEAUTY WAS EXPRESSED IN ART

In his essays from 1920, Kishida discussed three ways in which he believed Inner Beauty could be manifested in works of art. They were Beauty of Decoration (*sōshoku no bi*), Beauty of Realism (*shajitsu no bi*), and Beauty of Imagination (*sōzō no bi*). His sophisticated appropriation of *shasei* and *shai* is evident in the way he conceptualized these three types of beauty. Beauty of Decoration "does not represent any natural objects" and is therefore a direct translation of the artist's Inner Beauty into abstract form.[46] Beauty of Realism emerges when the artist recognizes beauty in nature that corresponds to his own sense of Inner Beauty and represents it in concrete form.[47] Beauty of Imagination is created by projecting intangible ideas and emotions onto visible objects in nature. Rather than faithfully representing natural forms, the artist relies on his memory and imagination to give expression to his sense of Inner Beauty.[48]

The Beauty of Realism, which to him was essentially the pursuit of textural beauty, represented "the most profound, most complex way of creating beauty" and hence the focal point of art-making for Kishida.[49] "Visual sensations such as color and blemishes" conveyed in a painting become "merged with the sense of touch" and arouse "mysterious, serene feelings" in the viewer. The artist could "recreate the mysterious aura of the object" and reach the realm of beauty beyond the physical shape only by pursuing this Beauty of Realism.

In realism at its purest, the more closely the work of art is based on the real color, shape, and line of the object, the more clearly it embodies beauty beyond shape and color. When the art object exudes [such] beauty, it has transcended the world of tangible reality.[50]

On the other hand, it was through decoration that an art object transcended to "the realm beyond form" and reached the ultimate goal of the visual arts:

the representation of Inner Beauty.[51] Kishida's ideas, especially his attempt to transcend physical likeness to capture the intangible essence of an object, are strikingly reminiscent of the close intertwining of *shasei* and *shai* often seen in premodern Chinese and Japanese art.

Kishida strove to combine realism, decoration, and imagination in his own art, claiming that although his style was primarily based on realism, he still wanted to create a painting in which all three components were "seamlessly merged together": "I do not mind if people called me a 'mystic' who originally started from realism. At the same time, I do not wish to see things from a realist standpoint only. I want to use my imagination and let it enhance the beauty of realism."[52] While any given work of art could combine three types of beauty in different proportions, he found an ideal combination of the three in the paintings by Emperor Huizong (1082–1135) of the Northern Song Dynasty (Figure 21.4). Judging from their composition, form, and style, he asserted that some of Huizong's works were the result of life sketches (*shasei*); however, he was also convinced that the artist probably altered his

Figure 21.4 Emperor Huizong, *Five-Colored Parakeet on a Blossoming Apricot Tree.* Northern Song Dynasty (960–1127), datable to 1110s. Ink and color on silk, 53.3 cm x 125.1 cm. Museum of Fine Arts, Boston. Available from: Museum of Fine Arts, Boston, http://www.mfa.org/collections/object/five-colored-parakeet-on-a-blossoming-apricot-tree-29081 (accessed July 6, 2015).

preparatory drawings to extract the profound beauty of the subject matter.[53] The Northern Song artist's work still "truly exemplif[ied] the way of realism," he asserted, because his motifs "derived from the beauty of nature" and embodied the artist's pursuit of "the most profound realm of beauty."[54]

THE "LACK OF REALISM" THEORY (1922)

Kishida further elaborated on the delicate balance between Inner Beauty and formal likeness in a 1922 essay entitled 'Shajitsu no ketsujo no kōsatsu' ('A Study of a Lack of Realism'). He continued to advocate realism as the basic principle of his painting theory but also contended that the artist needed to *restrain naturalistic representation* in order to express Inner Beauty. This is where *a lack of realism* came into play. He defined it as 'aesthetic denial of reality' and 'the denunciation of the pursuit of concrete beauty.'[55] Present in any work of art that "convey[ed] a sense of mysticity," a lack of realism could be the result of either a totally unconscious coincidence or a deliberately controlled effect.[56] Work by a technically deficient artist might look interesting, but it could not quite convey "beauty."[57] Alternately, the artist might intentionally pursue a lack of realism in search of more profound beauty. Such a lack of realism inevitably reveals the deepest core of the artist's character and therefore strikes the viewer with a profound afterglow of Inner Beauty.[58]

The "lack of realism" theory proves beyond doubt that Kishida appropriated traditional East Asian aesthetics. He rationalized his thought by addressing the dialectic between *shasei* and *shai*.

> It may be interesting if one could pursue realism to the fullest and still produce a masterpiece imbued with spirit resonance. But ... the relativist law of nature would not allow us to make the most of such resonance ... without sacrificing realism at all.[59]

Although he did not use the exact words, his comment on the dynamics between "realism" and "spirit resonance" is clearly a reference to the dichotomy of *shasei* and *shai*. He further explained that as realism diminished, "it would naturally give rise to stylization, such as simplification, emphasis, and quaintness, which would accentuate decorativeness and mystery."[60] Moreover, he embraced the avoidance of formal likeness prevalent in East Asian aesthetics.

> [It would be] dangerous to indulge in the satisfaction deriving from lifelike representation of the object ... . [Artists should not] stop pursuing a more profound level of artistic expression for fear of sacrificing the external likeness.[61]

It is unquestionable that the idea of realism in Chinese painting, which Kishida greatly admired, inspired these comments.

KISHIDA'S VIEW OF REALISM IN THE PAINTINGS FROM THE SONG AND YUAN DYNASTIES

Kishida Ryūsei's milestone essay, "A Discussion of Realist Paintings in the East and West with Reference to Paintings of the Song and Yuan Dynasties" (1924), shows that he recognized many of his artistic ideals in the paintings of the Song (907–1279) and Yuan (1279–1368) Dynasties.[62] He found the beauty in them to be entirely different from that in European art. They may seem "mundane and effortlessly done"[63] at the first glance because the painters prioritized the expression of infinity, quietude, and strength over sheer visual beauty,[64] but, in fact, they embodied a kind of beauty that "be[came] more and more resonant as one look[ed] at it time and time again."[65]

Kishida claimed that "pure realism was perfected over one thousand years ago in China" by none other than the Song and Yuan painters.[66] Although Western art was "infinitely more advanced than Eastern art in the portrayal of lifelikeness (*nyojitsukan*),"[67] Eastern art, particularly the paintings of the Song and Yuan Dynasties, had a "more profound realism" than Western art.[68] While these tableaux might lack visual accuracy, this was not due to technical deficiency but to conscious rejection of the "realistic rendition of color, shading, and dimensionality" in pursuit of a more profound realism.[69] These paintings embodied a superb example of "a lack of realism," an essential component to Inner Beauty. Although Kishida never clearly explained what he meant by 'pure realism' or 'profound realism,' one can safely infer from his descriptions that he regarded the aesthetic principles from the Song and Yuan Dynasties, which tended to favor spirituality over formal likeness, as the model for his own ideals of Inner Beauty and the Spiritual Realm.

Kishida also discussed how Chinese painting thrived while using a completely different set of techniques than Western art. Chinese painters considered the depiction of form through shading to often produce pedestrian work and obscure "the beauty of texture."[70] Instead of chiaroscuro, therefore, they often used flat-tone shading (*kuma*). This, he asserted, was because they knew from experience that "flat-tone coloring accentuated by delicate contour lines" had "austere beauty" and could "evoke profundity and mysteriousness much better than chiaroscuro."[71] Even this technique, however, was to be applied only in moderation. If the painting became too realistic, it would be considered vulgar in Chinese art.[72] What may seem like a deficiency or anomaly in Chinese art by the Western standards of beauty was in fact a conscious choice—in other words, a deliberate "lack of realism": "The old masters in China … preferred the profundity that is conveyed by flat-tone coloring and denied more realistic portrayal. They thus created the greatest, the most delicate synthesis of symbolism and realism."[73] For Kishida, the purposeful rejection of lifelikeness in Chinese art represented the best method of achieving his own artistic goal—"the synthesis of symbolism and realism."

Kishida's theories were by no means a mere pastiche of Chinese aesthetics. In fact, he challenged one of the most essential values in the world of Chinese art. He insisted that paintings based on *shasei* (*shaseiga*) were "artistically more meaningful" than the ambient, expressive monochromatic ink painting, which was usually considered the absolute canon of Chinese painting.[74] The high regard given to literati painting and monochromatic landscape painting in Sino-Japanese aesthetics, according to Kishida, was a creative misunderstanding of spirit resonance.[75] Like Shiba Kōkan and Takahashi Yuichi, he regarded Chinese-style ink painting as closer to calligraphy than to painting.

> [Monochromatic ink painting] pursues divine aura through the ambiance conveyed by ink and lines as well as the will of the brush (*hitsui*) … rather than strictly formal qualities. Some ink paintings do capture the shape of the object rather closely, but even then, the form is usually of secondary importance.[76]

He also argued that even the famed painting of gibbons by Southern Song Dynasty painter Mu Qi (thirteenth century) was focused on capturing the ambiance of majestic mountains rather than presenting a visually accurate image of the animals.[77] His admiration for paintings based on *shasei* and his downgrading of ink painting are consistent with his steadfast advocacy of paintings based on concrete reality as the "universal, orthodox route in the way of painting."

> When painting becomes detached from realism, its beauty tends to be simple and crude. Essentially, beauty is an idea that dwells in the human mind. Theoretically speaking, therefore, it could be represented simply by converting the idea into form and does not necessarily have to copy external objects. But we must not forget that our thoughts … acquire complexity through the stimulations of the external form.[78]

CONCLUSION

Kishida Ryūsei's idea of realism thus reflected the complex trajectory of modern Japanese art. He was an admirer of individualism embodied by Van Gogh and Cézanne, as were the authors of the popular Shirakaba School. His self-confessional prose fascinated aspiring young artists of the early twentieth century. He, however, eventually abandoned the expressive style, which dominated the contemporary art scene, in favor of a hyperreal style inspired by Northern Renaissance and classical Chinese art. As I have shown in this chapter, the traditional Chinese and Japanese aesthetic concepts provided the inspiration for Kishida's artistic goals. And yet, the driving force behind his seemingly anti-modern tendency was precisely a modernist interest. Unlike the pioneering oil painter, Takahashi Yuichi, he did not appropriate these traditional ideas in order to defend oil painting as a medium. His theory of realism chronicles his endeavor to enrich his own art by applying indigenous East Asian concepts to the Western-style medium. While evaluations of his success as an artist may vary from one art historian to another, it is evident to all that Kishida gave a new role to the ideas of *shasei* and *shai* in his treatises and, by extension, in modern Japanese art.

NOTES

1. I would like to thank A. Minh Nguyen, Judith Daniels, and Mary Hancock for their editorial assistance; Hong Kong University Press for permission to use a published translation of a poem by Su Shih; and Museum of Fine Arts (Boston), National Museum of Modern Art (Tokyo), Ōhara Museum of Art (Kurashiki, Japan), and Seiji Tōgō Memorial Sompo Japan Nipponkoa Museum of Art (Tokyo) for permission to reproduce the images in this chapter.
2. Japanese culture developed its own aesthetic sensibilities independent from China, but very little of that was converted to text until the seventeenth century.
3. See Mikiko Hirayama, "Japanese Art Criticism: The First Fifty Years," in *Since Meiji: Perspectives on the Japanese Visual Arts, 1868–2000*, ed. J. Thomas Rimer (Honolulu: University of Hawai'i Press, 2011), 257–80.
4. His essays have been published in a 10-volume collection, which is quite unusual for Japanese artists. See *Kishida Ryūsei zenshū*, 10 vols. (Tokyo: Iwanami Shoten, 1979–1980).
5. For the changes in the meanings of *shasei* and *shai* in Chinese art theory, see Shimada Shūjirō et al., "Nihon no kachōga no seiritsu to tenkai," in *Kachōga no sekai*, vol. 6, *Kyōha no ishō* (Tokyo: Gakushū Kenkyūsha, 1983), 117.
6. Ibid.
7. *Shajitsu* by itself usually denoted generic realism, whereas *shajitsushugi* (*shugi* means "ism") became established as the translation of realism by the early twentieth century.
8. Kishida Ryūsei, "Bika," in *Bi no hontai* (Tokyo: Kōdansha, 1985), 45–46. Henceforth cited as *BNH*.
9. Kishida Ryūsei, "Shajitsuron," in *BNH*, 93, emphasis mine.
10. The Shirakaba School published its own journal *Shirakaba* (*White Birch*), which was instrumental in introducing Post-Impressionism to Japan.
11. Shūji Takashina, J. Thomas Rimer, and Gerald D. Bolas, eds., *Paris in Japan: The Japanese Encounter with European Painting* (Tokyo and St. Louis, MO: Japan Foundation and Washington University in St. Louis, 1987), 278.

12. Nakamura Shigeo, *Chūgokugaron no tenkai* (Kyoto: Nakayama Bunkadō, 1965), 31.

13. Gu Kaizhi, "Essay on Painting (*Lunhua*)," quoted in Susan Bush and Hsio-Yen Shih, eds., *Early Chinese Texts on Painting* (Cambridge, MA: Harvard University Press, 1985), 24.

14. Nakamura, 33.

15. Such ideas derived from the Daoist belief that painting had the ability to bring out the spirit residing in the object through lifelike portrayal. Ibid., 31.

16. The Six Laws became widely known in China when Zhang Yanyuan (ninth century) reprinted them in *Records of Historical Painting*. Because Xie never clearly defined the Six Laws, they were subsequently reinterpreted numerous times. See Bush and Shih, 14.

17. Xie's view of spirit resonance is generally interpreted as reference to the spirit residing in the subject matter of a painting and in the finished painting rather than the artist's spirit. Ibid., 11.

18. Nakamura, 188.

19. Kawakami Kei, "Kodaikaiga no taisei," in *Tōyō bijutsu zenshi*, ed. Matsubara Saburō (Tokyo: Tokyo Bijutsu, 1981), 301.

20. Susan Bush, *The Chinese Literati on Painting: Su Shih (1037–1101) and Tung Ch'i-ch'ang (1555–1636)* (Cambridge, MA: Harvard University Press, 1971), 13.

21. Bush and Shih, 91. This idea was presented in *An Account of My Experiences in Painting (Duhua Jianwenzhi*, late eleventh century) by the painter Guo Joxu (active last half of the eleventh century).

22. Bush, 2.

23. Bush and Shih, 207.

24. The poem was written by Su Shi (1037–1101) on his contemporary Wen Dong (1018–1080). Ibid., 212. The text was published in *Early Chinese Texts on Painting*, ed. Susan Bush and Hsio-Yen Shih, 212. Copyrights © 2012 by Hong Kong University Press. Reprinted by permission of Hong Kong University Press.

25. Shimada et al., 117.

26. Kanō Yasunobu, "Gadō yōketsu," in *Nihon garon taisei*, vol. 4, ed. Toshinobu Yasumura (Tokyo: Perikansha, 1997), 17–18.

27. Nakabayashi Chikutō, "Chikutō garon," in *Nihon garon taikan*, ed. Sakazaki Shizuka (Tokyo: Arusu, 1927), 28.

28. Kōno Motoaki, "Edo jidai 'shasei' kō," in *Nihon kaigashi no kenkyū*, ed. Yamane Yūzō sensei koki kinenkai (Tokyo: Yoshikawa Kōbunkan, 1988), 401–03.

29. Nakabayashi, 28.

30. Kōkan's sources were imported paintings and prints, including *vedute* images brought from the Netherlands and paintings by Chinese *emigré* artist Shen Nanpin (active ca. 1720–1760).

31. Shiba Kōkan, "Discussions of Western Painting," in *Shiba Kōkan: Artist, Innovator, and Pioneer in the Westernization of Japan,* ed. Calvin L. French (New York: Weatherhill, 1974), 172.

32. Ibid., 176.

33. Ibid., 171.

34. Takahashi Yuichi, "Takahashi Yuichi rireki," in *Nihon kindai shisō taikei*, vol. 23, *Bijutsu*, ed. Aoki Shigeru and Sakai Tadayasu (Tokyo: Iwanami Shoten, 1989), 178. This excerpt is from Takahashi's memoir of a trip to Shanghai. The identity of Yi Xian is unknown.

35. Takahashi Yuichi, in *Takahashi Yuichi aburae shiryō*, ed. Aoki Shigeru (Tokyo: Chūō Kōron Bijutsu shuppan, 1984), 195.

36. Kishida Ryūsei, "Uchinaru bi," in *BNH*, 31.

37. Ibid., 29.

38. Ibid.

39. Kishida Ryūsei, "Bika: bijutsuhinteki yōso," in *BNH*, 40.

40. Kishida, "Shajitsuron,"92.

41. Kishida Ryūsei, "Bijutsuron," in *BNH*, 17.

42. Ibid., 17.

43. Kishida, "Shajitsuron," 93.

44. Ibid.

45. Ibid., 94–95.

46. Kishida Ryūsei, "Sōshokuron,"in *BNH*, 62.

47. Kishida, "Uchinaru bi," 33.

48. Ibid., 32.

49. Kishida Ryūsei, "Shajitsu no ketsujo no kōsatsu," in *BNH*, 151.

50. Kishida, "Bika," 45–46.

51. Kishida, "Shajitsuron," 84.

52. Kishida, "Uchinaru bi," 38.

53. Kishida Ryūsei, "Tōzai no bijutsu o ronjite Sōgen no shaseiga ni oyobu," in *Kishida Ryūsei zuihitsu shū*, ed. Sakai Tadayasu (Tokyo: Iwanami Shoten, 1996), 247.

54. Ibid., 248.

55. Kishida, "Shajitsu no ketsujo,"148.

56. Ibid., 147–48.

57. Ibid., 158.

58. Ibid.

59. Ibid., 153–54.

60. Ibid., 161.

61. Kishida, "Shajitsuron," 85.

62. The Song Dynasty consists of the Northern (960–1127) and Southern (1127–1279), but Kishida discussed paintings from both regimes without distinguishing between the two.

63. Kishida, "Tōzai," 228.

64. Ibid., 232.

65. Ibid.

66. Ibid., 248.

67. Ibid. He also added, "Eastern art never developed in this direction since life-likeness was considered vulgar" (ibid.).

68. Ibid., 224. It is important to note that Kishida used the word *nyojitsukan* to describe the naturalistic representation in Western art. *Nyojitsukan* implies precise recreation of both visual and tactile impressions of the object, much like what

Takahashi Yuichi strove to achieve in his work. This contrasting of *nyojitsukan* in Western painting with *shajitsu* in Chinese painting further demonstrates that Kishida's idea of realism in fact embraced what was customarily placed under the rubric of *shai* in Chinese and Japanese painting theories.

69. Ibid., 249.
70. Ibid., 252.
71. Ibid., 250–52.
72. Ibid., 249.
73. Ibid., 253.
74. Ibid., 241.
75. Ibid., 235.
76. Ibid., 241.
77. Ibid.
78. Ibid., 242.

Chapter 22

The Pan Real Art Association's Revolt against "the Beauties of Nature"

Matthew Larking

INTRODUCTION

In *Alois Riegl: Art History and Theory*, Margaret Iversen writes, "The intelligibility of a particular work of art requires some systematic framework in the same way that an utterance depends for its intelligibility on its being formulated in a public language."[1] One of the parts public languages played in the culturally broad field in which Japanese painting participated was that of the aesthetic and thematic corpus of *kachō fūgetsu*. This remains in the present, to varying degrees, a host of poetic and pictorial references deeply connected to the everyday. The concept of *everyday aesthetics* has gained considerable currency in recent years[2] in relation to a variety of Japanese artistic practices and the present chapter seeks to extend that discourse into relatively recent Japanese painting.

This chapter is concerned with the revolt against one public language of the everyday in modern Japanese painting (*nihonga*) in the middle of the twentieth century for further private, pictorial concerns that addressed very different perspectives on the range of meanings of the everyday. These predicated individualized aesthetics formed in the relationships between artist and society, a reaction to a perception of tradition, and the redeployment of tradition in the service of the contemporary at a moment of cultural upheaval following World War II. The first section briefly traces the development of *kachō fūgetsu* from its inauguration in Japanese poetry and painting inspired by Chinese precedents through to its marginally diminishing authority in the early twentieth century. The discussion here aims at setting forth the cultural territory that some early post–World War II Kyoto-based *nihonga* sought to supplant. The second section introduces the Pan Real Art Association (*Pan Riaru Bijutsu Kyōkai*) and their attitudes toward art in their early years along

319

with their artistic reaction to the aesthetics and themes of *kachō fūgetsu*. The third section addresses particular works of art in order to elaborate on Pan Real's pictorial engagements with postwar realities and the final section touches on the continuation of similar concerns in the present.

THE BEAUTIES OF NATURE

Kachō fūgetsu—literally, "flowers, birds, wind, and the moon" or, more generically, "the beauties of nature"—is a thematic corpus of usually nature-based subject matter which also includes the ceremonies and the rituals of everyday life carried out in accord with the changing seasons. The corpus of seasonal materials has been constituted differently across great spans of time though largely it has been accretive. In the tradition of East Asian painting, the genre is paramount to religious and landscape painting and these occasionally overlap.

The thematic corpus has its origins in China and it was through *waka* (classical poetry) in the Heian period (794–1185) and later poetry genres that the themes were transmitted to painting, resulting in its formative stages, as Haruo Shirane notes, "Heian-period four-season paintings, twelve-month paintings, and famous-place paintings—not to mention the scroll paintings (*emaki*) that depict Heian court tales."[3] These formats and themes continue to be propagated in the present to varying degrees.

Shiki-e (four-season paintings) depicted the characteristic seasonal transitions in landscape and accompanying flora and cultural activities appropriate to the time of year. *Tsukinami-e* (twelve-month paintings) further compartmentalized the seasons and each month became associated with the representation of particular flora, animals, insects, marine life, and activities such as elegant pursuits that were part of the converse with nature. The seasonal references were subject to change along with the cultural emphases of the times though an abundance of visual references were available for any single moment. Kobayashi Tadashi offers the following list on a set of *hanafuda* cards: January–pine and crane; February–plum blossom and bush warbler; March–cherry blossom; April–wisteria and cuckoo; May–iris; June–butterfly and peony; and so on.[4]

Meisho-e (pictures of famous locations) represented localities, usually at their seasonal best, and the mere mention of the name was enough to inspire a visual reference such as Yoshino with the image of spring or Tatsuta with autumn. While inspired by poetry in origin, painting itself could inspire seasonal verse and so there was reciprocation in aesthetic transmission. The practice of pasting *tanzaku* (vertical slips of poetry on paper) onto folding screens, for example, is thought to have begun in the thirteenth and fourteenth centuries and a later shift was for poetry to be painted directly on the folding screen.

The late thirteenth and fourteenth centuries added to the list of nature-based content the subjects of ink bamboo, apricot (*ume*), and orchid as practiced by Zen priests, and much of the early concern was with the representation of the idea (*shai*) that sought to capture the spirit of the artist or that of his or her subject rather than with the faithful representation of nature. This continued into the Muromachi period (1337–1573), and, again under the influence of Chinese painting precedents, there arose the trend for large-scale decorative wall painting in gorgeous colors featuring flowers and birds that continued through the Azuchi-Momoyama period (1573–1603). In the Edo period (1603–1868), the aesthetics of *kachō fūgetsu* continued to be propagated widely by the ubiquitous Kanō School of Painters and within various other lineages and by individuals such as Tawaraya Sōtatsu (?–ca. 1640) and what later came to be called 'the *Rinpa* School of Painting.'[5]

In the middle Edo period, a subsequent shift to capturing the lifelikeness of nature became evident. This was in part spurred by the influence of the Chinese merchant Shen Nanpin (ca. 1682–1795), who specialized in bird and flower painting and was resident in Nagasaki from 1731 to 1733. The heightened realism with which nature was depicted was one of the streams of influence that ran through the Maruyama-Shijō School that formed around its progenitor, Maruyama Ōkyo (1733–1795). This was widely influential upon the uptake of nature-based subject matter in Kyoto *nihonga* and elsewhere well into the twentieth century where practically all major early modern painters included it within their repertoire. As Haruo Shirane writes of a broad variety of nature-based subject matter in Japanese arts, the seasons had long been "a fundamental means of categorizing the world and everyday life."[6]

These representations of nature and the aesthetic consciousness surrounding them brought nature under control, making it elegant, poetic, and factitious. As Kenji Ekuan elaborates, "We say that everyone loves nature. But nature to which people are unable to attribute any significance or which has not been altered in any way by human beings represents a quality, or condition, quite unrefined and impossible for people to enter into."[7] That the corpus of pictorial content is nature refined and idealized owes much to its initiation in poetry as a form of "social communication and cultural expression" carried out among the aristocratic classes primarily within the major cities of Japan, even as it later came to permeate societal divisions in the Edo period through to the present.[8] Nature was, in a multitude of ways, commensurate with aspects of refined human nature. The representation of bamboo, butterflies, and a cat, for example, though apparently independent of a particular seasonal reference, was a subject for painting having the meaning of 'a man of virtue lives long' (*kunshi-chō-mei*).[9]

This pictorial content was auspicious and decorative, and while the themes of *kachō fūgetsu* were in accord with Japanese aesthetic concerns valuing temporal instability in the arts and, more abstractly, an aesthetics of impermanence, it could also turn in the reverse direction with the themes of "pine, crane, bamboo, and turtle," indicative of longevity and immortality.[10] A picture with the subject of a pine, for example, was appropriate as a gift for a sixtieth birthday and indeed various other occasions.[11] A *tanzaku* in the Nichibunken Collection by the Edo-period scholar Aida Rissei (d. 1848) relates part of the long cherished cultural value flush with human emotion in relation to a certain "longevity banquet" held in the shades of pines: "We can say we know the reason why those aged trunks endure: For a thousand years never ill, stout-hearted when times are hard."[12] While the subject matter was appropriate to the seasons, months, and individual days, such as the practice of associating the pine with New Year, carp with Boys' Day, and Hina dolls with Girls' Day, among the various other manifestations, each in turn gave way to a sequence of succeeding content as the seasons turned and so the cycle could be supposed to repeat *ad infinitum*.

The twentieth century inherited and perpetuated this poetic and visual vocabulary, though it gradually became evident that *kachō fūgetsu* was a corpus against which to revolt, to be replaced by an insistence on individual aesthetic concerns. The founding announcement by Yokoyama Taikan (1868–1958) and his colleagues for the Restored Nihon-Bijutsu-in (*Saikō Nihon Bijutsu-in*) in 1914, for example, stated: "In short, we refuse to create worthless copies of gourd paintings simply to curry favor" with the artists of old. "The new Japan is weary of 'old art,' which conservatively and stubbornly sticks to the old ways."[13] And then again in 1918 in Kyoto with the establishment of another *nihonga* group, the Association for the Creation of National Painting (*Kokuga Sōsaku Kyōkai*), the seemingly growing anachronism of *kachō fūgetsu* coined again by "gourds" was similarly addressed: "As for displaying the original characteristics of *nihonga* by relying on the traditions fused in nature, members may be conservative, but they would not imitate the people of the past who painted gourds as if restricting their own creative demand on grounds of a singular definition of *nihonga*."[14] The artists of each of these organizations, however, continued to turn out a steady flow of nature-based content.

In poetry, too, a gradual rejection and replacement became apparent:

Takahama Kyoshi (1874–1959) ... stressed in a famous lecture in 1928 that "haiku is literature that should describe flowers, birds, wind, and the moon [*kachō fūgetsu*]." This view, referred to as *kachō-fūei* (composing on flowers and birds), spurred an opposition movement in 1931 called the Shinkō haiku undō (New Haiku Movement), led by Kyoshi's disciple Mizuhara Shūōshi

(1892–1981) and others, who believed that human affairs and social engagement, including antiwar activism, should be the central subjects of haiku. The two directions—one toward nature and the other toward society—represent different sides of haiku.[15]

That shift in the character of the everyday, from nature represented by the corpus of *kachō fūgetsu* on the one hand, to society represented by individual aesthetic concerns founded upon everyday realities on the other, would arguably see one of its most distinctive forms shortly after World War II with the emergence of the Pan Real Art Association.

FORMATION OF THE PAN REAL ART ASSOCIATION

Pan Real was formed in Kyoto in March 1948 by Yamazaki Takashi (1916–2004) and Mikami Makoto (1919–1972) as the reimplementation of the wartime Rekitei Art Association (*Rekitei Bijutsu Kyōkai*) that had brought together various art forms such as *nihonga*, *yōga* (Western-style painting), photography, and *ikebana*.[16] By the time of their "first" exhibition in May, 1949, following their inaugural, poorly planned one of May 1948, Pan Real had reconceptualized itself as an *avant-garde* of *nihonga* complete with a vitriolic manifesto that sought to "gouge out the eyes" of the "conservative anachronisms of *nihonga* painting circles."[17]

The 'Pan' of their title was to be the equivalent to the character read 'han' (汎), as in 'pan-European,' meaning "relating to the whole or all of the parts." The 'Real' was not meant to be taken as realism in a narrow sense, but addressing societal realities in addition to the uptake of period developments in the arts.[18] This postwar polysemy of 'realism' included the nineteenth-century Realism of the French Salons, twentieth-century Social Realism, abstraction and Surrealism, literary influences such as Franz Kafka, and the existentialism of Albert Camus.[19] Pan Real likewise adopted the range of significations as integral to their pictorial revolt.

Fudō Shigeya (1928–) later gave further clarity to the group's name and their stance in relation to contemporary society. With the diminishing cultural isolation in the early postwar years, young artists became aware of Picasso's anti-fascist *Guernica* (1937), which offered them a model for the role of the artist working within contemporary society. This in turn led Pan Real members to doubt that *nihonga* had to be done in prescribed ways embodied in part by the corpus and aesthetics of *kachō fūgetsu*, and so they directed their artistic attentions toward very different everyday concerns.[20] As Fudō explained, throughout Pan Real's formative period, everyday society was flush with defeat in war, destruction, war crimes, starvation, occupation, hard labor, and ideological controversy.[21]

Pan Real's primary revolt was against the institutions of *nihonga* and these included not only the educational ones but also the public juried exhibitions, which their manifesto claimed were "feudalistic guild mechanisms constituting a stronghold of latent oppression."[22] *Kachō fūgetsu* was denounced in a supplementary explanatory article published in the May 17, 1949 issue of the newspaper *Yūkan Kyoto*. While the text carried the name of the official author of the Pan Real manifesto, Shimizu Junichi (1924–1988), the newspaper article was in fact written by Mikami.[23] He wrote that contemporary *nihonga* was deeply ensnared with the spirit of *kachō fūgetsu*, flush with coy sentiment and human emotion, and not simply the depiction of flowers and birds. Abandoning *kachō fūgetsu*, he wrote, was to result in the artist retaking recognition of one's own spirit. He suggested that the essence of the *nihonga* tradition could be more correctly inherited through emphasis on the subjectivity of the artist turning an eye to the everyday realities of society.[24] To do this, Pan Real sought to take stock of the immediate aftermath of World War II, to contemporize *nihonga* and expand its range of motifs and materials all the while retaining the idiom's identity while putting it under transformation by free incursion through the porous borders of *nihonga*'s conventionally posed binary, *yōga*.

As the art journalist Hashimoto Kizō recalled of the so-called "first" exhibition of 1949, for which as a *nihonga* exhibition there was an expectation that the themes and aesthetics of *kachō fūgetsu* be manifest, "there was not a single example of elegant *kachō-ga* (paintings of birds and flowers)."[25] Elsewhere he recollected of the same show: "Owing to the sweaty hot atmosphere of the young artists and the sordidness of the venue, it makes a shocking impression. The happenings of anti-artists today hardly bear comparison."[26]

PICTORIAL PROPOSITIONS FOR A NEW POSTWAR *NIHONGA*

Mikami's *F City Mandala* (1950) (Figure 22.1) was a work that the artist felt representative of his best early output,[27] as it fused the destruction of the town where he had grown up, his internal hopes for the future, and an amalgamation of his borrowings from Cubism, Surrealism, and the formal attributes of the transmigration of the soul found in Pure Land Buddhist painting. Swirling clouds flank the left and right of the picture and they disperse at the center to open onto a blue sky. An angel at left carries a white flower and two older faces hover at right, one looking out from the clouds to a vision of a pristine city, the other addressing the viewer. Mikami explained to a class reunion in 1967 that the decimated landscape at bottom, and the strewn buildings which dot it, was Fukui, the capital city of Fukui Prefecture, following the air raids

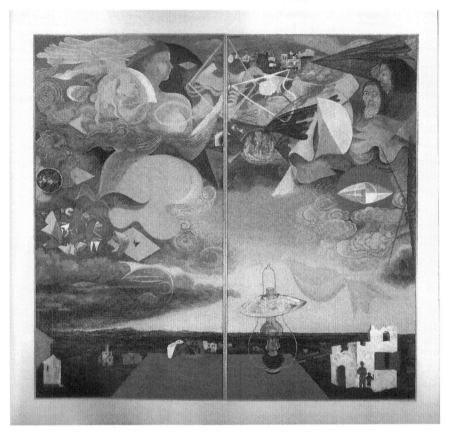

Figure 22.1 Mikami Makoto, *F City Mandala.* 1950. Mineral pigments on paper, paired screens, 181.7 cm x 182.0 cm. Fukui Fine Arts Museum, Fukui Prefecture, Japan. Reproduced with permission from Shimada Masahiro.

at the end of World War II. The face of the angel was that of his younger sister and the older faces on the right were painted while he thought of his parents. Mikami regretted those who waged war and the stupidity of it all. The picture was intended as a prayer for living in peace.[28]

Formally, the work is said to have taken its visual hint from the National Treasure of Japan *Amida shōju raigōzu* (*Descent of Amitābha and the Heavenly Multitude*) attributed to Genshin (942–1017).[29] The subject pictured the Amida Buddha with attendant deities descending from swirling clouds to carry the soul of the believer to the Pure Land and so was part of the deathbed rites and welcoming ceremonies for which Mikami was to turn to extremely personal circumstances.[30] The pristine city seen amidst the clouds at top, then, is envisioned as a celestial Buddhist paradise rising out of the smoldering ruins of Fukui.

Picasso was a well-noted stylistic stimulus to Mikami in the late 1940s and early 1950s, particularly, as Yaoyama Noboru has indicated regarding his neoclassicism and Surrealism.[31] While *F City Mandala* bears little formal resemblance to Picasso's *Guernica* (1937), it was indeed his version of that work as his Pan Real colleague Ohno Hidetaka (1922–2002) noted that Mikami had often said he had wanted to make such.[32] While the "look" of Picasso can be seen more clearly in earlier work, one can note the central lamp set upon the foreground table in *F City Mandala* as a compositional reversal of the light at top in *Guernica*. The painting, however, is a complicated collage of pictorial references, and in them one finds the miniature circular body form (potentially painted at a later date) writ large in Mikami's later *oeuvre*, as in *Moxibustion Kaleidoscope* (1966) (Figure 22.2), concerning his mistrust of Western medicine, the meridian points of moxa cautery, and the visible structures Western medicine discerns in nerves and blood vessels, in contrast to the invisible ones of Eastern medicine.[33] Mikami's long battle with pulmonary tuberculosis was part of the stimulus for his later stylistic subject matters.

Ohno Hidetaka's *Dongorosu* series utilizing jute bags and mineral pigments began from 1958, the year he ended his tenure with Pan Real. Two stimuli for the body of work's emergence were apparent. The first was the textiles of the Egyptian Copts that he had seen at an exhibition of Asian and African art.[34] The other concerned the textiles that wrapped the Chūson-ji mummified bodies that were exhumed briefly in 1950.[35] The suggestion first occurred of making prints using fabric that then evolved into using the sacking material itself as a kind of undulating low-sculptural relief surface that could be bunched and painted over resulting in works like *Collage No. 21 (Composition)* (1959) (Figure 22.3). Subsequent works shifted to minimizing the wrinkles in the fabrics and became more geometrical. The geometries became further insistent when the sacking came to be folded on top of a painted mineral pigment surface as a kind of sculptural origami. *Scarlet No. 24* (1964) (Figure 22.4), for example, has the sacking arranged into triangular configurations on a brilliant reddish background.

A concurrent concern was drawing primarily abstract circular forms with *sumi* ink and *gofun*, and these illustrated a collaboration with the American poet Cid Corman in the edition *Clocked Stone* (1959).[36] From 1961, these too took on a sculptural bent in that Ohno began to work up the circular forms in concrete which he then applied to *sumi* ink painted surfaces. He then colored the circular forms a dark brown recalling *Bizen* ceramic wares

Figure 22.2   Mikami Makoto, *Moxibustion Kaleidoscope.* 1966. Mineral pigments on paper, framed, 151.5 cm x 92.0 cm. Kyoto Municipal Museum of Art, Kyoto, Japan. Reproduced with permission from Shimada Masahiro.

such as *Seven Forms* (1961).[37] While pure abstractions, the pieces also admit further traditional Japanese readings because the differentiated circular forms, made as they are of cement, recall configurations of stones set in temple gardens.

Kimura Shigenobu observed that the forms in the early 1958 works of bunched fabric were largely irrational, though by the time they evolved into

328   *Matthew Larking*

Figure 22.3   Ohno Hidetaka, *Collage No. 21 (Composition)*. 1959. Mineral pigments
and fabric on board, framed, 144.5 cm x 174.0 cm. Kyoto Municipal Museum of Art,
Kyoto, Japan. Reproduced with permission from Ohno Emiko.

the scarlet, folded geometries beginning in 1962, they had become almost
entirely rational, while still carrying an organic scent. He noted further of
Ohno's abstractions in general that there is a harmonizing of polarities and a
resistance to the oppositional nature of binaries. Instead of plotting mineral
pigments (*nihonga*) versus oil paints (*yōga*) in the usual antagonistic and
essentialist binary relation, mineral pigments are combined very literally
with other materials and concrete. The "form" of Ohno's abstractions appear
Western, he wrote, though their "content" is Eastern.[38] Ohno's sculptural
painting of the late 1950s and early 1960s tends to straddle binaries rather
than divide into them, combining geometric abstraction with instinct, the
inorganic with the organic, the feel of tradition with the call of the contemporary. Readings of the works unify those things Western and Eastern, Kimura
says, without mediating them.[39]

Hoshino Shingo's (1923–1997) *Jintaku* series (rubbing from the human
body) began with a series of paintings in 1964 titled *Work in Mourning*,
provoked by his father's death in March the same year.[40] Observing the cre-
mation through a small window, the coffin split and he witnessed the soles

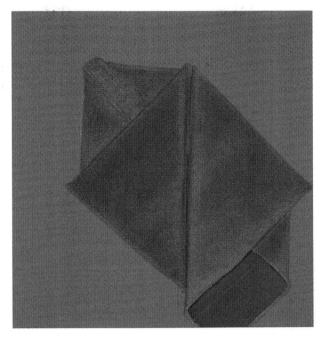

Figure 22.4   Ohno Hidetaka, *Scarlet (No. 24).* 1964. Mineral pigments and fabric on board, framed, 141.0 cm x 129.0 cm. Kyoto Municipal Museum of Art, Kyoto, Japan. Reproduced with permission from Ohno Emiko.

of his father's feet turning to ash. Overtaken by grief, he set to work in his atelier.[41] In the early works, the artist made rubbings of his hands and feet and affixed them to the painting surface. These carry the suggestion of a Buddhist inheritance, because "[a]t first there were no images of the Buddha; instead there were depictions of his footprint ... and other motifs that were relics testifying to the actual existence of the great Buddha."[42] The hand prints, too, could perform a similar symbolic function because they are reminiscent of the hand gestures, *in* (印), of Buddhist iconography, for which the character in its more general everyday usage indicates the authorial seal of the bearer.

The early *Jintaku* works featuring hand and feet rubbings were done in *sumi* ink, itself a "cremated" material, though in later works, Hoshino would incorporate most of his body, daubing paste over himself and pressing sheets of *washi* against him which when pulled away were sprinkled with grains of mineral pigment. After drying, the fragments were trimmed and collaged into coherent images of bodily poses that often look tortuously convulsed.[43]

The religious significance of these works is underscored by a number of references and in *Work from the Human Body* (1966), the centrally organizing upright torso is encircled by dozens of outstretched arms and myriad eyeballs as a modern day thousand-armed Kannon. The iconographical, compassionate significance of the deity was to see suffering with a thousand eyes and to assuage it with one thousand arms, and so the Buddhist iconography was turned to personal concerns that can be traced to the loss of his father. A further father figure appears in Hoshino's torso set against a cross in *Black Sacrifice* (1966), in which an array of arms circle up on either side to the horizontal bar in a welcoming embrace in the Christian sacrifice of the son for the father.

The *Jintaku* series can be read as Hoshino's autobiographical record of loss and pain that were variously forms of remembering, mourning, and celebrating the prominent figures in the artist's life including his mother, Pan Real colleague Mikami Makoto's early death from tuberculosis, and Hoshino's childhood friend and later fellow colleague in the Hitihito Association, Nakamura Masayoshi (1924–1977), who battled lung cancer. *Mikami* (1982), for example, incorporates a *trompe l'oeil* portrait of the artist on the tenth anniversary of his death above which Hoshino's collaged body lies limp. Hoshino was also to retrospectively associate the series with his visceral reaction to seeing the charred and agonizingly strewn bodies in his hometown of Toyohashi in 1945 following the aftermath of air raids on the city.[44]

Significantly, however, while Hoshino's mature body of work largely concerned mourning those close to him, the impression of the artist's own body was the record of a living one that sought to capture the feeling of flesh and its physical and psychological reactions to death.[45] The *Jintaku* series, then, can be understood in parallel to the Buddha's footprint, as testimony to actual existence.

COLLUDING CONTEMPORARY THOUGHT

These are some of the exemplary works that the Pan Real Art Association proposed as representing an engagement with contemporary life in its various manifestations in the postwar period to which the sentimental emphasis on the everyday corpus and aesthetics of *kachō fūgetsu* stands in distinct contrast. This substitution of a public language (*kachō fūgetsu*) for a variety of private languages (individualized aesthetics), in addition to an expanded range of materials and playing truant from conventional *nihonga* institutions, has, however, obscured the intelligibility of their distinctive bodies of work.

The aesthetics of *kachō fūgetsu* remained dominant in postwar *nihonga* and renunciation of them fundamentally hurt Pan Real economically, particularly in terms of reduced popularity. In exhibiting independently from the major *nihonga* exhibiting institutions exemplified by the national *Nitten*, Pan Real members also shunned the acclaim and financial rewards these connections could bring along with the sanctification of their art practices by a wider artistic and public audience.

In contrast, one of Pan Real's major early rivals, the Creative Art Society (*Sōzō Bijutsu*), which formed in 1948 (the same year as Pan Real), continued to perpetuate the tradition of *kachō fūgetsu*. Their formal innovations were far more influential upon the mainstream for it and these included reductionist abstraction to near color-field painting as a backdrop for birdlife or floral motifs. Shimomura Ryōnosuke (1923–1998) reflected that in inception, however, Pan Real never intended to sell works and it was enough that people would come to their exhibitions to see large-scale paintings that could not typically be accommodated within Japanese homes. Once exhibited and with the artists having no place to store the occasionally sprawling works, many early pieces were subsequently destroyed.[46]

Pan Real was not of course alone in revolting against the seemingly prescribed subject matters of "the beauties of nature" in *nihonga* in the postwar period, though they were the preeminent group to articulate their cultural reaction in writing and pictorial propositions for an expanded range of subjects. The revolt against "the beauties of nature," however, remains an ongoing concern within contemporary *nihonga*. As a progressive exponent of the idiom, Mise Natsunosuke (1973–) exclaims:

> These days I sometimes read "nihonga" as "nihongo" (Japanese language). ... There is no meaning at all in slavish obedience to conventional values and techniques represented by the "flowers-birds-wind-and-moon" (*kacho fugetsu*) type of painting ... . The Japanese spoken in Edo period (1603–1867) Japan was quite different from that spoken today ... . All I want to do is convey the nuances of my own way of painting *nihonga* (just as I would in speaking Japanese).[47]

Beginning with a very public language, literally his native one, and rejoining the verbal and visual reciprocations that gave rise to the aesthetics of *kachō fūgetsu*, Mise rejects the imposition of the past on the present. This also reflects the ongoing tensions implicit within recent *nihonga* concerning the propagation of a public visual language, or the rejection of it, for the articulation of personal voice.

NOTES

1. Margaret Iversen, *Alois Riegl: Art History and Theory* (Cambridge, MA: MIT Press, 1993), 13.

2. Yuriko Saito, *Everyday Aesthetics* (Oxford: Oxford University Press, 2007).

3. Haruo Shirane, *Japan and the Culture of the Four Seasons: Nature, Literature, and the Arts* (New York: Columbia University Press, 2012), 57.

4. Kobayashi Tadashi, "Within the Tradition of Nature over the Seasons," in *Nature in Japanese Art: From Sansui to Landscape*, ed. Aichi Prefectural Museum of Art (Nagoya: Aichi Prefectural Museum of Art, 2005), 23.

5. Kusanagi Natsuko, "Kachōga no dentō to ima—shajitsu hyōgen to seishin hyōshutsu no hazama de," *Nihonga wo manabu* 2 (1999): 13.

6. Shirane, xii.

7. Kenji Ekuan, *The Aesthetics of the Japanese Lunchbox*, ed. David B. Stewart (Cambridge, MA: MIT Press, 2000), 77. The Western painting tradition is not without its correspondences. See Rensselaer W. Lee, *Ut Pictura Poesis: The Humanistic Theory of Painting* (New York: Norton, 1967), 9.

8. Shirane, xii, 18, 203.

9. Wa-ei Taishō Nihon Bijutsu Yōgo Jiten Henshū Iinkai, ed., *A Dictionary of Japanese Art Terms: Bilingual [Japanese & English]: A Popular Edition* (Tokyo: Tokyo Bijutsu, 1990), 178.

10. Shirane, 21.

11. Paul Berry and Michiyo Morioka, *Literati Modern: Bunjinga from Late Edo to Twentieth-Century Japan* (Honolulu: Honolulu Academy of Arts, 2008), 198.

12. This work in the Nichibunken Collection may be viewed online: http://tois. nichibun.ac.jp/hsis/heian-jinbutsushi/Tanzaku/38/info.html (accessed June 23, 2017). The English translation comes from this website.

13. Saitō Ryūzō, *Nihon Bijutsuin-shi* (Tokyo: Chūō Kōron Bijutsu Shuppan, 1944), 211–12. The English translation used is from John Szostak, *The Kokuga Sōsaku Kyōkai and Kyoto Nihonga Reform in the Meiji, Taishō and Early Shōwa Years (1900–1928)* (Ph.D. diss., University of Washington, 2005), 255.

14. Tsuchida Kyōson cited in Shimada Yasuhiro, "The Art Scene of the Taisho Period and Bakusen," in *Tsuchida Bakusen: A Retrospective*, ed. Takeo Uchiyama (Tokyo: Nihon Keizai Shimbun, 1997), 37.

15. Shirane, 216–17.

16. Yamano Hidetsugu, Kawai Yuki, and Nagai Akio, foreword to *Nihonga no zenei 1938–1949*, ed. Yamano Hidetsugu, Kawai Yuki, and Nagai Akio (Kyoto: Kyoto Kokuritsu Kindai Bijutsukan, 2010), 7.

17. Shino Masahiro and Nakai Yasuyuki, eds., *Panriaru sōseiki ten—sengo nihonga no kakushin undō* (Nishinomiya City: Nishinomiya City Otani Memorial Art Museum, 1998), 2.

18. Ibid., 78.

19. Yamada Satoshi, "Sengo nihon no riarizumu ni tsuite—atarashii seiki no nihon bijutsu no tame ni," in *Sengo nihon no riarizumu 1945–1960*, ed. Nagoya-shi Bijutsu-kan (Nagoya: Nagoya-shi Bijutsukan, 1998), 8–11.

20. Fudō Shigeya, "Engankyō de miru furushōmon," in *Shōwa 20 nendai no nihonga—atarashii bi no sōzō wo mezashite*, ed. Naora Yoshihiro (Shimane: Shimane Kenritsu Bijutsukan, 1995), 83.

21. Ibid., 84.

22. Shino and Nakai, 2.

23. Fudō Shigeya, *Kahataredoki no shōzō: naki gayū ni sasagu—pan riaru bijutsu kyōkai keisei e no taidō* (Kyoto: Fudō Shigeya, 1988), 16.

24. Ibid., 17–18.

25. Hashimoto Kizō, *Kyoto to kindai bijutsu* (Kyoto: Kyoto Shoin, 1982), 215.

26. Hashimoto Kizō cited in Kimura Shigenobu, "Mikami Makoto no hito to sakuhin," in *Mikami Makoto gashū*, ed. Mikami Makoto gashū henshū iinkai (Tokyo: Sansaisha, 1974), 134.

27. Yaoyama Noboru, "Mikami Makoto sono hito to sono sekai," in *Pan riaru bijutsu undō no kishu—Mikami Makoto hyōron, nikki*, ed. Shimada Masashi (Fukui City: Fenikkusu Shuppan, 1995), 42.

28. Ibid., 43.

29. Kimura Shigenobu, "Mikami Makoto no seiri to shinri," in *Makoto Mikami ten: jiko gyōshi kara 'uchū' e*, ed. Amano Kazuo (Shinagawa: O Bijutsukan, 1990), 10.

30. Katayama Hiroaki, "Welcoming Descent of the Amida Triad," in *Omi: Spiritual Home of Kami and Hotoke*, ed. Executive Committee for the "Omi: Spiritual Home of Kami and Hotoke" Exhibition (Shigaraki: Miho Museum, 2011), 22.

31. Yaoyama, "Mikami Makoto," 44.

32. Ibid., 50–51.

33. Shimada Masashi and Inaki Nobuo, "Mikami Makoto wo kangaeru—sono sakuhin no naritachi ni tsuite," in *Pan riaru bijutsu undō no kishu—Mikami Makoto hyōron, nikki*, ed. Shimada Masashi (Fukui City: Fenikkusu Shuppan, 1995) (Supplemental, corrected text), 7.

34. Kimura Shigenobu, "Sokubutsusei e no shikō—dongorosu sakuhin wo megutte," in *Ohno Hidetaka* (Kyoto: Sanjō Gion Garō, 1985), unpaged.

35. Amano Kazuo, "Busshō no kanata ni …—Ohno Hidetaka no gareki ni sotte," in *Ohno Hidetaka-ten*, ed. Amano Kazuo (Shinagawa: O Bijutsukan, 1989), 15.

36. Kimura, "Sokubutsusei e no shikō," unpaged.

37. Ibid.

38. Ibid.

39. Ibid.

40. Yaoyama Noboru, "Wasurekataki deai—Mikami Makoto to Hoshino Shingo no [nihonga]," in *Ishiki no hida: Hoshino Shingo-ten—pan riaru bijutsu kyōkai no yōranki to tomo ni*, ed. Morita Yasuhisa (Toyokawa: Sakuragaoka Museum, 2008), 11.

41. Ibid., 10.

42. Katayama Hiroaki, "List of Works: 9, Footprint of Buddha," in *Omi: Spiritual Home of Kami and Hotoke*, ed. Executive Committee for the "Omi: Spiritual Home of Kami and Hotoke" Exhibition, 18.

43. Yaoyama, "Wasurekataki deai," 11.

44. Ibid.

45. Hoshino Shingo, "Pan riaru kara hitohito made," in *Mikami Makoto Hoshino Shingo II nin (futari) ten*, ed. Yaoyama Noboru (Fukui City: Fukui Prefectural Art Museum, 1985), unpaged.

46. Shimomura Ryōnosuke, *Tangan Fukugan* (Osaka: Tōhō Shuppan, 1993), 13–14.

47. Mise Natsunosuke, *Fuyu no Natsu L'Estate in Inverno* (Tokyo: Hatori Press, 2010), 117.

Chapter 23

The Aesthetics of Emptiness in Japanese Calligraphy and Abstract Expressionism

John C. Maraldo

NISHITANI'S AESTHETICS OF SENSORY EMPTINESS AND JAPANESE CALLIGRAPHIC ART

There is something contradictory about the whole notion of an aesthetics of emptiness. Aesthetics, from the Greek *aistetike*, refers to the world perceptible by the senses, and more narrowly considers what is beautiful in this world and what makes things beautiful. Emptiness (Sanskrit: *śūnyatā*) is the central Mahayana Buddhist teaching that all beings, all phenomenal forms, are empty of permanent, independent existence. The doctrine of emptiness describes precisely the lack of self-subsistent, substantial forms, and it points to the folly of attaching to forms as if they were abiding realities. The point would seem to be to avoid concerning oneself with sensible forms, beautiful or otherwise. Of course, we could always fall back on the famous formulation of the *Heart Sutra*, that emptiness is nothing but form and form nothing but emptiness. Many readers of this formula, while granting that we cannot have the one without the other, still place the emphasis on the emptiness of forms, not on the forms of emptiness. What sense would it make to speak of poetic and visual art practices as expressions of emptiness?

This sort of speaking is precisely what the twentieth-century Japanese philosopher Nishitani Keiji (1900–1990) engages in. He proposes not only that emptiness is ineluctable for the manifestation of forms—a point that was argued as early as the second century by the Indian philosopher Nāgārjuna[1]—but also that forms or phenomena are necessary for the manifestation of emptiness. And there is, he says, one phenomenon that is most apt to elicit the envisioning of emptiness: the vast and empty sky. Nishitani plays on the double meaning of the sinograph 空, which signifies both the Buddhist idea of emptiness and, in ordinary language, the sky. He suggests that the vast and empty sky is not merely a metaphor for emptiness, a visible phenomenon standing in for an invisible reality. There is something about the visible sky that intimately and not only metaphorically connects it to the idea of emptiness, in that a vast and empty sky 虚空 may be visible but it is without (particular) form. Nishitani suggests further that Buddhist emptiness, conveyed through the image of a vast empty sky, not merely expresses a certain doctrinal idea but also evokes a certain sensitivity. He calls this 'emotive emptiness' 情意的な空.[2] Nishitani refers to such emotive or sensory emptiness when he writes: "The form in which emptiness as a Buddhist doctrine has permeated the sensory world is Chinese and Japanese art. Particularly, this permeation appears in painting and poetry."[3] Nishitani's essay proceeds to explore expressions of such emptiness in Chinese and Japanese poems.

In the following discussion, I offer some illustrations in the realm of the visual arts. We can begin with the proposal that some artworks make manifest the space within which things occur, that such space is an example of emotive emptiness, and that the interplay between such space and occurring images exemplifies the "relation" between emptiness and form.

We must, however, immediately avoid a misunderstanding of this kind of talk. The emptiness formula of the *Heart Sutra*, after all, does not posit two independent items of relation, form and emptiness, but rather properly refers to the teaching that every form is empty of substantial, self-subsistent being, as is every other basic *skandha* or constituent of individual persons, that is, every feeling, perception, volition, and consciousness. Relating this teaching to the aesthetics of emptiness, we could say that the place within which visible things occur is not simply some independent, empty space surrounding an object. Understanding the matter that way would give us two perceptual items or images, an image without form and other images with form. It would also repeat the usual cliché that Chinese and Japanese landscape art emphasizes the empty space around the depicted objects more than the objects themselves. Such imagery takes the visual forms as one thing and the emptiness surrounding them as another, a preexistent, blank background or void upon which the objects are painted, drawn, or written. This imagery fails to appreciate the interactive relationship between visual forms and emptiness that Nishitani intimates.[4] Not only do forms or shapes need a surrounding space in order to appear as distinct forms or shapes, but, reciprocally, emptiness also becomes visible through these arts only in contradistinction to the forms. This observation, too, has become commonplace in discussions of Buddhist-inspired art,[5] and the paintings of the Japanese landscape painter Sesshū Tōyō (1420–1506) are often cited as examples. The French artist André Masson (1896–1987) observed that Sesshū found "space within space" in which everything springs from the lines that divide the surface.[6] The broken brushstrokes that characterize Sesshū's *haboku* style make visible and even accentuate the spaces they delineate, just as, in another sensory realm described in a haiku by Bashō, silence becomes audible only in interaction with the shrill cries of the cicada penetrating the rock.[7]

Reading Nishitani, however, I am inspired to take this commonplace observation further and relate the aesthetics of emptiness to time as well as space. The *Heart Sutra*'s emptiness doctrine, that is, that every form, feeling, perception, volition, and consciousness is without independent, substantial being, is also a statement about impermanence and lack of perduring being. Seen in this light, the doctrine implies that things as well as the acts of consciousness that register them are better described as events than as beings. Morita Shiryū (1912–1998), one of the founders of *avant-garde* calligraphy or *sho* 書 in Japan, says as much in a fascinating essay published as "Calligraphy and Abstract Painting" in 1971.

A brush, Morita writes, is not merely an object in the world, not just an instrument that people make and use, and not even an extension of the artist or the artist's body. It is also something that gives the artist her existence. Similarly, it is the activity of the artist that makes the brush a brush. Neither exists anywhere by itself; together, they form an indivisible whole or unity. The artist and her brush codefine and even cocreate each other, here and now, in a temporal totality Morita calls *place*. It is and she is only by virtue of this interactivity:

> If I as a tangible, finite human being stand over against a tangible, finite brush, then I and the brush mutually restrict one another and cannot become one. This shell called 'I' must split open, this hull must fall off, for the self to be released into a world that is formless and infinite. The self, released and unified with a place, becomes the totality of 'I' and my brush.[8]

Morita then describes the interrelation between the brush and the artist, and their lack of independent and perduring being, by alluding to Nishitani's reading of a famous cryptic passage in the *Diamond Sutra*. Adapting the *Sutra*'s passage, Nishitani speaks of fire not being fire, that is, not burning itself, and therefore being or manifesting as fire.[9] Morita writes,

> I am not I (but rather this place), and therefore I am I. The brush is not a brush (but rather is this place), and, therefore, it is a brush. As a calligrapher I transcend myself and am released from myself; this liberation continues to work within me. I am no longer restricted by myself. This is where I can truly become myself.[10]

The emphasis on emptiness and interdependence is obvious in Morita's essay, but equally significant is the definition of the world of the artist in terms of events rather than beings. Artists and brushes exist properly not as beings that preexist an artwork but as temporal events that emerge through its creation.[11]

Curiously, other than the mention of creating *sho*, Morita does not describe in this essay the artwork itself that is created in the interaction of artist and brush. For Morita, who privileges *sho* over other arts, it goes without saying that the *sho* artwork, too, is more event than thing. *Sho* comes about in the meeting of brush and artist (and ink and paper) in a way that traditionally emphasizes the temporality of the brush strokes, executed once and for all and (ideally) never redrawn or written over (Figure 23.1). The viewer, too, could be said to cocreate the work when she sees it, follows its strokes, and feels its power, delicacy, or expressed emotion. Morita could easily say that the artwork is an intersection of artist, brush, ink and paper, and viewer; all of these are interacting events and not independent beings.

It is somewhat ironic that Morita's *avant-garde sho* movement in Japan began to present calligraphic works as things that could be placed beside one another in art exhibitions, rather than hung and revered one at a time, one representing all, in temples and alcoves. Although the cocreation mentioned above might occur between a viewer and a work in an exhibition space as well as in a kind of sacred alcove space, the location might alter the perception of the artwork's temporality. I do not know whether a quiet time in front of a hanging scroll in an alcove is more conducive to the perception of fleeting brush strokes and emotive emptiness. If so, the altered space in *avant-garde sho* exhibitions evoked impermanence on a different scale. The exhibitions themselves were most often short-lived events. In any case, an event requires its place as much as a depicted form requires its surrounding space.

Figure 23.1 Mary Jo Maraldo, *Snow* 雪**.** 1994. *Sumi* ink on paper, 8 in. × 10 in. Collection of Mary Lance and Ben Daitz, Corrales, NM. Reproduced with permission from artist. © 1994 Mary Jo Maraldo.

Nishitani, perhaps appropriating his teacher Nishida Kitarō's language, writes of *place* or *ba* 場 as much as space in his article on emotive emptiness. Space or place—what is the difference? One often thinks of space 空間 as absolute, that is, as being by itself and sufficient unto itself, either an objective reality as Newton thought or a mental condition for experiencing the world, a form of sensibility in Kant's terms. Nishitani is well aware of these thinkers when he composes his piece. He writes tentatively of our perception of the empty sky 虚空 as "an eternally constant empty space ... the only 'eternal thing' we can see with our eyes."[12] Place, on the other hand—although Nishitani does not articulate this—implies the location of something within space. A place implies a relation whereas space can denote an absolute void. Place describes temporal and spatial context. The link to a temporal and spatial context is clearer when speaking of events than when speaking of things (beings or entities). In the perception of emotive emptiness in the arts, we shift not only from things to events but also from space to place. Instead of perceiving objects in space, we learn to perceive events and their places. Moreover, Nishitani would insist, our perception, too, is an event that takes place and cocreates us. The event of *sho* and other visual arts can be the creation of the space as well as of form, but always in this very place: the place of the interaction of viewer and work, as well as the stretch of paper, scroll, or canvas. Artists like Morita were well aware of creating space to let things/ events occur in a particular place.

AVOIDING ORIENTALISM BUT PRESERVING EMPTINESS: THE SPACE OF CONTENTION BETWEEN JAPANESE CALLIGRAPHIC ART AND ABSTRACT EXPRESSIONISM

The quotation from Nishitani that begins this chapter locates the form of emptiness in a wider but still particularized and differentiated geo-cultural place: the art of China and Japan. Yet, from a Buddhist perspective, there is no reason to confine expressions of emptiness to any particular geo-cultural area of art, much less to an artist's intent to show the interrelation of emptiness and form. Several art historians have made comparisons between Japanese calligraphic artists and European and American abstract expressionists who use brushstrokes and compose paintings in a way similar to the Japanese. A few scholars have gone on to scrutinize the comparisons and claims of influence. Certainly, today, scholars with a raised historical consciousness are aware of another context for discussing topics like the aesthetics of emptiness. This context is the historical issue of the cultural nationalism of artists, which includes both Orientalism—or Western stereotyping of Asian artists—and the reverse stereotyping of "the West" by Japanese artists. In this section,

I describe the Orientalist (or reverse-Orientalist) context and then suggest how we may remove Nishitani's insights from this kind of nationalist agenda. Artists like Morita, as Bert Winther-Tamaki demonstrates, did eventually appeal to principles like nondualism to valorize the East over the West.[13] But it is not necessary to follow their lead. I would like to suggest a way that avoids Orientalism yet still preserves the possibility of seeing space created by forms, and of perceiving the place and event of artistic creation, in non-Asian and non-Buddhist art.[14]

We may begin with a pair of artists who dipped into Orientalism and dis-illusionment with it: Morita Shiryū himself and the artist he featured in the fourth volume of his *avant-garde* magazine *Boku-bi* in 1951, Franz Kline (1910–1962). There came a time when Morita did insinuate that expressions of emptiness were the exclusive possession of the East and, particularly in the present age, of Japan. By the 1970s, he saw a profound difference between the calligraphic art of Japan and the works of Western abstract expressionists that seemed to emulate it. When asked on the one hand to compare Japanese *sho* and European ink drawings that mimicked signs, he said, "We [Japanese] regard ideographs not only as signs but [also] as something into which we pour our life and soul. So, I believe ideographs in our calligraphy are much more than mere signs ... . We *use* them not as mere signs but as something that signals our very existence."[15] When asked on the other hand to compare the Western work that seemed to approach ideographs and the kind of *sho* that moved away from them, Morita responded,

> In discussing this problem, I must touch on my favorite term, *ba,* literally "place."[16] A brush and the person who handles it are quite different things, but if the two unite as one, the element essential to the creation of calligraphic art emerges. I would like to call this other dimension *ba* ... . These two—[the artist's] will and brushwork—have been freed of each other, and yet become unified on a different level at a certain "place." ... Whether or not one seeks one's true self in *ba* makes a great difference in the creation of art. In short, as long as one seeks objects outside oneself, one cannot attain *ba* ... . [In Western action painting like Pollock's, one does not find] a true understanding of *mu,* "nothingness." I don't want to speak about my conception of *mu* apart from my idea of *ba,* but, since I want to relate my own experiences as fully as possible, just let me say that *mu* is in the paper as well as in the brush.[17]

Morita's response here not only echoes some of the more cryptic statements about artist and brush in the essay "Calligraphy and Abstract Painting," but it also clearly reflects his privileging of the Asian Buddhist background of his work.[18]

A few years after Morita's statement, the critic and interviewer Gordon Washburn presented an equally sweeping and Orientalist verdict of the difference between East and West, this time to valorize the heroic spirit of the Western artists as opposed to the detached nature of Asian, especially Zen, art:

> Whereas in Asian art we may find a cool elevation of spirit—a veritable levitation into apparent weightlessness ... in Western art the tendency is to uncover man's tormented soul and to trace his passionate pilgrimage in time. The Eastern approach is not a soul-striving, not a reaching for the stars, not a heroic adventure ... . we should compare the great black grids of Kline with the bold brushstrokes of the Japanese calligrapher Shiryū Morita—a typical West-East contrast. The great, thrusting girders in Kline's works shoot out of the canvas at its edges. They have nothing in common with the floating scolls [*sic*] of Morita that seem to find perfect accommodation within the rectangles of their frame. Kline's expansive images seem like enlargements of a titanic battleground—a section of a heroic context too large to be contained, even in his greatest canvases. We have only to turn to other Westerners in this linear vein ... to see that all offer a somewhat similar sort of statement, each of which is frankly personal and emotional in nature. The spirit of *mu* is not built into their approach to life.[19]

In his own Orientalism, Washburn, too, attributes the spirit of *mu* to the art of the East, as seen in Morita's art and Zen, and even in *ukiyo-e* woodblock prints. "What the Japanese call *mu* is everywhere present," Washburn claims.[20] His form of *mu*, moreover, is cool and tame, detached and contained, compared to the heroic, unbounded striving of Kline and his contemporaries. For Washburn, there is definitely no *mu* in the Western artists.

Franz Kline himself, after proclaiming the influence of Japanese artists like Kōrin, Sesshū, and Hokusai on his very early work and exclaiming his "passionate interest in calligraphy" in 1951, soon became disillusioned with any association with *sho*. He explicitly denied that his work was influenced by Japanese calligraphy and railed against the Orientalization of his paintings. Winther-Tamaki contextualizes and ultimately undermines Kline's denial.[21] One of Kline's statements near the end of his life is particularly revealing:

> The Oriental idea of space is an infinite space; it is not painted space, and ours is. In the first place, calligraphy is writing, and I'm not writing. People sometimes think I take a white canvas and paint a black sign on it, but this is not true. I paint the white as well as the black, and the white is just as important.[22]

Kline's statement ironically links him to Japanese calligraphy in three ways that concern the three questions of writing or not writing, background or figure, and "their [Japanese]" influence on "us" or "our [American]" influence on "them."

First, the distinction between writing and painting is difficult to make even in traditional Japanese "calligraphy." *Sho* can be translated as 'writing' or as

'drawing.' The difference is even harder to see in *avant-garde sho*, which
may not only be illegible to readers of Japanese but may also not represent
sinograms (*kanji*) at all. It often deliberately distances itself from writing, and
thus the very term 'calligraphy' can be very misleading. Many *sho* artists are
also *not writing*; they are no longer reproducing *kanji*.

Secondly, as Winther-Tamaki points out, American interpreters had
already claimed for Japanese art the prominence of background space that
Kline was claiming for his work in distinction from Japanese art. Some interpreters emphasized further the leveling of the difference between figure and
ground in Japanese art. Winther-Tamaki thinks that, despite Kline's claim
about painted space, "the effect of most of [his] black and white paintings ...
is that of black forms on a white ground."[23] But the issue is not necessarily
whether the background or the figure/object is the more prominent in either
East Asian or Kline's art. Indeed, perhaps as early as the 1890s, Ernest
Fenollosa called attention to the principle of *nōtan* 濃淡 or the reversibility
of contrasts like black and white at work in Japanese art (Figure 23.2).[24]

We can, I think, see the same principle at work in Kline's paintings, where
it is easy to shift from seeing black forms on white to seeing white forms on
black. Both black and white, after all, are painted in, as Kline says. The principle of *nōtan* is as visible in Kline's work as it is in examples of Japanese
calligraphic art (Figure 23.3).

Moreover, like Kline, some *avant-garde sho* artists have likewise worked on
painted surfaces. Morita's "Dragon Knows Dragon" (Figure 23.4), for example,
is silver lacquer brushwork on the black-lacquered surface of a folding screen.

It is well documented that Kline was a strong inspiration for Morita and
his friends in the late 1940s and early 1950s, although I do not know if their
later use of painted surfaces was due to Kline's influence, nor do I know if
earlier or traditional *sho* was ever done on inked or painted surfaces, except
on pottery or lacquerware. If we want to put it in nationalistic terms, it may
be a matter here of Americans influencing Japanese *avant-garde* calligraphic
artists rather than the other way around. In view of other elements of their
works, however, common features are evident, and this is my third point.
Despite the profound distinction that Kline wished to draw between his own
work and Japanese calligraphy, both can be viewed as not writing, as foregrounding neither white nor black, and as mutually influenced and influential.
Moreover, without wishing to "buddhacize" Kline's achievement, may we
not, in some of his works, see space created by forms or perceive the place
and event of artistic creation (Figure 23.5)?[25]

A relevant difference between Kline's work and *sho* would be how the
brushwork is executed—whether in one-time strokes that are never redrawn
or in strokes painted back and forth over the same surface. Brushstrokes done

Figure 23.2   Mary Jo Maraldo, *Big* 大. 2001. *Sumi* ink on paper, 8 in. × 10 in. Collection of Jerome and Maryanne Hellmann, St. Joseph, MI. Reproduced with permission from artist. © 2001 Mary Jo Maraldo.

once and for all would seemingly reflect more vividly the idea of impermanence and the uniqueness of an event. If so, this characteristic is hardly limited to Buddhist-influenced Japanese artists, however. The work of Mark Tobey (1890–1976) provides an example.

Tobey is often cited as an abstract expressionist deeply influenced by Zen and by Sino-Japanese calligraphy. A closer look, however, reveals a connection that is more distant in one sense but closer in another. Tobey did in fact learn calligraphy from a Chinese friend in Seattle in 1922, and a decade later traveled to China and Japan.[26] He spent a month in a Japanese Zen monastery in 1934.[27] He learned enough, however, to disavow any deep absorption of Zen or its arts on his part:

> I don't think that people [like me] get very close to the reality of Zen, though. You don't understand Zen in two years, or ten years. You don't know what Zen is in twenty years unless you're exceptional. You certainly don't find out right away. You have to give your life to know Zen.[28]

Figure 23.3 Franz Kline, *Untitled.* 1952. Enamel on canvas, 53 in. × 68 in. Metropolitan Museum of Art, New York. Reproduced with permission. © 2017 Franz Kline Estate / Artists Rights Society (ARS), New York.

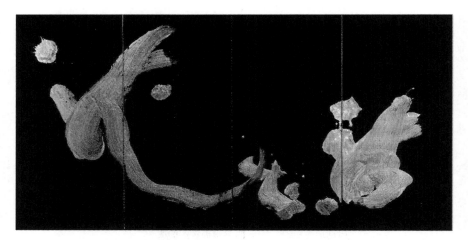

Figure 23.4 Morita Shiryū, *Dragon Knows Dragon (Ryu wa ryu wo shiru).* 1969. Four-panel screen, aluminum flake pigment in polyvinyl acetate medium, yellow alkyd varnish, on paper, 162 cm x 307 cm. Art Institute of Chicago, Chicago. Gift of Mr. and Mrs. Milton Fisher (1981.364). Reproduced with permission from the Art Institute of Chicago.

Figure 23.5 Franz Kline, *Ninjinsky.* 1950. Enamel on canvas, 45 in. × 35 in. Metropolitan Museum of Art, New York. Reproduced with permission. © 2017 Franz Kline Estate / Artists Rights Society (ARS), New York.

Tobey's religious life was much more influenced by the Baha'i faith, to which he converted long before his interest in Zen and which he continued to affirm until his death. When asked in 1971, "What attracted you most in Zen? Its relation to art? Was it, for example, the 'interior space,' or 'emptiness,' or 'accidental value'?" he replied, "I don't put much stock in that." He went on to resist talk of an "Oriental period" in his work and to deny that his paintings

346   *John C. Maraldo*

have the same point of departure as "these Zen ideas." What he assimilated from Oriental art, the only thing he as an American foreigner could take from it, he said, was its "rhythmic power": "I was most interested in the dynamics of creation."[29] In Tobey's own mind, then, his connection would not be with the spatial relationships in calligraphic art, a static idea of "emptiness" or "interior space," but with a more dynamic element. The rhythmic power displayed by Tobey's paintings, moreover, is not explained simply by the reversibility of form and surrounding space, of figure and ground. To be sure, this *nōtan* principle is evident in his work, and he played with it by painting white forms on a black background as well as black on white. But the rhythmic power is rather conveyed through brushstrokes that are executed once and for all, as in *sho* (Figure 23.6). And because Tobey's forms have no roots whatsoever in recognizable signs like sinograms, because they are not placed in any familiar context, it is perhaps even easier to see the work itself as a place, a context of its own, that displays the very event of artistic creation. Perhaps Tobey better than Morita has succeeded in manifesting the cocreation of brush and artist.

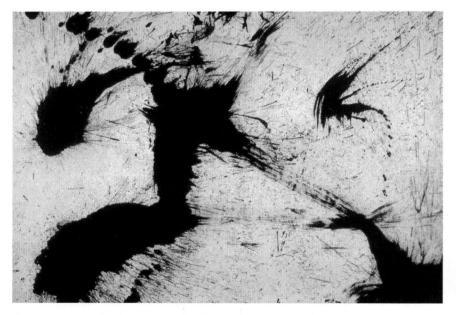

**Figure 23.6 Mark Tobey, *Space Ritual No. 1.* 1957. *Sumi* ink on paper, 29 in. × 38 in. Seattle Art Museum, Seattle, WA. Eugene Fuller Memorial Collection. Reproduced with permission from Seattle Art Museum.

I would like to consider, finally, an artist's work that is frequently celebrated for its Zen-like meditative spatiality but is probably not influenced by Zen culture, and is definitely remote from calligraphic art. The final paintings of Mark Rothko (1903–1970), designed for the chapel in Houston where they now hang, remarkably display both the interdependence of form and space, as well as the event of creation in awareness of a particular place.

Rothko's chapel paintings, done in the late 1960s, are enormous fields of grays, blacks, and variations of other hues, but without any depicted shapes or forms (Figure 23.7). (Even if the shades of blue in the original are not visible here, the image still gives a hint of the tonal variation.)

These paintings would seem to be depictions of the void itself, with only extremely subtle nuances in shading to arrest the attention of the viewer. One might see them as depicting Nishitani's empty sky at night time. In other words, one might see them as taking the surrounding space that allows individual forms to appear, and making that the visible phenomenon, the form of emptiness. In non-Buddhist terms, the paintings seem to have made what is usually a background into a foreground without depicting any figures. One student of Rothko's works, however, has also noticed the relation of space and form in the actual setting of the chapel, the concrete place for which Rothko intended the paintings. Sheldon Nodelman suggests several ways to

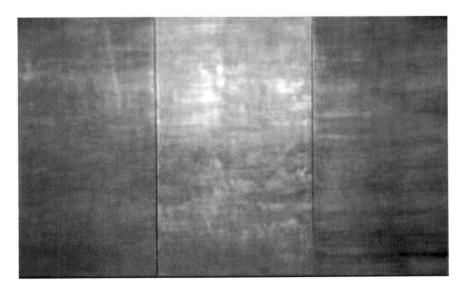

Figure 23.7   Mark Rothko, The Apse Triptych. 1965–1966. Oil on canvas, 180 in. × 297 in. Rothko Chapel, Houston, TX. Reproduced with permission. © 1998 Kate Rothko Prizel & Christopher Rothko / Artists Rights Society (ARS), New York.

Figure 23.8   Panorama of the Rothko Chapel. 1965–1966. Rothko Chapel, Houston, TX.
Reproduced with permission. © 1998 Kate Rothko Prizel & Christopher Rothko / Artists
Rights Society (ARS), New York.

view the paintings in their particular context through a "series of reciprocal
framings—motivated by the changing focus of the observer's gaze." One
might see the walls of the octagonal chapel as ground and each painting as
figure, "transforming the wall itself into a fictive space"; or one might frame
a painting by its edges, or by the surrounding wall, or the wall by the adjacent
walls, or all these by their periphery (Figure 23.8). Nodelman implies that the
walls do not constitute a separate space but can "appear as negative cutouts
of the paintings' shapes."[30]

In addition to this interdependence of form and space, Rothko's chapel
paintings may also elicit the kind of emotive or sensory emptiness of which
Nishitani speaks. This observation is not gratuitous; it reflects the way that
Rothko himself wanted his field paintings viewed. He denied that he painted
color fields for their own sake, and strove instead to open an immediacy and
create an emotive relationship with the viewer. "There is no such thing as a
good painting about nothing," he said.[31] Nodelman notes that Rothko

insisted that content was all-important; he had no interest whatever in form, in composition and color, for its own sake. He indignantly denied being a 'colorist.' The refusal of conventional and secondhand content ... was for him a necessary means toward the achievement of authentic and essential content, toward *'the elimination of all obstacles between the painter and the idea and between the idea and the observer.'*[32]

Later, Rothko emphasized, "I'm only interested in expressing basic human emotions ... The people who weep before my pictures are having the same religious experience I had when I painted them, and if you, as you say, are moved only by their color relationships, then you miss the point."[33]

I suggest that Mark Rothko's chapel paintings in their particular setting offer an example of work that, independently of Buddhist influence, evinces the aesthetics of emptiness that Nishitani and Morita describe. They allow us to sense and to feel the forms of emptiness, the interdependence of form and emptiness, and the place where the cocreation of artist and painting, painting and viewer, is at work.

CONCLUSION

Nishitani's creative interpretation of the Buddhist teaching of the emptiness lends itself to a deeper appreciation of the interdependence of space and form in aesthetics. Nishitani's "sensory or emotive emptiness" is evoked by the spatial and temporal context within which images occur. This aesthetic is displayed in visual arts like Japanese calligraphy and abstract expressionist painting where an interplay of space and form, and of artist and artwork, takes place. The *avant-garde* calligrapher Morita Shiryū in particular stressed the cocreation of artist and work that comes about in the place and activity of art-making. But a comparison and contrast of these two artistic traditions also shows that the provenance of visualized emptiness is by no means confined to East Asian art. The real contradiction regarding an aesthetics of emptiness is the view that one nation or tradition is the proprietor of its expressions.

NOTES

1. In chapter 24 of the *Mūlamadhyamakakārikā*, Nāgārjuna argues that without emptiness the phenomenal world would not manifest at all. Verse 19 of that chapter sums up this point: "A thing that is not dependently arisen is not evident. For that reason, a thing that is non-empty is indeed not evident." See David J. Kalupahana, *Nāgārjuna: The Philosophy of the Middle Way* (Albany, NY: State University of New York Press, 1986), 341.

2. Nishitani, "Kū to soku 空と即," in *Nishitani Keiji chosaku shū*, vol. 13 (Tokyo: Sōbunsha, 1987), 112. Marra translates this as 'sensory emptiness.' See Nishitani Keiji, "Emptiness and Sameness," in *Modern Japanese Aesthetics: A Reader*, trans. and ed. Michele Marra (Honolulu: University of Hawai'i Press, 1999), 180.

3. Nishitani, "Emptiness and Sameness," 180.

4. Nishitani describes this kind of relationship as "reciprocal permeation" and also calls it *egoteki* 回互的, which Marra translates as 'revolvingly reciprocal' and Jan van Bragt translates as 'circuminsessional.' See Nishitani, "Emptiness and Sameness," 197; and *Religion and Nothingness*, trans. Jan van Bragt (Berkeley, CA: University of California Press, 1982), 294–95, respectively.

5. Alan Watts was one who popularized this view: "One of the most striking features of the Sung landscape, as of *sumi-e* as a whole, is the relative emptiness of the picture—an emptiness which appears, however, to be part of the painting and just unpainted background. By filling in just one corner, the artist makes the whole area of the picture alive." See his *The Way of Zen* (New York: Penguin Books, 1957), 198.

6. See the 1969 interview by Takemoto Tadao in *Dialogue in Art: Japan and the West*, ed. Chisaburō Yamada (Tokyo: Kodansha International, 1976), 298.

7. Bashō's haiku reads *shizukasa ya / iwa ni shimi iru / semi no koe*: "such stillness / piercing the rock / the cicada's cry."

8. "Sho to chūshō kaiga 書と描象絵画" ("Calligraphy and Abstract Painting"), in *The Works of Shiryū Morita, Selected by the Artist* (Kyoto: Bokubi Press, 1970), 120–33. See my partial translation in *Japanese Philosophy: A Sourcebook*, ed. James W. Heisig, Thomas P. Kasulis, and John C. Maraldo (Honolulu: University of Hawai'i Press, 2011), 1201–02.

9. Nishitani, *Religion and Nothingness*,116 ff., 125 ff. Nishitani adapts the formula from the *Diamond Sutra*—"The Buddha is not the Buddha, therefore the Buddha is the Buddha"—from section 8 of Kumārajīva's Chinese version of the *Vajracchedikā Prajñāpāramitā Sūtra*.

10. Morita's formulation here was also most likely influenced by Hisamatsu Shin'ichi (1889–1978), a student (like Nishitani) of Nishida Kitarō, and a calligrapher and Zen teacher acknowledged by Morita as an inspiration for the new direction in calligraphy. See the 1972 interview of Morita by Takemoto Tadao in *Dialogue in Art*, ed. Chisaburō Yamada, 307. In "Calligraphy and Abstract Painting," Morita writes of the brush "blessed as the field from which we gain freedom and become our true [formless] selves." This last expression is clearly an echo of Hisamatsu.

11. For an elaboration on Morita's statement, see John C. Maraldo, "Four Things and Two Practices: Rethinking Heidegger *Ex Oriente Lux*," *Comparative and Continental Philosophy* 4, no.1 (2012): 69–70.

12. Nishitani, "Emptiness and Sameness," 179–80.

13. In his critical examination of the nationalistic context of postwar Japanese and American artists, Bert Winther-Tamaki, for example, credibly connects Morita's "East-versus-West" rhetoric to his "mentors," Hisamatsu Shin'ichi and Ijima Tsutomu. See Winther-Tamaki, *Art in the Encounter of Nations: Japanese and American Artists in the Early Postwar Years* (Honolulu: University of Hawai'i Press, 2001), 87.

14. My selection of three artists to show this possibility, among numerous other artists associated with abstract expressionism, is admittedly arbitrary. I would, however, include both artists undeniably influenced by Japanese calligraphic art and some not at all influenced by it.

15. From the interview with Morita, in *Dialogue in Art*, ed. Chisaburō Yamada, 310.

16. *Ba* 場 is the term translated as *field* in Nishitani's *Religion and Nothingness*, and differs slightly in connotation from Nishida Kitarō's famous notion of *basho* 場所, frequently translated as *place*.

17. From the interview with Morita in *Dialogue in Art*, ed. Chisaburō Yamada, 310–11. *Mu* 無 (*wu* in Chinese) refers to the nothingness celebrated in Zen Buddhist philosophy and echoes the famed *kōan* story about the Zen master Zhaozhou Congshen (778–897), who responded "not" or "no" (*mu*) to the question, "Does a dog have Buddha-nature?" Morita's relating of *mu* to *ba* may be an allusion to Nishida Kitarō's concept of *mu no basho* 無の場所, the place of nothingness.

18. Winther-Tamaki offers another quotation as evidence of Morita's cultural nationalism: "The West and Japan take completely different attitudes toward the sign, whether motif or word. The former deals with it as object, we by becoming the sigh itself as subject" (87).

19. Gorden Washburn, "Japanese Influences on Contemporary Art: A Dissenting View," in *Dialogue in Art*, ed. Chisaburō Yamada, 208–09.

20. Ibid., 208.

21. Winther-Tamaki, 58.

22. Cited in Winther-Tamaki, 60. The author takes the quotation of Kline from Katherine Kuh, *The Artist's Voice: Talks with Seventeen Artists* (New York: Harper and Row, 1962), 144. Contrary to the last point Kline makes in this statement, in fact he often painted forms on unpainted backgrounds, as in untitled works of 1947 and 1955.

23. Ibid.

24. See Dorr Bothwell and Marlys Mayfield, *Notan: The Dark-Light Principle of Design* (New York: Dover Publications, 1968), 78.

25. Kline is only one artist associated with abstract expressionism for whom these points hold. Consider Robert Motherwell's painting *Calligraphy* (1965–1966) or Pierre Soulanges's various versions of *Peinture sur papier* (1948–1950) and *Peinture* (1970).

26. Takemoto Tadao's 1971 interview with Tobey in *Dialogue in Art*, ed. Chisaburō Yamada, 303–04.

27. The various references to this sojourn (see, for example, Winther-Tamaki, 47) do not allow me to tell whether he actually stayed in a training monastery, a *senmon dōjō*, which would have been highly unusual for a foreigner at that time, or rather resided in a neighborhood Zen temple.

28. Takemoto Tadao's 1971 interview with Tobey in *Dialogue in Art*, ed. Chisaburō Yamada, 304–05.

29. Ibid.

30. Sheldon Nodelman, *The Rothko Chapel Paintings: Origins, Structure, Meaning* (Austin, TX: University of Texas Press, 1997), 164.

31. In 1943, Rothko and two other artists, Barnett Newman and Adolf Gottlieb, wrote to the *New York Times*: "It is a widely accepted notion among painters that it does not matter what one paints, as long as it is well painted. This is the essence of academicism. There is no such thing as a good painting about nothing. We assert that the subject is crucial and only that subject matter is valid which is tragic and time-less. That is why we profess a spiritual kinship with primitive and archaic art." "Mark Rothko: Myths and Symbols," National Gallery of Art, Washington, DC, accessed June 22, 2015, http://www.nga.gov/feature/rothko/myths2.shtm.

32. Quoted statements from Mark Rothko, *The Tiger's Eye*, no. 9 (October 1949), 114; cited in Nodelman, 304–05; my emphasis. In 1952, Rothko repeated, "The pro-gression of a painter's work, as it travels in time from point to point, will be toward clarity; toward the elimination of all obstacles between the painter and the idea, and the idea and the observer. As examples of such obstacles, I give (among others) mem-ory, history, or geometry, which are swamps of generalizations from which one might pull our parodies of ideas (which are ghosts) but never an idea itself. To achieve this clarity is, inevitably, to be understood." Cited in Susan J. Barnes, *The Rothko Chapel: An Act of Faith* (Houston, TX: Menil Foundation, 1989), 22.

33. Quotation from Selden Rodman, *Conversations with Artists* (New York: Devin-Adair, 1957), 8; cited in Barnes, 22.

Chapter 24

On Not Disturbing Still Water

Ozu Yasujirō and the Technical-Aesthetic Product

Jason M. Wirth

In a well-known and often analyzed passage from Heidegger's "Aus einem Gespräch von der Sprache zwischen einem Japaner und einem Fragenden,"[1] the inquirer tells his Japanese interlocutor that the "blinding confusion [*die Verblendung*]" is "growing" to such an extent that "one is no longer able to see how the Europeanization of the human and the earth is dissipating everything essential at its source" (*US*, 104). In one sense, this is a powerful indictment of globalization that now appears all the more prophetic. The Japanese interlocutor indirectly agrees by supplying what he deems to be a "fitting" example, namely, the film *Rashōmon* (1950), which first brought Akira Kurosawa to international attention, winning both the Academy Award for Best Picture and the Grand Prix at the Venice International Film Festival. The inquirer is puzzled and surprised. Did not *Rashōmon* introduce something distinctively Japanese about the film aesthetic? He had thought that the film allowed him to "experience the captivation of the Japanese world that led one to the enigmatic" (*US*, 104). The Japanese interlocutor disagrees on behalf of all Japanese, claiming that some of its scenes were too "realistic." The inquirer is quite sympathetic: such reliance upon the real is caught up in a decisive Occidental preference for the ideal over and against the real as the sensuous. The Japanese interlocutor, however, reveals that he is ultimately trying to make a more sweeping point: it is film as such that distorts the Japanese aesthetic, "that the overall Japanese world is imprisoned in the object-oriented character [*das Gegenständliche*] of photography and is specifically posited in its terms" (*US*, 105). The inquirer is quick to agree: "The East Asian world and the technical-aesthetic product of the film industry are not compatible with each other" (*US*, 105).

In a sense, the Japanese interlocutor is insisting that (a) film is just another form of photography; (b) as such, it is inherently objectifying; and (c) the

idea of a Japanese film is decisively oxymoronic: either there is the nonobjectifying Japanese aesthetic tradition or there is photographic image, moving
or otherwise, that captures ("imprisons") the world in the form of an object.
Although I do not mean to belittle the discussion between the inquirer and his
Japanese interlocutor, I will now seek to take film more seriously and in such
a way that I do not *ipso facto* consign some of the great Japanese cinematic
achievements to the prison of "the object-oriented character of photography."
Although one could make the same case by looking at photography more
carefully, I will make some modest gestures in this direction by turning to
the late work of Ozu Yasujirō, whose films did not come to the attention of
Western audiences as early or as dramatically as those of Kurosawa. I do so
to contest the claim that cinema as such is incompatible with the more rari-
fied Zen and Shinto values that one finds, as does the Japanese interlocutor,
in Nō drama (*US*, 106). This is not because one finds in Ozu's cinema the
superficial stylization of traditional Japanese gestures, Zen or otherwise. It
is because Ozu in practice attempted to rethink the possibilities of cinema
beyond their technological degradation into "the object-oriented character of
photography." Playing on the meaning of Dōgen's *Shōbōgenzō* (*Treasury of
the True Dharma Eye*), I would like to suggest that Ozu shows us a way to
open *the true cinematic eye* and, in so doing, displays not Zen themes and
Zen references—such gestures would only be set pieces—but rather a Zen
cinematic sensibility.[2]

Rather than engaging in a wide-ranging survey of Ozu's filmography,
I will concentrate primarily on his 1953 masterpiece *Tōkyō Monogatari*,[3]
which came out three years after *Rashōmon*. I will frame my discussion first
around a remarkable discussion of Ozu in Gilles Deleuze's *Cinema 2: The
Time-Image*. In a decisive passage, Deleuze argues that Ozu (unlike either
Kurosawa or Mizoguchi) is a master of the time-image (*l'image-temps*) and,
as such, a cinematic thinker of time from a Zen perspective. "Time is the
full, that is, the unalterable form filled by change. Time is 'the visual reserve
of events in their appropriateness,'"[4] an explicit allusion to the *Shōbōgenzō*.

Although there are some visual references to the Buddhist world (statues,
a temple) in *Tōkyō Monogatari*, there are no explicit references to Zen. Some
of the early establishing shots at the home of the aging married couple Shukichi and Tomi, who live in the relatively remote small city of Onomichi
(in the western part of Honshu island between Hiroshima to the West and
Okayama to the East), feature the famous Jōdō-ji as a backdrop. (Jōdō-ji is
neither a Jōdō Shin temple, as the name errantly implies, nor a Zen temple,
but rather a Shingon temple.) Prince Shōtoku (574–622), the almost mythic
founder of Japanese Buddhism and associated with the famous Hōryū-ji in
Nara, is reputed to be responsible for this temple, putting it, at least in the
cultural imagination, at the promising dawn of Japanese Buddha Dharma.

This symbolic birth temple of Buddha Dharma also hosts the funeral for Tomi at the end of the film, somehow connecting birth and death, what Dōgen, following the Buddha, called 'life's great matters.' It may also be worth remembering that Onomichi, touted by tourist councils in somewhat kitschy terms as 'Japan's hometown,' is in Hiroshima-ken, not far from the provincial capital that was obliterated eight years before the appearance of Ozu's film.

Without explicit references to Zen, what makes this a Zen film? It is certainly not a programmatic and nostalgic application of Zen culture and that may be a good thing. In contemporary Japan, Zen is chiefly associated with the funeral business (the Sōtō School reports that eighty percent of lay people visit Sōtō temples only for matters related to the funeral ceremony while less than twenty percent do so for reasons related to practice).[5] Funerals may be a good source of revenue for a temple, but it is hard to imagine that Dōgen would have championed such Dharma-commerce. In fact, the overwhelming majority of Zen students in Japan are the first-born sons of temple heads, training not to open the true Dharma eye but rather to inherit their father's temple. This is another marked contrast with Dōgen, who sternly insisted that those who speak of Zen as a school (*shu*) of any kind are devils: "Those who groundlessly refer to themselves in this way are demons who violate the Buddha way, enemies who are not welcomed by Buddhas and ancestors" (*Butsudō*, S, 502). No school, no culture, no language, no gender, no sutra, and no artwork has a monopoly on the Dharma. One can belong to a Zen school, practice lots of Zazen, and perform countless funerals, but in the end, it may only be true that one is just going through the motions because that was one's job. It is ironic, given his repudiation of the very idea of a Zen school, his complete dismissal of temple politics, and his radical critique of Japanese Buddhist culture (including the wretched treatment of women), that Dōgen is still considered, along with Keizan, to be one of the two patriarchs of Sōtō Zen. In fact, William M. Bodiford has shown that the Dōgen "hagiography" is a relatively recent, largely fabricated, and highly politicized campaign in Eihei-ji's rivalry with the competing head temple Sōji-ji.[6] The same worry could be extended to the degeneration of practice into the many various "schools" of practice (Zen or otherwise).

What makes *Tōkyō Monogatari* a Zen film invites us not only to rethink what we mean by 'Zen' but also to reconsider the possibilities of cinema as such. What is cinema? Of what powers is it capable? What is the Zen manner of cinema (as opposed to "the object-oriented character of photography")? In order to honor this question, we will follow Deleuze when he argues that this consideration means that we must also ask again, "What is philosophy?"—"Cinema itself is a new practice of images and signs, whose theory philosophy must produce as conceptual practice" (*C2*, 280). Certain works of cinema challenge us not to routinely draw from the stockpile of philosophical materials, but also to be productive and creative so that we can rise up to the philosophical demands of cinema. In such a practice, however, we are not once again subjugating the image to the priority of the concept, but rather using philosophy creatively to allow cinema to speak on its own terms. Ozu's cinema is not philosophy by other means. The autonomy of cinema, its attempts to do what only cinema can do, demands that thinking with images not be confused with conceptual analysis. Nonetheless, these are examples of films that ask philosophy to reconsider its traditional tasks and to enter into philosophical relationship with them, producing neither a philosophy of film nor film as philosophy, but rather a new hybrid relationship between the two. As such, in our own way, we find ourselves in the end taking up Heidegger's demand, beyond his own quaint conclusions about cinema, that we create space in language for what otherwise remains inaudible in the reduction of cinema to part of the ongoing globalization and "Europeanization of the human and the earth."

One must also concede that David Bordwell is right to insist on certain problems of speaking of Ozu in terms of Japanese aesthetics or Zen aesthetics (as the film critic turned director Paul Schrader does so effusively): "To speak of 'Japanese aesthetics' itself is to suggest that the tradition is more homogeneous than it is."[7] The Zen in Ozu is not necessarily based on any conceptual understanding of Zen or a commitment to any particular canonical practices. This should give us some pause in affirming Donald Richie's insistence, in his pioneering study *Ozu: His Life and Films*,[8] that Ozu "is the man whom his kinsmen consider the most Japanese of all film directors" (*O*, 1) and that Ozu had "the real Japanese flavor" (*O*, xi). Although this has now become a cliché, it does reflect that Ozu's films were not originally considered commercially suitable for Western import (*Tōkyō Monogatari* did not have its US premiere until 1972, almost twenty years after the film was made). Richie finds the key to Ozu's cinema in its pervading mood of *mono no aware*, the pathos of things, already mentioned fourteen times in the Heian-period *Genji Monogatari* (*O*, 52).

Although I sympathize with Bordwell's caveats about how this mood was largely reinvented by the eighteenth-century literary theorist Norinaga Motoori (1730–1801) as a selective and "nostalgic concept, shot through with a sense of loss" for the vanishing moral purity of the ways of yore (*OPC*, 28), Ozu films are poignant without being nostalgic, and even the inevitable family conflicts that characterize his films are not pleas for a return to the good old ways. Ozu's world is chaotic and the pain of dissolution is no more or no less meaningful than the joy of reconciliation or the discussion at the beginning of *Tōkyō Monogatari* between Shukichi and Tomi about the location of the air pillows that Shukichi forgot that he had already packed in his own suitcase. Richie tells us that *mono no aware* denotes "a serene acceptance of a transient world, a gentle pleasure found in mundane pursuits soon to vanish, a content created by the knowledge that one is with the world and that leaving it is, after all, in the natural state of things" (*O*, 52). I would defend Richie in one sense, namely, that for all of its limitations, gross overgeneralizations, and clichés, *mono no aware* has the virtue of sensitizing one to the temporality of Ozu's cinema. That being said, this may not be an entirely convincing articulation of the power of time in Ozu's cinematic eye. The wistful attunement to the vicissitudes of things risks reducing the problem of time to the problem of finitude, that is, birth and death as the "natural state of things."

In *Shōji* (*Birth and Death*), Dōgen tells us that birth and death (*saṃsāra*) are indeed the great matters, but "[t]here is nothing such as birth and death to be avoided; there is nothing such as nirvana to be sought ... . It is a mistake to suppose that birth turns into death. Birth is a phase that is an entire period in itself" (*S*, 884–85). This is not the plaintive mood of finitude and the consequent appreciation for the things occasioned by an awakening to their ephemerality. (Such is Keizo's realization when he confesses that "[n]o one can serve his parents beyond the grave" or Shige's complaint that "life is too short," but such is not the standpoint of Ozu's cinematic eye.) The "cherish-things-because-they-are short-lived" explanation assumes that things (*mono*) are entities and that, as such, they come, endure through time (whether too long or too short), and depart. From the perspective of time itself, however, there is no time that is not appropriate, no time that is too short or too long. Dōgen's famous fascicle *Uji* (*The Time Being*) counsels us to "see each thing in this entire world as a moment of time" (*S*, 105) and to "actualize all time as all being; there is nothing extra" (*S*, 107). Each thing is not a being *in* time, but rather time expresses being and being expresses time (in the sense of *dōtoku* 道得, to express the way of things without capturing it in language). There *is* no time in itself—it presents being but in itself it is not a being. Not only is there no being called 'time,' but time also prevents being from being itself all by itself. The illusion of being in itself is the illusion of *svabhāva* or "own-being" or "self-being" that Nāgārjuna and many of the Mahāyāna tradition's greatest teachers constantly exposed. Or as Deleuze says profoundly of Ozu: time is "the unchanging form in which the change is produced" (*C2*, 17; *C2F*, 27).

Of course, one might immediately protest, as some have, that Ozu explicitly dismissed any Zen reading of his films (see *O*, 256; *OPC*, 27). Although one does not have to be explicitly Zen (i.e., subscribe to some alleged Zen values and doctrines) to have a Zen sensibility, one does not even necessarily have to know that one's sensibility is Zen in order for it to be in some way Zen. Nonetheless, Kathe Geist gives us a fuller look at the comment in question: "They [foreign critics] cannot understand the life of salaried men, impermanence [*mujō*], and the atmosphere outside the story at all. That's

why they say it is Zen."[9] Geist identifies the irony in making reference to
mujō while dismissing Zen. *Mujō* speaks to the emptiness (*śūnyatā*) or lack of
intrinsic being in all things. Logically, Ozu is neither confirming nor denying
his work's Zen sensibility, but at the very least, he is saying that those who
attribute a Zen explanation to his films do so because they are clueless about
both his films and Zen. Certainly, *Tōkyō Monogatari* is not an exercise in
applied Zen, an illustration of Zen concepts, or the reactionary deployment of
traditional Zen artifacts. If this is a Zen film, it is so not because of its cultural
allusions or didactic intentions, but because with his lens Ozu tries to open
the true Dharma eye, much in the way that, holding up a flower, the Buddha
blinked and Mahākāśyapa smiled. The Buddha responded, "I possess the true
Dharma eye, the marvelous mind of Nirvana, the true form of the formless,
the subtle dharma gate that does not rest on words or letters but is a special
transmission outside of the scriptures. This I entrust to Mahākāśyapa."[10]
Ozu's cinematic eye, his very manner of seeing, is a Dharma eye.

Deleuze argues that Ozu produces images of time when "the action image
disappears in favor of the purely visual image of what a character *is*, and
the sound image of what he *says*, completely banal nature and conserva-
tion constituting the essentials of the script" (*C2*, 13–14; *C2F*, 23). Banality is not the place as it was, for example, in Kurosawa's *Ikiru* (1952), out
of which the decisive and dramatic action suddenly emerges. In *Ikiru*, the
banality of bureaucratic life is interrupted when Watanabe Kanji (Shimura
Takashi) is diagnosed with stomach cancer. This in turn produces a long,
brooding crisis—How will I live my final days under the shadow of my fast
encroaching death?—until the double paralysis (the dull, purposeless life
of a bureaucrat and the *aporia* that the sudden presence of the proximity of
death induces) is suddenly and decisively broken by Watanabe's decision to
build a playground, despite the overwhelmingly adversarial bureaucracy of
his own department.[11] Even during the long, often pompous and self-serving,
mostly sake-driven, speeches by Watanabe's colleagues at his funeral, the
self-deception that we saw to such dramatic effect in *Rashōmon* maintains its
inertia. Only Watanabe awoke to his death, albeit while his lips were barely
red, but his death serves as a *memento mori* challenging our own paralysis
and refuge in banality. As Deleuze said of Kurosawa more generally, "One
must tear from a situation the question which it contains, discover the givens of the secret question which alone permits a response to it and without
which even the action would not be a response."[12] Watanabe acted decisively,
activated by the dawning disclosure of the question, a question that does not
emerge enough for most of the mourners to puncture the banality of their
self-indulgent funeral speeches.

The situation is much different with Ozu, where "everything is ordinary
or banal, even death and the dead who are the object of a natural forgetting"

(*C2*, 14), something "close to a kind of Zen wisdom" where "nothing is remarkable or exceptional in life" (*C2*, 14)—"everything is ordinary and regular, everything is everyday [*tout est quotidian*]" (*C2*, 15; *C2F*, 25). There is, therefore, no "breathing space or encompasser to contain a profound question, as in Kurosawa" (*C2*, 15; *C2F*, 26). As a kind of intellectual experiment, we could imagine that Ozu's signature low angle, stationary shots (the famous "tatami" perspective, that is, the immobile view from the floor) are also the point of view of a person doing Zazen. In the latter, one is neither moving the body nor judging with the mind. Whether Ozu intended this or not is beside the point. From the stationary view from below as it gazes upon the noise and chaos of the quotidian, the lens presents itself as the opening of the true Dharma eye. It becomes like a mirror that in Mahāyāna famously does not discriminate in what it reflects, but receives all images equally. In receiving images without judgment, they are also received in the immensity of their original ambiguity.

Do we say that Ozu's films have many meanings or open meanings and that this produces the ambiguity that opens the space for the projection of personal interpretations? In a way I do not want to deny this, but this is only trivially true. *Mu* (無), for example, is not in itself meaningful; it is not an idea. It is the great sea out of which we make the tofu again and again. The *mu* that is the simple epitaph on Ozu's gravestone does not express a theory about either life or death. It is not a final statement of Ozu's artistic philosophy; rather, even death, which we believe is the most meaningful, albeit ultimate thing that will ever happen to us, is here no longer especially meaningful.[13] What haunts the concept of *mu* is *mu* itself as it haunts the concept as such by invoking the emptiness of its field, the sea out of which it emerged as a drop. That nothing is special means also that everything is special, although nothing is especially special. This is not because of some existentialist void, the disappointing whimper of a mere lack. If everything is special, then everything is worthy of cherishment—beyond high and low—and the great sea, already haunting the mirror of the camera lens itself, becomes the infinite compassion of Kannon with a thousand arms.

Zen Master Ummon famously counseled that "every day is a good day." Time is not divided up into a hierarchy of the high and the low, the good and the bad. The Buddha himself warned that "beliefs" are the origins of war. Deleuze, for his part, makes this kind of point when he borrows an interesting argument from Leibniz (who had an abiding interest in China):

> The world is made up of series which are composed and which converge in a very regular way, according to ordinary laws. However, the series and sequences are apparent to us only in small sections, and in disrupted or mixed-up order, so that we believe in breaks, disparities and discrepancies as in things that are out of the ordinary. (*C2*, 14; *C2F*, 24)

Everything happens in its time and, as such, in its *justesse* (how it happens
is how it should happen, how it is appropriate for it to happen), but since
we inevitably do not see events in their *justesse*, we confuse our lives and
exacerbate our pain. This is what the historical Buddha called the 'second
dart,' namely, the supplemental mental pain that physical pain causes us. We
think about our pain in the terms that pain sets for us and hence think painful thoughts about our pain. While there is no cure for the first dart, that is,
no cure for sickness, old age, and death, one can cultivate oneself so that the
attachment, aversions, and delusions that govern the second dart are pacified
(*EBD*, 91): "This is Ozu's thinking: life is simple, and man never stops com-
plicating it by 'disturbing still water'" (*C2*, 15; *C2F*, 25).

Strikingly, Deleuze explicitly connects this sensibility with Dōgen. There
is a small but critical typo in the English translation of *Cinema 2*. In the early
discussion of Ozu's cinema as paradigmatic of the time-image, footnote 30
incorrectly cites Dōgen while footnote 31 cites Antonioni, making it appear
as if the latter were suddenly making Zen pronouncements. The footnotes are
obviously off by one, something discernible even by considering the context
of Deleuze's analysis as it appears in the English translation. The correct reference to Dōgen refers to the following, quite remarkable passage:

> Time is the full, that is, the unalterable form filled by change. Time is "the visual
> reserve of events in their appropriateness." [*Le temps, c'est le plein, c'est-à-
> dire la form inalterable remplie par le changement. Le temps, c'est "la réserve
> visuelle des événements dans leur justesse."*] (*C2*, 17; *C2F*, 28)

Deleuze is not here referring to an actual line or passage by Dōgen, but
rather to the 1980 French translation of the Japanese title of Dōgen's *magnum opus*, *Shōbōgenzō*, of which the translators, Ryōji Nakamura and René
de Ceccatty,[14] made a small selection and provided philosophically expan-
sive (albeit controversial) translation choices. Their translation of the word
Shōbōgenzō is quite unusual and merits examination. The kanji 正 (*shō*) is
typically read 'right or true' but is here being read as *dans leur justesse*, that
is, 'in a fitting matter, in their appropriateness, suitability, propriety, or aptness.' Most strikingly,法 (*bō* or *hō*), which is the kanji for 'Dharma,' is read
as *les événements*, that is, 'the events, happenings, or occurrences,' although
such language should not automatically be ceded to Heidegger's *das Ereignis*. 眼 (*gen*) is the kanji for 'eye' and 蔵 (*zō*) is the kanji for 'treasury' or
réserve. Typically, one speaks of the eye as a true eye (as when it becomes
a Dharma eye and when one plucks out Bodhidharma's eyeball and makes it
one's own), but here the translators associate the eye with the treasury itself
(*la réserve visuelle*) and the true as the propriety of events, that is, things not
understood as entities but rather as occurrences of Buddha nature (Japanese:

busshō; Sanskrit: *tathāgatagarbha* and *Buddha-dhātu*), with no intrinsic natures, but in each occurrence proper and apt. The translators strictly demarcate their use of *l'événement* as a translation of *hō* (法), 'Dharma,' from Heidegger's *Ereignis*:

> *Hō* does not concern either being or presence … *hō* is a synchronic plane where events interlace, cling, and go 'on peregrination.' The proper is only the 'proper of the Buddhist event.' Every rapprochement with the texts that Heidegger devoted to the event (… the donation of the present is the proper of the event [*la donation du présent est le propre de l'événement*], *Die Gabe von Anwesen ist Eigentum des Ereignens*) is excessive. (*RVE*, 133)

From the standpoint of the Dharma, each event is as it should be. Contrary to the American director Paul Schrader's emphasis on the issue of a kind of Zen transcendence in Ozu's cinema ("a hierarchy from the Other-oriented to the human-oriented"[15]), Deleuze insists that there is "no need at all to call on a transcendence" (*C2*, 17; *C2F*, 28). Or if we insist on the language of alterity, otherness, and the transcendence of the nonhuman—for the Dharma is not found in the seeming obviousness of the quotidian world (what Mahāyāna called 'the dust of the *sahāloka* or *sahā* world,' the world of projections, discriminations, hierarchies, etc.)—then we would have to take more seriously how the Japanese director Yoshida Kiju understands the problem apropos of *Tōkyō Monogatari*:

> However, it is noteworthy that a phrase like "the view from the sacred other side" does not necessarily contain religious meaning. It is unclear whether Ozu-san believed in life after death. It is most convincing to think that he did not. In any case, as long as all human beings die in the end, it is simply word play to distinguish the world before and after death, calling them this side and the other side. We should only use these terms in order to enrich our ways of expression and communication. We can also talk about them more freely without any religious connotations.[16]

The other side is the perspective of absolute death on human events. In this respect, Yoshida sees the other side haunting the funeral scene: "Since Ozu-san refused to regard human deaths as sacred, this scene became unforgettable" (*OA*, 110). Yoshida speaks of the film as a "revelation" of "silence" that "drives" the audience "to silence" (*OA*, 88), a silence in which the other side is the haunting presence of the dead, "a chaotic world of human beings … filled with the gazes of the dead," which are the "only measures that human beings are given for the order of the world" (*OA*, 117). The images of our *sahā* world are brought into stark relief by the plane of immanence that is the absolute time of death, haunting everything, high and low, cherished and hated, wise and stupid. It is the time of the absolutely ordinary, vast emptiness with nothing sacred.

For Deleuze, Ozu's "everyday banality" is the opposite of the everyday experience of the everyday, the quotidian perspective on the quotidian. Sensory-motor relations, the pervasive habits of feeling, seeing, and thinking through which the quotidian appears as unimportant and upon which "movement-images" are able to work, "tend to disappear in favor of pure-optical situations, but these reveal connections of a new type, which are no longer sensory-motor and which bring the emancipated senses into direct relation [*un rapport direct*] with time and thought" (*C2*, 17; *C2F*, 28). This is Ozu's achievement: "to make time and thought perceptible, to make them visible and of sound" (*C2*, 18; *C2F*, 28). As Yoshida observes, regarding the opening and closing scenes of Onomichi overlooking the Inland Sea: "The two [scenes] look exactly the same, but their resemblance quietly indicates the sorrow of the passing time. It means that we can never retrieve time once it is gone" (*OA*, 88). The seeming similarity between the two shots serves to present the underlying absolute difference upon which the sensory-motor illusion of sameness operates. There is only the singularity of each moment.

This is at the heart of Deleuze's celebration of Ozu. "[O]psigns, empty or disconnected spaces, open on to still lifes as the pure form of time. Instead of 'motor situation—indirect representation of time,' we have 'opsign or sonsign—direct presentation of time'" (*C2*, 273; *C2F*, 357). Time is not *represented*, as it is in the motor situation, playing off our habitual and unthinking perceptions, but rather time as such *presents* itself because the images of the ordinary are no longer habitually ordinary and taken for granted. They are not repetitions of the same, but rather repetitions as the play of the pure difference of time itself. As in a sensory-motor cinematic narrative, we do not have periods of exposition that contextualize what will emerge as the important sequences (the so-called "money shots"). There is no expression of time that is more time or less time than any other expression of time. Hence, we have Tomi's death, Kyōko and Noriko's agreement that life is disappointing, Shukichi and Tomi's poignant estimation that their busy and annoyed children are nonetheless "certainly better than average," given equal weight with "the establishment of any dialogue whatever, apparently without a precise subject-matter" (*C2*, 14; *C2F*, 23).

We can see this detachment—not an indifference, but compassion without judgment for the whole folly of the human bungling of time—in the sequence in Atami where Shukichi and Tomi have been banished by their preoccupied children. First we see the great sea itself (with Hatsushima in the distance) and then a sequence of shots of their sleepless night while revelers drunkenly play mahjong and eat sushi. The bright moments after dawn find the couple on the Atami seawall (Figure 24.1), anticipating Shukichi's dawn viewing in the hours after Tomi's death, a repetition that presents repetition itself as the operation of difference or what Bordwell has called the 'parametric.' Repetition is not the representation of a coincidence. The couple against the backdrop of the great sea is then punctuated by a pair of maids gossiping about the status of the newlyweds whose mess they are cleaning. Shukichi and Tomi decide to return home, but as they stand up, Tomi is dizzy, presaging her imminent death. This is all against the backdrop of the great silent sea, reminiscent of the Buddha Sea that receives all streams equally, embracing beauty and ugliness, life and death, the important and the trivial. Again, this is not to say that the infinite nonentitative singularities that express the Buddha Sea are all sacrificed in a dark night where all Buddhas are black. The excessive concern with emptiness is the nihilistic and pernicious Zen *śūnyatā*-sickness (Japanese: *kūbyō*), as if one were evacuating the concrete and making some kind of headlong descent into pure—that is, merely abstract—emptiness. Ozu presents the nonseparation of form and emptiness, not the nihilistic and reactive emptying out of all forms.

We can also see the juxtaposition of the habitually dramatic (death) with the habitually banal (the seemingly unimportant activities that comprise most of our lives) in the sequences before, during, and after Tomi's death.

Figure 24.1 Shukichi and Tomi on the Seawall in Atami. *Tōkyō Monogatari* 東京物語. Directed by Ozu Yasujirō 小津安二郎. Shōchiku, 1953. Film.

For example, when Koichi learns that Tomi is seriously ill, he walks to the door and, in a scene that is not in the original script, bends down and whistles, as if to call a dog.[17] At the funeral, the priests slowly chant the *Daihishin Dharani*, a phonetic Japanese approximation of a Chinese transliteration of a Sanskrit or Pāli text whose meaning would not have been evident to anyone chanting it or to anyone at the funeral. The commercial ships still ply their way by Onomichi. Moths still flutter about incandescent bulbs. Despite Tomi's impending death, no one ever forgets to make sure that the mosquito coil is lit. Shukichi addresses the comatose Tomi, reassuring her that her children are coming to see her, but Ryū Chishū's performance and the screenplay indicate the obvious: "With these words he is really reassuring himself" (*TSS*, 228). What are the right words to address death when death itself stares back at us as an emptiness commanded or captured by no word?

Contrary to the worry about the prison of the "object-oriented character of photography," Ozu presents all images as visual and audio signs of death-time. In a scene not in the original script, Keizo apologizes to his dead mother for not being on time; Shige laments that "life is too short," as if either sibling could ever catch up with time. When would life be long enough? In the film's final exchange, a differential *repetition* of one of the film's opening exchanges, Shukichi tells his neighbor that Tomi "was a headstrong woman, but if I knew things would come to this, I would have been kinder to her when she was alive." Although we inevitably disturb the still waters of time—the pith of human affairs—Ozu's lens responds with a compassionate distance, as if it were the watch that joins Noriko with the absolute time of the dead, reminding us of one of the Buddha's own death words: "If you want to be free from suffering, you should contemplate knowing how much is enough" (*Haichi Dainin Gaku, S*, 772).

NOTES

1. Martin Heidegger, *Unterwegs zur Sprache* (Pfullingen: Neske, 1959). Henceforth cited as *US*. All translations from this work are my own responsibility.

2. I have generally relied on the recent edition of the *Shōbōgenzō—Treasury of the True Dharma Eye: Zen Master Dogen's Shobo Genzo*, ed. Kazuaki Tanahashi, trans. Robert Aitken et al. (Boston: Shambhala, 2013). Henceforth cited as *S*.

3. A translation by Donald Richie and Eric Klestadt of the original screenplay, written by Ozu Yasujirō and his screenwriter Kōgo Noda, can be found in *Contemporary Japanese Literature: An Anthology of Fiction, Film, and Other Writing Since 1945*, ed. Howard Hibbett (New York: Alfred A. Knopf, 1977), 190–237. Henceforth cited as *TSS*.

4. Gilles Deleuze, *Cinema 2: The Time-Image*, trans. Hugh Tomlinson and Robert Galeta (Minneapolis, MN: University of Minnesota Press, 1989), 17. Henceforth

cited as *C2*. Gilles Deleuze, *Cinéma 2: L'image-temps* (Paris: Les Éditions de Minuit, 1985), 28. Henceforth cited as *CF2*.

5. William M. Bodiford, "Zen in the Art of Funerals: Ritual Salvation in Japanese Buddhism," *History of Religions* 32, no. 2 (1992): 150.

6. William M. Bodiford, "Remembering Dōgen: Eiheiji and Dōgen Hagiography," *Journal of Japanese Studies* 32, no. 1 (2006): 1–21.

7. David Bordwell, *Ozu and the Poetics of Cinema* (Princeton, NJ: Princeton University Press, 1988), 27. Henceforth cited as *OPC*.

8. Donald Richie, *Ozu: His Life and Films* (Berkeley, CA: University of California Press, 1974). Henceforth cited as *O*.

9. Kathe Geist, "Buddhism in *Tokyo Story*," in *Ozu's* Tokyo Story, ed. David Desser (Cambridge: Cambridge University Press, 1997), 102. For the sake of consistency with the present chapter, I have emended the quote by replacing 'ephemerality' with 'impermanence' as a translation of *mujō*. Henceforth cited as *BTS*.

10. Quoted in Heinrich Dumoulin, *Zen Buddhism: A History*, vol. 1, *India and China*, trans. James W. Heisig and Paul F. Knitter (New York: Macmillan, 1988), 9.

11. Deleuze understood the question to be: "'What is a man who knows he is allowed only a few more months of life to do?' Everything depends on the givens." See Gilles Deleuze, *Cinema 1: The Movement-Image*, trans. Hugh Tomlinson and Barbara Habberjam (Minneapolis, MN: University of Minnesota Press, 1986), 191.

12. Ibid., 189.

13. Geist reports that Ozu commissioned a calligraphy of *mu* from a Chinese monk during his war service and that he held on to it for the rest of his life and "his tombstone in the [Rinzai] Zen temple Engakuji in Kita-Kamakura bears the single character *mu* as his only epitaph" (*BTS*, 102).

14. Dōgen, *Shōbōgenzō: La réserve visuelle des événements dans leur justesse*, ed. and trans. Nakamura Ryōji and René de Ceccatty (Paris: Éditions de la Difference, 1980). Henceforth cited as *RVE*. Translations from this text are my responsibility.

15. Paul Schrader, *Transcendental Style in Film: Ozu, Bresson, Dreyer* (New York: Da Capo Press, 1988), 6.

16. Yoshida Kiju, *Ozu's Anti-Cinema*, trans. Daisuke Miyao and Kyoko Hirano (Ann Arbor, MI: Center for Japanese Studies, University of Michigan, 2003), 103. Henceforth cited as *OA*.

17. The screenplay simply gives the following cue: "Koichi starts to leave" (*TSS*, 227).

Part VI

THE LEGACY OF KUKI SHŪZŌ

Chapter 25

Finding *Iki*

Iki *and the Floating World*

David Bell

IKI AND THE FLOATING WORLD

The term *iki* was used during the Tokugawa period to describe an elegant sensibility that emerged within the *ukiyo* "floating world" of Edo (today's Tokyo). *Iki* refers to a sense of urbane sophistication demonstrated in provocative relations between the opposite sexes. Kuki Shūzō suggests the closest Western equivalents may be located in the French expressions 'coquette,' 'raffiné,' and, especially, 'chic.' *Iki* exists in opposition to the conventional, boorish (*yabo*), or unrefined (*gehin*).[1] *Iki* suggests concepts like 'stylish,' 'fashionable,' or 'tasteful.' *Iki* finds subtly provocative expression in attitudes of countenance or posture, lightness of bearing, and self-contained urbanity. *Iki* is never loud, showy, or demonstrative. Hiroshi Nara describes *iki* as "urbane, plucky stylishness," characterized by "the ability to resign oneself quickly to inescapable destiny, an embodiment of *iki*, and a type of spiritual tension called *hari*."[2] He finds in *iki* qualities of cool elegance, subtle flirtatiousness, spontaneity, and suggestiveness.

Iki taste and refinement arises within the dualistic tensional relations between men and women, sustained through the maintenance of playful mutual provocation that resists consummation.[3] Kuki described three central and interdependent conditional moments of *iki*. The first was *bitai* or coquetry, the erotic tension generated in this sustained potential of sexual relations. *Bitai* is distinguished by qualities of playfulness, voluptuousness, raciness, and passion that would be lost if sexual congress were achieved.[4] The second moment of *iki* was *ikiji*, a sense of "brave composure."[5] Nishiyama Matsunosuke substitutes *hari*: "strength of character" characterized by "unimpeachable refinement," dignity, smartness, panache, or "affected bravado."[6] The third condition was *akirame*, a sense of urbane resignation.[7]

Nishiyama suggests *akanuke*, unassuming urbanity, or well-disposed indifference to fate.[8]

These three conditions are characterized by a sense of playfulness, "purposeless purpose,"[9] and capricious, lighthearted disinterest that sits in contrapuntal relation to resignation born of a depth of life experience and an awareness of *iki*'s "origin in the 'world of suffering' where 'one's body drifts in the light swirl of things, without floating free.'"[10] Kuki finds the synthesis of *bitai, ikiji*, and *akirame* manifest in the geisha of the Yoshiwara and later Fukagawa entertainment quarters of Edo. He clarifies the relational character of *iki* by positioning it (using a three-dimensional schematic) in tensional relation to other qualities: "refined" (*jōhin*) and "unrefined" (*gehin*); "showy" (*hade*) and "subdued" (*jimi*); "chic" (*iki*) and "conventional" (*yabo*); "sweet" (*anami*) and "astringent" (*shibumi*).[11] *Iki* is distinctly different from, but can be comprehended in its relations to, each of these values. *Iki*'s manifestation in characteristics of behavior and art is reflected in Kuki's arrangement of his analysis into two realms: the "natural" and the "artistic" expressions of *iki*.

Ukiyo, the floating world, describes attitudes and sensibilities informing diverse engagements within the amalgam of entertainments of tearooms and restaurants, poetry and literature (*uta-awase* poetry contests, *sharebon, ukiyo-zōshi*, and *kibyōshi* fiction), gambling, Kabuki theatre, and the licensed pleasure quarters. It might be more subtly appreciated as attitudes characterized by habits of pleasure, hedonism, elegant fashion and comportment, and knowing *tsū* sensibilities and tastes. Its careless indulgence suggests a lighthearted world: a construction that was confirmed in contemporary literary and pictorial representations of its diverse engagements.

The *kanazōshi* publication *Ukiyo monogatari* (*Tales of the Floating World*, ca. 1661) by Asai Ryōi (ca. 1612–1691) captures its ephemeral and evanescent flavor. Ryōi's opening section "On the Floating World" describes the shift from early Buddhist notions of *uki* as "sad" to one of *uki* as "floating" in "the delightful uncertainties of life in a joyous age when people lived for the moment, merrily bobbing up and down on the tides of uncertainty like a gourd in the waves."[12] The narrative follows the protagonist Hyōtarō (*hyō* means "gourd") through his indulgence in the worlds of gambling and sexual pleasures, and his inevitable decline into impoverishment, until finally he renounces the world, taking the name 'Ukiyobō.' The increasingly somber tone pervading the narrative brings the "floating" world of pleasure closer to the Buddhist notion of a world of suffering.[13]

Ryōi's melancholic synthesis of both "sad" and "floating" appreciations of *uki* turns on the *aware* pathos of a thirteenth-century passage by Kamo no Chōmei (1153–1216):

The flow of the river is ceaseless and its water is never the same. The bubbles that float in the pools, now vanishing, now forming, are not of long duration: so in the world are man and his dwellings ... . Which will be the first to go, the master or his dwelling? One might just as well ask this of the dew on the morning glory. Perhaps the dew may fall and the flower remain—remain only to be withered by the morning sun. The flower may fade before the dew evaporates, but though it does not evaporate, it waits not the evening.[14]

Like Ryōi's, Chōmei's lines reflect his retreat from the tragic events of his own world into reclusion and detachment from worldly engagement.

Four interrelating qualities inform *iki* engagements within the floating world. First, *iki* maintained the *knowing urbanity* of *tsū*. *Tsū* meant "knowledgeable person," relating to *daitsū* or "grand connoisseur."\ *Tsū* informed the *furyū* stylishness and refined, literate engagements of floating-world communities. Fujimoto Kizan's (1626–1704) *Shikidō ōkagami* (*The Great Mirror of the Art of Love*, 1678) recorded the ways its specialist knowledge informed the demonstration of taste on which entrée into the Yoshiwara depended—a "true ... Way of Love" founded on behaviors embracing decorous habits of personal appearance and deportment, modesty and propriety, and literary and artistic knowledge.[15]

Second was *resignation*, colored by sad acceptance, at once (for *yūjo* prostitutes at least) the inevitable legacy of the harsh actualities of floating-world life, and a reflection of *iki* and *ukiyo* origins in the Buddhist "world of suffering."[16]

Third, this sense of resignation informed attitudes of disinterested *detachment* generated from the impersonal engagements, harsh indentures, and inevitable transience of floating-world pleasures.

Urbanity, resignation, and detachment lay in relation to a fourth quality of lightness and play (*asobi*) that infused floating-world engagements and their representations in literature, song, and dance. Kuki saw *iki* as an engagement of disinterested amorous play of coquetry: "The purposeless purpose of *iki* will be objectified in the rhythm of the tremor of the lips."[17] It was realized in habits of postural coquetry (sidelong glances, light whimsical smiles), stylish speech, couture (casual suggestions of nudity in glimpses of ankles, wrists, or *décolletage*), or the characteristic lightness of demeanor and conversation of geisha entertainments.[18] Playful *iki* interactions between the sexes, albeit moderated by delicacy, decorum, and "a touch of sadness," maintained the impetus of *iki* relations: "A stylish posture is a light and easy pose that shows coquetry to the other sex while maintaining control and moderation."[19] Outside the pleasure districts, a sense of play informed social pleasures like bathing, theatre, dining, sightseeing, and shopping and informed the conventional means of pictorial depictions of the floating world.[20]

LOCATING *IKI* IN *UKIYO*: FOUR MOMENTS
IN THE FLOATING WORLD

It seems difficult to locate the refined provocations and delicate tensional relations of *iki* sensibilities in the *aragoto* bombast of Kabuki theatre, the vulgarity of popular songs, or the consummation of brothel-quarter pleasures. While *iki* is not realized in theatrical melodrama or physical gratification, it did, however, inform habits and manners of social intercourse in these worlds, as well as the representational forms they adopted in dramatic, literary, or pictorial constructions through which participants learned about and made sense of them.[21] It informed the "generic factuality" of a range of real-world settings—"ordinary pictorial sites" of theatres, restaurants, bathhouses, riverbanks, sake shops, and street scenes.[22] Suggestions of *iki* flavors of urbanity, resignation, and playfulness can be located in the "everydayness" (*nichijō-sei*) of Edokko (literally, "child of Edo") or *chōnin* (townsman) engagements in these generic settings.

Kabuki Expressions of Iki

However demonstrative they seemed on stage, Kabuki performances were constructed in tensional relations reflecting those of *iki*. These developed between *aragoto* "rough stuff" and softer *wagato* acting styles, and between Kabuki's realism and its *kabuku* eccentricity. Stage conventions founded on closely observed gestures and interactions of everyday engagements were translated into stage representations that emphasized the tensional distance between protagonists in frozen *mie* poses that preserved the spatial autonomy of each actor. Kuki offered the example of the relationship between the courtesan Agemaki and the playboy hero Sukeroku in the nineteenth-century play *Sukeroku yukari no Edo zakura* (*Sukeroku: Flower of Edo*).[23] The everyday setting of *Sukeroku* is the Yoshiwara brothel district. Sukeroku is represented as a playful *roué*—the *iki* lightness of his sophisticated, easy refinement, urbane wit, and fashionable demeanor is emphasized through their tensional juxtaposition with his dark alter ego Soga no Goro. Sukeroku is the embodiment of *iki* qualities of *hari* strength of character, *bitai* attraction, and *akanuke* urbanity.[24] His elegance is emphasized by its juxtaposition with the apparently *yabō* slapstick of many of his actions. The tensional dimension of *iki* is most evident in the relation between Sukeroku and Agemaki: between the synthesis of *tsū* confidence, cultivated taste, and playful self-indulgence of Sukeroku's playboy character and the chic delicate beauty, passion, and "brave composure" of Agemaki. The playful passion between Sukeroku and Agemaki is inevitably compromised by their necessary resignation to duty and fate.

These tensional relations of *iki* are generated through playful engagements of the Kabuki medium like the contrapuntal arrangement of figures in *hippari mie* group poses. The chic refinement of *iki* is established in Sukeroku's entrance dance in a melding of dance, music, costume, and gesture that demonstrates the "complexity of this aesthetic as ... an expression of fashionable style" in "displays of fashion and expressions of attitude" reflecting those of contemporary taste.[25] The dance exploits the understated power of *wagoto* "soft-style" movements and gestures to represent the contradictory qualities in Sukeroku's character and mission. They juxtapose his urbane accomplishment and fashionable ease against an inevitable resignation to fate. It is through the contrivance of these relations that *Sukeroku* develops its playfully inventive impetus. That sense of play is developed through the *kabuku* eccentricities of the play's narrative in juxtapositions of slapstick comedy and serious themes, between comic vulgarity and sophisticated stylishness, and in punning ambiguities of plays on words and situations. The rhythmic vitality and interplay of sound and movement in Sukeroku's dance alternates between erotic allure and a darker resignation to fate, investing the dance and the play with sensual provocation and a tempering resignation and pathos.

Literary Expressions of Iki

The word *iki* was used in Meiwa-era (1764–1772) literature to describe floating-world consciousness in elegant comportment, social intercourse, and refined taste.[26] Worldly, often humorous, *gesaku* popular literature like *kibyōshi* (illustrated "yellow covers") provided audiences with short, accessible, often satirical insights into less accessible domains of floating-world engagements. Santō Kyōden (1761–1816) draws prosaic observations of incongruous *ukiyo* juxtapositions of refined urbanity and coarse, *yabō* humor in his 1785 *kibyōshi Edo umare uwaki no kabayaki* (*Playboy, Roasted* à la *Edo*;[27] alternatively, *Spitchcock of an Edokko Lecher*). His narrative follows the experiences of Enjirō, the young, indolent, *yabō* son of a wealthy Edo merchant. Enjirō is a *hankatsū* (phony) would-be playboy who ventures into the brothel quarters to establish a reputation as a great man of the world. Vulgar and clumsy, he lacks the refined manners and taste to facilitate his entrée into this world. His boorish attempts to achieve notoriety and romance inevitably end in embarrassing failure. Kyōden's lively arrangements of text and image construct his passage in the manner of an amusing parody on a young man's folly. Despite its humor, Enjirō's humiliating failure and the work's representation of the empty aspirations of would-be Edo roués have melancholic undertones.

Kyōden constructs diverse insights into the everydayness of the floating world, especially brothel quarter, realities by locating Enjirō's misadventures in recognizable settings. These include *mizuchaya* street refreshment stands, *hikitejaya* teahouses (settings for arranging introductions and preliminary entertainments), *chaya no nikai* (second-floor brothel quarters), the brothel districts of Yoshiwara, Shinagawa, Fukagawa, and Shinjuku, and Kabuki theatres like the Kobikichō playhouse.[28] In the Yoshiwara, Kyōden locates Enjirō's ambitions in real places—Daimon, its main gate, Nakanachō, its main avenue, and real establishments like *Uwakimatsuya* ("Wanton Pines Teahouse"). These views include clear delineations of the requisite accoutrements of their engagements—smoking sets, sake warmers and trays of food, details of bedding and ablutions, candlestands and lamps that indicate nocturnal settings, and insight into practices like moxibustion.

Kyōden depicts real Kabuki stars, including Kōraiya (Matsumoto Kōshirō IV, 1737–1802),[29] and makes oblique references to Ichikawa Monosuke II (1743–1794) and the *onnagata* Segawa Kikunojō III (1715–1810)—both wildly popular during 1780s. He cites real figures from the pleasure quarters, including the great *oiran* Segawa and Utahime, Bokuga (Suzuki Uemon, proprietor of *Ōgiya* or "Fan House"), and Daikokuya the Overseer (personal name 'Sōroku'), who managed arrangements for liaisons.[30] He refers to different ranks of *yūjo*, from *oiran* high-ranking courtesans, through geisha, *odoriko* dancing girls, *jōrō* prostitutes, *jigoku* freelance prostitutes, *shinzō* attendants, and *kamuro* trainees. Kyōden presents geisha, courtesans, or *kamuro* in their finery with Hachijō silk and *shima-chirimen* striped crepe (he mentions the Yoshiwara fabric store *Nakaya*), elaborate *shimada* coiffures, and bared ankles and feet. The avoidance of direct engagement, averted eyes, or mouths covered with fans or sleeves are consistent with the resigned, disinterested detachment of the women of the quarters.

Kyōden's "real" floating world embraces the gambling and careless spendthrift ways of the Edokko denizens whom Enjirō aspires to imitate, the conventionality of extramarital sexual relations, the cheap romanticism and florid allusions of *meriyasu* sentimental ballads, and earthy *yabo* humor—for instance, *mimi no waki ni makuradako,* "you can instantly tell she's a former pro by her pillow-callused ears."[31] References to contemporary literature, theatre, and song draw ambivalent tensions between elegance and vulgarity. Discordant references to famous names like Yuranosuke, the doomed hero of *Kanadehon chūshingura*, allude to attitudes of "brave composure," resilience, and resignation to fate that characterized the real lives of women of the quarters. The sheer futility of Enjirō's pretense reflects the impossible distance between most Edo men and the elevated women of the Yoshiwara.

Allusions to *iki* sensibility inform Kyōden's representation of privileged knowledge and urbane carelessness as conditions of engagement in the quarters. He describes pretenses to fine taste in teahouse and brothel furnishings, screen paintings, lacquerware, bonsai, and gardens, in the accomplishment of refined skills like letter writing, as well as the status of fashionable dress and deportment and the arcane contrivances of brothel-quarter language. Enjirō's adoption of touts and tutors to assume this knowledge sits in ironic juxtaposition to *machi geisha* (town geisha) pretensions to Heian court fashion in the adoption of the elaborate *furisode*, knowledge of the classics (*Genji monogatari, Ise monogatari*, and their great lover heroes Genji and Narihara), and the subtle echo of the cloistered Fujiwara world in his surprised discovery (in fascicle 3) that one might get sunburnt walking out of doors.

Kyōden's narrative is suffused with a singular sense of play. It is generated through the ironic representation of the hopelessness of Enjirō's dream of passing from dilettante to urbane man of action. It is represented, pictorially, in Kyōden's arrangement of the indolent, slightly deformed Enjirō (his *hana-kuta* "squashed-nose" was associated with syphilis)[32] against the refined dress and carriage of *odoriko* geisha like Oen (a "seasoned coquette")[33] or the unfortunate Ukina. Above all, it is present in the representation of floating-world engagements as the location of playful indulgence in pleasures of food and drink, conversational wit, and the provocative relations between the sexes.

Brothel-Quarter Expressions of Iki

However contrived, Kyōden's fiction finds close accord with the actuality of brothel world transactions. Kuki emphasizes that *iki* was necessarily an *experiential* phenomenon, "a '*sense intime*' in the profoundest sense of the word."[34] Kuki emphasizes this "experiential" dimension of *iki* engagement in his explanation of the "natural" expression of *iki*.[35] The brothel districts of Yoshiwara and later Fukagawa provided settings for delicately modulated, witty, and teasing interactions between *tsū* clients and highly refined geisha. *Iki* sensibility is generated in human relations through subtly erotic intonations of voice, in the sidelong, downcast glance, in the delicately modulated balance between provocation and disinterest, or in lightly articulated movement and graceful disposition. As Kuki notes also, brothel settings implied an idealized sense of "distanced intimacy" in intimate views of women "carrying the recollection of recent nudity, and having just casually dressed in a simple bath robe, this pose completes the expression of coquetry and its formal cause."[36]

The tension between provocative display and disinterest was famously evident not in the nocturnal intimacies of the quarters, but in the rare, highly contrived, public displays of their attractions like the *oiran dōchū*. The early evening *oiran dōchū* promenade along Nakanochō to *ageya* destinations took place in the licensed quarters only three times a year in spring, summer, and autumn. A nineteenth-century observer of one of the last *dōchū* recorded the striking beauty of the women, their gorgeous finery, coiffures, elevated black-lacquered *geta*, and the extravagant accompaniment of attendants. It emphasizes the careful solemnity of its carefully choreographed pageant:

> It is difficult to give in words an adequate notion of the extraordinary effect of this procession. The costly and gorgeous clothes of the *yūjo*, silks of marvelous richness, and brocades blazing with scarlet and gold; the exaggerated bow of her *obi* tied in front ... the pyramidal *coiffure*, the face as white as snow, the eyelashes black, the lips vermillion, and even the toe-nails stained pink; the men-servants respectfully holding the tips of her fingers on each side and giving as much heed to every step as an acolyte might give to an aged Pope, her several woman-servants walking solemnly behind; a footman pushing back the crowd and another removing every twig or dead leaf from her path; her slow and painful *hachimonji*; her stony gaze straight before her, half contemptuous and half timid; the dense and silent crowd.[37]

For most, this was as close as they could ever get to a real relationship with the women of the quarters. Its painfully slow progress allowed their eyes to linger admiringly, while the *oiran* remained aloof. *Iki* tension developed between attraction to this alluring display and the disinterested detachment shown by each of the *oiran*:

> The courtesan in procession was not a normal human being: she was a figure on the stage of the Yoshiwara and had to maintain her composure throughout. She ignored all acquaintances, friends, and lovers. Addressed, she did not respond and kept her eyes straight ahead. At most she might smile slightly or nod.[38]

The *oiran dōchū* set the scene for a playful arrangement of attraction and resistance through the tensional relation of desire on the one hand, and the disengaged detachment of *oiran* countenance on the other. The coquettish suggestion of the possibility of a relationship was played out against the impossibility of gratification.[39] The tension was intensified by that sense of *ikiji* brave composure, "which sustains the tensional relationship of coquetry and polishes it."[40] Elegant disposition, light good grace or gravitas, and resigned sadness were inevitable reflections of powerless *yūjo* life in the "the hard and heartless floating world" of the brothel quarters.[41] Plucky (*hari*) composure and necessary resignation to a tangible world of suffering in the lives of women in the quarters echoed the resignation to *kugai,* the "world of suffering" of Buddhist spiritual ideals.

Ukiyo-e *Expressions of* Iki

This sense of composure and lightness of bearing, born of sad resignation to fate, informs the gently playful lightness of the figure compositions by Suzuki Harunobu (1725?–1770). Both his wanly floating, slim-waisted women and his delicately wrought geometries of pattern and color exemplify the "artistic expression" of *iki* more closely than those of later Bunka and Bunsei *bijin-ga*.

Harunobu's *Aki no kaze* (*Autumn Breeze*; Figure 25.1) represents contemporary Edo life on two levels. On one level, it is a commonplace representation

Figure 25.1   Suzuki Harunobu, *Aki no kaze* (*Autumn Breeze*). Ca. 1764. Color woodblock print, 7.5 in. x 10.7 in. Collection of author, Dunedin, New Zealand.

of everyday life: two young women walking on a path, their garments blown about by gusts of an autumn breeze. Harunobu observed real models to inform their movement with a degree of authenticity. On the other level, it is a *bijin-ga* representation of two anonymous young *yūjo* of the brothel quarters. The actuality of the scene is enhanced by its sense of grace and its light, dance-like movement, captured in an intimately witnessed moment of time— a real, public event that Edo audiences would have recognized.⁴²

The ambiguity between everyday and *ukiyo* contexts complements the delicate interplay of the two figures to invest the subject with a sense of *iki* suggestiveness. The coquettish hint of *bitai* potential is enhanced by the loose arrangement of clothing revealing glimpses of bare skin. This sense of provocation is countered by a vertically flowing sequence of spatial ambiguities in the space between their bodies and garments: sleeves and hems surge toward each other at one moment and are blown apart at another. Together with the expressionless, self-absorbed countenance of each woman, these ambiguities invest the composition with a sense of detachment consistent with *akirame* resignation of *iki* relations. The autumnal setting suggested by the *hagi* grass and chilly breeze provokes a sense of *aware*, an awareness of the sadness of things consistent with the fragility of beauty in the inevitable passage of time.

The "natural expression" of *iki* represented here is complemented by formal arrangements of line, color, and pattern consistent with those Kuki articulated as the "artistic expression" of *iki*. The woodblock print *nishiki-e* medium favored the clear, limpid linearity of Harunobu's finely articulated contours and the edges and folds of clothing. This *iki* sensibility of linear design is complemented by the *fūryū* "up-to-date" stylishness of their garments. The close, vertically disposed parallel stripes and complementary *obi* design of the figure at right especially inform that sense of the relational and intricate precision in which Kuki found expression of the "relational quality of coquetry" and qualities of "cool disinterest," "brave composure," and "resignation."⁴³ That cool disinterest is reflected also in the sobriety of Harunobu's color arrangements, in soft, weakly saturated variations of pale tea- and yellow-browns and their juxtaposition against the intense black garment of the figure at left. If the curving arabesques of the figures tend to disrupt the formal geometries of parallel stripes, the quiet delicacy of Harunobu's linear articulations and vertical disposition of their gentle movement emphasize the composition's sense of lightness and its figures' floating, indeterminate occupation of space.

The delicate tensional relations of Harunobu's design, the ambiguous social and sexual identities of his women, and the dance-like suspensions of time invest this composition with a gently playful sense of *iki* coquetry. This sense of *asobi* informed the inventive play of Harunobu's pictorial enterprise: though honed through close observation from life, both figures have been appropriated from earlier works by Ishikawa Toyonobu and Nishikawa Sukenobu,[44] and both were employed elsewhere by Harunobu himself in the regenerative and inventive play informing the development of other pictorial compositions. Harunobu's focus on the spirited world of the pleasure quarters, his playfully articulated interfigural relationship, and the ethereal lightness of bearing of his figures invest the composition with both a sense of grace and a suggestion of the "purposeless purpose" of *iki* play. This synthesis between the playful provocations of his subjects, the formalities of *nishiki-e* design, and the convincing sense of "everydayness" brings Harunobu's compositions as close as any others to a pictorial realization of *iki* in *ukiyo-e*.

CONCLUSION

Early in his thesis, Kuki seems to make a provocative claim, that *iki* manifests a Japanese aesthetic character: "a remarkable self-manifestation of the specific mode of being of Oriental culture, or rather, of the Yamato people."[45] The controversies provoked by this phrasing may lie in a confusion between two claims: that *iki* is the *representative* sensibility of Yamato culture[46] and that *iki* is a *distinctive* phenomenon of Yamato (especially Edo) culture, consistent with earlier *Yamato-e* focus on local genre subjects. *Iki* sensibility may color other instances of sensible and artistic engagements in Japanese settings, in *Yamato-e* and today, but its origins lie securely in experiential sensibilities specific to the *ukiyo* floating world. Certainly, the term was in use in Edo and the crystallization of floating-world refinement in *iki*-style, *iki*-gesture, or *iki*-taste seems to have been well established by the later eighteenth century. The tensional relations of floating-world habits—between elegant, restrained detachment and sexual gratification; between *chōnin* or clumsy *yabō* and urbane, stylish, articulate *daitsū* taste—were all described as everyday actualities in the theatre, popular literature, brothel quarter, and pictorial arts in forms that audiences could accept as valid reflections of real-world experiences.

Suggestions, or reflections, of *iki* experience informed and were constructed in the arts of Kyōden, Harunobu, and their contemporaries in refined syntheses of popular entertainment, document, and *iki* taste. Underpinning these syntheses is a sense of complementary tension (*kinchō*) between apparently incompatible qualities. The success of this tensional synthesis in both "natural" and "artistic" expressions of *iki* lies in the construction of a kind of *simultaneity*, an elusive positioning of "in-the-moment" or "in-between-ness" achieved in the suspended time and motion of compositions like Harunobu's *Aki no kaze*. This condition established a setting in which *bitai* coquetry could stand in intimate relation to disinterest, elegant refinement, or *iki* chic.

Simultaneity was the necessary condition for melding otherwise separate concepts of urbane coquetry, composure, resignation, or disinterest to inform *iki* experience. Without that condition, *iki* consciousness remained insubstantial or elusive.

This quality of simultaneity also forms a condition for the fusion of playful *asobi* and the sad resignation of *ikiji* and *akirame* and early appreciations of *ukiyo* as a world of sadness. This synthesis informs the disinterested play of Kuki's "purposeless purpose" in which both a playfully erotic provocation and a sense of lightly carried acceptance of fate by a "well-formed heart" can be melded in a single gesture, moment, or provocative phrase.[47] For Harunobu and Kyōden as much as for Kuki, situating these multivalent qualities within the everydayness of real, comprehensible, human activities in Edo floating-world settings gave *ukiyo* arts their capacity to generate a playful, albeit poignant, sense of *iki* experience as capable of provoking a sense of delight as it was of making sense of the subtle, complex, and sometimes discordant qualities of the floating-world milieu of Tokugawa-period Japan.

NOTES

1. Kuki Shūzō, *Reflections on Japanese Taste: The Structure of* Iki, trans. John Clark (Sydney: Power Publications, 1997), 53.

2. Hiroshi Nara, ed., *The Structure of Detachment: The Aesthetic Vision of Kuki Shūzō, with a Translation of* Iki no kōzō (Honolulu: University of Hawai'i Press, 2004), 1–2.

3. Kyūbun Tanaka, "Kuki Shūzō and the Phenomenology of *Iki*," in *A History of Modern Japanese Aesthetics*, ed. Michael F. Marra (Honolulu: University of Hawai'i Press, 2001), 318–19.

4. Kuki, *The Structure of* Iki, 37–38.

5. Ibid., 40.

6. Nishiyama Matsunosuke, *Edo Culture: Daily Life and Diversions in Urban Japan, 1600–1868* (Honolulu: University of Hawai'i Press, 1997), 54.

7. Kuki, *The Structure of* Iki, 41.

8. Nishiyama, *Edo Culture*, 54.

9. Kuki, *The Structure of* Iki, 42.

10. Ibid.

11. Ibid., 63–64.

12. Donald Keene, *World within Walls: Japanese Literature of the Pre-Modern Era 1600–1867* (New York: Holt, Rinehart and Winston, 1976), 156.

13. Ibid., 158.

14. Kamo no Chōmei, *Hōjōki* (*An Account of My Hut*), in *Anthology of Japanese Literature: From the Earliest Era to the Mid-Nineteenth Century*, comp. and ed. Donald Keene (Rutland, VT: Charles E. Tuttle Company, 1955), 197–98.

15. Donald Keene, *Landscapes and Portraits: Appreciations of Japanese Culture* (London: Secker and Warburg, 1972), 244.

16. Thorsten Botz-Bornstein, "'Iki,' Style, Trace: Shūzō Kuki and the Spirit of Hermeneutics," *Philosophy East and West* 47, no. 4 (1997): 564.

17. Kuki, *The Structure of* Iki, 77–79.

18. Tanaka, "Phenomenology of *Iki*," 337.

19. Ibid., 338–39.

20. Mary E. Berry, "(Even Radical) Illustration Requires (Normalizing) Convention: The Case of 'Genre Art' in Early Modern Japan," *Journal of Visual Culture* 9, no. 3 (2010): 353.

21. Ibid., 357.

22. Ibid., 356.

23. Kuki, *The Structure of* Iki, 40.

24. Jay Keister, "Urban Style, Sexuality, Resistance, and Refinement in the Japanese Dance *Sukeroku*," *Asian Theatre Journal* 26, no. 2 (2009): 222.

25. Ibid., 215–16.

26. Nara, *The Structure of Detachment*, 1.

27. Adam L. Kern, *Manga from the Floating World: Comicbook Culture and the Kibyōshi of Edo Japan* (Cambridge, MA: Harvard University Asia Center, 2006), 401.

28. Ibid., 408.

29. Ibid.

30. Ibid., 409.

31. Ibid., 363.

32. Ibid., 403.

33. Ibid., 406.

34. Botz-Bornstein, "'Iki,' Style, Trace," 563.

35. Kuki, *The Structure of* Iki, 71–83.

36. Ibid., 75.

37. Joseph Ernest de Becker, *The Nightless City: Or the History of the Yoshiwara Yūkaku* (New York: ICG Muse, 2000), 241–42.

38. Cecilia S. Seigle, *Yoshiwara: The Glittering World of the Japanese Courtesan* (Honolulu: University of Hawai'i Press, 1993), 228.

39. Kuki, *The Structure of* Iki, 38.

40. Tanaka, "Phenomenology of *Iki*," 327.

41. Kuki, *The Structure of* Iki, 41–43.

42. Berry, "'Genre Art' in Early Modern Japan," 347–50.

43. Kuki, *The Structure of* Iki, 87–89.

44. Timothy T. Clark, "*Mitate-e*: Some Thoughts, and a Summary of Recent Writings," *Impressions* 19 (1997): 19–20.

45. Kuki, *The Structure of* Iki, 33.

46. Leslie Pincus, *Authenticating Culture in Imperial Japan: Kuki Shūzō and the Rise of National Aesthetics* (Berkeley, CA: University of California Press, 1996).

47. Kuki, *The Structure of* Iki, 42.

Chapter 26

Iki and Glamour as Aesthetic Properties of Persons

Reflections in a Cross-Cultural Mirror

Carol Steinberg Gould

Iki is a precise, though cryptic, Japanese aesthetic category.[1] It embodies many of the concepts usually associated with Japanese aesthetics, among them those Donald Keene points to in his "Japanese Aesthetics,"[2] that is, "suggestiveness, irregularity, simplicity, and perishability." *Iki* applies both to the interior of persons, as well as to perceivable things. Thus, *iki* is, to put it in Western terms, primarily "an aesthetic property of persons,"[3] a concept I explain in this chapter and elsewhere.[4] Some aesthetic properties of persons have both an authentic and a contrived form. Contrived *iki* involves mimicking the external expressions of *iki*, for example, wearing clothes in colors such as plum and deep blue, a woman arranging her hair so as to show the nape of her neck, and speaking in a mezzo-soprano voice. Authentic *iki* involves making unself-conscious choices that express the *iki* of one's subjectivity. One with authentic *iki* would be chic and unconventional without deliberation.

Glamour is one of the few Western examples of an aesthetic property of persons with both authentic and contrived forms. Just as *iki* reflects principles of the Japanese aesthetic, so too glamour reflects principles of the traditional Western aesthetic. Glamour, however, is a more elastic category than *iki*. For example, its external manifestations are indeterminate, unlike those of *iki*. We cannot predict the colors that a glamorous person would choose, as we can with *iki*. In their authentic forms, both *iki* and glamour involve a rich subjectivity of their possessors. Many in the West confuse glamour with its contrived form, thus construing it as a type of bodily presentation. In its authentic form, however, glamour is not about the body. Similarly, *iki* is not about the body. Although Kuki has criteria for bodily and sartorial expressions ("objectifications") of *iki*, these are neither necessary nor sufficient conditions for *iki* so much as they are clear signs. As Kuki puts it,

[I]t is a grave error to base one's understanding of the structure of *iki* on its objective expressions. For *iki* does not necessarily exhibit all the nuances available to that expression. Objectification itself is subject to a number of constraints. That is why *iki* that has been objectified rarely embodies, both in depth and breadth, the entirety of *iki* as a phenomenon of consciousness. Objective expression is no more than symbolic of *iki*.[5]

One may thus variously express or manifest *iki*, Kuki tells us. But what is *iki*?

This chapter examines *iki* in the context of the Western notion of glamour and the more general notion of an aesthetic property of persons. I draw a distinction between authentic and contrived glamour and then a parallel distinction between authentic and contrived *iki*. My account aims to cast light on three matters: (1) the nature of *iki*, (2) its relation to the Western idea of glamour, and (3) the idea of an aesthetic quality that emanates from the person's subjectivity rather than from external props or accoutrements. My overarching argument is designed to illuminate the notion of an aesthetic property of persons and to show why *iki* would fall into this category.

Kuki Shūzō's *Iki no kōzō* (*The Structure of* Iki) is the definitive account of *iki*. Kuki understands authentic *iki* to be a mode of subjectivity, which he identifies with three subjective modes: coquettishness, *bushidō* bravery and determination, and a profound Buddhist insight into the fleeting finitude of life and all things. Kuki associates the second, especially, with a feminine attitude, with the *bushidō* feature as belonging to the woman in a heterosexual relationship. This focus leads to a serious, although *not* fatal, contradiction in his analysis, as I argue in this chapter. The contradiction will emerge between the *bushidō* and Buddhist elements of *iki*.

Iki arises from erotic life. Kuki's identification of the *bushidō* element with female erotic experience may betray some of his personal idiosyncrasies and intellectual views that are neither ethnic nor nationalistic. Nonetheless, our investigation of Kuki's concept of *iki* casts light on *iki* and the depth of the aesthetic, more generally. The comparison of *iki* and glamour, while illuminating *iki*, may also deepen our understanding of comparative aesthetics and of aesthetics *tout court*, particularly, as I suggest here, the scope of aesthetic properties.

I do not address the alleged political dimension of Kuki's analysis in this article, as others have already done so and the political dimension is arguably ancillary to his argument and its originality. In any case, it goes beyond the scope of this chapter. My focus is on Kuki as an ontological and aesthetic thinker. In describing *iki* as "rich in ethnic coloring," he means that it is colored with the philosophical ideas of Japanese Buddhism and the Japanese cultural ideal of *bushidō*, both of which he views as being at the core of

Japanese philosophy. As we shall see later in this chapter, as *iki* reflects some core Japanese philosophical and aesthetic ideals, so glamour reflects some traditional Western philosophical concepts.

As noted, authentic *iki* bears striking similarities to authentic glamour. Both categories have a twofold structure in their taking both an authentic and a contrived form; both have a certain gravitas, a maturity of character; both require an adult range of experience; both belong to persons who keep their own counsel; both suggest mystery; both embody their respective cultural traditions. Before probing these qualities more deeply, it will be helpful to consider the context of Kuki's work.

BACKGROUND TO KUKI'S *IKI NO KŌZŌ*

Stephen Light renewed Western interest in Kuki's *Structure of* Iki with the 1987 publication of his authoritative monograph on Kuki and Sartre along with some of Kuki's Parisian essays.[6] Since then, much has been written on Kuki and on his relation to various German and French philosophers. The current moment is an apt time in Anglophone philosophical aesthetics to explore Kuki's *iki*, for Anglophone aestheticians have a new interest in everyday aesthetics[7] and Continental philosophy. Kuki's work reflects the fusion of his distinctively Japanese sensibility and his then recent European influences. Despite the often-mentioned Heideggerian influence on him, Kuki's work reflects a profoundly French sensibility. Sartre is often credited with having been Kuki's French tutor. Jan Walsh Hokenson, with a nod to Light, discusses Kuki's involvement with French Philosophy, telling us that for a few months in 1928, Kuki and Sartre met weekly to discuss French philosophy from Descartes to Bergson.[8]

While attending Bergson's lectures, Kuki took to Bergson, finding him the most fascinating European philosopher. One can understand his attraction to French philosophy, more generally, given that its tradition of subjectivity is close to the Japanese emphasis on the experience of the phenomenal world. Moreover, Bergson's notion of intuition is close to the Zen concept of understanding a person or an artwork by intuitively becoming that other entity or experiencing the world from the way one intuits its vantage point. Kuki would go on to become a specialist in French philosophy and to publish influential works on Japanese philosophy.

Kuki related well to the French, earned their respect, and was invited to lecture at the exclusive intellectual gatherings at Pontigny in 1928. In Kuki's lectures, he pointed to the two fundamental elements of Japanese thought as Zen Buddhism and the ethos of *Bushidō* (though these are by no means exhaustive of Japanese thought). Both are reflected in his treatment of *iki*.

As insistent as Kuki is on analyzing *iki* as a Japanese phenomenon, Kuki's text exhibits a powerful French philosophical motivation. Although many scholars claim that Kuki's work shows primarily the influence of Heidegger, Thorsten Botz-Bornstein argues—rightly, I believe—that Kuki's work shows a far more definite affinity with French philosophy.[9] Kuki's evident admiration for Bergson supports Botz-Bornstein's thesis. Moreover, Kuki's treatment of *iki* reflects his observations of and gravitation toward French life and culture (and women), with its elegant aestheticism. In fact, he drafted his *Structure of* Iki while in France during 1925–1927.[10]

Yet Kuki betrays his own personal biases in his treatment of *iki* and, most saliently, in his identification of sexuality with heterosexuality. In the first chapter of his work, which is on the "intensional structure of *iki*," Kuki identifies the first feature of *iki* as "coquetry directed towards a person of the opposite sex,"[11] As he says,

> [C]oquetry is a dualistic attitude; … it puts a person of the opposite sex in opposition to the monistic self; and … it posits a possible relationship between that person and the self. *Iki* ranges through meanings like *namamekashisa* 'lusciousness,' *tsuyapposa* 'eroticism,' *iroke* 'sexiness,' and … these arise precisely from the tension implicit in the dualistic possibility.[12]

Coquetry, the first of the three "intensional" components of *iki,* is an attitude one adopts that creates a *frisson*, a sexual tension. This tension arises from an allure, a mystery, something hidden, and the coquette's suggestiveness. It is not aloofness, which is why in the same passage Kuki contrasts coquetry with elegance and assuming an aura of high class.

It is crucial that we note how odd it is that Kuki characterizes *iki* with heterosexual desire. Homoeroticism was not unknown among Japanese or European males of Kuki's time. In fact, from at least the Heian through the Edo period, homoeroticism was generally accepted within many important Japanese subcultures, even though homosexuals in most situations were expected to marry a woman. It was not until the Meiji period (1868) that Japanese attitudes began to shift, largely under Western influences. This tectonic shift was not rapid. Nor did it lead to annihilation of homoeroticism. Rather, it embedded it in a new cultural ecology.

Why would Kuki associate *iki* and flirtation solely with heterosexuality? Given that he noticed the dandies of Paris, some indisputably homosexual, this is especially puzzling. Let us consider a few facts about Kuki's life.[13] At twenty-three, Kuki converted to Roman Catholicism: whether this was for spiritual or aesthetic reasons is unclear. He never married, although he frequented the so-called pleasure quarters and red-light districts. His remaining single was unusual—even a man in a homosexual relationship would likely have married. Kuki's mother, who may have been a geisha or servant before her marriage, had a relationship with a close friend of his father's, an affair that seemingly had begun before Kuki's birth. Both men influenced Kuki profoundly. We cannot know whether these biographical details may have been psychoanalytically instrumental in Kuki's identification of desire with heterosexual desire.

GROUNDWORK: AESTHETICS OF PERSONS

In order to explain an aesthetic property of a person, we must stipulate some individually necessary conditions of what a person is: a person is a being who (1) has a right not to be objectified (among other rights), (2) has dispositions to have subjective reactions to act in and respond to the world in various ways, (3) has the capacity for self-reflection and self-actualization, (4) can experience the world in ways that are not merely instrumental, (5) is unique in her take on the world and is irreplaceable, and (6) possesses character whose dispositions and actions merit moral praise or blame.[14]

Note that these conditions contribute to a person's being an ethical agent and an aesthetic being. Conditions (2) and (3) are the groundwork for how we evaluate a person as an ethical being, while conditions (4) and (5) form the basis for our judgments of a person's aesthetic nature. To glean a person's ethical or aesthetic nature, we need to observe her for a period of time. Both are dispositional. We can aesthetically judge a person's bodily self after brief observation, whether the person appears attractive, decorative, or well-built, for example. Seeing an aesthetic property of a *person*, as with an ethical property, requires time, because we have to observe a person's reactions to the world and actions in the world.

As an exemplar, let us use glamour, which, in its authentic form, I define as a *nondeliberate* but active expression of a person's interior mode of existence. It does not conform to a socially prescribed norm of self-presentation (as contrived glamour does) and therefore must be recognized as creative. As I mention elsewhere,[15] George Eliot alludes to this quality in the opening lines of *Daniel Deronda*, where she describes Gwendolyn having the "secret form or expression" that gives "a dynamic quality to her glance." She evinces this in any setting, in any attire. Unlike *iki,* glamour is not a seductive or coquettish attitude. It arises from a quality of Gwendolyn's imagination, her original and sometimes surprising take on the world. It stands to reason that in a society like early-twentieth-century Japan, an original view of things would not be prized as it would in the West, which incorporates an atomic notion of the self. We discern it in a person's bearing, glance, and/or general mode of self-presentation.

Authentic glamour, then, is an imaginative projection of the self, attained partly through one's nonconscious way of being embodied. Being glamorous is not something one consciously tries to achieve. Rather, it emerges from one's subjective modes of being, which some third-person observers will discern intuitively. Someone with contrived glamour does try, albeit unsuccessfully, to be glamorous by using conventionally prescribed attire, vivid make-up, showy jewelry, luxurious cars, and so forth; yet authentic glamour "radiates from the complexity of an individual [person] ... as a particular expression of imagination and personal uniqueness."[16] This is why other people tend to project their own fantasies onto a glamorous person. That is, different people see the authentically glamorous person in light of their own unique individual deep desires. Authentic glamour, unlike contrived glamour, is morally neutral. Note, too, that unlike *iki*, it is not inconsistent with any particular type of body, clothing, or hairdo.

To return to aesthetic aspects of persons, we must view a person in the setting of her life's narrative. Each person's narrative is necessarily unique. Correlatively, a person's constellation of aesthetic properties will be unique. Note that to say each person's narrative or constellation of properties is unique is not to say that each is equally original. Some are more conventional than others. How do we perceive these properties in others? When we observe a person's glamour, we do so by perceiving her bodily reactions and behavior as her glamour emanates from her as she lives in the world over time. It is important to bear in mind that a person's aesthetic nature is different from that person's moral nature, although both emerge as the person exists in the world over time.

A person possessing aesthetic qualities is vastly different from an artwork that has them. Nonetheless, we ascribe such properties to artworks (and other perceptible things), and we often heap praise or contempt on artworks. With people, we may admire or dislike their aesthetic properties, but we are more apt to consider their moral properties of greater importance. As an aesthetic property of a person emanates from the person's perceived qualities, so the aesthetic properties of an artwork emerge from their first order perceptual qualities.

According to Sibley's groundbreaking analysis of aesthetic properties,[17] we must distinguish between attributing an aesthetic property to something or someone and judging that the thing or person has it. Someone might attribute edginess to a movement of a string quartet, but only because other trustworthy people have told him it is there. They may have given him reasons for it, but if he is tone-deaf and unmusical, then he will not be able to judge that for himself. This means that an aesthetic property is *not* reducible to a fixed set of perceived qualities, neither in a string quartet nor in a charismatic performer. A person's aesthetic properties, then, cannot be reduced to a set of things we perceive. Thus, one cannot manufacture glamour or *iki* by, for example, wearing certain garments or cosmetics or cultivating certain perceivable attributes such as a toned physique or a *refined* accent. Anyone motivated to do so can work on his strength of body or refinement of enunciation. It is akin to sexiness: one cannot acquire it from a cosmetic surgeon, make-up artist, or stylist. Note that judging a person's aesthetic properties is less direct than judging an artwork's. If we hear a melody as ethereal, for example, we hear the ethereality in the melody. By contrast, when we see a person's glamour or *iki*, we cannot observe it in her subjectivity; rather, we grasp it as it unfolds in her actions, words, appearance, and gestures.

Kuki depicts *iki* as an aesthetic nature of a person, one that can be eponymously attributed to a person's physical presentation (slender body, long facial structure, a subtle use of language, and a certain cadence of speech), the natural world (steady rain), or an artwork (contour lines in painting). *Iki*, however, is primarily a feature of an individual's subjectivity, which is presumably why Kuki begins his work by examining the "intensional structure" or subjective phenomenology of *iki*. That said, a woman in a bright red and gold suit, ablaze with expensive jewelry would not, could not, have *iki*. For a woman to have *iki*, it is neither necessary nor sufficient that she have the obvious signs of *iki*—that she be slender-bodied, long-faced, simply groomed with an informal hairdo and inconspicuous make-up, and elegantly attired in understated fabrics in blues, grays, and browns. Certain aspects of one's appearance, however, such as a gaudy suit, preclude *iki*.

A person needs more than such *signs* of *iki*; she needs a certain mode of subjectivity. Glamour, like *iki*, implies a certain personal complexity, which is one reason why children cannot have glamour; nor can they possess *iki*. It would be taboo to describe a child with either term. Like glamour, *iki* has a contrived form. Kuki describes *shibumi* ('astringent'), one of the terms related to *iki*. *Shibumi* refers to the taste of unripe persimmons, the opposite of *amami*, or sweet. Sweetness is a less nuanced sensation. One could associate *amami* with the taste of cotton candy or candy corn and the color baby pink; *shibumi* with light brown, deep blue, and plum. *Shibumi* implies what we might call 'an understated edginess that (like *iki*) cannot be manufactured.' Kuki views *iki* and *shibumi* as positive qualities, and he contrasts them with such terms as *jōhin* ('refined,' 'cultivated') and *hade* ('showy,' 'flashy'). The latter two terms, he tells us, "belong [to] the general human being," whereas *iki* and *shibumi* apply to the "particularized heterosexual being" because of their association with a type of sexual tension between a man and a woman in a private space.[18] 'Refined' and 'flashy' are less complex and more formulaic, whereas *iki* and *shibumi* are nuanced, spontaneous, and suggestive of a sensibility that arises from the sexual *frisson* between a particular man and a particular woman, who together inhabit a private, hermetic sphere, totally consumed by their passionate liaison and sealed off from others. But why "particularized heterosexual being"?

KUKI ON *IKI* AND SEXUALITY

Kuki's *The Structure of* Iki is complex and, in places, opaque, despite, or perhaps because of, its brevity. The work has four chapters: "The Intensional Structure of *Iki*," "The Extensional Structure of *Iki*," "Natural Expressions of *Iki*," and "Artistic Expressions of *Iki*." In explicating the intensional structure of *iki*, which is the primary feature of *iki,* Kuki avers that its meaning is tripartite, involving coquetry, pride and honor, and resignation or acceptance. As *iki* connotes eroticism, coquetry or flirtatiousness is essential. At first glance, it seems odd to conjoin coquetry with *bushidō* courage and monk-like, Buddhist resignation. But Kuki shows insight in pointing out that erotic interaction requires a certain *bushidō* quality, a sense of self-honor that will not allow a person to give herself to someone she finds boorish. *Bushidō* also includes feeling honorable and not desperate for erotic alliances. A person with *iki* keeps her own counsel, has a sense of her own worth, and has, as Kuki says, "a rather aggressive range of sentiments directed towards the opposite sex, showing a bit of resistance."[19] In his Pontigny lecture, "The Notion of Time and Repetition in Oriental Notions of Time," Kuki describes *bushidō* as "immanent, voluntarist liberation" and a determination "to truly live."[20] This is another type of bravery.

Iki requires, too, a Buddhist sense of *akirame*, the acceptance that erotic alliances weaken once consummated. This relates to *iki*'s origin in the floating world, which is transitory and ultimately meaningless. A resignation accompanies this insight, lightening the significance of the erotic connection and leading to a weightlessness, which Kuki conflates with stylishness. The acceptance of flux would make one appreciate style and the chic, with which some identify *iki*. Note that the coquetry of *iki* connotes bewitchment and mystery.[21]

Kuki asserts that *iki* takes two forms, one being a phenomenon of consciousness, the other one being behavior manifested in flirtatiousness or coquetry "that realizes itself by means of an idealism and unrealism." There seems to be a contradiction in the intensional structure of *iki:* Kuki claims that *iki* is primarily a mode of consciousness, which suggests it is a type of subjectivity whereby its possessor posits herself erotically in relation to another. Kuki claims that once the sexual attraction is consummated, the attraction vanishes. The coquette aims to conquer, but the conquest makes her the victim, for her mystery has evaporated, according to Kuki. Hence *iki* requires a sophisticated resignation that if one's charms are effective, she will lose them in relation to a particular other.

One finds here a contradiction in Kuki's explication of the sexual dimension of *iki*. The destruction of male desire after sexual union is inconsistent with *iki* as a phenomenon of consciousness. The consciousness of the other is ineluctably elusive. It is therefore inconsistent with a loss of mystery. If Kuki were to shift his assumptions about the loss of a woman's mystery after consummation and apply the Buddhist *akirame* to sexuality, he could avoid this contradiction. He presumes that after sexual union, the male will objectify the woman, for he has become acquainted with her body and her sexuality. *Iki* does not objectify the male, but only the female. Kuki writes:

> As Nagai Kafū says in his novel *Kanraku*, "there is nothing more pathetic than having a woman after trying to have the woman." He must surely have in mind the "boredom, despair, and aversion" arising from the disappearance of coquetry … For that reason, the main concern of coquetry—and the essence of pleasure—is maintaining a dualistic relationship, that is to say, protecting the possibility as a possibility.[22]

Iki, then, seems to be a woman's attitude of resignation (*akirame*) to the inevitable loss of her attractions once she has exercised her agency in a sexual liaison.

Kuki expands on *akirame* as resignation rooted in the knowledge of fate and of the fluidity of reality. This arises perhaps from the capriciousness of an intimate partner or the disappointment following intimate consummation. One grasps the suffering of being and the illusory nature of permanence. This gives one "a frame of mind that is light, fresh, and stylish," one that focuses on the present moment and the parade of artistic and social changes.

Kuki assumes, strangely, that fulfillment of desire brings boredom. But the resignation Kuki describes arises from one's perception of the inevitability of change. Before examining why this leads to a contradiction for Kuki, let us consider some basic tenets of Japanese Buddhism on which Kuki draws in delineating this distinctively Japanese notion of *iki*. For the Japanese Buddhist, as Kuki indicates, nothing is permanent. Reality is a stream of phenomena. Just as this would be true of ordinary things, it is equally so for the self. The self, like all other things, is in constant flux, violating the law of identity. It is not a fixed entity that persists through time and change. There are two famous passages in Dōgen's *Genjokōan* that express this notion:

> But the ocean is neither round nor square; its features are infinite in variety. It is like a palace. It is like a jewel. It only looks circular as far as you can see at that time. All things are like this.[23]

> Just as firewood does not become firewood again after it is ash, you do not
> return to birth after death.... Birth is an expression complete at this moment.
> Death is an expression complete at this moment.[24]

Dōgen, a canonical figure in Japanese Buddhism, points out in these passages
that the self is constantly in a process of existing anew. A self that desires
and achieves some measure of enlightenment becomes a different entity and
therefore must constantly strive for renewed enlightenment. Desire is never
conclusively fulfilled. The absence of an enduring self (or the presence of a
no-self) is at the heart of Buddhist philosophy.[25]

In a sense, then, the coquette and her admirer can never consummate an
attraction, for desire cannot be conclusively satisfied. Desire can be, and
would be, renewed. If desire is never conclusively satisfied, then this boredom or jadedness is not inevitable. Moreover, if the self is continually changing, it seems far more likely that desire would be renewed. Rather than losing
interest in a lover, one would seem to be in a constant state of desire. The
woman embodying *iki* would be a continuous mystery, for after each encounter, she would be someone different. In this way, too, *iki* is like glamour: it
conveys a sense of something one has that is unknown and compelling.

It is baffling, then, why Kuki would see consummation as leading to
objectification. For consummation of true attraction should ignite a deeper
appreciation of each other's subjective world in its particularity. We might
speculate that this is one reason why Japanese narratives find the process of
attraction more aesthetically interesting than the story of consummation. That
is, there is a sense in which a relationship, however brief, consists of a process
of getting to know someone who remains ineluctably elusive. This Sisyphean
process[26] could be quite exciting, even intoxicating, while it may also be a
source of the resignation in *iki*—authentic *iki,* one might say, conveys a melancholy enlightenment merged with a *bushidō* bravery and pride in one's own
mystifying continuous recreation.

Why does the person embodying *iki* feel melancholy resignation? Is it
because she knows that a lover who pursues her will lose interest after she
shares with him an erotic encounter? Kuki is inconsistent in suggesting this
while also describing this resignation as arising from "a state of mind ... that
has removed itself from any egoistic attachment to reality."[27] It may be that
a geisha, a concubine, or a woman or man working in the pleasure quarters
comes to the *iki* state of mind this way. But *if* it can only arise from what Kuki
terms 'decadence,' then the definition of *iki* is far narrower than Kuki clearly
intends it to be. This state of mind would be a professional liability, rather
than a philosophical insight, as he claims it is in describing it as "Buddhist,"
with its understanding of "transience" and "emptiness." He thus contradicts
his own analysis in asserting that *iki* requires a sense of possibility inherent

to attraction, which love, he tells us, precludes: once "actualized ... [it] is no longer a possibility." We could say that Buddhism entails possibility. As Dōgen puts it in the *Genjokōan,* "when Buddhas are truly Buddhas, they do not necessarily notice that they are Buddhas. However, they are actualized Buddhas, who go on actualizing Buddhas." Enlightenment does not persist, because the self does not persist. Moreover, at every subsequent moment, one's experience of enlightenment would be different, both numerically and qualitatively.

The contradiction bedeviling Kuki's work may arise from an extreme misogyny, which prevents him from granting a woman full personhood, given the conditions set forth earlier in this chapter. If a woman loses her *élan* in the eyes of a man with whom she has been intimate, then her lover has violated her right—as a "particularized heterosexual being"—not to be objectified and denied her uniqueness. In Sartrean terms, her lover makes her an object, thus denying her personhood and freedom. In the space of Japanese Buddhism, this would be a different kind of violation: it would be denying the ontological unity of all things and the deep unreality of a persistent ego. It may be that Kuki cannot allow for both the *bushidō* bravery and the insightful resignation that he posits as parts of the intensional structure of *iki.*

This makes it even more baffling as to why Kuki would see consummation as leading to boredom, unless it is a symptom of his own habitual objectification of women. It remains impossible to know someone even after consummation, for that person is inherently inaccessible. Authentic *iki* conveys a melancholy enlightenment merged with a *bushidō* pride in one's own mystifying uniqueness as a "particularized heterosexual being." Kuki's contradiction would dissolve were he to take a more egalitarian approach to sexual attraction and its endless possibilities of cathexis; for an egalitarian or nongendered analysis would make unnecessary the resignation of the woman who is no longer desired. On such an analysis, *iki,* like glamour, would then apply equally to men and women—as it should.

IKI AND GLAMOUR: JAPANESE AND WESTERN AESTHETICS

Having compared *iki* and glamour, let us briefly contrast these two aesthetic categories. *Iki* reflects several principles at the heart of Japanese philosophical aesthetics. First, the traditional Japanese notion of the self is a "we-self," a collective notion. *Iki,* Kuki emphasizes, is relational in that it concerns one's relation to a member of the opposite sex (or, we might describe it as a feature of one's consciousness toward a potential sex partner). *Iki* would be conceptually impossible in a solipsistic world. This eroticized *iki* self exists only in relation to another; it emerges from "we-ness." Glamour, however, bestows mystery on its possessor, who appears to inhabit an unknown, unique world. This manifests the Western notion of selfhood as a unique, private subjectivity, an atomic self.

As an aesthetic category, *iki* is distinctly Japanese. Consider *iki* in light of the general characteristics that Keene has distilled. (1) *Iki* exemplifies *suggestiveness*. Coquetry suggests a relationship or, as Kuki says, "to come as near as possible, and at the same time making certain that nearness stops short of actual touch." *Iki* is also suggestive of the aftermath of the relationship, as Kuki avers variously. (2) *Iki* embodies *irregularity*, which may include imperfection and asymmetry. Consider a minor expression of *iki*, such as hair in a bun with random loose tendrils. Kuki describes *décolletage* as "symboliz[ing] *iki* because it breaks the equilibrium of the garment slightly and suggests a possible pathway to the woman's flesh." He contrasts this with the Western custom of a woman exposing her back, shoulders, or even part of her breasts. (3) Expressions of *iki* also exemplify *simplicity*, for instance, muted colors, simple, transparent make-up, and fabrics of horizontal stripes, or interiors in which contrasting materials express the duality inherent in *iki*. *Iki* cannot be loud, fussy, or elaborate in pattern. (4) Most obviously, *iki* instantiates *perishability*, which is at the heart of the traditional Japanese aesthetic experience. The essential Buddhist element of *iki* arises from *iki* requiring a sense that while a type of pleasurable connection is developing, that pleasure will die before it ever occurs. Kuki describes an *iki* woman as "smiling in a minor key." *Iki* is the personal embodiment of the *wabi-sabi* aesthetic (which itself expresses Keene's four principles).

While glamour betokens maturity and evocativeness, it does not instantiate the *wabi-sabi* aesthetic. Glamour conveys a sense of liveliness, rather than impending death. It does not require an awareness of perishability, nor does it require a *bushidō* spirit. The glamorous person is intriguing and mysterious, in part because others do not know what imagined world she may envision. Glamour is compatible with a wide range of personal aesthetic choices, none of which is necessary (or sufficient) for glamour. Kuki's reductive approach cannot work for glamour.

CONCLUSION

Despite its problems, Kuki's study reveals an understanding of the ontology of aesthetics, especially its application to persons, as well as to artworks, nature, and artifacts of everyday life. His study affords us a glimpse into the Japanese notion of *iki*, which signifies the traditional Japanese attitude toward life as aesthetic. Glamour, *iki*'s Western twin, has the same structure as it did centuries ago. Were Kuki not to confine *iki* to a certain social status and fixed set of reactions to its possessors, it, like glamour, would become more visible across cultures and subcultures, for *iki* is fundamentally a way of living and being with respect to potential erotic partners and the world, more generally. Even if this is distinctively Japanese, it does not mean that Kuki, a Francophile, wrote his work with nationalistic rather than aesthetic and philosophical concerns.

NOTES

1. For helpful discussions and questions on this chapter, I am grateful to Mara Miller and David Levine. I owe special thanks to A. Minh Nguyen.

2. Donald Keene, "Japanese Aesthetics," in *Japanese Aesthetics and Culture: A Reader*, ed. Nancy G. Hume (Albany, NY: State University of New York Press, 1995), 27–41.

3. I use the term 'property' for convenience. Strictly speaking, 'category' is more precise for *iki*. I follow the spirit, if not the letter, of Mara Miller, "Japanese Aesthetics and Philosophy of Art," in *The Oxford Handbook of World Philosophy*, ed. William Edelglass and Jay L. Garfield (Oxford: Oxford University Press, 2011), 317–33; and others, who seek to avoid imposing inappropriate Western metaphysical constructs on Japanese concepts.

4. Carol S. Gould, "Glamour as an Aesthetic Property of Persons," *Journal of Aesthetics and Art Criticism* 63, no. 3 (2005): 237–47; and "Towards a Theory of the Aesthetic Properties of Persons," *Suplemento de Contrastes* 17 (2012): 157–69.

5. Hiroshi Nara, *The Structure of Detachment: The Aesthetic Vision of Kuki Shūzō, with a Translation of* Iki no kōzō (Honolulu: University of Hawai'i Press, 2004), 56.

6. Stephen Light, *Shūzō Kuki and Jean-Paul Sartre: Influence and Counter-Influence in the Early History of Existential Phenomenology* (Carbondale, IL: Southern Illinois University Press, 1987).

7. See, for example, Yuriko Saito, *Everyday Aesthetics* (New York: Oxford University Press, 2008); Andrew Light and Jonathan Smith, eds., *The Aesthetics of Everyday Life* (New York: Columbia University Press, 2005); Thomas Leddy, *The Extraordinary in the Ordinary: The Aesthetics of Everyday Life* (Peterborough, ON: Broadview Press, 2012); Christopher Dowling, "The Aesthetics of Daily Life," *British Journal of Aesthetics* 50, no. 3 (2010): 225–42; and Kevin Melchionne, "The Definition of Everyday Aesthetics," *Contemporary Aesthetics* 11 (2013), accessed June 18, 2015, http://www.contempaesthetics.org/newvolume/pages/article. php?articleID=663.

8. See her masterful *Japan, France, and East-West Aesthetics: French Literature, 1867–2000* (Madison, NJ: Fairleigh Dickinson University Press, 2004).

9. Thorsten Botz-Bornstein—in his "Contingency and the 'Time of the Dream': Kuki Shūzō and French Prewar Philosophy," *Philosophy East and West* 50, no. 4 (2000): 481–506—argues that Kuki's work displays the powerful influence of French

philosophy, despite the abundant scholarly treatments of Kuki as a German-influenced thinker. I agree with Botz-Bornstein. I believe Kuki synthesized elements of Japanese thought and French philosophy. One could speculate that Kuki influenced the young Sartre.

10. See Yamamoto Yuji, *An Aesthetics of Everyday Life: Modernism and a Japanese Popular Aesthetic Ideal, "Iki"* (MA thesis, University of Chicago, 1999), accessed June 18, 2015, http://yuji.cosmoshouse.com/works/papers/aes-every-e.pdf.

11. Nara, *Structure of Detachment*, 19.

12. Ibid.

13. See Hiroshi Nara, "Capturing the Shudders and Palpitations: Kuki's Quest for a Philosophy of Life," in Nara, *Structure of Detachment*, 95–129.

14. I discuss these criteria in more depth in my "Towards a Theory."

15. Gould, "Glamour," 246.

16. Ibid.

17. Frank Sibley, "Aesthetic Concepts," *Philosophical Review* 68, no. 4 (1959): 421–50.

18. Both 'general human being' and 'particularized heterosexual being' occur on page 24 of Nara's *The Structure of Detachment*.

19. Ibid., 20.

20. Light, 50.

21. Kuki suggests the word 'chic' as close in meaning to 'iki.' He points out that one possible origin is 'chicane' in its meaning of "intricate trickery" as a kind of sophistry (Nara, *Structure of Detachment*, 16). This would make its origin similar to that of 'glamour,' which arises from earlier terms for "occult knowledge" or "power with magic spells" (see Gould, "Glamour," 238).

22. Nara, *Structure of Detachment*, 19.

23. Kazuaki Tanahashi, ed., *Moon in a Dewdrop: Writings of Zen Master Dōgen*, trans. Robert Aitken et al. (New York: North Point Press, 1995), 71.

24. Ibid., 70.

25. For an extensive treatment of this issue, see Gereon Gopf, *Beyond Personal Identity: Dōgen, Nishida, and a Phenomenology of No-Self* (Surrey, UK: Curzon Press, 2001).

26. In his first lecture at Pontigny, Kuki dismisses the Greek attitude toward Sisyphus as superficial, because the Greeks do not know how Sisyphus himself experiences it. See Light, 49.

27. Nara, *Structure of Detachment*, 22.

Chapter 27

Scents and Sensibility

Kuki Shūzō and Olfactory Aesthetics

Peter Leech

Of his years studying philosophy in France during the 1920s, the Japanese philosopher Kuki Shūzō (1888–1941) offers a poignant recollection. "When I was in Paris," he writes, "I liked Guerlain's *L'Heure Bleu* and [Houbigant's] *Quelques Fleurs* out of the perfumes available for ladies. It also happened that I sprinkled the inside of my vest with Guerlain's *Bouquet de Faunes.*"[1] Now it is unlikely that Kuki's sprinkling was a conscious act of defiance in the face of the faintly unsettling observation by Alexandre Dumas that in Paris, "[a]part from the philosophers, everyone smelled nice."[2] But the passage certainly attests to Kuki's personal refinement and signals the philosophically unique olfactory inflection I discern in his writings. My aim here is to explore this inflection in the hope of illuminating certain phenomenological characteristics of Japanese aesthetics.

Immediately, though, it should be said that my contention is not that Japanese culture gives greater aesthetic prominence to the sense of smell than is the case in the West. (Actually, as we shall see, the *reverse* is often true.) But the peculiar nature of smell, I propose to argue, acts as a conceptual fulcrum in determining deep-lying issues of aesthetics in general and Japanese aesthetics in particular. The first section of the chapter—*The Scents of Kuki*—seeks to demonstrate this point.

What is further remarkable about Kuki's thought, though, is that it so readily traverses cultural and philosophical diversity. Drawn to aesthetic delicacies (equally Japanese and French), Kuki is also simultaneously drawn to a strict aesthetic architectonic (equally Japanese and German). It is the latter which I seek particularly to emphasize in a second section—*Kuki, Kant, Iki*—for it is undeniably clear that Kuki's thought consistently turns around Kant's, both epistemologically and aesthetically.

In a final section—*The Contingent and the Aesthetic*—my particular focus is aesthetic resistance to the idea of contingency. Importantly here, I want to dispel an orthodoxy of Kuki studies that he is motivated by a "philosophy of contingency."[3] While it is certainly true that Kuki is *exercised*—just as Kant was—by the idea of the contingent, the principal aim for both seems to me to identify a philosophical and aesthetic *harness* for what may otherwise seem merely contingent. This, of course, is exactly *why* our sense of smell can assume prominence. For, among the senses, the evident peculiarity of smell *is* its contingent and uncontrolled nature.

That Kuki is so preoccupied with the olfactory is perhaps nowhere clearer than in his gnomic conclusion to one of his last essays. In a reflection on his cross-cultural engagements with both Japanese and Western aesthetics, Kuki finally declares, "I indeed have the smell of the traditional [Japanese] past. My love for tradition, however, is not as faint as a scent."[4] This curious passage forms a suitable epigraphic guide to the argument I now propose to develop.

THE SCENTS OF KUKI

Kuki Shūzō's arrival in Paris in 1924 marks a definitive moment in his cultural and aesthetic development. Nothing prior could have prepared him for the *chic* of Parisian life and his immediate fascination—represented in my opening quotation—with the fragrances of Paris. And his response to this is dramatic. Suddenly, the student of philosophy turns to an outpouring of verse, which is perhaps most remarkable for its abundant invocations of olfactory imagery and metaphor.

A complete survey of Kuki's poems during this period would be excessive, but a few instances may suffice. So, for example, from the collection *Parī Shinkei* (*Paris Mindscapes*, 1925–1926), "Seafood Restaurant" offers Kuki's gourmet encomium to the great Parisian establishment Prunier:

> A scent more fleeting than a dream
> Like breathing at the bottom of the sea.[5]

From the collection *Nihonshi no ōin* (*Rhyme in Japanese Poetry*, 1931), there is the more extended metaphor in "A Stroll" in reference to the bibliophile Latin Quarter:

> Where does the heart dwell?
> The old bookstores stand in a row,
> Letting the fragrance of past wisdom flow,
> Isn't that boulevard St. Michel?[6]

But it is not just wisdom that, for Kuki, has a fragrance. In *Haben [Parī Yori]* (*Fragments from Paris*, 1927), there is a particularly striking olfactory imagery of the morally good:

Good,
Smell the fragrance
Evil,
Let the flower bloom.[7]

The reference here is to Charles Baudelaire's infamously decadent collection of poetry *Les Fleurs du Mal* (*The Flowers of Evil*, 1857). And it is perhaps at this point that Kuki first begins to recognize his own inner tension between the Baudelairean aesthete on the one hand and the philosophical aesthetician on the other. So, for instance, in *Tanka 134* of his *Parī Shōkyoku* (*Sonnets from Paris*, 1926)—and, as we shall shortly see, this is not the only occasion where his poetry makes reference to Kant—Kuki writes,

"The Flowers of Evil"
And "The Critique of Practical Reason"
Go shoulder to shoulder jeering
At each other.[8]

In this, there could be no more succinct evidence of what I earlier noted as Kuki's ready traverse of cultural and philosophical diversity.

But we must pause here to consider an important question: why is it that Kuki, on reaching Paris, might have become so absorbed in the scents of the city? Setting aside the likelihood that Kuki was personally an aesthete of fragrance (indeed, perhaps, a *synaesthete*, prone to express general experience in the olfactory imagery and metaphors of his poetry), there is one clear answer. As a native of Japan, Kuki would have been startled by the public wearing of perfumes. For it is a curious fact that very rarely in Japan—even now—would one encounter a scented woman or man, and indeed it is often explicitly proscribed in workplaces and educational institutions. As the perfume critic Chandler Burr observed of Japanese culture: "Scent on your skin? Bodily pollution, my Japanese friends called it."[9]

There is, though, one clear instance that comes to mind of a place for the olfactory in Japanese aesthetic culture: namely, *kō* (incense) and *Kōdō* (the Way of Scent). No Western visitor to the great department stores of Tokyo or Kyoto could fail to notice the extent of retail counters devoted to exquisitely packaged *senko* (small, delicately fragranced sticks of incense, quite unlike the cruder form of joss sticks more familiar in the West from their origin in Chinese and Indian culture).

The special refinement of *Kōdō,* however, is that during the Tokugawa rule it was developed as a complex aesthetic "game" (*kō-kwai*), replete with the same elaborate kind of etiquette and rules as the tea ceremony itself, and with the same purpose of reflective discernment.[10] For what is most striking about *kō-kwai* is the characterization of the sensory activity held to be involved. The fragrances are not "smelled"; oddly, they are said to be "listened to" (*monkou*). And what this immediately portends, and is a matter for later discussion, is a Japanese aesthetic proclivity for attentive analysis, which, of course, smells themselves generally do not permit; commonly, they come to us—indeed may overcome us—"whole," with no discernibly discrete elements.

There are two further instances from the intensity of Kuki's Parisian poems that act as a prelude to the following section. Kuki's major work *Iki no kōzō* (*The Structure of* Iki, 1930) also had its origins in Paris in the form of a draft, *Iki no honshitsu* (*The Essence of* Iki, 1926). But when in *Tanka 87* from *Parī Shōkyoku* (*Sonnets from Paris*), Kuki first introduces the problematic concept of *iki,* strikingly it *is* as a fragrance.

Furusato no	My heart smells
"Iki" ni niru ka o	A fragrance similar to
Haru no yo no	The [*iki*] of my homeland
Rune ga sugata ni	In the figure of Renée
Kagu kokoro ha na	On a spring night.[11]

The second instance is more philosophically remarkable. Again in *Parī Shōkyoku,* in *Tanka 123,* Kuki writes,

Kokoro iu	The heart says,
"Konogoro itashi"	"Lately it hurts!"
Yaya arite	After a while
Tamashii no iu	The soul says,
"Kanto ni kaere"	"Go back to Kant."[12]

It is this imperative to "go back to Kant" that I now take up.

KUKI, KANT, *IKI*

For Kuki, to "go back to Kant" is in fact, quite literally, to return to his early philosophical education. As an undergraduate at Tokyo Imperial University in 1909, he first encountered the work of Immanuel Kant through the eccentric German aesthetician, Raphael von Koeber.[13] It appears though that Kuki did not complete his doctoral studies and withdrew in 1921 to embark for

France, arriving first in Nice. From there, Kuki travelled to Germany in order to study Kant at the University of Heidelberg under Heinrich Rickert.[14] Thus, Kuki's early studies seem to have implanted an intimate intellectual familiarity with the philosophy of Kant.[15]

The question, however, is *why,* as a Japanese thinker, Kuki might have entertained the poetic imperative to "go back to Kant." It is, of course, a profound hazard for a non-Japanese commentator to offer observations of Japanese culture, but there is at least one point that might be made. Insofar as Japanese aesthetics may be said to find its origins in *Chadō* (The Way of Tea, manifest in *chanoyu*, the tea ceremony), its most obvious feature is the overwhelming ubiquity of rules (*temae*), from the simple act of cleaning a teacup to the manner in which a tea master should walk. In a phrase that, I fancy, would have appealed greatly to Kant, there is a "moral geometry" in *chanoyu*. The phrase is from Okakura Kakuzō's celebrated *The Book of Tea* (1906) and is situated in his claim that

[t]he Philosophy of Tea is not mere aestheticism ... It is moral geometry, inasmuch as it defines our sense of proportion to the universe. It represents the true spirit of Eastern democracy by making all its votaries aristocrats in taste.[16]

However, in turning to more formal aspects of philosophy, Kuki's fascination with the olfactory is a significant departure from the generally Kantian cast of his thought.

Importantly, and unlike Kuki, Kant was robustly dismissive of our sense of smell, both aesthetically and epistemologically. Thus, in a passage from the *Critique of Aesthetic Judgment,* he resents as "annoying"

the practice of regaling oneself with a perfume that exhales its odours far and wide. The man who pulls his perfumed handkerchief from his pocket gives a treat to all around, whether they like it or not, and compels them, if they want to breathe at all, to be parties to the enjoyment.[17]

It might further be observed that the claim here is neither peculiar to Kant nor even to eighteenth-century sensibilities. As Luca Turin, a legendary twenty-first-century scientist and critic of scent, once put it, "the woman who sits next to you at a concert wrecks the evening by wearing half an ounce of [Dior's perfume] *Poison.*"[18] For the moment, though, let me simply mark as a matter for later consideration the possibility (for both Kant and Turin) that a smell may be overpowering or, as I put it a moment ago, that it may "overcome" us.

What is more immediately curious—and it has to be said philosophically unsatisfactory—is Kant's construction of the epistemology of smell in the

anthropological writings of his last years. The terminology employed by
Kant in these discussions is surprisingly imprecise and unstable. The three
"highest" senses of sight, hearing, and touch are variously described as
"outer," "objective," or "mechanical." By contrast, both smell and sensory
taste are, for Kant, "lower" senses described as "inner," "more subjective
than objective," "chemical," or "inside the body."[19] What appears to inform
Kant's thought here is his conviction that the two lower senses have virtually no cognitive value—especially smell, which he characterizes as "taste at
a distance."[20] At best, they may act as an *invitational* or, more particularly,
an *avoidance* alert to the source of the sensations. Beyond that, Kant also
appears to take the view that the two senses are "involuntary" (which is what
I take him to mean by their 'chemical' origin 'inside the body'), and are
therefore not open to the reflective discernment that characterizes authentic
aesthetic judgment.

Now, so far, such claims may seem unexceptional and largely a matter of
common sense. Of course, the mere whiff of soured milk or rotting meat will
act as a motive for immediate disposal if not, indeed, the involuntary act of
retching. But Kant goes further and more perplexingly in a passage from his
posthumously published "Reflections on Anthropology."[21] "All sensations,"
Kant contends,

> have *Benennungen* of their own, e.g. for sight red, green, yellow, for taste sweet,
> sour, etc., but smell cannot have proper *Benennungen*; rather, we borrow the
> *Benennungen* from other sensations, e.g. it smells sour, or has a smell of roses
> or carnations, it smells like moschus. These are all *Benennungen* from other
> sensations. Hence we cannot describe smell.[22]

There are real problems with this passage, in which I have substituted Kant's
original term *Benennungen* for the translators' word 'appellations.' Literally translated, the German *Benennungen* means "names," but I assume that
Kant's translators have wisely substituted 'appellations' to evade the obvious
philosophical awkwardness of saying that *sensations* can be said to have
"names" rather than the descriptions that we employ to identify them. But
there are two deeper and more direct problems.

The first of these is that Kant is plainly wrong to conclude, "Hence we cannot describe smell." Of course, we can. Among the descriptive adjectives we
use are, for example, *acrid, dank, fetid, fusty, musty, pungent, putrid, rancid.*
And while it is true that we seem to have many more adjectives for disagreeable smells than for those that are agreeable, we do regularly describe smells
as *fresh, clean, sweet, astringent.*

The second problem is Kant's contention that the *benennungen* of smells
are "borrowed from other sensations." Well, it *is* true that we do frequently

resort to simile in order to describe a smell, as in 'smells *like* moschus' (deer musk). But Kant seems to forget that while something *other* than the flowers may have "the smell of roses or carnations," what clearly does have *just* that smell *are* roses and carnations.

Further, when, for instance, I describe the distinctive smell of white free-sias as "peppery," I am not invoking the sense of taste, far less sight, sound, or touch. What I discern in the flower is the *smell* of green peppercorns, and even if blindfolded, I could determine precisely that I was smelling a *white* freesia rather than one of the more vibrantly-hued variations of the flower.

Now it may be that Kant is relying on the widespread and apparently uncontentious belief that smell *is* the most primitive sense, which in our developed, antiseptic world has lost much of its evolutionary value. When we say that smells "dog" us—in the sense that we cannot, as it were, avert our noses from an offensive smell just as we may avert our eyes from an offensive sight—we mean at least that smells tend to follow us around like a persistent dog. But there is the further sense that smells can render us *like* dogs, who—no matter how well-trained—simply cannot be diverted from a scent source (often, of course, to the frustration of the dog owner, though also to our general amusement in watching the sheer enthusiasm with which a sniffer dog used for security purposes at airports will attempt to detect olfactory traces of drugs, explosives, or cash).

But it is obviously not the case, at two different levels of reasoning, that our sense of *pleasant* smells has been degraded or lost. At the first (and lower) level, were this to be the case, then the fragrance industry (responsible for producing perfumes, household and car deodorizers, and whatnot) would not be as rampantly and globally profitable as it is. Nor would house-selling agents advise the cynical strategy of having the lingering smell of baking bread emanating from a kitchen oven in order to seduce potential buyers. Here, however, a plausible objection is that these facts alone hardly entail the possibility of an aesthetic dimension to our olfactory sense. On the contrary, our being drawn to pleasant smells—as much as we may be repelled by those that are unpleasant—exactly signals what I identified a moment ago as the "involuntary" in Kant's phenomenology of smell.

However, at the second (and higher) level, it is also true that a reflective discernment of smells can—indeed *must*—be cultivated. Most obviously, this is so with *parfumeurs* who—at least in France—generally undertake several years of initial training not in Paris but around the town of Grasse in the Alpes-Maritimes region, inland from the French Riviera. The microclimate of Grasse is especially propitious for scented flower- and herb-farming, and there are said to be more than 2,000 natural aromas there that an aspiring "nose" is required to discriminate. Similarly, refined chefs will rely as much on their sense of smell as on their sense of taste. A chef unable to determine simply by smell that a dish had an excessive quantity of garlic or verbena, say, would not sustain employment in any *haute cuisine* restaurant.

Again, though, it might be objected that these examples of olfactory discernment are too specialized to count as other than exceptional. But, in relation to Japanese aesthetic culture in general and to Kuki Shūzō in particular, what may seem exceptional in the West is perfectly ordinary in Japan. Though I referred earlier to the practice of *Kōdō* and "listening to" the fragrances of incense, there is a far more everyday Japanese practice that may be observed in even the most modest *udon* or *ramen* noodle shop. On being presented with a noodle soup, Japanese diners will first bring the bowl to the nose in order to inhale the smell and linger over the inhalation. (By contrast, in Western fast-food equivalents, the practice would more likely be taken as an act of gustatory *suspicion* rather than of appreciation.) Then, on ingesting the dish, the noodles are sucked into the mouth with loud slurping noises that, again in the West, would be regarded as a vulgarity. But there is a clear olfactory purpose to this slurping. That is, by inhaling oxygen while you eat, the fragrance of the soup is sustained and so enhances the taste of it.[23]

However, while I may so far have been able to suggest that Kuki was an olfactory aesthete—perhaps even an olfactory *synaesthete*—and while I may so far have been able to link the suggestion to aspects of everyday Japanese culture, what I have yet to demonstrate is that his primary contribution to a Japanese aesthetics in *Iki no kōzō* may *itself* be founded in a conception of the olfactory. It is to this matter that I now turn.

The persistent and fundamental problem of *Iki no kōzō* is, of course, how to translate the word *iki*. Published translations include 'chic,' 'detachment,' and 'stylishness.'[24] There really is no stable English equivalent and perhaps this point serves to underpin Kuki's own claim that "the study of *iki* can only be constituted as the hermeneutics of ethnic [i.e., Japanese] being."[25] Now it is not so much to my purpose here to offer a translation of *iki*, though a superseded idiom in English may serve—namely, 'cool,' indicating something like "refined disinterest" (in the correct, Kantian sense) or "detached stylishness."[26] However, none of these translations so far suggests an *olfactory* quality of *iki*—a "fragrance" such as Kuki poetically proclaims he detects in the figure of Renée in *Tanka 87*. Yet there is a peculiar quality of the diagram (Figure 27.1) that Kuki himself provides to illustrate the complex structure of *iki* which is intriguing.[27]

What comes to mind with such a diagram is Okakura's thought of a "moral geometry." But my further intuition is that Kuki's structure of *iki* may best be construed on architectonic analogy with the Aristotle's Square of Oppositions (Figure 27.2) with which Kuki—and indeed Kant—would undoubtedly have been philosophically familiar.

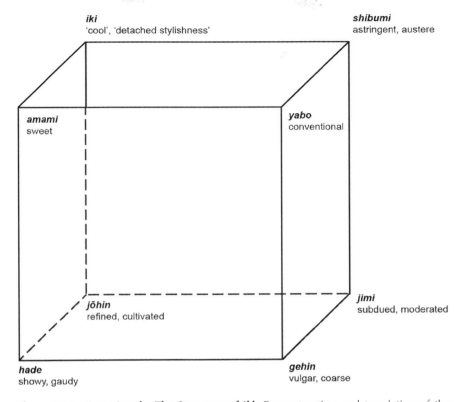

Figure 27.1   Peter Leech, *The Structure of* Iki. Reconstruction and translation of the diagram published in Kuki Shūzō, *Iki no kōzō* (Tokyo: Iwanami Shoten, 1979), 44. 2013. Digital image, 7.7 in. × 6.9 in.

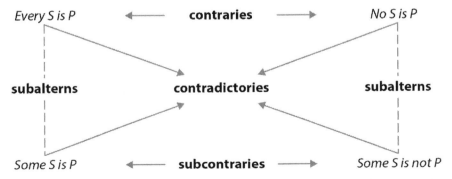

Figure 27.2   Peter Leech, *Aristotle's Square of Opposition*. 2013. Digital image, 7.7 in. × 3 in.

Now, of course, Kuki is not concerned with propositions but with concepts and his diagram has a cubed form. Nonetheless there are, I find, useful points of parallel with the reconstructed structure of *iki* in Figure 27.1. So, for example, Kuki's *iki* might be held to be a contradictory of *gehin* (vulgar, coarse), and *shibumi* (astringent, austere) a contradictory of *hade* (showy, gaudy)—that is, neither pair of properties can simultaneously be the case. Or with Aristotle's subalterns, an instance of *iki* might entail that it is also *jōhin* (refined, cultivated), or an instance of *amami* (sweet) might entail that it is also *hade*.

But the peculiarity of the diagram is that the concepts employed are not in any obvious way *visual*. While Kuki's *text* in *Iki no kōzō* is heavily weighted toward visual exemplification, it is difficult to discern how the concepts of the correlative diagram might apply visually. What could be meant, for instance, by saying that a painting or sculpture was *shibumi*, *amami*, or *jimi*?

In fact, I find it more natural to think of these concepts and the others as descriptors of smells. For instance, in the plague of so-called celebrity perfumes we now endure (in which popular singers or actors give their name to a scent), most that I have encountered could indeed be described as *hade* (showy) or as *gehin* (vulgar), and I fervently hope for such reasons *not* to encounter *Someday by Justin Bieber*. On the other hand, fragrances such as Annick Goutal's *Eau d'Hadrien*, with its intense citric notes, might well be described as *shibumi*, or the softer tones of Hermès's *24 Faubourg* as *jōhin*. And one can only suppose, from my opening quotation, that in Guerlain's *L'Heure Bleu* and *Bouquet de Faunes*, Kuki had found the olfactory essences of *iki*.[28]

A more perplexing question remains. Insofar as it may be right to construe the diagrammatic structure of *iki* as—so to speak—"fragranced," and whatever Kuki's personal preoccupation with the sense of smell may be, can any useful philosophical purchase be found for aesthetic analysis and for Japanese aesthetics itself through consideration of the olfactory? I believe it can and it is to this matter that I now finally turn.

THE CONTINGENT AND THE AESTHETIC

As I observed earlier, an inviting feature of Kuki Shūzō's writings is that we encounter a philosopher articulate in his embrace of the quite different aesthetic cultures of Japan and Europe. More specifically, I suggested, Kuki appears drawn both to a structured aesthetic architectonic, which might be said to be equally Japanese and German, *and* to a more delicate aesthetic phenomenology, which might be said to be equally Japanese and French.

However, there is one fundamental philosophical concept that, as I have already indicated, requires closer analysis: namely, what might be held to be the "contingent" aspects of the olfactory. Earlier, I noted Michael F. Marra's claim that Kuki espouses a "philosophy of contingency."[29] But I can make no sense here of the idea of a *philosophy* of contingency. What could this conceivably *be*? A "philosophy" of what merely *happens*? It is more accurate to say that Kuki was *exercised* by the concept of contingency, but on two counts, I contend that Marra fails to recognize the precise origin of his concern.

On the first count, Marra's reading of Kuki's poem "Gūzensei" ("Contingency") fails to observe the nature of the philosophico-mathematical problem with which Kuki is actually dealing: namely, the fifth of Euclid's ten axioms in his *Elements,* the so-called Parallel Axiom (or Parallel Postulate). Formally, this reads: "If two straight lines are crossed by a third in such a way that the interior angles on one side are less than two right angles, then the two lines will meet if produced on that side."[30] Informally, this is, of course, the idea that parallel lines will never intersect, and Kuki's poem reads at the relevant point,

> The principle that two parallel lines do not intersect
> To the intersection of parallel lines don't you object?
> With this, contingency is fulfilled.[31]

Here, Kuki is clearly aware of the profound problem with Euclid's Parallel Axiom. From Proclus in the fourth century until attempts in the nineteenth century to establish an alternative, non-Euclidean geometry, mathematicians had been agitated that the Euclid's Parallel Axiom was *not* a self-evident or necessary truth (and thus not an "axiom" at all). It was merely a contingent fact about parallel lines that they did not intersect, and therefore something that could be otherwise. But what Kuki poetically contends is that, of course, we *do* object to the possibility that parallel lines might intersect, and that his slightly odd notion of a contingency "fulfilled" effectively reintroduces the idea of necessity: a species of "contingent necessity," so to speak.

Now the idea of a "contingent necessity" may seem to be a logical solecism, but, on my second count, its origin for Kuki should be evident. That is, once again, Kuki's imperative to "go back to Kant" is at work, and what is readily recognizable is Kant's introduction, alongside necessary *a priori* truths and contingent *a posteriori* truths, of the category of *synthetic a priori* truths, in respect of which it might very loosely be said that "contingency is fulfilled." As a matter of fact, early in his *Critique of Pure Reason,* Kant, like Kuki, employs another fundamental Euclidean principle to *demonstrate* his very conception of a synthetic *a priori* proposition. As Kant puts it:

That the straight line between two points is the shortest, is a synthetic proposition. For my concept of *straight* line contains nothing of quantity, but only of quality. The concept of the shortest is wholly an addition, and cannot be derived, through any process of analysis, from the concept of the straight line.[32]

Thus, the principle that the shortest distance between two points (on a Euclidean plane) must be a straight line is a synthetic *a priori* proposition, just as Euclid's Parallel Axiom is.

In returning to the aesthetic context of Kuki's *iki,* however, it seems to me plain that what Kuki is attempting to overcome—certainly in what I claimed as the Aristotelian form of the diagrammatic structure of *iki*—is the belief that in making aesthetic judgments we *are* operating in the realm of pure contingency. That is, that we cannot appeal to rules in forming any aesthetic judgment. Yet, it might immediately be objected here, was this not exactly Kant's fundamental contention in his *Critique of Aesthetic Judgment*?

But such an objection is only pertinent if what is thought to be at issue is the *formation* of an aesthetic judgment. It is not, however, the case where the issue is the manifestation of aesthetic creativity (what Kant calls the 'genius' of fine art). Kant here is vigorous in his argument that a genuine aesthetic creativity cannot come about by mere chance or contingency. As he claims,

> [T]here is still no fine art in which something mechanical, capable of being at once comprehended and followed in obedience to rules, and consequently something academic, does not constitute the essential condition of the art ... . Now, seeing that originality of talent is one (though not the sole) essential factor that goes to make up the character of genius, shallow minds fancy that the best evidence they can give of their being full-blown geniuses is by emancipating themselves from all academic constraint of rules, in the belief that one cuts a finer figure on the back of an ill-tempered than of a trained horse.[33]

It is exactly this principle that, I contend, is so apparent in Japanese aesthetic culture: it *is* the "moral geometry" that, as I noted, Okakura identifies in the multiple rules (*temae*) of the tea ceremony. And it is this same kind of aesthetic rule that is ubiquitous elsewhere in Japan, from *ikebana* to the humble *bento* box.[34]

Still, there *is* a fundamental problem when we consider the phenomenon of smell. For we can, so to speak, gain no cognitive purchase on the structure of smells. The point is nicely made by the great British art critic Adrian Stokes in his delightfully entitled essay "Strong Smells and Polite Society." Stokes writes that "[w]e swallow smells whole, as it were," and adds that

> [w]e are little interested in the composite nature of smells, their parts and correspondences. We tend to think of each olfactory experience as unrelated ... Consequently, for this reason alone, there is no art of smell, since art depends upon

an additive or balancing process between parts. To see or to hear is to observe details, dovetailing, whereas the sub-divisions of smell are vapid.[35]

It is around this point that we may begin to see why Kant in particular (though interestingly not Kuki) was so aesthetically dismissive of smell. With smell, there appears to be no "academic constraint of rules" that would "constitute the essential condition of ... art."[36] This is the point that Stokes echoes, but at the same time adds a telling qualification to the claim that "we swallow smells whole, as it were": namely, that "in doing so we may become enveloped or possessed."[37] It is this experience of envelopment or possession—the possibility, as I said earlier, of being "overpowered" or "overcome" by a smell—that, I want finally to suggest, locates the olfactory at the outer limit of a Kantian aesthetic.

Of the five senses, it is smell that most nearly approaches the contingent condition of what Kant understood as the "sublime." That is, strong odors will overpower us in their inescapability and in our incapacity to avert attention *from* or engage in any reflective negotiation *with* them. These are the lessons we learn from Kant himself, from Turin, and from Stokes in their remarks on smells. But Kant expresses the point more formally in a passage from his "Analytic of the Sublime" in the *Critique of Aesthetic Judgment*, where he contends that an object that provokes the feeling of the sublime "may appear, indeed, in point of form to contravene the ends of our power of judgment, to be ill-adapted to our faculty of presentation, and to be, as it were, an outrage on the imagination."[38]

Such "ill-adaptation" and "outrage" is, of course, precisely the problem we generally have with the olfactory. Insofar as smells typically envelop or possess us, overpower or overcome us, our first philosophical instinct is to set aside olfactory sensibility as having neither epistemic nor aesthetic value, which is, of course, exactly the instinct that I have argued we find with Kant. Yet with Kuki Shūzō's thinking we must pause. For Kuki, it insistently seems, there is more to smell than meets the nose.

CONCLUSION

In the strange metaphorical acknowledgement I cited earlier, Kuki declares himself to have "the smell of the traditional [Japanese] past." We may now, I hope, see how literally this may be meant. While it is no part of my argument that Japanese aesthetics construes the olfactory as a *paradigm*, what is evident and culturally unusual is the attention given to smell. Negatively, of course, the Western habit of scenting the body is regarded as a "pollution." Yet, as I have indicated, there *is* in Japan the high tradition of *Kōdō* and the reflective discipline of "listening to" scents. Even in Japanese everyday life,

I noted, there is the distinctly non-Western convention of reflectively pausing before eating in order to register the fragrance of a dish.

But Kuki extends his metaphor by adding that his love for tradition "is not as faint as a scent." The argument of this chapter might here be construed to articulate this proposition in two different respects. In the first, my contention was that Kuki's diagrammatic structure of *iki* and the concepts he employs has a surprising olfactory character: it is as if, against the commonplace view of the fleeting nature of scents, there *were* in fact a structural logic such as we may discern in the diagram of the structure of *iki*. In the second respect, Kuki's own imperative to "go back to Kant" may be said to constitute a counter to his philosophical mentor's derogation of smell and to philosophy's neglect of olfactory sensibility in general. In so doing, my claim is that Kuki Shūzō defies the idea of the "faintness" of scent and, with the delicacy of his own olfactory aestheticism, suggests a bolder presence in the phenomenology of Japanese aesthetics itself.

NOTES

1. Kuki Shūzō, "Oto to nioi: Gūzensei no oto to kanōsei no nioi" ("Sound and Smell: The Sound of Contingency and the Smell of Possibility," 1936), in *Kuki Shūzō: A Philosopher's Poetry and Poetics,* trans. and ed. Michael F. Marra (Honolulu: University of Hawai'i Press, 2004), 273–74. Henceforth cited as *KSPPP.* Kuki incorrectly identifies *Quelques Fleurs* as a perfume created by Lanvin rather than by Houbigant. I should acknowledge here the major debt that studies of Kuki in English owe to the late Michael F. Marra's scholarship and translation, though I have had occasion to dispute his interpretations. See Peter Leech, review of *Kuki Shūzō: A Philosopher's Poetry and Poetics,* translated and edited by Michael F. Marra, *Bulletin of the School of Oriental and African Studies* 68, no. 2 (2005): 42–44.

2. Alexandre Dumas, "Les Parfums," in *Le (Petit) Moniteur Universal du Soir,* October 16, 1868; quoted in Alain Corbin, *The Foul and the Fragrant: Odor and the French Social Imagination* (Cambridge, MA: Harvard University Press, 1984), 76.

3. Michael F. Marra, "Worlds in Tension: An Essay on Kuki Shūzō's Poetry and Poetics," in *KSPPP,* 17.

4. Kuki Shūzō, "Dentō to shinsu" ("Tradition and Progressivism"), in *KSPPP,*285.

5. Kuki Shūzō, "Seafood Restaurant," in *KSPPP,* 47.

6. Kuki Shūzō, "A Stroll," in *KSPPP,* 112.

7. Kuki Shūzō, "The Negative Dimension," in *KSPPP,* 51.

8. Kuki Shūzō, *Tanka 134,* in *KSPPP,* 93.

9. Chandler Burr, "Display It, Don't Spray It," *New York Times Magazine,* May 1, 2005, accessed June 24, 2015, http://www.nytimes.com/2005/05/01/magazine/display-it-dont-spray-it.html?_r=0. It is certainly not that Japan *lacks* a cosmetic industry. Shiseido, the largest Japanese cosmetic corporation, was actually founded in 1872, only half a century later than those of Paris. But in Japan it is still the case

that Shiseido's products focus on skincare and make-up rather than fragrance. As Burr reports, while the focus on scents of Western cosmetic brands is around fifty percent, in Japan the estimated figure remains a surprisingly low fifteen percent.

10. The best and most detailed account of *kō* and *kō-kwai* remains Lafcadio Hearn, "Incense," in *In Ghostly Japan* (Rutland, VT: Tuttle Publishing, 2005), 19–45.

11. Kuki Shūzō, *Tanka 87*, in *KSPPP*, 83. Kuki's term, *iki*, is preserved in Japanese here. Marra translates Kuki's *iki* as 'stylishness' without further comment.

12. Kuki Shūzō, *Tanka 123*, in *KSPPP*, 91.

13. For a detailed chronology of Kuki's life, see Hiroshi Nara, *The Structure of Detachment: The Aesthetic Vision of Kuki Shūzō, with a Translation of* Iki no kōzō (Honolulu: University of Hawai'i Press, 2004), 171–75. Raphael von Koeber (1848–1923) was appointed to teach philosophy at Tokyo Imperial University in 1893, following posts at the universities of Berlin, Heidelberg, and Munich. A talented pianist, Von Koeber had a special interest in Kantian aesthetics and the aesthetics of music, but was more often identified in Tokyo by his peculiarly shabby appearance and dress.

14. Heinrich John Rickert (1863–1936) was Professor of Philosophy at the University of Heidelberg from 1915 to 1932. Among his major publications was *Kant als Philosoph der modernen Kultur* (*Kant as Philosopher of Modern Culture*) (Tübingen, BW: Mohr, 1924).

15. Given Rickert's Kantianism, I remain unconvinced by an orthodoxy of Kuki studies that his time at Heidelberg displaced Kuki's focus from Kant to the work of Husserl and Heidegger. See, for example, Marra, "Worlds in Tension," 9–10.

16. Okakura Kakuzō, *The Book of Tea* (Tokyo: Kodansha International, 1989), 29–30.

17. Immanuel Kant, *The Critique of Judgement, Part One: The Critique of Aesthetic Judgement*, trans. James Creed Meredith (Oxford: Oxford University Press, 1952), 196. Henceforth cited as *CAJ*. The context of the passage is equally interesting, and indeed prophetic for our own times, in further denouncing music insofar as "it scatters its influence abroad to an uncalled-for extent (through the neighborhood), and thus, as it were, becomes obtrusive and deprives others ... of their freedom" (*CAJ*, 196). It is socially depressing that it is almost impossible now to find restaurants—in fact public places and events—where one can comfortably converse with friends against the relentless competition of amplified music.

18. Luca Turin, *The Secret of Scent: Adventures in Perfume and the Science of Smell* (London: Faber and Faber, 2006), 15. For an excellent account of Turin's role in the science of smell, see Chandler Burr, *The Emperor of Scent: A Story of Perfume, Obsession, and the Last Mystery of the Senses* (London: William Heinemann, 2003).

19. Immanuel Kant, *Kant: Anthropology from a Pragmatic Point of View*, trans. Robert B. Louden (Cambridge: Cambridge University Press, 2006), 45–50.

20. Ibid., 50.

21. Immanuel Kant, "Reflexionen zur Anthropologie," in *Kants gesammelte Schriften*, vol. 15, ed. Königlich Preussischen Akademie der Wissenschaften (Berlin: Walter de Gruyter, 1923). Regrettably, the text is not included in *The Cambridge Edition of the Works of Immanuel Kant: Opus postumum*, ed. Eckart Förster, trans. Eckart Förster and Michael Rosen (Cambridge: Cambridge University Press, 1993),

but is partially translated in Winfried Menninghaus, *Disgust: Theory and History of a Strong Sensation,* trans. Howard Eiland and Joel Golb (Albany, NY: State University of New York Press, 2003).

22. Kant, "Reflexionen zur Anthropologie," cited in Menninghaus, 111. For further commentary on Kant on smell, see Christopher Turner, "Leftovers / Dinner with Kant: The Taste of Disgust," *Cabinet* 33 (2009), accessed June 24, 2015, http://cabinet-magazine.org/issues/33/turner.php.

23. The Japanese comedy film *Tampopo,* directed by Jūzō Itami (Tokyo: Itami Productions, 1985), had a remarkably warm and popular reception in Western cinemas, though I suspect that the communal soup-slurping scene in the noodle shop was found comical simply because it seemed so definitively non-Western.

24. The two current English translations of *Iki no kōzō* are Nara, *op. cit.*; and Kuki Shūzō, *Reflections on Japanese Taste: The Structure of* Iki, trans. John Clark (Sydney: Power Publications, 1997). Marra's translation, 'stylishness,' occurs, as noted above, in his rendering of Kuki's poem, *Tanka 87,* in *KSPPP,* 83.

25. Kuki, *Reflections on Japanese Taste,* 118.

26. A problem here is that the word 'cool' in English is generationally migratory. 'Cool,' among my own current students, seems to be a form of assent or affirmation rather than a form of uncontrived and detached stylishness.

27. Figure 27.1 is my own reconstruction and translation from the diagram published in Kuki Shūzō, *Iki no kōzō* (Tokyo: Iwanami Shoten, 1979), 44.

28. An especially useful source for the characterization of fragrances is Luca Turin, *Parfums: Le guide* (Paris: Hermé, 1992).

29. Marra, "Worlds in Tension," 17.

30. Euclid, *The Thirteen Books of Euclid's Elements,* 3 vols., trans. Sir Thomas L. Heath (New York: Dover, 1956), 1:154.

31. Kuki, "The Negative Dimension," 52.

32. Immanuel Kant, *Critique of Pure Reason,* trans. Norman Kemp Smith (London: Macmillan, 1968), 53.

33. Kant, *CAJ,* 171. I have argued this particular point at length in relation to Japanese aesthetic culture in my "Freedom and Formula: An Inter-Cultural Problem of Western and Japanese Aesthetics," in *The Pursuit of Comparative Aesthetics: An Interface Between East and West,* ed. Mazhar Hussain and Robert Wilkinson (Burlington, VT: Ashgate 2006), 233–48.

34. The "marvelous discipline" of the *bento* box is intriguingly discussed in Kenji Ekuan, *The Aesthetics of the Japanese Lunchbox,* ed. David B. Stewart (Cambridge, MA: MIT Press, 2000).

35. Adrian Stokes, "Strong Smells and Polite Society," in *A Game That Must Be Lost: Collected Papers* (Cheadle: Carcanet Press, 1973), 24.

36. Kant, *CAJ,* 171.

37. Stokes, 24.

38. Kant, *CAJ,* 91.

Selected Bibliography

100 Key Words for Understanding Japan (Nippon o Shiru Hyakusho): SUN Special Bilingual Issue. Tokyo: Heibonsha Ltd. Publishers, 1993.

Addiss, Stephen, Gerald Groemer, and J. Thomas Rimer, eds. *Traditional Japanese Arts and Culture: An Illustrated Sourcebook*. Honolulu: University of Hawai'i Press, 2006.

Allison, Anne. "The Cultural Politics of Pokémon Capitalism." Paper Presented at the Media in Transition 2: Globalization and Convergence Conference, Massachusetts Institute of Technology, Cambridge, MA, May 10–12, 2002.

———. "Cuteness as Japan's Millennial Product." In *Pikachu's Global Adventure: The Rise and Fall of Pokémon*, edited by Joseph Tobin, 34–52. Durham, NC: Duke University Press, 2004.

Anderson, Richard L. *Calliope's Sisters: A Comparative Study of Philosophies of Art*. Englewood Cliffs, NJ: Prentice Hall, 1990.

Anesaki, Masaharu. *Art, Life, and Nature in Japan*. Rutland, VT: Charles E. Tuttle Company, 1973.

Arima, Michiko. "Creative Interpretation of the Text and the Japanese Mentality." In *The Empire of Signs: Semiotic Essays on Japanese Culture*, edited by Yoshihiko Ikegami, 33–55. Amsterdam: John Benjamins, 1991.

Avella, Natalie. *Graphic Japan: From Woodblock and Zen to Manga and Kawaii*. Mies, Switzerland: RotoVision, 2004.

Bell, David. *Hokusai's Project: The Articulation of Pictorial Space*. Folkestone, UK: Global Oriental, 2007.

Berry, Mary E. "(Even Radical) Illustration Requires (Normalizing) Convention: The Case of 'Genre Art' in Early Modern Japan." *Journal of Visual Culture* 9, no. 3 (2010): 347–59.

Berthier, François. *Reading Zen in the Rocks: The Japanese Dry Landscape Garden*. Translated by Graham Parkes. Chicago: University of Chicago Press, 2000.

Blocker, H. Gene and Christopher L. Starling. *Japanese Philosophy*. Albany, NY: State University of New York Press, 2001.

413

Bordwell, David. *Ozu and the Poetics of Cinema.* Princeton, NJ: Princeton University Press, 1988.

Borggreen, Gunhild. "Cute and Cool in Contemporary Japanese Visual Arts." *Copenhagen Journal of Asian Studies* 29, no. 1 (2011): 39–60.

Botz-Bornstein, Thorsten. "'Iki,' Style, Trace: Shūzō Kuki and the Spirit of Hermeneutics." *Philosophy East and West* 47, no. 4 (1997): 554–80.

Bownas, Geoffrey and Anthony Thwaite, trans. and eds. *The Penguin Book of Japanese Verse.* London: Penguin, 1964.

Brandt, Kim. *Kingdom of Beauty: Mingei and the Politics of Folk Art in Imperial Japan.* Durham, NC: Duke University Press, 2007.

Bullen, Richard. "Refining the Past." *British Journal of Aesthetics* 50, no. 3 (2010): 243–54.

Carlson, Allen. "On the Aesthetic Appreciation of Japanese Gardens." *British Journal of Aesthetics* 37, no. 1 (1997): 47–56.

Carter, Robert E. *The Japanese Arts and Self-Cultivation.* Albany, NY: State University of New York Press, 2008.

Cheok, Adrian David. "Kawaii/Cute Interactive Media." In *Art and Technology of Entertainment Computing and Communication*, edited by Adrian David Cheok, 223–54. London: Springer, 2010.

Clark, John. "Sovereign Domains: *The Structure of 'Iki.'*" *Japan Forum* 10, no. 2 (1998): 197–209.

Clark, Timothy T. "*Mitate-e*: Some Thoughts, and a Summary of Recent Writings." *Impressions* 19 (1997): 7–27.

Dale, Peter N. *The Myth of Japanese Uniqueness.* London: Routledge, 1986.

Davis, Darrell William. *Picturing Japaneseness: Monumental Style, National Identity, Japanese Film.* New York: Columbia University Press, 1996.

De Bary, Wm. Theodore, Donald Keene, George Tanabe, and Paul Varley, eds. *Sources of Japanese Tradition.* Vol. 1, *From Earliest Times to 1600.* 2nd ed. New York: Columbia University Press, 2002.

De Bary, Wm. Theodore, Carol Gluck, and Arthur Tiedemann, eds. *Sources of Japanese Tradition.* Vol. 2, *1600 to 2000.* 2nd ed. New York: Columbia University Press, 2002.

Desser, David. *Ozu's Tokyo Story.* Cambridge: Cambridge University Press, 1997.

Dōgen. *Master Dōgen's Shōbōgenzō, Book 2.* Translated by Gudo Nishijima and Chodo Cross. London: Windbell Publications, 1996.

———. *Shōbōgenzō: Zen Essays by Dōgen.* Translated by Thomas Cleary. Honolulu: University of Hawai'i Press, 1986.

Ebersole, Gary L. *Ritual Poetry and the Politics of Death in Early Japan.* Princeton, NJ: Princeton University Press, 1989.

Ekuan, Kenji. *The Aesthetics of the Japanese Lunchbox.* Edited by David B. Stewart. Cambridge, MA: MIT Press, 1998.

Fujiwara, Teika. "Maigetsushō." In *The Theory of Beauty in the Classical Aesthetics of Japan*, translated and annotated by Toshihiko Izutsu and Toyo Izutsu, 79–96. The Hague: Martinus Nijhoff, 1981.

Gill, Robin D. *Cherry Blossom Epiphany: The Poetry and Philosophy of a Flowering Tree*. Key Biscayne, FL: Paraverse Press, 2006.

Grilli, Peter. *Pleasures of the Japanese Bath*. New York: Weatherhill, 1992.

Haft, Alfred. *Aesthetic Strategies of the Floating World:* Mitate, Yatsushi, *and* Fūryū *in Early Modern Japanese Popular Culture*. Leiden: Brill, 2012.

Haga, Kōshirō. "The *Wabi* Aesthetic Through the Ages." In *Japanese Aesthetics and Culture: A Reader*, edited by Nancy G. Hume, 245–78. Albany, NY: State University of New York Press, 1995.

Hahn, Tomie. *Sensational Knowledge: Embodying Culture Through Japanese Dance*. Middletown, CT: Wesleyan University Press, 2007.

Hakuin, Ekaku. *The Zen Master Hakuin: Selected Writings*. Translated by Philip Yampolsky. New York: Columbia University Press, 1971.

Hammitzsch, Horst. *Zen in the Art of the Tea Ceremony: A Guide to the Tea Way*. New York: St. Martin's Press, 1980.

Hasegawa, Yuko. "Post-Identity Kawaii: Commerce, Gender, and Contemporary Japanese Art." In *Consuming Bodies: Sex and Contemporary Japanese Art*, edited by Fran Lloyd, 127–41. London: Reaktion Books, 2002.

Hattori, Dohō. "The Red Booklet." In *The Theory of Beauty in the Classical Aesthetics of Japan*, translated and annotated by Toshihiko Izutsu and Toyo Izutsu, 159–67. The Hague: Martinus Nijhoff, 1981.

Hayashiya, Tatsusaburō, ed. *Kodai chūsei geijutsuron* (*Ancient and Medieval Theories of Art*). Tokyo: Iwanami Shoten, 1973.

Heine, Steven. *A Blade of Grass: Japanese Poetry and Aesthetics in Dōgen Zen*. New York: Peter Lang Publishing, 1989.

———. *A Dream Within a Dream: Studies in Japanese Thought*. New York: Peter Lang Publishing, 1991.

Heisig, James W. *Philosophers of Nothingness: An Essay on the Kyoto School*. Honolulu: University of Hawai'i Press, 2001.

Heisig, James W., Thomas P. Kasulis, and John C. Maraldo, eds. *Japanese Philosophy: A Sourcebook*. Honolulu: University of Hawai'i Press, 2011.

Herrigel, Eugen. *Zen in the Art of Archery*. Translated by R. F. C. Hull. New York: Pantheon Books, 1953.

Hirota, Dennis, ed. *Wind in the Pines: Classic Writings of the Way of Tea as a Buddhist Path*. Fremont, CA: Asian Humanities Press, 1995.

Hisamatsu, Shin'ichi. *Zen and the Fine Arts*. Translated by Gishin Tokiwa. Tokyo: Kodansha International, 1971.

Huey, Robert N. *Kyōgoku Tamekane: Poetry and Politics in Late Kamakura Japan*. Stanford, CA: Stanford University Press, 1989.

———. *The Making of* Shinkokinshū. Cambridge, MA: Harvard University Press, 2002.

Hume, Nancy G., ed. *Japanese Aesthetics and Culture: A Reader*. Albany, NY: State University of New York Press, 1995.

Ienaga, Saburō. *Japanese Art: A Cultural Appreciation*. Translated by Richard L. Gage. New York: Weatherhill, 1979.

Iida, Yumiko. *Rethinking Identity in Modern Japan: Nationalism as Aesthetics.* London: Routledge, 2002.

Ikegami, Eiko. *Bonds of Civility: Aesthetic Networks and the Political Origins of Japanese Culture.* Cambridge: Cambridge University Press, 2005.

Inaga, Shigemi. *Questioning Oriental Aesthetics and Thinking: Conflicting Visions of "Asia" under the Colonial Empires.* Kyoto: International Research Center for Japanese Studies, 2010.

Isozaki, Arata. *Japan-ness in Architecture.* Translated by Sabu Kohso. Edited by David B. Stewart. Introduction by Toshiko Mori. Cambridge, MA: MIT Press, 2006.

Iwabuchi, Koichi. *Recentering Globalization: Popular Culture and Japanese Transnationalism.* Durham, NC: Duke University Press, 2002.

Iwaki, Ken'ichi. "The Logic of Visual Perception: Ueda Juzō." In *A History of Modern Japanese Aesthetics*, translated and edited by Michael F. Marra, 285–317. Honolulu: University of Hawai'i Press, 2001.

Izutsu, Toshihiko, and Toyo Izutsu. *The Theory of Beauty in the Classical Aesthetics of Japan.* The Hague: Martinus Nijhoff, 1981.

Kamo, no Chōmei. *Hōjōki (An Account of My Hut).* In *Anthology of Japanese Literature: From the Earliest Era to the Mid-Nineteenth Century*, compiled and edited by Donald Keene, 197–212. Rutland, VT: Charles E. Tuttle Company, 1955.

Karatani, Kōjin. "Japan as Museum: Okakura Tenshin and Ernest Fenollosa." Translated by Sabu Kosho. In *Japanese Art after 1945: Scream against the Sky*, edited by Alexandra Munroe, 33–39. New York: Harry N. Abrams, 1994.

———. *Origins of Modern Japanese Literature.* Translated and edited by Brett de Bary. Durham, NC: Duke University Press, 1993.

———. "Uses of Aesthetics: After Orientalism." In *Edward Said and the Work of the Critic: Speaking Truth to Power*, edited by Paul A. Bové, 139–51. Durham, NC: Duke University Press, 2000.

Kasulis, Thomas P. *Intimacy or Integrity: Philosophy and Cultural Difference.* Honolulu: University of Hawai'i Press, 2002.

———. *Zen Action / Zen Person.* Honolulu: University of Hawai'i Press, 1981.

Katō, Shūichi. *Form, Style, Tradition: Reflections on Japanese Art and Society.* Translated by John Bester. Berkeley, CA: University of California Press, 1971.

Kawabata, Yasunari. *Japan, the Beautiful, and Myself: The 1968 Nobel Prize Acceptance Speech.* Translated by Edward G. Seidensticker. Tokyo: Kodansha International, 1969.

Keene, Donald, ed. *Anthology of Japanese Literature: From the Earliest Era to the Mid-Nineteenth Century.* New York: Grove Press, 1955.

———. *Dawn to the West: A History of Japanese Literature.* New York: Columbia University Press, 1999.

———. "Japanese Aesthetics." In *Japanese Aesthetics and Culture: A Reader*, edited by Nancy G. Hume, 27–41. Albany, NY: State University of New York Press, 1995.

———. *Landscapes and Portraits: Appreciations of Japanese Culture.* Tokyo: Kodansha International, 1971.

————. *World within Walls: Japanese Literature of the Pre-Modern Era 1600–1867.* New York: Holt, Rinehart and Winston, 1976.

Keister, Jay. "Urban Style, Sexuality, Resistance, and Refinement in the Japanese Dance *Sukeroku.*" *Asian Theatre Journal* 26, no. 2 (2009): 215–49.

Kelts, Roland. *Japanamerica: How Japanese Pop Culture Has Invaded the U.S.* New York: Palgrave Macmillan, 2006.

Kern, Adam L. *Manga from the Floating World: Comicbook Culture and the* Kibyōshi *of Edo Japan.* Cambridge, MA: Harvard University Asia Center, 2006.

Kerr, Alex. *Lost Japan.* Melbourne: Lonely Planet Publications, 1996.

Kikuchi, Yuko. *Japanese Modernisation and* Mingei *Theory: Cultural Nationalism and Oriental Orientalism.* London: Routledge, 2004.

Kindaichi, Kyōsuke and Sueo Sugiyama. *Ainu geijutsu (Ainu Art).* Sapporo, Japan: Hokkaido Publication Project Center, 1993.

Kinsella, Sharon. "Cuties in Japan." In *Women, Media, and Consumption in Japan,* edited by Lise Skov and Brian Moeran, 220–54. Honolulu: University of Hawai'i Press, 1995.

Koma, Kyoko. "Kawaii as Represented in Scientific Research: The Possibilities of Kawaii Cultural Studies." *Hemispheres* 28 (2013): 103–16.

Koren, Leonard. *Wabi-Sabi for Artists, Designers, Poets and Philosophers.* Berkeley, CA: Stone Bridge Press, 1994.

Kuki, Shūzō. *Reflections on Japanese Taste: The Structure of Iki.* Translated by John Clark. Sydney: Power Publications, 1997.

Kusanagi, Masao. "The Logic of Passional Surplus." In *Modern Japanese Aesthetics: A Reader,* translated and edited by Michele Marra, 148–67. Honolulu: University of Hawai'i Press, 1999.

LaFleur, William R. *The Karma of Words: Buddhism and the Literary Arts in Medieval Japan.* Berkeley, CA: University of California Press, 1983.

Lebra, Takie Sugiyama. *The Japanese Self in Cultural Logic.* Honolulu: University of Hawai'i Press, 2004.

Lee, O-Young. *The Compact Culture: The Japanese Tradition of "Smaller Is Better."* Translated by Robert N. Huey. Tokyo: Kodansha International, 1991. Originally published in 1984 by Kodansha International as *Smaller Is Better: Japan's Mastery of the Miniature.*

Leech, Peter. "Freedom and Formula: An Inter-Cultural Problem of Western and Japanese Aesthetics." In *The Pursuit of Comparative Aesthetics: An Interface Between East and West,* edited by Mazhar Hussain and Robert Wilkinson, 233–47. Aldershot, UK and Burlington, VT: Ashgate, 2006.

Lippit, Seiji M. *Topographies of Japanese Modernism.* New York: Columbia University Press, 2002.

Lopes, Dominic McIver. "Shikinen Sengu and the Ontology of Architecture in Japan." *Journal of Aesthetics and Art Criticism* 65, no. 1 (2007): 77–84.

Marceau, Lawrence. *Takebe Ayatari: A* Bunjin *Bohemian in Early Modern Japan.* Ann Arbor, MI: Center for Japanese Studies, University of Michigan, 2004.

Marra, Michael F., trans. and ed. *A History of Modern Japanese Aesthetics.* Honolulu: University of Hawai'i Press, 2001.

————, ed. *Japanese Hermeneutics: Current Debates on Aesthetics and Interpretation.* Honolulu: University of Hawai'i Press, 2002.

————. *Kuki Shūzō: A Philosopher's Poetry and Aesthetics.* Honolulu: University of Hawai'i Press, 2004.

Marra, Michele, trans. and ed. *Modern Japanese Aesthetics: A Reader.* Honolulu: University of Hawai'i Press, 1999.

————. *Representations of Power: The Literary Politics of Medieval Japan.* Honolulu: University of Hawai'i Press, 1993.

————. *The Aesthetics of Discontent: Politics and Reclusion in Medieval Japanese Literature.* Honolulu: University of Hawai'i Press, 1991.

Matsumoto, Koji. "Japanese Spirituality and Music Practice: Art as Self-Cultivation." In *International Handbook of Research in Arts Education*, edited by Liora Bresler, 1425–38. New York: Springer, 2007.

Matsuo, Bashō. *The Narrow Road to the Deep North and Other Travel Sketches.* Translated by Nobuyuki Yuasa. London: Penguin, 1966.

McCullough, Helen C., trans. *The Tale of the Heike.* Stanford, CA: Stanford University Press, 1988.

Miller, Mara. "'A Matter of Life and Death': Kawabata on the Value of Art after the Atomic Bombings." *Journal of Aesthetics and Art Criticism* 74, no. 2 (2014): 261–75.

————. "Aesthetics as Investigation of Self, Subject, and Ethical Agency in Postwar Trauma in Kawabata's *The Sound of the Mountain*." *Philosophy and Literature* 39, no. 1A (2015): A122–A141.

————. "Beauty, Religion, and Tradition in Post-Nuclear Japanese Arts and Aesthetics." In *Artistic Visions and the Promise of Beauty: Cross-Cultural Perspectives*, edited by Kathleen M. Higgins, Shakti Maira, and Sonia Sikka, 57–75. Dordrecht: Springer, 2017.

————. "Denis Dutton's *The Art Instinct* and the Recovery of Ainu Aesthetics." *Philosophy and Literature* 38, no. 1A (2014): A48–A59.

————. "Japanese Aesthetics and Philosophy of Art." In *Oxford Handbook of World Philosophy*, edited by Jay L. Garfield and William Edelglass, 317–33. Oxford: Oxford University Press, 2011.

————. "Japanese Aesthetics and the Disruptions of Identity after the Atomic Bombings." *Kritische Berichte: Zeitschrift für Kunst- und Kulturwissenschaften* 38, no. 2 (2010): 73–82.

Miller, Mara and Koji Yamasaki. "Japanese (and Ainu) Aesthetics and Philosophy of Art." In *Oxford Handbook of Japanese Philosophy*, edited by Bret W. Davis. Oxford: Oxford University Press, forthcoming.

Minami, Hiroshi. *Psychology of the Japanese People.* Translated by Albert R. Ikoma. Tokyo: University of Tokyo Press, 1971.

Miner, Earl Roy, Robert E. Morrell, and Hiroko Odagiri. *The Princeton Companion to Classical Japanese Literature.* Princeton, NJ: Princeton University Press, 1988.

Mitukuni, Yoshida, Tanaka Ikko, and Sesoko Tsune, eds. *Tsu Ku Ru: Aesthetics at Work.* Hiroshima: Mazda Motor Corporation, 1990.

Miyoshi, Masao. *Accomplices of Silence: The Modern Japanese Novel.* Berkeley, CA: University of California Press, 1975.

Mizuhara, Sonohiro, Naoki Kaneko, Yasuo Kuwahara, Tomoko Matsuo, and Michiko Fukaya, eds. *Japan Is Beautiful: Kawabata Yasunari and Yasuda Yukihiko.* Translated by Rumiko Kanesaka, Brian Smallshaw, Fujisato Kitajima, Mark Frank, and Yoko Araki. Tokyo: Kyuryudo Art Publishing, 2008.

Morris, Ivan I. *The World of the Shining Prince: Court Life in Ancient Japan.* New York: Knopf, 1964.

Motoori, Norinaga. *Motoori Norinaga shū (Collected Works of Motoori Norinaga).* Edited by Yoshikawa Kōjirō. Vol. 15 of *Nihon no shiso (Thought in Japan).* Tokyo: Chikuma Shobo, 1969.

Munroe, Alexandra, ed. *Japanese Art After 1945: Scream Against the Sky.* New York: Harry N. Abrams, 1994.

Murase, Miyeko. *Bridge of Dreams: The Mary Griggs Burke Collection of Japanese Art.* New York: The Metropolitan Museum of Art, 2000.

Nanbō, Sōkei. "A Record of Nanbō." In *The Theory of Beauty in the Classical Aesthetics of Japan,* translated and annotated by Toshihiko Izutsu and Toyo Izutsu, 135–58. The Hague: Martinus Nijhoff, 1981.

Nara, Hiroshi, ed. *The Structure of Detachment: The Aesthetic Vision of Kuki Shūzō, with a Translation of* Iki no kōzō. Honolulu: University of Hawai'i Press, 2004.

Nihon koten bungaku taikei (Outline of Classical Japanese Literature). 100 vols. Tokyo: Iwanami Shoten, 1958–1968.

Nihon koten bungaku zenshū (Complete Works of Classical Japanese Literature). 51 vols. Tokyo: Shōgakukan, 1970–1976.

Nishitani, Keiji. "The Japanese Art of Arranged Flowers." Translated by Jeff Shore. In *World Philosophy: A Text with Readings,* edited by Robert C. Solomon and Kathleen M. Higgins, 23–27. New York: McGraw Hill, 1995.

Nishiyama, Matsunosuke. *Edo Culture: Daily Life and Diversions in Urban Japan, 1600–1868.* Honolulu: University of Hawai'i Press, 1997.

Nitobe, Inazō. *Bushidō: The Soul of Japan.* Rutland, VT: Charles E. Tuttle Company, 1969.

Odin, Steve. *Artistic Detachment in Japan and the West: Psychic Distance in Comparative Aesthetics.* Honolulu: University of Hawai'i Press, 2001.

———. "Intersensory Awareness in Chanoyu and Japanese Aesthetics." *Chanoyu Quarterly* 53 (1988): 35–44.

Ōe, Kenzaburō. "Japan, the Dubious, and Myself." In *Japan in Traditional and Postmodern Perspectives,* edited by Charles Wei-Hsun Fu and Steven Heine, 313–25. Albany, NY: State University of New York Press, 1995.

Ōgi, Fusami. "Gender Insubordination in Japanese Comics (*Manga*) for Girls." In *Illustrating Asia: Comics, Humor Magazines, and Picture Books,* edited by John A. Lent, 171–86. Honolulu: University of Hawai'i Press, 2001.

Ohashi, Ryōsuke. "*Kire* and *Iki.*" Translated by Graham Parkes. In *Encyclopedia of Aesthetics,* vol. 2, edited by Michael Kelly, 553–55. New York: Oxford University Press, 1998.

Oka, Hideyuki. *How to Wrap Five Eggs: Japanese Design in Traditional Packaging*. New York: Harper & Row, 1967.

Okakura, Kakuzō. *The Book of Tea*. Rutland, VT: Charles E. Tuttle Company, 1956.

———. *The Ideals of the East*. Rutland, VT: Charles E. Tuttle Company, 1997.

Ortolani, Benito. *The Japanese Theatre: From Shamanistic Ritual to Contemporary Pluralism*. Rev. ed. Princeton, NJ: Princeton University Press, 1995.

Parkes, Graham. "Japanese Aesthetics." In *The Stanford Encyclopedia of Philosophy*, Spring 2017 Edition, edited by Edward N. Zalta. Accessed August 26, 2017. https://plato.stanford.edu/archives/spr2017/entries/japanese-aesthetics/.

———. "The Role of Rock in the Japanese Dry Landscape Garden: A Philosophical Essay." In François Berthier, *Reading Zen in the Rocks: The Japanese Dry Landscape Garden*, translated by Graham Parkes, 85–155. Chicago: University of Chicago Press, 2000.

———. "Ways of Japanese Thinking." In *Japanese Aesthetics and Culture: A Reader*, edited by Nancy G. Hume, 77–108. Albany, NY: State University of New York Press, 1995.

Pilgrim, Richard B. *Buddhism and the Arts of Japan*. Chambersburg, PA: Anima Books, 1981.

Pincus, Leslie. *Authenticating Culture in Imperial Japan: Kuki Shūzō and the Rise of National Aesthetics*. Berkeley, CA: University of California Press, 1996.

Rath, Eric C. and Stephanie Assmann, eds. *Japanese Foodways, Past and Present*. Urbana, IL: University of Illinois Press, 2010.

Reeve, John, ed. *Living Arts of Japan*. London: British Museum Publications, 1990.

Richie, Donald. *A Lateral View: Essays on Culture and Style in Contemporary Japan*. Berkeley, CA: Stone Bridge Press, 1992.

———. *A Tractate on Japanese Aesthetics*. Berkeley, CA: Stone Bridge, 2007.

———. *Ozu: His Life and Films*. Berkeley, CA: University of California Press, 1977.

Rimer, J. Thomas and Yamazaki Masakazu, trans. *On the Art of the Nō Drama: The Major Treatises of Zeami*. Princeton, NJ: Princeton University Press, 1984.

Saito, Yuriko. *Aesthetics of the Familiar: Everyday Life and World-Making*. Oxford: Oxford University Press, 2017.

———. *Everyday Aesthetics*. Oxford: Oxford University Press, 2007.

———. "Japanese Aesthetics: Historical Overview." In *Encyclopedia of Aesthetics*, vol. 4, edited by Michael Kelly, 4–12. 2nd ed. New York: Oxford University Press, 2014.

———. "Japanese Aesthetics of Packaging." *Journal of Aesthetics and Art Criticism* 57, no. 2 (1999): 257–65.

———. "The Japanese Aesthetics of Imperfection and Insufficiency." *Journal of Aesthetics and Art Criticism* 55, no. 4 (1997): 377–85.

———. "The Moral Dimension of Japanese Aesthetics." *Journal of Aesthetics and Art Criticism* 65, no. 1 (2007): 85–97.

———. "Representing the Essence of Objects: Art in the Japanese Aesthetic Tradition." In *Art and Essence*, edited by Stephen Davies and Ananta Ch. Sukla, 125–41. Westport, CT: Praeger Publishers, 2003.

Sandrisser, Barbara. "On Elegance in Japan." In *Aesthetics in Perspective*, edited by Kathleen M. Higgins, 628–33. Fort Worth, TX: Harcourt Brace College Publishers, 1996.

Sarashina (AKA Takasue no Musume). *As I Crossed a Bridge of Dreams: Recollections of a Woman in Eleventh-Century Japan (Sarashina nikki, Sarashina Diary).* Translated by Ivan Morris. New York: Penguin Classics, 1989.

Sartwell, Crispin. *The Art of Living: Aesthetics of the Ordinary in World Spiritual Traditions.* Albany, NY: State University of New York Press, 1995.

———. *Six Names of Beauty.* London: Routledge, 2004.

Schrader, Paul. *Transcendental Style in Film: Ozu, Bresson, Dreyer.* New York: Da Capo Press, 1988.

Sei Shōnagon. *The Pillow Book of Sei Shōnagon.* Translated and edited by Ivan Morris. New York: Columbia University Press, 1967.

Seo, Audrey Yoshiko, and Stephen Addiss. *The Art of Twentieth-Century Zen: Paintings and Calligraphy by Japanese Masters.* Boston: Shambhala, 1998.

Shikibu, Murasaki. *The Tale of Genji.* Translated by Edward G. Seidensticker. New York: Alfred A. Knopf, 1976.

Skov, Lise. "Fashion Trends, Japonisme and Postmodernism: Or 'What Is So Japanese about *Comme des Garcons?*'" In *Contemporary Japan and Popular Culture*, edited by John Whittier Treat, 137–68. Honolulu: University of Hawai'i Press, 1996.

Sokoloff, Garrett. "By Pausing before a *Kicho*." In *Aesthetics in Perspective*, edited by Kathleen M. Higgins, 620–27. Fort Worth, TX: Harcourt Brace College Publishers, 1996.

Surak, Kristin. *Making Tea, Making Japan: Cultural Nationalism in Practice.* Stanford, CA: Stanford University Press, 2012.

Suzuki, Daisetz T. *Zen and Japanese Culture.* New York: Pantheon Books, 1959.

Suzuki, Tomi. *Narrating the Self: Fictions of Japanese Modernity.* Stanford, CA: Stanford University Press, 1996.

Tachibana no Toshitsuna. *Sakuteiki (Records of Garden Making).* In *Sakuteiki: Visions of the Japanese Garden*, translated by Jirō Takei and Marc P. Keane, 153–204. Boston: Tuttle Publishing, 2001.

Takeuchi, Melinda. *Taiga's True Views: The Language of Landscape Painting in Eighteenth-Century Japan.* Stanford, CA: Stanford University Press, 1992.

Tanahashi, Kazuaki. *Brush Mind: Text, Art, and Design.* Berkeley, CA: Parallax Press, 1990.

Tanaka, Kyūbun. "Kuki Shūzō and the Phenomenology of *Iki*." In *A History of Modern Japanese Aesthetics*, translated and edited by Michael F. Marra, 318–44. Honolulu: University of Hawai'i Press, 2001.

Tanizaki, Jun'ichirō. *In Praise of Shadows.* Translated by Thomas J. Harper and Edward G. Seidensticker. New Haven, CT: Leete's Island Books, 1977.

———. *The Makioka Sisters (Sasameyuki, 1943–1948).* Translated by Edward G. Seidensticker. New York: Alfred A. Knopf, 1957.

———. *Seven Japanese Tales.* Translated by Howard Hibbett. New York: Putnam, 1981.

———. *Some Prefer Nettles.* Translated by Edward G. Seidensticker. London: Vintage, 2001.

Tansman, Alan. *The Aesthetics of Japanese Fascism.* Berkeley, CA: University of California Press, 2009.

Treat, John Whittier. "Yoshimoto Banana Writes Home: The *Shōjo* in Japanese Popular Culture." In *Contemporary Japan and Popular Culture*, edited by John Whittier Treat, 275–308. Honolulu: University of Hawai'i Press, 1996.

Tsuji, Nobuo. "Ornament (Kazari)—An Approach to Japanese Culture." *Archives of Asian Art* 47 (1994): 35–45.

Tsunoda, Ryusaku, Wm. Theodore de Bary, and Donald Keene, eds. *Sources of Japanese Tradition*. 2 vols. New York: Columbia University Press, 1964.

Tyler, Susan C. *The Cult of Kasuga Seen Through Its Art*. Ann Arbor, MI: Center for Japanese Studies, University of Michigan, 1992.

Ueda, Makoto. *Literary and Art Theories in Japan*. Cleveland, OH: Case Western Reserve University Press, 1967.

Varley, H. Paul. *Japanese Culture*. 4th ed. Honolulu: University of Hawai'i Press, 2000.

Vincent, Keith. "Nihon-teki miseijuku no keifu" ("The Genealogy of Japanese Immaturity"). In *Nihon-tekisōzōryoku no mirai: Kūru japonorojii no kanōsei (The Future of the Japanese Imagination: The Potential of Cool Japanology)*, edited by Azuma Hiroki, 15–46. Tokyo: NHK Books, 2010.

Viswanathan, Meera. "Aesthetics, Japanese." In *Routledge Encyclopedia of Philosophy*, vol. 1, edited by Edward Craig, 79–91. New York: Routledge, 1998.

Walker, Janet. *The Japanese Novel of the Meiji Period and the Ideal of Individualism*. Princeton, NJ: Princeton University Press, 1979.

Washburn, Dennis C. *The Dilemma of the Modern in Japanese Fiction*. New Haven, CT: Yale University Press, 1995.

Yamamoto, Tsunetomo. *Hagakure: The Book of the Samurai*. Translated by William Scott Wilson. Tokyo: Kodansha International, 1979.

Yamasaki, Koji. "Indigenous Peoples and Museum Materials—Lessons from Preparing for the Ainu Cultural Exhibition." In *Teetasinrit Tekrukoci: The Handprints of Our Ancestors: Ainu Artifacts Housed at Hokkaido University—Inherited Techniques*, edited by Koji Yamasaki, Masaru Kato, and Tetsuya Amano, 92–96. Sapporo, Japan: Hokkaido University Museum / Hokkaido University Center for Ainu and Indigenous Studies, 2012.

Yamasaki, Koji, Masaru Kato, and Tetsuya Amano, eds. *Teetasinrit Tekrukoci: The Handprints of Our Ancestors: Ainu Artifacts Housed at Hokkaido University—Inherited Techniques*. Sapporo, Japan: Hokkaido University Museum / Hokkaido University Center for Ainu and Indigenous Studies, 2012.

Yanagi, Sōetsu. *The Unknown Craftsman: A Japanese Insight into Beauty*. Adapted by Bernard Leach. Tokyo: Kodansha International, 1989.

Yano, Christine R. *Pink Globalization: Hello Kitty's Trek across the Pacific*. Durham, NC: Duke University Press, 2013.

Yasuda, Ayao, ed. *Nihon no geijutsuron (Theories of Art in Japan)*. Tokyo: Sōgensha, 1990.

Yoda, Tomiko. *Gender and National Literature: Heian Texts in the Constructions of Japanese Modernity*. Durham, NC: Duke University Press, 2004.

Yokoi, Yūhō and Daizen Victoria. *Zen Master Dōgen: An Introduction with Selected Writings*. New York: Weatherhill, 1976.

Yoshida, Kenji. "Aboriginal Peoples and Museums—New Attempts to Realize Self-Representation in the 'Message from the Ainu' Exhibition." In *Message from the Ainu: Craft and Spirit*, edited by Foundation for Research and Promotion of Ainu Culture, 146–55. Tokushima, Japan: Association of Tokushima Prefectural Museum, 2003.

Yoshida, Kenkō. *Essays in Idleness: The* Tsurezuregusa *of Kenkō.* Translated by Donald Keene. New York: Columbia University Press, 1967.

Index

abstract expressionism, 339, 351nn14, 25
acceptance, xliii, li, lxxi, 6, 38, 356, 371, 380, 390
An Account of My Hut, 259, 293, 380n14
actor-agent theory, 150
Addiss, Stephen, xv, xxvi–xxvii
aesthetic appreciation, xxxvii, liii–lviii, 20, 93–99, 101–2, 104, 105nn6, 12, 106nn22, 25, 108n40, 176, 195
aesthetic category, 383, 394
aesthetic contemplation, 49, 52–58, 194
aesthetic cultivation, lv, 68, 121–22, 133
aesthetic egalitarianism, xxx, xxxii, xliv
aesthetic experience, xxv, xxx–xxxi, xxxiii, xxxv–xxxvii, xlii, xliv, lii, liv, lvii, lxiv–lxv, lxxiii, 45–47, 49, 52–53, 56, 58, 94, 104, 110, 121–23, 129, 130–31, 133–34, 155, 159, 161–63, 165n31, 166n32, 203, 269, 270
aesthetic expression, 37, 63, 67–68, 131–32, 211, 230
aesthetic paradigm, 121, 130, 133, 136n72
aesthetic property, lxxii, 383–84, 387–89, 395n4

aesthetic sensibility, xxx, xxxvi, li–lii, 19, 21–22, 65, 89, 277, 315n2
aesthetic value, xxx–xxxi, xxxiii–xxxvii, xliv, lii, lv, 32, 36–38, 121–22, 130, 143, 144–45, 148, 197, 275, 286, 292, 409
aesthetic welfare, 69–70
aestheticization of death, xxxix, lvi
aesthetics of alienation, 213
aesthetics of daily life, 395n7
aesthetics of disaster, 285
aesthetics of emptiness, l, lxviii, 335–52
aesthetics of fascism, 180
aesthetics of imperfection, xxxiii, xxxvii–xxxix, lxvi, 133, 294, 394
aesthetics of implication, xxxiii, xxxv–xxxvi
aesthetics of insufficiency, xxxviii, 38
aesthetics of suggestion, xxxiii–xxxvi, lxx, lxxii, 22, 296, 369, 371–72, 376, 378–79, 383, 386, 394
aesthetics of the everyday, xliv, 43n31, 319, 332n2, 385, 395n7
aesthetics of the indistinct, l–li, 17–27
African-American, 208, 210–18, 219nn20, 23, 31
agency, 150, 201, 269, 274–75, 278–79, 280n4, 391
aidagara, 252

425

438 *Index*

Contributors

Stephen Addiss is Tucker-Boatwright Professor Emeritus of the Humanities and Professor Emeritus of Art at the University of Richmond in Richmond, Virginia. He has exhibited his ink paintings and calligraphy in China, Japan, Korea, Singapore, Taiwan, Austria, England, France, Germany, and many venues in the United States. He is also the author or coauthor of more than 30 books and exhibition catalogues about East Asian art, including *The Art of Haiku* (Shambhala Publications, 2012), *Zen Sourcebook* (Hackett Publications, 2008), *Old Taoist* (Columbia University Press, 2000), *How to Look at Japanese Art* (Harry N. Abrams, 1996), *Haiga: Haiku-Painting* (University of Hawai'i Press, 1995), *Tao Te Ching* (Hackett Publications, 1993), *The Art of Zen* (Harry N. Abrams, 1989), and *Tall Mountains and Flowing Waters* (University of Hawai'i Press, 1987).

David Bell is associate professor at the University of Otago College of Education in Dunedin, New Zealand. He teaches the theory, curriculum, and pedagogy of visual arts education and has contributed courses in Japanese art history to the program of art history and theory. His research interests and publications embrace the arts of Edo-period Japan, aesthetic education, and museums as sites for aesthetic and transcultural learning.

Thorsten Botz-Bornstein was born in Germany, studied philosophy in Paris, and received his PhD from the University of Oxford. He has been researching in Japan and worked for the Center of Cognition of Hangzhou University in Hangzhou, China as well as at Tuskegee University in Tuskegee, Alabama. He is currently associate professor of philosophy at Gulf University for Science and Technology in Kuwait City, Kuwait.

Richard Bullen is senior lecturer in art history and theory at the University of Canterbury in Christchurch, New Zealand. In 2009, he curated an exhibition of *ukiyo-e*, "Pleasure and Play in Edo Japan," at the Canterbury Museum in New Zealand and edited the accompanying publication. He has published on aspects of the tea ceremony in *The British Journal of Aesthetics* and *Studies in the History of Gardens and Designed Landscapes*. He is currently engaged in a major research project on the Canterbury Museum's Rewi Alley Collection of Chinese Art.

Allen Carlson is professor emeritus of philosophy at the University of Alberta in Edmonton, Canada. His research interests include environmental philosophy and aesthetics, especially the aesthetics of nature and landscape. He has published numerous articles and several books, including *Nature and Landscape: An Introduction to Environmental Aesthetics* (Columbia University Press, 2009), *Aesthetics and the Environment: The Appreciation of Nature, Art and Architecture* (Routledge, 2000), and, with Glenn Parsons, *Functional Beauty* (Oxford University Press, 2008).

Robert E. Carter is professor emeritus of philosophy at Trent University in Ontario, Canada. Trained at Tufts University, Harvard University, and the University of Toronto, he is the author, coauthor, or editor of twelve books, and nearly one hundred articles and reviews. His books include *The Kyoto School: An Introduction* (State University of New York Press, 2013), *The Japanese Arts and Self-Cultivation* (State University of New York Press, 2008), *Encounter with Enlightenment: A Study of Japanese Ethics* (State University of New York Press, 2001), *Becoming Bamboo: Western and Eastern Explorations of the Meaning of Life* (McGill-Queen's University Press, 1992), and *Dimensions of Moral Education* (University of Toronto Press, 1984). Dr. Carter has visited Japan on nine occasions to teach and research, living in Japan for two years as visiting professor at Kansai Gaidai University in Osaka, Japan. He has also been visiting professor at the University of Hawai'i at Mānoa in Honolulu, Hawai'i. He is a poet and a musician, currently playing trumpet in two big bands.

David E. Cooper is professor emeritus of philosophy at Durham University in Durham, England. He has been visiting professor at universities in North America, Europe, and Asia, and the chair or president of many learned societies, including the Aristotelian Society, the Mind Association, the Friedrich Nietzsche Society, and the Philosophy of Education Society of Great Britain. His books include *Senses of Mystery: Engaging with Nature and the Meaning of Life* (Routledge, 2017), *Sunlight on the Sea: Reflecting on Reflections* (David E. Cooper, 2013), *Convergence with Nature: A Daoist Perspective* (Green Books,

2012), *A Philosophy of Gardens* (Oxford University Press, 2006), *The Measure of Things: Humanism, Humility, and Mystery* (Oxford University Press, 2002), and *World Philosophies: An Historical Introduction* (Blackwell, 1996).

Cheryl Crowley is associate professor of Japanese language and literature at Emory University in Atlanta, Georgia. She completed her master's degree at the University of Pennsylvania and her PhD at Columbia University. She has published on Japanese literature in *Monumenta Nipponica, Early Modern Japan: An Interdisciplinary Journal, The U.S.-Japan Women's Journal, Japanese Language and Literature*, and *The Japan Studies Review*. Her book, *Haikai Poet Yosa Buson and the Bashō Revival*, was published by Brill in 2007.

Timothy Unverzagt Goddard is assistant professor of Japanese studies at the University of Hong Kong (HKU), where he teaches Japanese literature, film, and cultural history. He received his AB in East Asian studies from Harvard College, and his MA and PhD in Asian languages and cultures from the University of California, Los Angeles (UCLA). His research interests include modernism, colonialism, urban space, and visual culture. Prior to his arrival at HKU, he was visiting lecturer in the department of Asian languages and cultures at UCLA. He is currently at work on a book manuscript based on his PhD dissertation, "*Teito* Tokyo: Empire, Modernity, and the Metropolitan Imagination," exploring literary, visual, and architectural representations of Tokyo as an imperial capital.

Carol Steinberg Gould is professor of philosophy at Florida Atlantic University in Boca Raton, Florida. She publishes widely in aesthetics, ancient Greek philosophy, philosophy of psychiatry, and, more recently, Japanese philosophy. From 2011 to 2013, she was a scholar for a program at the New York-based Aquila Theatre Company called 'Ancient Greeks / Modern Lives: Poetry-Drama-Dialogue,' a major initiative funded by the National Endowment for the Humanities. She coedited *Ethics, Art, and Representations of the Holocaust* (Lexington Books, 2013). More recently, she has been writing a book on the aesthetic properties of persons. The work is a foray into both ontology and everyday aesthetics. In line with her interests in embodiment and the philosophy of psychiatry, she has also written and spoken on the ethics of women in ground combat.

Mikiko Hirayama is associate professor of Asian art history and director of Asian studies at the University of Cincinnati in Cincinnati, Ohio. Her research focuses on Japanese art criticism of the Meiji, Taishō, and early Shōwa periods, especially the issues of realism and the expressions of national identity in

Western-style painting (*yōga*). She is one of the contributors to *Art and War in Japan and Its Empire: 1931–1960* (Brill, 2013) and *Since Meiji: Perspectives on the Japanese Visual Arts, 1868–2000* (University of Hawai'i Press, 2011). Her articles have been published in periodicals such as *Monumenta Nipponica* (2011), *History of Photography* (2009), and *Art Journal* (1996).

Matthew Larking is assistant professor in the faculty of global and regional studies at Doshisha University in Kyoto, Japan. His principal interests lie in the formations and trajectories of Japan's modern painting movements, particularly *nihonga* (modern Japanese-style painting), *yōga* (Western-style painting), the Japanese uptake of literati painting, *nanga/bunjinga*, and their interrelations. In addition to scholarly work, he has been writing as an art critic for the national newspaper, *The Japan Times*, since 2002.

Peter Leech was the founding appointment in art history and theory at the University of Otago, New Zealand in 1991, following positions in philosophy at several universities in Europe and North America. His research in aesthetics and art theory has been widely published internationally and includes a suite of papers since 2005 on Japanese aesthetics. He has held several international visiting professorships, most recently at the Ibero-American University (Universidad Iberoamericana) in Mexico City, Mexico (2011), and is currently completing a book entitled *The Painting of Philosophy*.

James McRae is professor of philosophy and religion and vice-chair of the faculty at Westminster College in Fulton, Missouri. He is a coeditor, with J. Baird Callicott, of *Japanese Environmental Philosophy* (Oxford University Press, forthcoming in 2017) and *Environmental Philosophy in Asian Traditions of Thought* (State University of New York Press, 2014), and he coedited *The Philosophy of Ang Lee* (University Press of Kentucky, 2013) with Robert Arp and Adam Barkman. An avid martial artist for over two decades, he is an instructor in Jeet Kune Do, Jiu-Jitsu, and Judo.

John C. Maraldo is Distinguished Professor Emeritus of Philosophy at the University of North Florida in Jacksonville, Florida. He earned a DPhil. from the University of Munich with a dissertation published as *Der hermeneutische Zirkel: Untersuchungen zu Schleiermacher, Dilthey und Heidegger* (Karl Alber, 1974), and then spent several years in Japan studying Japanese philosophy and Zen Buddhism. He has been guest professor at Kyoto University in Kyoto, Japan and the Catholic University of Leuven in Leuven, Belgium. In 2008–2009, he held the Roche Chair in Interreligious Research at Nanzan University in Nagoya, Japan. He is a coeditor, with James W. Heisig and Thomas P. Kasulis, of *Japanese Philosophy: A Sourcebook* (University of Hawai'i Press, 2011) and, with James W. Heisig, of *Rude Awakenings: Zen, the Kyoto School, and the Question of Nationalism* (University of Hawai'i Press, 1995), and the author of numerous works on Heidegger, the Kyoto School, Buddhism, and comparative philosophy.

Mara Miller, a philosopher, Japanese art and literature specialist, and artist, is a visiting scholar at the Center for Biographical Research at the University of Hawai'i at Mānoa, where she also teaches premodern Japanese literature for the Department of East Asian Languages and Literatures. She earned her doctorate in philosophy from Yale University, her master's degree from the University of Michigan's Center for Japanese Studies, and her bachelor's degree from Cornell University. The author of *The Garden as an Art* (State University of New York Press, 1993), *The Philosopher's Garden* (forthcoming), and six dozen scholarly articles, she is completing *Terrible Knowledge and Tertiary Trauma*, a book on why we should teach about the atomic bombings of Hiroshima and Nagasaki, why we don't, and how we should use art to do so.

Hiroshi Nara is professor of Japanese and chair of the department of East Asian languages and literatures at the University of Pittsburgh in Pittsburgh, Pennsylvania. His most recent publications include *The Structure of Detachment: The Aesthetic Vision of Kuki Shūzō* (University of Hawai'i Press, 2004) and an introduction to and an English translation of Watsuji Tetsurō's *Koji junrei—Pilgrimages to the Ancient Temples in Nara* (MerwinAsia, 2012).

A. Minh Nguyen is professor of philosophy and Asian studies, inaugural director of the interdisciplinary Asian studies program (which program he cofounded), associate director of the honors program, and inaugural coordinator of national and international scholarships and fellowships (which office he cofounded) at Eastern Kentucky University in Richmond, Kentucky. He earned a bachelor's degree in mathematics, a master's degree in philosophy, and a doctoral degree in philosophy from Columbia University. A Vietnamese-born specialist in the philosophy of mind and theory of knowledge, he also works in the areas of Chinese thought and Japanese aesthetics while maintaining an abiding interest in ethics and political philosophy. His work has been published in a number of philosophical, literary, and interdisciplinary journals, including *The Journal of Philosophical Research*, *The Journal of Value Inquiry*, *The Kenyon Review*, *Evolution and Cognition*, *Dialogue*, and *Think*. He received the 2002 Rockefeller Essay Prize from the American Philosophical Association.

Steve Odin has been teaching Japanese and East-West comparative philosophy in the department of philosophy at the University of Hawai'i at Mānoa since 1982. He has been visiting professor at Boston University in Massachusetts as well as Tohoku University and the University of Tokyo in Japan. Also, he has been a recipient of grants from the National Endowment for the Humanities, the Fulbright Program, and the Japan Foundation, and other awards to fund research in Japan. His publications include *Artistic Detachment in Japan and the West: Psychic Distance in Comparative Aesthetics* (University of Hawai'i Press, 2001), *The Social Self in Zen and American Pragmatism* (State University of New York Press, 1996), and *Process Metaphysics and Hua-Yen Buddhism: A Critical Study of Cumulative Penetration vs. Interpenetration* (Sri Satguru Publications, 1995). His most recent book is *Tragic Beauty in Whitehead and Japanese Aesthetics* (Lexington Books, 2015).

Graham Parkes is a native of Scotland. He taught Asian and comparative philosophy for thirty years at the University of Hawai'i at Mānoa, then for seven years as professor of philosophy at the National University of Ireland, Cork, where he founded and directed the Irish Institute for Japanese Studies, and now as visiting professor of philosophy at East China Normal University in Shanghai. He has published extensively in the field of Japanese thought and culture, and is the author of the entry on Japanese aesthetics in *The Stanford Encyclopedia of Philosophy*, an online reference work.

C. Michael Rich studied for his PhD under Edwin McClellan at Yale University and has written about and translated works by Mori Ōgai and Mishima Yukio. He saw his first nō play in 1983 and began studying nō performance in 2004 in Kyoto under *Kanze-ryū shitekata nōgakushi* Katayama Shingo, Tamoi Hiromichi, and Ōe Nobuyuki. He studied *kotsuzumi* and *ōtsuzumi* in Kyoto and performed in more than thirty nō plays with professional and amateur nō actors and musicians in Japan and the United States. Since 2009, he has invited *Kanze-ryū shitekata nōgakushi* Asano Atsuyoshi to Kentucky as visiting artist-in-residence at the University of Kentucky and Georgetown College and to teach workshops and give performances. Rich currently teaches Chinese and Japanese languages and cultures at Eastern Kentucky University, where he is associate professor of Chinese and Japanese.

J. Thomas Rimer is professor emeritus of Japanese literature at the University of Pittsburgh. His recent publications include the following edited volumes: *The Columbia Anthology of Modern Japanese Drama* (Columbia University Press, 2014), which he edited with Mitsuya Mori and M. Cody

Poulton; and *Since Meiji: Perspectives on the Japanese Visual Arts, 1868–2000* (University of Hawai'i Press, 2011).

Yuriko Saito is professor of philosophy at the Rhode Island School of Design in Providence, Rhode Island. Her research fields are Japanese aesthetics, everyday aesthetics, and environmental aesthetics, and she has published a number of journal articles and book chapters on these subjects. Her *Everyday Aesthetics* (hardback 2007, paperback 2010) and *Aesthetics of the Familiar: Everyday Life and World-Making* (hardback 2017) were both published by Oxford University Press.

Roy Starrs teaches Japanese and Asian studies at the University of Otago in New Zealand. He has published widely on Japanese literature, art, and culture. His most recent books include *Modernism and Japanese Culture* (Palgrave Macmillan, 2011) and, as editor, *Rethinking Japanese Modernism* (Brill, 2011), *Politics and Religion in Modern Japan: Red Sun, White Lotus* (Palgrave Macmillan, 2011), and *When the Tsunami Came to Shore: Culture and Disaster in Japan* (Brill, 2014).

Akiko Takenaka is associate professor of Japanese history and associate department chair at the University of Kentucky in Lexington, Kentucky. She specializes in the social and cultural history of modern Japan with a research focus on memory and historiography of the Asia-Pacific War. She is the author of *Yasukuni Shrine: History, Memory, and Japan's Unending Postwar* (University of Hawai'i Press, 2015).

Meera Viswanathan is associate professor emerita of comparative literature and East Asian studies at Brown University in Providence, Rhode Island, where she specialized in classical and modern Japanese literature and aesthetics, medieval European literature, and comparative literature. She has published essays on Japanese court poetry and its relationship to social structures, on the modern philosopher Kuki Shūzō and his theory of *iki*, on the leitmotif of the *yamamba* (mountain witch) in Japanese literary history, and on the problem of value and relationship in early-twentieth-century Japan as it plays out in the work of the philosopher Watsuji Tetsurō and the novelist Natsume Sōseki.

Jason M. Wirth is professor of philosophy at Seattle University in Seattle, Washington, and works and teaches in the areas of Continental philosophy, Buddhist philosophy, aesthetics, and Africana philosophy. His recent books include *Commiserating with Devastated Things: Milan Kundera and the Entitlements of Thinking* (Fordham University Press, 2015), *Schelling's*

Practice of the Wild: Time, Art, Imagination (State University of New York Press, 2015), *The Conspiracy of Life: Meditations on Schelling and His Time* (State University of New York Press, 2003), and the coedited volumes (with Patrick Burke) *The Barbarian Principle: Merleau-Ponty, Schelling, and the Question of Nature* (State University of New York Press, 2014) and (with Bret W. Davis and Brian Schroeder) *Japanese and Continental Philosophy: Conversations with the Kyoto School* (Indiana University Press, 2011). He is associate editor and book review editor of the journal *Comparative and Continental Philosophy*.

Koji Yamasaki is associate professor at Hokkaido University's Center for Ainu and Indigenous Studies in Hokkaido, Japan. He collaborated with others to curate the 2009 exhibit *Teetasinrit Tekrukoci: The Handprints of Our Ancestors: Ainu Artifacts Housed at Hokkaido University—Inherited Techniques* and to author the catalogue. He specializes in cultural anthropology and museum studies. His collaborative research with the Ainu people focuses on modern meanings and uses of museum materials.

Michiko Yusa is professor of Japanese thought and intercultural philosophy in the department of modern and classical Languages at Western Washington University in Bellingham, Washington. Her major publications include *Zen and Philosophy: An Intellectual Biography of Nishida Kitarō* (University of Hawai'i Press, 2002) and *Japanese Religious Traditions* (Prentice Hall, 2002). Her most recent work is an edited volume, *The Bloomsbury Research Handbook of Contemporary Japanese Philosophy* (Bloomsbury, 2017). While the main focus of her research remains the philosophy of Nishida Kitarō, her research interests extend to intercultural philosophy, women philosophers, women's spirituality in Japanese Buddhism, women Christian mystics, Raimon Panikkar's thought, and the Zen philosophy of peace.

About the Editor

A. Minh Nguyen earned a bachelor's degree in mathematics, a master's degree in philosophy, and a doctoral degree in philosophy from Columbia University. He is currently professor of philosophy and Asian studies, director of the Asian studies program, associate director of the honors program, and coordinator of national and international scholarships and fellowships at Eastern Kentucky University.

Made in the USA
Coppell, TX
24 December 2021

69996099R00289